# Lockheed Martin's
# Skunk Works

by

## Jay Miller

**Aerofax**
an imprint of

**Midland Publishing Ltd.**

# In Memory of Alvin H. Parker

This revised edition published 1995 by:
**Midland Publishing Ltd.**
24 The Hollow, Earl Shilton
Leicester, LE9 7NA, England
ph.: (01455) 847815 fax.: (01455) 841805

First published in 1993 by:
**Aerofax, Inc.**
708 Viewside Circle
Arlington, TX 76011

United States trade distribution by:
**Specialty Press Publishers & Wholesalers Inc.**
11481 Kost Dam Road
North Branch, MN 55056 USA
ph.: 612 583-3239; toll free ph.: 800 895-4585
fax.: 612 583-2023

A NASA ER-2 has recently been equipped with a dorsal antenna and associated radome to allow imagery transmission to ground receiving stations in real time via Tracking Data and Relay Satellites (TDRS) using NASA's new Starlink system. This equipment is similar in most respects to the Senior Span U-2S systems operated by the Department of Defense.

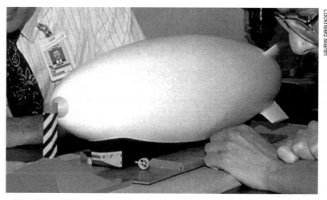

The Skunk Works is presently studying a new airship that could lead to a new global transportation system. The proposed heavy lifter, with a length of 1,160 feet and a diameter of 290 feet, would have a speed of 75 knots, a payload of 1.1 million pounds, and a range of 4,000 to 6,000 n. miles. It's interesting to note the dirigible Hindenberg was 804 feet long and 135 feet in diameter.

# Lockheed Martin's
# *Skunk Works*

by Jay Miller

# Contents

# Acknowledgements

As I noted in the first edition of this book, *Skunk Works* was the result of one man's efforts more than any other...Richard Abrams, then Director of Flight Test for Lockheed's Advanced Development Company (LADC— which is better known to the lay-world as the *Skunk Works*). Dick, whose own credits—both as a flight test engineer and as an author—were lengthy and notable, was one of those rare individuals who combined a love of work with a love of history...particularly in the field of aerospace. This book was essentially Dick's idea, and without his perseverance and foresight, it almost certainly would never have come to pass.

Less than a year following the publication of *Skunk Works*, Dick Abrams died. It was a sudden and tragic loss for us all. We who had been privileged to be his friends and co-workers were stunned and frustrated. I can only hope that *Skunk Works*, in some way, perpetuates the legacy of skill, wisdom, and dedication to craft Dick so unerringly represented.

Not long after Dick's demise, another close friend--and one of Lockheed's most notable helmsmen--was lost when the great engineer Ben Rich died during early 1995. Ben, a man whose friendship I treasured and whose knowledge I greatly admired, was a rarity among corporate aerospace leaders; he was one of the few who could lay claim to a long legacy of hands-on involvement with the hardware with which he was so closely associated. He was a legend among legends...and I will be a long time in missing those crack-of-dawn phone calls and the sound of Ben's mildly raspy, but always upbeat voice.

Among the many aerospace companies this author has had the privilege of working with over the years, Lockheed—now Lockheed Martin—stands head and shoulders above its peers in terms of responsiveness to its public and its relationship with the media. In the case of this book in particular, there were many Lockheed employees and associates who assisted without hesitation at every turn. They include: Ed Baldwin, ADP (ret.—special thanks); Ward Beman, Lockheed (ret.); Ellen Bendell, Communications, LADC; Keith Beswick, Director of Flight Test, LADC (ret.); Buddy Brown, LADC; Debbi Burch, Administrative Services, LADC; Dick Burton, Flight Test, LADC; Fred Carmody, Manager, LADC Field Operations, Beale AFB; Irv Culver, Lockheed (ret.); Rus Daniell, ADP (ret.); Cal Davis, Flight Test, LADC; Terri Day, Flight Test, LADC; Bob Driver, Graphic Arts Coordinator, LADC; Jim Eastham, Test Pilot, ADP (ret.); Hal Farley, Jr., Chief Test Pilot, LADC (ret.); Jim Ghezzi, Program Security, LADC; Jack Gordon, now President, LADC;

Gary Grigg, Director-Program Development; Pete Harrigan, Director-Employee Communications, Lockheed Corporation; Willis Hawkins, Lockheed Corporation (ret.); Eric Hehs, Editor, Code One; Sherrie Laveaux, Flight Test, LADC; Tony LeVier, Lockheed Chief Test Pilot (ret.); Denny Lombard, Public Information Photographer, LADC; Sol London, Employee Communications Editor, LADC (ret.); April McKettrick, Lockheed Corporation; Sherm Mullin, President (ret.), LADC; Bob Murphy, ADP (ret.); Bill Park, Chief Test Pilot, ADP (ret.); Tom Pugh, Flight Test, LADC; Jim Ragsdale, Director of Communications, LADC; Jeff Rhodes, Public Relations Representative, LASC; John Rowett, Coordinator, Administrative Services, LADC; Lou Schalk, Test Pilot, ADP (ret.); James Sergeant, Lockheed Martin, Ft. Worth; Steve Shobert, Program Security, LADC; Eric Shulzinger, Lockheed Corporation; Gene Souza, Program Security, LADC; Rich Stadler, Manager of Public Information, LADC (ret.); and Denny Thompson, V.P. Business Management, LADC.

Others, of course, have given generously of their time and materials. Among those deserving of special mention are: Shelly Abrams, Dick's wife; Holmes Anderson; David and Krin Anderton; Joyce Baker, History Office, Air Force Flight Test Center, Edwards AFB; Bob Baldwin; Glen Best; Walter Boyne, Director of the National Air & Space Museum (ret.); Tom Copeland, President, Aerofax, Inc.; Tim Cullum; Ronnie Day; Al Dobyns; Bill Esquilla, Global Group; Jeff Ethell; Jay Everett, Vice President, Aerofax, Inc.; Charles Fleming (special thanks for drawings); Rene' Francillon, Ph.D.; James Goodall (special thanks); Mike Haggerty, USAF; Dick Hallion, Ph.D., USAF Historian, Bolling AFB; Chuck Hansen; Nancy Johnson, widow of Clarence L. "Kelly" Johnson; Randy Jolly, Aero Graphics; Harry Kent; Tony Landis (special thanks); John Mallozzi; J. C. "Cam" Martin, Chief, External Affairs, NASA Dryden; Frank McCurdy, C-130 specialist; Jerry Moore (cover designer); Carol Osborne, Osborne Publisher, Inc.; Ed Petrushka; Chris Pocock (special thanks); Mick Roth; Pat Sharp, Dept. of the Air Force; Earl Shellner, Maj., USAF, Chief, Public Affairs, 49th FW, Holloman AFB; James Stevenson; Jim Wolf, Global Group; and James Young, Ph.D., Chief Historian, Air Force Flight Test Center, Edwards AFB.

To Susan, Anna, and Missy, my thanks with love...

Jay Miller
August, 1995

*Perhaps the most celebrated attack aircraft in history, the* Skunk Works' *precedent-setting F-117A embodies virtually all contemporary combat aircraft disciplines. Optimised to meet various low-observables criteria, it is a bizarre, yet practical design.*

# Preface

*"I'll try to use at least 17 percent nouns and verbs, which I have found over a long period of time means you're saying something. And I'll try to control the use of personal pronouns, to which I'm addicted."*

**Clarence L. "Kelly" Johnson**

---

Having authored more than a few books and over a thousand articles about a myriad collection of esoteric aviation subjects, I've come to a point in my professional career wherein it is difficult for me to get excited writing about anything but the most extraordinary. Aerospace journalism is a time-consuming and laborious process, and it becomes ever more tedious as the subjects of greatest interest are slowly eliminated from a long list of preferences.

However, over the course of what now is many years work, there has remained for me one subject of exceptional intrigue, and one about which I have often aspired to write...Lockheed's enigmatic and historically significant Advanced Development Company (LADC)...world-renowned as the *Skunk Works*. Undeniably the most famous operation of its kind ever, it has become a symbol, both real and imagined, of all that is good about the US aerospace industry and its extraordinary technology.

But writing about the *Skunk Works* was not something undertaken casually. In fact, over a period of many years' observation, I had concluded...accurately...that no worthwhile description of the *Skunk Works* and its fabled management, engineering staff, and hardware could be successfully accommodated without the direct intercession of the *Skunk Works* itself.

This was not, after-all, your average aircraft company. The *Skunk Works* had for decades immersed itself in the blackest of "black" world projects and its reputation for such involvement automatically curtailed the writing of an accurate history without their assistance. Too much of what the company had done in the past remained covered in a veil of secrecy. No matter how intense or persevering the research, there simply was no recourse but to depend upon hearsay and rumor unless LADC and its various "customers" agreed to cooperate.

Fifty years is a long time for a corporate entity to remain not only functional, but financially viable. It was just this type of milestone, to be celebrated during 1993, that led LADC and several of its "customers" to a decision permitting the *Skunk Works* access I needed. Discussions with the company resulted in a commitment to make this book happen, and within weeks, I was on my way to California for the initial research effort.

Within the constraints of security, I was given privileges which, to my knowledge, had never previously been permitted anyone from the "white" world. As I discovered, LADC's long-hidden legacy was far more profound than anything I had imagined. It immediately became apparent that, given the mid-year deadline of this project, much of the hardware insights and technical data at my disposal would have to be set aside for use at a later date. Accordingly, related books on noteworthy *Skunk Works* aircraft will be forthcoming as time permits.

Regardless, the book you now hold in your hands is a testament to an extraordinary body of work, perhaps unmatched in the history of aviation, and certainly unmatched by any other sub-division of a major US aerospace company. It does not represent production quantities of vast proportions, nor a single performance spike in the time line of aerospace history, but rather a high level of business acumen and technology that remains the standard by which all other aerospace companies and their products are judged. This, then, is the story of the *Skunk Works*—from its inception during 1943, to the present—and with some insight into its future.

Jay Miller
September 1993

---

## A Note on Sources

This book describes the history of an institution that has been intimately involved in many projects directly or indirectly associated with national security interests. Accordingly, many of the *Skunk Works'* early aircraft programs have only recently arrived at a point in time wherein it is finally possible to discuss them in public...and with any degree of authority. Other programs, particularly those of a more recent vintage, remain sensitive, and therefore beyond the scope of this book to describe.

In order to accommodate the author's request for access to previously unpublished information, a number of unique documents were released for reference for the first time ever. Among these were "logs" kept by "Kelly" Johnson and other intimates describing the day-to-day activities inside the *Skunk Works* and, in particular, the trials and tribulations of individual aircraft programs. Excerpts from these logs, coupled with miscellaneous other declassified hardware documents, represent the majority of the previously unpublished textual material found in this book. Their insights are, without doubt, the most detailed yet unveiled for public consumption.

Readers are asked to understand that most, if not all of the "log" quotes are the entries as they were written. No grammatical, technical, or historical changes of any kind have been made that would effect the import of the wording.

Finally, it should be mentioned for the benefit of the more astute readers—and Lockheed employees who were intimately involved with select *Skunk Works* projects—that there are minor omissions and purposeful oversights in select chapters. Items of continuing sensitivity either have been selectively edited or consciously deleted at Lockheed's request. Noteworthy among the latter is U-2 production data. Due to continuing US Government security restrictions, the Lockheed Advanced Development Company is unable to verify the accuracy of the U-2 production information in this book.

Any mistakes or errors of fact are totally the responsibility of the author.

Jay Miller

---

*The* Skunk Works *was born as a result of the XP-80. Test pilot Tony LeVier (right) sits on* Lulu Belle's *wing with ground crew at Muroc.*

*The most recent aircraft the* Skunk Works *has been involved with is the YF-22A...a technology demonstrator for the forthcoming F-22A.*

Lockheed's C-23 was one of the company's earliest military aircraft and was developed from the Altair. It was operated by the Army for some seven years.

Charles Lindbergh and his wife Anne flying in their Lockheed Sirius...which was specially designed for them by Lockheed's chief engineer, Gerald Vultee.

Wiley Post and his famous Lockheed Vega, the Winnie Mae, are seen shortly after landing at Floyd Bennet Field at Brooklyn, New York on July 22, 1933 at 11:59 p.m. Post and the Vega had just circumnavigated the globe in a record seven days and eighteen hours.

# Chapter 1:

# LOCKHEED BEFORE THE *SKUNK WORKS*

*"I would like to make an added point that comes home to me very clearly, having been involved in some 44 aircraft development programs, and 20 in the Skunk Works. I've seen time and again where the United States industry—the aircraft industry, or any other you want to choose—has demonstrated that when it knows what it is going to produce, it can't be beat."*

**Clarence L. "Kelly" Johnson**

As with all accomplished companies of its ilk, Lockheed takes great pride in its success and in the simple fact it not only has persevered, but has succeeded during a time when many other similar companies have failed. With a history that can be traced back to 1913, Lockheed is a rare survivor in a field littered with the debris of the mismanaged and politically inept. This success is directly attributable to the guidance provided by the likes of such gifted corporate chiefs as Carl Squier (who was never a chairman of the company), Robert and Courtlandt Gross, Dan Haughton, Bob Haack, Roy Anderson, Larry Kitchen, and Dan Tellep. These men, married to a corporate philosophy that has remained flexible enough to weather a variety of bankruptcy (1932), cash flow (1971), and questionable ethics (1975) assaults, have successfully guided Lockheed through tumultuous storms that would have sunk lesser corporate ships.

Lockheed's history is lengthy, and from a corporate perspective, typically complex. Like most major capitalist organizations, it has had good and bad fiscal years while persevering in an industry notable for its financial instability and a roller coaster business climate. Through good times and bad, over a period now spanning some eight decades, nearly sixty distinct aircraft types have kept Lockheed's widely distributed production facilities operating with noteworthy consistency.

Lockheed's founding fathers, three brothers by the name of Malcolm, Allan, and Victor Loughead (the latter a half-brother from their mother's previous marriage), by 1912 had developed a mutually strong interest in aviation. This was at a time when such pursuits still were considered borderline insanity. Victor, the oldest, already had acquired modest fame as the author of *Vehicles of the Air* (published in 1909 by The Reilly and Britton Company of Chicago)...a general reference book describing how to build, fly, and maintaining early aircraft. Victor's enthusiasm led to Allan and Malcolm developing similar aviation affinities. When they became old enough, the two joined forces and under the aegis of their Alco Hydro-Aeroplane Company embarked on the construction of a small, single-engine "hydro-aeroplane" referred to as the Model G.

Alco proved short-lived; by 1913 it had failed and the biplane had been placed in storage. Allan and Malcolm were forced to find conventional employment working for others.

The two brothers again teamed during 1916. With the help of outside investors, they resurrected the Model G biplane and formed the Loughead Aircraft Manufacturing Company. This venture resulted in one F-1 flying boat (later modified to land plane configuration), two license-built Curtiss HS-2L flying boats, and the development of the advanced, but unsuccessful S-1 sport biplane. Unfortunately, this modest output, coupled with the end of World War One, was not sufficient to keep the fledgling Santa Barbara, California company afloat. During 1921 it was liquidated.

Ever persevering, Allan, during 1926 con-

*Hall Hibbard and "Kelly" Johnson during the war years. Hibbard, who eventually became Lockheed's chief engineer, had joined the company during 1932 as an assistant to Richard von Hake.*

vinced backers to invest in a second Loughead aircraft company. This time, tired of the constant mispronunciations and in recognition of the new start, he changed the Loughead spelling to the phonetically more palatable *Lockheed*. The new company, now based in Hollywood, California, embarked rapidly on a major production program that would hold it in good stead for the following three-and-a-half years.

Under the able engineering not only of Allan Loughead, but also of the great John K. "Jack" Northrop—who had sporadically worked with the various Loughead operations since the F-1 flying boat of 1916—such aircraft as the inimitable *Vega, Air Express,* and *Explorer* rolled from the company's small production line with amazing regularity. Approximately a year after moving to Burbank during 1928 with about 50 employees, the reputation of Lockheed's products had caught the attention of the rapidly expanding Detroit Aircraft Corporation...which then was attempting to become the General Motors of the aircraft industry. A buy-out offer, much to Allan Loughead's chagrin, was accepted by Lockheed's board of directors, and some four months prior to the infamous stock market collapse of October 1929, the company—along with eleven others of similar persuasion— became a Detroit Aircraft subsidiary.

Allan Loughead, disassociating himself from the Detroit operation, went on to form Loughead Brothers Aircraft Corporation and Alcor Aircraft Corporation. Unfortunately, neither met with success. By the late 1930s, Allan, Malcolm, and the oft-forgotten Victor had moved on to other lines of work. It was not until three decades later that a Loughead brother again was directly involved with the company he had helped found; during 1969, Allan signed-on as a part-time Lockheed consultant.

Lockheed's initial successes with the *Vega* and other such aircraft of the early 1930s, were followed by those of the *Air Express, Sirius,* and several other similar models. These were all dependable, high-performance, all-wood monoplanes known for their quality construction and reasonable cost.

Jack Northrop's decision to leave the company and form his own during March of 1928 led to his replacement by another soon-to-be-noteworthy-aviation-pioneer, the talented Gerald Vultee. His tenure would see the birth of the *Orion* and *Altair* series, and unfortunately, the destructive effects of the Depression. Though sales continued at a rapid clip, they proved insufficient to offset the drain created by parent Detroit Aircraft Company's deteriorating financial situation. On October 27, 1931, Detroit capitulated, and along with it, its Lockheed subsidiary. The latter struggled on with a skeleton crew until June 16, 1932, but was forced to terminate operations during a vain attempt to complete two more *Vegas* (these aircraft were, in fact, eventually completed, but not under the auspices of Lockheed Aircraft Company).

The failings of the Detroit Aircraft Company's finances were not enough to totally discount its Lockheed subsidiary's unqualified successes. Accordingly, some five days after final foreclosure, San Francisco-based broker Robert Gross and a small group of investors walked out of the U.S. District Court in Los Angeles in sole possession of Lockheed's existing assets--then estimated to have a value of $129,961--for a total cost of $40,000.

This was gutsy action at a time when the country was in the terrible grip of the most devastating depression in its history. But it highlighted Gross's far-sighted thinking...and his tenacious approach to business.

The investment in Lockheed was not foolhardy. The born-again Lockheed Aircraft

*Loughead brothers' 1913 Model G was the first successful tandem tractor seaplane manufactured in the US. It was first unveiled at the Panama Pacific International Exposition in San Francisco during 1915.*

Corporation was quick to rejuvenate extant orders that had existed prior to the Detroit debacle. Orders for a significant number of *Vegas, Orions,* and at least one *Altair* started things off in proper fashion...thanks to the magnificent salesmanship of Carl Squier who had come onboard from Detroit Aircraft.

Heading the new operation as president and general manager was the newly-hired Lloyd Stearman who, in his own right and like Northrop and Vultee before, eventually would become a historically significant US aviation personality. Working with him was chief engineer Robert von Hake and a then-unknown assistant chief engineer by the name of Hall Hibbard.

Knowing the future of the company did not lie with its old products, Gross, Stearman, von Hake, and Hibbard embarked on a plan to design and build a new twin-engine, all-metal transport to meet the needs of the fledgling US air transport industry. Though initially concluding a single engine suitable, they later became convinced twin-engine configurations were where the key to Lockheed's future lay. Following initial design work, a 1/20th-scale wood and metal (engine cowls) wind tunnel model of the proposed Lockheed Model 10 *Electra* was built and delivered to the University of Michigan for testing. There, a Prof. Edward Stalker was asked to evaluate the advanced twin and assess its performance and stability characteristics.

After considerable wind tunnel study, Stalker's review concluded that, typical of aircraft of the period, the Model 10 had good potential performance while being marginally within the somewhat arbitrary stability limits then considered satisfactory for an aircraft of its type. Surprisingly, a somewhat precocious Stalker understudy, Clarence L. "Kelly" Johnson (then doing post-graduate work in aeronautical engineering), who had participated in the generation of the aircraft's tunnel test data, contrarily had concluded its longitudinal and directional control problems were, as he put it, "bad", at best.

In a somewhat remarkable chain of events, Johnson, during 1933—a year prior to the initiation of the Model 10 tunnel tests—had applied to Lockheed for an engineering job. He had not been turned down, but instead had concurred when von Hake recommended that he first return to Michigan and complete his master of science degree in aeronautical engineering. Von Hake also told Johnson that though Lockheed still was in the throes of its post-bankruptcy start-up, there might be an open engineering position if and when forthcoming aircraft programs began to gather momentum.

Johnson took von Hake at his word; shortly after the conclusion of Stalker's Model 10 tunnel study, he returned to Lockheed's Burbank, California offices... master's degree in hand...and again asked for employment. Cyril Chappellet (one of the major shareholders in the new company) and Hibbard were the people who actually hired Johnson—as Lockheed's 36th employee. It would be looked back upon as perhaps the single most important personnel transaction in the aircraft manufacturer's history.

"Kelly's" debut shortly after his arrival was anything but auspicious. In a meeting with Chappellet and Hibbard during the course of one of his first days at work, he told the engineering group their new Model 10 was only marginally stable. Bluntly, he told the group he did not agree with Prof. Stalker's conclusions. He felt a better and safer aircraft could be designed.

These comments came as somewhat of a shock to Hibbard. A day after listening to Johnson's matter-of-fact declaration, he cornered the neophyte engineer and orally reviewed his academic credentials in a face-to-face confrontation. He felt certain he could repudiate the Model 10 disparities that had been brought to light. Hibbard would recall, years later, he came close to firing Johnson on the spot. Several months after the encounter, and after concluding Johnson's claims might have some merit, he told the young engineer to return to Michigan and solve the Model 10's stability shortcomings.

Johnson drove to Michigan with the large Model 10 wind tunnel model awkwardly squeezed into the back passenger compartment of his car. Some 73 tunnel runs followed, this number being necessary to narrow the sources of difficulty. The idea of attaching "controllable plates" to the horizontal tail tips surfaced while run number 72 was underway. These auxiliary surfaces, tested during run number 73, "worked very well", particularly after the destabilizng wing root fillets were removed. The next step improved control even further. Full, twin vertical tail surfaces now replaced the "plates", supplementing the original fuselage-mounted vertical tail. Superb directional control resulted. It was concluded later the original vertical tail was unnecessary...and it was removed.

Johnson, who until the Model 10 assignment had been working as a tool designer at Lockheed, returned from Michigan somewhat a hero and most importantly a "full-fledged member of the engineering staff". In solving the Model 10's problems, he had set the company and its product line on the path to financial success. The Model 10 would give birth to several perturbations including the Model 12 (a scaled-down Model 10) and the highly successful Model 14. Consequently Johnson would be partially responsible for the financial latitude implied in the prototyping of the Model 22...which later would become world-renowned as the P-38 *Lightning*.

Even in consideration of the several short-term successes realized during the period from 1934 to 1937, Lockheed's future, by 1938, again had begun to look bleak. Placing most of its eggs in a single basket, a concerted effort under the aegis of corporate representative Kenneth Smith resulted, on June 23, 1938, in the consummation of a contract for between 200 and 250 Model B14L (bomber version of the Model 14) *Hudsons* for the British Royal Air Force. At the time, this was the largest order ever placed with an American manufacturer by a foreign military service. Lockheed suddenly was back on its feet...this time for good.

During 1937, Lockheed formed a wholly-owned subsidiary under the AiRover name with the intent of tasking it with the development of a new commercial aircraft family. By 1938, AiRover had become the Vega Airplane Company. The exigencies of the forthcoming war eventually curtailed full exploration of Vega's initial charter, and the operation eventually became a major production facility for Lend-Lease aircraft, Lockheed-built B-17 *Flying Fortresses*, and other miscellaneous combat aircraft types. Later, during November of 1943, the encumbrance of having Vega as a separate entity under the Lockheed corporate umbrella was eliminated when the division was absorbed fully by Lockheed Aircraft Corporation.

The Japanese attack on Pearl Harbor on December 7, 1941, brought Lockheed into the forefront of major world-class aircraft manufacturing companies. Orders for virtually every aircraft the company had in test or production, including the P-38, the Model 14 (and derivatives such as the *Lodestar, Ventura,* and *Harpoon* ), and the forthcoming *Constellation* increased almost exponentially. Between July

*The successes realized by the sale of* Vegas *to private, commercial, and military customers allowed the company to move from Santa Barbara to a new home in Burbank, California.*

1, 1940 and August 31, 1945, the company produced no less than 19,077 aircraft for the war effort. This figure represented 6.6% of all US production during that period and some 9% of the airframe weight total. By the end of World War II Lockheed was the fifth largest manufacturer of aircraft in the US.

Some seventy percent of the aircraft produced during this period rolled from production lines at Lockheed 's main Plant B-1. A mile away, at Burbank's Union Terminal facility (acquired by the company during 1940), the remaining approximately thirty percent rolled from Plant A-1. Concurrently, work also expanded into a number of considerably smaller satellite facilities referred to as "feeder plants", and modification and service centers were opened near Grand Prairie, Texas and Van Nuys Airport, California. Parts, overhaul, and maintenance facilities also came together in several European countries. By mid-1943, the company worldwide employed over 94,000 people.

The war catapulted Lockheed into the upper echelons of financially successful aircraft production companies. Accordingly, it was able to indulge research and development initiatives that otherwise would have been all but impossible during more austere times. Most notably, as early as 1939, Hall Hibbard and "Kelly" Johnson had become somewhat infatuated with jet propulsion theory. This power-plant concept, already being exploited with considerable efficacy on the other side of the Atlantic, had been placed on the back burner in the US primarily because of the exigencies of the war. By 1944, however, this was no longer the case. Money was made available for studies and hardware development. Working with Hibbard and Johnson were Phil Colman, Willis Hawkins, and Gene Frost--on airframe development--and the far-sighted Nathan Price on propulsion.

This team--a precursor to the soon-to-be-born *Skunk Works*--over a period of six months generated a variety of design studies that eventually resulted in the definitive L-133 jet-propelled, canard-configured fighter. Of all-steel construction and with an estimated maximum speed of 600 mph, it was to be powered by two Lockheed-designed and built L-1000 (XJ-37) axial-flow turbojets of 5,500 pounds thrust each.

Both the futuristic aircraft and the amazingly advanced jet engine eventually would become less than footnotes in the history of the company, but not before several major components of the L-1000 were built and tested by the Menasco engine manufacturing company which had won an "auction engineered by the US Government...which had decided it was a restraint of trade for power-

*Lockheed's founders on June 6, 1932 (l. to r.): Ron King, Asst. Treas.; Carl Squier, V.P., Sales; Lloyd Stearman, Pres.; Robert Gross, Chmn./Treas.; Cyril Chappellet, Sec.; and Hall Hibbard, V.P./Chief Eng.*

*"Kelly" Johnson with a (wire-supported) Model 10 tunnel model at the University of Michigan. Noteworthy is the single vertical fin and rudder assembly...one source of the aircraft's directional stability problems.*

*Lockheed's first production* Constellation *was the military C-69. The first aircraft, with the Lockheed manufacturing number 049-1961, would play a key role in long-term development of the type.*

plants to be manufactured by airframe companies.

As it was, the L-133 and L-1000 experience, though seemingly non-productive at the time, eventually would bear Lockheed significant fruit. Both concepts were extremely advanced for the early 1940s, even in light of parallel German and English efforts, and the axial flow engine in particular would prove prescient from a technology standpoint. More importantly, the small but signiicant experience base resulting form the maverick airframe and engine would hold the company in good stead when the Air Force finally realized a legitimate need for a jet-propelled fighter.

*Orders for the P-38* Lightning *as a result of Allied involvement in World War Two helped elevate the company out of the morass of the Depression.*

*Hall Hibbard, a graduate of the Massachusetts Institute of Technology, was Lockheed's unheralded engineering genius for over four decades.*

*Though never to reach the hardware stage, the extremely futuristic L-133 jet fighter would come to exemplify the kind of forward thinking approach to engineering so often found in Lockheed, and in particular, Skunk Works products. Its canard configuration was forty years ahead of its time.*

*Even more exotic than the airframe it was proposed to power, the L-1000 axial flow turbojet engine, the product of Lockheed's Nathan Price, was expected to propel the L-133 to speeds well in excess of 600 mph. Its axial flow design was years in advance of any other jet engine then available to US aircraft manufacturers.*

# Chapter 2:
# *SKUNK WORKS* PRELUDE

*"It was interesting at that time, we could trace back ten different times when the Army Air Corps and the Air Force had gone to the prototype development approach and then swung back to other more complex management systems. This goes all the way back to McCook Field operations."*

**Clarence L. "Kelly" Johnson**

Jet engine technology in the form of propulsion for aircraft had gone through a relatively long and laborious gestation by the time it was successfully applied to Germany's Heinkel He 178, the world's first successful jet-powered aircraft. Ernst Heinkel's company had initiated jet propulsion studies as early as 1936 under the aegis of a neophyte engineer by the name of Hans von Ohain. Young and brilliant, von Ohain had been invited to join the Heinkel team and to indulge his theories of jet propulsion that had surfaced while he pursued an engineering diploma at the University of Gottingen.

Concurrent with von Ohain's work, and in fact preceding it, was a similar effort undertaken by another young and brilliant engineer, Flight Lieutenant Frank Whittle of Great Britain. Though other British countrymen had begun exploring the attributes of jet propulsion during the same 1920s time period, it was Whittle who first concluded the gas turbine and its pure jet thrust were a practical means of aircraft propulsion. Whittle's January 1930 patent predated all other practical attempts to develop a jet engine and thus later gave credence to his "inventor of..." claims.

Regardless, Whittle's efforts, unlike those of von Ohain, were not given significant government support until after the modest successes realized by his privately funded model "U" engine of 1937. This jet, which ran for the first time on April 12, set precedent for all following Whittle engines and served as a testbed in developed form until it was all but destroyed on February 22, 1941. By that date, Whittle had acquired sufficient private sector financing to form Power Jets Limited...a company with the singular purpose of producing the Allies' first successful jet engines.

In the meantime, von Ohain's work, actively funded by the Nazis, had met with considerable success. His first demonstration engine, the HeS 1, had run for the first time during March of 1937. Producing some 550 pounds thrust, it led almost immediately to an improved successor, the HeS 3. This engine, in its developed 1,100 pound thrust HeS 3b form, became the first flight worthy jet engine in history. Around it, the Heinkel company designed the simple, high-wing He 178 testbed aircraft.

Following its first flight in the capable hands of Heinkel test pilot Erich Warsitz at the company airfield at Marienehe on August 27, 1939, the He 178 was used not only to study the jet engine as an aircraft propulsion unit, but also to convince Nazi and Luftwaffe leaders of the jet engine's viability. Its success in the propaganda department later was manifested in the extraordinarily rapid development of such superb operational combat aircraft as the Messerschmitt Me 262 and the Arado Ar 234, and in turn, in the attempted development of a plethora of jet-powered combat types that included the highly advanced Messerschmitt P.1101, the Henschel Hs 132, the Junkers Ju 287, and the Heinkel He 162. Though these were all the German jet aircraft types to reach

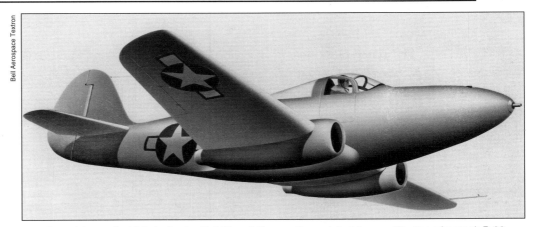

One of the earliest jet studies by Bell Aircraft Corporation entailed the modification of a stock P-39 *Airacobra. The reciprocating engine behind the cockpit was replaced with two wing-mounted jet engines.*

Bell Aerospace Textron

the hardware stage, they represented only the tip of an iceberg in relation to what was on Germany's drawing boards at the end of the war. Only the cessation of hostilities prevented German development of a stable of combat jets that could have drastically changed the outcome of the war.

On the other side of the Atlantic, US work on jet powered aircraft had been slow to develop. The reasons were manifold, but in essence they all boiled down to unstoppable momentum in the form of an industrial complex committed to more conventional (i.e., reciprocating engine powered) aircraft forms. With the war balance slowly swinging in favor of the Allies as a result of massive production runs and relatively skilled manpower, it was difficult to suddenly bring on-line a propulsion system that not only was then little-understood, but decidedly unproved. Though the jet engine's performance advantages were assumed to be significant, no Allied service had yet operated one in combat, and only limited experimentation had taken place outside the laboratory. In general, the military's mindset was positive but the demands of the war dictated concentrating production on weapons and equipment that then represented known quantities.

Royal Air Force Intelligence Report No. 2256, written by Wing Commander G. E. F. Proctor, recounted the first known Allied encounter with the Luftwaffe's stunningly successful Messerschmitt Me 262 jet fighter. On July 25, 1944, Flt. Lt. A. E. Wall (pilot) and Pilot Officer A. S. Lobban (navigator) while flying an unarmed reconnaissance variant of the agile de Havilland *Mosquito* over Munich Germany, noticed an approaching enemy aircraft approximately 400 yards astern and closing fast. The *Mosquito* had been circling at 30,000 feet while taking oblique photographs of important Munich targets. When the enemy machine was spotted, Wall immediately applied full power and dove, also slowly rolling to his left. As he leveled off at 28,000 feet, he noted a true airspeed of 412 mph...which he assumed to be sufficient to outrun any known German aircraft at that altitude. Looking aft, however, Wall quickly discerned the mysteri-

ous German fighter as having no difficulty remaining in trail. Accordingly, he hurriedly initiated a turning dogfight to avoid almost certain disaster.

Five times Wall turned into the attacking Me 262, but was unable to gain an advantage. Though succeeding on at least three occasions in getting on the jet's tail, the unarmed *Mosquito* proved slower than its adversary and only marginally more maneuverable. It was only by diving into cloud cover that the Royal Air Force aircraft and its crew were able to escape the frustrating battle. When Wall and Lobban returned to their home base at Fermo near Ancona, Italy, they spent little time equivocating over the capabilities of the long-rumored German jet...they were convinced its performance capability was something the Allies could not easily or safely ignore.

In fact, Allied intelligence sources had been monitoring German jet and rocket aircraft activity for many months. Reconnaissance flights had acquired glimpses of the secret Me 262 on several occasions, and related aircraft, such as the rocket-powered Messerschmitt Me 163, had been observed as well. So little was known about these advanced machines and their performance envelopes, intelligence personnel were hard-pressed to provide Allied combat crews even minimal information. It was not until initial Allied encounters were more thoroughly assessed that it was possible to acquire some insight into the German jets and what they might provide in the way of a threat.

US intelligence agencies had been closely monitoring the Allied reports and consequently had served to awaken appropriate military commanders to the potential threat. In turn, available information pertaining to jet engine technology was reviewed with renewed interest, including indigenous US research that had been undertaken during the preceding two decades. Most of the latter concerned turbo-supercharging of conventional reciprocating engines (turbosuperchargers, which were high-pressure/high-speed air compressors, stemmed from technology that was directly applicable to the compressor sections of jet engines), but in 1936, a seminal paper directly

**11**

*The first Bell XP-59 arrived at Muroc Army Air Field during September of 1942. It had been loaded aboard a special freight car in Buffalo, New York and had been escorted by armed guard the entire trip. The General Electric Type I-A centrifugal flow jet engine also was transported by train.*

related to jet propulsion entitled, "The Gas Turbine as a Prime Mover for Aircraft", was prepared and released by Wright Field. The following year, during February, General Electric sent a related study to Wright Field entitled "Gas Turbine Power Plants for Aeronautical Applications". The latter still viewed the propeller as the primary propulsion force, but the resulting integration of turbines and propellers almost certainly was one of the earliest US studies relating to what eventually became known as turboprop engines.

General Electric's ascent to the preeminent position of US gas turbine technology leader came about with little conscious effort on behalf of the company. The acquisition of such noted engineering minds as turbosupercharger designer Sanford Moss and similarly oriented Dale Streid gave the company a technological advantage not fully appreciated until after the war. Streid, whose initial jet engine pessimism was reversed upon being exposed to the rudimentary work then being undertaken by Frank Whittle, wrote a prescient paper during September of 1939 entitled, "Airplane Propulsion by Means of a Jet Reaction and Gas Turbine Power Plant".

In fact, Streid and Mosse had been fortunate to be privileged to events at British Thomson-Houston...a company founded by and then still associated with General Electric...and not inconsequently under contract to Whittle's Power Jets, Limited to build and statically test prototype jet engines. By 1939, enough progress had been realized to convince the British Air Ministry that research funding was appropriate. Accordingly, a contract was let for a prototype engine, the 855 pounds thrust W.1, to power a proposed jet-powered research aircraft to be built by Gloster under contract SB/3229 dated February 3, 1940, and designated E.28/39.

During March of 1941, following receipt of a preceptive letter dated February 25 from General H. *Hap* Arnold (who earlier had been briefed by intelligence personnel on jet-powered aircraft developments in Germany), then Deputy Chief of Staff for Air, Vannevar Bush, Ph.D. (then chairman of the National Advisory Committee for Aeronautics), formed a "Special Committee on Jet Propulsion" under the chairmanship of Will Durand, Ph.D. , ex-chairman of the NACA and a noted proponent of turbosupercharging (and, notably, one of Sanford Mosse's professors at Cornell University). Working with Durand as committee members were representatives from the Army Air Corps, the Navy Bureau of Aeronautics, the National Bureau of Standards, Johns Hopkins

University, the Massachusetts Institute of Technology, Allis Chalmers, Westinghouse, and General Electric.

Establishment of the Durand Committee led to the birth of preliminary jet engine proposals from the three engine manufacturers, with Allis Chalmers offering a rudimentary ducted fan; Westinghouse offering a high-performance turbojet; and General Electric offering a turboprop. The following July, the NACA approved initial development work by the three manufacturers, and during September, the Durand Committee recommended that all three engine projects be funded by the two primary military services. Accordingly, the Navy took control of the Allis Chalmers and Westinghouse programs and the Army took over the General Electric.

During April of 1941, while meeting with British military commanders in England, Gen. Arnold was given the opportunity to see the Gloster E.28/39 testbed aircraft while it was undertaking high-speed taxi tests and short "hops" into the air at the Hucclecote airfield (the first of two prototypes was successfully flown for the first time one month later at Cranwell, on May 15, 1941) and review in detail the Whittle jet engine. The display impressed Gen. Arnold. He immediately requested that information pertaining to the aircraft and its unique propulsion system be provided his technical staff in London for detailed review.

Upon returning to the US the following month, Gen. Arnold immediately arranged a meeting with Brig. Gen. Frank Carroll, then Chief of the Engineering Division at Wright Field, and Brig. Gen. Oliver Echols, then representing the Air Staff of the Army Air Force's Headquarters in Washington, D.C. During the briefing that followed, Gen. Arnold impressed upon Carroll and Echols the importance of what he had seen and emphasized that US involvement was not only required, but mandatory. Concurrently, he advised the US State Department of British jet engine developments and requested it assist in the establishment of diplomatic intercourse that would permit the acquisition and dissemination of jet engine information and technology in the US.

By early September of 1941, the receipt of British jet engine technology, insights, drawings, and hardware via the technical team assembled under command of Gen. Arnold had resulted in a decision to build a copy of the Whittle jet engine. Almost by default (i.e., as a result of its in-depth knowledge of turbosuperchargers), General Electric (Schenectady, New York and Lynn, Massachusetts) was the unanimous choice to build the engine, and Bell

Aircraft Corporation (Niagara Falls, New York)—also by default (in part due to its proximity to General Electric)—was picked to build the airframe.

The British government agreed to provide rights to the US Government and also to provide a single complete engine (the W.1X used during the E.28/39's initial taxi tests) and one of the two E.28/39s (later found to be unnecessary). Bell, after submitting and getting approval for its aircraft design, received a contract on September 30, 1941 for three Model 27 aircraft with the military designation XP-59A.

On October 1, 1942, one year to the day after the sample Whittle engine departed England as bomb bay cargo aboard an Army Air Corps Consolidated B-24 *Liberator*, the prototype Bell XP-59A, powered by two General Electric I-A centrifugal-flow jet engines, flew into US aviation history. With Bell chief test pilot Robert Stanley in the cockpit, the XP-59A successfully completed its first test hop (to an altitude of twenty-five feet) from the dry lake bed at Muroc Army Airfield in California.

The Army Air Force, deeply enmeshed in World War Two, had placed relatively little emphasis on the development of the P-59 as a legitimate combat aircraft. Like the Gloster E.28/39 that had preceded it, the US jet had been conceived primarily as a testbed to serve as a proof-of-concept vehicle for the jet engine. Combat capability was only a distant second priority.

Even the P-59's engine installation had been sublimated to the point wherein aerodynamics had taken a back seat. Mounted beneath the wings on either side of the fuselage centerline, the engines generated insurmountable aerodynamic drag figures that would have been unacceptable in a more conventional combat machine. On the positive side, the engine installations and their associated nacelles provided easy access for maintenance (important with a prototype of this kind), permitted the use of short exhaust pipes (thus improving engine efficiency), and overcame concerns related to asymmetry in the event of a single engine failure (as a result of their proximity to the fuselage centerline).

The three prototypes had, in fact, been followed by thirteen YP-59As for use in service trials. In turn, these were followed by some twenty production P-59As and thirty P-59Bs (out of an original order for eighty)...which effectively represented the final total number of P-59 aircraft built. Beginning on February 5 and ending on February 18, 1944, three of the YP-59As were used to evaluate the type as an air combat platform, being flown against a

*Bell's XP-59 was a simple and utilitarian design that succeeded admirably as a testbed, but failed as an advance in fighter design. Performance was abysmal, even by reciprocating engine standards, and the War Department found little to argue with when it was suggested that a more advanced jet fighter be developed.*

Republic P-47D *Thunderbolt* and a Lockheed P-38J *Lightning*.

Unfortunately for the three first-generation jets, their performance against their considerably older, reciprocating engine-powered stablemates was abysmally poor. In mock air combat, the P-47 and P-38 proved faster in level flight, capable of higher maximum altitudes, faster in a dive, and with a higher rate of climb. In only one part of the envelope did the P-59s prove only marginally superior...and that was in turn radius.

The Army Air Forces Board overseeing this fly-off later reported:

"After careful analysis of all tests conducted by the Material Command Service Test Agency, the Proving Ground Command, and the Army Air Forces Board, it is not believed that the P-59 airplane is operationally or tactically suited for combat nor is it believed that any modifications to this aircraft, short of a completely new design, would improve its combat suitability..."

It concluded by noting:

"...although the aircraft is not suitable for combat, there is a requirement for a limited number of subject airplanes to be utilized for jet training and for general Air Force familiarization. The Army Air Forces Board is further of the opinion that use of jet propelled aircraft will become widespread in the immediate future and that the P-59, although unsatisfactory for tactical use, is an excellent aircraft for purposes of conducting research on jet power plants and pressure cabins. The P-59 will also make an excellent training ship in that its low wing-loading makes the airplane very safe for transition flying and the fact that it has two engines is an added safety factor. "

Some three weeks after the Muroc evaluations, Gen. Arnold made it official; the P-59A would not become the Air Force's first full-production jet fighter. Its poor performance when pitted against contemporary US combat aircraft did not justify operational deployment. More importantly, intelligence data describing the rapidly evolving German jet aircraft initiative was giving every indication a fleet of fighters with performance capabilities far in excess of those being realized by the Bell P-59 was hurriedly being created.

Consequently, it already had been concluded a newer, considerably more capable fighter was needed in order to maintain even simple parity with the new enemy jets. Bell's machine, even in lighter, redesigned form, could not possibly compete with what the Luftwaffe was about to field. What Gen. Arnold also knew, but few others had been privileged to know, was that Lockheed, some eight months earlier, had been given the go-ahead on a new jet fighter unquestionably capable of meeting the Luftwaffe threat head-on. While word of the P-59's demise began to spread, the new Lockheed fighter's flight test program was secretly gathering momentum at Muroc.

*At Muroc, the three prototype XP-59s were not initially assigned serial numbers--or any other form of identification--in order to maintain their secrecy. The aircraft were maintained on site by Bell personnel.*

*The second production Bell P-59A. This model differed somewhat from the prototypes and the pre-production series aircraft in having an extended ventral fin, a revised vertical fin, and other changes.*

13

*The XP-80 at Muroc Army Air Field immediately prior to its first flight on January 8, 1944. Rounded tips to increase aerodynamic efficiency were installed on the wings and tail surfaces after the aircraft's fifth flight.*

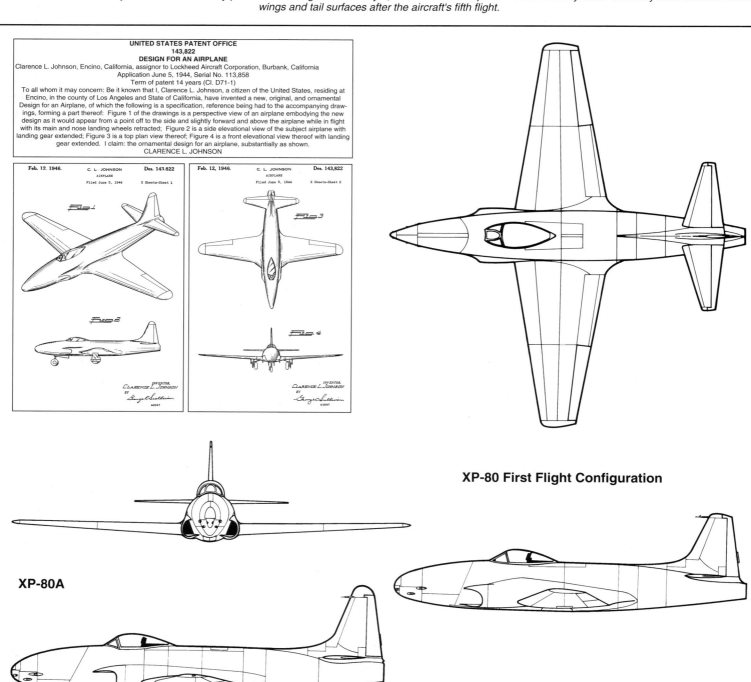

UNITED STATES PATENT OFFICE

143,822

DESIGN FOR AN AIRPLANE

Clarence L. Johnson, Encino, California, assignor to Lockheed Aircraft Corporation, Burbank, California

Application June 5, 1944, Serial No. 113,858

Term of patent 14 years (Cl. D71-1)

To all whom it may concern: Be it known that I, Clarence L. Johnson, a citizen of the United States, residing at Encino, in the county of Los Angeles and State of California, have invented a new, original, and ornamental Design for an Airplane, of which the following is a specification, reference being had to the accompanying drawings, forming a part thereof: Figure 1 of the drawings is a perspective view of an airplane embodying the new design as it would appear from a point off to the side and slightly forward and above the airplane while in flight with its main and nose landing wheels retracted; Figure 2 is a side elevational view of the subject airplane with landing gear extended; Figure 3 is a top plan view thereof; Figure 4 is a front elevational view thereof with landing gear extended. I claim: the ornamental design for an airplane, substantially as shown.

CLARENCE L. JOHNSON

**XP-80 First Flight Configuration**

**XP-80A**

Drawn by Charles Fleming

## Chapter 3:

# BIRTH OF A LEGEND

*"To come in then with a proposal to our management that we go on into a jet aircraft program—that was a little hard! Mr. Gross said, 'Kelly, you've been bothering me now for seven years for an engineering experimental department. I don't think much will come of this, but take it on."*

**Clarence L. "Kelly" Johnson**

On May 17, 1943, the Army Air Force held a conference in Washington, D.C. attended by Gen. Frank Carroll, Col. Howard Bogart, Col. Marshall Roth, Col. Ralph Swofford (later replaced by Lt. Col. Jack Carter), and Capt. Ezra Kotcher all of the Air Technical Service Command, and Hall Hibbard and Nate Price of Lockheed Aircraft Corporation. During this meeting, Hibbard and Price were briefed on the status of jet propulsion development (primarily in Britain) and were invited to submit a fighter proposal around Maj. Frank Halford's deHavilland H.1B *Goblin* centrifugal flow turbojet engine (later, when licensed-built by Allis-Chalmers in the US, it would be officially designated J36).

At the time, the *Goblin* was considered the best and most powerful jet engine immediately available to the Allies, and the only powerplant capable of challenging what now was perceived as a rapidly growing German jet threat. Because of this, the highly sensitive drawings and specifications for the *Goblin*, first provided Bell Aircraft Corporation for their proposed XP-59B study, had been transferred upon Air Force directive to Lockheed...which received them on March 24, 1943.

Two months later, Hibbard and Price were queried during the May 17 meeting as to whether Lockheed might consider designing and building a jet fighter around the British powerplant. Due in part to the interest shown in jet propulsion by Hibbard, Johnson, and Price with their L-133/L-1000 studies during the preceding three years and their associated attempts to sell both to the Air Force (Lockheed Report No. 2571 entitled, "Design Features of the Lockheed L-133" dated February 24, 1942 had been circulated at Wright Field to no avail), it was a foregone conclusion that Lockheed's response would be favorable...and it was.

On the day of this decision, word was immediately relayed back to Burbank where Johnson quickly initiated a preliminary design effort. On June 15, Johnson and several associate engineers hand-carried the initial XP-80 proposal and two associated reports (No. 4199, "Preliminary Design Investigation" and No. 4211, "Manufacturers Brief Model Specification") to the Air Technical Service Command. This package then was reviewed by the ATSC and Air Force Headquarters in Washington, D.C. and on June 17, 1943, an official "go-ahead", approved by Gen. Oliver Echols, was issued through Gen. Carroll.

Action now was taken to process a letter contract for one prototype aircraft...which was issued as Authority for Purchase No. 329678 dated June 17, 1943. Along with it was Lockheed's original June 15, 1943 price quote for $524,920...which later would be modified to the reduced figure of $515,018 in consideration of a cost fixed fee compromise. Letter contract No. W535 ac-40680 was approved on June 24, 1943 and was followed by the formal contract

*The full-scale forward fuselage mock-up of the XP-80 was the only mock-up assembly scheduled or completed. It served primarily to permit the proper assessment of cockpit and nose compartment details.*

on October 16 for what the Air Force now referred to as Project MX-409.

On October 25, 1943, Authority for Purchase No. 361433 was initiated asking for a contract Supplementary Agreement with amendments as follows:

Item 1: One aircraft; estimated cost, $495,210

Item 2: One high-speed wind tunnel model; estimated cost, $21,205

Item 3: One 1/3-scale wind tunnel model; estimated cost, $30,470

Item 4: One free-spinning model; estimated cost, $3,531

Item 5: Flight tests; estimated cost, $69,404

Item 6: Engineering data; estimated costs included in Item 1

Total estimated cost, $619,820

Fixed fee of 4% on Items 1 and 5, $22,584

Total cost, $642,404

Delivery dates, as a result of these amended costs, also were modified somewhat and included the decidedly early completion of the aircraft itself on November 11, 1943. Notably, because of the expedited design, manufacture, and flight test of the aircraft, the Authority for Purchase eventually became Supplementary Agreement No. 1 to the contract.

At Lockheed, the new L-140 project, started in the middle of an incredibly intense production program that was geared to meet the massive generic needs of a burgeoning world war, received only minimal corporate attention. Robert Gross, then company president, and Hall Hibbard, chief engineer, assigned the pro-

*XP-80 forward fuselage had progressed rapidly following initiation of construction. This was what it looked like on September 4, 1943. Exposed intake tunnel is noteworthy.*

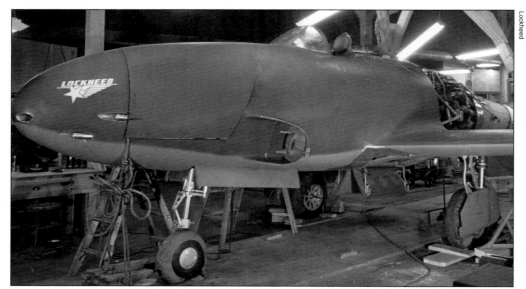

*XP-80 nears final assembly on November 13, 1943. Engine has been installed and the aircraft has been painted. Protective canvas wheel covers are noteworthy.*

ject to Johnson because of his strong interest in jet propulsion, his established organizational skills, and because he was the most competent of the many young engineers on the company's expansive staff.

Johnson, in his autobiography, noted the *Skunk Works'* beginning as follows:

"For some time I had been pestering Gross and Hibbard to let me set up an experimental department where the designers and shop artisans could work together closely in the development of airplanes without the delays and complications of intermediate departments to handle administration, purchasing, and all the other support functions. I wanted a direct relationship between design engineer and mechanic and manufacturing. I decided to handle this new project just that way."

On June 18, the first entry in the XP-80 log noted that "Reports Number 4199 & Number 4211 given to Art Viereck and Don Palmer for study". Concurrently, things remained hectic on the bureaucratic side. Johnson had been burdened with the creation of the entire operation, inclusive of hiring personnel, overseeing engineering, and reviewing construction. By Monday, June 21, the organization chart had been initiated. The day's log entry also included the following:

1. 150 days to flight date starting June 23.

Can't take "no" for an answer.
2. Engine will be here about July 15.
3. Separate purchasing set-up.
4. About 20 engineers.
5. About 80 shop men.

6. Secrecy of paramount importance.
7. 10 hours a day 6 days a week—no Sundays.
8. Shop layout discussed.
9. Engineering personnel discussed, list from Walt Jones.

On June 19, the principles upon which the XP-80 project would be operated were set down by Don Palmer. In time, these would be embodied in the 14 basic operating rules of the *Skunk Works* that "Kelly" Johnson drew up a decade later, during the early 1950s:

**(1)** Centralization of authority and responsibility.

(a) Project engineer is fully responsible for all decisions subject only to next higher authority. This includes design, materials, strength, weight, production design, costs, procurement of materials.

**(2)** Everything possible will be done to save time in accomplishing the ultimate results.

(a) Project engineer will devise ways and means as required to avoid delays. These ways and means will be implemented by management without decentralization of control or authority.

**(3)** After decisions have been made, there will be no changes without the consent of higher authority than the Project engineer.

**(4)** Information will be passed on to the

## XP-80 EXPERIMENTAL GROUP

**H.L. HIBBARD**
*Vice President*
*Chief Engineer*

**C.L. JOHNSON**
*Chief Research*
*Engineer*

**W. BEMAN**
*Aero and Wind Tunnel*
*Division Engineer*

**E.D. PALMER**
*Special Projects*
*Engineer*

**A.M. VIERECK**
*Managing Engineer*
*Experimental Dept.*

**R. THOREN**
*Flight Test*
*Division Engineer*

**W.P. RALSTON**
*Assistant*

**L.F. HOLT**
*Assistant*

*23 Engineers*
*and Draftsmen*

*105 Shop*
*Mechanics*

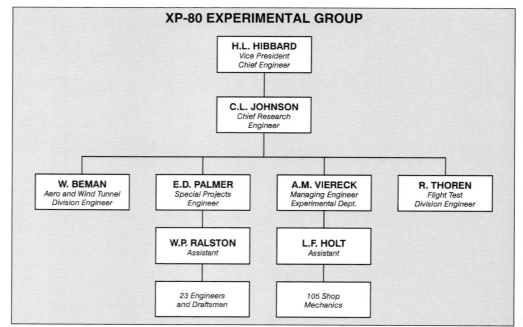

*A deHavilland Halford H.1B turbojet is off-loaded at the* Skunk Works *for XP-80 installation.*

*XP-80 cockpit instrumentation was conventional, even by jet fighter standards. Shown is the instrument panel and a gunsight installed in the full-scale XP-80 mock-up.*

*The XP-80 undergoing static engine runs at Muroc on January 5, 1944...some three days before its first flight. Installed thrust was measured using a simple, but accurate scale attached to the aircraft by a pulley and cable system.*

shop in the most direct and simplest manner. Advance information will be released at the earliest possible time for material procurement, tooling and shop make-ready.

(a) Layouts on paper or metal will be used extensively.

(b) Sketches shall be used wherever possible

(c) The airplane shall serve as the basic mock-up and parts may be designed on the spot and made to fit.

(d) A wood mock-up of the section forward of the pilot's seat and above the main landing gear will be required.

(5) A purchasing set-up working directly for the project and no other shall be made. This set up shall cooperate with the established purchasing department but shall be allowed to operate without the red-tape and policy encumbrances thereof. Keynote—get the stuff.

(6) A separate stock room shall be established and means shall be set up to get project materials into stock directly upon receipt.

(7) Receiving, fabrication, assembly, and final inspection shall be one group of men (one man).

(8) Special parts, materials, shapes, fastenings, shall be avoided wherever possible. Parts and materials from stock shall be used even at the expense of weight within reason. The chance of delay in delivery it too great.

(9) Records of all information going into the manufacture of the airplane are to be kept by the men who develop and transmit the information. This includes changes as necessitated by the fabrication and assembly of the parts.

(a) Prints of layouts and design aid templates shall be retained and kept up to date on the spot. Only the minimum number of prints will be made.

(b) Sketches shall have either carbon copies or prints made of them, same for all written information and instructions.

(c) Parts made to fit the ship shall be duplicated except where no complications would result should another airplane have to be built.

(10) Each engineer on this project shall be designer, shop contact, parts chaser and mechanic as the occasion demands.

(a) Engineering shall always be within a stone's throw of the airplane.

(b) There shall be but one object—to get a

good airplane built on time.

(c) Any cause for delay shall immediately be reported to C. L. Johnson in writing by the person anticipating the delay.

Engineering under Johnson's direction embarked rapidly on the basic necessities for designing and manufacturing the experimental jet fighter. Underscoring the objectives of simplicity and efficiency, the L-140 "Drawing Room Manual" stated that "Any type of drawing may be used provided it contains sufficient information to build the part or assembly. No 'system' of any kind is required other than clearness. Conventions should be used to represent such items as bolts, fasteners, etc. Freehand work is encouraged but important parts should be drawn to scale. Explanatory notes should be used wherever they will add to the clearness or reduce drafting time."

On June 22, the log included the fact that "Johnson, Viereck, 'E.O.' Richter, Jim Lidd and Palmer met and settled arrangements to be made at the W/T (wind tunnel). Space to be 28 x 40 at head of stairs to accommodate engineers. Will be ready tomorrow a.m. Walter Jones & Palmer rounded up powerplant engineers to get the picked men. Henry Rempt will not be available until July 4 but this is considered OK. He has to go to Dayton on the XP-49. Wally Bison was picked for materials man. We still need a hydraulics man. The business manager is to be Fred Kerr. At 4:00 p.m. CLJ addressed assembled engineers, outlined airplane and program. The men appeared to be 100% and 'rarin to go'. Arrangements have been made with J. Harrison to get the equipment over there for 7:00 a.m. tomorrow morning. Willis Hawkins, Viereck, Bill Ralston, and Palmer met in the evening to break down the airplane and discuss design and construction. A preliminary breakdown was made which will be expanded later as required. Hawkins read 'principles' as set down June 19 and concurred as have Johnson, Jones, Viereck, and 'Finn' Thrane."

The new facility took over space that had been assigned to wind tunnel model construction. This area became the new L-140 area machine shop. In order to get enough tools to execute the project, a local tool shop was literally bought out.

The following day, June 23, the log matter-of-factly noted:

"The 150 days starts today. Full crew of engineers reported except for Art Bradley

(hydraulics) who is on vacation until next Monday. Henry Rempt will spend 1-1/2 days here and then go to Dayton on the XP-49 until July 5. Work was assigned according to breakdown prepared last night. All mock-up items have first priority. Bob Holland will make up fuselage lines on vellum 1/4 size to be used immediately on mock up and preliminary design—this drawing will absorb changes if any and a set of 1/2 size lines on metal will be prepared for use full size in shop for blocks, etc. These lines will be reproduced on vellum full size for eng. layout use. Al York is working with Ed Posner on aerodynamic loads. Virgil Moss and Johnny Johnson are on balancing loads—Dave Hill on landing gear. Henry Danielson on wing contours, Irv Culver on fuselage. The boys started on 2 copies of specification and preliminary design report and were sketching etc. by 9:00 a.m. Palmer, Johnson, Hawkins went over airplane in 'Kelly's' office and noted 40 odd changes and notes. Later in the day, these were communicated to the men (about 1 p.m.). These notes were recorded in Design Notebook 1320. Viereck has succeeded in buying some wood-working tools which will be delivered tomorrow about noon. Larry Holt is to back Viereck up on night shift. The Engineering purchasing agent is to be appointed tomorrow at 2 p.m. We already have work for him, for instance— procure *Mustang* stick for mock-up. 'Kelly' has wired Col. Swofford for 6 guns and information on radio. GFE list to be prepared for 'Kelly' to phone in tomorrow at 8:00 a.m. Personnel is as follows: Palmer—project engineer;

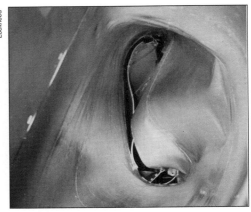

*An intake duct failure on November 18, 1943 caused a serious and unscheduled delay.*

*Lockheed logo was painted on both the vertical tail and the nose of the XP-80. It bore no serial number and had national insignia on the fuselage sides and the conventioinal wing positions.*

Ralston—assistant project engineer; York—stress; Hill—stress; Moss—stress; Johnson—stress; Irv Culver—fuselage; Dick Boehme—fuselage; Danielson—wing; Charlie Sowle—wing; Gordon Brown—cockpit & controls; Phil McLane—cockpit & controls; Joe Szep—empennage & aft fuselage; Joe Newcomer—empennage & aft fuselage; Wavey Stearman—powerplant; Hill—landing gear; Bradley—hydraulics; Rempt—electrical & radio; Holland—loft; Bison—materiel; Kerr—business management; Ed Fife—weight and balance (1/2 time). Phones 2639, 2994 and 2847 (Viereck) were installed about 4 p.m." Joining later would be Len Bohacek and Gerry Gossett. Eventually, twenty-three engineers and one-hundred-five shop personnel would make up the P-80 team.

For the next five months, work on what the Air Force now was officially referring to as the XP-80 was both intense and, for those who participated in its design and construction, fulfilling. The log covering this period is filled with insights into the highs and lows of an extraordinary event-in-the-making. On June 25, for instance, a footnote says,"We gain a day today because contract wasn't signed until yesterday. Got *Mustang* stick about 5 p.m." Another entry, dated June 28, giving some insight into the highly secretive nature of the project and its the physical plant environmental failings notes, "Windows were installed yesterday, much better." Still another, on June 29 states, "Culver and Dick Boehme squeezed every bit of tank possible into fuselage and got 151 gallons. This permits elimination of 2 outboard interspar tanks and cleans up the wing struc-

ture considerably!" This elation was offset the next day when it was noted, "We find today that preliminary design mistook imperial for US gallons. We await decision on whether outer interspar tanks go back in."

Putting extraordinary pressure on Johnson and his L-140/XP-80 team at Lockheed was the Air Force requirement the aircraft be completed in 180 days or less. Exacerbating this challenge was the fact that only a mock-up *Goblin* engine initially was made available. This relatively crude replica, arriving on July 10, was "safely stowed away in the mock-up room covered up with canvas. It had been taken off the Air Transport Command ship at Sacramento and was sent down by Army truck. Someplace along the line the top of the big box was lost and it wasn't covered until it arrived at Lockheed Air Terminal where personnel covered it up with paper."

On August 24, 1943, the British Air Commission in Washington, D.C. notified the Air Force (and Lockheed) that a real, albeit non-flyable *Goblin* was being shipped to California. Then, on September 21, Gen. Carroll was informed this engine had not been shipped as promised due to "a part change necessitated by overheating the engine during a test run". On October 1, an additional delay was reported due to a high tail pipe temperature that could not be accounted for by the British. Finally, on November 2, 1943, the long-promised non-flyable "installation engine" arrived.

Some four months earlier, on July 20, the official mock-up committee had convened at Lockheed to review the abbreviated XP-80

wood replica that had been built during the preceding four weeks. Basically consisting only of the forward fuselage section, it contained an accurate facsimile of the cockpit, framework for the windscreen, the nose and armament bay detail, wing root stubs, and other appropriate appurtenances. The committee met at 10 a.m. and stayed until 5:45 p.m. meeting again on each of the following two days. When it was all over, eighteen changes had been determined necessary, all "more or less minor".

The facility in which the XP-80 was being designed and built—and the one which would be looked back upon as the first home of the *Skunk Works*—was a temporary lean-to with a frame built from salvaged shipping crate wood. The roof was a canvas tent. Located near the wind tunnel at Plant B-1, it was unairconditioned, poorly lit, and extremely cramped. On one occasion, on July 26, the log noted, "No work started as yet to relieve heat in lean-to. Men are complaining (100° F.)." The following day the problem apparently was corrected as it was noted, "Engineering air cooler installed—makes it much more comfortable here."

By August 12, the aircraft was beginning to take shape, "Progress as of today is 68.7% complete engineering. The wing is still our toughest problem. Rib 40 is about done..." On the 16th it was noted that "Mr. Hibbard came in later to make sure the progress pictures were not faked!" And the next day, the entire XP-80 team was told that they could all attend the first flight of the aircraft if they could "get it done in 140 days!"

On August 24, a review of the aircraft's structural stress analysis was undertaken, and it was concluded that nothing unsatisfactory had been discovered. Everything that had surfaced as a problem had been "taken care of." On the same day, it was noted, "the stabilizer is started, wing still not skinned—fuselage about 1/2 skinned".

On August 31, a meeting in "Kelly's" office attended by Col. Bogart, Col. Swofford, Col. Don Keirn, and Palmer outlined future P-80 considerations from the standpoint of production aircraft. It was agreed that the basic armament configuration then assessed for the aircraft would not be changed until the Air Force determined the best weapon combination; the second P-80 would have extended range and be pressurized; and the third aircraft would have all its predecessors' features plus the forthcoming General Electric I-40 engine, high-lift flaps, an armament upgrade, increased wing area, 22-inch nose gear tire, increased tail surface area, higher gross weight, "further cleanup for production", and wing tip fittings for drop tanks or bombs. These issues were further defined on September 11 when a policy decision concerning the two proposed follow-on aircraft was made. On the same day, the XP-80's stabilizer was completed and the aft fuselage section and jig were moved out of the way for initiation of wing mating. That night, the 80th day, the wing was put in position under the aircraft during the night shift and the mating process was initiated.

It should be mentioned here that illness proved a personnel difficulty of considerable impact during the course of the extremely labor intensive XP-80 venture. With skilled personnel in extremely short supply, even minor ailments such as head colds and flu were sicknesses that had considerable impact on the aircraft's production schedule. On September 14, it was noted in the XP-80 log that three men were sick and that in total, some 20 man

*A month before its first flight, the painted and polished XP-80 sits on the dry lake bed at Muroc Army Air Field northeast of Los Angeles. Upper surface was dark blue green and lower was medium gray.*

*XP-80 was a very clean design with relatively low frontal area. Quality of Skunk Works workmanship only enhanced the impression of refined aerodynamics. In truth, typical of a Skunk Works product, the XP-80 was a relatively simple and highly practical aircraft.*

days had been lost to illness to date.

By October 7, the remaining engineering work on the XP-80 consisted of five small items and significant miscellaneous contact work with the shop. Included were the service manual and stress reports. "Plumbing is being done mostly by direct contact. Record pictures will be taken. Wing tanks being fitted. Ailerons being fitted. Flap (one side) was operated today. Fillets on wing are coming along well. Canopy is assembled and will be ready for final fitting in a few days. No word on shipment of powerplant yet. Field equipment is progressing OK. Nose landing gear is being put together, probably hang tomorrow. We will use 19-inch aircraft tire as vendor disappointed us on 16-inch low pressure wheel. Guns have been dunked in cosmoline so we won't have to disturb them until firing tests. CLJ gave permission to short some of the armament compartment work in favor of jobs effecting flight date. There are 133 jobs to go and 25 days—should average six a day and eight would be better at this stage. Watching this very closely."

The lack of engine availability remained a serious, if not overwhelming concern. On October 11 it was noted in the log, "No word on engine as yet. CLJ to contact Ralph Swofford tomorrow. There are twenty-six jobs dependent on the arrival of the engine. Only four of these can be worked with the mock-up. The engine is definitely delaying us from here on in."

As it turned out, the availability of the much-needed *Goblin* engine remained unknown and talk turned to using a considerably less powerful and decidedly out-of-date General Electric I-16 (on April 10, 1945, a joint Army-Navy conference officially renamed this engine J31) for initial flight trials. This option, promoted by the Air Force, was never seriously considered by Lockheed, but the ninth *Goblin*, originally intended as the first flight worthy engine for the XP-80, was damaged during testing and now was scheduled to be replaced by the tenth which was scheduled for shipment on October 22.

Finally, on October 25, word was received "the engine is all inspected and boxed and on the dock waiting for an airplane which is promised for October 29th weather permitting. This ship will come clear thru to California. There will be further discussion as to whether we deliver ship to Muroc with or without engine. There will be a mechanic furnished with the engine."

Arrival of a non-flyable engine in no less than five separate crates on the afternoon of November 3 finally cleared the way for completion of the aircraft. Minor difficulties arose with the Lockheed-built engine mount and the tachometer shaft, but these were quickly rectified over a period of ten days while the aircraft was primed and painted. Finally, on November 13th, the XP-80 was disassembled and moved outside from its weather-worn lean-to for the first time. A crane loaded it aboard a flat bed truck for the seventy-mile trip northeast to Muroc and a day later it was off-loaded using a ramp. Reassembly was initiated immediately and on November 17, the *Goblin* engine was powered-up for the first time.

The engine lit on the first try. Measurements were taken to determine installed thrust and no major difficulties were encountered (the *Goblin*, only a pre-production prototype powerplant, had a static thrust rating of 3,000 pounds at 10,500 rpm; as installed in the XP-80, this thrust dropped to 2,460 pounds at 9,500 rpm).

No further runs were undertaken on the 17th, but on the 18th, the engine again was statically tested with the aircraft in a "tied down" position. Unfortunately, on this second run, at about 8,800 rpm, the intake ducts, stressed to withstand 4 pounds per square inch pressure, collapsed "sucking cleco's and other stuff into the engine and damaging the leading edge of the impeller". Upon initial examination, the duct damage, attributed to faulty load distribution, did not seem severe. The failure was quickly evaluated and a solution developed in the form of a 12 psi duct, and a cursory examination of the engine indicated that only minor rotor damage had occurred.

Three days later, however, the night shift, examining the engine in greater detail, discovered a 3-1/2 inch crack in the impeller—which was determined to be material failure, and not the result of the duct incident. This was a serious defect; the engine could not be operated safely. Suddenly, the still unflown XP-80 was without propulsion; there was no spare engine and attempts to acquired a new engine or replacement parts initially proved fruitless. On November 27, a deHavilland representative informed Lockheed that a new engine would be shipped on December 11 and would arrive on December 15. The damaged engine was, in turn, to be shipped back to England for repairs.

Frustratingly, on December 9, word was received via Maj. Terhune that the number eleven *Goblin* engine had disintegrated during a static test. Accordingly, delivery of a replacement engine to Lockheed would be delayed

*January 8, 1944...the first flight day. To the right, walking in the long coat and stocking cap, is "Kelly" Johnson. Visible on the hill are most of the Skunk Works personnel who worked on the XP-80.*

Static testing of the deHavilland-built Halford engine following installation in the XP-80 was conducted inside a hangar at Muroc in consideration of security and the bitter cold desert winter.

until December 22. On December 11, the team at Muroc packed their engineless aircraft and all associated equipment and moved to Hangar 20B. By the 14th, they were again "organized and going".

While the team waited for the new engine, miscellaneous checks were run on the airframe and work continued on minor subassemblies and pre-design for the second and third aircraft, which now were beginning to take shape around a new General Electric engine called the I-40 (on April 10, 1945, a joint Army-Navy conference formally renamed this engine the J33).

On December 28, a wire to Johnson arrived indicating the new *Goblin* engine would be delivered to Muroc that afternoon at 5:30 p.m. The following day, the engine was uncrated and prepared for installation by Guy Bristow (of de Havilland), Bradley, Harold Benson, and Palmer. Two days later, it was statically tested for the first time, reaching 5,000 rpm. The log entry for December 30 noted that the "generator is out, the throttle is out of rig, but all else is OK." On New Year's Eve, 1943, the engine was run to maximum thrust at 9,600 rpm without problems. The generator had been repaired and everything was in place for initiation of taxi tests.

Having taken a day off for New Year's, no additional work was completed until January 2, 1944. The log entry for that day states, "Gang went back to lake to put on tail and complete

drains, etc. Tail will now stay on. Tentative schedule is taxi January 3, inspect January 4, fly (if lake is dried out) maybe January 5." On the same day, Johnson also quietly cleared the way for full-scale engineering for the L-141 (XP-80A)...except for its wing. This was good news for the *Skunk Works* team, as they had begun to run out of things to do. Culver, York, Sowle, and Bojens were assigned to the project between what remained of their L-140 duties.

These improved aircraft, officially referred to by Lockheed as L-141s and by the Air Force as the XP-80As, as their design evolved, began to differ markedly from their predecessor. They had a fuselage of greater length, twenty-five percent greater design weight, new intake ducts, a new engine installation, improved landing gear, and numerous other major and minor changes. New design features included a detachable fuselage-tail assembly; a quick-change engine installation; control surface hydraulic boosters; combined cockpit pressurization and cooling; wing-tip fuel tank and bomb carrying capability; fuselage dive brakes; an automatic fuel transfer system; short-chord control surfaces; precision contour control and special finish; a high acceleration type armament installation; jet engine water injection system; internal radio antennas; and an automatic emergency fuel system. In effect, they were new aircraft emulating the XP-80 in basic configuration only.

The pilot chosen to fly the XP-80—by now bearing the mutually agreed to, but unofficial nickname *Lulu-Belle*...also from an Al Capp character—during its first flight, was noted Lockheed chief test pilot Milo Burcham. A veteran of many hours test flying and time at the controls of a wide variety of combat aircraft types, he was an ideal choice for the risky business of getting the new jet into the air safely for the first time. Taxi tests were successfully completed on January 3 on the strip in front of the Muroc hangars. The only concern was a tendency for the aircraft to "go back on its tail".

On January 6, Johnson proposed the following Saturday, January 8, as the first flight date. Problems with the dry lake bed being partially flooded dictated moving flight operations to the north end of Muroc and it was there that *Skunk Works* personnel would be brought from Burbank in order to observe the first flight from a near-by embankment. That afternoon, Milo shot touch and goes in a P-38 on the north end of the lake to confirm its suitability.

The log entry for January 8, 1944 would go down as one of the most important in Lockheed's already stellar history:

"January 8, 1944 Flight date!! 3 bus loads (about 140) of L-140 men left plant 5 at 5:30 a.m. and arrived at Muroc at 8:00 a.m. Lt. Weist got us all to the north ridge by 8:30 a.m. where a fine view of the flight could be had. Others present were Mr. Robert E. Gross, Cyril Chappellet, Charlie Barker, K. Smith, Cols. Bogart and Marcus Cooper and others. Col. Bogart spoke to the men on the fine job they had done etc. His talk was enthusiastically received. The ship had been brought to the north side the night before and all was ready at 8:30 a.m. when a run up was made. The ship was fueled and Milo took off at 9:10 a.m., circling once and landing 6 minutes later. Ailerons very sensitive (15-1 ratio) and landing gear wouldn't retract. Scissors switch was out of adjustment. After a fix was made, he took off again for a 20 minute flight, climbed, stalled, rolled, zoomed, buzzed the field to everyone's delight—positively fastest ship we've seen, rolls about 360° per second. A marvelous performance. Landed with partial flaps. Something wrong with flap actuator. 'Absolutely a new sensation in flying'. Maneuverability terrific. Milo had hit speeds in excess of any P-38 dive he had ever made! Cockpit is quiet, no nibble no buffet. Everyone greatly impressed and enthusiastic about the whole thing. The men 'went wild' and repeat-

A flight test photo panel was installed in the ammunition compartment. Instrument readings were recorded by a 35 mm camera during flight.

Six .50 caliber machine guns were installed at all times. The photo panel was removed in order to load ammunition containers for gun firing tests.

edly expressed their gratitude for being able to see the first flight. Had sandwiches and beer in Mint Canyon on the way home and "Kelly" & Milo made short talks on how the airplane flew and answered questions. All in all, everything went off fine and it was indeed a great day and will be long remembered by all those who were fortunate enough to be present. (Airplane put in hangar until Monday, January 10, 1946)."

Burcham would later describe the historic first flight in his postflight report:

"During the descent, I worked the speeds up slowly. The airplane felt good. I reached a maximum of 490 indicated airspeed and everything felt good. The cockpit ws quiet and there were no shrieks from the canopy. Visibility is good. Maneuverability seemed normal as far as I investigated. I noticed some effect on rudder forces, as I had to hold light left or right rudder, depending on the speed. I made a low pass across the field with full power, 9,500 rpm, and reached 475 indicated airspeed. After pulling up I made a series of rolls, in both directions. The airplane rolls extremely well, and has a very fast rate of roll."

By January 15, Burcham had conducted five flights on the XP-80 for a total of 1.67 hours of flight time. The primary objective of these flights was to obtain preliminary impressions of the XP-80's flying characteristics as well as information regarding its climb and level flight performance capabilities. A significant amount of flight time also was devoted to evaluating the aircraft's stall characteristics and high-speed performance.

By this time, the XP-80 had reached speeds of nearly 500 mph and was judged by Burcham to be a generally stable aircraft at these flight conditions. This high-speed capability was much greater than that of any reciprocating engine fighter in any service in the world at the time. At low speeds, however, the aircraft had rather unpleasant stall characteristics; with the flaps down, the pilot had very little warning of an impending stall, and the aircraft invariably rolled sharply to the right once stalled. This unsatisfactory characteristic was soon corrected by the addition of wing fillets which had been developed during wind tunnel tests.

Other less serious problems at this time included high longitudinal stick forces, overly sensitive lateral control, an unsatisfactory fuel management system and poor engine reliability and performance.

On the 17th, Johnson ordered the ship "laid up" for seven to ten days to accomplish changes that early flight testing had mandated as necessary. These included addition of the afore-mentioned leading edge fillets: rounded tips were installed on wings and tail surfaces; stabilizer incidence was changed by raising leading edge by 1-1/2°; elevator tab made servo (1° tab for 2° elevator); fuel system was completely revised with transfer pumps, no selector valve, small fuel filter, no bulge tank, and automatic switching device in fuselage tank; engine burner nozzles were balanced for more even jet temperatures; aileron booster valve centering spring was removed, and control valve flow characteristics were altered...15:1 boost ratio.

By February 7, all of these modifications had been completed, and on February 10, the XP-80 was airborne again on its sixth flight with Burcham at the controls, primarily to evaluate the aircraft's stall characteristics with the new leading-edge wing fillets installed; they did eliminate the tendency to roll to the right as

*Nicknamed* Lulu Belle, *the XP-80 spent much of its early flight test career at Muroc Army Air Field being flown by Air Force, Navy, and other service pilots.*

had been observed during previous stall tests.

On February 12, the first Army familiarization flight (the XP-80's eighth flight) was flown with a Capt. W. A. Lien at the controls. This was the beginning of a joint test program involving Army and Lockheed personnel to accurately estab lish level flight speed performance of the XP-80, and to determine the more important aspects of its flying characteristics. Unfortunately, the engine installed at the time time was restricted to less than 75% (9,500 rpm) of the design thrust rating. In spite of this, the XP-80 earned the distinction of being the first jet aircraft in America to exceed a level flight speed in excess of 500 mph. The highest speed measured during this series of flights was 506 mph at an altitude of 20,000 feet. By March 29, a total of 19.6 hours of flying time had been logged during 28 flights.

Gun firing tests were conducted during the first part of April. Ground firing tests consisted of firing 2,200 rounds from each of the six nose guns. During these tests the ejection compartment filled with empty cases and links, due to the fact the ejection doors were too small, and the guns stopped firing when the ejection chutes became filled. Gun adjustments were also very difficult to make due to close quarters in the gun bay.

Aerial firing tests were conducted during the next four XP-80 flights and consisted of firing approixmately 1,200 rounds per gun during level flight, pushovers, pullouts, climbs and dives, and banks and turns. The ejection doors were enlarged before these tests were started, and no stoppages were encountered during the exercise. Most importantly, the guns continued to fire throughout the range of

normal accelerations from a positive 7.5 gs down to a negative value of 1.5 gs. The joint program was concluded on April 13, and by this time 32 flights had been flown on the XP-80 for a total of 22.6 hours of flying time.

During early 1944, the British Air Commission completed additonal tests on the *Goblin* engine and decided to release a revised and improved version cleared for operation at 9,800 rpm. A new H-1 engine was shipped to Lockheed for installation; it arrived at Muroc during late April and was cleared for flight on May 26. Additional flight tests were undertaken with it shorlty afterwards, but due to excessively high tail pipe temperatures, no stabilized runs were possible.

On May 31, the new H-1 engine was restricted to operation at a reduced thrust rating because of reported explosions of the type in Great Britain. This restriction proved relatively short lived but only the original 9,500 rpm rating was reinstated within days of the restriction. Regardless, high tail pipe temperatures continued to plague the aircraft.

The only major engine failure occurred during a ground run after flight 9 on February 14. Excessive heat was noted on the aft fuselage and later inspection of the engine showed that two stator blades had been completely burned away. Inspection of the burner in front of these two blades revealed that the burner orifice had loosened and turned sideways, allowing a large excess flow of fuel to that burner can. A locking device was designed and installed in all burner nozzles, and no more trouble was experienced from this cause.

XP-80 spin tunnel model tests were initiated January 21, 1944, at the NACA's Langley

*Late in its career the XP-80 was used as an introductory trainer for neophyte jet fighter pilots. The rapid delivery of large numbers of jet fighters--and their complementary trainers--eventually led to its retirement.*

XP-80 at the beginning of its restoration process at the Smithsonian Institution's National Air & Space Museum's Paul E. Garber facility at Silver Hill, Maryland.

Field facility. At no time did this model attain a steady spin condition. After losing its intial launching momentum the model oscillated violently in roll and pitch. Some five months later, on June 24, Lockheed test pilot Tony LeVier was tasked with performing the actual XP-80 spin tests. Not surprisingly, these duplciated the earlier spin tunnel test results...almost exactly. Spins were very violent with large amplitude oscillations and high rotation speeds. LeVier noted the "airplane had a violent whipping action accompanied by flopping over on its back and righting again, thus, nothing approaching a steady spin was encountered." A total of 26 spins were undertaken; fifteen right and eleven left.

Following the spin program, the XP-80 was relegated to exhibition, training, and miscellaneous minor test work. From August 8 through August 18, 1944, following the delivery of the two XP-80As and, later, the YP-80A, the XP-80 was transferred from Lockheed to the 412th Fighter Group for use in tactical evaluations of the jet fighter in simulated combat. Activated just under a year earlier, on November 29, 1943, the 412th consisted of experienced combat pilots whose mission was to conduct tests and provide a detailed evaluation of the Bell P-59 and the Lockheed P-80. Later, they were tasked with training pilots to fly the new jet fighters. Composed of the 29th, 31st, and 445th Fighter Squadrons, the 412th was assigned at various times to Muroc, Palmdale, Bakersfield, Santa Maria, and March Field before being inactivated on July 3, 1946.

During May of 1945, after serving with the 412th, and following another short tenure at Muroc to allow time to repair a severe fuel leak, the XP-80 was ordered transferred again, this time to the Army Air Force Training Command at Chanute Field, Illinois. This order was rescinded shortly afterward, primarily because it was realized by the Air Force the aircraft was the only P-80 that could accommodate the still viable *Goblin* jet engine. Work as a *Goblin* testbed kept the aircraft on duty—though not in service—at Muroc until June 10,

1946...the termination date of its military tenure.

In truth, the aircraft had been little utilized during its last nine months at Muroc Army Air Field. The high tail pipe temperature problems had prevented any worthwhile research using the aircraft. And its usefulness had been superseded by newer aircraft with newer and more powerful engines. Accordingly, on November 8, 1946, the XP-80 was delivered to the Museum Storage Depot at Park Ridge, Illinois. An Army Air Force form at the time noted, "Change from experimental to obsolete and remove from the book."

On May 1, 1949, the Smithsonian Institution's National Air Museum (as today's National Air & Space Museum then was called) took custody of the Park Ridge depot, which then contained some 115 aircraft and over 160,000 miscellaneous items. During the early 1950s, all aircraft in this collection, including the XP-80, eventually were disassembled, crated, and shipped to the Museum's storage and restoration facility at Silver Hill, Maryland. From then until late 1976, it remained in long-term storage, initially outdoors, then later in one of the several large Silver Hill (now called the Paul E. Garber Preservation and Restoration Facility) storage buildings.

During 1976 it was decided to restore the XP-80 for museum display purposes. This effort, typical of those methodically undertaken by the NASM, was not a simple refurbishment, but rather a complete and highly detailed renovation of the airframe and its propulsion and miscellaneous subsystems to their original configuration at a given point in the aircraft's operational career.

The XP-80 was completely disassembled by NASM personnel and all parts were reconditioned or replaced as necessary using original materials and techniques wherever possible. The Allis-Chalmers-manufactured license-built copy of the original deHavilland "*Goblin*" engine also was refurbished, though to a lesser extent. Its general configuration had been found to be quite good and little work was

required to make it display-worthy.

External markings were meticulously researched in light of the long period of time the XP-80 had been in relatively unprotected storage. Virtually all of the original paint had deteriorated and gone through a color shift, and as a result, visual review of the extant colors failed to provide accurate color references. Eventually, however, it was concluded the aircraft had utilized lusterless Federal Standard (F.S.) 595A 34092 green on its upper surfaces and F.S. 595A 36440 gray on its lower. The green upper surface color was highly unorthodox. Because of the green color, the aircraft was sometimes jokingly referred to as the *Green Hornet*.

Restoration of the XP-80, the *Skunk Works*' first aircraft, was completed during May of 1978. Just short of 4,850 man-hours were required to bring it up to NASM display standards.

---

### The *Gray Ghost* and the *Silver Ghost*:

*"In three hours, General Frank Carroll and his advisors gave us a letter of intent to go do two things: to build a turbojet engine; and to build a prototype of a fighter."* Clarence L. "Kelly" Johnson

As noted earlier in this chapter, once design work on the XP-80 had progressed to the point of near-completion, follow-on work was solicited and obtained by Lockheed (via Johnson) in the form of a contract to build two pre-production series XP-80A aircraft. These initially were referred to in-house at Lockheed as L-140s, but by December of 1943 were identified as L-141s. These machines, though superficially resembling their predecessor, were in fact totally new airframes with only moderate XP-80 commonality.

Work on follow-on P-80 aircraft had been initiated as early as August of 1943, when on the 31st of that month, a meeting in "Kelly's" office with Cols. Bogart, Swofford, Keirn, and Don Palmer had confirmed the Air Force's interest. During the meeting it also was agreed the new aircraft would be pressurized and have improved range. Perhaps most importantly, they would be powered by the 4,000 pound thrust General Electric I-40 jet engine...which later would be officially designated J33.

The Air Force had become concerned about the availability of the *Goblin* engine as deHavilland had not been able to keep up with initial orders, even as early as 1944. Accordingly, though the I-40 was somewhat larger and heavier than its British stablemate, it was picked as the new fighter's powerplant based on General Electric's promise it could have the new engine in full production by the time Lockheed needed it.

The increased size of the I-40 dictated major changes in the basic XP-80 configuration. The fuselage length grew from 32 feet 10 inches to 34 feet 6 inches and wingspan increased from 37 feet to 38 feet 10-1/2 inches (though the span was greater, a narrower chord resulted in slightly less total wing area). The landing gear were made considerably stronger to accommodate the weight increase from 8,916 pounds to 13,780 pounds (which was due in part to an increase in internal fuel capacity from 285 to 485 gallons). Noticeably, a taller vertical tail surface was added to maintain required directional stability. Other changes included a detachable fuselage/tail assembly to permit easy engine access and

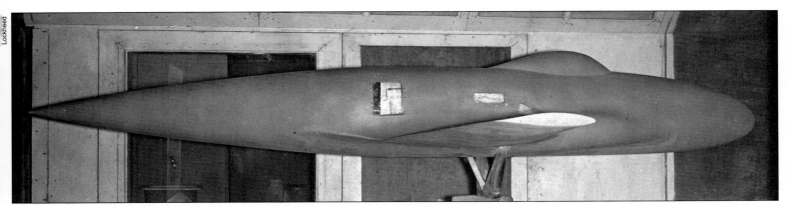

*The XP-80A wind tunnel model illustrates the major differences between this definitive configuration and that of the XP-80. The stretched and aerodynamically refined fuselage of the former permitted the introduction of the considerably more powerful General Electric I-40 turbojet engine.*

quick-change capability; control surface hydraulic booster units; combined cockpit pressurization and cooling; the ability to carry either drop tanks (165 gallon) or bombs on the wing tips; fuselage dive brakes; an automatic fuel transfer system; short-chord control surfaces; precision contour control and special surface finish; a high acceleration-type armament system (the quantity of ammunition carried was increased from 200 to 300 rounds per gun); a jet engine water injection system; internal radio antennas; and an automatic emergency fuel system.

On January 2, 1944, six days prior to the first flight of the XP-80, full-scale engineering on the L-141s was initiated by Johnson. On January 12, Johnson mentioned to the small engineering team that the Air Force had expressed interest in a series of YP-80As after the two L-141s (officially designated XP-80As by the Air Force) were completed.

On January 13, it was noted that the L-141 design was "shaping up." Numerous questions remained to be settled, however, including whether the wing should be redesigned and/or whether the engine could be moved to offset changes in center of gravity resulting from fuselage growth. Finally, during a January 21 meeting in "Kelly's" office, Jones, Viereck, Ralston, and Palmer were told to go ahead with "two L-141s and eight YP-80s plus 1 static test article".

Importantly, this meeting signaled the beginning of the end for the original *Skunk Works* team, as it also was noted that "Bill Ralston is to head up a project group of about 5 picked men to separate from the parent project in 2 months. This will be under the Jones organizational tree and will be responsible for the 9 YP-80 airplanes. *This plan of splitting off pieces of the Engineering Experimental project as required and replenishing as necessary is established as the standard course of events*

*where a model is to go into production."*

Thus a precedent was set that would be followed for the next ten years; a small core of hand picked engineers and builders would be utilized to design and hand craft prototypes outside the bounds of the normal company bureaucracy, and if and when a follow-on pre-production or production contract ensued, a spin-off group would be shed from the original prototype team to carry the aircraft into and through production. New recruits from the main Lockheed operation, concurrently, would be drafted to fill in gaps whenever and wherever necessary in the elite prototype team. Philosophically, this would keep a constant flow of "fresh blood" moving through the *Skunk Works*, and thus provide ever changing perspective and intellectual growth on behalf of the design and engineering team.

Like the XP-80 before, the Air Force had asked for and received from Johnson a commitment to complete the two XP-80As in a fixed number of days. Because of the modest lead-time that already had been gained through the manufacture of miscellaneous sub-assemblies and pre-contract engineering, it now was possible for Johnson to promise two aircraft in no less than 120 days.

On January 24, 1944, the log noted it was day number one on the L-141. "Meeting in Hibbard's office with CLJ, Mort Bach, Dick Maurer, Vierreck, Ralston, Palmer to get off to a good start on this combined program of 13 YP-80s and 2 L-141s. Ralston will keep log book on YP-80. Having trouble getting men, need 5 for YP-80 and 4 for 141. This can cause delay if we don't get them within a few days." The next day, the amount of time allocated for construction was amended when it was noted, Johnson..."gave us five extra days (125 in all) on the L-141. These are to show on the shop calendar.'

On January 28, one of the more important

mechanical aspects of the XP-80A and all subsequent P-80 series aircraft was approved. "Culver's scheme for breaking tail away at engine trunnion station is OK by C. L. Johnson." This simplified a number of structural problems and saved about 75 pounds. On January 31 it was noted the L-141s were officially to be designated XP-80A by the Air Force. Additionally, the new I-40 engine scheduled for the two aircraft was run up to 75% rpm. After five hours running time, "it was torn down and everything was OK".

By March, construction of parts for the two pre-production aircraft was progressing with considerable speed. Engineering now was 54% complete and bulkheads were in place in the main fuselage jig. Engine exhaust pipe cooling problems discovered by General Electric had dictated increases in diameter and this adversely affected all *Skunk Works* engineering work that had taken place prior to the decision. This in turn forced a delay on the completion of the empennage, which put pressure on the entire team from the standpoint of being able to meet the delivery date. On March 16, the first skin was fitted to the fuselage of the first XP-80A.

On April 1, it was noted that engineering was 83.5% complete. The landing gear doors, lower fillet, hydraulics, and electrical systems represented most of the remaining work on the XP-80As. In the shop, the fuselage skinning was about 90% complete except for the empennage, which was only framed. The aft wing framing was about 50% complete and the stabilizers and fins were ready for installation.

On April 22, the wing and fuselage of the first XP-80A were mated. As noted in the log, there was "no trouble at all...final check shows tips differ by 1/8 inch fore and aft and by .14 inch vertically. Incidence is off by 8 minutes as near as we can measure." Four days later, Johnson sat in the mock-up and critiqued the

*The* Gray Ghost *in the paint bay at Lockheed's Burbank plant prior to delivery by truck to Muroc Army Air Field.*

*The* Gray Ghost *being loaded aboard a flat bed trailer for the nearly 90 mile trip to Muroc. Empennage was removed but carried on same trailer.*

*XP-80A (the Gray Ghost) caravan on its way to Muroc on June 11, 1944. Fuselage was carried perpendicular to trailer centerline in order to leave room for empennage and aft fuselage. Canvas covers protected the aircraft from prying eyes and any potential environmental catastrophies.*

instrumentation layout. The mock-up was to become a "permanent institution to be inherited by WPR and strictly kept up to date".

The following day, the first I-40 engine arrived and was immediately uncrated and installed in the aircraft. The installation went smoothly, but some distortion was noted in the mount assembly and corrective action was

*Like the XP-80, the XP-80A was statically tested in a tied down state while attached with cables and pulleys to a mechanical thrust measurement scale.*

taken to fix it.

On May 2, in an effort to keep things busy in the *Skunk Works*, Johnson arranged to have the P-38L *Pathfinder* program moved over from the main plant. Thirty-five days were allocated for prototype construction! This relatively little-known P-38 modification (referred to inside the *Skunk Works* as *Snooty*) involved

the installation of an AN/APS-15 radar in the aircraft nose gun bay and a dielectric fairing mounted in place of the standard metal nose cone. This "most secret" mod later led to the successful development of the P-38M night fighter.

By this time, the decision had been made to send the first YP-80A (technically, the fourth P-80 aircraft) to the NACA. This ship, though only beginning to enter the preliminary stages of construction during May of 1944, was to be equipped with a special "dive tail" designed to accommodate heavy dynamic loads. Drawings for this tail were sent to the Materiel Center and the tail itself was modified to incorporate pressure leads at Langley Field.

Finally, on June 3, 1944, the first XP-80A was virtually complete. Painted in light gray lacquer—which gave rise to its nickname of *Gray Ghost*—and missing only its insignia and final touch up, it was almost ready to fly. Caravan arrangements for transporting it from Burbank to Muroc were made, and a departure time of midnight was scheduled. In fact, the caravan did not leave Burbank until 3:20 a.m. the following morning. Interestingly, for the first time, the Air Force allowed publicity

*An unhelmeted Tony LeVier, Lockheed's chief test pilot, during an early test hop in the Gray Ghost. Quality of Skunk Works' team workmanship is readily apparent in superior finish. Visible in the background is Muroc Army Air Field's North Base facility.*

*The remains of the* Gray Ghost *following its loss to engine failure on March 20, 1945. Lockheed test pilot Tony LeVier escaped, though not without serious back injuries. The engine problem eventually was traced to a metallurgical anomaly in a turbine wheel.*

movies to be taken of the P-80's shipment...though the film could not be released without Air Force permission.

Six days after its arrival at Muroc, and 138 days after it had been officially started, the first XP-80A took to the air for the first time on June 10. Lockheed had picked its well-known P-38 test pilot, Tony LeVier, to make this initial flight.

He had been informed of this decision on May 30. Checked out over a period of several days in the XP-80, he had logged scant few hours of jet time by the advent of the XP-80A's first flight.

As stated in the log, "Flew today!! Wobbly takeoff down wind but toward lake. Thirty-five minutes later LeVier returned and landed on

lake with one flap down! Bless the boost! Thrust limited to 2,600 pounds. Airplane rolled in hangar to be analyzed Tuesday as everyone is dog tired. No. 1 (XP-80) with Jim White piloting put on a good show. Big crowd including both Gross's and Hibbard. Quite a few 'outsiders' from production, etc. Lt. Weist was somewhat upset by size of crowd and errors in

*The* Silver Ghost *was built from the start with an abbreviated back seat to accommodate a flight test engineer or observer.*

*The* Silver Ghost, *like the XP-80, was equipped with a flight test photo panel in the gun bay. As with the XP-80, a camera filmed the instrumentation.*

*The XP-80A structural test specimen. This was built by the Skunk Works to verify airframe integrity. Very little structural testing had been undertaken with the XP-80 due to the high-priority placed on its expedited construction and initiation of flight test.*

*The XP-80R was the highly modified XP-80B prototype. Major external changes included a redesigned canopy with reduced frontal area, high recovery intakes, sharp wing leading edges, and a virtually flawless finish. The improved second configuration is illustrated.*

list. Picnic was enjoyed by all."

As Tony recalled the flight, everyone was having a picnic but him, "Once airborne, I realized this aircraft was not only unstable in pitch, but the heat pouring into the cockpit was almost unbearable. I knew at that moment that I hadn't asked for enough of a bonus for that flight! When I reduced power at liftoff, the aircraft would hardly accelerate, and it took several minutes before I obtained 260 VI (velocity indicated) to commence my climb. Struggling to 10,000 feet over Muroc Dry Lake, I proceeded to run off the list of test items on my knee pad. As I started the flaps-down test, the plane began to roll upside down. Unable to correct the split-flap condition, I said, "Nuts to this. I'm getting down before I lose the whole can of worms! Using almost full right stick, I made a fast flat approach and landed on the dry lake bed safely. "

Obviously, the first flight had not been extraordinarily successful. Instability resulting from a too-far-aft center of gravity had surfaced within moments of LeVier's getting airborne, and hot air (325° F) had blown into the cockpit as a result of a faulty cockpit pressurization valve. The latter remained a problem for the next several flights and though partially corrected through modification of the existing system, it remained an on-going frustration until an improved pressurization/cooling system could be introduced.

Additionally, the I-40 engine still was a "green" powerplant. The fuel system was inadequate and undependable, there was a five hour limitation on the turbine, and 11,000 rpm could be utilized only for takeoff...with a further reduction to 10,500 rpm at liftoff. Fuel consumption was also astronomically high.

Other problems surfaced during subsequent flight testing, including a duct rumble that proved disquieting to the pilot...and to some observers on the ground. Considerable wind tunnel research was required to uncover the problem which eventually was traced to a stagnant air layer on the inside wall of each duct. The problem was eliminated by adding boundary layer bleed slots inside each intake. This solution also eliminated the "snaking" anomaly.

Another problem with considerably more serious implications was that of aileron "buzz". A high-speed problem that was found to occur at approximately 0.80 Mach, it increased in intensity relative to aircraft speed. Concerns were raised that such occurrences could potentially destroy the ailerons if sustained for even moderate periods of time.

Full-scale wind tunnel and flight test studies were conducted both by Lockheed and the NACA to identify the problem. It eventually was determined that compressibility was the culprit. Many solutions were studied and it quickly was discovered that increasing cable tension was an effective means of stopping the buzz.

Unfortunately, the *Gray Ghost* was to have a short flight test career. On March 20, 1945, its I-40 engine disintegrated in flight and the aircraft came apart. As its pilot, Tony LeVier, recalls, "It was...the most horrifying experience of my whole flying career. I was just leveling off from a dive to make a maximum speed test (560 mph) at 10,000 feet mean sea level to check duct redesign. My final check of all systems had been made, and I was cinching up my seat and shoulder harness another notch, when the aircraft suddenly started to shake and pitch downward. I immediately pulled back to check the tuck, when the nose yawed left violently and the earth and sky became a blur as the plane tumbled out of control toward the ground. Unable to extricate myself from the plane, and with but a few thousand feet between me and the ground, I thought I had bought the farm. As suddenly as it had started acting up, however, the plane slowed and the wild tumbling subsided. I fought my way out of the cockpit, plummeting like a brick in one of the small emergency parachutes of that era. I hit the ground with such force that my back broke.

"When we examined the aircraft wreckage, it was soon apparent what had happened; the whole tail was missing. I can say with all sincerity that there is nothing worse for an aviator than to lose his tail! The failure finally was traced to a turbine disc manufacturing procedure."

In fact, the failure revealed a metallurgical

*Following the abortive speed record attempt at Muroc during October of 1946, the XP-80R was returned to the* Skunk Works *for further refinement.*

*The original configuration of the XP-80R included flush, "NACA"-style intakes, the small canopy, and the super smooth finish. Laminar flow airfoil is readily apparent in this view.*

anomaly that was over a year and at least one additional accident in being analyzed. According to Johnson, "...the turbine wheel was not found for a year, even after a most extensive and highly scientific search. A farmer finally picked up a large piece six miles to one side of the flight path."

Apparently, when the General Electric I-40's turbine wheels were cast, they were made by slicing a single ingot into several pieces. As it turned out, the turbine wheel made from the ingot piece that had been at the ingot top contained virtually all of the ingot's impurities. These had slowly risen during the cooling process. The impurities weakened the disc, unknowingly at the time making it unsuitable for jet engine use. Once the problem was uncovered, the upper portion of each ingot simply was cut off and recycled.

Prior to Tony's accident, another noted Lockheed test pilot also had experienced an engine failure, but with fatal results. XP-80 first flight pilot, and chief Lockheed test pilot Milo Burcham, during a routine test hop in the third YP-80A on October 20, 1944, had just departed the Burbank airport when he reported a flame-out. It was his first YP-80A flight...and his last. During an attempted emergency landing, he slammed into a gravel pit and was killed instantly.

Johnson personally participated in the accident investigation and later concluded the primary cause to be a sheared fuel pump drive shaft. Contributing was a faulty overspeed governor which failed to limit engine rpm. The drive shaft failure had resulted in loss of fuel pressure which in turn, starved the engine. An electrically driven fuel pump was quickly developed that would assure fuel flow, even in the event of primary fuel pump failure. Sadly, on August 6, 1945, Maj. Richard Bong, a Medal of Honor winner and the highest scoring U.S. ace of World War 2 (and to the present day), was killed in a P-80A while attempting to takeoff to the south from the Van Nuys, California airport, also apparently as a result of fuel pump failure. A post-accident investigation, according to Johnson, indicated that Bong had forgotten to turn on the electric back-up pump prior to takeoff, even though his ground crew had warned him to do so.

The second XP-80A and the last of the P-80 series aircraft actually to be built under the

*A water injection system was utilized to increase the mass flow, and thus the thrust of the original Allison J33-A-17 engine during the October 1946 speed record runs. The water tank is visible in the gun bay.*

aegis of the *Skunk Works*, was completed in late July of 1944 and moved to Muroc by truck. With Tony LeVier at the controls, this aircraft, purposefully left unpainted so that its performance could be compared to that of the painted *Gray Ghost*, was successfully flown for the first time on August 1. Nicknamed *Silver Ghost* in consideration of its bare metal finish, it was the first "two-seat" P-80 family member as it was configured with a somewhat cramped, instrumented flight test engineer's position in the area behind the pilot normally occupied by a fuel cell. Interestingly, with the onset of flight test and the surfacing of the duct rumble anomaly, this position was temporarily filled by Johnson. During the course of several flights, Johnson accurately assessed the problem, simply by listening to the unusual intake sounds. Later, he participated in other test projects utilizing this aircraft.

The *Silver Ghost* was optimized to serve as an engine testbed. Accordingly, it was heavily instrumented with equipment for recording engine thrust, intake ram pressure, fuel consumption, exhaust temperatures, and related propulsion system data. Relatively late in its career it was used to test the Westinghouse J34 afterburning turbojet engine scheduled for use in the then-forthcoming XF-

90. In this configuration, the *Silver Ghost's* dorsal fin was used to accommodate instrumentation and afterburner fuel lines...though the latter unit was never installed.

### The XP-80R:

At least one other important P-80 project became the *Skunk Works'* responsibility before the rapidly diminishing team moved on to other things. On November 11, 1945, a Gloster *Meteor* Mk.4 of the Royal Air Force set a new world speed record of 606.25 mph. This, one of the first records of its type to be set by a jet-propelled aircraft, gave rise to an Air Force interest in breaking the record using a slightly modified P-80A. Following a study of the P-80 aircraft by Johnson and various Lockheed and Wright Field engineers, it was concluded a stock P-80A, with minimal modification could attain a speed of 615 mph at the required 100 meter maximum sea level altitude. Additional work, such as incorporation of flush intakes, squared wing tips, a sharp wing leading edge, and water-alcohol injection for the engine might permit a speed of 635 mph...which then would put the record temporarily out of British reach.

Gen. "Hap" Arnold, after assessing the proposed speed record attempt and the time

*Bearing few markings and an extraordinary surface finish, the XP-80R was completed by the* Skunk Works *during late September of 1946 and prepared for its assault on the world's absolute speed record. At the time, the record was held by a British Gloster* Meteor *F.4.*

*With revised intakes offering improved mass flow and a more powerful 4,600 pound thrust Allison Model 400 (a special version of the J33 with water-methanol injection) the XP-80R was used for a second, successful, world speed record assault.*

and money required, arranged for the Air Force to allocate $75,000 toward the project. Two P-80As were to be utilized. One would be slightly modified and equipped with a water injected Allison J33 engine; the other would be extensively modified per the recommendations of Lockheed.

High-speed runs through a specially laid-out speed trap using the slightly modified P-80A, with Maj. Kenneth Chilstrom at the controls, were undertaken during early 1946 at Muroc. The flights, though conducted under the scrutiny of representatives from the *Federation Aeronautique International* (FAI) and having the intent of setting a new world speed record, also had the secondary objective of testing the water injected J33. The aircraft was extensively refinished for the record attempt. All gaps in surface panels were filled with a putty-like material and the entire aircraft was meticulously painted, rubbed, and waxed. Flight control cables were tensioned to 400 pounds.

Additionally, the guns were removed from the engine bay and replaced with a 110 gallon fuel tank to make up for the loss of wing fuel tank space now set aside for engine water. Water injection provided a considerable short period thrust increase when used judiciously.

In effect, it cooled and thus volumetrically reduced the compressor section air...consequently increasing mass flow. The resulting additional thrust was cheap and safely acquired, though totally dependent upon the

amount of water that could be carried.

Lockheed modified the engine to accept a fourteen-nozzle water spray ring, but limited its use to 11,500 rpm or above due to the possibility of flame drowning. In total, six engines were assigned to the speed record project, each to be assessed with the intent of improving the J33's operational dependability and performance.

During the course of Chilstrom's numerous passes through the Muroc speed trap, it became apparent that breaking the British record would not be easy. A maximum speed of 596 mph appeared to be the P-80A's limit, and to go above that would require the extensive modifications assessed earlier by Lockheed's *Skunk Works* team. Complicating things was yet another British speed record set by Group Captain E. M. Donaldson in a Gloster *Meteor* F.4. The new speed record of 616 mph suddenly made it doubtful that even the modified P-80A could be a serious record contender. And the P-80A was not the only US aircraft in the running. Republic's new XP-84, a similarly straight wing first-generation jet fighter, was proving its mettle at Muroc by running the speed trap at speeds in excess of 600 mph--and thus becoming officially the fastest US aircraft.

By October of 1946, considerable pressure was being placed on both Lockheed and Republic to tweak their respective aircraft and break the British-held record. It had been over two decades since the US last claimed posses-

sion and it was apparent that the new jets offered the only reasonable opportunity to regain it...if all the proper conditions could be met. Col. Albert Boyd, tasked by Gen. Arnold, confronted both engineering teams with the challenge.

Republic's attempts during October of 1946 proved premature, primarily because the XP-84's General Electric J35 engine water injection system was insufficiently developed. As a result, it was decided to table, for the time being, the XP-84 record attempt.

This left Lockheed's *Skunk Works*-modified P-80, now referred to as the XP-80R, as the only US record hope. Johnson had personally overseen the extensive modifications which included high-recovery, very low-drag intakes, modified and sharpened wing leading edges, clipped wing tips, covered and sealed gun ports, a reduced profile windshield and canopy, and most importantly, the addition of an upgraded Allison J33-A-17 engine.

Practicing, the XP-80R, with Col. Boyd in the cockpit, on October 2 and 4, 1946, went through the Muroc traps at what at first appeared to be record speeds. Unfortunately, though initial computations indicated an equivalent ground speed of 620 mph, a recalculation some twelve hours later lowered this to a considerably less-encouraging 600 mph. Even following installation of a fresh engine, the earlier speed could not be broken. Discouraged, Lockheed and the Air Force elected to cancel the official record attempt scheduled for October 5.

Johnson, after analyzing the speed run results and examining the aircraft, concluded the primary problem lay with the flush intakes. Though offering low drag, they also had poor ram characteristics. Accordingly, new intakes were designed and installed. Though appearing conventional, they were in fact larger and considerably more efficient than their production equivalent. Coupled with a still more powerful Allison engine (the 4,600 pound thrust Model 400...later officially designated J33-A-23), and the other modifications that already had been developed for the aircraft, it was correctly assumed that little else could be done to make the XP-80R, now nicknamed *Racey*, any aerodynamically cleaner or more efficient.

Some nine months after the failed October

*The revised conventional intakes were larger and considerably more pronounced than the original flush, NACA-type intakes. Though offering more drag, the engine thrust increases offset the penalty.*

record attempt, the XP-80R was back at Muroc with Col. Boyd in the cockpit. On June 19, 1947, everything--including the weather--was at last in place for the ultimate attempt. Guided by reddish smoke flares set off at each end of the course, Boyd passed through the traps four different times per the F.A.I. requirement. Speeds of 617.1, 614.7, 632.5, and 630.8 mph were officially logged, giving an average speed of 623.8 mph...and giving the US its first official world speed record in almost a quarter century.

With the completion of the second XP-80A and the initiation of production on what now was a total of fourteen YP-80As (inclusive of one static test article and the single XF-14 reconnaissance variant), the P-80 program moved out of the *Skunk Works* and into the mainstream production process at Lockheed's Burbank facility. Planning and manufacture of the YP-80A, according to a report issued by Chuck Wagner on March 19, 1954, started "upon completion of the organization of Department 28-10" during early February of 1944. This department was created specifically for the purpose of producing the YP-80A. Building 175 at Plant B-1 was selected and production operations were started in the assigned area. The building contained 103,500 square feet of which 72,500 square feet was closed off and used specifically for YP-80A production.

The P-80, formally named *Shooting Star* by company executives Robert Gross and Hall Hibbard, would go on to have a long and successful career not only in the US military, but in the air forces of Brazil, Chile, Columbia, Ecuador, Uruguay, and Peru, as well. It would lay claim to the first jet versus jet air combat victory in history (the destruction of a MiG-15 over Korea on November 7, 1950 by Lt. Russell Brown) and amass an extraordinary record as a fighter, fighter/bomber, and recon-

*With Albert Boyd in the cockpit, the XP-80R makes a pass through the speed traps at Muroc Dry Lake on June 19, 1947. A new world speed record of 623.738 mph resulted.*

naissance platform during the course of the Korean War. Afterwards, though outdated, it performed yeoman's duty with various Air Guard and Air Reserve units, being finally phased out of US service during 1958. In total, including prototypes and production aircraft, some 1,732 P-80s were built.

As just one of their several significant legacies, the XP-80 and the two XP-80As left behind the consummated reality of one of "Kelly" Johnson's long held dreams...an experimental department where the designers and shop artisans could work together closely in development of airplanes without the delays and complications of intermediate departments to handle administration, purchasing, and all other support functions. He aspired strongly to

have a direct relationship between the design engineer, the mechanic, and manufacturing, and he wanted a chance to prove it would work. The P-80 project provided that opportnity...and served as the seed for what would grow into the world's most famous and mysterious aircraft manufacturing institution.

*The first production batch of P-80As, including 44-85004 (shown), consisted of 208 aircraft. Most of these original machines were delivered painted light gray over-all. The P-80 eventually proved a successful fighter and would lay claim to the first jet-versus-jet aerial combat victory.*

**Model 75 Saturn/1946**

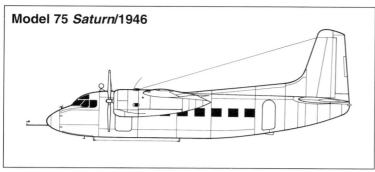

**XR6O-1/XR6V-1 Constitution/1946**

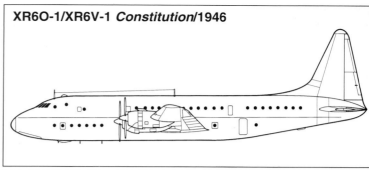

**TP-80C/T-33A/1948**

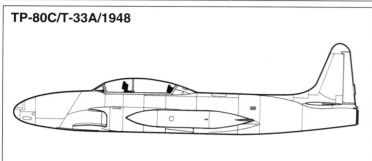

**YF-94/1949**

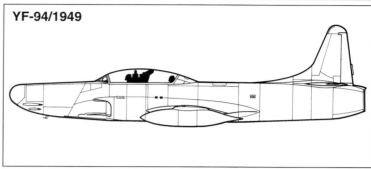

**XF-90/1949**

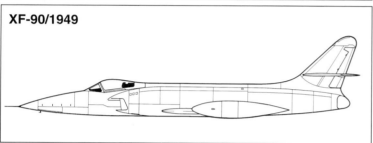

**YF-94C/1950**

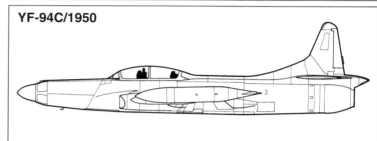

**X-7A/1951**

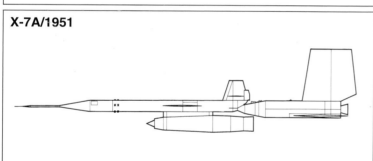

**L-245/1953**

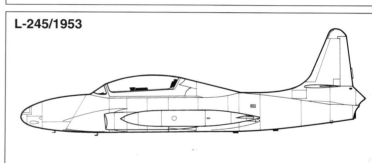

**XFV-1/1953**

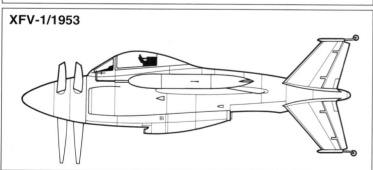

**R7V-2/YC-121F/1954**

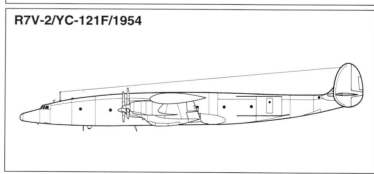

**RB-69A/1954**

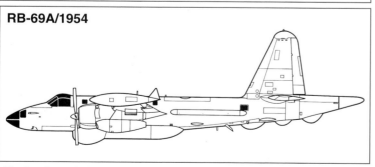

**YC-130/1954**

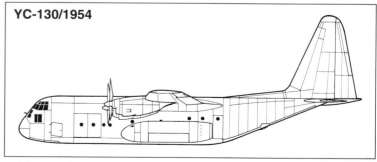

*The interim period between the XP-80 and the U-2 was highly productive for Lockheed, but remains a gray area for the Skunk Works. In reality, the Skunk Works did not exist in tangible form, but was instead more of a philosophy than an entity. Significant aircraft built during these ill-defined years under the aegis of "Kelly" Johnson and his preliminary design organization include the above, which are shown in chronological order. Drawings are by Charles Fleming.*

# Chapter 4:

# The In-Between Years

*"...when they don't know what they're going to build, nobody can clobber it as well as American industry. We demonstrate that yearly."*

**Clarence L. "Kelly" Johnson**

In any retrospective describing the history of the *Skunk Works* it is necessary to "confront" the period from 1945 to 1954 with some trepidation. By late 1945, the *Skunk Works*, as it then existed, had served its purpose and effectively had ceased to exist as a separate entity within the corporate umbrella of the Lockheed Aircraft Company. Regardless, "Kelly" Johnson had not let the successes of the XP-80 program be absorbed by the ever-threatening corporate bureaucracy. Having seen the attributes of the unencumbered design and manufacturing system he and his *Skunk Works* teammates had created, he was determined to retain its operating philosophy for future endeavors.

By the time the P-80 was handed off to Lockheed's Department 28-10 for expansion into a production program, several other aircraft had been brought onboard under the *Skunk Works* operating philosophy for future execution. These projects, the prototypes for the Model 75 *Saturn*, the XR6O-1 *Constitution*, the T-33 and T2V-1 *SeaStar*, the F-94 *Starfire*, the XF-90, the RB-69, the X-7, the R7V-2/YC-121F *Constellation*, the XFV-1, and the YC-130 *Hercules*, would not all be brought to life at once under the *Skunk Works* umbrella, but rather would arrive with surprising regularity over a period of some nine years. This steady work flow kept the *Skunk Works* alive *philosophically*, but did little to retain any coherent core group that could accurately refer to itself as *the Skunk Works*.

Significantly, during this period, none of these aircraft would be created in a true *Skunk Works* atmosphere, but rather would utilize various aspects of the *Skunk Works* approach to prototyping. In every instance, some aspect of design, engineering, or construction was handled by what now is looked back upon simply as the vestiges of the old XP-80 approach. In many cases, the engineering talent was the same as that utilized for the XP-80, only now it was operating under the aegis of Lockheed-California Company, rather than independently under the aegis of the *Skunk Works*.

Keeping it all alive was "Kelly" Johnson who was, at times, the only physical manifestation of what remained of the original *Skunk Works*. Often working on several projects at once, he rarely distinguished between Lockheed aircraft being "done in the *Skunk Works*", and aircraft that were not. It was truly a unique period...and one that will forever remain a gray area in the Advanced Development Projects history. Ben Rich, retired LADC President, today refers to it as the time of the *Skunk Works* "fast action shop"...its singular purpose was to create or assist in the development of prototypes quickly and quietly and with minimal outside help or interference.

## Model 75 *Saturn*:

*"Then we had our* Saturn, *a small transport airplane, on which we made the most complete market survey we've made on anything up until recently. And it was to be a low cost-per-airplane-mile airplane, it was good—but it was a complete failure because it faced 10,000 C-47s that were available at half the cost, and were better in terms of several other regards— larger, mainly and available quickly."* Clarence L. "Kelly" Johnson

Not blind to the attributes of being the first out of the blocks in any competitive venture, Lockheed's management, headed by President Robert Gross, initiated a major study to determine airline requirements for what was assumed to be a rapidly approaching post-war era. Though the outcome of the war, in early 1944, still was somewhat in question, the general consensus was that the time was ripe to look to the future. In effect the company had nothing to lose...and everything to gain.

During 1944, teams of Lockheed market research analysts and sales engineers led by Carl Squier and Leonard Schwartz traveled some 22,000 miles in four months gathering and assimilating data in an attempt to accurately assess future airline needs. They interviewed farmers, merchants, bankers, businessmen, and housewives. Most significantly, they spent a considerable amount of time querying airline representatives, and in particular the regional carriers and trunkline operators.

The resulting data was fed to Lockheed's engineering staff which already was anticipating considerable commercial success with proposed post-war civilian versions of the C-69 *Constellation*. Because of the size and performance of the latter, heavy emphasis was placed on development of a smaller aircraft to service the needs of feeder-type airlines. The resulting configuration, born under the company designator L-146, was an intermediate-sized twin, promoted by Lockheed to prospective customers as being able to..."bring air travel to Main Street...and to the world's byways." It was, the promotional literature claimed, "Designed to do the big business of the little airline and the little business of the big airline".

By the fall of 1944, the basic configuration for the L-146 had been chosen by project chief engineer, Don Palmer (under chief of preliminary design, Willis Hawkins)...who not coincidentally, was intimately involved in the *Skunk Works* as project engineer on the XP-80. Under the guiding hand of Palmer (and later, his L-146 replacement, F. A. Smith), the project was committed to mock-up and hardware execution. In the XP-80 log for June 7, 1944, it

Lockheed

*One of the lesser-known commuter aircraft of the past half-century, Lockheed's attractive but notably unsuccessful* Saturn *was simply too expensive for the post-World War 2 market. Though Lockheed conducted a thorough market analysis, sales failed to materialize in numbers sufficient to merit production.*

*A typically advanced Lockheed design, the high-wing* Saturn *preceded similar configurations--such as the Dutch Fokker F.27--by over a decade when it took to the air for the first time on August 8, 1947.*

*Particularly noticeable were the* Saturn's *two-blade propellers. Large aircraft of this type often utilized relatively powerful engines which generated enough torque to merit use of a three-blade design.*

*The* Saturn's *high wing permitted the fuselage to serve as a pendulum. This helped stabilize the aircraft in flight and improved the ride and passenger comfort.*

was noted, "Saw CLJ briefly—he OKs the tentative Hawkins-Palmer plan on the L-146 mock-up. We can set up the manpower to suit current conditions. All instructions to shop are to emanate from Palmer's group. Engineering work to be charged to preliminary design and be directed by Hawkins—so far, Holland and Culver are on L-146—more men later."

During the autumn of 1944, an International Air Conference held in Chicago was duly attended by representatives from virtually all the free world's airlines. Not surprisingly, it proved a major vending opportunity for Lockheed. The L-146, commercially promoted as the *Saturn*, proved a sales success. Conditional sales contracts for no less than 500 aircraft at $85,000 each were garnered within months of the aircraft's unveiling, and there was every appearance it was on its way to airliner stardom.

Consequently, work accelerated at Lockheed. On June 12, 1944, construction of the mock-up was formally initiated when five full- and part-time personnel were assigned to the project in a hangar next to the XP-80

area...which was the original *Skunk Works*. Three days later, the XP-80 log noted, "At present, Culver, Holland, and Stewart are on it. Fuselage structure is all rough planned and aft body plan is done. Forward body plan will be done by end of week so Ralph Hicks can start mock-up and 1/10 size lines check model."

The exigencies of war slowed work on the Model 75 (the production model designation) but did not kill enthusiasm for the project. By the middle of 1945, the first of two prototypes was entering construction and a second aircraft was planned. Eventually, no less than 189,600 man hours was expended on their design and construction.

In many ways, the *Saturn* was the first commercial transport to be in a position to take advantage of the technology advances emanating from the war years. Engine exhaust gases were utilized to provide jet thrust, the wing was a laminar flow design, and construction materials consisted of state-of-the-art aluminum alloys that heretofore could be found only on the most advanced military aircraft. Per its commercial objectives, it was optimized to

operate in and out of undeveloped airfields independent of elaborate maintenance facilities and long runways. It was designed to carry 14 passengers in two rows or with a quickly moveable bulkhead dividing passengers from cargo, up to 3,000 pounds of cargo or any intermediate combination of the two. The individual passenger seats were luxuriously upholstered and the hammock-type chairs were constructed of tubular steel.

Palmer's group had remained conscious of the more plebian aspects of rural airport life and had designed the *Saturn* accordingly. The low fuselage was configured to enable trucks to drive up to the cargo door for direct loading and unloading. And passengers could enter or exit the aircraft with little difficulty also as a result of the low-set fuselage. An integral step positioned just below the cabin door could be folded down for use as needed. Passengers, if required, could handle their own baggage, passing it into a storage space in the main cabin. And for maintenance access, the entire nose section could be swung back as "easily as opening a door"...affording access to all controls and the instrument panel. Most notably, the main landing gear doors, powerplants, engine cowls, elevators and tabs, and wing flap assemblies were interchangeable from right to left or from aircraft to aircraft...thus reducing the need for large parts inventories.

Complicating design of the L-146 somewhat was the Civil Aviation Authority's decision to revise its performance requirements for twin-engine aircraft in the event of engine failure. Clearing a 50 foot obstacle during takeoff with a full load and one engine out presented serious difficulties, and in order to meet the C.A.A. mandate, a redesign with more powerful engines was required. Regardless, the first aircraft, officially designated Model 075-77-01, was completed by *Skunk Works* personnel and equipped with two 600 hp Continental GR9-A nine-cylinder radials (developed from the Wright R-975). Rolled out during early June, it took to the air from Lockheed's Burbank facility for the first time on June 17, 1946 with company test pilot Tony LeVier at the controls with Rudy Thoren, Lockheed's director of flight test in the copilot's seat.

During the ensuing flight test program, LeVier discovered the aircraft to have poor stall characteristics, a noticeable lack of power, and engine cooling problems. A leading edge strake cured the stall problem, but the inadequacies of the Continental engines could not be overcome. Accordingly, two 700 hp seven-cylinder Wright 744C-7BA-1s replaced the GR9-As on the first aircraft and also were mandated for the second and all production examples. In modified form, the first aircraft took to the air with the Wright engines for the first time on August 8, 1947. Subsequently, its performance proved adequate and most of the earlier configuration's failings appeared to have been overcome.

Though well executed and decidedly attractive, the *Saturn*, as Carl Squier later noted, was "ill-starred almost from the beginning. It ran up against one setback after another. When the war ended, we found ourselves confronted with supplier strikes, tooling troubles, and rising costs. As design progressed, the airplane got heavier and more complicated. We had to increase its price to $100,000 a copy. And our analysis of the potential market didn't prove out."

Additionally, Squier and Schwartz's survey had not foreseen other adverse developments.

*Two-blade propellers are particularly distinctive in this view. Wide landing gear stance gave* Saturn *excellent ground stability.*

Saturn's *proximity to the ground and low stance were purposefully designed-in to provide easy cargo and passenger access.*

As noted in the October 1957 issue of Lockheed's corporate magazine "Of Men and Stars", "Airport construction lagged in smaller cities where Lockheed had hoped the *Saturn* would serve profitably. Many regional carriers had little backing and weren't prepared for lean years. There were failures and consolidations. And the biggest handicap of all in this shrinking market was availability of war surplus transports. They could be readily converted to commercial operations, they could be bought for one-fourth to one-third as much as the *Saturn*, and they could do the job adequately if not so well. By February 1946 the War Assets Administration reported sales of more than 31,000 aircraft usable in civil aviation—including scores of Lockheed *Lodestars*."

By late 1947, the handwriting was on the wall. The *Saturn* was not going to be a successful venture and there was no reason for Lockheed to throw any more money into its development. In spite of its relatively low operating costs and its better maintenance characteristics, it could not compete against $25,000 Douglas C-47s and similarly cheap C-54s. Flyaway costs of the *Saturn* were now expected to be between $100,000 and $130,000. Taking advantage of tax write-off options, the two prototypes were released to reclamation crews to be chopped up as scrap.

### Model 89/XR6O-1/XR6V-1 *Constitution*:

*"The* Constitution *was a Navy project— actually started out as a program for* Pan American Airlines *at 184,000 pounds gross weight. In this project we used the* Skunk Works *engineering methods, but we used conventional shop practices. The aircraft was good, but we never got the 5,500 horsepower turboprop engines it was designed for. It ended up one of the world's most underpow-*

*ered airplanes."* Clarence L. "Kelly" Johnson

By far the largest Navy transport of its day, the Model 89 *Constitution* (supposedly, the Model 89 number was chosen because the Constitution of the US was ratified in 1789) came to life as a study project calling for a larger follow-on to the Lockheed Model 49 *Constellation* almost a year before the official birth of the *Skunk Works*. The original specification, as outlined by Hall Hibbard and "Kelly" Johnson, called for an aircraft capable of carrying a 20,000 pound payload over a range of 4,500 miles while cruising at between 250 and 275 mph at 25,000 feet. Top speed would be over 300 mph.

The war had brought with it a need to move large masses of personnel and equipment to distant combat zones as rapidly as possible. Several aircraft companies, including Lockheed, elected to respond to this need by designing and building large transport aircraft capable of spanning the globe while carrying massive payloads.

Concurrently, *Pan American Airways*, long a proponent of long-range, heavy, overwater-capable transports, had been tasked by the War and Navy Departments with the burden of servicing the long range transport needs of the military. With both services' blessings, Pan American proposed to several aircraft manufacturers that they study the possibility of building large, ultra-long-range transports for intercontinental delivery of men and equipment to combat zones around the world. Ideally, these aircraft also would later be adaptable to commercial configurations in peacetime. The resulting Boeing (C-97), Convair (C-99), and Douglas (C-74) projects eventually were assigned to the Air Force while the Lockheed project, formally designated XR6O-1, fell under Navy jurisdic-

tion.

Lockheed's Jack Real, working for some fifteen months with *Pan American's* Andre Priester, served as just one of several liaison's between the company and the airline in an attempt to provide a more realistic perspective on the proposed new transport and its operating requirements. The formal signing of a Navy contract during the spring of 1943 for what initially was a $111,250,000 order for fifty aircraft was pared back to $27,000,000 and two aircraft following V-J Day in late-1945.

Working with Pan American engineers and Comdr. E. L. Simpson, Jr., representing Navy interests, Hawkins was in charge of preliminary design and Pulver became project engineer. Joining them were Art Flock, assistant project engineer; Jack Real, a flight test engineer; Herb von Streain, production superintendent; and George Prudden, supervisor of final assembly. In total, a small group of some fifteen Lockheed personnel, including Holley Dickinson on wing design, were pulled from the P-38, P-49, P-58, P-80, PV-2, P2V, and R50 projects and assigned to the Model 89. This team later was expanded to 40 prior to the production order cancellation.

By the middle of 1942, some 28 different configurations had been examined to determine which would be most suitable for the new aircraft. Eventually the choices were narrowed to one, a conventionally configured four-engine transport of mid-wing design. To be powered by four new Wright "turbine propeller" (turboprop) engines of approximately 5,500 horsepower, it was to have a pressurized doubledeck/double-lobe fuselage (shaped in cross-section like a figure 8) and be capable of carrying up to 204 military passengers in its maximum density configuration. A less packed normal configuration would provide seating for

*The* Constitutions *were built in a newly-constructed six-story building at Lockheed's Burbank airport facility. To the right is the second airframe.*

*The two* Constitutions *were not completed until some fifteen months after the end of World War Two. By then, their original mission had lost its priority.*

33

*The* Constitution *was enormous by any standard. Unfortunately, it was completed at a time when its load-carrrying abilities were no longer needed.*

*Somewhat underpowered and possessing serious range limitations, the two* Constitions *had limited usefulness as military transports.*

168. Post-war configurations optimized for the airlines would be configured to carry 51 seated passengers and 58 passengers in sleeper births, along with 11 crew members. In a mixed passenger/cargo configuration, passengers would be carried on the upper deck and cargo on the lower (two cargo hoists were installed on either side of the lower 106 inch x 76 inch cargo doors; these could handle loads up to 10,000 pounds) though it would remain possible to accommodate passengers there, as well. As one Lockheed promotional piece pointed out, the aircraft would be "roomy enough to hold a Pullman car, a boxcar, and a flatcar, with space left over for a passenger bus."

The aircraft was in fact, huge. The wings were so thick a catwalk was installed permitting crew members access to the engines in flight (on one occasion, an outboard engine oil system gasket failed and it became necessary to shut down the engine and feather the propeller; a crew member accessed the broken gasket, replaced it, cleaned up the residual oil, and refilled the oil tank; the propeller then was unfeathered and the engine restarted without any further difficulty). Total fuel capacity was a then-phenomenal 9,780 gallons.

On November 26, 1943, Hall Hibbard and "Kelly" Johnson filed a joint patent application for the Model 89, which noted that it was a "new, original, ornamental design". The patent

was granted on April 10, 1945...more than a year before the first aircraft's first flight.

The sheer largess of the Model 89 required the construction of an entirely new facility at Lockheed's Burbank plant. Approximately 60 feet tall, 414 feet wide, and 303 feet deep, the $1,250,000 Building 309 pioneered cantilever bridge-type steel girder construction.

Many innovations were built-in to the new Model 89, not the least of which was a passenger entrance through the nose wheel well and a 3,000 pounds per square inch hydraulic system that required the power of no less than 13 pumps. This hydraulic system, among other things, powered the booster units for the control surfaces.

The space- and weight-saving four-wheel, truck-type tandem main landing gear, requiring an estimated 50,000 engineering man-hours to bring to fruition, was equipped with special wheel assemblies that both aerodynamically (flapper vanes on the tires) and electrically (via flat, pancake-type individual 2 hp electric motors) pre-rotated the tires to a speed of 80 mph prior to touchdown.

The lack of urgency caused the Navy to cancel development of the Wright turboprop engine. The Pratt & Whitney R4360-18 *Wasp Major* was substituted. Its power rating of only 3,000 horsepower left the aircraft considerably underpowered. This change led to a long ges-

tation and a first flight that did not occur until over a year after the war had ended. The first aircraft, completed and statically tested during the summer, finally was flown for the first time on November 9, 1946 with Joe Towle as pilot, Tony LeVier as co-pilot, Rudy Thoren as flight test engineer, and Jack Frick and Dick Stanton as assistant flight test engineers. The initial hop, the takeoff of which was observed by nearly 10,000 spectators, provided initial insights into the aircraft's performance capabilities. A top speed of 303 mph and a recorded cruising speed of 269 mph were observed, with a leisurely 2 hours and 17 minutes being taken to cover what was normally a straight-line distance of about 70 miles from the Lockheed Air Terminal to Muroc Army Air Base. Following two touch-and-goes at Muroc, the aircraft returned to Burbank.

Earlier, Robert Gross, departing from Lockheed's long-standing practice of naming its aircraft after heavenly bodies, had officially named the aircraft the *Constitution*. "It seemed fitting", he explained later, "that the largest plane we had yet produced should be named after America's Constitution, a symbol of our nation's greatness and strength. Secondly, there was the Navy ship *Constitution*—'Old Ironsides'—with its historical interest and naval tradition."

Some 44 hours into the flight test program it was firmly concluded takeoff performance was marginal with the extant engines (they generated only 2,770 horsepower on a 90° F day, instead of the advertised 3,000 horsepower), a decision was made to upgrade to more powerful versions. Accordingly, R4360-22Ws, capable of generating 3,500 hp with water injection, replaced the R4360-18s. These also were installed in the second Model 89 as well. Concurrent with the engine upgrade, smaller propellers were installed; 4-bladed 16 feet 8 inch units replaced the original 4-bladed 19 feet 6 inch Curtiss Electrics when fatigue cracks were discovered in fuselage skin and select stringers exposed to the propeller plane.

The flight test program, upon completion and utilizing both aircraft, logged 618 hours. During flight test the first aircraft was equipped with 54 tanks carrying 1,100 pounds of water each on its upper deck. By pumping their contents fore and aft, the aircraft center of gravity could be altered quickly over a wide range, thus permitting exploration of the center of gravity envelope.

Interestingly, the Model 89 had been designed to mount three 1,000 pound thrust Rocket Assisted Takeoff (RATO) units in the upper surface of each wing. The RATO units were fired just before the landing gear retraction cycle was started. It took 14 seconds to retract the landing gear and 15 seconds to expend the RATO units. RATO increased the aircraft's sea level rate of climb from 180 feet per minute to 540 feet per minute at 184,000 pounds gross weight with "one engine inoperative, the propeller wind milling, and the landing gear in the extended position".

*Both* Constitutions *were literally hand-built by Lockheed personnel at the company's Burbank facility. Workmanship was superb in every respect. Polished aluminum finish was spectacular.*

*Operational Navy service deminished the luster of the original polished aluminum. Near the end of their careers, the two* Constitutions *served as a Navy promotional and recruiting tools.*

Constitution's *enormous size and weight required a unique landing gear consisting of two main struts in tandem with two wheels per strut.*

*Mounting tubes were placed in the upper surface of each wing root section to accommodate a total of six RATO units for improved takeoff performance.*

The *Constitution* was designed to meet Civil Aeronautics Authority #4 standards. At 184,000 pounds, it could takeoff in 3,000 feet and clear a 50 foot obstacle in 5,000 feet. At its maximum normal landing weight of 160,000 pounds, it could clear a 50 foot obstacle and stop in 2,300 feet.

On February 2, 1949, the first XR6O-1, as the type officially was designated by the Navy, was delivered to Transport Squadron VR-44 at NAS Alameda, California. Six months later, the second aircraft, which had flown for the first time on June 9, 1948, also was delivered to VR-44...though after it initially had been flown at the Naval Air Test Center, Patuxent River, Maryland to satisfy Navy flight test requirements.

This second *Constitution*, unlike the first—which was outfitted for test work and cargo transport—was given an upper-deck VIP interior or capable of seating up to 92 passengers. It had a crew of 12 including a captain, a pilot, a copilot, a flight engineer, an assistant flight engineer, a radio operator, a navigator, two flight orderlies, and three relief crewmen. It also was capable of carrying 40,000 pounds of cargo in the 7,375 cubic foot lower deck space. Aft of the crew quarters was a spacious galley. This permitted the serving of 300 hot meals per flight. On the forward bulkhead, above the forward spiral staircase (there was also a central spiral staircase) was a permanent glass case containing a scale model of the original USS *Constitution*.

Following their initial acceptance tests, the two aircraft were used for a regular twice-weekly shuttle from Moffett Naval Air Station (San Francisco) to Patuxent Naval Air Station (Washington, D.C.,) with a fuel stop in Olathe, Kansas. Passenger loads of 100 or more were commonplace. Eastbound flight time was 11.7 and westbound was 13.9 hours.

Oftentimes the two *Constitutions* were used by the Navy for promotional purposes. Large and imposing, they were a strong crowd draw at airshows. One tour during 1949 saw the first aircraft stop in no less than twenty-three cities for periods of up to three days at a time. Readily visible and painted in huge letters on the aircraft's side were the words, "Your Navy, Land and Sea".

During 1950, the aircraft had the honor of being the first to present full-length inflight motion pictures when the world premier of the movie "Slattery's Hurricane" was reviewed over New York City at an altitude of 10,000 feet. During another flight from the east to west coast, the Navy football team reviewed inflight films of their games and those of their forthcoming opponent, the University of Southern California (USC won). On still another occasion, the aircraft served as a radio station for Arthur Godfrey when he presented a live, one-hour performance with his entire cast while flying over New York City.

In service, the two aircraft suffered from several major performance deficiencies, not the least of which was insufficient range. Though utilized sparingly for transporting cargo and personnel between the US mainland and Hawaii, they often had to be flown with a substantially reduced payload in order to have adequate fuel reserves. Additionally, the aircraft were noticeably underpowered. This, coupled with a cooling problem that forced the use of drag-inducing partially open cowl flaps on virtually every long-range mission, led to several Lockheed proposals calling for a variety of potential powerplant upgrades. A long list of advanced piston, compound, and turboprop engines were proffered for the Model 89, but none came to fruition.

During 1950, the two XR6O-1s were redesignated XR6V-1s to bring them in-line with then-contemporary Navy designation standards (V was the new letter designator assigned to Lockheed-manufactured aircraft for the Navy being built at what had been the Vega facility; O was the predecessor plant designator referring to the original Lockheed facility). During the 1951/1952 time period both aircraft were cycled through Lockheed for a major overhaul program. The following year, however, they were deemed too expensive to operate and placed in long-term storage at the Navy's storage and disposition center at Litchfield Park, Arizona. Two years later, in 1955, they were declared surplus and sold for $98,000 to the highest bidder.

As civil transports, the two *Constitutions* were to have been utilized by their private sector owners as heavy freight haulers. Upon receipt the first aircraft, initially owned by George Crockett of *Alamo Airways*, was flown to Las Vegas, Nevada. The second aircraft was flown to Opa-Locka, Florida where, during 1966, it was seriously fire damaged during an aborted attempt to fly it to South America. Due to the exorbitant cost of a proposed mandatory flight test program, neither aircraft was granted an Approved Type Certificate by the Federal Aviation Administration. As a result, the two became noteworthy derelicts at their respective home airports. The Las Vegas aircraft eventually served as a billboard and the Opa-Locka aircraft was considered for restaurant duty once it fell under the ownership of Executive Terminal Associates. Finally, the two behemoths simply fell into severe disrepair. During 1969, the Las Vegas aircraft was sold for scrap. Public concern over the "eyesore" the Opa-Locka aircraft supposedly represented led to its scrapping just over a decade later.

Though to have been convertible to commercial air transport use, the two *Constitutions*, by the advent of their respective first flights, were hopelessly out of date and decidedly underpowered. *Pan American*, after the war, had only half-seriously reviewed Lockheed's proposed Model 189, which was the projected commercial *Constitution*. To have been powered by four 3,500 hp Pratt & Whitney TSB3-G versions of the original R4360, it would have been capable of accommodating 129 day pas-

*Insufficient power proved the* Constitutions' *Achilles Heel. Proposals to upgrade their engines or replace them with turboprops were never brought to fruition.*

TP-80C full-scale forward fuselage and cockpit mock-up. Cockpit contained fully-detailed instrument panels and seats.

The first TP-80C under construction at Burbank. Dimensional changes resulting in the two-seat cockpit arrangement were relatively few and simple.

sengers or 109 night passengers and a crew of fifteen. *Pan American* and several other solicited airlines eventually rejected this, and the Model 289 (to have been powered by four 5,500 shaft horsepower Wright *Typhoon* turboprop engines, it would have had a takeoff weight of 240,000 pounds and the ability to carry up to 154 passengers plus crew) and the similar—though reciprocating-engine-powered—Models 389 and 489 (with the ability to carry up to 168 passengers and with a gross weight increased to 195,000 pounds), as well.

Other studies using various Wright, Allison, and Pratt & Whitney engines also were offered, but to no avail. Finally, a turboprop version powered by British-build Armstrong-Siddeley *Pythons* was studied, but eventually rejected. As Lockheed Vice President Cyril Chappellet later would lament, "Even if we could have hung bigger engines on it, the Model 89 faced a dim future in the commercial market. *Pan American*, though seriously interested at first, reappraised its operations at the end of the war and decided the airplane was too big for immediate traffic needs."

### T-33 and T2V *SeaStar:*

*"From that came the T-33 and then a series of derivatives for interceptors. The T2V was a Navy program, a carrier based airplane. And we made as many of those as the Navy had engines for. It was a success."* Clarence L. "Kelly" Johnson

Lockheed's P-80 *Shooting Star*, as production accelerated and operational service time began to accumulate, was not long in developing a track record not in keeping with Lockheed's long tradition of safe and dependable aircraft. The fighter's difficulties lay not

with the basic airframe, but rather with the immaturity of jet engine technology. "Kelly" Johnson, in his early essay, "Development of the Lockheed P-80A Jet Fighter Airplane", acknowledged this when he noted:

"It is natural that service experience with such a new type as the P-80, involving so many new features, would bring to light a host of new problems. The lack of propeller slipstream on takeoff and in low speed maneuvers has been confusing to pilots trained in conventional aircraft. The lack of dependable means for preventing engine overspeeding has overstressed turbine wheels in many cases. Even in cases where overspeeding has not been present, turbine wheels have failed with disastrous results. In one case, the pilot landed safely after the wheel split and flew through the sides of the fuselage. During an early Lockheed test, Mr. Tony LeVier had a wheel fail at 540 mph. This cut the whole aft end of the airplane off. There is *no* practical means of providing a guard to absorb the energy from a large split turbine wheel to prevent it from doing extremely great damage. The wheel must be designed to be practically infallible even after losing a number of blades. So far, blade losses have been few and not at all dangerous. They generally go out of the tail-pipe. Reliable governing is an absolute *must* to prevent wheel failures."

By 1947, the P-80's attrition rate was nearing epidemic proportions. Not only had Lockheed's chief test pilot, Milo Burcham, been killed in a P-80 accident, but the highest scoring US ace, Richard Bong, had lost his life in a *Shooting Star*, as well. These and other P-80 crashes had left little room for argument when it came time to discuss the attributes of a trainer version of Lockheed's first-generation jet. There remained, however, considerable difficul-

ty convincing the Air Force—during what were rapidly becoming extremely austere post-war times—to allocate the funds necessary for prototype development. As it were, new P-80 pilots were arriving at their operational assignments having been exposed to a curriculum that included time in North American T-6s, North American P-51s, and unbelievably, static operating time in older P-80s that were kept on the ground by mounting their landing gear in large concrete blocks!

Lockheed's V. F. "Mac" Short, in 1945 a vice president in charge of military relations, had argued—almost from the beginning of the program—that a trainer version of the P-80 was necessary to transition pilots from reciprocating engine aircraft into the new world of jet propulsion. From 1945 to 1947, he consistently pushed for the development of a two-seat P-80 and argued its case with the Air Force at every opportunity.

Company president Robert Gross and chief engineer Hall Hibbard eventually capitulated to Short's logic. Essentially agreeing to his argument "ground instruction is not enough—student pilots still have to solo without jet experience in the air", they elected to allocate $1,000,000 in corporate funds to design, build, and flight test a prototype two-seat P-80. It was assumed the hardware expense would eventually bear fruit in the form of an Air Force contract.

During May of 1947, several members of the original *Skunk Works* P-80 team under the direction of Don Palmer initiated preliminary design and development work on the new Model 580. Three months later, with the Air Materiel Command's approval, a single P-80C was pulled from the P-80 production line and set aside for a special *Skunk Works* team to modify to the new two-seat configuration. In the interim, a full-scale forward fuselage mock-up was completed and approved, and necessary hardware drawings were made.

Typical of a *Skunk Works* effort, a high level of secrecy surrounded the modification endeavor, though in this case primarily to keep knowledge of its existence from leaking into the advanced planning departments of other, competing aircraft manufacturing companies. The market for jet trainers, though in a state of infancy, was expected to grow with considerable rapidity during the coming years and Lockheed's corporate offices aspired to be the first to offer such an aircraft to the Air Force and Navy.

With Palmer leading a small team of fourteen, the P-80C fuselage was partially disassembled and the task of lengthening it to accommodate a second, slightly elevated seat

The first TP-80C early in its flight test program. This aircraft would become a veritible *Phoenix* rising from the ashes as it would serve later as the prototype YF-94.

Lockheed's TP-80C prototype, 48-356, would result in one of the most successful production programs in the history of the company.

The L-245 differed markedly from the actual production aircraft, particularly in the design of its empennage and associated tail surfaces.

and associated dual controls was begun. A 29 inch plug was inserted forward of the wing and another 12 inch plug was inserted aft. Consequent to this, the fuselage fuel tank capacity was reduced from 207 to 95 gallons. This was compensated for by replacing the standard self-sealing tanks in the otherwise unmodified wings with considerably more capacious nylon cells. These, when coupled with the normal tank complement, gave an internal fuel capacity of 353 gallons...which was only 72 gallons less than that of the single-seat fighter. Additional fuel could be carried in optional 165 gallon jettisonable tanks hung from the wing tips—which on production aircraft were replaced later by 230 gallon centerline-mount tip tanks.

Though early P-80s had not been ejection-seat equipped, by the advent of the new two-seat configuration such emergency egress systems were becoming mandatory on all high-performance combat aircraft. Accordingly, the new TP-80C, as the trainer P-80 now officially was designated, was reengineered to incorporate two Lockheed-designed ejection seats to accommodate the crew. These sat under a stretched single-piece Plexiglas canopy that, unlike that of the sliding unit found on the single-seat P-80, was hinged at its aft end and electrically raised and lowered (or in an emergency, manually) upon crew command.

Limited armament in the form of two .50 caliber machine guns with 300 round per gun was retained, primarily to accommodate gunnery training requirements. These later would be complemented on select production aircraft by the addition of hot wing stores stations.

The TP-80C prototype was rolled out quietly at Burbank during early March of 1948, and following static and taxi testing, was successfully flown for the first time on March 22, with Lockheed's Tony LeVier at the controls. During follow-on testing, it quickly became apparent the new trainer was an exceptional aircraft—and every bit the equal of its single-seat predecessor. In fact, during performance trials, it was discovered the two-seat configuration, due primarily to its improved fineness ratio, was slightly faster in climb, cruise, and maximum speed at all comparable engine settings.

The Air Force agreed on April 7, 1948 to acquire twenty production TP-80Cs for service testing. Consequent to this, Lockheed elected to send the aircraft on a month-long tour of Air Force bases..."taking aloft everyone from generals to green cadets". On June 11, 1948, the designation of this and the twenty subsequent production examples was changed to TF-80C and on May 5, 1949, to T-33A.

The TF-80C prototype proved an exceptional sales tool. During the course of the month-long promotional tour of Air Force bases

and Naval air stations, sales chief Carl Squier acted as an advance man. The aircraft, piloted by Tony LeVier, flew from facility to facility with considerable rapidity and relative ease. Squier, forced to use whatever transportation was available, traveled by car, chartered aircraft, and airline...and was rarely more than "one jump in advance of LeVier and his mechanic. I was never so tired in my life. I was losing sleep night after night. And Tony maddened me because he'd step out of that jet job at each new stop fresh as a daisy".

Following a LeVier demonstration at the Patuxent River Naval Air Station flight test center, Navy interest in the two-seat P-80 was piqued. Though the need for a jet trainer was never in question, the Navy, like the Air Force, was hesitant to allocate scarce acquisition funds. During early 1948, fifty essentially stock Air Force F-80Cs had been acquired to complement an initial three aircraft that had been used to study the feasibility of jet fighters in Navy service. During the course of assimilating these single-seat *Shooting Stars*, the resulting high attrition rate quickly removed any doubt that may have persisted concerning justification for the trainer.

A year after the arrival of the single-seat aircraft, an initial order for twenty-six Navy TF-80Cs—which in the interim had become T-33As—was placed. Upon delivery to the Navy, these officially were designated TO-2s and became the first of an eventual total of 699 of their type to enter Navy service.

Though the standard T-33 configuration was sufficient for most conventional Navy training requirements, the special needs associated with carrier operations were not so easily addressed. Johnson and select engineers who then were the core of what remained of the original *Skunk Works*, were well aware of the aircraft's failings in this part of the envelope. During October of 1952, as the T-33 production program continued to gain momentum and orders, the corporate offices agreed to support

a design study exploring the attributes of an improved version.

Johnson, in particular, aspired to upgrade the working environment of the instructor, and therefore the instructor's efficiency. Additionally, there was a general consensus that the approach and stall speeds of the standard T-33 were somewhat high for neophyte aviators, and definitely high for safe carrier training operations. In order to address part of the former problem, Johnson proposed to elevate the instructor's (aft) ejection seat some six inches and totally reconfigure both the windscreen (making it single-piece) and the canopy...all to improve forward visibility. In order to improve low speed performance and stability, leading edge slats were to be added to the wings, boundary layer control (BLC) was to be added to the flaps, and the horizontal and vertical tail surfaces were to be increased in size, and thus in area.

The BLC system was somewhat progressive for its day as the technology was relatively new and—because of expense—had never previously been applied to an operational aircraft. The system functioned using bleed air from the engine compressor section. Air was collected by a circular manifold from engine compressor chambers and discharged over the top of the flap leading edge along the entire flap span. The improvement in performance was expected to come in the form of a 4 knot reduction in landing speed, a 7 knot reduction in takeoff speed, and a 15% reduction in pattern speed when compared to similar figures for the standard T-33A.

Other changes were more subtle, but nevertheless noteworthy. The fuel system was to provide for single point high pressure refueling...which was expected to reduce refueling time to one-third that of the T-33. The landing gear also was redesigned to accommodate expected carrier landing loads. A sink-rate more than twice that of the T-33 was to be standard and the gear itself was to be capable

Instructor pilot's elevated rear seat was optimized to permit superior forward vision. In particular, this was expected to appeal to the US Navy, where forward vision was critical to aircraft carrier operations.

*One of the most significant changes found on the L-245--when comparing it to its predecessors--was the leading edge slat system installed for improved low speed stability.*

of absorbing five times the energy required of its Air Force sibling.

After reviewing "Kelly's" projected figures and improvements, the corporate offices concurred a prototype should be funded. By now referred to by the temporary design designation L-245, it was decided to acquire from the Air Force an uncompleted T-33A, and use this aircraft for the demonstrator airframe. Unofficially referred to by the still-unused Air Force designator, T-33B, the privately funded trainer was assembled by a small *Skunk Works* team at the Burbank facility and rolled out during late November of 1953.

Civil-registered N125D and strikingly painted in a non-military gold and white color scheme, the new aircraft, piloted by Tony LeVier, became airborne for the first time on December 16, 1953, at Lockheed's Burbank facility. During the preliminary test flights that followed, it became apparent that directional stability had been adversely affected by the

new, "humped" canopy configuration. Accordingly, the aircraft was grounded temporarily while an extended dorsal fin was added and other minor changes were made.

Though optimized for Navy service, the L-245 nevertheless was demonstrated to the Air Force during early 1954. Feeling the T-33 was adequate for its needs, the latter shied away from the new trainer, which then left the only serious production hope in Navy hands. Fortunately, preliminary trials utilizing Navy pilots resulted in extremely favorable reviews, and the Navy, desperately in need of a carrier-suitable jet trainer, awarded Lockheed a contract during May of 1954 for eight Model 1080-91-08s, officially designated T2V-1. Unlike the L-245 demonstrator, these aircraft would be equipped with non-jettisonable tip tanks, a retractable arrestor hook, and a generally strengthened airframe and landing gear. In addition, the nose landing gear was to be hydraulically adjustable in order to raise the

nose for improved carrier takeoff performance.

Between June 3 and June 7, 1954, the L-245 was formally evaluated by Navy pilots from the Naval Air Test Center at Patuxent River, Maryland. Shortly afterwards carrier suitability trials were conducted aboard the USS *Antietam*. The L-245 was then returned to the *Skunk Works* team for modification. Under the supervision of Johnson, it was modified to conform to the production aircraft standard. A hydraulically-adjustable nose landing gear, an arrestor hook, a revised tail cone, and other similar upgrades were incorporated. Painted in conventional Navy training unit colors, but still bearing its civil registration, the modification was completed during November of 1954 and it was flown shortly afterwards. Simulated catapult takeoffs and arrested landings, were conducted at the Naval Weapons Center, China Lake, California, and the resulting data was utilized to determine the final design features of the actual production aircraft. The first of the latter flew for the first time on January 20, 1956.

Unfortunately, the father of the two-seat P-80, V. F. "Mac" Short, did not live long enough to witness the extraordinary success of his offspring. During August of 1948, he died of a heart attack at his Lockheed desk...content only in knowing that his basic battle had been won. Some 5,691 T-33s of all kinds eventually were manufactured by Lockheed. An additional 656 aircraft were manufactured by Canadair in Canada, and 210 aircraft were manufactured by Kawasaki in Japan. Additionally, well over a thousand Lockheed manufactured T-33s eventually found their way into the air forces of over twenty countries around the world, many under the aegis of the Mutual Defense Aid Program. In all, the Navy bought 150 T2V-1s (redesignated T-1A on September 18, 1962) before the Lockheed production program ended during 1959.

### F-94 *Starfire*:

*"At this time, right after World War II, there was a whole stable of prototype airplanes, starting with the F-87, F-88, F-90, F-91, and a bunch of bombers. We had lots of prototypes then."* Clarence L. "Kelly" Johnson

The apparent failures during 1948 of several first-generation all-weather jet interceptors, including the Curtiss XP-87 *Blackhawk* and the Northrop XP-89 *Scorpion*, set the stage for yet another perturbation of the basic XP-80 airframe. With trainer, production fighter, and navalized versions either under development or being delivered to operational units, the standard P-80, by the beginning of the 1950s, gave every impression of being a true "Jack of all trades". In truth, it had suffered through considerable teething difficulties and had survived only because of perseverance on the part of its parent company and its superb engineering staff. By the advent of the somewhat unexpected Air Force need for an all-weather interceptor, most of the *Shooting Star's* initial failings had been overcome and it was generally well-understood from an aerodynamic and mechanical standpoint.

Observing the *Blackhawk* and *Scorpion* difficulties, the Air Force, under the aegis of a General Operational Requirement issued on October 8, 1948, elected to explore the attributes of extant alternative aircraft that might be utilized in the interim until the failings of the planned production aircraft could be corrected. Pressure to bring an effective all-weather jet

*The first T2V-1. This aircraft was developed as a result of the Navy's favorable impression of the L-245 and the performance and safety improvements it offered over other then-extant carrier trainers.*

interceptor into the operational inventory as rapidly as possible had surfaced the preceding year when the emerging post-war Russian long-range strategic bomber force first unveiled a facsimile reproduction of the venerable Boeing B-29 *Superfortress*. This aircraft, eventually attributed to the Tupolev design bureau and formally designated Tu-4, was code-named *Bull* by the West.

The appearance of the Tu-4 during the 1947 Soviet Aviation Day display at Tushino near Moscow proved a turning point in the benign image presented by the Russians during the immediate post-war years. Possession of B-29 technology explicitly implied a long-range bomber capability that had not been predicted to occur by Western intelligence bureaus until years later. This, coupled with the aggressive nature of the Russian dictator, Joseph Stalin, and the predicted development of a Russian nuclear weapon (which in fact came to pass with the detonation of a crude device during August of 1949), provided the US government, and in particular, the Air Force, with the incentive needed to actively pursue acquisition of an interim all-weather interceptor to fill the gap that occurred with the failure of the XP-87 and the delayed introduction of the XP-89.

Hall Hibbard, "Kelly" Johnson, Rus Daniell, and several other Lockheed engineers had proposed advanced derivatives of the P-80 to the Air Force on several occasions between 1945 and 1947. Among these were studies calling for aircraft equipped with radar and advanced weaponry, including air-to-air missiles. These were reviewed with a modicum of interest and accordingly, cost justifications remained elusive...until the Tu-4 revelation.

During March of 1948, after exploring several alternatives—including the Navy's new Douglas XF3D-1 *Skyknight*—the Air Force approached Lockheed with a request that a interceptor feasibility study, utilizing the TP-80C airframe, be initiated immediately. The envisioned interim interceptor would be required to accommodate the Hughes-developed E-1 fire control system and, in the aft crew compartment, a radar operator and his equipment instead of an instructor pilot.

The first of its kind, the E-1 was ordered during June of 1948 when the Air Force requested the AN/APG-3 radar be adapted to the Northrop F-89; by contract amendment dated November of 1948, the requirement was extended to include a "new Lockheed interceptor". The resulting modified AN/APG-3 was redesignated AN/APG-33 and the entire system, including the A-1C gunsight, during 1949, became the E-1 fire control system.

Design and engineering of the new P-80

*The prototype YF-94 was the first TF-80C, 48-356, modified with a new nose, an afterburner-equipped engine, and miscellaneous upgraded subsystems.*

derivative—ordered by the Air Force on October 14, 1949—was assigned by Johnson to a *Skunk Works*-style team led by Rus Daniell. The resulting remake of the original TP-80C incorporated the new radar in an enlarged Lock-foam (a first-generation dielectric material developed by Lockheed) nose radome while permitting retention not only of the original two .50 caliber machine guns, but an additional pair of machine guns in the same compartment, as well. Hughes, supervising the installation and intimately involved in the design and reconfiguration process, found the modification considerably more difficult than originally anticipated. Repackaging the fire control system—which originally had been created for use as a gun-laying radar in the Convair B-36 heavy bomber—was not an easy task.

During November of 1948, the TP-80C (by now officially referred to as the TF-80C) was endorsed by Sec. of Defense James Forrestal. During January, Lockheed was given a letter of intent for the modification of two TF-80Cs to the interceptor configuration (under the initial designation of XTF-80C).

The initiation of detailed design for what was referred to in-house at Lockheed as the Model 780 revealed the need for substantial changes to the basic two-seat trainer. In light of the additional weight of the AN/APG-33 and associated E-1 fire control system, the standard Allison J33 turbojet engine was determined to have insufficient thrust to meet the specified minimum performance requirements. Daniell's team therefore called for use of the J33-A-33 which, though similar dimensionally to the original engine, was equipped with a single-stage afterburner. The engine had a dry thrust rating of 4,000 pounds and a afterburner rating of 6,000 pounds. Conveniently, the

increased engine length and weight were offset in terms of center of gravity by the weight of the radar and fire control system.

The addition of the radar system dictated a major redesign of the TF-80C's nose. In a successful attempt to retain most of the original P-80's weapons complement, the radar and associated electronics were placed forward and above the gun bay which remained capacious enough to accommodate four .50 caliber machine guns and ammunition boxes with 300 rounds per gun. Other changes included an increased-area vertical tail and the loss of 30 gallons in fuel tank capacity as a result of tank redesign to accommodate the radar system and operator's space requirements. With only a total internal fuel capacity of 318 gallons, it became mandatory for the Model 780 to almost always be flown with underwing (later, centerline) tip tanks. These (in their first iteration) had a 165 gallon capacity which gave the aircraft a total fuel capacity of 648 gallons.

Concurrent with the work on the Model 780 and in light of increasing interest in afterburners and their proposed use in then-forthcoming Lockheed fighter designs such as the P-80D and E and the XP-90, Lockheed and the Solar Corporation undertook a major afterburner design study by modifying a Westinghouse J34 and equipping it with a Solar afterburner. This combination, in turn, was installed on the second XP-80A, which, as noted in Chapter 3, had been built as a jet engine testbed.

Use of the XP-80A for afterburner research during December of 1948 proved an enlightening experience...not only for Lockheed, but also for their test pilot, Tony LeVier. On the first flight following modification, LeVier found the J34's afterburner impossible to light. After several attempts utilizing standard

*Prototype YF-94 equipped with centerline tip-tanks. Rear cockpit appears to be covered for flight test purposes.*

*The Lockheed-funded, civil-registered (N34C) L-188 prototype for what was to become the F-94C Starfire.*

The prototype F-94C, 50-955, was the original L-188 demonstrator with a military serial number. As acquired by the Air Force, the aircraft initially was assigned the YF-97A designator. During September of 1950 this was changed to YF-94C.

procedure, he elected to accelerate engine rpm to near 100% and then abruptly shove the throttle into afterburner. This injected a large amount of fuel into the burner section and caused an enormous burst of hot flame. The latter instantaneously moved downstream to the afterburner fuel nozzles...which then ignited. This technique was developed into the "hot streak" afterburner ignition method at a later date and became a fairly standard, if not somewhat unorthodox method for afterburner lightoff.

Still not convinced LeVier's was the method of choice, on the ninth afterburner flight

Solar engineers asked him to attempt an afterburner light after closing the exhaust nozzle "eyelids". These worked as promised, but the subsequent overheating of the hot section literally melted parts of the assembly and all but destroyed the engine. LeVier's emergency landing was successful but the airplane required considerable down time for refurbishment. On the positive side, Solar and Lockheed became considerably more aware of the sensitivity of afterburner fuel flow and relight requirements.

Concurrent with the test flying of the XP-80A, construction of the two Model 780 proto-

types got underway in a secluded area at Lockheed's Plant B-1. Two TF-80Cs, the prototype and the eighteenth production aircraft, were pulled for the project and stripped to their basic structures for modification. Some 75% of the original aircraft were utilized, with the remaining 25% to be made up of totally new parts.

Typical of a *Skunk Works*-type effort, the first Model 780 was ready for roll-out in no less than fifteen weeks. Initially referred to as an ETF-80C and then as an ET-33A (with the "E" prefix for Exempt, rather than Experimental), it and its stablemate to follow were generally— but not officially—acknowledged to be designated YF-94 (interestingly, subsequent modifications to the second aircraft resulted in it being formally redesignated YF-94 during April of 1950, EYF-94 during January of 1953, and finally EYF-94A during September of 1954; this aircraft still carried the last mentioned designation when it was dropped from the Air Force inventory during February of 1956).

When completed, the first of the two prototype Model 780s only superficially resembled the forthcoming production aircraft. The Hughes radar had not been installed, the engine was a conventional J33 without afterburner, and the highly classified aft cockpit was bare of virtually all functional radar-related equipment. Hughes, in fact, was having difficulty in meeting its radar delivery schedule and it appeared that initial Model 780 flight tests, for the foreseeable future, would have to be conducted with lead weights in place of the planned electronics. Due in part to these delays, Russ Daniell went to the trouble of exploring other radar options, even proposing that a competing Westinghouse radar be utilized in place of the Hughes AN/APG-33. When Hughes finally delivered the first E-1 system for installation, these efforts were discontinued.

The first Model 780, upon completion, was trucked to nearby Van Nuys airport for initiation of flight tests. Van Nuys was less populated than Burbank, and it was assumed that flight testing could be accomplished with less impact on the surrounding population. Following a short series of static and low and high speed taxi tests, on April 16, 1949, Tony LeVier, with

The YF-94C prototypes, of which there were two, were the first of the F-94 family to be equipped with swepth horizontal tail surfaces and power-boosted elevators.

flight test engineer Glenn Fulkerson in the radar operator's position, piloted the aircraft into the air for the first time.

Installation of an afterburner-equipped J33, shortly afterwards, quickly underscored the testy nature of such propulsion system technology. Flame-outs proved commonplace, and consistent inflight relights were elusive. Eventually, a concerted effort involving engineers from Allison, Solar, and Lockheed led to the development of a dependable afterburner flame-holder.

As flight characteristics of the two Model 780s—during early 1949 officially redesignated YF-94A and named *Starfire* by Lockheed—had proven benign, and the afterburner anomalies finally had been overcome, the actual production program was consummated without difficulty per the original contract. The first production F-94A took to the air on July 1, 1949, and was officially accepted by the Air Force on December 29. It eventually would be followed by 853 other *Starfires*—and make claim to being the Air Force's first all-weather jet fighter.

"Kelly" Johnson, not one to be content with past achievements, on February 24, 1949, during an F-94A mock-up review, proposed an F-94B for study in Lockheed's preliminary design department. The following March 17, as this study progressed, he proposed for the first time the development of a rocket nose for a fixed air-to-air rocket installation. This was the result of a general trend in fighter design which seemed to be heading in the direction of all-rocket armaments. Though it would not be incorporated in the F-94B as built (as a result of an Air Force decision made during August of 1949), it would surface again as the armament complement for the F-94C.

Lockheed pursued the advanced, rocket-equipped F-94 configuration under the in-house L-188 designator, but concurrently pursued follow-on Air Force orders for a less sophisticated F-94 referred to as the Model 780-76-12. This proposed *Starfire* retained the gun armament, the E-1 fire control system, and the J33-A-33 engine, but added a significant number of subtle improvements that included a 1,500 pounds per square inch hydraulic system (in place of the 1,000 pounds per square inch system of the F-94A), increased rear cockpit headroom, a more effective pressurization system, a high-pressure oxygen system, and windshield anti-icing and de-fogging. Additionally, to accommodate bad weather landings, a Sperry-developed Zero Reader would be provided the pilot along with an AN/ARN-5B glide path receiver, a RC-105D localizer receiver, and a AN/ARN-12 marker beacon receiver. In an attempt to improve range and endurance, this model also would be equipped with 230 gallon Fletcher tip tanks (later also retrofitted to most F-94As).

The nineteenth F-94A, redesignated YF-94B, was modified in production as a result of engineering work conducted under the direction of Rus Daniell. Meeting the Model 780-76-12 specification, it was not the ultimate rocket-equipped interceptor Lockheed aspired to build, but it was a good interim compromise until stronger Air Force interest could be generated.

The YF-94B flew for the first time with Lockheed's Tony LeVier at the controls on September 29, 1950—and as expected, performed identically to its predecessor. By the advent of this aircraft, F-94 performance figures and over-all capability were being challenged, and in some cases, eclipsed by newer aircraft rolling from competitors' production lines. Hibbard and Johnson were well aware of this

*As first built, the YF-94C, as the YF-97A, was primarily an aerodynamic and propulsion system testbed. It initially was flown with a Rolls Royce Tay in place of the production Pratt & Whitney J48.*

*The first YF-94C was modified to incorporate a production standard nose, spoilers for roll control, and an enlarged vertical tail for improved directional stability.*

and had continued to promote development of an advanced F-94 to the Air Force.

With corporate support, Johnson continued to actively pursue the advanced F-94/L-188 configuration (not the one represented by the YF-94B) and eventually settled on a design that offered an all-new wing with a noticeably reduced thickness/chord ratio, a swept horizontal stabilizer, redesigned and considerably more effective speed brakes, increased internal fuel capacity, an all-rocket armament, and the improved E-5 fire control system coupled with the more powerful 250 kW AN/APG-40 radar. Most importantly, the US license-built version of the British Rolls Royce *Tay*, the Pratt & Whitney J48, was to replace the Allison J33. This engine would provide no less than 30% more thrust than its predecessor in afterburner.

During July of 1948, the Air Force was briefed by Johnson on the upgraded version of the L-188—which would eventually be referred to as the F-94C. The initial reaction, in part to the expected availability of the Northrop F-89, was not favorable. Hibbard and Johnson, though modestly disappointed, returned to Lockheed and embarked on a major effort to convince corporate officers to let them build a prototype of the ultimate F-94. They rationalized, convincingly, that having actual hardware to drive home their arguments would turn the Air Force in their favor.

Accordingly, minimal corporate funding was allocated, and in order to keep costs under control, a single F-94A, produced without government money, was pulled from Lockheed's production line and set aside for the reincarnation. Civil registered, and equipped temporarily with a non-afterburning Rolls Royce *Tay* turbojet, this aircraft, with Tony LeVier piloting, took to the air for the first time on January 19, 1950, flying from the Van Nuys airport.

Follow-on flight tests did not go smoothly. The aircraft's high thrust and conservative aerodynamics allowed it to fly only cautiously in the upper right hand corner of its performance envelope. It suffered from "Dutch roll", "Mach tuck" (at 0.84 to 0.85 Mach), aileron buzz, reduced elevator effectiveness at high Mach, poor directional stability, and unsatisfactory low-speed handling. Though LeVier later would often refer to the F-94C as his favorite

aircraft, this description was not applicable during the early days of flight test.

Changes incorporated in the prototype, and later applied to the production series to correct performance and handling deficiencies, included the following: removal of the wing root extension fillet (a carry-over from the wing design of the original XP-80) to improve low speed approach and stall characteristics; incorporation of a power-boosted, swept horizontal tail to eliminate high-frequency vibration at high Mach numbers; the addition of dampers to correct aileron buzz; the addition of spoilers to increase roll rate and control; the redesign of the drag chute compartment door to eliminate shock stall at high Mach numbers; an increase in the vertical fin area in order to improve directional stability at high Mach; and supplementing the dive brake complement with additional dive brakes on the empennage sides.

Johnson's perseverance finally paid off one month after the prototype's first flight. Ongoing difficulties with a radar-equipped North American F-86 derivative and the Northrop F-89 had convinced the Air Force that lengthy delays before service introduction of these aircraft were inevitable. Accordingly, once again they were forced to go with an interim aircraft...and the F-94 was the only viable option. The L-188 testbed now was bought by the Air Force and assigned a serial number. Temporarily referred to as the YF-97, it was repainted and, over a period of several months,

*F-94C nose mock-up with tubes for twenty-four 2.75-inch folding-fin air-to-air rockets.*

F-94D EIGHT GUN NOSE

CAL. 50 M-3 GUN

*The YF-94D nose gun bay full-scale mock-up. This advanced F-94 version was to have been a single-seat ground attack aircraft with increased range and improved external stores capability.*

slowly brought up to near-production standard with the installation of an afterburner, the larger centerline tip tanks, and a production standard nose.

Concurrent with the acquisition of the YF-97, a fully militarized prototype YF-97 equipped with the improved Hughes E-5 fire control system (which consisted of the AN/APG-40 radar and the AN/APG-84 computer) and the more powerful Pratt & Whitney J48-P-3 (6,000 pound thrust dry and 8,000 pound thrust with afterburner), also was ordered on July 21, 1950. This aircraft later would be upgraded to production configuration when its original nose was replaced with the standard rocket-armament configured nose and its associated fire control system. With the order for the YF-97, the Air Force also ordered 388 production aircraft (Model 880-75-13s). Initially designated F-97As, these were formally redesignated F-94Cs on September 12, 1950.

Flight tests confirmed that the YF-97, though not as fast as the F-86D and F-89A, was a significant improvement over the earlier F-94A and F-94B. This, unfortunately, was offset by the myriad problems besetting the Hughes fire control system, the autopilot, the drag chute (a first for an operational fighter), the fuel dump system, and the engine and its associated afterburner. The J48, in fact, failed its 150-hour qualification test and was not able to successfully pass until May of 1952. Even after this, problems with the fuel burner nozzles and the afterburner remained unresolved for a considerable period of time.

Progressively, however, deficiencies were corrected by Lockheed and Pratt & Whitney. In addition to corrective changes, Lockheed introduced two improvements which altered the appearance of the aircraft; the rounded radome of early production aircraft was replaced by a more pointed unit, and, beginning with the 100th production aircraft (but later retrofitted to earlier aircraft), armament was doubled by mounting a 12-rocket pod on the leading edge of each wing. Finally, to minimize horizontal tail buffeting, which had progressively worsened from the F-80 through the F-94A/B into the F-94C, Lockheed introduced a box fairing covering a portion of the fuselage located at the junction of the tail surfaces.

Although requiring much time and delaying the F-94C's entry into service by nearly two years, the various airframe, system, and powerplant modifications and improvements resulted in the Air Force obtaining a potent interceptor. True, the F-94C was not as fast at high altitudes as other all-weather fighters then being procured by the Air Force, but at low altitudes it was the best of the lot. Furthermore, once modifications eliminated engine flame-out when all 24 rockets were salvoed, the closed breech installation of its armament rendered the *Starfire* substantially more accurate than the F-86D and F-89D which had open-ended rocket installations.

In the end, its limited range was the aircraft's major shortcoming. This, however, was not due to a design oversight; being the ultimate development of a relatively small 1943 design, the F-94C did not have the internal volume required for greater fuel capacity.

The first nine production F-94Cs were accepted by the Air Force during Fiscal Year 1952. The last 225 *Starfires* were accepted during Fiscal Year 1954. Eventually, the F-94C went on to have a lengthy and modestly successful Air Force service life.

### The XF-90:

*"The XF-90 was the only airplane to defeat the atom bomb. It's military requirement concept was poor, and it was ten years before the engine for which it was designed was available. It didn't come out good."* Clarence L. "Kelly" Johnson

During mid-1945, "Kelly" Johnson realized the P-80 configuration had serious limitations in terms of maximum speed, range, and firepower, and along with a select group of engineers from the XP-80 project began to set their sights on considerably more advanced aircraft configurations. Information gleaned from captured German files on swept wing technology proved particularly alluring and over a period of several months, some sixty-five different configurations exploring swept wings were given serious scrutiny. Encompassed in this study were V-tailed, W-winged, tri-engine, and numerous other then-unorthodox approaches.

On August 28, 1945, the Air Technical Service Center released a request for new fighter design proposals. Johnson responded less than two months later, on October 15, with a twin-engine design powered by two of Lockheed's L-1000 axial flow turbojets. The following month, from November 27 through 30, Johnson was at Wright Field formally

*Two F-94Bs, 51-5500 and 51-5501, were modified to serve as F-94D weapon system testbeds. Each was equipped with the elongated F-94D nose and associated gun complement.*

*The proposed production F-94D would have superficially resembled the F-94C but would have incorporated an increased-area wing, the revised nose, and a single-seat cockpit.*

 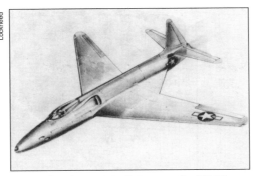 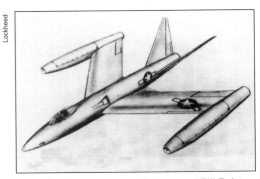

*Numerous configuration studies--some verging on the bizarre--for what eventually became the XF-90 were conducted by Lockheed's Don Palmer and Bill Ralston prior to settling on the relatively conventional swept-wing design that was actually built.*

proposing the L-153, as the new aircraft was called. This configuration was reviewed with considerable interest, but the response to the Lockheed powerplants was less than enthusiastic. On January 11, Johnson proposed an alternate configuration powered by two General Electric TG-180s. A month later, still another engine was suggested, this being the Westinghouse Model 24C.

By early April, the new aircraft (inclusive of designs being submitted by other manufacturers) was being referred to by the Air Force as the XP-90 and was defined as a fixed-wing, twin-engine, Westinghouse-powered aircraft. The Air Force specification, like the aircraft's mission, proved vacillatory and it became difficult for Johnson and his team to settle on any one design. Regardless, a Phase I study contract was awarded to Lockheed and a $25,000 work order was issued on June 7. The official contract for two Model 90 aircraft was signed on June 20, and as a result, on August 29, intensive work was begun in preliminary design reevaluating what had transpired to that point. A substantial number of configurations were studied with the final design being a variable-geometry aircraft having a 25,000 pound gross weight.

While the initial work was being reviewed at Wright Field, on September 12, 1946, a decision was made by Johnson to have Willis Hawkins "start a study of a delta wing bi-motor". Once the basic design had been settled, a wind tunnel model was built and initially tested during January of 1947.

On November 18 through 22, the improved, variable-geometry XP-90 configuration was presented to Wright Field personnel by Hall Hibbard and Johnson. The two Lockheed engineers also took the opportunity to open discussion on a delta wing configuration, presenting facts and figures to Gen. Lawrence Craigie and the others who were present. This generated considerable interest, much to Hibbard and Johnson's surprise, and two days later, a similar response was received from the Navy during a presentation in Washington, D.C.

As a result of the Air Force and Navy interest in the delta wing, on December 2, Johnson proposed to Hibbard that the conventional XP-90 be shelved and work continued on only the delta wing configuration. It was suggested by Johnson that the company push hard for prototype funding so that actual hardware could be manufactured and flight tested at the earliest possible date. Accordingly, work on the variable-geometry XP-90 was stopped.

On February 3, 1947, Lockheed received a letter from Wright Field "authorizing our designation of the delta wing version of our studies as the XP-90." It also was noted on this date that, "no work was done on the variable sweep-

*This tailed-delta wind-tunnel model was studied with considerable intensity and considered the most likely hardware candidate until very late in the XF-90's design history.*

*Full-scale mock-up of the XF-90 (note XP-90 on nose). Though aesthetically pleasing, the actual aircraft proved overweight and underpowered by the time it was finally built and flown.*

back version after December 1, 1946".

On February 19, "Kelly" Johnson noted in the XP-90 log, "Just about ready to call our first group together for a conference on starting the mock-up. The weight situation is considerably out of hand, and every effort must be made to get about 1,000 pounds out of the airplane. We have arbitrarily established a normal gross weight of 21,000 pounds, landing weight of 17,500 pounds, and over-load takeoff of 25,000 pounds. This last weight is about 500 pounds short of what I believe to be the actual weight, but we are unable to make the range at higher weights".

Wind tunnel work on the delta wing planform now was well underway at Pasadena's California Institute of Technology. On April 8, "Kelly" noted, "Went over wind tunnel tests and found an error in interpretation on effect of sharp leading edge. The airplane was completely out of bed with no apparent solution to rolling instability at high angles of attack and in regard to directional stability at high angles. The sharp leading edge which I had proposed in a previous memo will apparently correct both of these deficiencies quite readily. In addition, I requested tests again on leading edge devices to lead to the elimination of the trimmer."

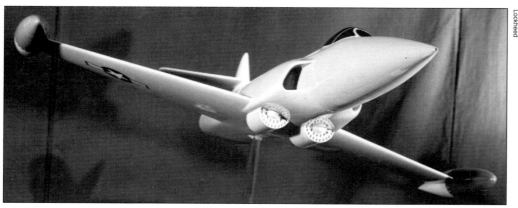

*Rotating 2.75-inch folding-fin air-to-ground rocket canisters were just one of several different armament systems studied for the XF-90. The wing tip pods also were optimized to carry both fuel and missiles.*

*Static testing of the XF-90's ejection seat was conducted at Lockheed using a functional seat, an anthropomorphic dummy, and a large safety net.*

*The first of two XF-90s was delivered by truck to Edwards AFB during late May of 1949. There it was reassembled in preparation for its first flight.*

*XF-90 field maintenance was undertaken as necessary at Edwards AFB in the hangars allocated to Lockheed by the Air Force for use during the flight test program.*

The following day it was stated, "The fuselage size is much too small and its drag considerably out of hand. While a droppable nose is being studied, I would consider this mainly to be a production feature and will take steps to provide an ejection seat for jumping at low altitude without dropping the nose and a P-80 type canopy as the present proposed canopy will not release in its existing form."

As wind tunnel work progressed over the following month, the rapidly evolving numbers continued to give every indication that the delta wing XP-90 was leading to a dead-end street. Drag and weight figures were untenable, and there appeared to be no solutions in sight. From April 21 to May 16, the various reports emanating from the wind tunnel remained negative. As Johnson noted, "The delta wing version of the airplane gets entirely out of hand because of high weights, poor trimability at high lifts, and high drag. Numerous versions of the airplane were tested, but the most probable configuration resulted in the use of wing tip trimmers and wing tip verticals. No progress report was written on May 1 because of lack of decisions on the airplane."

On May 19, Johnson rendered a final verdict, "I wrote a memo to Hibbard suggesting we discontinue the delta wing version and make a conventional type incorporating Fowler flaps and extending leading edge with one or two engines. We decided to call General Craigie to inform him of the situation and propose a visit about the middle of June to sum up the state of development."

The decision, however, was not all Johnson's. Other members of the team, including Willis Hawkins, Jack Weaver, and Phil Colman, disagreed with the termination and as a result, additional wind tunnel tests were conducted. Afterwards, during a period from June 23 through July 11, Johnson prepared "Lockheed Report No. 6178" wherein the delta wing configuration was compared to the standard fixed wing. Johnson's conclusions remained the same...the fixed wing was the better of the two aircraft to carry through to development.

This decision was not a light one. As Johnson noted, "It will be extremely difficult to go to Wright Field and change our mind for the third time on this configuration, but I feel at least that we have thoroughly evaluated what the XP-90 should be with the possible exception of powerplants where I have still recommended to Mr. Hibbard that we use a single I-40 type with tailpipe burning."

On July 14, Hall Hibbard and Johnson carried the report on the delta wing XP-90 to Wright Field and presented it. "It was extremely well received, and in spite of its being an unpleasant job to admit our early mistakes, they took it in grand fashion and on July 16 gave us permission to go forward with the conventional airplane. We stirred up a considerable amount of interest in the I-40 engine and pointed out emphatically the dependence of the airplane on tailpipe burning."

The Wright Field support led to a renewed XP-90 effort. The project, in its swept wing Model 90 form, now was turned over to Don Palmer and a decision was made to investigate Allison and Westinghouse engine options. On July 23, it was determined that 13-1/2 months would be required for first flight and that two prototypes could be built on the contract balance of $4 million. Eight days later, 36 personnel, including Bill Ralston as Palmer's assistant, were assigned to the project.

As design and initial construction work got underway, it became readily apparent that one of the major unknowns was the powerplant. The aircraft, because of its weight, was going to be highly dependent upon afterburning engines in order to meet its performance goals. The I-40 engine was still experimental, and little was known about its afterburner and associated dependability. Accordingly, beginning on September 8, 1947, Johnson "got up a proposal on afterburning on XP-80A-2" and later carried it to Wright Field for consideration. Tentatively approved by the Air Materiel Command during December, this resulted in the afterburner research flight test program one year later as noted in the F-94 section of this chapter.

By December 2, 1947, the full-scale XP-90 mock-up was completed and made ready for

Air Force inspection. This took place over a period of four days, ending on December 6, and as Johnson noted, the inspection was "very successful". Concerns had been expressed about the six 20 mm cannon armament, and in particular, shell ejection damage, but over-all, the review had gone without any major difficulty.

Beginning on March 3, 1948, Johnson went to Washington D. C. and Wright Field in order to present proposals for ground attack and reconnaissance variants. The former was considered a mandatory capability in order for a production contract to be authorized, and the latter was a configuration in which considerable interest had been expressed.

As work progressed on the XP-90 prototype, Johnson became more and more aware of how difficult it was to keep intact the XP-80-type *Skunk Works* environment around the new aircraft. On March 17, he noted, "Having trouble keeping the P-80 experimental system on the '90. Considerable discussions on letter of agreement with manufacturing. They are proposing such changes that all advantages of an engineering experimental setup would be lost."

On April 15, this dilemma apparently was resolved by a modified letter of agreement between the manufacturing and engineering departments. "It is now much more acceptable as it eliminates such features as free access of the manufacturing people to the design area and incorporation of production changes in the prototype airplane. This was a very rough deal."

By early May, the two prototype XP-90s were starting to take shape. Changes in propulsion, basic mission objectives, and miscellaneous hardware requirements seemed to plague progress at sporadic intervals, and as a result, a hoped-for September first flight date proved impossibly optimistic. In the interim, new missions for the aircraft continued to surface. During August, for instance, queries concerning making it into a night fighter were received. Johnson responded with a quick study offering a configuration equipped with an articulated Martin nose turret, but noted, "I do not feel this to be a good design."

By mid-August the aircraft was still mired in engineering and manufacturing difficulties. Morale was at an all-time low, and many of the elite team's personnel were getting worn down by the intense work schedules and the seemingly impossible deadlines. Transfers to other Lockheed departments were becoming more commonplace and Johnson was beginning to have problems keeping qualified team members on staff. On October 20, he noted, "Had session with Ralston and Palmer about morale of Engineering Group. Pressure has been so intense for so long that many of the old gang want to make changes to other groups no longer working on prototype development. This has been a long tough job."

On November 4, the wing and fuselage of the first aircraft were mated. As noted by Johnson, there were "no difficulties". The first flight date, however, remained very much undetermined, and it appeared that the spring of 1949 was a best guess.

On February 1, 1949, all plans for the production F-90 (the "P" designator had been changed to "F" during June of 1948) were stopped due to a "probability that no production order will be granted until F-88, F-90, and F-93 are evaluated. Starting to reduce engineers on project." Work at a reduced pace continued,

*The XF-90 pioneered the use of high-strength 75ST aluminum alloy...which was nearly 25% stronger than 24ST aluminum alloy then serving as the industry standard.*

however, and on February 7, the company agreed to finance Johnson's proposed development of an all-weather fighter nose for the second aircraft using company funds.

On May 10, the engines were run for the first time on the partially completed first aircraft. A wing fitting failure curtailed further ground testing on the following day, but on May 13, a Friday, the aircraft was successfully taxied for the first time. These tests were continued through May 17 and eight days later, the XF-90 was partially disassembled and loaded aboard a truck for the trip to Muroc.

Finally, on June 3, after numerous high speed taxi runs, "we flew the airplane for thirty minutes." An official first flight in front of some 300 personnel took place the next day at 9:00 a.m. The aircraft, as it had been on its first flight, was piloted by Tony LeVier, who kept it airborne for some 30 minutes. Chasing him in a TF-80C was Lockheed test pilot "Fish" Salmon...with Johnson in the back seat. As Johnson noted, the flight was "a great success, but could not go to high speed because of rudder nibbling."

From June 4 through July 29, the aircraft completed a total of 17 flights. The non-afterburning Westinghouse XJ34-WE-11 engines proved very underpowered and RATO was required for almost every takeoff. Low speed buffeting was encountered and eliminated, but

a rudder compressibility anomaly at Mach 0.82 was not so easily overcome.

From August 19 to September 6, the first XF-90 was grounded in order to install the afterburners and change the rudder. The flight testing that followed proved inconclusive, however, as afterburner problems were rampant and solutions were not easily or quickly developed. These difficulties adversely affected the flight test program and were bearable only because the competitors' aircraft—in what now had become a tight race for a still ill-defined "penetration fighter/ground attack aircraft" requirement—also were having serious difficulties.

By September 29, the date of the first flight with tip tanks in place, the first aircraft had accumulated eighteen hours of flying time. On October 6, Johnson noted, "Still running ground thrust tests on afterburners. Rudder buffets in spite of longer cord and smaller trailing edge angles." As the trouble continued, Johnson's frustrations and his log notes escalated in exasperation, "More of the same kind of trouble. Having difficulty getting to altitude without afterburning and making very short flights when afterburning. Talking to Tony on bonuses."

Ironically, similar difficulties were befalling the competition. Though not one to revel in their misfortune, Johnson never failed to critically observe what they were doing. On

*During the course of the fly-off entailed in competing with McDonnell's XF-88 and North American's XF-93, the XF-90 carried and dropped 1,000 pound bombs and fired its six 20 mm machine guns.*

*RATO capability was demonstrated on several occasions and was found to dramatically improve the aircraft's takeoff performance...particularly on hot days and when the aircraft was heavily loaded.*

45

*The XF-90 was a large aircraft, particularly when compared to its F-80* Shooting Star *predecessor. The XF-90 weighed approximately twice as much as the P-80A.*

November 22, he noted, "McDonnell have sent their first airplane back to St. Louis for extending the fuselage and fixing the ducts. Their second plane crashed attempting to land with one engine and stalled out at 50 feet. Battle of the 88, 90, and 93 is very intense, and here we are full of problems."

The XF-90's problems were manifold and not easily resolved. The aircraft, though never intended as a true "envelope expander", was nevertheless—and somewhat inadvertently—a technology testbed. Lessons being taught would eventually pay-off in later years...though in 1949 this was a difficult thing to see. And Johnson, in his usual fashion, refused to give up on an aircraft he truly believed in. On December 20, this perseverance was never more visible than when he noted..."Having trouble with wing slots not opening at high g; locked them out and then encountered terrific buffeting. Am going to try revision to center aileron section at leading edge. Made complete stall studies in flight and followed all maneuvers in the TF-80. Testing is getting tough with Tony, Fish, and myself all having California flu and not doing a good job at high g's."

Three days later he noted, "The first (wind

tunnel) test with my revised leading edge showed extremely important improvements. Center section stall is delayed 5° to 6° and basic wing lift increased 10%. Hope this works full scale. Had Palmer start construction of this modification. Also decided to revise aileron boost to get a better balance between high and low speed flight."

On January 4, Lockheed received a letter from the Air Materiel Command stating that April of 1950 would be the date for the formal XF-90 evaluation at Muroc. The Lockheed fighter would be actively compared to the McDonnell XF-88 and North American XF-93. This immediately increased the pressure on Johnson, Palmer, and the rest of the team and forced the renewal of effort to correct the XF-90's seemingly innumerable problems. From February 20 through April 20, this work resulted in general elimination of engine roughness caused by tailpipe misalignments, cockpit noise resulting from open gun blast tubes, and directional oscillations caused by closed exhaust nozzle "eyelids". In the interim, during test flights, LeVier had inched the speed of the aircraft upward, eventually achieving Mach 1.12 in a shallow dive.

On May 22, Phase II testing, involving a

detailed Air Force examination using Air Force test pilots, was initiated. Col. Richard Johnson, Capt. Newman, and several other pilots were assigned to the various Lockheed, McDonnell, and North American aircraft. As Johnson noted in the log, "We had no formal warning as to what this (Phase II) would be, but it has developed into quite a rat race. Evaluation will be done in three parts, which are performance testing, handling characteristics, and tactical evaluation. About 14 pilots will be checked out in the airplane."

The evaluation progressed in spurts mixed with both frustration and humor. On May 25, Johnson noted, "Greatly worried. Capt. Newman got lost on his first flight, landing at wrong end of Muroc. I got him by radio and directed him to our base." And on June 1, in frustration he wrote, "Getting increasingly more information on what the evaluation is to be. I am greatly afraid that we will not be given credit for having a full strength unrestricted airplane, while others will get the benefit in performance and not be sufficiently penalized. I will write a letter, trying to emphasize this fact. Capt. Newman landed at the main base at extremely high speed, and locked the brakes. It completely burned out a tire and two inches of iron from the wheel, going off the runway at a high speed. Have robbed No.2 airplane of its wheels and tires and plan to continue at once."

On June 5 through 9, the log gave additional insights into the intense competition, "Making excellent progress on Phase II. Fighting daily battles to keep airplane running. Fuel tank troubles probably will cost us our ability to finish performance testing this week. Have not been able to get data on our own airplane from Air Force, but have been very successful in getting complete story by radio. The Air Force pays no attention whatsoever to their own regulations on giving out performance data by radio, and on having their airplanes chased during critical tests. Expect to check out more pilots next week, but will make a desperate effort to have some kind of a training program. North American had the XF-93 blow up on June 6th, and are hauling it back to the factory. While it was an afterburner fuel leak, the pilot disregarded North American's instructions and started another takeoff after landing. Very lucky not to kill himself. Both North American and I expect we will lose at least one of the three airplanes in checking out all these pilots on all three airplanes."

Fortunately, that was not to happen, but unfortunately, the competition was to bear little fruit, not only for Lockheed, but for the two other competitors, as well. Johnson, in reviewing the Phase II tests noted, "The Evaluation was extremely poorly organized and only at the end of it did Col. Dorr Newton, who was officially in charge of the whole program, arrive. He is a fine fellow who was very cooperative. Had several explosions, a fire, and lost all turbine buckets on one engine during test. The airplane proved many of our design features and flew well. Performance of our men was extremely good. We were visited by different maintenance and inspection groups, as well as those looking into producibility. An extremely busy time."

On July 18 through 22, Johnson flew to Wright Field and then to Washington, D.C. attempting to promote new versions of the XF-90. Among these were a variety of single engine configurations including the Model 190-33-02 powered by an Allison J33-A-29 and the Model 390-35-02 powered by a General

*Lockheed proposed many different F-90 configurations and options to the Air Force, including this photo-reconnaissance version depicted in model form.*

Electric J47-GE-21. A twin engine upgrade, the Model 290-34-03 also was proffered, powered by two Westinghouse J46-WE-2s. None of these would come to fruition, primarily because of the relatively poor performance of the first prototype. Additionally, intake and structural modifications required to accommodate the single engine arrangements were too expensive and too complicated to be justified.

On July 25, Johnson got the first strong hint that the penetration fighter program was not likely to be funded. "In spite of my visit last week, we received instruction today to discontinue flying both airplanes and store them at Muroc. This is apparently due to the money aspect of the problem and not to future plans for the type." The latter statement was typical Johnson optimism, but not a realistic assessment of the situation. Though he remained, on July 29, convinced the XF-90 had won the Phase II fly-off, on August 23, the final verdict was reached, "They threw out completely all penetration fighters. Apparently the rules of war have changed and they are more interested in the ground attack versions. In fact, the 90 has been evaluated as a ground attack and not a penetration fighter. We have decided that I should take a trip next week to find the latest thinking in fighter airplanes. "

On August 28, Johnson noted, "Took a trip to Wright Field and Washington again. The picture is extremely confused. I am sure we could build our prototype 90 ground attack airplane if we wished, but information which we have collected on the Russian airplanes, plus the long delay that would now result before getting into production, makes the 90 obsolete. I cannot recommend building it to face airplanes four and five years from now that will have 15° more sweep, half the weight, and one-third the range. Couldn't stand that. Have recommended we drop the airplane in a memo to Hall (Hibbard) and Bob (Gross) on 9/5." A final note, on September 6, stated, "Dissolved 90 project permanently". On September 11, 1950, the McDonnell XF-88 was declared the "competition" winner.

In truth, the XF-90 had been marked for failure from birth. With an ill-defined Air Force specification, a weight problem stemming from an attempt to meet a poorly understood mission requirement, and powerplants that could not possibly have compensated for the excessive structural over-kill, the XF-90's operational prospects were virtually non-existent. On the positive side, Lockheed and the various *Skunk Works* engineers who conceived and built the XF-90 pioneered the use of 75ST aluminum (some 25% stronger than the commonly used 24ST aluminum), verified the viability of the unusual horizontal tail/vertical tail structural/control system mix, and indirectly participated in the improvement of the jet engine afterburner.

Late in the program, when refitted with the afterburning Westinghouse XJ34-WE-15 engines, both prototypes showed improved performance, but not enough to overcome that of their primary competitor, the McDonnell XF-88. Though none of the penetration fighter contenders would enter production on their own merits, the developed XF-88 , in the form of the F-101 *Voodoo*, would eventually have a long and eventful Air Force career.

As to how, according to Johnson, the XF-90 "defeated the atom bomb", suffice it to say the second aircraft still exists. Used as a test specimen during the 1952 atomic bomb tests at Frenchman's Flat, Nevada, it survived three

*Full-scale wooden mock-up of the original delta-wing X-7 configuration. Small size of wing and vertical tail surfaces are noteworthy. Engine nacelle is visible attached to ventral pylon.*

massive blasts with remarkably little damage. Recent interest in recovering it for museum display has been discouraged, primarily because it remains highly radioactive. The first XF-90 was sent to the NACA's laboratory in Cleveland, Ohio and there used as an exemplary structural test specimen. Its final disposition is unknown.

XF-90 research, development, test, and evaluation costs totaled at $5.1 million. The estimated unit price for the first 170 production F-90s was estimated to be $670,000. "Kelly" Johnson lamented that price was "as much as the early *Constellations*!"

### The X-7:

*"X-7 was a ramjet test vehicle. Made a good many of those things. It was designed to fly at speeds up to Mach 4.0 at over 93,000 feet altitude. It tested the engine for the Bomarc. It was an engine-test research vehicle."* Clarence L. "Kelly" Johnson

Post-war analysis of available technology and the attempted assimilation of the massive quantity of data accessed as a result of Nazi Germany's capitulation found the US aerospace industry in an envious, but extraordinarily complicated position. The sheer mass of data suddenly laid at the feet of US academicians and technocrats during 1946, coupled with the opportunity for research into virtually every facet of the aerospace sciences, at times proved overwhelming. There seemed to be no limits. Though funding was always an issue of significant contention, the post-World War Two perspective on military spending for research seemed to be one of blind benevolence...and as a result, many obscure programs were given what amounted to blank checks.

Though not necessarily falling into the lat-

ter category, propulsion system projects created to explore virtually every form of jet, rocket, turboprop, reciprocating, and ramjet power surfaced in overwhelming numbers. Strong military support for these myriad undertakings brought many of them to fruition, including a significant number optimized to explore the attributes of powerplants for supersonic aircraft. This was particularly significant in light of the fact the first supersonic flight—on October 14, 1947—had yet to take place.

On December 6, 1946, as a result of this research, Lockheed representatives responded to an Air Force proposal calling for the construction and flight test of an unmanned testbed for purposes of aerodynamic and propulsion system research at very high speeds. A letter of intent, TSEON-7 dated January 1, 1947 was received one month later. As the Wright Field-designated MX-883 project, the Air Force request was reviewed by several members of the advanced design department staff.

As a result, during 1947, Lockheed, under the auspices of an engineering exercise headed by Willis Hawkins, conducted a brief preliminary design analysis to determine the characteristics of a pilotless vehicle designed to serve as a flying testbed for the Marquardt XRJ-37MN-1 ramjet engine. This study became the Model L-171 and it indicated that a satisfactory vehicle could be produced to fulfill the requirements outlined in Army letter TSEON-7 of January 1, 1947. Two L-171 configurations evolved and both met the criteria as outlined:

(1) Ramjet inlet would not be influenced by the test vehicle at speeds above Mach 1.

(2) Speeds of Mach 2.3 to 3.0 would be attainable.

(3) Lowest drag coefficient would be at Mach 3.0.

(4) Sufficient fuel would be provided for

*Small-scale models of the original X-7 delta configuration were drop-tested from a specially modified Lockheed P-38. Aerodynamic data gathered from these tests led to wing configuration change.*

*The X-7s were built under the aegis of a Skunk Works-like operation but were actually the program that led to the creation of the company's Lockheed Missiles & Space Division.*

*The second X-7 during the course of pre-flight inspection and review. A functional Marquardt ramjet is positioned underneath. Flight test instrumentation was densely packed in the fuselage.*

*The X-7 was a relatively small research vehicle with limited range and endurance. It was, however, a precedent-setting design in terms of its telemetry and performance monitoring capability.*

*All initial X-7 launches utilized a Boeing B-29 as the carrier aircraft. A special pylon assembly was built under the left wing between the Superfortress's two Wright R3350 engine nacelles.*

three minutes operation at Mach 3.0 at 50,000 feet (this would be in addition to the fuel required to accelerate to Mach 3.0).

(5) Sufficient control would be available to perform an 8 g turn at Mach 3.0.

(6) Powerplant and instrumentation would be recoverable after each flight.

(7) All components subjected to ram air would be capable of withstanding temperatures in the 800° to 900° F range.

Two designs eventually surfaced, the L-171-1 and the L-171-2. Only the latter was used for aerodynamic analysis and launch methods studies. Launching from both air and ground were considered. Air launching proved the more practical option as the ramjet could be functioning at ignition speed without the need to carry or consume additional fuel. Two booster types were explored...solid fuel and liquid fuel. Both were designed to accelerate the L-171, after launch, to about Mach 2.4.

The L-171 made sense, but suffered from a lack of versatility. Its design complicated the issue of engine variety and its small size (length of the L-171-1 was only 15 feet 3.5 inches) curtailed the internal carriage of sufficient fuel quantities. As a result of the latter, the short projected flight endurance severely limited data acquisition opportunities.

These failings forced Lockheed to set the L-171 aside for a more utilitarian approach to the Air Force requirement. From the preliminary design work of Irv Culver, configuration and engineering guidelines for the new flight test vehicle emerged. Prominent among them was the desire to recover, intact, a test engine after flight for post-flight examination and, if possible, to reuse it; the need to generate and record large quantities of data (the telemetry technology developed during the course of the X-7 program, overseen by "E. O." Richter, was to be precedent-setting; it would hold Lockheed in good stead for many years to come); and a realization that conventional flight test methods of mounting an engine on an existing airframe would be ill-advised (the high maximum Mach numbers envisioned as a result of using ramjet engines dictated that a dedicated airframe be developed). This was the final concept accepted by the Air Force; development was initiated, accordingly.

Hawkins' engineering team worked steadily on the project for many months. Having a development program continue under the umbrella of the preliminary design department was unusual, but the X-7 did not require the secrecy of a *Skunk Works* program and it didn't fit a normal project organization. It could, however, use the *Skunk Works* operating philosophy. Thus it was left in preliminary design. As Willis Hawkins put it, "they couldn't find a better place to put us".

Among the design decisions made during this period were: the aircraft would have to be air-launched (available off-the-shelf rocket assisted takeoff units did not then have enough thrust and operating endurance to get the test vehicle from ground level to the altitude and speeds required); it would have to be parachute recovered for post-flight analysis and re-use; the engine being tested would have to be under-slung (an engine buried in the wing or fuselage would limit internal fuel capacity and discourage the testing of a variety of powerplant configurations); and it would have to have an extremely thin, straight (though tapered) wing to avoid the high-Mach aeroelastic problems inherent in swept wings and the drag problems associated with delta wings.

Work on the final X-7 configuration began with the launching of several 1/3-scale, uncontrolled, free-flight models with a shock-cord slingshot. This later advanced to the use of a rudimentary launching pad at Muroc Air Base, California. Still later, various instrumented scale models were dropped in free-fall from a Lockheed P-38 (piloted by Fred Jenks...who later would become X-7 program manager) and later, a Boeing B-29.

In addition to aerodynamic information, the scale model program produced a great deal of miscellaneous data and gave Lockheed engineers significant hands-on experience with actual flightworthy hardware. It also permitted a preliminary look at launch techniques (causing Lockheed to choose a B-29 as the carrier aircraft—based on its payload capacity, its performance, and its availability) while providing time and experience to develop a dependable telemetry system.

In choosing the B-29 as the X-7's primary launch platform, Hawkins' engineering team had been cognizant of the fixed dimensions of the tandem boost system that had been chosen as the means to accelerate the research missile up to ramjet ignition speed. The large, Allegheny Ballistics Laboratory 105,000 pound thrust solid fuel booster required elephantine aerodynamic surfaces for directional stability. These eliminated any possibility the X-7 would fit into the B-29's bomb bay; the bomber's massive wing spar carry-through structure could not be modified to provide the necessary dimensional clearances. A folding vertical fin was considered, but this eventually was discarded in favor of a pylon-mounting arrangement installed under the B-29's port wing. The pylon was a rather complex, high-drag, wire-braced structure which was assembled by Lockheed personnel and laboriously bolted in place.

Another modification permitted the attachment of RATO bottles. Engineering studies backed by wind tunnel data indicated the B-29/X-7 combination would create a marginal B-29 power situation during takeoff. In order to ensure safe flight in the event of engine failure, RATO unit mounting assemblies were attached to the B-29 aft-fuselage and RATO was used at the beginning of every X-7 mission.

During late 1950 and early 1951, the first of the X-7s was assembled in a small production facility in Plant B-6 at Burbank. The initial test vehicles, per the original specification outlined by Hawkins, were small, simple, and rugged. Designed for multiple use, they were equipped with a ground penetration spike and a staged and reefed parachute system for recovery. A split surface drag brake was mounted on the trailing edge of the vertical fin permitting variation of vehicle drag characteristics throughout its flight envelope. A 14-channel telemetry system was provided that measured engine and vehicle performance values. The trapezoidal mid-wing had a 4% thickness/chord ratio. Wing tip horn-balanced ailerons were used for roll control and an all-moving slab stabilator was mounted midway up the vertical fin, providing pitch control. There was no rudder.

The first full-scale X-7A-1 flight took place on April 26, 1951. Following a clean release over the Air Force missile test range near Alamogordo, New Mexico, a 5-second free fall was followed by booster ignition. Unpredicted pulsations during the 5 second booster burn caused the separation charge (made of gun powder) to fire prematurely. This backed the booster off its connector a few inches, unlocking the pin that held it in roll alignment with the

*Large solid-fuel booster unit was essentially an enormous RATO bottle with wings. Both the booster and the X-7 were designed to be parachute recoverable.*

X-7. The booster then rolled approximately 90° and almost instantaneously displaced the majority of the aerodynamic loads to one stabilizing fin. As the fin collapsed, the entire assembly pitched up and disintegrated.

Most of this activity had taken place in front of the B-29. It was with some surprise that the crew found themselves having to penetrate a rapidly expanding debris cloud . Fortunately, this took place without serious damage to the B-29.

During the post-accident investigation it was found that an inertia separation activation switch had failed. This was redesigned, and during November a second X-7A-1 flight was attempted. This missile, following launch, had a successful booster ignition and at first seemed to be heading for a smooth flight. However, just as separation began, one of the booster stabilizing fins failed and there was another spectacular disintegration.

The fin failure eventually was traced to an aeroelastic problem related to insufficient stiffness. Redesign was undertaken and all extant and new boosters were modified accordingly. Concurrent to this, the complete booster assembly underwent a number of significant design changes...all resulting in improved dependability.

Three flights with dummy X-7s followed, these verifying the integrity of the modifications. On the third flight, which was considered the most successful, the X-7 was boosted without problems and successfully separated. Unfortunately, the Marquardt ramjet failed to ignite properly and no appreciable thrust was generated. The recovery system worked as designed, however, and some 30 miles downrange from the launch point the missile was retrieved.

Additional flights now were consummated with significant regularity. By January of 1954, fourteen had been attempted and the majority had met with at least some measure of success. The first two had been conducted with smaller ramjet engines in the 20 inch diameter family. Built by Wright and Marquardt, they were followed in short order by the Marquardt 28 inch series which were under development for the forthcoming Boeing *Bomarc* (*Bo*eing and *M*ichigan *A*eronautical *R*esearch *C*enter)— a project that could trace its origins back to May 1945, when Boeing entered the guided missile field with its Ground-to-Air Piloted Missile. This latter weapon, when merged with the technology resulting from the General Electric *Thumper* (MX-795), and the University of Michigan Aeronautical Research Center's *Wizard* (MX-794) programs, gave birth to the antecedents of what was to become the *Bomarc* during 1950. This large and complex weapon then would become the only Air Force development project in the field of long-range, surface-to-air guided missiles from 1950 through 1953.

*Bomarc's* primary mission was the "air defense of the continental US" and its Air Force function was to "augment and later replace manned interceptors". It was effectively an area defense missile, while those of other services were limited to point defense. Thus, while the Army's *Nike* could provide close support for a city or for an industrial site, *Bomarc* was designed to hit invading aircraft and missiles at 80,000 feet and at distances of up to 200 miles from its launch site. This was at least 30,000 feet higher and 175 miles farther than the same specifications for the *Nike*.

Initial *Bomarc* tests, by late 1951, had been discouraging. Propulsion system failures, control system anomalies, and other difficulties had led to numerous unsuccessful launches,

*Large size of X-7/booster combination dictated the under-wing arrangement for transporting the research vehicle to altitude. Propeller tip clearances and related concerns are noteworthy.*

*The most advanced of the standard X-7 configurations was the X-7A-3. This aircraft offered improved performance in the form of increased range, increased endurance, and higher maximum speeds.*

and it was apparent the program would be many years in gestation unless progress could be made on several technology fronts at once.

The X-7, at this time, surfaced as a logical device for flight testing at supersonic speeds the Marquardt ramjets that were so critical to the *Bomarc* during cruising flight. As early as August 1951, R. E. Marquardt, president of the company bearing his name, referred to the X-7 as "insurance" for the Boeing program. By May of 1952, Boeing had been directed to furnish three unguaranteed Marquardt engines for X-7 flight tests. A development lag at Marquardt prevented the scheduled July delivery of the first engine, and it was several months before it was finally delivered.

The first 28 inch ramjet was flown on an X-7 at Holloman AFB, New Mexico on December 17, 1952, and resulted in ten seconds of burning, a rough blow-out, and "minor damage" to the engine. The next flight, on February 2, 1953, was only slightly more successful. On April 8, the tenth flight, the ramjet burned for some 20 seconds and the vehicle reached an altitude of 59,500 feet and a Mach number of 2.6. Unfortunately, the lean limiter stuck and the thrust decayed before maximum performance could be attained. A September 12 flight initially appeared equally promising but failed to generate significant flight time.

*Recovery procedures included use of the X-7's nose spike for ground penetration upon contact.*

Another flight on December 8 failed when the ramjet's graphite exhaust nozzle malfunctioned. The nozzle later was replaced with an all-metal unit.

Though not appearing successful, these initial *Bomarc*-related X-7 flights actually were quite productive in that they consistently revealed design failings in the Marquardt ramjet engines or related systems. By the end of 1953, though only a few truly successful flights had been logged, Boeing was asking the Air Force for additional flight time and more X-7s.

The majority of the initial X-7 flights were dedicated to exploring the performance parameters of the various Marquardt ramjet configurations being considered for the *Bomarc*. Though at first scheduled only for the X-7A-1 model, work on this project eventually passed into the domain of the X-7A-3 and even spilled over into the later and more advanced X-7B and XQ-5 series. During later years, 36-inch diameter ramjets were tested under the X-7A-3s and for a while, there was talk of flight testing a monstrous 48-inch engine for another, unspecified program.

Little known, but significant contributions to still other important ramjet-powered aircraft were made by the X-7, particularly under the aegis of its later perturbations. Most notable of these was the RJ43-MA-11 propulsion system found in the D-21 drone described in Chapter 11. These engines, which required high supersonic speeds for ignition, were unique in the fact they were capable of functioning for up to two hours at maximum thrust. At a cruising speed of Mach 3.25, the operating dynamics of this powerplant remain unparalleled in the history of conventional ramjet propulsion systems.

During 1954, concurrent with the official founding of the Lockheed Missile Systems Division (this eventually became the Lockheed Missiles and Space Company) on January 1, Willis Hawkins and the X-7 engineering staff were moved from the advanced projects office at Burbank to their own facility...a 77 acre site at Van Nuys that had served as a Lockheed production flight test facility. Within a year, employment jumped from 250 to 1,250.

As noted in the January 1958 issue of "Of Men and Stars", "At about the same time, differences of opinion rose about the basic administrative and operating policies in connection with design and development of unmanned weapons. Unable to reach agreement on the relative roles of research scientists and aeronautical engineers, two top level Lockheed missile managers left the company. Taking over

as temporary vice president and Missile Division general manager was Hall Hibbard. Taking over as director of research laboratories was Louis Ridenour—an internationally known nuclear physicist, radar authority, and electronics expert. Hawkins remained as the assistant general manager for engineering and development. During November of 1956, Eugene Root, Lockheed's corporate director of development planning, became a vice president and the missiles division general manager. Herschel Brown became assistant general manager for administration. And as 1958 began, D. J. Gribbon—formerly executive assistant to D. J. Haughton, Lockheed's executive vice president—became director of the Missile Division's manufacturing branch."

The Van Nuys facility, surprisingly, was outgrown in less than two years. Lockheed, believing in its rapidly growing missile division, bought 275 acres at Sunnyvale, California and a few months later, leased 22-1/2 acres at Stanford University in Palo Alto, some seven miles north. On the two sites, construction was initiated on $30 million worth of laboratory, experimental, research, and manufacturing buildings. Test facilities later were operated at Holloman AFB, New Mexico, Alamogordo, New Mexico, and later at the Air Force Missile Test Center at Patrick AFB, Florida.

Concurrent with the move to Van Nuys, the new company embarked on a program to develop an advanced X-7 derivative called the X-7A-3. In order to accommodate the performance requirements of newer and faster aircraft and powerplants, it was decided to upgrade the basic X-7A-1 by enlarging it (by some 3 feet in length), improving its command responses, diversifying its test instrumentation package, increasing the capacity of its instrumentation, refining its aerodynamics, strengthening its airframe, and completely revising its booster design. Importantly, a new on-board wing-mounted camera system would permit twice the film coverage of its predecessor while permitting the use of new infrared film techniques.

The new Thiokol 50,000 pound thrust (each) twin booster arrangement for the X-7A-3 was tested in model form. The test program, referred to as "Mum" (in deference to a well known underarm deodorant of the same name...and the physical similarities of the booster unit placement at the wing root) successfully verified the system's integrity and cleared the twin boosters for operational use.

A new launch aircraft also was obtained. A Boeing B-50, offering improved high-altitude performance and the ability to lift considerably heavier payloads than its predecessor was assigned to the program by the Air Force. The change to the new booster system also cleared the way for bomb bay carriage as the dimensional constraints no longer existed.

The most noticeable change in the X-7A-3 was its new wing. Offering increased area, a greater taper ratio, a much finer thickness/chord ratio (the wing was only 2 inches thick at the root), and faired upper surface camera pods which resembled thick wing fences, it was effectively a total redesign of the original planform.

For the remainder of the X-7's flight test program, the basic vehicle configuration remained essentially unchanged. From May 1955, until the final flight on July 20, 1960, approximately 100 missions were flown. During the final flight test stages, airframes #20, #33, and #43 logged the most flights and

*Full-scale mock-up of the XFV-1 included a detailed model of the gun-aiming radar in the propeller spinner fairing, the ports in the wing tip pods for the gun barrels and casing ejection, and the various ventral access doors to permit engine and systems maintenance.*

flight time, with 31 missions completed between them. All three survived flight testing and were in flyable conditions when the program was terminated.

The X-7 set many world speed and altitude records for air-breathing vehicles during the course of its ten years of service. Some of the more significant included a maximum speed of Mach 4.31 (2,881 mph) using a 36 inch diameter ramjet; a maximum altitude of 106,000 feet; a maximum flight time for type of 552 seconds; a maximum distance for type of 134 miles; and a maximum number of flights per vehicle of 13. The latter aircraft was nicknamed *Ol' Methuselah*.

During the 130 X-7 flights eventually logged, many test items and projects were parasited onto the basic vehicle. A few of these included the modification of one X-7's wing to accommodate no less than 300 thermocouples to record temperature data; and the experimental use of $H_2O_2$ fuel additives and boron-based high energy fuel. The latter was tested on three different occasions. Though the results were favorable, the logistics of handling the extremely toxic propellant proved formidable. Besides being dangerous to inhale—even in minute quantities—it also was hypergolic.

The X-7A-1 and X-7A-3 series were followed by five X-7Bs. Intended to test guidance and control systems in the same way the X-7A tested powerplants, the X-7B program was terminated just as the flight test program was getting underway. Twelve X-7B flights were completed prior to cancellation.

A relatively unmodified version of the X-7A-3, known as the XQ-5 (Air Force System 427L) and given the name *Kingfisher*, was developed for use as a dedicated high-speed target drone. Somewhat surprisingly, the XQ-5's performance proved significantly higher than that of the surface-to-air weapons it was designed to test, and it is doubtful that any were destroyed by "enemy" action. This situation eventually affected the XQ-5's operational career as a *Bomarc* and *Nike* anti-aircraft missile systems target...as it literally performed its

way out of a job.

Approximately 80 of the 130-plus X-7/XQ-5 flights attempted were successful either partially or completely. Problems of bewildering variety surfaced during the course of the flight test program, including range safety concerns, ineffective radar control, malfunctioning autopilots, simple human error, and poor design, but the missile's enviable performance envelope eventually became an item of considerable pride for Lockheed's fledgling Missiles and Space Company.

---

**The XFV-1:**

*"Our first Navy program was next, the XFV-1, a tail-sitting airplane for direct takeoff and landing from a small area on any Navy ship. It was supposed to back down onto the deck. We did excellent in terms of cost and weight, but this aircraft was a failure. It was a failure because we had a bad powerplant, and we couldn't look back over our shoulder when flying the thing and judge height. We could practice on clouds all day, but this is the only airplane we ever built which we were afraid to fly ourselves in the final tests."* Clarence L. "Kelly" Johnson

The rapid advances in propulsion and aerodynamics realized by the US aviation industry following the end of World War Two tentatively cleared the way for the realization of many long-sought solutions to problems almost all directly attributable to low power-to-weight ratios. Particularly sensitive to this long-standing short-coming were vertical takeoff and landing aircraft such as helicopters and a whole host of fighter and cargo configurations.

During 1947, the Air Force and Navy initiated feasibility studies calling for the design and development of several different vertical takeoff and landing (VTOL) aircraft types, including fighters. The Navy, in particular, found VTOL appealing primarily because of the inherent deck space limitations and the associated short-comings of steam catapult and

arresting gear systems utilized on most then-extant aircraft carriers.

Lockheed, under the aegis of funding provided by the Navy, pursued its own VTOL fighter study with considerable energy, even going so far as to build small, semi-scale models of VTOL aircraft powered by reciprocating model airplane engines. These small wooden U-control models served to verify the most basic tenets of VTOL fighter design and encouraged the company to pursue a full-scale testbed contract.

By 1950, the Air Force- and Navy-supported VTOL studies had resulted in a decision to pursue specific mission requirements and additional research funding was allocated. Among the several projects given Navy financial support was one calling for the development of a VTOL-capable fighter. This aircraft was to be optimized to operate off platforms mounted on the afterdeck of ordinary cargo ships.

Lockheed's Art Flock, during August of 1950, had been appointed project engineer on the Model 81 VTOL fighter developed in preliminary design in response to the Navy convoy fighter initiative. During early 1951, the Lockheed proposal—along with those of Convair, Goodyear, Martin, and Northrop—was expeditiously reviewed by the Navy. It was concluded the Convair proposal had the most merit, while the Lockheed and Martin proposals remained worthy of further exploration. The Lockheed and Martin proposals were then further reviewed to assess which of the two should be provided prototype funding. When it was determined the Lockheed aircraft would be the less expensive to develop, the Martin aircraft was eliminated as a contender.

Korean War pressures by now had given rise to increased Congressional funding for such programs and on April 19, 1951, a contract for two (plus one static test article) of Lockheed's Model 81 aircraft (initially designated XFO-1) was issued along with a similar contract for two Convair Model 5s (designated XFY-1). These prototypes were to be capable of upgrading in production form to operational

*Fuselage of the first XFV-1 under construction. It was designed to be relatively lightweight in order to attain the mandatory high thrust-to-weight ratio required for vertical takeoff and landing.*

*The first XFV-1 under construction at Lockheed's Burbank facility. The temporary fixed landing gear, including the tail wheels, already was attached in preparation for the first taxi tests and first flight.*

ticated gearbox and turning two three-blade contra-rotating Curtiss-Wright *Turboelectric* constant chord propellers.

The XT40, a first-generation turboprop, gave the fully-loaded XFV-1 a power-to-weight ratio of approximately 1.2 to 1. Fuel, totaling some 508 gallons, was carried in fuselage, wing, and tip tanks, with the latter also serving to accommodate—in the proposed production aircraft—either four 20 mm cannon or forty-eight 2.75 inch folding fin aerial rockets evenly divided between each. In the two prototype aircraft, the wing tip pods were to house instrumentation, with recorders and other equipment mounted in the spaces normally allocated weapons.

The production aircraft, referred to as the Model 181 by Lockheed and officially designated FV-2 by the Navy, besides having armament, also would have differed in being equipped with the considerably more powerful Allison T54-A-16 engine, having a bullet-proof windscreen, being provided armor plate in appropriate places, and being equipped with air-to-air radar in the forward, non-rotating portion of the propeller spinner. The engine change would have dictated a revised engine air intake and cooling system intake arrangement and as a result, would have created distinctive changes in the basic configuration of the aircraft.

During early 1953, the first XFV-1 was completed at Lockheed's Burbank facility with an interim 5,850 equivalent shaft horsepower XT40-A-6 engine in place of the more powerful YT40-A-14 scheduled for actual flight tests. Modified to incorporate a temporary V-strut supported main landing gear permitting conventional takeoffs and landings, the aircraft, shortly after roll-out, was ground and taxi tested at Burbank and later, Edwards AFB, while awaiting receipt of the flightworthy engine, a propeller, and a propeller spinner. The test program was under the immediate supervision of Ernie Joiner.

In addition to the main gear, the aircraft also was equipped with a pair of small, bolt-on, castoring tail wheels attached to the lower two tail surfaces. Each main gear wheel was equipped with a single disc brake, these providing both asymmetrical steering and conventional braking as needed.

Lockheed test pilot Herman "Fish" Salmon was assigned to the aircraft as chief test pilot. On December 23, 1953, during the course of a high-speed taxi test at Edwards AFB, the aircraft inadvertently became airborne for the first

convoy escort fighters once flight testing had been completed.

Art Flock's Allison XT40 turboprop-powered aircraft, created with the assistance of "Kelly" Johnson, was designed to sit vertically on a cruciform tail equipped with a castoring, load-bearing wheel and associated shock absorber assembly at each tail surface tip. The somewhat stubby, but nevertheless attractive fuselage was essentially a fairing for the XT40 and cockpit, with the former consisting of two Allison T38 turboprops mated through a sophis-

*Static and taxi tests were conducted with the propeller spinner fairings off to prevent overheating of transmission assembly and facilitate maintenance.*

*Size of Curtiss-Wright* Turboelectric *contra-rotating propellers was in marked contrast to the aircraft's relatively diminutive fuselage and wings.*

*The XFV-1 on its special ground handling trailer. This portable unit was designed to raise or lower the XFV-1 from its normal vertical takeoff and landing attitude. In the lowered (horizontal) position the aircraft and its systems could be more easily accessed for maintenance.*

time. Salmon landed moments after leaving the ground. No serious problems were encountered. Because the engine was not flight rated, it would be another seven months before a first official flight could be consummated. Finally, however, on June 16, 1954, with Salmon in the cockpit, the first XFV-1, in conventional mode, completed its first official flight. A total of twenty-two flights accumulating 11 hours and 30 minutes of flying time were completed during a ten-month period from June of 1954 through March of 1955 (see Appendix J).

In the performance of these flights Salmon investigated the handling characteristics of the XFV-1 great detail. In the execution of thirty-two transitions from horizontal flight to hovering attitude, it was learned that minimum buffeting occurred by zooming into the vertical position and holding it with the application of power. Constant altitude transitions were also made but resulted in buffeting from 120 knots down to 70 knots with the maximum amplitudes reached at 90 knots. Handling ease in roll and translation was readily demonstrated during hovering flight. The transitions from vertical to horizontal flight were easily acomplished without altitude loss by application of available power.

Development of a full-swiveling pitot-static head for installation on the left wing tip pod boom aided materially in indicating both airspeed and direction of motion to the pilot at all aircraft attitudes. Through lack of reliable vertical rate indication the pilot was unable to always maintain vertical rates within the requirements necessary for adequate control and found that control loss occurred at descents of approximately 800 feet per minute. Prompt application of power regained control with slight altitude loss.

All flights (sometimes chased by Lockheed's Lou Schalk in a North American T-28) were made with the auxiliary landing gear installed. This added a weight penalty of over 700 pounds and prevented investigation of the handling characteristics in the design speed range over 250 knots because of the increased

drag. Alhough all takeoffs and landings were made in the horizontal attitude, simulated vertical takeoffs were performed at safe operating altitudes.

Satisfactory aircraft characteristics at all flight attitudes were demonstrated during the test program. Excellent performance of the control system and a lack of structural, hydraulic, or electrical system problems gave every indication the aircraft was capable of performing its VTOL design mission.

With flight safety stressed during all testing, a cautious approach was made to the vertical flight phase near the ground. Recurrent service problems and major breakdowns of the Allison T40 and the Curtiss-Electric C(6L8)65S contra-rotating propeller indicated that safe operation could not be assured with this installation.

A review of the program's progress now indicated a continuous inability to sustain flight operations sufficiently to retain pilot experience as a result of repeated delays for major component breakdowns. Therefore, since the installationof the engine and propeller did not show the high degree of reliability required, the XFV-1 program was terminated.

The XFV-1, and its competing design, Convair's XFY-1, proved incapable of accommodating any Navy fighter role. With anticipated maximum speeds of only 580 mph, it was readily apparent neither type would be competitive in any envisioned future air combat scenario, and the risks associated with the unknowns of VTOL operations at sea were too great to merit production funding.

Adding to the conviction the two VTOL fighters were doomed was the fact the 7,100 equivalent shaft horsepower Allison YT40-A-14 became a still-born project and never saw the light of day as a flightworthy powerplant. Accordingly, Lockheed and Convair were advised at an early stage of testing to view their respective prototypes as research vehicles.

The axe formally fell on June 16, 1955. The second XFV-1 thus became an uncompleted airframe and sat for a while at Burbank

before disposition. Eventually it was given to NAS Los Alamitos, California where it was used as a gate guardian until December of 1979. It then was donated to the Naval Aviation Museum in Pensacola, Florida and placed on permanent display as a primary example of mid-1950s VTOL technology.

The first aircraft was grounded on the day the Navy canceled the program. Hiller Aircraft, then working on several VTOL aircraft projects, requested and received the XFV-1 and promptly began a review of its propulsion and control system arrangement. During this process, the aircraft was disassembled and its XT40 engine and associated gearbox assembly recovered for use in the company's forthcoming X-18 tilt-wing VTOL cargo aircraft. It was used during the course of the Hiller aircraft's abbreviated flight test program at Edwards AFB that spanned from the end of 1959 through July of 1961.

### The R7V-2/YC-121F:

*"And there was the Navy version, R7V-2. We had poor performance in the Skunk Works there, because we tangled with 17-7 stainless steel, which required a million parts in very thin gauges that were very difficult to assemble. We had to do them over twice. And this was a failure. It was a failure even in the experimental phase because of the high cost. The airplane flew good and all that, but never went into production."* Clarence L. "Kelly" Johnson

Wartime development of Lockheed's aesthetically pleasing *Constellation* transport proved a far-sighted venture for a company that at the time was better known for long-range fighters and light bombers. Lockheed, under the guidance its progressive management and engineering staffs had predicted the post-war years to be highly conducive to the development of long-range, high-speed reciprocating engine airliners and they designed their Model 49—initially known in military guise as the C-69—accordingly. With the 1945 cessation of

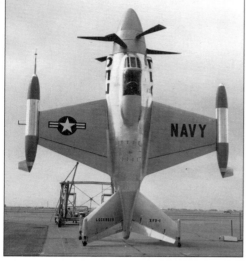

*XFV-1 never took-off vertically as per its orginal design specification.*

*Drag generated by temporary fixed landing gear adversely affected maximum speed of the XFV-1. The aircraft never flew without the temporary gear in place.*

*Proof positive the XFV-1 successfully converted to vertical flight and back during its test program.*

*Though its flight test program was abbreviated, the XFV-1 proved a reveiling and far-sighted technology exercise for Lockheed and its advanced engineering department staff.*

hostilities, the military orientation of the C-69 was changed rapidly to commercial. Sales to airlines were solicited, and a large number of aircraft were sold. Even the famous entrepreneur, financier, and pilot Howard Hughes, then the majority stock holder in *Trans World Airlines*, participated in formulating the design parameters of the post-war *Constellation* airliner. Interestingly, Hughes--before US anti-trust laws were changed--imposed a restraint on Lockheed requiring the company not to sell *Constellations* to other airlines if TWA bought them. Only Eastern was allowed to acquire the type in the US...because it was a "north/south" airline. Lockheed thus was forced to emphasize *Constellation* sales to foreign customers.

The *Constellation* was unquestionably the most technologically and aerodynamically advanced airliner in the world at the time of its debut. Fast, reliable, economically palatable, and simply pleasing to look at, it had only one failing...it was offered to the airline industry in competition with commercial versions of the ubiquitous Douglas C-54. The latter, one of the most dependable and numerous US military transports of World War Two, though lacking the *Constellation's* aesthetics, was an extremely dependable, good performing, and commodious aircraft with a ready supply of experienced pilots.

Though undeniably a commercial success by the end of its production history, the *Constellation* nevertheless ran a distant second to the Douglas DC-4, DC-6, and DC-7 commercials in terms of sales. The Douglas airliners outsold the popular Lockheed aircraft because they were uncomplicated, affordable, and backed by a sales team that was highly competitive in the national and international marketplace. Regardless, development of the *Constellation* went through many successful iterations, culminating in the truly magnificent Model 1649 *Starliner*. A grand total of 856 *Constellations* (including both commercial and military variants) were completed by the time the last aircraft rolled from the Burbank production line during late 1958.

Hall Hibbard and "Kelly" Johnson, two key players in the development of the *Constellation*—which had come to life during 1938 as the Model 44 *Excalibur*—continued to explore development options of the basic

*The four turboprop* Constellations *were ordered as R7V-1s but became R7V-2s following conversion. Two of the aircraft were then delivered to the Air Force as YC-121Fs.*

*The biggest failing of the turboprop-powered* Constellations *was their timing; they became available at the same time pure-jet transports--such as the Boeing 707--were arriving in the marketplace.*

design throughout its lengthy production history. The advent of jet engines during the course of World War Two had led Lockheed to many indirectly related studies of jet-powered commercial transports, including perturbations of the basic *Constellation* design incorporating jet engines as auxiliary and/or secondary powerplants. Some of these studies also explored the attributes of turboprop engines and in some cases called for their use as reciprocating engine replacements.

Unfortunately, though a small number of turboprop engines had been developed by US powerplant manufacturers during the immediate post-World War Two years, none were considered worthy of commercial air transport application. Costs were prohibitive, dependability was questionable, and operating economics remained hard to justify in light of the expected marginal increases in performance.

When the Air Force canceled the 5,000 equivalent shaft horsepower Wright XT35 turboprop during late 1947, one of the most promising of the several commercially applicable turboprop powerplants died on the vine. Concurrently, however, Wright moved ahead with its R3350 *Turbo-Cyclone/Turbo-Compound* reciprocating engine series, which later went into production for the Lockheed P2V-4 *Neptune* anti-submarine warfare aircraft. This engine, utilizing three "blown down" turbines interfaced with the exhaust ports and in turn directly geared through three fluid couplings to the engine crankshaft, thus was able to convert about 20% of the available engine heat energy—normally lost in the exhaust gases—to power.

The R3350, though acquired in considerable numbers for several military aircraft and both the commercially-successful *Super Constellation* and the DC-7, remained only an interim powerplant option as far as the airlines were concerned. Looking to the future for more fuel efficient and less maintenance-intensive propulsion, the turboprop continued to lure, but with few offerings to fill the need.

Engine manufacturers were not oblivious to the airline's wishes. In England, D. Napier and Son Ltd., a small but successful engine manufacturer that had begun experimenting with turboprop engines of their own design during the early 1950s, during 1955 and 1956 reengined a Convair 340 with two 3,200 equivalent shaft horsepower NE1.I *Eland* turboprops. Later, this same aircraft was converted to two NE1.6 *Elands* of 3,500 equivalent shaft horsepower. Concurrent to this, a Convair 440 also

was converted to the Napier engines in the US.

The successes realized by these initial commercial turboprop testbeds were watched closely by the airline community. In short order manufacturers, including Lockheed, began studies of their own aircraft powered by the pioneering Napier engine. First among these was the forthcoming Model 188 *Electra* which Lockheed envisioned as their *Constellation* follow-on and the first production turboprop Lockheed commercial transport.

In Latin America, the small airline *Panair do Brasil* announced their intention to reengine as many as eleven of their early Model 049 *Constellations* with Napier *Elands*. It was stated at the time that such reengining would not only improve payload and range capabilities, but also would give the aircraft a cruising speed 50 mph faster than its reciprocating engine predecessor.

Unfortunately, the *Panair* plans failed to bear fruit when it was discovered Douglas DC-7Cs could be bought for less money while providing performance roughly comparable to that predicted for the turboprop *Constellation*. *Eland* conversions of the *Constellation* continued to be explored by various airlines, but during July of 1961, Napier was acquired by Rolls-Royce and the *Eland* shortly afterwards was discontinued.

On July 27, 1949, the British de Havilland *Comet*, the world's first commercial jet airliner, took to the air for the first time. Viewed with a mixture of awe and curiosity by the airline industry, it nevertheless heralded a major turning point in the history of air transport. Though plagued by a series of calamitous explosive decompression accidents, and thus doomed to a relatively abbreviated production history, it served to provide a prescient view of air travel's powerplant future. Concurrently, it also signaled the beginning of the end for the reciprocating engine airliner as a viable transport entity.

Lockheed, faced with the dilemma of having to design a totally new all-jet transport or, at a more leisurely pace, to slowly move in that direction via the conversion of extant products such as the *Constellation* to turboprop power, elected to choose the latter. Conveniently, the airlines proved equally conservative, electing to continue buying reciprocating engine airliners until viable turboprops could be developed for extant airframes. Lockheed even went so far as to structurally stress the newer *Constellation* airframes to accommodate the projected power increases represented by a conversion to turboprop propulsion. Allison's T38, rated at

3,500 equivalent shaft horsepower, already had flown on a modified Convair 240 on December 29, 1950, and it was proposed by *Eastern Airlines* that this engine, or a developed version, be utilized to upgrade their fleet of older *Constellations*.

The prototype *Constellation*, nicknamed "Old 1961" had been bought back by Lockheed from Howard Hughes during early 1950 and had been converted to the first *Super Constellation*. As such it served Lockheed as a testbed for a large number of *Constellation* programs, not the least of which were a series of engine upgrades and improvements. Included was an early 1954 installation in the number 4 position of a single 3,750 equivalent shaft horsepower Allison YT56 turboprop engine turning a three-blade Curtiss turbo-electric propeller with broad chord blades. This powerplant, scheduled for use in the forthcoming Lockheed C-130 transport, first flew on April 29, 1954. As such, it became the first turboprop-powered Lockheed airliner...though it still had a DA-1 *Turbo-Compound* R3350 in the number 1 position and two standard R3350s in positions 2 and 3.

Once military test requirements had been met, the YT56 engine was reconfigured to meet the commercial Allison 501D-13 specification that was planned for the forthcoming Lockheed L-188 *Electra* turboprop airliner. Some 207 hours of flying time were logged in this form, it being replaced during the first few months of 1957 with a true Allison 501D-13 and an Aeroproducts 606 four-blade propeller.

As interest in turboprop conversions to the *Constellation* continued to grow, so grew the variety of turboprop engine options. During 1955 and 1956, Lockheed seriously considered utilizing the Rolls-Royce RB.109 *Tyne* and the earlier-mentioned Napier *Eland* turboprops on the *Super Constellation*, and options calling for pure jet auxiliary propulsion systems were studied with equal enthusiasm.

"Old 1961" by the end of the 501D-13 program in 1958, had outlived its usefulness at Lockheed. Initially placed in storage, it later was bought by California Airmotive. Its subsequent career there proved short, and having been depleted of all its serviceable parts, it was scrapped.

Development of the penultimate Model 1049 *Constellation* by Lockheed considerably increased interest in turboprop propulsion not only by the airlines, but by the military, as well. This aircraft was ideally suited to turboprop power, and was designed from the start to be physically compatible with such propulsion if and when it became available. As a result, Lockheed's Hibbard and Johnson elected to set up a special team as an adjunct to ongoing special projects efforts specifically to explore the attributes of such propulsion systems on four dedicated testbeds. Two aircraft would serve each of the military services.

As originally designed, the *Super Constellation* had been stressed to permit the future installation of suitable turboprop engines if ever the opportunity should arise. Accordingly, when the Air Force and Navy agreed to finance the conversion and flight testing of four such aircraft, the primary concerns proved to be systems integration, rather than structural. Concurrent with the service's interest and support, the airlines, including Eastern (then under the direction of famed World War One ace Eddie Rickenbacker), also aspired to see built a turboprop version of the ubiquitous *Constellation*.

*In service, the R7V-2s and YC-121Fs spent most of their operational careers powered by four Pratt & Whitney YT34-P-12A turboprops driving three-blade propellers.*

During November of 1951, a Model 1149 had been studied by Lockheed as a turboprop conversion of the Model 1049, and the following year, preliminary design work under the auspices of Johnson and Don Palmer had been undertaken exploring the attributes of the Pratt & Whitney T34 and *Super Constellation* combination. Two aircraft on the Navy's R7V-1 production line then were moved into a special area and converted to accommodate the YT34-P-12 turboprop engines and their associated three-blade, square-tipped, 15 foot diameter, 2 foot chord Hamilton Standard Turbo-Hydromatic propellers. In this configuration, and now designated R7V-2, the first aircraft—nicknamed *Elation*—made its first flight on September 1, 1954.

Two additional R7V-1s also were pulled from Navy production and modified with 5,700 equivalent shaft horsepower Pratt & Whitney T34-P-6 turboprops and transferred to the Air Force. These two aircraft were officially redesignated YC-121Fs (originally they were referred to as C-134s). The first of these made its first flight on April 5, 1955.

The two YC-121Fs, in addition to having the more powerful T34-P-6 engines, also were equipped with two 600 gallon wing tip tanks to give a total fuel capacity of 8,750 gallons. And like the two R7V-2s, there also was provision for two 500 gallon underwing tanks...though in fact these were never fitted. Both the R7V-2s and the YC-121Fs had a maximum takeoff weight of 150,000 pounds, a payload of up to 36,000 pounds, and cruising speeds of 440 mph. The latter made them the fastest propeller driven transports in the world at the time of their debut.

At the beginning of 1956, an R7V-2 piloted by Lockheed's Roy Wimmer reached a speed of 479 mph in a dive from 25,000 feet to 8,000 feet at a 20° angle. The dive, conducted as part of a rapid descent test, involved relatively low throttle settings. During this same period, this same aircraft took off at a record gross overload weight of 166,400 pounds—which was nearly twice the gross takeoff weight of the *Constellation* prototype flown for the first time just thirteen years earlier. During the tests, the R7V-2 carried a full fuel load plus 30,000 pounds of water in special cabin tanks, lead ballast totaling 7,800 pounds, and 8,214 pounds of test equipment.

In production form, the R7V-2 and YC-121F would have had the same interior configurations as the operational R7V-1 and C-121C. Up to 106 passengers could be accommodated during overland flights; up to 97 passengers could be carried during over water flights; or 73 stretcher cases plus four medical attendants could be carried in either circumstance. Up to 36,000 pounds in the pure freight mode could be carried by either model.

Of the two R7V-2s, one was used by Lockheed for performance, stability, control, and powerplant trials, and the other was used for radio, air-conditioning, pressurization, electrical, and other miscellaneous systems testing. With the YC-121Fs, they joined four other Air Force testbed aircraft powered by T34s, a pair of Boeing YC-97J *Stratofreighters* and a pair of Douglas YC-124B *Globemasters*.

In spite of this experimental fleet, interest in the T-34 had waned by 1954 and along with it, interest in the turboprop powered transports. Though work on the single-shaft, 13-stage axial flow compressor/three-stage turbine T34, initiated under a Navy contract in 1945, had been on-going for over ten years by this time, newer powerplants had superseded it in performance and specific fuel consumption figures. It eventually was to be found on only one production aircraft, the Douglas C-133 *Cargomaster*...originally scheduled to replace the venerable C-124.

In spite of the T34's age, Lockheed, encouraged by the successes of the four prototypes, proposed two airliner *Constellations* with civil T34s (5,500 equivalent shaft horsepower Pratt & Whitney PT2F-1 *Turbo-Wasps*) for propulsion. Referred to as the Models L-1249A in freighter configuration and L-1249B in passenger configuration, they were to be much the same over-all as the standard commercial *Super Constellation*. The primary differences lay in the engine nacelle attachment points...which were to be modified specifically for the new engines; and in the landing gear design...which was to be strengthened in order to accommodate the 150,000 pounds maximum takeoff weight. Performance was expected to include a maximum speed of 449 mph and a cruising speed of 368 mph at 25,000 feet Maximum payload was estimated to be 40,918 pounds. To increase range, two 600 gallon wing tip tanks were an option and provision for two 500 gallon underwing tanks was to be provided. The wingspan would have been reduced to 117 feet before tip tank installation (with tanks in place, span would have been 126 feet). Absolute range with all four tanks in place would have been 4,150 miles.

The Model 1249 was expected to be able to fly from London to Moscow and back in seven hours, or to Cairo in six hours with a load of 32,000 pounds, or San Francisco or Los Angeles to Honolulu in under six hours, or New York to London in 8-3/4 hours with a stop at Gander. Though Lockheed pushed sales of this version with considerable vigor, even offering to convert older Model 1049s to the 1249 configuration, they met with no success and the project was abandoned.

Following the afore-mentioned tests of the Allison 501D-13 engine on "Old 1961", an R7V-2 during 1956 was bailed to Lockheed by the Navy and reengined with four 3,750 equivalent shaft horsepower Allison 501D-13s turning Aeroproducts 606 four-blade propellers. This aircraft then was committed to a 1,000 hour flight test program intended to develop the forthcoming engine and associated systems for the *Electra* and its proposed Navy anti-submarine warfare variant, the *Orion*. As with the T34 installation, the 501D-13s exhausted over the wing trailing edges, but through pipes of smaller diameter. The cowling shape for the new engines also was revised, in part due to the Allison engine's propeller reduction gearing being offset beneath its power section.

Along with two Military Air Transport Service 1700th Squadron Convair YC-131Cs equipped with 3,250 equivalent shaft horsepower Allison YT-56s, the modified R7V-2 embarked on an intensive flight test program to determine the operational suitability of the new turboprop engine. By July of 1958, approximately a year after it had first flown with the new engines, it had logged more than 750 hours of engine development time...averaging no less than 8 hours a day in simulated airline service.

After completion of their respective flight test programs, the four turboprop *Constellations* were dismantled and their parts utilized to keep other *Constellations* in flyable condition. These rebuilds, though expensive, cost less than half the price of buying two totally new aircraft, yet resulted in essentially new aircraft in terms of airframe life. The biggest rebuild problem was adaptation of the differing electrical systems to a uniform Model 1049H standard.

In a final attempt to give new life to the military turboprop *Constellation* program, Lockheed, during mid-1957, won a Navy contract for a new version of the airborne early warning (AEW) radar-equipped WV-2. The resulting CL-257, which had been proffered to the Navy during January, was formally designated W2V-1 and equipped with the APS-70 radar in a large dorsally mounted "saucer"-type rotating radome. Based on the *Super Constellation* and its 150 foot span wing, it was to be powered by four Allison T56 turboprop engines complemented by two Westinghouse J34 turbojet engines in wingtip pods. Gross weight was increased to 175,000 pounds. Though first flight tentatively was scheduled for late 1959 or early 1960, only a month after the contract was awarded, the Navy found itself in a budget squeeze and the W2V-1 was abandoned.

Though modestly successful, the turboprop *Constellation* program proved too little, too late. The jet age, by the mid-1950s, had filtered down to the airline industry, and with the advent of the de Havilland *Comet*, the Tupolev Tu-104, and the Boeing 707, it was apparent the future lay in pure jet airliners. Turboprops continued as viable engine options for smaller, short-legged commuter aircraft, but their use on transcontinental and intercontinental airliners proved economically unjustifiable.

---

**The RB-69:**

One of the least known of the *Skunk Works'* many efforts, the RB-69 program was initiated under the aegis of a CIA contract calling for an aircraft to monitor and document electromagnetic emissions and transmissions in denied territories. The project was begun during 1954 with "Kelly" Johnson overseeing program manager Luther McDonald...who effectively ran it until 1957 when Fred Cavanaugh took over after being pulled from the P2V program.

McDonald, in order to meet the CIA's mission profile, had proposed the use of Lockheed's venerable P2V *Neptune,* then the longest ranged twin-engine aircraft in the world. Under the auspices of a *Skunk Works*-type engineering and manufacturing environment, five new P2V-7s and two older Navy P2V-7s became RB-69s (a designation purportedly "plucked out of thin air") and were secretly rolled out at Burbank with Air Force markings during 1955. Delivery flights were made to Edwards AFB North Base where flight testing was accomplished in considerable secrecy. Referred to by the CIA as *Project Cherry* or later, *Wild Cherry,* the objective was to build an aircraft that could safely penetrate denied airspace, gather intelligence data, and return...all without being easily detected by defensive systems.

US pilots hired by the CIA to fly the RB-69, like their U-2 counterparts to follow, went through a "sheep dipping" exercise that effectively erased their real identities and replaced them with backgrounds that were totally fictitious...right down to their contrived names. Each aircraft carried a crew of twelve, including a pilot, a copilot, a flight engineer, a radio operator, and eight electronic intelligence personnel to operate the various sensor systems. Later Taiwanese missions were flown with a crew of fourteen.

After going through a rigorous training program at Palmdale, California and Edwards AFB North Base (later, some training was accomplished at Eglin AFB, Florida), both US and foreign pilots embarked on the first operational missions of the program. These were flown out of Weisbaden in Germany during 1955 and 1956. Because of their knowledge of the local terrain and eastern European languages, Czechoslovakian or Polish crews often manned the two RB-69s undertaking the Russian missions. A mix of penetration and border surveillance flights were flown. One of the first objectives was the collection of power grid data. This was acquired by flying over western Russia's power lines.

The aircraft were equipped with a variety of unique systems, including the first viable terrain avoidance radar (built by Texas Instruments) and a Singer-manufactured Doppler radar for navigation...which worked with considerable effectiveness over land, but not over water. One of the first traveling wave tube-type noise jammers, from Applied Technology Inc. (ATI), was part of the active countermeasures complement as well but was not considered reliable. As Cavanaugh said in an interview that took place many years after the fact, "If they lasted for an 8 hour mission we couldn't believe it!"

In later years the aircraft were given deception jammers, a large side-looking-airborne-radar (SLAR) by G.E. (it was not installed until late in the program), a Doppler radar in its tail, an ATI developed $K_u$ band ELINT receiver, and a massive assortment of miscellaneous other jammers, sensors, and related equipment. At one time, an AN/APR-3 jammer was part of the aircraft's complement. No armament was carried, though it is claimed aft-facing AIM-9 air-to-air missiles could be mounted on wing pylons if necessary. Camera systems for photographing marks of interest were manufactured by Fairchild. Mercury arc lights for camera work were mounted in tip pods...but these were not used operationally.

When the European operation was com-

*The variety of sensors carried by the various RB-69s differed considerably from aircraft to aircraft. Even bomb bay configurations were changed to accommodate different mission requirements.*

*The seven RB-69s initially participated in peripheral and penetration flights around and into the Soviet Union and were flown out of Germany.*

promised by a US officer (he reportedly was entrapped by a female KGB agent), the Weisbaden missions were terminated. Chinese operations then became highest priority.

In China, the RB-69s—flown with Taiwanese markings in place of US insignia—replaced a variety of aircraft (Douglas A-26s, Boeing B-17s, and Consolidated PB4Ys) that had been used to drop espionage agents and supplies inside Chinese borders. Electronic intelligence and leaflet dropping missions also were flown with considerable regularity.

Insertion missions, wherein agents were parachuted from the RB-69s (usually at night) often included the use of a special cargo container. Mounted in the aircraft's bomb bay and designed to accommodate survival gear, communications equipment, or anything else necessary for successful execution of a mission, this all-wood container (designed so that it could be easily destroyed and thus eliminated as evidence of the insertion process) was tested over the El Centro range in California before being placed in Taiwanese service.

The operating squadron in Taiwan was the 34th Squadron. Nicknamed the *Bats,* it had been involved in earlier operations utilizing

Douglas A-26s, Curtiss C-46s, Douglas C-47s, and miscellaneous other aircraft types. With these aircraft and the RB-69, most missions were flown at night and at low altitude (usually below 1,000 feet).

Crews were hand-picked by the Taiwanese Air Force and rigorously trained by the CIA in the US. Headquarters for the operation were set up at Hsinchu AB in Taiwan in a special area set aside for covert operations under the auspices of the 8th Fighter Wing (nominally).

The Chinese operation began during early 1957 and continued for the following seven years. Perimeter missions ran along the coast but penetration flights into China were made. These went as far as Peiping and Kwangchow. Missions sometimes were flown from S. Korea. A few, possibly not having anything to do with Chinese operations, were flown from the US Johnson Island protectorate in the Pacific Ocean. From 1958 through about 1964 there were 81 penetrations of Chinese airspace.

Unfortunately, the aircraft sporadically were intercepted. On one notable occasion an RB-69 was caught flying over Xian. This aircraft was attacked by four MiGs near mountainous terrain. During the ensuing chase one of

*Several, though not all, of the RB-69s were equipped with side-looking-airborne-radar (SLAR) systems for terrain mapping of unfriendly territory. This was one of the first operational uses of this system in history.*

*The majority of surviving RB-69s wound up in Taiwanese Air Force service and were repainted in Taiwanese markings following their delivery to the Taiwanese mainland.*

the MiGs flew into a mountain and was destroyed. The RB-69 escaped.

Chinese defenses steadily improved during the course of the RB-69's Taiwanese tenure and on June 11, 1964 one was lost to enemy activity over the Shantung peninsula. As many as four other RB-69s apparently were lost by the time the aircraft was removed from Taiwanese service.

The Chinese, frustrated by the RB-69s unfettered night penetrations of Chinese airspace, eventually perfected a night illumination system that successfully exposed the aircraft long enough for fighters to make visual identification and attack. This required that large numbers of Ilyushin Il-28s and Shinyang J-5s be sent aloft to drop flares. These lit the entire night sky and in so doing, exposed the RB-69s and permitted their interception and destruction. The successes thus realized proved instrumental in the 1964 CIA and Taiwanese decision to remove the type from operational service.

### The YC-130 *Hercules*:

*"Then comes the YC-130. The first two prototypes were built using partial Skunk Works methods. It was then taken and moved down to Georgia, who took it on, and went into production that is now heading for a total of 1,500 airplanes. I think the concept was good, it demonstrated our ability to hand it off to another production organization who took it on and made it work."* Clarence L. "Kelly" Johnson

On February 2, 1951, the Air Force Tactical Air Command issued Request for Proposals to the Boeing, Douglas, Fairchild, and Lockheed aircraft companies calling for a medium weight turboprop-powered transport capable of meeting the specifications and performance criteria outlined in any one of three General Operational Requirements it included. The particular GOR to which Lockheed elected to respond, SS-400L, which had grown out of the air transport failings that had surfaced during operations by the Far East Air Forces Combat Cargo Command at the beginning of the Korean War, called for the aircraft to accommodate four typical missions, referred to as "airhead", "resupply", "logistical support" and "troop carrier".

The "airhead" mission required the aircraft to carry a 25,000 pound payload to ground forces holding a position in enemy territory while retaining a combat radius of 1,100 nautical miles without refueling; it was to be flown at a maximum altitude of 1,000 feet at high speed. The "resupply" mission required the aircraft to carry 37,800 pounds of cargo over a distance of 950 nautical miles and back without refueling, or 25,800 pounds of cargo over a distance of 1,300 nautical miles one way (if refueling was conducted at the delivery point, ranges with the two payloads then would become 1,500 nautical miles and 2,520 nautical miles, respectively). The "logistic support" mission required a range of 1,700 nautical miles while carrying a 37,800 pound cargo (this would be accommodated without tactical equipment and with a limiting load factor of 2.5 g rather than 3 g). In the "troop carrier" configuration, the aircraft would be required to accommodate 64 paratroops or 92 ground personnel.

The Air Force demanded a quick response to the RFP and within days of its release, Art Flock had been assigned as chief project engineer with Willis Hawkins as general supervisor. Hawkins at the time also was in charge of Lockheed's preliminary design department. *Skunk Works* operating proce-

dures would be utilized as appropriate to expedite design and prototype development. Working with Hawkins were Eugene Frost, Eldon Peterman, Dick Pulver, and Flock...all veterans of earlier *Skunk Works* projects under Johnson's guidance.

Assigned the Temporary Design Number L-206 and later becoming the Model 82, the new transport rapidly evolved under Flock's direction. As its configuration matured, so grew the preliminary design group's conviction it was creating a logical yet utilitarian aircraft capable not only of achieving, but superseding the basic GOR objectives which specified payload/range requirements eight times that of any then-extant design.

Additionally, it became apparent the new performance requirements defined substantial improvements over existing transports in other areas. One-engine-out capabilities over the drop zone were increased by factors of 1.5 to 2.0. Dependable controllability and stability at low speeds were essential. Design payload/range capabilities were multiplied by a factor of 8. Moreover, exceptional takeoff and landing performance would be required in order to meet the new assault transport requirement.

Equipment and structural demands showed improvements of similar magnitude. Throughout the operating range, an 8,000 foot pressure altitude for both crew and cargo compartments was now required. An integral ramp and rear door operable in flight for heavy equipment drops were specified. The limit flight-load factor was increased to 3. Excellent crew visibility would be absolutely necessary. The clear cargo volume asked for resembled a railroad box car (40 feet x 10 feet x 9 feet). The cargo floor had to be at the level of standard truck beds. And the landing gear was to be capable of enabling aircraft operations in fields of clay, sand, or humus.

Simplicity, reliability, and rugged construction became the preliminary design team's philosophy along with economy of manufacture, operation, and maintenance.

The resulting transport's cargo bay was 41 feet long, 10 feet 3 inches wide, as low as 9 feet high (at the point of the wing carry-through structure) and only 3 feet 5 inches above ground level, due in part to mounting the high lift wing (with an aspect reatio of 10) high on the fuselage. At its forward end, just ahead of the propeller disc line, cargo could be loaded through a 6 foot 8 inch wide by 6 foot high fuselage cut-out equipped with an upward swinging door. At its aft end, it was equipped with a two-segment rear door whose forward segment was hinged at its forward end and designed to swing down to a maximum of 13° and thus serve as an entry or exit ramp. The smaller rear segment was hinged at its aft end and designed to swing up into the aft fuselage, thus providing increased clearance for cargo loading and unloading. Paratroop doors were provided on both sides of the fuselage just forward of the aft cargo hold door.

In consideration of the rough field requirement in the GOR, Gene Frost, deputy director of preliminary design, spent a considerable amount of time agonizing over the design of the landing gear. In the end, the high-wing configuration dictated an encapsulated gear assembly attached to the fuselage sides in faired-in pods. This proved an engineering windfall, as it simplified the retraction mechanisms, left the cargo hold unaffected volumetrically, and had little impact on the aircraft's drag. The tandem wheel assemblies, equipped with high-flotation

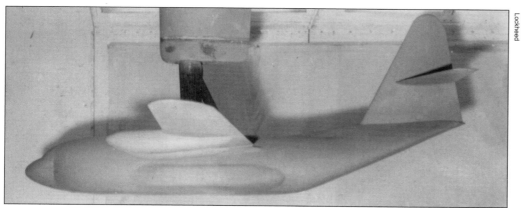

*One of many C-130 wind tunnel models; this configuration sported cruciform-type tail surfaces. Model was inverted in wind-tunnel and has been turned right-side-up for illustration purposes.*

*Full-scale wood and metal mock-up of the C-130 was built at Lockheed's Burbank facility during 1951 and later transported to Marietta, Georgia following transfer of C-130 production to that plant. The two prototype YC-130s were generally true to the basic design features defined in the mock-up.*

tires, retracted vertically into the pods and thus eliminated any geometrically complex strut assemblies. Consequently, it became possible to build a strong landing gear while keeping weight to a minimum.

The advent of efficient turboprop engines, in particular Allison's by now extremely dependable 3,750 equivalent shaft horsepower T56-A-1 (turning Curtiss-Wright *Turboelectric*, full-feathering, reversible, three bladed propellers), proved a major windfall for the Model 82. The related decision to equip the aircraft with four instead of two engines permitted improved safety, allowed for significant increases in gross weight and payload weight, and eased the task of meeting speed, climb, and range requirements. Additionally, pressurization of the entire fuselage, at the time somewhat of a novelty, became an achievable goal due to the excess power available.

In addition to conventional materials and processes, a number of new ones were utilized in the new Lockheed transport in order to obtain increased performance and serviceability. Bonding allowed the use of lighter gauge metals. Approximately 100 thin-gauge aluminum assemblies were used. Typical applications involved the joining of doublers and stiffeners to skins of wing and empennage trailing-edge assemblies. The use of metal bonding was restricted to relatively flat panels in order to minimize production problems during the period when shop techniques were being developed. Even so, a number of production problems arose and were solved by close coordination between engineering and manufacturing.

The Model 82 also became one of the first aircraft to benefit from the use of a new aluminum alloy...A78S-T. Most usage was in the form of plate and extrusions for primary structure, particularly integrally stiffened skins. Such use allowed a 7% increase in stress factors over 75A-T. Approximately 210 individual A78S-T parts were designed into the aircraft including a number which weighed over 100 pounds each.

During the course of design development and mock-up construction, inputs from external sources was invited and reviewed. Air Force and transport personnel were brought in from virtually every segment of the industry. Each was asked to critique the new aircraft and recommend changes or improvements. The resulting information was carefully assessed by Flock and his team and where appropriate,

incorporated into the actual aircraft. Additionally, Lockheed representatives associated with the Model 82's development visited facilities that could provide insight into operational requirements and usage.

Interestingly, by this stage of the Model 82's development, Johnson had begun to have doubts about its ability to succeed. Unhappy with its rather proletarian aesthetic qualities, he had reached a point where he refused to sign-off the paper proposals being submitted to the Air Force...forcing his boss, company vice president Hall Hibbard, to overrule him.

Regardless, the proposals, upon completion, were submitted to the Air Force during April of 1951. Lockheed's aircraft weighed 57,500 pounds empty and had an all-up weight of 108,000 pounds including a 25,000 pound payload. An alternate gross weight of 124,200 pounds was achievable with load factors reduced from the design 3 g. Predicted performance for the aircraft exceeded the requirements in almost every important part of the envelope.

Because of Korean War pressures, the Boeing, Douglas, Fairchild, and Lockheed pro-

posals were quickly evaluated by the Air Force. On July 2, five months after first receiving the RFP, Lockheed was informed its proposal had been picked for prototyping over those of the competition. On July 11, Contract AF 33 (038)-30453 was awarded Lockheed calling for the construction and flight testing of two Lockheed Model 82s...formally designated C-130 by the Air Force. In short order the company officially named the new transport *Hercules* in concert with its tradition of naming aircraft after stars and constellations.

Some three years later, the second YC-130, the first of the two prototypes to be declared flightworthy, was cleared for its initial hop. Accordingly, on August 23, 1954, with Stanley Beltz as pilot, Roy Wimmer as copilot, Jack Real as flight test engineer, and Dick Stanton as flight engineer, it departed the Burbank airport at 2:45 p.m. on its first flight. Sixty-one minutes later it landed safely at Edwards AFB. Johnson and a small crew had flown chase in a P2V *Neptune*.

The number one YC-130, crewed by Roy Wimmer (pilot), Joe Ware (co-pilot), and Jack Real flight/flight test engineer, took to the air on

*The nearly square cross-section of the C-130's cargo compartment was 41 feet 5 inches long. An Army ton-and-a-half truck tests clearances during 1951 using the C-130 full-scale mock-up at Burbank.*

*The second YC-130, 53-3397, was the first of the two prototypes to fly. The first aircraft, 53-3396, was being used as a static test (structural) article at the time.*

*Both prototypes were powered by Allison T56-A-1 turboprops. This same engine, albeit in more advanced and considerably more powerful versions, would go on to power every single C-130 ever built.*

*The two YC-130s, 53-3396 and 53-3397, during a formation flight. The peculiar nose configuration of the YC-130s and initial production C-130As would later be replaced by the familiar radome-equipped nose.*

*The two YC-130s were to become the only two Hercules to be built at Lockheed's Burbank facility. A decision to the produce the aircraft in Marietta, Georgia led to all C-130 assets being transferred there.*

January 21, 1955, having served as a static test article while the number two aircraft would be used to accomplish the initial flight test tasks. This first flight lasted about an hour and involved a takeoff from Burbank and a landing at Palmdale.

As predicted, early flight test work with the two "roman nosed" aircraft proved very encouraging. Pilots reported good handling characteristics and considerably better-than-expected performance. Due in part to the fact the basic mission weight of 108,000 pounds had been 5,000 pounds lighter than guaranteed, cruising speed was some 20% higher, takeoff distances were some 25% lower, ceiling and initial climb rates were some 35% higher, landing distances were some 40% shorter, and single-engine-out climb rates were a stunning 55% higher than predicted.

These figures, coupled with the other obvious attributes of what was rapidly becoming widely admired as a most remarkable aircraft, gave the Air Force confidence its decision to support the program had been a good one. Remarkably, the service had committed to an initial buy of seven C-130As under contract AF33(600)-22286 dated February 10, 1953, approximately a year-and-a-half prior to the aircraft's first flight.

Predating the latter event, the Air Force had requested Lockheed to reopen an Air Force-owned manufacturing facility in Marietta, Georgia in order to meet an expected Korean War-fanned increase in aircraft production capacity. Initially, it was proposed this facility, which had been built for Bell Aircraft Corporation during World War Two—and which had initially been used to manufacture Bell-built models of the Boeing B-29—would be utilized to refurbish a large fleet of B-29s then in storage at Pyote AB some forty miles west of Odessa, Texas. Following the success of this operation, and the follow-on production of some 394 Boeing B-47 *Stratojets*, Lockheed announced, during October of 1952, its decision to shift production of the C-130 to this facility under the direction of Al Brown. Brown moved temporarily from Marietta to Burbank and along with a team of Marietta engineers, worked side-by-side with their Burbank associates as the prototype aircraft were assembled.

As part of the transfer of C-130 assets that followed completion of the two prototypes, the fifty-ton full-scale C-130 wooden mock-up also was moved to Marietta. Placed onboard an Army barge, it was shipped via the Panama canal to Savannah, Georgia and then moved by two flat-bed trucks the remaining distance to Marietta. Beginning with the third *Hercules*...which was the first production C-130A...all following C-130's rolled from the Marietta production line. Only the first two YC-130s would lay claim to having been built in Burbank.

On March 10, 1955, the first production C-130A was rolled out at the Marietta, Georgia facility. On April 7, 1955, with Bud Martin as pilot, Leo Sullivan as copilot, and Jack Gilley, Chuck Littlejohn, and Bob Brennan as flight test engineers, it took off on what would become the first flight of the first Georgia-built *Hercules*. By the summer of 1955, the two prototype YC-130s had been joined by three production examples and flight test work at Edwards AFB was progressing rapidly. During July, the third C-130A demonstrated a ground takeoff roll of only 900 feet and the ability to land in 600 feet—both with a payload in excess of eight tons.

*Though "Kelly" Johnson retained considerable reservations concerning the viability of the C-130 as a production military transport, his concerns proved unfounded. Over 2,000 have been built during the nearly forty years of production that have ensued since the type's first flight.*

Some thirty-seven years after the first flight of the production aircraft, on May 15, 1992, Lockheed delivered the 2,000th production *Hercules*, a C-130H, to the Air Force. This transport, representing one of the most successful aircraft production programs ever, is only the most recent heir to a legacy that now lays claim to a seemingly endless list of accomplishments.

*So-called "Roman-nose" YC-130 configuration was continued into the initial batch of production C-130As. Many of these aircraft later were retrofitted with the better-known protruding radome-equipped nose which provided room for a larger antenna.*

*Full-scale XF-104 mock-up was not only an accurate and highly detailed rendition of the actual aircraft, but also a masterpiece of woodworking and a testimonial to the art of carpentry. Original intake configuration that preceeded the later half-cone design is noteworthy.*

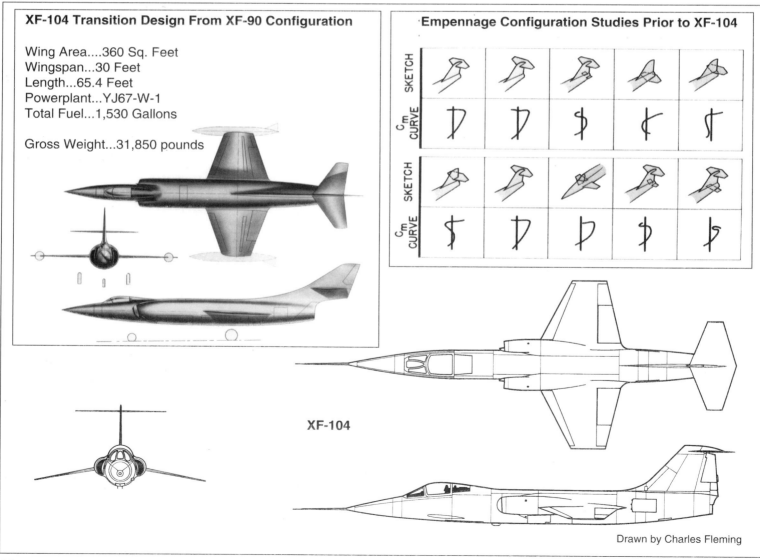

### XF-104 Transition Design From XF-90 Configuration

Wing Area....360 Sq. Feet
Wingspan...30 Feet
Length...65.4 Feet
Powerplant...YJ67-W-1
Total Fuel...1,530 Gallons

Gross Weight...31,850 pounds

### Empennage Configuration Studies Prior to XF-104

XF-104

Drawn by Charles Fleming

62

# Chapter 5:
# THE XF-104 *STARFIGHTER*

*"Next the F-104, we consider that the cost and performance of that model excellent. And I guess after some 2,500 of them having been built around the world, we consider the F-104 series a success."*

**Clarence L. "Kelly" Johnson**

A post-World War 2 malaise in western fighter development evaporated on May 1, 1950 with the crossing of the Yalu River and entry into air combat near the Manchurian border of six MiG-15s. With the realization the Soviet Union had in operational service a world-class, swept-wing, jet-powered fighter, US and other western air forces were rudely awakened to the fact they had been remiss in not actively pursuing transonic, state-of-the art advances of their own. Nothing the west had to offer—with the possible exception of the untried North American F-86 *Sabre*—was a match for the agile and fast MiG bureau aircraft. "Kelly" Johnson, one of the many engineers made aware of the MiG-15's superior performance and miscellaneous other attributes, later would note that during the Korean War, "there was universal criticism of our American fighters in regard to their capabilities in ceiling and high-altitude maneuverability, as well as their complexity from a maintenance point of view."

During the 1949/1950 period, Lockheed's preliminary design team was endeavoring to create a successor to the respected, but performance-limited F-80. As noted in Chapter 4, one ill-fated attempt to develop a *Shooting Star* follow-on was the over-built and under-powered XF-90. Concurrent with Lockheed's conclusion this heavy penetration fighter would not be placed in production, various company personnel, including Johnson, met with and purposefully interviewed fighter pilots who had flown in Korea in an attempt to gain insights into what future fighters should have in the way of desirable capabilities and features.

These insights were reviewed by Johnson and others in preliminary design and then interfaced with relevant technical data from Lockheed's then-secret X-7 ramjet-powered research vehicle program. Information from the various X-7 flights pertaining to configurations, aeroelasticity problems, and supersonic aerodynamics was used to assess the possibility of building a low-aspect-ratio, thin, straight wing aircraft that would have excellent flight characteristics in the Mach 2 to 3 speed range.

An effort then was made to convert the XF-90 into a supersonic configuration. A 3% thickness/chord ratio wing then was attached to a modified XF-90 wind tunnel model. This proved revealing, but not a sufficient advance to merit investment in full-scale hardware.

Other studies led to the design of the Lockheed Model 205 which had an air intake mounted above and behind the cockpit. To this point, *Skunk Works* efforts had concentrated on aircraft in the 25,000 to 45,000 pound gross weight class. The afore-mentioned interviews with US pilots in Korea, however, when coupled with Air Force foreign technology insights, led to the conclusion an extremely light aircraft in the 15,000 to 18,000 pound gross weight category might be more suitable. Concerns surfaced immediately, however, over

*The first XF-104 under construction at Lockheed's Burbank facility. The Starfighter would prove to be the smallest of the 1950s and 1960s vintage "Century Series" fighters.*

whether such a small aircraft could provide the performance required...while carrying suitable armament and all the associated miscellaneous equipment necessary for air combat against larger foes.

Johnson explained that there were two schools of thought on this matter, "The large airplane exponents claimed that equal speed, range, and fighting power could not be obtained in a smaller airplane because such fixed items as the pilot size, canopy size, engine thrust per square foot of frontal area, and fixed equipment item weights were a smaller percentage of the large airplane weight than of the smaller one. Likewise, the fuselage cross section and size, in general, would be

unfavorable for the smaller airplane, resulting in lower ratios of lift-to-drag and thrust-to-drag, even if the same percentage of fuel weight could be carried. There was not in existence a small engine which had as good thrust to weight ratios or specific fuel consumption as the larger engines then available. These factors were all true at the time; so it was necessary to make some rather major advances on practically all of these fronts before a successful lightweight fighter could be developed."

The Korean War became a major proving ground for rapidly evolving jet fighter design philosophies. When Lockheed began reviewing the accumulated data from the afore-mentioned interviews, it became apparent Air Force

*Completed XF-104 mock-up. Forward fuselage included a complete cockpit with ejection seat and manually retractable nose landing gear. Side-hinged canopy later would be seen on U-2 spin-off.*

*The first XF-104 was delivered to Edwards AFB by truck from Burbank during late January of 1954. Following reassembly, it was taxi tested in preparation for its first flight.*

*The first XF-104, 53-7786, shortly after its arrival at Edwards AFB and while being off-loaded from its transport truck. Empennage and tail surfaces had been removed to facilitate carriage.*

*Static ground tests were undertaken at Edwards AFB during late January and early February of 1954. Special intake screens were provided to protect the aircraft's engine from foreign object damage.*

*The XF-104 first was flown powered by a Buick-manufactured version of the Wright XJ65-W-6. This engine provided a maximum of 10,200 pounds thrust with afterburner.*

pilots flying F-80s, F-84s, and F-86s had constantly espoused the attributes of lighter aircraft to enhance altitude, speed, and acceleration performance. At the same time, they criticized over-complexity and the tendency to "add-on" components and capabilities that simply weren't needed. In turn, this ignited arguments both for and against stripped versus fully-equipped aircraft. Neither side gained noticeable ground while the war in Korea raged on.

In the interim, Lockheed's L-205 Temporary Design Designation study, offered to the Air Force in prototype form as the Model 99 during late 1950, was awarded a development contract. The following January, however, preliminary work was halted when reservations concerning its capabilities in light of expected advances in enemy aircraft surfaced during an initial Air Force review. This was followed, during May of 1952, by a new contract calling for two 12,000 pound class Wright J67-powered prototypes. When it was discovered the Air Force demanded to have all patent and production rights rescinded to the US government, Lockheed refused to sign the contract and the project died.

By this time, too, the preliminary design team had presented the Air Force with the first of its lightweight fighter design studies, and this had garnered enough interest to merit further review and a change in priorities. After many discussions with Air Force personnel concerning the attributes of lightweight versus heavyweight aircraft, Johnson and his team requested funds to build a lightweight, "completely equipped" fighter in order to explore its feasibility and operational applicability. An unsolicited proposal, for the CL-246, was delivered to Gen. Donald Putt's office in the Pentagon during November of 1952. When reviewed by Gen. Don Yates and Col. Bruce Holloway, it quickly generated enough interest to merit the release of a hurriedly fabricated General Operational Requirement to the US aircraft industry and by the middle of December, competing designs had been received from North American (NA-212), Northrop (N-102), and Republic (AP-55). During January, Lockheed's CL-246 was picked over its competitors for prototyping, and on March 12, Letter Contract AF33(600)-23362 was issued by the Air Force calling for the construction and initial flight testing of two XF-104 (Weapon System WS-303A) aircraft.

Johnson later would recall, "The design aim was to produce a supersonic fighter that would have a performance capability in excess of Mach 2 and combat altitudes of over 60,000 feet. This performance could not be expected with the initial engine installation—the (non-afterburning) Wright J65—but could be exceeded with the General Electric J79. It was necessary to use the latest form of armament, consisting of the T-171 (the so-called 'Gatling gun'), which was the equivalent of four to six older type 20 mm guns but which was substantially lighter and more compact. It was evident that major steps must be taken in the provisions for advanced radar and gunsights."

A *Skunk Works*-type mode of operation was instituted at Lockheed to expedite development and construction of the two prototypes. As a result, chief project engineer Bill Ralston was able to have the full-scale mock-up completed and ready for inspection on April 30 and the first completed aircraft out of the shop some 355 days after the project was formally started. During this period, an extensive wind tunnel program was undertaken using not only

*The second XF-104, 53-7787, was virtually identical to the first. Both were equipped with J65 engines and equipped with the distinctive non-half-cone equipped intakes. The XF-104s were somewhat smaller and lighter than the definitive F-104A and had lower maximum speed and altitude capabilities.*

*Taxi tests of the first XF-104 were conducted with little difficulty by Lockheed's Tony LeVier. Noteworthy in this view is the extended right speed brake.*

*The first official flight of the first XF-104 took place at Edwards AFB on March 4, 1954 with Tony LeVier at the controls.*

Lockheed's own facilities, but those of the NACA as well.

The initial proposal had been created in Lockheed's preliminary design deparment under Hall Hibbard and "Kelly" Johnson. Willis Hawkins and Gene Frost were head and deputy design managers using support from Phil Colman as head of aerodynamics. Dick Heppe, Jim Hong, and Ben Rich worked for Colman. Ed Baldwin, Dick Boehme, Henry Combs, Rus Daniell, and Ken Pitman were assigned to preliminary design. These latter all became permanent members of the XF-104 team under Don Palmer. Irv Culver, the chief designer of the X-7, was essentially the concept design leader in the preliminary design department. Other team members under Art Vierick were involved in the actual prototype construction process.

The effort resulted in a stunningly small but efficient aircraft. Johnson later would summarize the design process as follows: "In laying out the basic arrangement, I proposed a symmetrical design for the attachment of the wings to the ducts and the ducts to the fuselage. It seemed evident that this form would give minimum drag while providing other arrangement advantages such as better clearance for the wing tip tanks and ability to carry the inlet air ducts directly to the engine. With a wing span of only seven feet outside of the ducts, it was considered feasible to attach the wings to rings forming the outside contour of the duct without any normal carry-through structure. After several structural engineers threatened to commit suicide, it was eventually determined that this could be done without any undue wing weight or fuselage weight penalty. A basic drag reduction of some 12% appeared to result from the midwing approach compared to low wing designs.

"One of the first problems that seemed apparent from the basic layout of the airplane was that the span of the vertical tail above the centerline of the fuselage was practically equal to the wing semi-span and with the high hori-

zontal tail position the vertical tail was very effective. It was evident that the rudder was, therefore, a good aileron, and that adverse roll would occur with rudder deflection. This indicated some amount of negative dihedral or 'cathedral' would be necessary, but it was difficult to determine the proper amount. At this time, the NACA at Ames Laboratory had modified a propeller-driven airplane to vary the lateral stability artificially by 'black boxes', so that different apparent amounts of dihedral could be evaluated and pilots' opinions gathered on what was a desirable relation between dihedral effect and a given amount of directional stability.

"A phone call to Mr. Smith J. DeFrance obtained his immediate concurrence in running a series of tests trying to simulate the desirable degree of cathedral which it would be necessary to employ for the F-104. Lockheed computed the characteristics required to simulate 0°, 5°, and 10° cathedral, and Mr. Tony LeVier, our engineering test pilot, visited Ames to evaluate the problem on the NACA aircraft. He was not told in advance what angles of cathedral were to be simulated, but he was told by radio what settings to try on the 'black box'.

"He was first given a setting of 0° dihedral,

whereupon he said over the radio, 'My God, what did you give me here?' The airplane was very difficult to fly. He was then given several other settings, with the result that a minus 10° was chosen to give good characteristics for the F-104 configuration. Throughout all phases of testing the F-104, such typical cooperation was obtained from the NACA.

"A major problem in the concept of the airplane was the flutter and aeroelastic characteristic encountered with a 3% thick wing. This wing was only three-quarters as thick as the thinnest research wing, and about 82% as thick as those flown at the time on the X-7 test vehicle. There were many unknowns, and still are, in the predictions of flutter, particularly in the transonic speed range, as well as at supersonic speeds. It was necessary to find some cheap means of testing empirically various wing and tail configurations to insure freedom from flutter. It seemed that the use of 5-inch HVAR rockets might be appropriate, using camera means to obtain flutter data, and a parachute for recovery of the camera. This study was actually undertaken prior to getting a contract on the XF-104, and was carried on initially for the larger fighters for which we had no Air

*The prototype Starfighters were thrust limited to about Mach 1.75. Mach 1.79 was achieved by the second aircraft on March 25, 1955...this being the highest speed reached by either prototype.*

*Design of the XF-104's horizontal and vertical tail surfaces required a significant engineering effort. Many variations were studied before the classical T-tail was chosen. Though heavier (due to structural considerations), it provided the aerodynamic elements considered necessary for effective stability and control.*

*The XF-104's distinctive extremely thin, trapezoidal wing was considered ideal for achieving high Mach numbers while retaining some semblence of low-speed stability and control.*

Force contract.

"When a private organization tries to go out and buy 5-inch rockets, they rapidly find out such armament cannot be purchased without government sanction. One day, when I was visiting a General in Baltimore, I made the problem known to him. The General immediately turned to his aide and said, 'send a message to General so-and-so in Korea and tell him to stop shooting 5-inch rockets for one morning and send them to 'Kelly'.' By the time I returned to California, some four-hundred odd 5-inch rockets had been delivered to Lockheed for implementing studies of flutter. There was no red tape in that operation, until we found out ourselves we lacked proper storage facilities for the rockets, an area in which to fire them, and several similar items. Edwards AFB solved these problem by providing the necessary facilities.

"A group under Mr. Ford Johnston was able in a very short time to do some excellent basic research on the flutter of the F-104 configuration, including such factors as tip tanks and tails. One dollar in every eight spent on the XF-104 program was spent on flutter and aeroelastic problems. Later, the tail surfaces and aft fuselage were mounted on a sled and tested to high speeds on the Edwards AFB sled facility. These precautions resulted in our having encountered no flutter problems on the aircraft to date.

"The problem of flight controls was solved by the application of irreversible boosters on the stabilizer and ailerons, and various damper devices were evaluated for providing the optimum gun platform at all speeds. The basic stability of the airplane is so good that perfectly safe flight can be maintained without any of the yaw, pitch or roll dampers in operation. The use of these devices, however, gives the airplane superior stability and damping, which is no doubt necessary for effective use of any supersonic airplane as an effective armament platform. An interesting problem developed in trying to fit an irreversible booster into the thin wing. This was solved by a 'piccolo' design involving multiple operating cylinders imbedded in what amounts to a solid piece of dural, which is practically a structural part of the airplane."

While the two prototypes were under construction in the *Skunk Works'* Burbank facility, Johnson and Ralston's team began to evaluate the over-all problem of producibility. The rapid prototype development system inherent in *Skunk Works* type operations does not always

*Because of their diminutive size, the XF-104s had limited internal volume and thus a low fuel fraction. The resulting range and endurance shortcomings were corrected to some extent through the use of wing tip-mounted jettisonable fuel tanks.*

allow sufficient time for incorporation of desirable production features. A program therefore was proposed to—and accepted by—the Air Force whereby for the sum of $400 thousand, a producibility study for the production airplane would be made concurrently with prototype development. A special group of about twenty employees—made up of production, structural, and cost analysis engineers—was set up in an area separate from the experimental group. This team was given duplicates of the prototype drawings as soon as they were released to the experimental shop. It was tasked with investigating the cheapest, lightest, and most maintainable form in which to produce each part of the production airplane. Constraining it was a requirement there would be no increases in weight or drag and likewise no adverse maintenance features. They were completely free to study any component manufacturing method available to industry.

Prior to making the final production drawings, all phases of the producibility report were reviewed by engineering, tooling, and cost personnel, and the best specific design was chosen for large scale production. In select cases, as many as twenty alternative designs were evaluated. Methods of building the wing, for instance, included the use of castings, forgings, honeycomb structure, heavy plate structure with column supports, and many other variations. When the meeting was concluded, there was complete agreement a good compromise had been reached between performance, weight, and producibility requirements.

Reaching a definitive CL-246 configuration was not a simple, one-step process. Problems with pitch-up, when first encountered by Lockheed in wind tunnel tests, led to some ninety-eight configuration modifications before the XF-104's first flight. It was possible in many cases to eliminate pitch-up, but always at a cost in other characteristics that were totally unacceptable. The use of a low tail, for instance, in almost every case eliminated pitch-up, but when it did, normal longitudinal stability, directional stability, drag, weight, and/or overall combat utility were severely compromised. Attempts were made, unsuccessfully, to use boundary layer control on the wing, fuselage, and canopy, but these proved ineffective, as well. Eventually, an artificial warning system was chosen over potential aerodynamic solutions and the first prototype for this system was bench tested during October of 1953.

A minor, but nevertheless potential problem with the CL-246 was roll coupling. The aircraft, though innately stable, was found to encounter roll coupling in low or negative g conditions. Inertia coupling could be encountered at roll rates of 180° per second at Mach numbers between 1.4 and 1.6. During the XF-104's flight test program, some 350 rolls—carried through three total revolutions in most cases—at altitudes ranging from 10,000 feet to 40,000 feet were made. Over-all it was concluded pilots had no need to be concerned with roll coupling, but under certain extreme conditions they should be aware of its possible occurrence.

The two XF-104s were powered by a single 10,500 pound thrust non-afterburning Wright J65-B-6 engine (license-built British Armstrong Siddeley *Sapphire*—the specific engines used in the XF-104s were manufactured by Buick). Because of its relatively low thrust rating, a sophisticated air intake design was not required. When the definitive General Electric J79 was chosen for the production air-

craft, however, speeds were obtainable that dictated a more complex intake design. Considerable wind tunnel testing was conducted in Lockheed's and various NACA wind tunnels in the course of developing the intake which consisted of a fixed cone in front of the duct and a variable by-pass arrangement to allow a certain percentage of the air entering the duct to flow between the engine and the fuselage skin and finally out an augmentor arrangement around the afterburner. Not only was excellent ram obtained using this arrangement, but an aerodynamic nozzle was formed allowing proper expansion to take place behind the afterburner and a good thrust coefficient to be generated.

Emergency egress also was a serious problem during the course of CL-246 design development. Every effort was made to develop the least complicated and safest ejection seat arrangement known at the time. Downward ejection was chose for a number of reasons. There was a much more reliable tie-in between the seat and lower escape hatch than can generally be obtained with ejectable canopies. Downward ejection also insured missing the horizontal and vertical tail, each having a leading edge with a .01 inch radius. Additionally, downward ejection allowed for a better instrument panel position and also permitted lower escape g's.

The decision to choose the downward ejection system was due in part to the experience base generated by other high-speed fighters then entering Air Force service. A *Skunk Works* group under the direction of Irv Culver investigated the possibility of reducing the air loads on the pilot and preventing tumbling of the seat so that the speed envelope for safe

escape could be improved. By making use of a skip flow generator, small retractable vanes alongside the seat to provide roll damping, and vertical vanes for yaw stability, a substantial improvement in ejection seat capability was obtained and verified during sled tests at Hurricane Mesa, California. Wind tunnel tests showed the application of the skip-flow generator to be very important in reducing the drag of the occupied seat and the airload on the pilot.

Studies involving the development and use of encapsulated ejection systems also were conducted. Johnson, however, felt the sacrifices required to develop a capsule were unwarranted and also concluded capsules did not provide a higher degree of safety. Control system disconnect problems, as well as capsule stabilization problems presented many difficulties as well as performance, simplicity, and maintainability sacrifices. Downward ejection therefore became the method of choice, but not without concerns for emergency egress situations during takeoff and landing.

Electronics were of considerable importance during CL-246 design and development as their size and weight directly impacted the size and weight of the completed aircraft. In the case of the gunsight, it was recognized at an early date that radar was required to extend the pilots vision in search, as it would be absolutely impossible, at the high speed the aircraft was expected to achieve during intercept, to depend on normal vision alone. A proposal was made to the Air Force whereby the development of a lightweight radar and gunsight would be undertaken, and this was approved. The RCA MA-10 (military designation was AN/ASG-14) fire control system evolved, weighing less than half the weight of

*XF-104's minimal wing was equipped with leading edge flaps, trailing edge flaps, and conventional ailerons. Leading edge was sharpened to a radius of .01 inch.*

*Both XF-104s in formation near Edwards AFB. These aircraft differed markedly from their General Electric J79-powered successors not only in terms of performance, but dimensionally, physically, and structurally, as well.*

other fighter radar and gunsight units. Complementing the radar was an infrared system sensitized to engine heat emissions.

The first of two XF-104 prototypes when completed at Burbank during late January of 1954, was loaded aboard a flat-bed trailer and trucked to Edwards AFB North Base. There, on February 28, with Lockheed's Tony LeVier in the cockpit, this aircraft successfully completed a short hop which was more of a high-speed lift-off than a legitimate first flight. Four days later, on March 4, the aircraft became fully airborne for the first time, again with LeVier at the controls. A landing gear malfunction kept the initial flight short, but the aircraft was recovered without difficulty.

XF-104 flight testing progressed rapidly between January and the arrival of the second aircraft nearly a year later. Though the J65's thrust limits—rather than structure or aerodynamics—dictated maximum speed capabilities, performance nonetheless proved exceptional. Arrival of the second aircraft—which was the first to be equipped with the General Electric M61 rotary cannon— also heralded the installation of the considerably more powerful afterburning Wright J65-W-7 (which also was

retroactively installed in the first XF-104). On March 25, 1955, with Lockheed test pilot Ray Goudey at the controls, this aircraft achieved a speed of 1,324 mph (Mach 1.79)...which was the highest attained by either of the two prototypes.

Unfortunately, the second XF-104 was lost not long after its record setting flight. On April 18, with Lockheed's Herman "Fish" Salmon at the controls, an explosive decompression event, caused by loss of the ventral ejection seat hatch fairing, was mistaken for a gun failure. As Tony LeVier, on an earlier flight in the same aircraft had run into gun difficulties, Salmon's hurried assessment of the problem was not without justification. His downward ejection was successful, but the second XF-104 was a complete write-off.

Flight testing with the first prototype continued without let-up and during November of 1955, the Air Force officially accepted the aircraft. The XF-104 flight test program eventually spanned three years before the surviving aircraft was grounded.

The prototype *Starfighter* program, though marred by the loss of the second aircraft, was successful enough to generate a initial follow-

on production order for seventeen service test YF-104As and six production-standard F-104As. In turn, 147 F-104As were manufactured by Lockheed for Air Force service (both Aerospace Defense Command and Tactical Air Command) with another 26 two-seat F-104Bs supplied as well. Seventy-seven single-seat F-104Cs and twenty-one F-104Ds also found their way into Air Force service.

The F-104 program eventually evolved into four separate phases as follows:

(1) Lockheed's California facilities manufactured single and two-place aircraft for the Air Force including those for the Military Assistance Program and for the German Air Force (1956-1966).

(2) Lockheed's California facilities manufactured "knockdown" assemblies for licensee use (1961-1967).

(3) Worldwide manufacture of single-place aircraft by licensees Germany, Belgium, the Netherlands, Italy, Canada, and Japan.

(4) Coproduction manufacture of two-place aircraft by Lockheed's California facilities and licensees Germany, Belgium, the Netherlands, and Italy (1964-1968).

Foreign *Starfighter* sales proved difficult to

*The prototypes, like the initial production F-104As, were equipped with downward-firing ejection seats. Early studies by Lockheed had indicated the Starfighter's estimated maximum speed performance would make upward firing seats impractical and potentially dangerous.*

*Both XF-104s had provisions for General Electric's then-new M61-A-1 rotary-barrel cannon. With a firing rate of 6,000 rounds per minute, the Vulcan, as it was tradenamed by GE, was the ideal complement to the F-104's extraordinary speed.*

obtain at first, but eventually proved the most lucrative market. NATO countries, following an intense competition between Lockheed and several other manufacturers, eventually picked the attractive F-104 as the fighter to meet its defense needs during the 1960s and 1970s.

A grand total of no less than 2,579 *Starfighters* were built, with 434 single-seat and 741 two-seat aircraft being built by Lockheed; 1,243 single-seat and 48 two-seat aircraft being built by NATO's European consortium; 340 single-seat being built by Canada; and 207 single-seat aircraft being built by Japan.

"Kelly" Johnson, in summarizing the F-104 in a paper released on June 18, 1957, presciently noted, "It is very difficult to see where added high speed is worthwhile, and it appears that the development of armament, radar, and fire control systems is the most fruitful field for our research efforts over the next five years".

*The XF-104s' fixed-ramp intakes were the product of the powerplant choice and the realization the prototypes would not be capable of achieving speeds requiring more sophisticated intake technology.*

*The two XF-104's proved the progenitors of a long line of Starfighters totaling in excess of 2,500 aircraft. At the time, this represented Lockheed's most successful post-World War Two aircraft production program.*

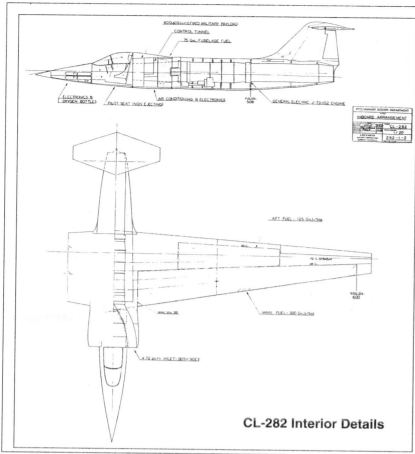

**CL-282 Interior Details**

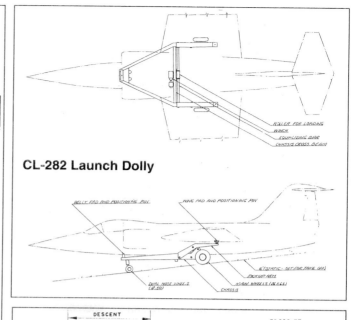

**CL-282 Launch Dolly**

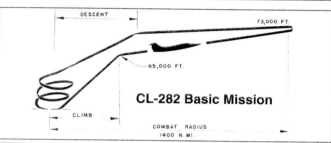

**CL-282 Basic Mission**

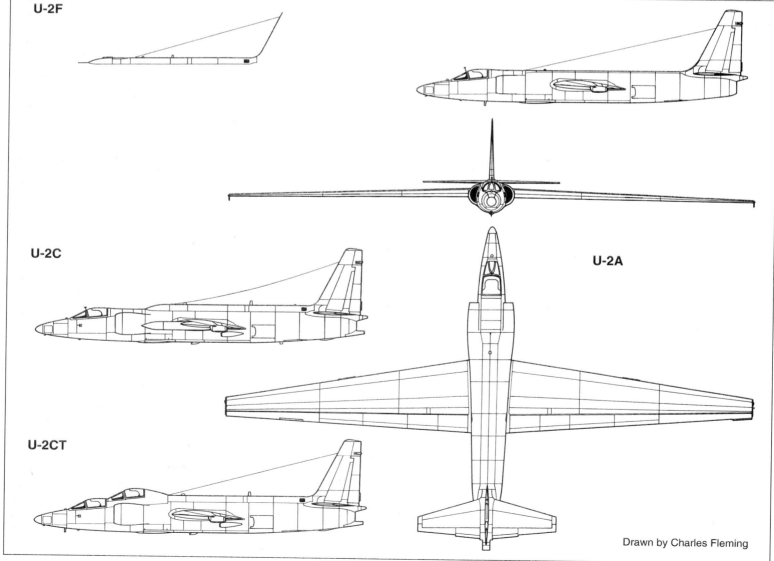

**U-2F**

**U-2C**

**U-2A**

**U-2CT**

Drawn by Charles Fleming

# Chapter 6:
# *AQUATONE* AND THE U-2...
## The Skunk Works Reborn

*"The U-2s. We underran our contract on that, and gave back the government over 20 percent of the first contract. It was a success. It was the first time when the Skunk Works went into production. Because of security and other reasons, we, for the first time, made more than two of anything, and we made the complete line of the U-2s and the other versions that have come from it."*

**Clarence L. "Kelly" Johnson**

High-altitude strategic reconnaissance philosophy was first articulated during late 1952 when an Air Force Major by the name of John Seaberg—then Assistant Chief of New Developments Office, Bombardment Branch, at Wright Field near Dayton, Ohio—placed on paper ideas he had for achieving sustained flight at ultra-high altitudes. Seaberg—who because of the Korean War had been called back to active duty following a stint as an aeronautical engineer at Chance Vought's Grand Prairie, Texas facility—had noted the new generation of turbojet engines—with their inherent high-altitude performance potential—could be mated to an aircraft with an extremely efficient high-aspect-ratio wing and achieve cruising altitudes far in excess of any aircraft then in service.

The ramifications were multiple and far-reaching. It was obvious that an aircraft operating at the altitudes Seaberg predicted possible would make detection extremely difficult and interception virtually impossible. Reconnaissance and weapons delivery were two ideal mission candidates for an aircraft with such unique performance potential.

Soon after organizing his ideas and presenting them to his superior, William Lamar (then Chief of the New Developments Office), Seaberg began to formalize a proposal calling for a high-altitude reconnaissance aircraft. By March of 1953 a formal specification had been created. Following review, it was approved for release to select aircraft companies.

"I immediately moved out on the preparation of the planning and program documentation we needed to get higher level support for starting a development effort which had been generated at the grass roots level", Seaberg later would recall. "There was no Air Force requirement at the time. The first document I produced was a standard format paper stating the objectives, the approach, the payoff or potential value to the Air Force, and schedule/cost estimates. We requested $200,000 to contract for design studies. We talked to no one in industry until months later when we got positive reactions from the Air Research and Development Command (ARDC). "

All three of the queried companies—Bell Aircraft Corporation of Niagara Falls, New York; Fairchild Aircraft Corporation of Hagerstown, Maryland; and Martin Aircraft Company of Baltimore, Maryland—responded by sending representatives to Wright Field. On July 1, 1953, study contracts—to run through December 31—were let to each. The new project, by now officially identified as MX-2147, also was given the classified codename of *Bald Eagle*.

Seaberg would recall, "Bill Lamar and I talked it over and decided that we should not consider any of the larger prime contractors like Boeing, Convair, North American, Douglas,

*The only known surviving photograph depicting one of the original U-2 full-scale mock-ups. This was the cockpit, windscreen, and canopy mock-up. Noteworthy is the fixed crew seat...which was not ejectable.*

and Lockheed. But rather go to two of the smaller contractors because we did not envision large production and we felt we would get higher company priority out of Bell/Fairchild, who also had some very innovative engineers and had done things like it before. So we called each of the three contractors in and asked if they would be interested, which they were. We talked to no other contractors. "

Only the Bell and Fairchild teams had been asked to submit proposals calling for the design and construction of a totally new aircraft. Martin had been asked to take their B-57 (which had been developed in Great Britain by the English Electric Company as the *Canberra* for Royal Air Force service) twin-engine attack bomber and examine the possibility of improving its already exceptional high-altitude performance (several stock B-57s already were in Air Force use as specialized reconnaissance air-

craft flying *Sneaky Pete* missions in the Far East) through a major redesign effort. The B-57 was a pressurized, readily adaptable high-altitude aircraft, and it conveniently resembled some of the early configurations drawn by Seaberg while working on the original project requirements. Seaberg considered the B-57 option an interim, near-term solution to the mission requirement, but not a definitive configuration.

By January of 1954, the three companies had completed their studies and submitted them to Wright Field for evaluation. Martin, as requested, proposed a big-wing version of the B-57 under the in-house Model 294 designator; Fairchild offered their single-engine M-195 calling for an over-the-fuselage intake and a stub-boom-mounting for vertical and horizontal tail surfaces; and Bell, under project chief Richard Smith, proffered their Model 67, a twin-engine,

*Approximately mid-way through the U-2A production program, construction of airframes was shifted from Burbank to a newly acquired, low-profile facility in Oildale, near Bakersfield, California.*

71

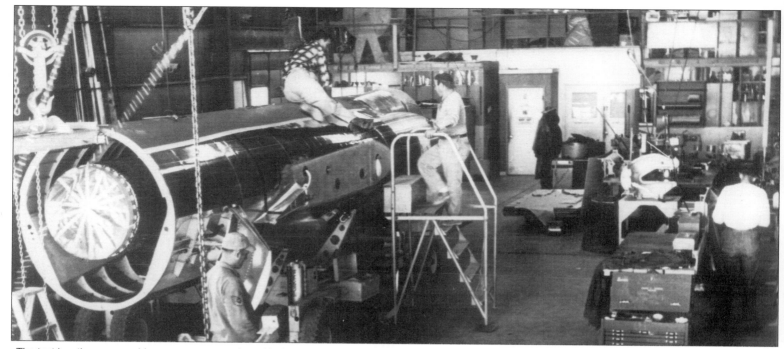

The test location reassembly process was conducted inside one of several hangars specially built for the U-2 program. The U-2 was a simple, yet highly sophisticated aircraft requiring little unorthodox capability or equipment for maintenance and support.

Virtually all U-2s, including the prototype, were delivered from Burbank to the test location by Air Force Douglas C-124 Globemasters.

The first U-2, Manufacturing No. 341, at the test location prior to its first flight. The "001" tail number is the only external identification visible.

rather fragile-looking aircraft that was the essence of lightweight airframe design.

Although the powerplant type to be used in the new high-altitude aircraft was undecided at the beginning of the studies, in-house research conducted by Pratt & Whitney under the auspices of the Air Force convinced the Wright Field engineering team that the new Pratt & Whitney J57 axial flow turbojet engine had the best potential for achieving the high-altitude performance required. Proposed modifications to the stock J57 were expected to permit a sustained operating thrust representing some 7% of the available sea level total at the desired cruising altitude. Though far from being an impressive figure, even by the standards of 1954, it was sufficient in the rarefied atmosphere above the tropopause to keep any one of the three proposed aircraft in sustained horizontal flight. Though other powerplants (i.e., the General Electric J73 and Wright J67) would be considered during the course of the program study period, the J57 was never seriously contested and all three submissions stipulated its use (with high-altitude modifications, the original designation for the specific J57 model involved was the J57-P-19; later this designation would become J57-P-37).

By March of 1954, evaluation of the three contenders had been completed by Seaberg and other engineers at Wright Field. Preparation of a detailed report with a recommendation calling for hardware procurement then was begun for submission to higher headquarters. The Martin and Bell proposals had been chosen as the most suitable for the mission, with the former serving as an interim aircraft and the latter as the long-term operational type. Fairchild's proposal was never in serious contention.

Seaberg later would recall the decision making process as follows: "I had the data evaluated by the Wright Field labs during January/March 1954. I prepared an analysis, picked Martin and Bell as preferred, wrote an abbreviated development plan, and prepared a concise briefing for the higher headquarters."

During mid-March, Lt. Col. Joseph Pelligrini, attached to a reconnaissance unit at Air Research and Development Command headquarters, visited Wright Field and met with Seaberg and several of his aides. Pelligrini was impressed with the on-going high-altitude reconnaissance aircraft program, but felt the delays involved with the design and development of a totally new aircraft could more easily be rationalized if acquisition and service integration of an interim aircraft could be expedited. The proposed B-57 modification, by now tentatively referred to as the B-57D, appealed to Pelligrini. He recommended Seaberg send a list of necessary B-57 modifications to ARDC headquarters in no more than seven days following their meeting. Pelligrini was confident the proposed B-57 modification could provide a fast way to meet the urgent Air Force intelligence requirement in Europe.

The first U-2 differed in many minor details from its successors. The wing tip skids were of a more abbreviated configuration, there was no drag chute housing, and the canopy sunshield was different.

The following month, Seaberg met with ARDC representatives at ARDC Headquarters in Baltimore, Maryland and gave a briefing on the three aircraft studies to Air Force commanders. Among those attending was Lt. Gen. Thomas Power who had just succeeded Lt. Gen. Donald Putt as ARDC commander. Power was impressed by the content of Seaberg's presentation and requested that he give the same briefing the following day at Strategic Air Command headquarters in Omaha, Nebraska.

This presentation, too, generated serious interest and it now was apparent Seaberg was gaining strong support and that the project had a good chance of proceeding to the hardware stage if political and technological pitfalls could be tactfully avoided. During May of 1954, Seaberg again was asked to make a presentation, this time to Air Force headquarters in Washington, D.C. Afterwards, Seaberg received immediate approval to forge ahead with the B-57D and tentative approval to consummate the Bell Model 67. The latter, because it was a totally new aircraft in need of significantly more time for development, was delayed temporarily while further studies were conducted to determine viability and performance advantages.

On May 18, 1954, some two weeks after returning from Washington, D.C., a new proposal for a high-altitude cruise aircraft, from Lockheed's preliminary design organization arrived on Seaberg's desk for review.

Johnson's own insights into the beginnings of the aircraft are only thinly recounted in his U-2 log: "December 1953, We started an investigation of wing area modifications and stripping procedures to modify the F-104 airplane to get the maximum possible altitude for reconnaissance purposes.

"February 1954, I was told of Air Force interest that would be developed with an airplane having the characteristics we were finally able to obtain on the F-104A study.

"March 5, 1954, I had about four men work up Lockheed Report #9732, describing the CL-282 high-altitude aircraft. This was a complete report, still tying the high-altitude airplane to the F-104. This report was sent to Gen. Bernard Schreiver early in March 1954. He was extremely interested and asked Lockheed to prepare a specific proposal."

In the report, Phil LeVeille of Phil Colman's preliminary design group wrote, "This report presents information on the design of an aircraft capable of flight at an average altitude of 73,000 feet with a combat radius of 1,400 nautical miles. The objective of the design is to accomplish this performance with a relatively small airplane and with a non-jettisonable military payload of 600 pounds. The airplane has a normal takeoff gross weight of 13,768 pounds including 4,966 pounds of fuel which is sufficient for the basic mission. With an overload gross weight of 14,815 pounds, the radius is increased to 1,720 nautical miles. It is a conventional turbojet design except for the relatively high aspect ratio of 10.0 and wing area of 500 square feet. The airplane has no landing gear; takeoff being accomplished by the use of a ground cart. Due to the design shape of the bottom of the fuselage a belly landing can be accomplished without damage to the airplane. The wing design is entirely new. Otherwise the airplane configuration is identical to the Lockheed XF-104 Day Fighter except for the removal of a straight 62 inch section of forward fuselage. This makes very minor local changes

*Purportedly taken by "Kelly" Johnson (who was flying chase in a Douglas C-47), this photograph is one of the few to depict the U-2's first flight on August 4, 1955.*

in the loft lines. The detail parts are lighter and somewhat different than in the XF-104 in order to incorporate the maximum possible structural simplification and efficiency. This simplification is made possible by the elimination of all requirements pertinent to the XF-104 not necessary for this design, such as fighter load factor, armament, landing gear, etc. However, the nature of the detail design is such as to utilize the maximum of XF-104 design and manufacturing experience. All basic tool jigs and most detail jigs for the XF-104 are used for the CL-282."

Johnson, not long after the report's release, wrote, "Early in April, 1954, I presented Lockheed letter LAC/156876 and a full description of the CL-282. This proposal covered our construction of 30 airplanes, Lockheed taking complete responsibility for the whole program, including servicing of the airplanes in the field."

Seaberg had heard of Johnson's Report No. 9732 for several weeks prior to its arrival. "It descended to my level when I got it in the mail on May 18, 1954, requesting my evaluation. You can see from this timing, that in the preceding month I had briefed three levels of General officers and received their approval to proceed with my recommended program."

Johnson had acquired the confidence of many high ranking military personnel. He was accustomed to dealing with them at all levels of the bureaucracy. It was almost inevitable, as far as Seaberg was concerned, that someone

in the Pentagon would take the liberty of telling Johnson about the classified high-altitude reconnaissance aircraft proposal.

Seaberg and his fellow Wright Field engineers spent three weeks evaluating the Johnson proposal. Given the Temporary Design Number CL-282, it consisted of a slightly-modified XF-104 fuselage and associated vertical and horizontal tail surfaces. Most noticeable, however, was the deletion of the XF-104's distinctive, trapezoidal-shaped wings and their replacement by a high-aspect ratio wing of extraordinary span. Designed into the latter were four integral fuel tanks complemented by a fifth tank in the fuselage. Together these provided a total fuel capacity of 925 gallons.

The powerplant proposed for the Lockheed aircraft was the General Electric J73-GE-3 non-afterburning turbojet with a sea level thrust rating of 9,300 pounds. In a serious break from the norm—a distinctive characteristic of almost all Johnson-initiated aircraft designs—the CL-282 did away with conventional landing gear (he had, in fact, pioneered this approach during the 1930s with the specially built—for Wiley Post—Lockheed *Vega*, the *Winnie Mae*). Early in the CL-282 design effort, Johnson had concluded that the proposed aircraft, in order to achieve its altitude objectives, would have to be extremely light...and the landing gear design would have to be innovative. He settled on the idea of replacing the conventional wheeled landing

*An unidentified Lockheed test pilot boards a U-2 prior to takeoff. The flight appears to be a high-altitude mission in consideration of the partial pressure suit being warn by the pilot.*

CIA U-2As at the test location. This photo was taken during early 1956 as preparations for deployment to the first operating location in England were underway. Noteworthy are the NACA logos visible on every U-2's vertical tail...verifying that the NACA (and later, NASA) front was in full force, even at this early date.

By mid-1956 U-2As had been delivered in sufficient quantities to merit operational deployment. Aircraft were flown in bare-metal finish with only NACA logo and fictitious i.d. numbers on their vertical fins.

The Type A camera system consisted of three Fairchild HR-732 24-inch cameras on a single support unit. Cameras, carried in the U-2A's "Q-bay", could be operated simultaneously, singly, or in combination.

gear by allowing the aircraft to land on its reinforced lower fuselage (essentially a skid). Though not new, this was nevertheless novel...and highly functional. A jettisonable, reusable, wheeled dolly would be used for takeoff.

Other CL-282 features included an unpressurized single-seat cockpit and a 600 pound sensor system payload. The latter was to be carried in a 15 cubic foot bay behind the cockpit. Wingspan was 70 feet 8 inches; length was 44 feet.

After a thorough but rushed review, Seaberg and his staff rejected the CL-282. The choice of powerplant, the unpressurized cockpit, and serious range deficiencies were all major stumbling blocks. The J73 was an unknown (and eventually unsuccessful) turbojet and its capabilities at extremely high altitudes were considered seriously deficient. Because of the tremendous thrust losses suffered by turbojet engines at the cruising altitude being proposed for the new reconnaissance aircraft, it was determined the J73's loss would be too great to provide the required performance. They strongly supported use of the Pratt & Whitney J57 in any contending aircraft design and because of this, they felt the CL-282 should be disqualified. Additionally, the CL-282 could not easily be modified to accommodate the preferred engine. Seaberg later would summarize the reviewing team's position by noting, "The evaluation letter I wrote (during late June of 1954) did recommend not buying the Johnson design. As far as I know, this position was accepted all the way up the line to the Gen. Putt level."

Johnson, after receiving word of the negative report would note, "May 1954, Air Force was proceeding with the Martin *Canberra*, and they are not too impressed with our CL-282 proposal." And still later, he would write, "June 7, 1954, received a letter which turned down our proposal on the basis that it was too unusual, that it was a single-engine aircraft, and that they were already committed to the Martin program."

### CIA:

When the Air Force informed Johnson of its decision to eliminate the CL-282 from contention, Johnson decided to pursue funding through other channels. Concurrently, a redesign of the CL-282 to accommodate the J57 was undertaken. Johnson's addressed not only other opportunities in the Pentagon, but later, as it turned out, other government offices as well. Trevor Gardner, the Air Force's Assistant Secretary for Research and Development, had agreed to meet with Johnson not long after the Air Force had turned down the CL-282. Gardner, who interfaced with the CIA, later would present Johnson's proposal to a CIA study committee.

Johnson's timing could not have been better. Numerous sources had begun to input data into the US intelligence community indicating the Soviet Union was moving ahead quickly with an extensive family of liquid-fuel, nuclear warhead-equipped intercontinental ballistic missiles. By the time Johnson began his attempt to sell the improved CL-282 to the CIA, the Soviet ICBMs had become an issue of extraordinary national concern. The CIA, fully briefed on the Air Force's high-altitude reconnaissance aircraft program, had become enamored with the idea of using the platform for more pressing national security needs of this type.

During mid-1954, as a fall-out over the ICBM fear, the Department of Defense, with President Eisenhower approving, formed a number of advisory groups to examine various aspects of military planning and weapons in the US and around the world. James R. Killian, then president of the prestigious Massachusetts Institute of Technology, became chairman of one of these committees, which was tasked with the responsibility of determining the possibility of a surprise attack by the Soviets. On November 18, 1954, the Killian Committee was briefed by John Seaberg on the three contending configurations proposed by Bell, Fairchild, and Martin. Lockheed's aircraft also was discussed, but only as a "walk-on" entry.

The Seaberg briefing took place in the office of Lt. Gen. Putt, Air Force deputy chief of staff for development. Seaberg recalls he was not introduced to the fifteen or so distinguished scientists making up the majority of the Killian Committee, but he recalls there were a number of prominent faces in the crowd. "Nobody announced who they were (tight security measures were really starting to close down). But from the technical questions I got I could tell there were aerodynamicists, propulsion, optics or camera, and other experts in the group. Dr. Edwin Land may have been there, but I really met him as an individual much later (1957 or 1958). This group was aware of Johnson's proposal by the time of this meeting. What I did was present the results of my comparative analysis of all four designs. I showed the relative high altitude performance capabilities of all four. I pointed out that aerodynamically the Bell, Fairchild, and Lockheed designs were close. Martin's B-57, being a modification, was not quite as capable. I stated that, in my opinion, the J73 would not be good enough to do the job in Johnson's airplane. And further, I overlaid a curve showing that with the J57 installed, it would then be competitive with the Bell and Fairchild designs."

The Killian Committee was indeed well aware of Johnson's CL-282. As it turned out, Gardner—one of those who had been tasked with assembling the list of names used to assemble the Committee in the first place—had taken the proposal to Committee members and given them his own summary of its capabilities. Still other panel members who were acquaintances of Johnson's through other channels

*Civil-registered N803X, this CIA U-2C was equipped with the intermediate size intakes predating the final large intake configuration. Noteworthy is infrared signature-reducing "sugar scoop" under exhaust.*

had been briefed by him directly.

Because of Johnson's ability to move freely within the confines of the DoD and intelligence communities, his long-standing friendship with the CIA's Philip Strong proved an important foot in the door during the critical decision making period that led to the program hardware contract. While work on the Bell Model 37 and Martin RB-57D moved ahead rapidly under the direction of the Air Force, Strong and another CIA associate, Richard Amory saw, with a little prompting, that Lockheed's CL-282 had merit and might indeed prove to be an exceptional sensor system platform if matched with the proper engine.

Strong and Amory, tasked with the gathering of intelligence related to the Soviet missile test facility at *Kapustin Yar*, had spent considerable time trying to coerce the Air Force into flying over the site on a one-shot reconnaissance mission. Unsuccessful, they concluded the CIA must establish a reconnaissance capability of its own, independent of the military. A trip to California by Strong to meet with Johnson during late 1953 gave birth to the CL-282 study initiated that December.

On November 19, 1954, Johnson would make the following log entry, "I met with the Government Advisory Board. They wanted to

be reassured that our proposal was technically feasible. They believed my story that we could make such an airplane in the time mentioned and also asked why Lockheed seemed to be the only one who could do this job. Gen. Putt answered graciously that we had proven it three times.

"I was impressed with the secrecy aspect and was told that I was essentially being drafted for the project. It seemed, in fact, that if I did not talk quietly, I might have to take a leave of absence from my job to do this special project.

"I returned to Burbank in the evening, with instructions to talk only to Robert Gross. He agreed that we must do the project."

Two days later, Johnson met with Gross and Hibbard at Gross's home. "I proposed that Engineering Experimental do the job, in spite of the large number of airplanes involved. This was accepted."

As it turned out, this was a momentous decision. In one master stroke, Johnson, with Gross's blessing, had transformed the virtually non-existent *Skunk Works* into not only a full-scale advanced design and engineering team, but a production facility, as well. Secrecy had mandated the change. Whereas the XP-80 had been a prototype effort only, the mandates

*CIA U-2As at Atsugi, Japan, during 1957. Closest aircraft represents what almost certainly is the world's first legitimate exercise in low-observables technology; it is covered with radar absorbent materials.*

*One of the more unusual camouflage schemes seen on the U-2 was this simple "polka-dot" pattern applied to CIA U-2C, N805X. Many different camouflage patterns were applied to the early model U-2s in response to the various operating locations to which they were assigned.*

*"Polka-dot" pattern apparently was used to test reconnaissance satellite sensors; but regardless, it had little if anything to do with protecting the aircraft in its high-altitude operating environment.*

of the confidentiality requirement for the new reconnaissance aircraft had dictated the need for an umbrella of secrecy to ensure the security of the production program and operational service.

Less obvious was the precedent unknowingly being set by Lockheed's on-going intimate relationship with the aircraft even after it was to enter operational service. At the time of contract consummation, it was not yet fully recognized that Lockheed's participation would be for the life of the aircraft...and that conventional methods of field support would not be sufficient. The CIA, because of its status as a civilian agency, its lack of experience in the support and operation of a major aircraft program, and its basic belief in Lockheed, had subordinated the reconnaissance aircraft's sustenance to the *Skunk Works*. It proved a wise and progressive decision...and one that would set precedent for many aircraft programs to come.

After the meeting with Gross and Hibbard, Johnson spent the next two days redesigning the CL-282 to accommodate a less unconventional landing gear, the J57, and a larger camera bay. Means for improving performance also were explored.

Dr. Edwin Land, a renowned authority on optics, an engineer, inventor of the Polaroid instant photo camera and process, and an influential non-government personality, during August of 1954 was shown a drawing of the CL-282, apparently by Trevor Gardner. At the time, he requested an opportunity to meet and talk with Johnson. As head of the Project 3 Intelligence Group of President Eisenhower's technical capabilities panel, he had considerable sway over activities within the intelligence community. The Land Group was the smallest of the three groups making up the President's panel, consisting of five members and himself.

From November 29 through December 3, Johnson undertook organization of the *Skunk Works* team that would design and build the new aircraft. Dick Boehme was recruited as project engineer to put the engineering unit together that eventually included Ed Baldwin, Phil Colman, and Gene Frost (interestingly, Colman and Frost never would become part of the actual *Skunk Works* team but instead would remain in Lockheed advanced design). Art Viereck, then Engineering Experimental

*CIA U-2F, N807X, departs Lockheed's facilities at Van Nuys airport in California on a test flight. Aircraft is carrying two 100-gallon external tanks. Fairings for inflight refueling receptacle are visible on dorsal spine.*

Division Manager, came onboard to guide the construction effort...as he had on so many projects before.. Some fifty select engineers, initially operating out of a small conference room located in Lockheed's engineering building and later operating out of a small, confined design room in Plant B-6 (adjacent to the experimental manufacturing area) building in the main Lockheed facility at Burbank, were now involved in the secret project.

"These men were put on a 45-hour week," Johnson would write in his log, "and I am spending half my time on this project. Talked to each man on the project to impress them with the necessity for speed and secrecy. It is extremely difficult to pull these engineers from other projects at this time, particularly in that I cannot tell anyone why."

During December of 1954, the Land Group met in a committee member's 1953 Ford automobile to discuss which of the various high-altitude aircraft proposals (Bell, Martin, Fairchild, or Lockheed) would be suitable for a reconnaissance mission over denied territory. More than an hour was spent in discussion while driving around Washington. One of the committee members, Allen Donovan, argued in favor of the Johnson aircraft. By the end of the meeting, a decision had been reached...the Lockheed design would be recommended to the President to fill the needs of the US intelligence community.

The Killian Committee, influenced strongly by the resulting recommendation, had become convinced the Lockheed CL-282, with the afore-mentioned powerplant change, would be ideal for the proposed intelligence-gathering mission. The Committee's opinion was soon delivered to Secretary of Defense Charles Wilson and Central Intelligence Agency Director Allen Dulles. During late November, convinced of the program merits, Wilson and Dulles decided to brief President Eisenhower. Eisenhower would recall later, "Back in November 1954, Foster Dulles, Charlie Wilson, Al Dulles, and other advisors had come to me to get authorization to go ahead on a program to produce twenty special high-performance aircraft at a total cost of about $35 million. A good deal of design and development work had already been done. I approved this action."

At this time, the CIA's director, Allen Dulles brought Richard Bissell, an economist who had taught at both Yale and MIT, in to direct the CIA side of the new program. Bissell recalled, "Towards the end of November (1954), I was summoned one afternoon into Allen's office and I was told, with absolutely no prior warning or knowledge, that one day previously President Eisenhower had approved a project involving the development of an extremely high-altitude aircraft to be used for surveillance and intelligence collection over 'denied' areas in Europe, Russia, and elsewhere. And Allen, after perhaps 15 minutes of explanation of the background of this undertaking told me that in half an hour I was to go over to the Pentagon and present myself in Trevor Gardner's office. When I arrived, Trevor Gardner, Gen. Putt, Gen. Irvine, and several others were already there. We were to decide between us, how the project was to be organized and run. My most vivid recollection of this meeting is of the telephone call put through at the end by Trevor Gardner to "Kelly" (Johnson) in which he gave him a go-ahead on a program to develop and produce 20 aircraft."

Eisenhower had agreed the funding and

*Very few U-2s were modified with inflght refueling receptacles. This U-2F, N802X, utilized by the CIA, is equipped with a refueling receptacle at the front end of its abbreviated dorsal spine.*

*A U-2F takes on fuel from a Boeing KC-97L. When refueling, U-2Fs (and the single U-2H) were usually flown with flaps in the gust relief position. Speed brakes were used to precisely control airspeed.*

direction of the project, to be codenamed *Aquatone*, would be through the offices of the CIA rather than the Air Force, with Richard Bissell to direct it. Though some Air Force money was to be utilized in the acquisition of J57 powerplants, the service's main job (with

Jean Kiefer working under Bissel as chief liaison between the service and the CIA) initially would be to act as a front and contract with Lockheed for aircraft development. The special engines would be mixed with a contract for conventional J57s ordered to meet the needs

*U-2F, N800X, on final approach. Aircraft is equipped with large ventral antenna. Slipper tanks on wing leading edges offset range loss resulting from weight increases due to systems growth.*

of Boeing B-52, North American F-100, and Convair F-102 production. Because of the sensitivity of the project, the Air Force would handle its part directly from headquarters.

At a later date, the Air Force was expected to absorb U-2 (as it now officially was designated) assets, these coming both directly from Lockheed and also from the CIA inventory. Additionally, a decision was made to create a publicity cover by releasing information stating the aircraft to have been developed as a high-altitude research tool for use primarily by the National Advisory Committee for Aeronautics (NACA). Funding for the new aircraft, the contract for which was signed on December 9, 1954, was to come from the CIA's secret Contingency Reserve Fund. Eventually, some $54 million would be allocated, with $8 million being returned by Lockheed following a 15% cost underrun (then, as now, an almost unheard-of occurrence...and said to be directly attributable to Johnson's unique management skills and techniques).

Earlier on November 9, 1954, Trevor Gardner had visited with Lockheed President Robert Gross and Johnson at Lockheed's Burbank facility. Following a review of the full-scale U-2 mock-up, Gardner gave official confirmation of project approval and a directive to go ahead with prototype construction. As both parties knew that Bell's Model 67 (by now officially designated X-16 by the Air Force as a cover) was moving along with considerable rapidity, it was agreed the completion date and first flight of the new Lockheed aircraft would have to be expedited.

Johnson promised the first *Aquatone* aircraft would be in the air no less than eight months after the first metal was cut. Finished drawings already were being delivered from the *Skunk Works* engineering team and actual construction of the first aircraft was scheduled to begin in early January. "Kelly's Angel", as some already were calling the new aircraft, had begun to take wing.

While *Aquatone* gathered momentum at Lockheed, construction of its Air Force counterpart, the Bell X-16, had begun during September of 1954. During the following twelve months, work progressed smoothly,

though with little visible urgency. *Aquatone* remained unknown to the Bell team assembling the new aircraft. It also was unaware of the complicated chain of events taking place in Washington, D.C. Once the decision by Eisenhower to turn over the Air Force mission to the CIA had been consummated, the X-16's purpose was eliminated and its funding could no longer be justified.

The death of the X-16 occurred during October of 1955, some two months after Lockheed's *Aquatone* aircraft had taken to the air for the first time. Though a relatively small contract, the X-16 had been important to Bell's economic future at a time when the company had few other major projects on its ledger. Loss of the contract proved a serious economic blow to Bell and one from which the company would not soon recover.

During November of 1954, with the new reconnaissance aircraft approved for production, Johnson and his 25 engineers and 81 shop personnel began putting in 100-hour work weeks in order to meet the promised 8-month first flight deadline. From a design standpoint, the new aircraft was technologically demanding. Weight and drag were overriding design considerations. Every aspect of the airframe, structure, and external shell was governed by its relationship to the basic empty weight of the aircraft and total aerodynamic drag at cruising altitude. On December 10, the design was frozen and on December 20, Johnson noted in his log, "Working like mad on airplane. Initial tunnel tests successful." One week later, construction of tooling was begun.

At this time, a flight test crew consisting of five engineers, five pilots, and twenty mechanics, plus an all-purpose man and two part-time engineers were transferred to the small *Skunk Works* team. On January 10, 1955, fabrication of parts for the first aircraft (including a single static test article) was initiated.

Among the unique weight-related accomplishments of the design program were the following: wing weight was kept to an almost unbelievable 4 pounds per square foot; the landing gear was a bicycle arrangement with the heaviest component consisting of a single main strut (jettisonable pogos mounted mid-

span on each wing were provided for balance); the tail assembly was attached at the center fuselage by only three bolts; the side-opening canopy was manually operated; the control system was unboosted; hydraulically actuated systems were kept to a minimum; there was no cockpit pressurization; and there was no ejection seat.

The CIA had agreed to the acquisition of an initial batch of twenty aircraft. These were to be built at the Burbank plant and later in a plant at a small town called Oildale, near Bakersfield, California and then transported to a newly constructed flight test location.

On March 15, 1955, wind tunnel testing was completed and the design was determined to be aerodynamically suitable for its flight envenlope. On May 21, 1955 Johnson noted, "Number one fuselage out of jig. Having a tough time on wing. Put almost everybody on it."

On June 29, he followed with the comment, "Terrific drive to finish airplane." On July 8, static testing of the deciated airframe was begun. These would be completed on September 21.

On July 15, Johnson would wearily note, "Airplane essentially completed. Terrifically long hours. Everybody almost dead." Five days later he would write, "Airplane turned over to inspection for final check." And the next day, "Airplane disassembled and loaded in loading carts."

On July 24, 1955, Johnson was able to report transport of the prototype aircraft to the flight test location. "We came down to the plant at 4:00 a.m. and loading operations were started at daybreak. Took about three hours to load into the C-124." Concerns over the C-124's ability to land on a wet surface led to a hurried assessment, "We landed on the runway and after quick inspection, decided that it would be safe to land the 124 if we let lots of air out of the tires. It was up to me to determine whether the 124 should come in. Two hours later it landed in a cloud of dust, using reversing propellers, making a beautiful landing. We unloaded the bird on schedule into the semi-completed hangars and assembled it." *Skunk Works* personnel flown in from Burbank initiated the reassembly process almost immediately.

Due to the security surrounding the project, an official designation had yet to be allocated. In-house at the *Skunk Works* and generally at the CIA it was known simply as the *Angel*. The CIA also referred to it more formally as the "Article" and the first aircraft was officially referred to as "Article 341". Additionally, as part of the program cover-up, pilots were referred to as "drivers" and the test location was referred to as "home plate".

Two days were required to get the all-aluminum aircraft back together and prepared for initial static engine runs and taxi tests. Pulled backwards from its metal hangar by a truck and

*Air Force U-2A, 56-6692 of the 6512th Test Group at Edwards AFB. This aircraft was equipped with the original Pratt & Whitney J57.*

*All U-2Cs were equipped with the Pratt & Whitney J75. Some later were equipped with "sugar scoop" exhaust, and other subtle changes.*

trailer unit, it was positioned just outside the hangar for the first engine tests. Being a prototype, Article 341 differed in detail from its successors to follow. Among the differences were: a canvas sunshield mounted on support cords (later aircraft would have the sunshield painted on the inside of the canopy); skid fairings that extended to the wing tip trailing edge; no drag chute housing above the engine exhaust port; no glass dome ahead of the windscreen or underneath the nose (for driftsight); no tracking camera dome or fairing; no fairing on the main landing gear door; and no bolt access panel forward of the empennage section break line.

Static engine runs were initiated on July 27 and were followed on July 29 by preliminary taxi tests. The runs were made about 100 yards to one side of the single north/south runway on the test location's lakebed. As Lockheed test pilot Tony LeVier later would recall, "Johnson had requested that the first run be made at a speed of 50 knots. After entering the aircraft and strapping in, I started the engine and signaled that all was in the green in the cockpit. The first run was in a northerly direction, roughly parallel to the runway. The aircraft was manually aligned by tow truck. I advanced the throttle and watched as the airspeed indicator wound rapidly to the 50 knot mark. The throttle then was retarded and the brakes gently applied."

LeVier noticed immediately that the brake response was poor and commented to that effect when Johnson and the other team members drove up in a chase car. "Johnson claimed the brake problem was due to the fact the brakes had not yet been broken-in. He told me there was nothing to worry about."

On the second taxi run, which Johnson requested be made at 70 knots, the aircraft was aimed in a southwesterly direction. As the aircraft accelerated, LeVier watched intently as the airspeed indicator wound around to the requested speed. He was not aware Article 341 had become airborne. As he retarded the throttle and looked outside the cockpit, he began to work the ailerons in order to develop some feel for how the aircraft might perform during flight...and specifically, how it might handle during landing. It was only then that he realized the control responses were real—and that the aircraft was actually thirty-five feet above the lakebed.

LeVier's lack of depth perception caused by the lakebed's smooth surface and a decided lack of runway markings, had failed to give him any visual indication that he was actually airborne. The realization of flight occurred after the throttle had been retarded.

As many Angel pilots later would discover, the J57 was not an engine noted for its quick throttle response at low airspeeds. Nevertheless, LeVier now slammed the throttle forward in an effort to accelerate and keep the aircraft from stalling. Buffeting had started. As LeVier quickly determined, he was headed for trouble unless a quick recovery could be made. Seconds later, the Angel settled back to earth, hitting the lakebed hard and blowing both main gear tires before bouncing back into the air one or two more times as the engine surged to life. LeVier retarded the throttle again, and this time the aircraft stayed on the ground. Brake application netted little response. The roll-out extended for almost a mile before the flat tires brought the aircraft to a halt.

The brakes now burst into flame directly under the fuel tank. Johnson would recall, "We were following in radio trucks, and finally got an extinguisher on the brakes. No harm done. Airplane was subjected to terrific test. Pogo sticks worked real well."

A debriefing session followed, at which time LeVier placed heavy emphasis on the extremely poor brakes. Additionally, the lack of external references in the form of runway markings were noted as being a serious problem. That evening the brakes were repaired while the runway marking request went undecided.

On the morning of August 4, 1955, Johnson, Ernie Joiner, Glen Fulkerson, Bob Murphy, and several other Skunk Works personnel watched as LeVier climbed into Article 341 in preparation for its first real flight. Given the call sign "Angel 1", the aircraft was to be chased by a company-operated C-47 with Johnson and test pilot Bob Matye (who was soon to become the second Angel test pilot) as observers. "Customers" also had been brought in from Washington, D.C., and they arrived at the test location by transport just prior to LeVier's takeoff.

LeVier recalls, "Prior to the first flight I had several conversations with Johnson concerning the landing technique to be utilized. Because of its unique zero track landing gear, Johnson insisted the Angel be landed main gear first. I disagreed, and told him it should be stalled-in with the tail wheel touching first." Johnson argued against this, insisting the Angel's high-aspect-ratio wing differentiated it from the landing characteristics of such bicycle gear equipped aircraft as the swept wing B-47 (pilots of which, LeVier had interviewed at some length in order to prepare for the first Angel flight). In the end, Johnson prevailed and at takeoff, LeVier promised to attempt to land the aircraft main gear first.

LeVier recalls the first takeoff and climb, taking place at 3:55 p.m., went perfectly and that he encountered no problems or difficulties during the ascent. Leveling at 8,000 feet, he spent 45 minutes cycling the landing gear, deploying and retracting the flaps, exploring stability and control characteristics, checking engine temperatures and exhaust pressure ratios, and practicing power-off stalls. There were no malfunctions of any kind.

As LeVier entered final approach, he could see Skunk Works and various government personnel lining up on one side of the landing area. As he crossed the threshold and cut the throttle, the aircraft began to settle in a nose-level-main-gear-first attitude. Flying on one side in the chase C-47 were Johnson and Matye, watching as the aircraft approached for touch-down. As LeVier had predicted, the Johnson landing technique did not work. The Angel touched, skipped, and then bounced into the air again, never once giving any indication it wanted to stop flying.

After going around the pattern again, a second approach, flare, and touchdown attempt netted the same result. Three more attempts followed including one in which LeVier tried to "spike" the main gear onto the runway by pushing the control wheel forcefully forward and aerodynamically driving the aircraft onto the lakebed. It did not work.

By now, Johnson was getting frustrated and was in almost constant radio contact with LeVier. To make matters worse, the sun was rapidly disappearing over the horizon and a summer rain shower was closing in almost as fast as the darkness. Under this pressure, LeVier decided to take matters into his own hands. The sixth attempt would be in the form of a conventional tail wheel landing.

Several days earlier, while preparing for the first flight, LeVier had placed two strips of tape on the canopy parallel to the horizon (this had been accomplished with the aircraft elevated to a level flight attitude while sitting statically on its ground transport dolly). Now, while watching these canopy marks closely, he glided over the threshold at approximately 75 knots and let the aircraft settle into a controlled stall. Almost in unison, the tail wheels and main gear contacted the lakebed. Though the aircraft porpoised momentarily, it quickly settled into a smooth rollout and uneventful full-stop after LeVier activated the gust control setting on the flaps. The latter effectively reduced wing lift and consequently killed the Angel's desire to fly. By 4:35 p.m., the first flight was over. Johnson would mark the occasion by drinking "...beer, of all things."

The initial brake repair did not solve the brake problem encountered during the initial taxi trials. For the next six days, work on the brakes was undertaken in-between flights. A "double" brake system was installed prior to a test flight on August 10. "They worked fine, " Johnson would note later, though one tire went flat during the landing roll-out.

LeVier completed a total of twenty flights in the Angel before being transferred back to the F-104 and other Lockheed flight test programs on September 1. His Angel work had completed Phase I testing and included exploration of the aircraft's stall envelope; exploration of the aircraft's maximum g (2-1/2 positive and 1-1/2 negative); and its speed capability up to maximum Mach number (0.85). Additionally, LeVier became the first pilot to take the aircraft to 50,000 feet. The latter required the use of a partial pressure suit. This had forced LeVier to go through the Air Force's high-altitude training program. When he completed the curriculum at the age of 42, he was at the time the oldest pilot to do so.

During this initial flight test period, the Air Force, at Johnson's recommendation, assigned the innocuous U-2 designator to the aircraft as its formal military alias. In the meantime,

*All-black Air Force U-2C departs Lockheed's Van Nuys facility following systems upgrade. Many U-2s eventually found in the Air Force inventory had begun their operational careers under the aegis of the CIA.*

*U-2F, 56-6680, equipped with rams horn antennas. Several U-2s were modified to this configuration and used operationally during the course of the Vietnam war.*

Article 341 and the other aircraft being delivered with some rapidity, were adorned with very few markings. In fact, while being tested at the location, the aircraft bore no markings at all except for call numbers and the NACA logo, on their vertical fins.

LeVier's position at the test location now was filled by Lockheed test pilot's Bob Matye and Ray Goudey. They became the second and third pilots to fly the U-2, respectively, and their responsibilities covered all aspects of the flight test program. Other Lockheed test pilots followed, including Bob Schumacher and Bob Sieker. Schumacher proved instrumental in clearing the U-2 for maximum altitude operation and in proving the viability of the aircraft's early sensor system payloads. Additionally, Schumacher, during 1963, became the first pilot to fly the U-2 from an aircraft carrier.

The flight test program during the remaining months of 1955 progressed smoothly. On October 18, Johnson noted the aircraft had reached design altitude and the third aircraft had been delivered to the test location. December 1 marked the U-2's first year anniversary which Johnson duly noted, "We have built four flying airplanes, have the ninth airplane in the jig, and have flown over our design altitude any number of times. We have trained crews and are developing the Bakersfield factory. It's been quite a year..."

By the beginning of the following year, four of the first five aircraft had been delivered to the test location. By March 31, total flight time on the nine aircraft fleet was 1,042: 33 hours. Altitudes considered incredible for 1955 were now being achieved by the U-2s on an almost routine basis. On one occasion, three consecutive altitude flights made by Matye broke, by significant margins, the then-extant world altitude record for class of 65,890 feet set by British test pilot Walter Gibb in an English Electric *Canberra* during August of 1955. On June 1, Johnson noted in the log, "Three missions over 10 hours (5,060 statute miles) and up to 74,500 feet with -31 engine."

By the end of 1957, two pilots had been killed and four aircraft had been damaged or destroyed. On April 4, 1957 the company lost Robert Sieker when the faceplate on his helmet failed while the aircraft was at altitude. Deprived of oxygen, he was unconscious in less than ten seconds. As reconstructed later, it appeared Article 341, modified for participating in a series of radar cross section tests under project *Rainbow*, had stalled at 65,000 feet and quickly entered a flat spin. Sieker apparently recovered in the denser atmosphere of low altitude. Though he attempted to manually egress the aircraft, he did not have enough height to deploy his parachute.

It was three days before the wrecked U-2, with Sieker's body lying fifty feet away, could be located. While flying a search mission, Lockheed test pilot Herman "Fish" Salmon and Ray Crandall spotted the remains. Within an hour, a helicopter team had reached the crash site. It later was determined a face mask clasp had failed. Johnson, upon learning of the accident cause, redesigned the clasp to prevent additional failures. Additionally, he concluded an ejection seat might have saved Seiker's life...and he recommended to the CIA and the Air Force that all existing U-2s, as well as all those forthcoming, should be ejection seat-equipped.

During early 1956, the first small group of six CIA pilots, specially selected following a grueling interview/schooling/test program conducted in Washington, D.C., arrived at the location to undergo U-2 flight training. All had undergone a CIA process called "sheep dipping" wherein their military backgrounds were disguised and their full-time employment was listed officially as being with private industry—in this case, Lockheed Aircraft Corporation (where they purportedly worked as "flight test consultants"). Additionally, they were given the unique privilege of being able to apply their time spent with the CIA toward their normal military advances and retirement.

The flight training program proved to be a fairly rapid process with piloting difficulties encountered primarily during landing instruction. The U-2 was an extremely difficult aircraft to land, particularly for pilots who had flown only aircraft with tricycle landing gear utilizing power-on approaches. Fortunately, the CIA had consciously picked pilots with above-average proficiency and all six of the original group mastered the landing technique by the end of the flight training period. By April of 1956, the initial flight test and training objectives had been accomplished and the six pilots and their aircraft were ready to embark on the first operational sorties of the program.

President Eisenhower, during mid-1955, still retained grave reservations concerning the proposed overflights of denied territory. Eisenhower, however, strongly believed in the undeniability of evidence in photographs. Upon the recommendation of Nelson Rockefeller and a study committee he chaired, Eisenhower proposed—in a last ditch effort to reconcile the differences between the Soviet Union and the US—during a Geneva Summit on July 21, 1955, that an "Open Skies" plan be considered by all participating countries.

This proposition stated that all participating countries would present to each other blueprints of their respective force structures. These would be used as reference and base line data for a limited number of annual reconnaissance overflights by each of the participating adherents. These flights would be used to verify blueprint claims and provide assurance to each country that all military activity was being kept at an equitable level.

Though obviously surprised by the Eisenhower proposal, the Soviet Union's Summit delegation reacted favorably to the idea and agreed immediately to confer with Party Secretary Nikita Khrushchev. Unfortunately, Khrushchev's reaction proved markedly reserved. He refused to accept or deny the proposal. When "Open Skies" were approved by majority vote in the United Nations one month later, Russia's neutrality dealt it a fatal blow.

During June of 1956, with the first group of CIA pilots in final preparation and some ten U-2s available for operational sorties, Richard Bissell and Allen Dulles arranged a meeting with President Eisenhower to discuss the overflight option. Secretary of State Foster Dulles and Eisenhower aide, Col. Andrew Goodpaster also attended. The conclusion was simple; with the death of "Open Skies" overflights were authorized...but only for an initial ten day period.

With the official sanction in hand, Bissel quickly returned to his CIA office and relayed the information to the U-2 operations team already in England. The first flight was tentatively scheduled for July 1.

In preparation for what now was referred to as *Operation Overflight,* the first two U-2s had been disassembled and air freighted to RAF Lakenheath, England on April 30, 1956. There the first of three CIA detachments, was formed under the spurious 1st Weather Reconnaissance Squadron, Provisional (WRSP-1) designator. In reality, the unit—a strange mix of CIA employees, Air Force personnel, and contracted civilians—was known simply as "Detachment A". A hangar on the far side of the Lakenheath airfield, remote from the majority of the main base activities, was set aside by the RAF for U-2 activities. The first U-2 flight from this facility took place on May 21.

As things turned out, no operational missions were flown from England during this period. Due to less than ideal foreign relations with the British government, "Detachment A" was forced, on June 15, to move operations closer to the Soviet border. Germany, through diplomatic liaisons, agreed to permit operations from Wiesbaden (despite the move to Germany, the British were kept apprised of U-2 activities; a CIA aircraft visited the Royal Aircraft Establishment at Farnborough during November of 1956 and British links to the program later became intimate during May of 1958 when four Royal Air Force pilots, John MacArthur, David Dowling, Michael Bradley, and Christopher Walker were sent to train in the U-2 with the Air Force at Laughlin AFB, Texas).

"Detachment A's" new location, from a security standpoint, was hardly an improvement over Lakenheath. Wiesbaden was a large town and the air base was only fifteen miles from the city of Frankfurt. Conveniently, however, it was close to *Camp King*, the CIA's major West German intelligence gathering facility. There, reports from agents and defectors from behind the Iron Curtain were sifted and analyzed and then used to form the basis for U-2 overflight requests.

On June 19, 1956, CIA pilot Carl

Overstreet departed Wiesbaden on the first operational flight. After overflying Warsaw, Poland and returning via Berlin and Potsdam, he landed without incident and delivered to the US intelligence community the first-ever surreptitiously taken U-2 photos. The results were spectacular. The quality of the imagery generated by the Type B folded-optics camera was everything the CIA had hoped for. Resolution, contrast, and quality were far beyond anything previously seen.

The development of the optical sensors for the U-2 had, in fact, been an amazing story unto itself. During May of 1951, the Air Force had set up a special study group at Boston on the aerial reconnaissance problem. Codenamed *Beacon Hill*, it had been chaired by Carl Overhage who—as a result of this team—had fortuitously brought Dr. Edwin Land, Allen Donovan of the Cornell Aeronautical Laboratories, and Dr. James Baker together for the first time.

Baker, of Harvard University and an astronomer by training, was one of the leading lens designers in the US during the 1940s and 1950s. At the same time, he was head of the intelligence systems panel for the Air Force. Later, he would be one of those who recommended the construction of the U-2.

As the person who conceptualized the Type B camera and its lenses and later personally inspected and checked each, Baker, more than any other single individual, gets credited with the creation of this most incredible optical device. He recently recounted the Type B camera's history as follows:

"The roots of the project go way back because there was a *Beacon Hill* study group in 1952 which covered a large number of subjects including aerial reconnaissance and what it might do for us in respect to our adversaries. In those days we were thinking of looking over fences instead of flying over them. A lot of our studies in 1952 were based on very long focal length things.

"I made a trip to Fort Worth, I guess it was, walking up and down the very long fuselage of one of the very big aircraft, the biggest was the B-36, thinking what a tremendous telescope could go into that thing; you could look over a fence 150 miles away. Even so, slant range photography was highly limited. We talked about it and the various ways.

"There was also at the time and preceding the "B" camera (the special project) a panoramic camera that was developed in the open which took 13 foot wide—horizon to horizon—panoramic strips, transverse to the line of flight film 18 inches wide and with a focal length of 48 inches. Well, as the special project was being discussed and planned in 1954, that kind of equipment that preceded was too cumbersome...too heavy and we had to decide what would be the most reliable compromise in terms of total coverage in terms of focal length, in terms of keeping it in focus under adverse conditions, the vibration, film processing and all that.

"Our group discussed all aspects of it, and finally, during the late months of 1954, I decided on a sequence of cameras, "A", "B", and "C" which were lightweight and compact and had the attribute of large coverage. The "A" systems were primarily drawn from Air Force stock. We had these refurbished and optimized to do their very best primarily just to get started. The "B" system was the first camera for the special project that was planned. Optical design was carried out, I believe, during

*U-2A, 56-6953, landing at RAF Ulpper Heyford during 1962. It is equipped with a particulate sampler in the Q-bay. The scoop assembly is visible on the left side of the fuselage ahead of the main landing gear.*

the early months of 1955 back in Cambridge, Massachusetts. However, the decision to cover horizon to horizon by a series of stop and shoot shots from left to right was made I guess maybe in a time period from October to December of 1954. We decided on having a single mirror in the camera...in spite of the rotation of field...because of wanting a supreme optical quality. In spite of the difficulty in keeping two mirrors lined up in a straight line and the ghost lighting this kind of photography introduces, we felt that high resolution was the supreme requirement and second to that was to get maximum coverage.

"The coverage involving the seven shots initially was thought to be planned for an 18 inch wide film; then we decided that when you wind a mile of film from one spool to the other you'd have a lot of trouble with the center of gravity so we decided to have two 9-1/2 inch size films moving in opposite direction to keep the c.g. fixed as the picture taking proceeded. That was what came about in the "B" system so the rest of it was a matter of simply seeking high technical excellence both in the optical design and in fabrication.

"The computers of the time—and there were some big ones not available to us—but we had the IBM CPC (Current Program Calculator) which by modern standards is something of a coffee grinder—in any case, the design work, being highly secret, had to be concealed from everyone in my group and everybody else in the area, so I carried on a rather normal schedule during the afternoons—-I was always a night owl so I didn't work much in the mornings—afternoons and evening and after everyone went home I put all the ordinary work away and then I would get started on the secret work.

"In those days because I couldn't use an

assistant to help me run the computers, I had them under some guise teach me how to run it during the daytime, and then I took over and started using the computer by myself during the night. So this is part of that little written-of portion of the history of how do you do unusual things when you look usual.

"In any case the design work was very well completed by May or June of 1955 and the Perkin Elmer Corporation took over the fabrication of the lenses and ordered the optical glass from the German shop people I suppose under the guise under some routine Air Force program to preserve secrecy. I had several of these lenses in my own laboratory after the parts were coming through. I put them together and did the fine figuring to get the image quality up to the maximum I was hoping for and to make sure that it all agreed with calculations. So over a period from 1955 and part of 1956, we were producing and checking and testing the various units as they came through.

There was also a "C" camera which had a focal length of 180 inches. And this was an interesting battle between "Kelly" Johnson, and myself and Dr. Land as to how big a camera we could fit into the rather dwindling space that "Kelly" was allowing us. He needed more and more room for batteries and other components; I needed more and more room for a 180 inch camera so we fought over the details of that. The consequence was the camera was more complicated than it needed to be but "Kelly" reminded me the airplane needed to fly before it could carry a camera. So it was just a question of compromise. The "C" camera was finished a couple of years later at a time when the "B" system already had been doing useful work on a big scale. And I believe the "C" system which was, with its 180 inch focal length v/s 36 inch, was meant for spotting; it was of looking

*Air Foce U-2A equipped with a particulate sampler in place of the right wing leading edge slipper tank. Gray markings were commonplace late in the U-2A/U-2C's operational career.*

Lockheed

*When they first entered operational Air Force service, the U-2s were left unpainted. Because of the care taken in assembly by* Skunk Works *personnel, the aircraft were truly magnificent to see. By the early 1960s, CIA aircraft already had transitioned to the type's better-known all-black paint scheme.*

for technical intelligence of things on the ground that were of special interest. I believe it could have been used, but the time period went by.

"The "B" system then turned out to be the work horse and I believe it certainly justified its existence. So, the "A" system was temporary, the "C" system was too much, and the "B"system did all the work."

The Type B camera was indeed a work horse. It was simple in design, construction, operation, and maintenance. It combined a large format (18 inch x 18 inch) and long focal length lens (36 inches) with a very large film capacity. These features—with the exotic diffraction-limited lens—enabled the Type B to provide very high resolution stereo coverage (five head position combinations were possible) of up to one million square miles during a single mission. Actual operational reliability averaged nearly 98%...or well over 10 million in-flight cycles. The 9-1/2 inch-wide thin-base film load was in the form of two 6,500 foot rolls. The film traveled in opposite directions across the platen. Complete data was imaged on both halves of each frame so that locating and matching them was not difficult. Lens aperture

was f/8 and ground resolution was 12 inches.

After a three week pause dictated by ongoing political considerations, U-2 operations were resumed. This second flight, with Harvey Stockman at the controls of Article 347, became the first to achieve the actual mission objectives of the aircraft...overflights of the Soviet Union. After departing Wiesbaden, Stockman flew over East Berlin, across northern Poland via Poznan, and into Belorusskay as far as Minsk. There he turned left to head north over Leningrad.

Not surprisingly, though Overstreet's flight had been conducted with little or no radar tracking by the Russians, Stockman's was much more closely followed. In fact, attempts by Soviet Air Force fighters to intercept his high-flying U-2 not only were observed by Stockman through the ventral driftsight, but also were recorded by the aircraft's electronic intelligence sensors. Turning back over the Baltic coasts of Estonia, Latvia, and Lithuania, he returned without further incident to Wiesbaden and made a safe landing. Stockman had been airborne for eight hours and forty-five minutes.

The next day, Carmen Vito boarded the

same U-2 and took-off to attempt the first overflight of Moscow. The mission plan called for an overflight of Krakow, Poland, then a turn east to Kiev, then another turn north towards Minsk, and then on to the Soviet capitol.

As it turned out, this third operational mission received considerable attention by the Soviet military. Interceptors were sent aloft in large numbers and vain attempts were made to shoot Vito down. Even more threatening were at least three SA-1 surface-to-air missile sites...which, surprisingly, were not activated. After violating Moscow's airspace, Vito changed course toward the Baltic coast and within a few hours and in spite of clouds and generally unsatisfactory weather conditions, was back on the ground at Wiesbaden . Like the one before, this mission—though long and circuitous—provided exceptional imagery of heretofore forbidden territory.

The photographs generated by these first three flights verified the great surveillance potential of the U-2 and its sophisticated camera. Most importantly, the ability to gather usable information using a high-altitude photographic platform was finally verified. The efforts of many long-frustrated strategic reconnaissance proponents were at long last vindicated.

By now, Soviet diplomatic circles were impacted. The U-2 flights had been tracked with little difficulty by Russian radar, and the Soviet government was embarrassed by the ease with which the aircraft were able to penetrate Russian airspace. The military repercussions were great...and in a communiqué dated July 10, 1956, the Soviet Ambassador to the US in Washington was asked to deliver a formal protest to the US Government and request that the overflights cease. In responding, US diplomats denied that any *military* aircraft had been involved in such activity. This was, of course, true...as the CIA was a *civilian*, and not a military agency.

Though these events proved relatively incidental, Eisenhower was sensitive to the

Robert Mikesh via Rene' Francillon

*The High-Altitude Sampling Program (HASP) took U-2s to many countries across the globe. Some of the earliest HASP missions were flown out of Laaverton, Australia, where this particular HASP U-2A is seen.*

*The highly flexible nature of the U-2's airframe permitted a large number of exotic and sometimes extraordinary modifications to be undertaken with little difficulty. Project TRIM, designed to explore the infrared signatures of ascending missile exhaust plumes...and other similar events...was just one of many examples.*

long-term political ramifications implied by continuing use of the U-2. Accordingly, he insisted on remaining in control and requested that each flight from mid-1956-on be conducted only after receiving his personal approval.

Johnson and the *Skunk Works* had been kept apprised of the U-2's successes and miscellaneous hardware problems as its operational career began to unfold. During June of 1957, he noted in the log, "Program continues at a high level of activity for us, between the normal operation, various packages, and the move to Muroc, which took place on June 10."

The Air Force, which also had begun receiving its first U-2s, had moved to Del Rio, Texas. The service's first program manager had been O. J. "Ozzie" Ritland, special assistant to the Deputy Chief of Staff, Development., and its second, Col. Leo Geary.

On June 28, according to Johnson, the Air Force lost two aircraft in one day. "In one, the pilot flew over his house to show off to his wife and dragged a wing 1,000 feet on the ground before he cartwheeled and was killed. On the other, it appears that an altitude blowout and/or oxygen failure cost us another life"

Johnson and the *Skunk Works* team had been briefed on the aircraft's vulnerability to radar and had been given all available information pertaining to Russian radar technology and its impact on the systems used to track the U-2. Johnson now attempted to reduce the U-2's radar signature. Schemes including stringing wires of various dipole lengths from each horizontal tail tip to each wing tip and from the nose to the vertical tail, and the incorporation of a metallic grid known as a *Salisbury Screen* covered in *Eccosorb* (a microwave absorbent coating made of foam rubber) were tested on Article 341. None proved effective across the entire spectrum of Russian radar frequencies.

After a thorough analysis, including operational deployment during 1958, Johnson concluded the drag and stability penalties were not justifiable; the only real solution lay in making radar absorption and attenuation an integral part of the aircraft's design and construction...which it was too late to do with the U-2.

During late May of 1956, the second CIA pilot class had entered U-2 training at the location, completing the course during August. From there, they had been shipped to Incirlik Air Base, near Adana, Turkey where they became "Detachment B". The unit comprised about 100 personnel...including a then-unknown pilot by the name of Francis Gary Powers. There were up to seven pilots and five aircraft available, with those figures varying from week to week.

With the advent of "Detachments" B in Turkey and C in Japan, U-2 activity increased but actual overflights of denied territories were kept to a minimum. Eisenhower remained concerned about the political ramifications and was cautious when approving penetration missions. Regardless, monthly flights, highly dependent upon weather conditions over the various target areas, were flown. A U-2 crash killing CIA pilot Howard Carey on September 17, 1956 near the German town of Kaiserlautern forced a short overflight cessation, but after several weeks of quiet, they were resumed.

During February of 1957, the last CIA U-2 pilot class finished its training at the test location and was dispersed to the three "Detachments". By now, "Detachment A" had been moved again, this time to a remote airfield at Giebelstadt in the hills south of Wurzburg, Germany. Not long afterwards it was merged with "Detachment B", now at Incirlik.

When CIA aircraft required major servicing or major subsystems upgrades, they were ferried or shipped back to the US where the *Skunk Works* accommodated the work at Edwards AFB North Base. Later, Lockheed Aircraft Services at the Van Nuys airport near Los Angeles did the required maintenance. Lockheed also had a service operation at the test location, and later, at Warner Robins AFB in Georgia. The latter eventually became the main logistics support depot for the U-2.

CIA U-2 operations continued in sporadic fashion throughout 1957, 1958, and 1959. Some thirty Russian overflights were completed during this thirty-six month period, with the vast majority of the other missions consisting of peripheral "snoops" or training sorties. Among the overflight objectives, a seismic sensor system was developed under the project codename *Purple Flash* that could be dropped from altitudes of over 70,000 feet and permanently implanted around nuclear test sites such as that at Lop Nor.

The peripheral missions were considered less risky than direct overflights and in many cases, resulted in intelligence that was as good as or better than that gathered by overflying the target directly. With the various improved sensors developed for the U-2 program, close proximity to a target was not always necessary. Usable imagery could be acquired from oblique angles at ranges approaching 100 miles, and electronic intelligence systems were equally sensitive.

At the beginning of the U-2 program, CIA, DoD, and Lockheed personnel all had estimated the aircraft's overflight life to be about two years. Beyond that, anti-aircraft improvements almost certainly would offset the aircraft's extraordinary altitude capability. The likelihood of an aircraft loss would be great after that time.

At the end of two years, however, no discernible improvement in Soviet anti-aircraft

Project Seeker *resulted in the U-2A being carrier qualified during 1963 in order to accommodate an urgent need to sample French nuclear explosions in the South Pacific. Trials were conducted successfully aboard the US Navy carrier* Kitty Hawk *before the operational missions were flown.*

*Four U-2As were modified to be carrier capable. Three were redesignated U-2G and one was redesignated U-2H. These aircraft had tail hooks, wire guides at the wing tips and ahead of the tail wheel, and a nose protection bumper and wheel assembly (the latter was retractable). The U-2H was inflight refuelable.*

capability had been detected. And though attempted intercepts by Russian fighters (i.e., MiG-19s and MiG-21s) and surface-to-air missiles (i.e., SA-1s and SA-2s) had been documented on numerous occasions, the U-2's ability to cruise above 70,000 feet continued to keep it well out of harm's way.

During 1958, the Soviets began to gather momentum in their efforts to develop an effective U-2 countermeasure. The SA-2, an improved surface-to-air missile eventually codenamed *Guideline* by the west and equipped with a warhead that had a kill pattern with a diameter of about 400 feet, was pushed into service, and for the first time, threatened the U-2's high altitude dominance. Though the estimated 2% probability of kill was low, for the first time the U-2 was forced into taking the new SA-2 launch sites into consideration. Accordingly, they were given a wide birth of up to 30 miles.

During December the first major U-2 upgrade was initiated by the *Skunk Works*. Johnson would note it in the log as, "...we reworked five U-2 aircraft into U-2C models,

using Pratt & Whitney J75 engines in place of the J57. We increased the absolute ceiling between 2,000 and 5,000 feet On one day in August, we had three airplanes at one time over 75,000 feet This was done at an expense of 300 to 500 miles in all out range."

The following March 1, he would continue, "The U-2 with the J75 engine is performing well. There have been several important missions run and it is living up to all our expectations. Have just about come to the end of our development flight testing, and I think it's necessary to get Goudey another job. It seems that, after about fifteen years, my old flight test group is tired of staying in the desert. Will have to set up a new one for the other project."

By the end of its third year of operation, the U-2's intelligence gathering ability had become the single most important tool in the entire US intelligence community arsenal. U-2 flights and their resulting imagery and electronic intelligence had revealed the fallacy of the Soviet jet bomber threat; had attenuated the impression Soviet ICBM technology was far advanced over of its western counterpart; and

had underscored the general shortcomings of Russian technology in general.

CIA U-2 operations were not confined to the Soviet Union during this period. During late September of 1956, Gary Powers flew across the eastern Mediterranean and gathered intelligence data on the positions of British and French warships as they prepared to aid the forthcoming Israeli invasion of Egypt. Further flights followed during the Suez crisis and later, during crises involving Syria, Iraq, Saudi-Arabia, Lebanon, and Yemen...all to gather intelligence data on military activities and the eternal warring between these various Mid-Eastern countries. Additionally, U-2 overflights of the Chekiang and Kaingsi Provinces in China began on December 6, 1958.

During September of 1959, Russian Premier Khrushchev visited the US allegedly to improve relations between the Soviet and US governments. This was reciprocated by an invitation to President Eisenhower to visit the Soviet Union during 1960. In the interim, it was agreed there would be a summit in Paris involving British and French participation. Hopes were high that a new era of cooperation between the "superpowers" was about to begin.

Surprisingly, though there had been a lull in U-2 activity—particularly overflights—during the course of Khrushchev's US visit, the forthcoming Paris summit did not merit similar consideration. Eisenhower, during January of 1960, approved flights for the first quarter of the year without being cognizant of their potential summit impact. Long before the Paris gathering, scheduled for May 14, U-2 mission profiles had been finalized by Col. Stanley Beerli (the CIA's U-2 director of mission planning and the immediate past commander of "Detachment A") and passed to the CIA for review. Secretary of State Christian Herter became the first to connect the significance of the overflight dates and their proximity to the date of the forthcoming summit, and he relayed the information to Allen Dulles. Upon further review, it was determined the missions, depending upon the weather, could be flown any time up to two weeks prior to the May 14 meeting.

On April 9, 1960, an overflight of Lop Nor by a CIA U-2 revealed that major work on a Russian ICBM project was moving along much faster than expected. The importance of this discovery led to a decision to schedule another flight over the same target area as quickly as possible. The mission was hurriedly approved and tentatively scheduled for late April or early May, depending on the weather.

Francis Gary Powers had flown some

*To protect the nose following a trap aboard an aircraft carrier, the U-Gs and the U-2H were equipped with special retractable nose landing gear. Noteworthy is the extended spoiler ahead of the flap leading edge.*

*Late in their careers, U-2Cs based in England were painted in subdued camouflage patterns and colors to assuage British citizens' fears the aircraft still were involved in covert spying activities.*

twenty-seven CIA U-2 missions following his arrival at Incirlik and "Detachment B" during mid-1956. Though the majority of the flights had been of the peripheral variety, some had penetrated Soviet airspace. Because of scheduling, Powers had been assigned the follow-up reconnaissance mission after the flight of April 9. Three attempts on April 28, 29, and 30 were made to launch, but it wasn't until May 1 that the weather over the target was good enough to accommodate photography requirements.

May 1, known as International Labor Day, was a major Soviet holiday. For this reason it was considered a "safe" day for the Powers mission. It was assumed the defensive anti-aircraft systems would not be at peak readiness and radar and other observation facilities would be minimally manned. Powers' targets were Sverdlovsk and Plesetsk, two major ICBM test sites and also the locations of some of the Soviet Union's heaviest anti-aircraft missile concentrations.

Powers' mission had been scheduled in conjunction with another, peripheral flight in the hope the latter would create a diversion, of sorts, for Soviet anti-aircraft defenses. Powers flight was to originate from a base near Peshawar, Pakistan and terminate 3,788 miles later at Bødo, Norway. The diversionary flight was to leave from Incirlik.

Powers' U-2, Article 360, had developed a reputation for being somewhat of a "hangar queen" during the course of its operational career. It had been plagued with a number of small, but seemingly unsolvable problems, not the least of which was its engine's susceptibility to compressor stalls and flame-out at altitude. Apparently, they were not considered serious enough to merit Powers' using a different aircraft.

On May 1, both flights took-off on schedule. Shortly afterwards, Powers leveled-off at 67,000 feet. Penetration of Soviet airspace followed and the aircraft soon was flying over denied territory. The mission went routinely in every respect until it passed over Sverdlovsk. During the course of the photo run, while still at altitude, Powers was stunned to feel and hear what seemed to be a dull explosion beneath and somewhat behind his aircraft. At the same instant, the sky turned bright orange. Seconds later, the U-2's right wing dropped. Powers responded by turning the control yoke left. Momentarily, this brought the U-2 back to a wings level position, but the nose then began to pitch downward—apparently because the horizontal tail had been adversely impacted by the explosion. Powers now realized something was terribly wrong. At the same moment, the U-2 pitched forward violently and both wings separated as the primary wing structure became overloaded.

Powers would recall later that his first rational thought while the aircraft was coming apart around him was that he should trip the sensor system destruct switches (located on an extension on the left side of the instrument panel; these activated a 70-second timed delay in a special pyrotechnics system). In later interviews, he would not be able to recall whether he had succeeded. In truth the concern was academic...as virtually everything aboard the U-2, including the Type B camera, would be damaged almost beyond recognition upon ground impact.

By now Powers' faceplate had frosted over and his partial pressure suit was fully inflated. What remained of the U-2 had entered an inverted flat spin. Centrifugal forces were

Air Force and CIA U-2s were painted black primarily to reduce their visibility at their normal operating altitude. The dull finish also reduced reflectivity. Radar, however, had little trouble tracking the aircraft.

pushing Powers forward...into the instrument panel. His legs were pinned as a result. This precluded use of the ejection seat as his legs would be severed at the knees if the handles were pulled. Realizing this, Powers struggled to regain proper seating position.

As Powers wrestled against the forces of the spin, he began to realize ejection was not necessary in order to egress the aircraft. The canopy could be manually released. Glancing at the unwinding altimeter, he noted he was descending through 34,000 feet. He immediately reached up and pushed open the canopy. He then unlatched his seat belts. As the last one released, he was thrown forward and half out of the cockpit. Almost instantaneously he realized he had failed to disconnect his oxygen hose...and that it was keeping him anchored to the aircraft.

An exhausting attempt to reenter the cockpit followed. When this failed, Powers began pulling on the hose in an effort to make it break. His incessant jerking finally snapped a connector. Finally, at 15,000 feet, he was free. Moments later, Power's parachute, released by a barometric sensor, opened.

During 1965, *The Penkovsky Papers* were translated into English and published in the US by Doubleday & Co. Authored by Oleg Penkovsky, a colonel who had worked for years in Soviet intelligence, the book provided some insight into the downing of Powers' U-2. Penkovsky claimed 14 SA-2s had been fired in a shotgun-type attack, and that *shock waves* generated by the explosions had led to the U-2's structural failure. The Soviet military's post-incident investigation failed to reveal any indication of physical contact by any of the SA-2s, and there apparently was nothing to indicate the aircraft had been hit by shrapnel. Penkovsky also claimed a Sukhoi Su-9, interceptor attempting to intercept and destroy the U-2, had been destroyed accidentally by one of the 14 SA-2s.

Powers was captured after landing in the middle of a farm field. Four days later, as the

political importance of the shoot-down began to dawn on the international community, the destruction of the U-2 became front page news around the world. What had once been the US's most secretive clandestine reconnaissance operation was now one of the world's most highly publicized.

Johnson had taken the Powers loss matter-of-factly. On May 1, in the U-2 log, he had simply noted, "We lost J75 airplane #360 flown by Francis G. Powers, west of Sverdlovsk." A month later, apparently after reviewing available information on the shootdown, he wrote, "I do not know now what will happen to the U-2 program. We are moving the Air Force IRAN (inspect and repair as necessary) program to Burbank next week and are studying various means of operating detachment airplane out of Muroc. We are going into refueling, drones, and the carrier operation once again."

Due to Powers' ensuing trial as an espionage agent—which was publicized with considerable vigor by the Soviet news agencies—the incident remained in the international spotlight for months after its occurrence. Though the political and diplomatic events are beyond the scope of this book to recount, it is important to note that the associated repercussions led to the immediate cessation of U-2 overflights and also the retraction of all U-2 operations world wide.

With the U-2 effectively deactivated, the US intelligence community found itself in a difficult position. U-2 successes, like an addictive drug, had led to an over-dependence on the system. By the time Powers was lost, fully 90% of all hard photographic data on Soviet military developments was being generated from the aircraft's overflight imagery. Withdrawal was painful.

Powers was eventually released, but only after spending nearly two years in prison (he had been sentenced to ten) and only after US agents completed negotiations with the Soviets calling for a-spy-for-a-spy-trade. During 1958, the FBI had apprehended Soviet spy Rudolf

Two U-2As were modified to the U-2CT configuration to serve as dedicated trainers. A second cockpit and associated controls and instrumentation were installed in the area normally referred to as the "Q-bay".

Miller collection

*Several U-2As were permanently assigned to Edwards AFB for test and research purposes. These aircraft tended to sport colorful markings and a variety of unusual appurtenances.*

Abel who had been the chief operative for the Soviet secret police (KGB) in the US for nearly a quarter century. Though one of the all-time biggest spy figures ever caught by the US government, it was decided to exchange Abel for Powers as a sign of serious intent. On February 10, 1962, Powers and Abel silently walked past each other on the German Glienicker Bridge...each returning forever to his homeland and neither ever to set foot on the other's soil again.

Johnson, who had been unwavering in his support of Powers throughout the overflight ordeal, hired him as a test pilot on the U-2 program not long after his return. Several years later, after retiring from the *Skunk Works*, Powers, during 1976, became a traffic news reporter flying a helicopter for a Los Angeles television station. Returning to Van Nuys Airport on August 1, 1977, after covering a brush fire, his helicopter ran out of fuel and crashed in an Encino field in the San Fernando Valley. Powers, along with his cameraman passenger, was killed instantly .

Powers, an Air Force captain when he left to fly the U-2 for the CIA, was buried in Arlington National Cemetery. In 1987, he was posthumously presented the Air Force Distinguished Flying Cross for his U-2 operations and a citation commending him for his May 1, 1960 flight into "denied territory".

Contrary to popular belief, the U-2's career did not abruptly end on that fateful May 1, 1960 day. Though "Detachment B" was withdrawn along with "Detachment C" at Atsugi, Japan, the U-2's usefulness as a sensor system platform was far from over. As the dust began to settle following the Powers incident, all U-2 Operating Locations (OLs) were quietly deacti-

vated and the aircraft and crews were returned to the US mainland.

Air Force U-2 activity, which had been sublimated to that of the Central Intelligence Agency, now was on the rise. Though CIA missions remained significantly more sensitive, the majority of the sampling missions now were being flown by Air Force aircraft. Somewhat surprisingly, while U-2 exposure to publicity was being downplayed by the CIA, the Air Force, during 1962, made a point of notifying the press of the deployment of three aircraft to RAF Upper Heyford in England.

Miscellaneous U-2 development work, even in light of the Powers incident, had continued at the *Skunk Works*. On June 24, 1960, Johnson had presented a proposal calling for the conversion of six aircraft to accommodate inflight refueling. An initial test by the Air Force on October 26 through 28, verified the U-2 could safely be flown behind a KC-135. Approval for initial conversion followed and on May 4, Johnson noted in the U-2 log, "Have developed in-flight refueling for the U-bird and can take aboard about 900 gallons from a KC-135." On October 5, he followed with the note, "We have completed the refueling program including night refuelings, with the project pilots at the Edwards AFB North Base. These tests have gone very well, but now we have to have a means for bringing the U-2 and the tanker together. Digging hard for beacons and other devices."

Lesser known, and much later in the program, Johnson also proposed a U-2 tanker. This occurred during December of 1964. No hardware resulted, but the idea of refueling at 70,000 feet remains intriguing.

It was a CIA U-2, and not an Air Force air-

craft which, on August 29, 1962, brought back the first photos of the Russian military build-up in Cuba. The CIA at this time had been flying two missions a month over the island. This rate was increased to one a week once suspicions of intermediate range ballistic missile (IRBM) activity began to increase. The Air Force now lobbied the President for approval to take over the mission that had been so rigidly controlled by the CIA. Knowing a U-2 follow-on already was undergoing flight test, the CIA did not counter the Air Force argument with any intensity. This—coupled with miscellaneous bureaucratic issues that included an on-going feud with the President over how many Cuban overflights were necessary per week—cleared the way for a formal transition of responsibility.

On October 9, the Air Force received approval to begin Cuban surveillance. Two Air Force pilots from the Strategic Air Command's 4080th Strategic Reconnaissance Wing were assigned the mission. CIA U-2s were used because, unlike their Air Force counterparts, they were equipped with the latest electronic countermeasures equipment.

Until October 9, the primary justification for the continuing dichotomy in the Air Force/CIA U-2 operation had been the so-called "theory of plausible denial". This held that if a military aircraft and pilot were shot down over unfriendly territory, the overflight could be construed as an act of war; a CIA aircraft and pilot, on the other hand, if lost, were not only "civilian", but also "officially disownable" by the US Government. A foreign country would be hard-pressed to declare war over a "civilian" intrusion. As this argument was beginning to crumble, the Air Force saw an opportunity to gain control of an assignment it had long coveted. When the Air Force agreed to meet President Kennedy's overflight frequency requirement—which had been denied by the CIA—Kennedy made the fateful decision to task the Air Force with the Cuban surveillance mission. This opened the door to wider Air Force participation and essentially led to the beginning of the end of CIA U-2 operations.

There was one assignment, however, that was retained by the CIA long after the Air Force took over the majority of U-2 activity. Due to its political sensitivity and its direct relationship with the intelligence community, the Nationalist Chinese U-2 operation in Taiwan was kept under CIA control throughout its history. A source of valuable intelligence about Communist China's nuclear weapons and missile test programs, it produced the first hard data on the status of the Communist Chinese military establishment. Interestingly, as a cover for the Taiwanese-operated U-2s, dummy contracts with the Nationalist Chinese (Taiwan) were drafted by Lockheed "formalizing" the transfer of the aircraft to the Taiwanese government. In fact, the aircraft remained fully under the control of the CIA. The contracts were signed by "Kelly" Johnson and Chang Kaishek.

Nationalist Chinese U-2 operations continued unabated—with both CIA and Nationalist Chinese pilots flying missions—until October of 1974, when the Nixon accords with the Communist Chinese led to a cessation of all Chinese overflight activity. All CIA U-2 operations, including the facility then being utilized at Edwards AFB North Base, were downgraded and, shortly afterwards, phased out of service.

The end of the CIA's U-2 mission was a boon to the Air Force's. All CIA U-2s and support equipment were brought in from the various CIA OLs and transferred to Air Force juris-

Lockheed

*Smokey Joe was just one of the the many programs involving the Edwards AFB U-2 fleet. Infrared monitoring equipment--including a "pickel barrel" sensor--and a second crew position were placed in the Q-bay.*

diction. This created somewhat of a dilemma as all equipment acquired by the CIA had been left unmarked and unidentified. The Air Force inventory system, highly dependent upon identification numbers and other means of inventory control, found the unmarked gear virtually impossible to absorb!

Less than a year after the Cuban missile crisis had come to a satisfactory conclusion, and before the CIA had gotten out of the U-2 business, a proposal surfaced at the *Skunk Works* requesting that studies be conducted exploring the possibility of operating the U-2 from aircraft carriers. Johnson responded to this during early May of 1963 and by June 24, he was progressing rapidly on the design of a carrier-compatible configuration. On July 17 he noted in the U-2 log, "The Navy visited here, and we discussed a test with the U-2 aboard the *Kitty Hawk*. At this time also discussed ability to put an A-12 aboard a large new carrier."

On August 4, 1963, a CIA U-2 was flown from Edwards AFB to North Island Naval Air Station at San Diego. After being loaded onto a "low boy" trailer, it was hoisted aboard the carrier USS *Kitty Hawk* (CV-63). The following day, Johnson noted: "Steamed out of San Diego to a point south of San Clemente Island. I wrote the flight card and briefed about 20 Navy personnel on what we wanted to do. They were all extremely cooperative, but it seems that the captain on the bridge didn't get word of what we wanted to do, so we had several instances of going too fast or too slow or in the wrong direction. With all of this, the aircraft took off, with Schumacher flying, in 321 feet, with no difficulty whatsoever. Carrier speed was 24 knots with a 6 knot wind. Made three approaches, flying through turbulence aft of the carrier...no problem whatsoever. But it was difficult to spot the airplane down. On third approach, Schumacher bounced, hit hard on the right wing tip, and picked the thing up just before coming to the end of the angled deck. After one more fly-by to see that all the parts were on, he flew home."

The political and logistical ramifications of this test were great. Operating Locations, as the various remote staging bases for the U-2 were called, were difficult to acquire and even more difficult to maintain. If aircraft carriers could be proved suitable for U-2 operations, they could eliminate all but the most remote OLs.

During January the *Skunk Works* tasked itself with development of a modification package that could be applied to any or all U-2s in order to make them carrier compatible. The three modified aircraft, formally referred to as U-2Gs, were equipped with: a stronger aft fuselage and empennage (three longerons were added); a faired tail hook ahead of the tail wheel and attached to the engine mounts and wing attachment points; a cable deflector ahead of the tail wheel assembly; a redesigned main landing gear strut assembly that could easily be unlocked and rotated to permit sideways movement of the aircraft (in order to ease deck handling difficulties); a fuel dump system for quick off-loading of fuel in an emergency; and later, cable guards for the wing tip skid plates. Almost as an afterthought, Johnson also added a spoiler on the top surface of each wing, "which, in conjunction with more flap angle, made the bird very docile to land at a precise spot."

During early 1964 Schumacher, "Deke" Hall, and several other CIA pilots completed a

Miller collection

*U-2A, 56-6721, spent most of its career at Edwards AFB configured with a second seat in the original "Q-bay". This aircraft now is displayed at March AFB, California in its original single-seat configuration.*

brief checkout in the Navy's North American T-2 at NAS Monterey, California. This was followed by T-2 carrier qualification flights from the USS *Lexington* (AVT-16) in the Gulf of Mexico, and then a return to U-2 operations at Edwards AFB.

On March 2, the U-2G was flown by Schumacher to the USS *Ranger* (CV-61) off the Pacific coast of California where two days of testing ensued. "It was a hard job for two days," Johnson would recall, "one of the greatest problems being light load takeoffs, which gave the airplane a tendency to drift into the bridge because it went so high so soon. Overall, tests were successful, although the project pilots had trouble. One of them dropped a wing but still took off."

The U-2Gs were turned over the CIA and used to carrier qualify a small cadre of five CIA pilots. The CIA already had several targets planned requiring carrier operations and expeditious training was mandatory. During May of 1964, a single U-2G was loaded aboard the USS *Ranger* and prepared for a mission under *Project Seeker*. The French, as it turned out, were about to test a nuclear bomb at Mururoa, a ten-mile-long strip of coral thousands of miles from any other land mass in the Pacific Ocean. The U-2G became the US intelligence community's only dependable insight into this significant test. It also provided a quick and accurate assessment of French nuclear weapons technology when follow-up particulate sampling missions brought back radioactive materials from the debris cloud.

Noteworthy was the modification of one U-2G to the U-2H configuration. This aircraft, in addition to the tail hook and other modifications, also was one of the few U-2s to be equipped with an inflight refueling receptacle. This made it perhaps the heaviest of all "first generation" U-2s, and thus one of the weakest performers. Much of its life was spent at Edwards AFB North Base where it was used for training and equipment test work.

By 1974, the CIA's interest in the U-2 centered on Taiwanese operations and the intelligence that resulted. Air Force control of the program had become almost total, however, and in light of the gradually improving quality of

intelligence being gathered by reconnaissance satellite systems operating under CIA direction, was sufficient to merit a total release of assets. With the transfer of the last items in the CIA's U-2 inventory to the Air Force, the CIA's U-2 chapter was quietly closed.

---

**Air Force:**

As noted earlier, the Air Force had been intimately involved with the high-altitude reconnaissance aircraft program since its inception during 1953. Though adding the U-2 to its inventory would not occur until after the CIA had placed it in service, Air Force money had been spent on the aircraft's development and it was an invisible but high priority item in the Air Force budget.

Nearly all CIA U-2 pilots had come from Air Force rosters. And in the beginning, the three CIA units were combined Air Force/CIA operations in which the Air Force (and Lockheed) provided almost all logistical support.

RB-57D operations had preceded the U-2's Air Force introduction and as a result, the service already was familiar with the idiosyncrasies of high-altitude aircraft and their systems. The Strategic Air Command's 4080th SRW had been flying the RB-57D above 60,000 feet for some two years by the time the first Air Force U-2's were delivered to Laughlin AFB, Texas on June 11, 1957—over a year after the type had been first accepted by the CIA.

The 4080th SRW's operating squadron at Laughlin was the 4028th SRS. This unit normally was equipped with approximately fifteen aircraft, and pilot strength was about twice that number. During September, five more U-2s were delivered with dedicated gas and particulate sampling systems in place of the more common accommodations for optical and electromagnetic sensors. These aircraft, later referred to sporadically as WU-2As, had a "hard nose" containing a small intake-and-valve assembly for the sampling mission.

The five WU-2As became the first Laughlin-based aircraft to be assigned a long term Air Force project. Known as HASP (High Altitude Sampling Program), it was to take no

Miller collection

*A single U-2A, 56-6722, was modified to the HICAT (High-altitude Clear Air Turbulence) configuration and equipped with a gust sensing probe under the nose and other associated equipment.*

*NASA's use of the U-2 was strictly a paper exercise until April 2, 1971, when the Air Force agreed to provide the Administration with two U-2Cs for research purposes.*

less than five years to complete and involve some 45,000 flying hours (almost all in U-2s).

Sponsored by the Defense Atomic Support Agency, HASP had been initiated during 1954 to determine the role played by the stratosphere in the world-wide distribution of fission products resulting from nuclear explosions. This eventually resulted in the most detailed and extensive study of radioactive material in the stratosphere ever conducted. During what became known to the 4028th as *Operation Crow Flight*, over 150 million cubic feet of stratospheric air were sampled.

The first HASP deployment was to Ramey AFB, Puerto Rico. After a short stay there, the HASP U-2s undertook the first of what was to be a long series of temporary duty assignments to miscellaneous Operating Locations throughout the world. During September of 1958, three aircraft went for a year to Ezeiza AB near Buenos Aires. During 1960, they returned to Buenos Aires for a two month stay. The northern hemisphere was covered by operations out of Eielson AFB, Alaska and Minot AFB, North Dakota. The first of at least six HASP detachments to Australia was made during October of 1960 when three aircraft operated out of RAAF Laaverton near East Sale, Australia. Another three aircraft were assigned to Laaverton one year later but flew out of RAAF Avalon. These flew the very last HASP missions during February of 1965.

Typical HASP flights lasted seven-and-one-half hours at cruising altitudes between 50,000 and 70,000 feet. In addition to particulates and gases, the U-2s gathered information about cosmic radiation, ozone accumulation, and upper atmospheric jet streams.

The 4028th operated alongside RB-57Ds of the 4025th SRS. Both squadrons mounted sensitive reconnaissance missions in addition to the more public HASP flights, in conjunction with missions being flown by CIA U-2s. Because of its serious wing fatigue problem, the RB-57D was forced into early retirement from strategic reconnaissance and was prompt-

ly replaced by the U-2. The U-2, already deeply immersed in sensitive surveillance programs, thus took over the secret *Toy Soldier*, *Green Hornet*, and *Sky Shield* missions.

During July of 1962 the first of an increasingly ominous series of intelligence reports describing a rapidly growing Soviet presence in Cuba began circulating within the confines of the US intelligence community. Noticeable increases in the number of military shipments to Cuba were perhaps the most obvious build-up signs, though in-country observers also had reported the number of Soviet military personnel on hand had grown dramatically.

Unfortunately, a supposed Cuban propensity for exaggeration cooled any strong US concern about a military build-up. Thus, for a few weeks following the initial flurry of reports, no action was taken.

Reports of a much more insidious nature, bearing descriptions of very large missiles began appearing with considerable regularity during early August of 1962. John McCone, the director of the CIA, after reviewing the most recent data, decided to take the information directly to President Kennedy. On August 22, he told Kennedy the Cubans were receiving intermediate range ballistic missiles.

The President, oftentimes skeptical of the intelligence community data delivered to his office daily, did not react with any urgency to McCone's report. He asked for additional proof of Cuban aggression before taking any action. On August 29, a CIA U-2 brought back photos verifying the existence of at least two active advanced surface-to-air missile sites with at least six under construction. Most alarming was the fact these sites were laid-out in the same Star-of-David pattern that had been photographed in Russia surrounding IRBM and ICBM launch facilities.

On September 8, a Navy P-2 tracked and photographed the Soviet freighter *Omsk* northeast of Cuba. The boat was carrying an unusual—but unidentifiable—cargo which looked suspiciously like crates for IRBMs. President

Kennedy, now becoming concerned McCone's earlier assessment might have some merit, requested that U-2 overflight frequency be increased to a rate of one mission per week. Difficulties with the State Department slowed execution of the frequency increase request and as a result, IRBMs landed without incident on Cuban shores on September 8...and nothing was done about it.

With the lifting of the overflight moratorium during the first week in October, CIA U-2s resumed penetration of Cuban airspace. On October 10, President Kennedy approved, for the first time, overflights by Air Force pilots. Two pilots from the 4080th, Maj. Rudolph Anderson and Maj. Steve Heyser went to McCoy AFB and there checked-out in CIA U-2s. Other 4028th pilots followed over the ensuing several weeks.

Bad weather prevented the consummation of the first Air Force overflight for several days, but finally, on October 14, Heyser took off and headed toward Isla de Pinos and then flew north toward the Cuban mainland. The run from San Cristóbal, perhaps the most critical part of the mission, lasted no more than five minutes. When it was over, Heyser set course for McCoy, and as it turned out, a memorable page in US history.

Heyser's film, shot at approximately 7 a.m., contained the first images verifying beyond any doubt the arrival of Soviet IRBMs on Cuban soil. Upon processing in Washington, D.C. by the National Photo Intelligence Center, the images were hurriedly analyzed and then delivered to the President's office and the State Department. By October 16, word of the stunning discovery had spread throughout the intelligence community and the Department of Defense.

Stepped up U-2 overflight activity now was ordered by the President and additional low-altitude surveillance was undertaken by Air Force RF-101Cs. On October 17, new photos indicated MRBM launch sites and associated equipment were under construction at Sagua la Grande, Remedios, and Guianajay. Additionally, there were indications SS-4 *Sandal* IRBM sites also were under construction.

U-2 overflight activity now was accelerated again, this time to a rate of six or seven flights a day. The 4080th logged some twenty sorties between October 14 and October 22, each mission being followed by supporting film transportation flights to Washington.

On October 22, 1962, President Kennedy made his now-famous speech revealing publicly that Cuba had acquired an extensive offensive weapons capability including MRBMs and IRBMs. In an unquestionably threatening tone, Kennedy declared that *any* Cuban missile launch would be regarded as an attack by the Soviet Union on the US and that massive retaliatory action would result. He also declared a "naval quarantine" of Cuba until all Soviet offensive weapons were removed from the Island.

U-2 overflights continued at a very high daily rate with most emanating from either McCoy AFB, Florida or Laughlin AFB, Texas. Due to the proximity of the island, flights direct from Laughlin proved well within the range of the aircraft. Many missions later were flown from Barksdale AFB (referred to as OL-19) near Shreveport, Louisiana. Between October 22 and December 6, no less than 82 Air Force U-2 missions were undertaken.

With SA-2s and MiG-21s in Cuban ser-

*NASA was fully responsible for all maintenance and support of its U-2Cs during the course of their service with the Administration. Such activity took place at NASA Ames, California facility.*

vice, the overflight assignment was not without danger. On October 27, while overflying the Cuban naval installation at Banes, Maj. Rudolph Anderson was shot down by an SA-2. This loss led to significant changes in overflight policy. Surface-to-air missile sites, from the date of Anderson's downing, were given priority consideration during flight planning. Consequently, electronic countermeasures equipment was reevaluated and improved.

Much later, two other Air Force pilots would lose their lives while flying the Cuban overflight mission, though not to enemy action. Capt. Joe Hyde disappeared near the southwest Florida coast in the Gulf of Mexico on October 20, 1963. And Capt. Robert Hickman, flying out of Barksdale AFB, Louisiana, became incapacitated during 1966 when he apparently lost consciousness at cruising altitude; his aircraft was found several days later in a remote forest area of Latin America.

On October 24, 1962 US patrol aircraft over the Atlantic noted that a number of Soviet merchant ships bearing what appeared to be military cargoes bound for Cuba had stopped in mid-ocean and turned around. On October 26, communications with the Soviets indicated they would begin dismantling the Cuban missile sites. On October 28, this was confirmed. The Cuban missile crises, due in no small part to the photographic intelligence provided by the U-2 surveillance program, had come to an end.

Frequent Cuban overflights continued. They still were in progress when President Kennedy, remarking, "I must say gentlemen that you take excellent pictures..." presented on November 26, 1962, an Outstanding Unit Award to the 4080th Wing during their temporary assignment to Florida. This was, in fact, the second such award received by the 4080th which had first been honored during March of 1960.

On July 12, 1963, the last U-2 left Laughlin AFB for the 4080th's new home in the desert at Davis-Monthan AFB near Tucson, Arizona. In spite of numerous training and operational accidents that had destroyed at least a dozen aircraft and ten pilots, unit strength remained at some 20 U-2s. HASP missions continued to keep things busy. Interspersed among them were a number of classified missions that often

required the 4080th's unique services at a distant OL.

At the very end of 1963, a new chapter for the 4080th began when President Johnson approved Air Force U-2 reconnaissance missions over Vietnam. During March of 1964, following the abrupt termination of HASP (caused by the international agreement to discontinue above-ground nuclear weapons testing), all HASP aircraft were reconfigured to accommodate conventional optical and ELINT sensor payloads. These aircraft were deployed under the codename *Dragon Lady* to Bien Hoa base near Saigon. Within a matter of days they had embarked on their first operational sorties. This U-2 effort would continue for the following twelve years.

In Vietnam, the U-2s were expected to provide covert surveillance of N. Vietnam's border areas and its Vietcong infiltration routes. Less obviously, it also was tasked with helping to develop a contingency list of targets inside N. Vietnam itself, should the war be escalated.

With unmanned, remotely piloted vehicles taking over many overflight duties early in the war, the U-2's mission primarily became one of stand-off surveillance. Though improvements in the aircraft also had been introduced by this time, including engine upgrades and more sophisticated electronic countermeasures systems, its age was beginning to show.

In the *Skunk Works*, Johnson and his engineering team had not been blind to the performance degradation being brought on by heavier payloads and the inability of engine improvements to compensate. On February 2, 1965, Johnson noted in the U-2 log that he was "making an investigation of ways and means to re-establish performance for the U-2. It is now so heavy and decked-out with so much external gear that it has lost approximately 50% of its range and several thousand feet in its cruising altitude. In spite of the most valiant design efforts, we are not able now to beat the original performance."

### U-2R:

Johnson's concerns—and the performance improvement studies that resulted—in effect heralded the arrival the U-2R. At one time referred to as the WU-2C and the U-

2N...and formally identified inside Lockheed as the CL-351...this aircraft was a totally new design based on the original U-2 configuration, but enlarged by approximately one-third. Many U-2 successor studies had been conducted in the *Skunk Works* following the successes of the original aircraft, but none had resulted in any major performance improvements. As Johnson would note on October 12, 1965, "Wrote a memo to Merv Heal to start a new study on the U-2 to optimize for a new J75 engine. Basic approach is to reduce the wing loading to what we had on the J57 and get back our 25 to 1 L/D ratio. Told him to give up effort on our previous designs. It's extremely difficult to beat the original U-2."

On January 18, 1966 he stated, "I presented the U-2R study to Albert Wheelon and others in the program office. This design is the result of a year's preliminary design and tunnel testing, where we made a complete circle and ended up merely enlarging the present U-2 to take advantage of a 20% power increase which has developed since September of 1965. All the various efforts to sweep the wings, use the Whitcomb flap, or change aspect ratio did not result in improved performance to any important degree. Going back to the original concept, where we can fly at a lift coefficient of 0.6 to 0.7, gives us an airplane with a 7,000 mile range unrefueled and a few thousand feet more altitude. However, it also includes much better installation of equipment."

On February 9, 1966 he noted, "We made a proposal quoting costs and schedules for 25 airplanes." During March he wrote, "Summarizing our accidents up-to-date, we have reached a plateau of hours, flights per accident and, of the original aircraft, we are now down to 21. There is no sign of metal fatigue or the usual problems of aging of the aircraft, as they have been well maintained and overhauled often."

A bigger and better U-2 now began to move forward inside the *Skunk Works,* though with minimal engineering effort. On May 17, 1966, however, this changed, "Had the engineering project organized under Ed Baldwin, with Fred Cavanaugh as his deputy, and now have about 30 people working on the engineering phases. Spent an afternoon on the boards,

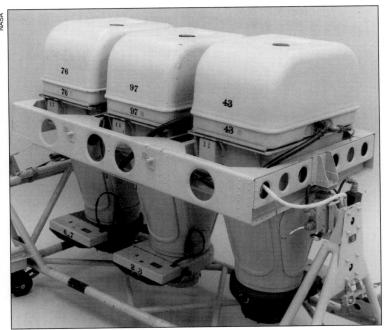

*The Type A camera system had an image motion compensation system which rocked all three Fairchild HR-732 24-inch cameras simultaneously.*

*The Type B camera was a workhorse. Its 36-inch folded-optics lens was the highest resolution device of its kind in the world at the time of its debut.*

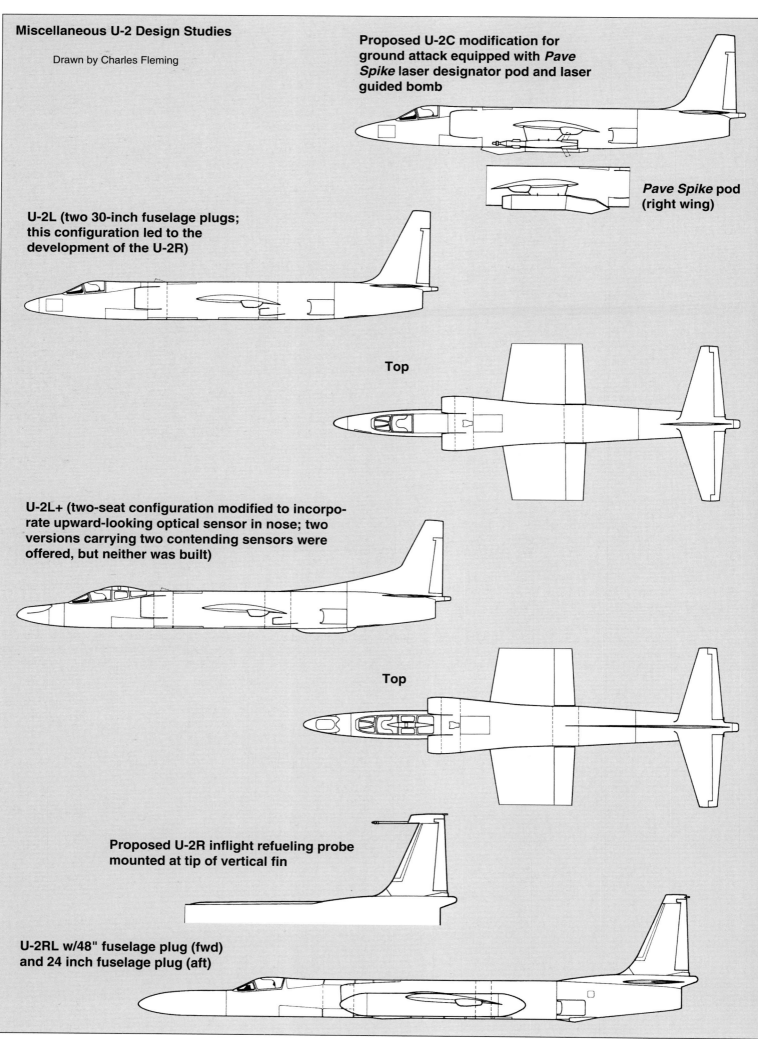

**Miscellaneous U-2 Design Studies**

Drawn by Charles Fleming

**Proposed U-2C modification for ground attack equipped with *Pave Spike* laser designator pod and laser guided bomb**

***Pave Spike* pod (right wing)**

**U-2L (two 30-inch fuselage plugs; this configuration led to the development of the U-2R)**

**Top**

**U-2L+ (two-seat configuration modified to incorporate upward-looking optical sensor in nose; two versions carrying two contending sensors were offered, but neither was built)**

**Top**

**Proposed U-2R inflight refueling probe mounted at tip of vertical fin**

**U-2RL w/48" fuselage plug (fwd) and 24 inch fuselage plug (aft)**

*The first U-2R on its first flight on August 28, 1967 following takeoff from the Edwards AFB North Base facility. Lockheed test pilot Bill Park was at the controls. The U-2R, though bearing the legacy and renowned designation of its predecessor, was in fact a totally new aircraft.*

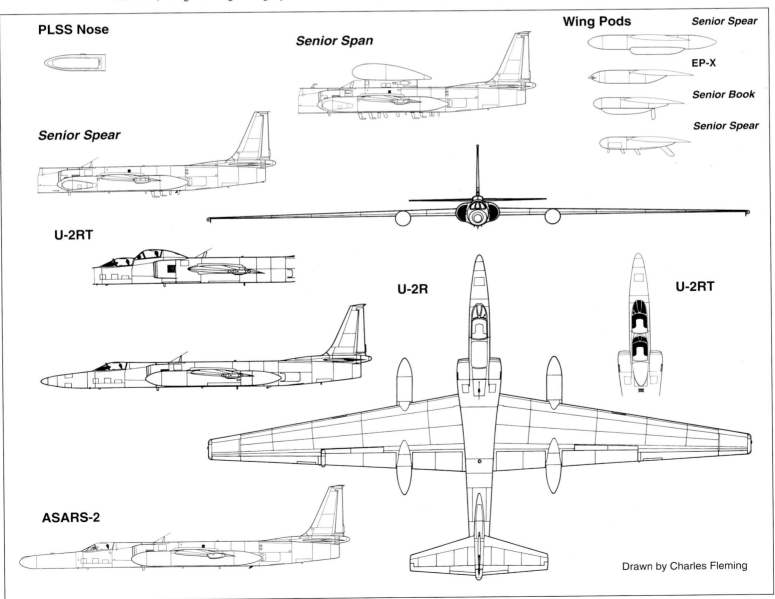

**PLSS Nose**

*Senior Span*

**Wing Pods**

*Senior Spear*

*Senior Spear*

**EP-X**

*Senior Book*

*Senior Spear*

**U-2RT**

**U-2R**

**U-2RT**

**ASARS-2**

Drawn by Charles Fleming

Another view of the first U-2R during the course of its first flight. The aircraft was flown without paint and bearing only its civil registration. Camera port is visible in nose.

and also had a meeting of those who might be involved, to lay out the ground work for the new model. Will make sure that we get better maintainability, electrical system, and service provisions in this airplane. "

The funding situation changed on August 15. "For the past several months, we have continued to do basic engineering on the U-2R. We have been funded for three months study effort, at about $100,000 a month. In July and August we put in almost an equivalent sum of Lockheed money to build a wind tunnel model. There is interest in the bird as a type."

Finally, on September 19, 1966, the Air Force—with the CIA standing quietly in the background—approved construction of one group of U-2Rs and a single static test article. Johnson would note, "Plan to build them in Building 351. Have increased the work force in engineering and have gone over the production plan." Ten days later, giving some indication as to how rapidly the aircraft was evolving, he would write, "Went over electrical systems and antennas, which are very elaborate. I do believe we can get them inside the contour. "

In the meantime, the older operational U-2As and U-2Cs were being attrited with considerable rapidity. On October 8, 1966, Johnson would be given a brief on the status of the U-2 fleet and would write, "We are now down to 18 operational birds from the original fleet."

The U-2R mock-up review took place on November 29, 1966 and few changes were recommended. The first-generation U-2 experience had provided ample opportunity for shortcomings to be acknowledged and analyzed, and this assimilated data had been applied from the very beginning to the new air-

craft. There was little a mock-up review could do to supersede this information resource.

On January 18, 1967 the Air Force approved the construction of more U-2Rs including a static test article. It already had been decided that some of these would be assigned to the CIA and be used in conjunction with the China surveillance program still ongoing in Taiwan. The other aircraft would go straight to the Air Force to supplement what was left of the small and over-burdened first-generation U-2 fleet.

Johnson continued to monitor the status of these early aircraft and on February 8, 1967 noted, "The airplane is now so heavy that the margin between stall buffet and compressibility is only 6 knots at high altitude. We really need the U-2R."

Between Johnson, Cavanaugh, Baldwin, and Ben Rich on propulsion, the new aircraft had evolved into a totally new design offering a 23 feet increase in wingspan (the NACA 64A airfoil remained unchanged, though at one time a supercritical airfoil had been studied); some 400 square feet of additional wing area; a lower wing structural weight of 3 pounds per square foot; an improved L/D of 27 to 1; a totally new and enlarged fuselage providing a substantial increase in internal volume for sensor system and electronic countermeasures system payload (and also permitting the elimination of the protruding oil cooler intakes and the "sugar scoop" modification to the exhaust nozzle); revised and enlarged horizontal and vertical tail surfaces; folding wing tips to permit aircraft carrier accommodation; proper stressing for a tail hook; hydraulically actuated roll (outboard) and lift (inboard) spoilers; a zero-zero ejection seat; a

larger retractable leading edge stall strips; and beefier landing gear to accommodate the large increase in weight. Later, accommodations for large wing-mounted sensor pods (referred to as "super pods") were retrofitted.

The powerplant was the same J75-P-13B found in the U-2C, but it did have miscellaneous internal changes providing improved dependability and some thrust increase. The larger wing also provided a major increase in internal fuel capacity, giving the aircraft an unrefueled range well in excess of 3,000 miles.

The program progressed smoothly, but, as Johnson noted on March 17, "We set up the static test program in a meeting with Dick Boehme, Ray McHenry, Pete Gurin, Ed Baldwin, and Loren Cass. The airplane is coming along quite slowly. This is basically because I have insisted on much better tooling than on prior models and, while it will take us longer to get started, we will get much better airplanes. I am constantly amazed at the size of the airplane as the various pieces begin to come through. We are getting very good workmanship and we appear to be in a sound position on scheduling."

On April 19, he wrote, "The fuselage skins are going on the cockpit area. The wings are beginning to take shape. There are no major problems. The aircraft weight is about 800 pounds over the design goals, about half of it due to added customer equipment." Two months later, he would note, "The first airplane is coming along slowly. Workmanship is dandy. It impresses you with its size. We have the first team on the airplane, and they are doing a really professional job. Nevertheless, it will be a struggle to meet our flight date, as always."

Finally, on August 28, 1967, following several days of static ground tests and taxi tests at the Edwards AFB, North Base facility, the U-2R was flown for the first time, "At 7:58 a.m. Bill Park made the first flight in the U-2R. Schumacher and I chased him in a Twin-Bonanza. There was a good turnout of Headquarters and Air Force people. The aircraft flew well. A very successful day."

On February 1, 1968, the second U-2R arrived at North Base and was immediately incorporated into the flight test program. Approximately one year after the initiation of these tests, the aircraft was declared ready for service introduction. This took place during late 1968 with the beginning of operational CIA-supported and orchestrated flights out of Taiwan. All of the first six aircraft were operated by the CIA, though only two were assigned the Taiwan mission. Two more went to McCoy

A U-2C (left) and a U-2R on the ramp at North Base. The two aircraft were markedly different. Though the U-2R was essentially a one-third bigger version of the U-2A/C, it represented a major improvement in mission capability, payload capacity, range, and crew comfort.

AFB in Florida to fly missions over Cuba and the remaining aircraft stayed at North Base to serve as trainers or undergo maintenance. The first and second Air Force pilots to fly the aircraft, Jack Fenimore and Robert Birkett, respectively, also began flight training at North Base about this same time. They would be on hand when the first Air Force aircraft was delivered during 1969.

The ongoing war in Vietnam, in the meantime, had kept the remaining first-generation aircraft extraordinarily busy. During 1966, the U-2 operating units had been involved in an orgy of renumbering undertaken by SAC in order to preserve some of its more famous unit designators. In consequence, the 4080th was redesignated the 100th SRW and the 4028th became the 349th SRS.

OL-20, assigned to Vietnam, completed no less than 1,000 missions during 1968 and during 1970, it achieved full squadron status as the 99th SRS around the time that the operation was moved—on July 11—to U-Tapao in Thailand. During the ensuing intensive *Linebacker II* aerial bombardment of North Vietnam during the closing months of 1972, U-2 flights were codenamed *Olympic Torch*. With the aforementioned RPVs, it took part in pre- and post-strike reconnaissance activity.

By now a lot of 99th SRS flying time was being devoted to the *Senior Book* program which, with the help of the RPVs, collected intelligence by electronic means from mainland China while remaining at high altitude outside Chinese airspace. *Senior Book* U-2s, modified for what was referred to as "minimally manned" configurations confined the pilot's role to handling the aircraft controls. The payload was exercised remotely.

The phasing-in of the U-2R over Vietnam led to the phasing out of the remaining Air Force U-2Cs. These aircraft, as they were returned to the US mainland, were rapidly removed from the active inventory and placed in storage at Davis-Monthan AFB, Arizona. Johnson's log for 1968 would note, "As of September 30 not much going on with the U-2C. The fleet is gradually degenerating and is down to about fourteen to fifteen usable airplanes.

Three years later, on April 1, 1971 he would summarize the status of the first-generation aircraft by noting, "The U-2Cs have been placed in storage at David Monthan AFB. From time to time there are discussions of using them for NASA programs and other things. This is the last comment in the Log of the U-2."

The Navy, following the successful carrier trials of the U-2A during 1963, had retained its interest in the aircraft and the various options it represented but had not pursued acquisition of a dedicated Navy configuration. A query from the Navy, however, during the fall of 1967 caused the *Skunk Works* to initiate preliminary design studies for the U-2R as a Navy aircraft. These continued into 1969, and by August, a contract covering the cost of actual hardware trials had been signed.

By late September land carrier trials of the U-2R had been successfully completed and *Skunk Works* test pilot Bill Park had been sent to Pensacola, Florida for carrier training with the Navy. Actual carrier trials, aboard the USS *America* (CVA-66) got underway during late November of 1969. As described by Park, the U-2R carrier trial history was as follows:

"The purpose of the landings was to demonstrated the carrier suitability of the U-2R.

*U-2R is seen on the special ground handling trailer at the Skunk Works facility at Palmdale developed to facilitate moving the aircraft during maintenance and systems upgrade events.*

*Test mating the U-2R's aft fuselage and forward fuselage at the Skunk Works Palmdale facility. The Pratt & Whitney J75 engine has yet to be installed.*

Having no experience in carrier landings, I first went to Pensacola for training in the regular T-2B syllabus. I think the most impressive part of the program down there was the students themselves, making carrier landing and cat shots with so little flying experience. I remember after we came back from the carrier, some of the kids asked me what I thought of it. They, of course, were all excited. We, here I was, the big-time test pilot trying to maintain my image, so I said something like, 'Oh nothing to it!' Hell, I'd never seen anything like it in my life!"

Continuing on to the training and preparation phase of the U-2 itself, Park returned to

*U-2R wing nearing final assembly. The wing is "wet" and serves as the aircraft's primary fuel tank. Special sealing procedures had to be developed in consideration of the U-2R's weight limitations.*

*The first TR-1A was rolled out at Lockheed's Palmdale facility during July of 1981. Structurally identical to the U-2R, it differed only in being optimized to carry equipment of a more tactical nature than its U-2R sensor system platform stablemate.*

*In service, all U-2Rs are painted dull black over-all. Serial numbers, spurious or not, are invariably seen in bright red paint on the vertical fin. National insignia are never present.*

*U-2R antenna complements, such as this* Senior Book *configuration for collecting intelligence vary considerably from aircraft to aircraft and are highly dependent on target emitters and mission objectives.*

California and worked with a Navy LSO (Landing Systems Officer) flying FCLPs (Field Carrier Landing Practice) while experimenting with various approaches, using flaps, no flaps, speed brakes, etc. A 45° flap setting was finally selected and an approach speed of 72 knots with 20 knot wind over deck was used for the *USS America* landings. The U-2 has no angle of attack indicator so the approaches were flown relying solely on indicated airspeed and

'feel'.

On the day of the actual carrier trials, Park departed Patuxent River, Maryland and immediately turned east toward the *USS America* located several miles offshore in the Atlantic. Arriving over the boat, he discovered the tailhook would not extend. He was forced to return to Patuxent River to have the safety pin removed.

A quick turnaround soon had the U-2R

back over the ship. A rather anticlimactic series of landings and waveoff demonstrations was then made. "I flew standard approaches and took a cut for the landings with no problem," stated Park. "The airplane demonstrated good waveoff characteristics and I felt at the time that landing could be made without a hook. We required very little special handling and even took the airplane down to the hangar deck. The outer 70 inches of the wings fold and by careful placement on the elevator we could get it in with no problem. One of the things that amazed me was the stability of the ship. The sea was fairly rough but the ship was as smooth and stable as could be."

Four other pilots later were qualified to fly the U-2R from carriers, but little use of this capability was made. As it was, the U-2R's extraordinary unrefueled range made carrier capability all but unnecessary. Among the various US and allied bases, there were few spots on the globe that could not be reached by the U-2R on one load of fuel.

During late 1972, the Navy again initiated a program to explore the U-2R's capabilities...this time as a ship tracking platform. Two U-2R's were loaned to the Navy by the CIA. Interest in using the aircraft for the Navy's EP-X (electronics patrol-experimental) study led to the two being delivered initially to North Base for the modification effort. The program ran for a year. The majority of the test missions were flown off the southern California coast.

The EP-X requirement called for real-time monitoring of maritime and naval ship activity from high altitudes. A forward looking RCA return beam vidicon camera, a UTL ALQ-110 ELINT receiver, and a forward-looking RCA X-band radar (with a range of up to 150 miles; this unit later was replaced by a more capable Texas Instruments AN/APS-116 radar), among other monitoring devices, replaced the more conventional sensor packages. The test program, though modestly successful, did not lead to a follow-on order and the two modified aircraft eventually were returned to Air Force standard.

One final Navy study was generated by the *Skunk Works* before Navy interest turned to other concerns. The U-2R for a while was proffered by the *Skunk Works* in the anti-shipping role. Equipped with anywhere from four to

*Extraordinary high-aspect-ratio wing of the U-2R permits superb high-altitude performance while providing the stability necessary for high-resolution photo reconnaissance. Range also is exceptional ; the U-2 can be gathering intelligence over virtually any spot on earth in a matter of hours.*

fourteen wing pylons and capable of carrying a variety of air-to-surface ordnance, it also had a second crew member position in the Q-bay normally reserved for sensors. Like so many of the U-2 variations before it, this armed model went no further than paper studies and a wind tunnel model.

The last of the original U-2Rs was delivered from the *Skunk Works'* Palmdale facility during December of 1968. As Johnson would note in the log, "We are rapidly running out of work on this program."

By the time of its twentieth anniversary, the Air Force's 100th SRW and its predecessor, the 4080th SRW, had received no less than six Outstanding Unit Citations. This enviable record went with the 100th during March as it moved from Davis-Monthan AFB to Beale AFB, near Sacramento, California. This move was the product of post-Vietnam era budget cuts. The Air Force had elected to consolidate its unique U-2 and SR-71 stables at the Beale facility under the 9th Strategic Reconnaissance Wing umbrella. The old wing and squadron numbers (100th and 349th/350th, respectively) now were assigned to the Boeing KC-135 *Stratotanker* units already at Beale. The 99th would become the designator for the relocated U-2 squadron. This activity officially was completed during October of 1976.

Not all Air Force U-2 missions during the 1970s were military in nature. SAC received and executed various requests from the Forestry Service and the Department of Agriculture, and on numerous occasions participated indirectly in similar non-military high-altitude sensor system-dependent programs such as geothermal energy monitoring, flood control, hurricane surveillance, and tornado damage assessment. Many of these requests were accommodated during normal training flights.

Now that the U-2 squadron was established at Beale AFB alongside that for the SR-71, it became easier to identify which missions were best allocated to each of the two thoroughly dissimilar aircraft—which were nevertheless in the same over-all business. As the Air Force rapidly was losing interest in the complex and expensive *Compass Cope* RPV program, the prospects for increased U-2 employment rose.

*Their versatility and conventional maintenance requirements permit U-2Rs to operate from remote sites around the world. As a result, they can respond to national security needs at a moment's notice.*

*Compass Cope*, an extremely long-range, high-altitude unmanned reconnaissance drone program, had come about as a result of the successes enjoyed by remotely piloted vehicles over Vietnam. The quality of imagery being generated and the quality of the various other intelligence formats gathered, was on par with that being collected by manned systems...at considerably less risk to the controller. Additionally, space and support system normally allocated a pilot or crew member could be utilized for additional sensors, more fuel, or simply a lighter (and thus higher performing) airframe.

Certain elements in the Air Force had become enamored with this approach to intelligence gathering, and had managed to argue, successfully, that such advanced systems were worthy of prototyping. Funding for such programs necessarily had to be bled from other, on-going programs such as the U-2R...and as a result, they became an economic threat to Lockheed.

During January of 1975, upon "Kelly" Johnson's retirement, Ben Rich became the new *Skunk Works* vice president and general manager. Rich and the *Skunk Works* shortly afterwards proposed to the Air Force a U-2R RPV that, it was presumed, could compete with the Teledyne and Boeing *Compass Cope* submissions. The program called for the development of an ultra-high-altitude, ultra-long-range (and thus ultra-long-endurance) remotely-piloted-vehicle that could do basically everything the U-2R could do...but without a man in the cockpit.

Because it was based on an aircraft already in production, Lockheed argued the U-2R RPV could be built cheaper and quicker than either of the Teledyne or Boeing products—while being equally capable. *Compass Cope's* demise during 1977 ended Rich's competitive concerns...and consequently, killed any further interest in an unmanned U-2R spin-off.

During August of 1976, the 99th SRS began detaching U-2Rs to RAF Mildenhall in

*Both optical and electromagnetic sensors are standard payloads for the U-2R. The aircraft's exceptional loiter capability makes it an ideal platform for either.*

*U-2R at Akrotiri, Cyprus. Aircraft is equipped with Senior Spear wing pods. Typical of U-2Rs, this aircraft bears no national insignia. Snoopy on tail is noteworthy.*

*An early production U-2R prior to delivery. Wing-mounted super pod option permitting transport of additional sensors did not surface until the advent of the TR-1A program.*

eastern England with considerable regularity. The detachment became permanent during 1979, with at least one U-2R and two SR-71As on station at all times. These aircraft, usually configured for electronic means of intelligence gathering, flew missions from Mildenhall at very regular intervals. Many of the missions lasted ten hours or more and involved peripheral surveillance along borders of the various eastern European countries and the Soviet Union.

During early 1978, a year after it had been proposed to the Air Force, the first details of the new TR-1A were released. A new-production U-2R with changes in secondary internal systems (i.e., electrical), it was to be adapted to carry a Hughes Advanced Synthetic Aperture Radar System (ASARS) and a UPD-X side-looking airborne radar. The latter, with a range of 50 miles, was optimized for use in the often-times-overcast European theater.

During July of 1977, Lockheed won a full-scale four year development contract for the ill-fated passive Precision Emitter Location Strike System (PLSS). Tested in prototype form on several of the U-2Rs operating in and out of Mildenhall during the period from 1977 through 1980, PLSS was a direct descendent of the earlier *Pave Onyx* and *Pave Nickel* programs offering increases in processing speed and accuracy. The program was canceled during

1987.

As the Iranian crises deepened during 1979 and the US began to expand its military presence in the Indian Ocean, a U-2R was detached to Diego Garcia and there utilized in the Iranian and Indian Ocean surveillance role. Direct overflights provided intelligence of inestimable value in helping the US make decisions of both tactical and strategic importance.

On November 16, 1979, after nearly a twelve year lapse, the U-2 was ordered back into production by the Air Force. The initial *Skunk Works* contract for $10.2 million, called for the refurbishment of the Palmdale, California (Air Force Plant #42) facility's U-2R production tooling that had been in storage at Norton AFB, California since 1969...and the creation of whatever new tooling might be required.

The first TR-1 production contract, for $42.4 million, was for an initial batch of three aircraft, two TR-1B trainers for the Air Force, and an ER-2 (TR-1A) for the NASA. Ultimately, a total of thirty-seven were manufactured on the TR-1 production line, including an additional trainer and another ER-2 for the NASA. The trainers would join the two older U-2CTs that had been in service since the late 1960s.

Following roll-out from Lockheed's Palmdale, California facility during July of 1981, the first TR-1A took to the air for the first time on August 1, with *Skunk Works* test pilot Ken Weir at the controls. Pilot introductory work using the first two aircraft was undertaken later that year and by April of 1982, six TR-1As had been delivered to Beale AFB. The first TR-1B was completed at Palmdale the following January, and after preliminary ground checks, was flown first on February 23 with Lockheed test pilot Art Peterson at the controls.

At the end of March 1981, the British government announced that a TR-1 Wing would be based at RAF Alconbury in England starting in 1983. The support structure for the new outfit, in the form of the 17th Reconnaissance Wing and the 95th Reconnaissance Squadron had officially come into being earlier, on October 1, 1981.

The last TR-1 was delivered to the Air Force from Palmdale on October 3, 1989. Since then, many changes in US military force structure have taken place, including the abolishment of the Strategic Air Command. Though still operating from Beale AFB, California, the 9th Wing now is part of the Air Combat Command. A Detachment, equipped with U-2Rs, still operates from RAF Alconbury north of London, England. During 1991 the Air Force announced that all TR-1-designated aircraft would henceforth be designated U-2R (the TR-1B trainer would be designated U-2RT).

The U-2R and TR-1 were critical contributors to *Desert Shield* and *Desert Storm* operations. They flew with a variety of sensors for high resolution photography, radar mapping, and low light observations. Intelligence agencies, field commanders, the Pentagon and even the President used this information to identify military targets, estimate enemy troop strengths, and make battle damage assessments. Occasionally, U-2R and/or TR-1 products were used to brief news media. The U-2R and TR-1 aircraft flew over 400 sorties and over a thousand hours while deployed to Saudi Arabia. Perhaps the most important post-production improvement ever to be made to the U-2R came about during 1988 under the Production Engine Improvement Program (PEIP) when a *Skunk Works* proposal calling

*U-2R with Nationalist Chinese markings (visible just aft of the extended speed brake). An undisclosed number of U-2Rs were flown by Nationalist Chinese pilots on missions over China and similar countries.*

*Originally referred to by the codename* Senior Stretch, *the* Senior Span *U-2R is optimized to transfer collected data to ground-based analysis centers. The large dorsal fairing contains a small dish antenna permitting transmission of data to virtually any spot on earth equipped with appropriate receiving gear.*

*Several U-2Rs have been converted to the* Senior Span *configuration. Transmission antenna is visible in opened dorsal fairing.*

*Most recent* Senior Span *configuration combines advanced synthetic aperture radar system (ASARS...mounted in nose radome) with data link capability.*

for the replacement of the increasingly insupportable Pratt & Whitney J75-P-13B non-afterburning turbojet with the General Electric F118-GE-101 non-afterburning turbofan (a derivative of the Northrop B-2's F118-GE-100) was approved for demonstration by the Air Force. Flight tests of the 19,000 pound thrust F118 (initially designated F101-GE-29) equipped U-2R began during July of 1989 at Lockheed's Palmdale, California facility with Skunk Works test pilot Ken Weir at the controls. Testing of the prototype engine was completed during 1993 after several phases of engine, airstart system, and airframe compatibility improvements. Since that time, production retrofits have been initiated at Palmdale under a regular depot maintenance program that includes adding a hydrazine airstart system and new electrical power generation systems.

As originally flown, the prototype F101 powered U-2R had no emergency airstart capability. As a result, following the first flight at Palmdale, subsequent first-phase flight testing was accomplished at Edwards AFB in order to be in proximity to the dry lakebeds for emergency landing in the event of engine flameout. Early during the program the aircraft was fitted with a fuel-air stored energy airstart system (Sundstrand-Turbomach) which allowed further testing to be accomplished at Palmdale. During a later phase of flight testing, a hydrazine system (Allied Signal) replaced the fuel-air system.

A production configured reengined U-2R completed its qualification phase of flight test at Palmdale during late 1993. Three U-2Rs incorporating the engine and other upgrades were officially delivered to the Air Force from Palmdale to Beale AFB, California on October 28, 1994. The upgraded aircraft are officially designated U-2S in the single-seat configuration and U-2ST in the two-seat (trainer) configuration. A total of 37 U-2Rs will be brought up to the new standard by the time the retrofit program ends during 1998. NASA's ER-2s also will be upgraded, starting in 1996.

Other upgrades being incorporated into the fleet include: lightweight composite components; a global positioning system; a digital autopilot and air data system; and a variety of reconnaissance sensor improvements. With the significant modernization programs completed and in work, the U-2S will continue to be a highly cost effective and capable reconnaissance asset for the foreseeable future.

### Edwards Air Force Base:

During the late 1950s, while Gary Powers and other CIA pilots were flying U-2s across the Iron Curtain on their secret missions, another group of U-2 pilots nearly ten-thousand miles away was helping perfect the reconnaissance systems of the future in the California desert. They worked for the 6512th Test Group of the Air Force's Air Research and Development Command (ARDC) and their modified U-2As flew from Edwards AFB while supporting a variety of test programs that served to explore the viability of the intelligence community's proposed reconnaissance satellite system.

*The first U-2S at the time of delivery to the Air Force on October 28, 1994, from the* Skunk Works' *U-2 modification facility at Palmdale. This particular aircraft, 80-1071, was first flown on July 25, 1983.*

*The first U-2ST, seen departing Lockheed's Palmdale facility for Beale AFB on October 28, 1994, was originally delivered as a U-2RT.*

*The* Senior Spear *pod system and associated antenna farm is one of the most visually impressive of the many sensor packages capable of being carried by the U-2R.*

*Three U-2RTs (originally TR-1Bs) were built as dedicated U-2R trainers. These aircraft, like the U-2CTs that preceeded them, had two seats and appropriate controls.*

*Two U-2Rs were placed on loan to the US Navy under the EP-X program. The configuration involved significant sensor system modifications but no major airframe changes other than a new nose radome.*

*Senior Lance involved modification to U-2R 68-10339. A Goodyear-developed synthetic aperture radar was installed in the Q-bay and its antenna was housed in a zippered, inflatable ventral radome.*

These programs had been redirected and expanded during 1958 in response to fears the Soviets were opening a significant lead in space. The Soviets already had successfully orbited *Sputnik 1* two months ahead of America's *Explorer 1*, and the missile used to launch the Russian satellite obviously was powerful enough to lift significantly heavier and potentially more lethal payloads.

At this time, Lockheed was in the forefront of the rapidly accelerating US effort to gain a foothold in space. They were prime contractors on the *Agena* second-stage rocket (a product of the Project *Suntan* effort) used to propel satellites into precisely defined orbits, and they also led the team of contractors responsible for developing some of the earliest US reconnaissance and early warning satellites including *Discoverer*, Satellite and Missile Observation System (SAMOS), and Missile Defense Alarm System (MIDAS).

Early tasks for the Edwards-based U-2s concerned work directly related to the *Discoverer* data capsule recovery system. The problems associated with successfully retrieving from orbit a sensor system capsule were enormous and they took many years to overcome.

The service of an entire squadron of Fairchild C-119 (and later, Lockheed C-130) recovery aircraft eventually were required to support the operational requirement of the program. These aircraft were based primarily on Hawaii, and their sole responsibility was the recovery of reconnaissance satellite sensor system payloads.

The Edwards U-2s assisted in perfecting the esoteric art of capsule recovery by carrying mock-up capsules to altitudes of approximately 70,000 feet and ejecting for the practice recovery session below. The dummy capsules, weighing approximately 300 pounds, after being ejected from the U-2 were lowered by parachute for the recovery process. The entire event often was photographed by a chase U-2 flying overhead.

When the actual *Discoverer* launches got underway during 1959, U-2s flew at high cruising altitudes in the recovery zone to photograph and track the reentry vehicles as they returned from space. This work proved of vital importance as it not only helped perfect the art of mid-air capsule recovery, but also permitted the reentry data to be used in the search for suitable *Titan* and *Minuteman* ICBM warhead reentry vehicle shapes.

Three Lockheed U-2Ds were modified to support the MIDAS program in Project *Low Card*, which later was renamed *Smokey Joe*. These aircraft carried an airborne optical spectrometer in a special rotating "pickle-barrel" housing atop the fuselage, behind the cockpit. The cylinder-shaped installation contained a forward-facing lens which could be used to scan for missile exhaust plumes. An observer was carried in the reconfigured Q-bay to monitor incoming data and aim the sensor.

The MIDAS satellites were supposed to provide extended warning from space of a Soviet ICBM attack. Edwards U-2Ds were detached to Patrick AFB, Florida and Ramey AFB, Puerto Rico from where they were used to test MIDAS sensors. US missiles launched from Cape Canaveral were used as practice targets. MIDAS proved unsuccessful and during 1962 the program was terminated. The SAMOS satellite series, also underway at this time, had faired somewhat better. Some excellent photo-reconnaissance results were obtained, including imagery that verified Soviet missile activity first documented by earlier U-2 overflights.

Though the U-2 branch at Edwards, known formally as the 6512th Test Group became known as the *Smokey Joe* detachment for its MIDAS support flights, it also performed many other research tasks, as well. With its now expanded fleet of five aircraft and eight pilots, the assignment became more diverse and included a variety of projects. Among the many were airborne tests of the SAMOS cam-

*Maintenance on U-2Rs at the Skunk Works Palmdale, California facility. Visible in the background are several SR-71As undergoing similar maintenance.*

eras and tests of NASA's *Tiros* and *Nimbus* weather-reporting satellites. During early *Tiros* development, U-2s flew over and photographed at precisely the same time-track of *Tiros* so that a comparative evaluation of the data being returned from the satellite could be made.

Project *Rough Rider* was a thunderstorm research program in which large cumulonimbus clouds were penetrated by test aircraft at various flight levels. *Smokey Joe* U-2s participated in this project by flying above the cloud formations being investigated below by other program aircraft. Late in the project, an instrumentation package developed by the Cambridge Research Laboratories also was carried by U-2s to measure disturbances of the electrical field caused by such thunderstorms. Data obtained with this sensor package was used to assist in the development of a tornado warning system.

The phenomenon of clear air turbulence (CAT) became an issue of considerable concern during the 1960s as a result of a series of aircraft accidents directly attributable to its occurrence. A comprehensive investigation program was initiated to determine its cause and define its characteristics. During 1963, one of the Edwards U-2s was heavily modified under the Hi-Altitude Clear Air Turbulence (HICAT) program to carry extremely sensitive turbulence measuring equipment and associated recording gear.

HICAT research was conducted over several years and took the uniquely marked U-2 initially to Puerto Rico, Alaska, and Panama. The program was extended during 1965, and with improved instrumentation, during October of 1966 visited Fiji, New Zealand, and Australia. The following March it flew missions out of Great Britain.

Although U-2 research flight activities at Edwards were scaled-down during the late-1960s, two aircraft continued to serve the Air Force Flight Test Center in a variety of roles until they were returned to Lockheed during 1978. At that time, they were the last U-2s still flying powered by the original Pratt & Whitney J57 turbojet engine.

### NASA:

As has been mentioned elsewhere in this chapter, NACA's initial involvement in the U-2 story came about at an early stage when the CIA elected to fabricate a cover attributing the aircraft to a NACA mission. Being a civilian agency, NACA's guise would be difficult to destroy in the event of an accident...or so the CIA assumed. This would be compounded by

The most recent advanced synthetic aperture radar system utilized by the U-2R is referred to as ASARS-2. Its avionics are cooled by a heat exchanger visible as an air intake above the nose cone.

the fact the U-2's configuration and stated mission would give every appearance of being non-aggressive.

The U-2 was, in fact, unveiled behind this facade on May 7, 1956, when Dr. Hugh Dryden, then NACA director, issued a six-page press release stating the U-2 to be a new aeronautical research tool developed for the study of turbulence and meteorological conditions. The Dryden release also stated the NACA was running the U-2 program with the technical assistance of the Air Force's Air Weather Service.

The May 7 release, issued on May 22, was followed by another which covered the apparently innocuous transfer of the U-2s to Europe. Great pains were taken to point out the fact the operation was a non-military affair using "civilian planes with civilian pilots". Heavy emphasis was placed on the fact the aircraft were being used for meteorological studies. At the location where the aircraft were flight tested and where the training program was being conducted, most of the U-2s could be seen with the NACA logo on the vertical fin.

As the U-2 overflight effort gathered momentum, it became more and more difficult for the NACA—and later, with the name

The Precision Location Strike System (PLSS) was an unsuccessful attempt to accommodate a tactical military need that remains unfulfilled to this very day. Utilizing a sophisticated radar ground mapping radar, it was designed to accurately locate and track threats and relay the information to friendly attack aircraft.

Initial U-2R carrier trials, using N812X, took place aboard the carrier USS America (CVA-66) during November of 1969.

U-2R modifications were similar to those of the earlier modified U-2As. Most significant was the addition of a retractable tail hook.

**U-2R Carrier/Arresting Gear**

change during 1958—the NASA, to maintain the long-transparent U-2 cover.

The destruction of Gary Powers' aircraft near Sverdlovsk brought an end to the NACA/NASA cover. Within days of Powers' loss, hurriedly written NASA media releases attempted to explain the agency's position in more believable terms. On May 6, 1960, as the Gary Powers debacle emerged like a huge storm on the US diplomatic front, a CIA U-2 was moved from North Base to Edwards AFB main base and placed on display for the media. Visible on its tail was a hurriedly painted NACA logo and a fictitious Air Force serial number.

Hugh Dryden, subsequently, was asked to make a statement to a Senate finance committee. It was noted there had been some 200 flights since 1956 which had carried NASA and Air Force Air Weather Service instrumentation. The flights had logged some 264,000 miles with no less than 90% of the flight time being spent at altitudes above 40,000 feet. Forty-percent of the flight time had been above 50,000 feet. Some of the mileage (which later was raised to 315,000) was almost certainly logged totally by the Air Force with no NACA/NASA involvement whatsoever. In fact, the NASA weather reconnaissance salient that

emanated from the original CIA master plan was undertaken as a by-product of the intelligence flights, rather than as an independent activity.

NASA's work with the U-2 was strictly a CIA paper exercise from 1955 through 1970. However, on April 2, 1971, NASA was at last approved to use the aircraft for scientific purposes. Two U-2Cs, one arriving on June 3 and the other on June 4, were placed on permanent loan by the Air Force. Part of the batch originally operated by the CIA, they were two of the three aircraft that earlier had been modified for carrier trials as U-2Gs.

Johnson would note in the U-2 log, "NASA is interested in using two U-2Cs for the Earth Resources Program. We proceeded to modify the aircraft for their mission and set up a field organization to provide them not only maintenance, but pilots. I hired Marty Knutson, Bob Ericson, Jim Barnes, and "Chunky" Webster to do the flying. They are based at Moffett Field, California but will deploy all over the United States."

NASA's U-2Cs, initially referred to as Earth Resources Survey Aircraft, formed the nucleus of what soon became the NASA High Altitude Missions Branch (HAMB) under the auspices of the Ames Astronautics Directorate. They were assigned the responsibility of conducting data collection flights to support a variety of earth resources projects...particularly the then-forthcoming Earth Resources Technology Satellite program. Importantly, they also participated in numerous disaster assessment flights documenting the effects of wind, rain, and fire.

Besides generating photo imagery, NASA's U-2Cs carried a number of sensor system experiments. Studies ranged from astronomy to stratospheric sampling and earth observation. The aircraft were deployed to locations as diverse as Honolulu, Hawaii; Fairbanks, Alaska; Wallops Island, Virginia; Loring AFB, Maine; and Howard AFB, Panama. They were used to measure the distribution and extent of ozone, nitric oxide, and aerosol particulates in the atmosphere.

The U-2Cs flew missions other than those sponsored by the NASA, as well. Client-supplied and funded projects were carried as often as contracts were obtained. Client's equipment was, of necessity, designed to be accommodated in the U-2C's Q-bay or one of the several other sensor compartments available on the aircraft.

The U-2C's Q-bay was pressurized and heated. It held a maximum of 750 pounds of equipment and was provided with top and bottom hatches that were easily removed by means of external latches. Two wing pods also were available for sensor transport. Each was capable of carrying up to 300 pounds of equipment. An additional 100 pounds of equipment could be supported in the upper fuselage in the

Armed U-2s, including the U-2R, have been studied with considerable intensity by the Skunk Works almost from the inception of the aircraft. This model represents a proposed Navy anti-ship configuration.

*One of the more radical armed U-2s included this U-2R (wind tunnel model) with no less than fourteen underwing pylons for weapons carriage. The weapon variety was extraordinary. Additionally, fixed pods could accommodate sensors, laser designators, or anything else suitable for an envisioned combat role.*

dorsal canoe.

Lockheed's role in the new NASA U-2 operation was not limited to overhauling the aircraft; it secured a contract to provide pilots, physiological support, and maintenance crews. This echoed practices that had been on-going for the CIA from the beginning of the original overflight program.

Marty Knutson, who would guide NASA's U-2 team for the following two decades...and in fact would remain a NASA U-2 pilot until electing to ground himself during 1984...would become project manager. Still later, former CIA pilot and reconnaissance manager Jim Cherbonneaux would be hired to serve as head of the HAMB, and pilots Dick Davies, Jerry Hoyt, and Doyle Krumrey would become part of the team. In turn, they would be joined by Jim Barrilleaux and Ron Williams, among others.

During their long tenure with the NASA, the two U-2Cs were used at a rate of approximately 100 flights per year per aircraft. On June 10, 1982, they were complemented by the arrival of the first ER-2. This aircraft, a demilitarized TR-1A, had been a line item in the NASA budget for some time and had first flown from Palmdale on May 11, 1981 with *Skunk Works* test pilot Art Peterson at the controls. It was in fact, the first aircraft built on the TR-1 production line. It flew its first operational mission two days after its Moffett Field arrival.

The ER-2 offers a marked improvement in payload capacity, endurance, and range over its two U-2C stablemates and also is considerably more comfortable to fly due to its larger and better-equipped cockpit. Payload capacity is in excess of 3,000 pounds and range is in excess of 3,000 miles. Maximum altitude capability is claimed by the NASA to be 78,000 feet

During June of 1987, a long-pending decision to retire the two U-2Cs was consummated with the grounding of NASA 708 after reaching its 10,000th flying hour. It was temporarily replaced by a TR-1A on loan from the Air Force. NASA 708 eventually became a static display item at the Ames visitor's center alongside a one-third scale model of a NASA space shuttle. The remaining U-2C, NASA 709, soldiered on for another two years, but during

April of 1989, it also was removed from the NASA inventory. It sits in the midst of the Warner-Robins AFB, Georgia, museum.

Noteworthy is the fact that NASA U-2 pilot Jim Barnes retired several months prior to the retirement of NASA 709. At the time, he had logged some 5,760 hours in U-2s...which was, and probably still is, the record for type.

Today, two ER-2s and a single TR-1A make up the NASA Ames high-altitude stable. As noted above, the first ER-2 was delivered on June 10, 1981. It was followed by the loaned TR-1A on June 3, 1988, and by the second ER-2 on March 1, 1989.

*NASA's first ER-2, 80-1063/NASA 706, was the first of the final production U-2R (TR-1A) batch to fly. The NASA now has two ER-2's.*

*The ER-2s are stationed at NASA's Ames, California facility where they participate in a wide variety of earth resources and other research programs. These aircraft recently have been redesignated U-2ER.*

The first JetStar, N329J, almost certainly at the end of its first flight on September 4, 1957, with Skunk Works test pilot Ray Goudy and copilot Bob Schumacher at the controls. The flight, which was accomplished without any serious problems, began and ended at Edwards AFB, California.

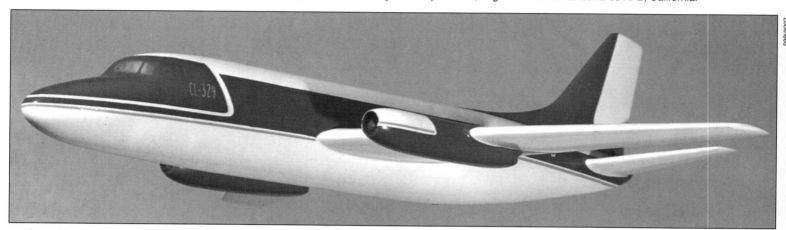

One of the many studies leading up to the definitive, aft-engine, CL-329 JetStar. Superficially resembling a small Boeing 737, this configuration faired-in the engine nacelles into the wing leading edges. Though acceptable, this layout soon was superceded by a more progressive rear engine arrangement.

Drawn by Charles Fleming

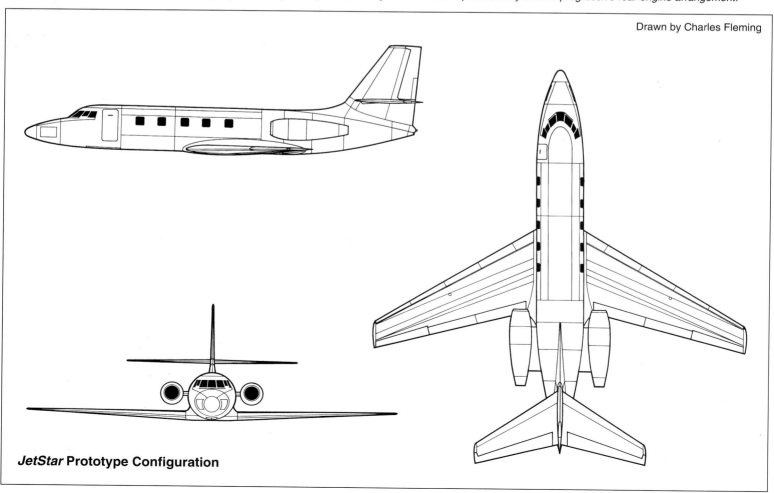

**JetStar Prototype Configuration**

# Chapter 7:
# THE *JETSTAR*

*"The JetStar—made two of them. They were a success as far as the prototypes went. When it was handed over to our Georgia division—here is a case where it wasn't handed over good. It was almost completely redesigned, went to four engines instead of two. The cost almost killed us in the end. But as far as the prototype part of the program goes, it went well."*

**Clarence L. "Kelly" Johnson**

During the latter part of 1955 it became apparent to the Air Force that its aging and somewhat eclectic utility transport and twin-engine training aircraft fleet was in need of replacement with contemporary hardware. Many of the aircraft then in use for these missions could trace their origins back to the pre-World War 2 period. All were powered by reciprocating engines.

Compounding the Air Force's problem was a post-Korean War funding shortfall that severely restricted new aircraft acquisitions. Nevertheless, the service elected to move ahead with long-term plans under the aegis of its UTX (Utility Trainer Experimental) and UCX (Utility Cargo Experimental) specifications. In order to do this, it required that the companies submitting proposals also be willing to fund the their respective prototypes using their own money. Concurrent with its August 1, 1956 Request for Proposals, the Air Force made it understood that, if funding constraints were lifted, it would order up to 300 of the winning design.

Making the new aircraft doubly enticing for manufacturers was the prospect of corporate and commercial sales beyond those to the military. The public market was thought to be sizable and, in the long run, a sufficient justification for three companies to support development internally. North American moved ahead with an aircraft to accommodate the UTX requirement and Lockheed and McDonnell tackled what at first appeared to be the more lucrative, but larger and heavier UCX specification.

"Kelly" Johnson later would note, "With the military as a ready prospect for such a sizable order, we pulled out all the 'stoppers'. We assembled our technical teams, studied the requirements, drew up plans, designed and built."

While the new Model CL-329 was conceived, engineered, and flown in less than eight months, Lockheed had in fact spent some $7 million during the preceding thirteen years studying large jet-powered transport aircraft that involved technology advances directly applicable to its forthcoming utility/training aircraft. As early as 1944, preliminary design

studies had been undertaken to evaluate the application of turbojet engines to commercial airliners. During 1948, earlier studies were discarded in favor of one incorporating four engines in a large, flat pod mounted behind the wing. This was designed with four heavy fore and aft longerons which acted as firewalls and which also could withstand a gear-up landing without suffering serious damage. A great deal of study was put into this design, and many wind tunnel tests were run to evaluate its attributes...versus those of conventional configurations with standard engine nacelles or wing engine pods.

During 1951 and 1952, the engine package was split and moved above the wing. Additionally, engines were staggered at each nacelle. By this time, the design was known in-house at Lockheed as the L-193. A mock-up of the engine installation and cockpit was built and wind tunnel tests of a version with an air intake located above and slightly forward of each wing trailing edge—leaving ample room for a boundary layer bleed system—indicated very satisfactory intake conditions and drag figures.

The basic problem of wing planform had been resolved by this time. Because it was desirable to cruise close to Mach 1 while carrying a large volume of fuel, the swept wing was found superior to a thin straight wing or a delta.

Johnson noted later that he had "certain basic objections to the use of the normal pylon-mounted nacelles, particularly in a low-wing aircraft". He felt there was too little experience with gear-up landings in aircraft that were designed so that the engines became the first parts to contact the ground.

After lengthy analysis, Johnson and the rest of his advanced design team noted the following advantages to a rear engine mounting versus pylon mounting:

(1) Substantially greater safety, particularly in a crash landing.
(2) Substantial advantages in cabin and exterior noise (the fuselage shields some noise effects for many angles around the aircraft).
(3) Excellent drag characteristics.
(4) Protection of the inlets from stones and

ground objects, particularly when the inlet is kept forward of the tailing edge of the wing.

(5) Improved maximum lift, due to the use of uninterrupted flap span.

(6) Substantially simpler systems, in terms of control routing, length of air ducting, electrical leads, etc.

(7) Favorable balance, which results in placing much of the fuselage ahead of the wing, so that more passengers obtain a good view.

(8) When properly placed over the wing, the wing acts as a guide vane to direct the inlet flow. For a change of angle of attack of the aircraft of approximately 19°, the change of angle of attack into the nacelle is less than 3°.

(9) the high location of the inlet in a protected location provides safety to the ground crew members when walking around the aircraft when engines are running.

(10) The ditching characteristics are improved by not having the nacelles located where they can dig into the water.

(11) A failed turbine wheel cannot go through the pressurized area of the fuselage or fuel tanks.

(12) The offset thrust after losing an engine is very low, so that an improved one-engine-out climb and control are available. Holding in a traffic pattern can readily be done with one-half of the normal powerplants out of operation, as all aircraft flight characteristics remain essentially unchanged.

They also noted contradicting arguments in favor of pylon-mounted wing nacelles as follows:

(1) The engine weight is not available for reducing wing bending moments and acting as a flutter counter-balance.

(2) Lighter structural weight with wing nacelles is claimed.

(3) When the double fuselage pod is used, a failure of a turbine disc in one engine might knock out the other.

While design development of the L-193 progressed smoothly during 1953, attempts were made by Lockheed to elicit interest, and possible sales, from the various airlines. Some, such as *Pan American* and *Air France*, reacted favorably, but no orders were received.

*One of the distinct disadvantages of the underwing engine placement was their susceptibility to foreign object damage.*

*The prototype JetStar was flown unpainted, bearing only its civil registration (N-329J) and the company name above the cabin windows.*

*"Kelly" Johnson played a key role in the design of the JetStar and considered it one of his more successful efforts.*

*The prototype JetStars were powered by two Bristol Orpheus turbojets. The second aircraft later would be reengined with four Pratt & Whitney JT12As.*

This unexpectedly poor commercial response, coupled with the significant financial risk entailed in the development of the 280,000 pound jet airliner, proved the deterrent that initially kept Lockheed out of the large turbojet passenger aircraft market.

When, during 1956, the Air Force informed industry there was a military requirement for a small jet transport to meet its UCX and UTX specifications, Johnson and his *Skunk Works* team, with corporate approval, immediately initiated preliminary design studies based on a small-scale L-193 variant. In particular the attributes of the jet flap principle and its ability to improve takeoff and landing characteristics were explored. While there was apparently an improvement in maximum lift available, the over-all outcome of the study showed there were insufficient benefits to warrant application of this propulsion/lift system to the aircraft proposal Lockheed eventually would submit to the Air Force.

The Air Force letter inviting manufacturers to present utility transport designs specified the desired payload, range, field length performance, certain items of radio, and various equipment. The UCX specification, which Lockheed had elected to pursue, called for a four-engine aircraft capable of carrying ten passengers and a crew of two for a distance of 1,500 nautical miles at a cruising speed of 435 knots at altitudes up to 45,000 feet. At overload weight and using external tanks, a range of 2,200 nautical miles against a 70 knot headwind was required. The latter was the hardest requirement to fulfill, because, including the required reserves, an equivalent still air range of over 3,200 statute miles had to be obtained.

The smaller UTX transport was to be a twin-engine aircraft, roughly half the size of the UCX, in the same basic performance category, but with reduced range. Both aircraft would have to be capable of meeting military and Civil Aeronautics Authority structure and performance requirements.

Lockheed decided to built two prototypes to the UCX specification in its special projects department. Johnson had concluded that, in order to expedite development of the aircraft, *Skunk Works* operating procedures would have to be applied. A schedule of eight months was determined necessary to accommodate initiation of construction through first flight. It was considered of primary importance to demonstrate a flight article in advance of any competition and to have a long background of development testing prior to going into production. Johnson felt "the best way to control cost and get a good product was by using a *few* good people and a tight schedule..."

The major stumbling block, from the very beginning of the program, was availability of an American made, small, lightweight jet engine. The General Electric J85 and Fairchild J83 still were under development and were not expected to be flight rated until long after the prototype airframe was ready to fly. Accordingly, Johnson decided that in order to get the CL-329 into the air at the earliest possible date, it would be necessary to power it with British-built 4,850 pound thrust Bristol *Orpheus* 1/5 turbojets. Two of these engines, which were scheduled to enter production in the US as the Curtiss-Wright TJ37A1, produced the same amount of thrust as four of the General Electric or Fairchild engines.

Johnson later would express extraordinary admiration for the *Orpheus*, "They were so good that it was decided at an early date to make all *JetStars* from serial number two up capable of using either two *Orpheus* engines, four J85s or J83s or, four Pratt & Whitney JT12A units. The design flexibility of the fuselage pod mounting is so good that this could be done at a built-in weight penalty of only 35 pounds. Whenever any of the small engines are available, a four-engine *JetStar* can be built. The *Orpheus* version, however, is fully competitive in performance (except with one engine out) and will be offered to those who want its lower cost, simplicity, and, at least for some time, its better reliability."

The day Johnson got the go-ahead on the CL-329, he had a red and white sign posted in the *Skunk Works* Burbank shop (Plant B-6) that stated, "First flight 9 a.m., Sept. 4, 1957—241 days left." Design work was initiated on January 7, 1957. Eventually some 350 personnel, including project engineer Dick Boehme and shop superintendent Art Viereck, were involved in design and construction.

During the 241 days Johnson had allocated to build the first CL-329, the *Skunk Works* team accomplished many significant design breakthroughs, not the least of which was that for the aircraft's tail. Utilizing features developed for the XF-90, the horizontal tail was rigidly attached to the vertical fin. The fin, in turn, was attached to fuselage by a pin through the rear spar, while an actuator raised and lowered the fin leading edge to change the stabilizer trim setting and, coincidentally, the fin sweep angle. This design gave a very clean intersection with no leakage and allowed a better structural condition for taking out asymmetrical tail loads.

In order to meet range requirements, two sets of external tanks were developed. These were mounted at the wing mid-span position. The smaller tanks had a 300-gallon capacity and the larger tanks had a 700-gallon capacity.

Following roll-out on August 1, the first CL-329, by now formally named *JetStar*, was disassembled (the wings and tail section were removed) and transported by truck to Edwards AFB where it was reassembled—over a period of a week—in preparation for its maiden filght. "The aircraft arrived at Edwards just one week prior to the first flight, and we worked around

*The second JetStar was registered N329K. It was virtually identical to the first and was similarly equipped with Bristol Orpheus engines when first flown.*

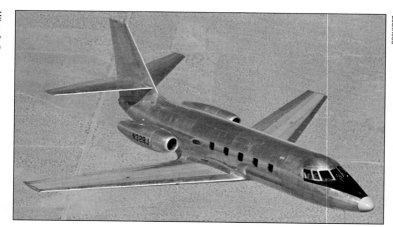

*All initial flight test work on the JetStar prototypes took place at Edwards AFB. Few problems were encountered and the test program went smoothly.*

the clock doing final assembly and the necessary preflight checkouts and engine runs," recalled flight test engineer Bob Klinger during a recent interview, "I remember the speed brake was installed for the first time at 3 a.m., just six hours before the first flight." The seats made it in just ten *minutes* before the first taxi runs.

Chosen for the first flight were Ray Goudey, pilot; Bob Schumacher, copilot; and Ernie Joiner as flight test engineer. All three were veterans of the *Skunk Works'* U-2 flight test program.

On the morning of Wednesday, September 4, 1957, the first *JetStar* taxied out onto the Edwards AFB dry lakebed. A short distance off the *JetStar's* wingtip was a chase T2V-1 piloted by Tony LeVier. Sitting in the back seat was "Kelly" Johnson.

At 8:58 a.m., the *JetStar* became airborne for the first time. It had met Johnson's September 4 first flight deadline and had beaten by two minutes the predicted 9:00 a.m. departure time. The aircraft was airborne for 39 minutes.

Flight testing of the CL-329 went well. Air Force Phase II testing was completed during February of 1958 using the first aircraft, and it was determined that the *JetStar* had excellent flight and performance characteristics. During some 300 hours of flight time, the first aircraft reached altitudes as high as 52,000 feet, speeds of 630 mph, Mach numbers of 0.92 clean and 0.90 with the large external tanks installed, and stall speeds of under 100 mph. Eventually, some 600 hours of testing were logged by both prototypes prior to the decision to commit the aircraft to production.

Ray Goudey, during a 1993 interview, looked back on his experiences with the prototype JetStar with considerable fondness. In recalling the aircraft, he noted, "I continued to fly it on and off until August 12, 1982, when its last flight was made delivering it to Canada. I accumulated 403 hours in one of the best aircraft I have flown." Goudey flew over 70 Lockheed aircraft types prior to his retirement from Lockheed.

On June 17, 1958, the first *JetStar* embarked on a promotional trip to demonstrate its transcontinental range and high cruising speeds. As Johnson later recalled, "I was along on its long-range flight demonstration. We flew at 40- to 50-thousand feet from Edwards AFB, California to McChord AFB, Washington, to Westover AFB, Massachusetts, McCoy AFB, Florida, and finished up back home at Edwards AFB. In all, we covered 6,700 miles in 18 hours. At 20,000 feet the

two-jet *JetStar* could hit a level speed of 610 mph."

The promotional trip, referred to by Lockheed as the "Home Run" flight, resulted in landings at bases strategically located at each "corner" of the US. *Skunk Works* personnel who participated in the flight included Ray Goudey, pilot; Bob Schumacher, copilot; Ernie Joiner, flight test engineer; Jerry Carney, shop manager, Bob Klinger, flight test engineer; and Johnson.

Unfortunately, though the demonstration tour proved a success, a national recession dictated the Air Force delay its plans to acquire the aircraft for operational service. Concurrent with this decision, during November of 1958, Lockheed's corporate offices elected to move JetStar production to Marietta, Georgia. This eliminated Burbank, and consequently, the *Skunk Works*, from the *JetStar* picture. And as a result of the Air Force's intransigence concerning four engines versus two (and its insistence that any engine used be of US manufacture and origin), during January of 1959 Pratt & Whitney JT12A turbojets were selected to power the *JetStar* in its production configuration. Four engines—per the original Air Force specification—would be used with two mounted in each of two fuselage-mounted pods.

The four-engine configuration first was tested using the second prototype JetStar. This aircraft in modified form, flew for the first time during January of 1960. The Pratt & Whitney engines proved a good, though expensive choice, and a decision to fit them to all production aircraft killed any further plans to equip the JetStar with the TJ37.

*Skunk Works* involvement with the *JetStar* had come to an end during mid-1958. Production and further development of the aircraft had been transferred to Lockheed's Marietta, Georgia division with little difficulty. During May of 1958 it had been announced the *JetStar's* unit price was expected to be $1 million per aircraft . Production then was expected to begin at Marietta on July 1 with first roll-out then scheduled for November of 1959. Production was expected to accelerate to 10 aircraft per month about two years after the initial Air Force go-ahead. These predictions would prove woefully optimistic.

On October 31, 1958 the *JetStar* was picked by the Air Force over North American's NA-246 submission to meet the requirements of the UTX specification...which Lockheed had not originally planned to accommodate. During October, the Air Force announced its plan to acquire the Lockheed aircraft under the designation T-40A. Shortly afterwards, however, it

withdrew the initial decision and awarded the contract to North American...for what became the T-39A *Sabreliner*. Eventually, two-hundred and eleven trainer and light transport *Sabreliners* would be acquired by the Air Force and Navy...while Lockheed's *JetStar* starved for orders. It was not until June of 1960 that an initial Air Force order for five *JetStars* (to serve as navigation aids checkers for the air traffic control system) finally arrived. The first of these, by now referred to as C-140A by the Air Force, was delivered during April of 1961.

On August 29, 1961, the *JetStar* was awarded a fully approved Type Certificate by the Federal Aviation Agency in accordance with Parts 4b and SR 422B of the Civil Air Regulations. This Type Certificate signified that the *JetStar* met all requirements established for the certification of civil passenger transport aircraft, and meant that fail-safe structural features and performance safety margins required in airline transports were included in the *JetStar*. Initial *JetStar* deliveries finally occurred during September of 1961.

By January of 1962, Lockheed, having spent $100 million on the *JetStar* program, was facing an $80 million loss. This was attributable to the Air Force's initial indications it would buy some 300 aircraft when in fact, by mid-January of 1962 it had bought only sixteen. Total sales, including corporate (a Navy order for two UV-1s eventually was canceled), then totaled only 43 aircraft. At the then current roll-out rate of two aircraft per month, it was taking Lockheed about nine months plus interior installation time to build a *JetStar*. It was estimated that 300 aircraft would have to be sold in order for the company to break even.

When *JetStar* production ended during 1980 with the delivery of the 204th and last aircraft to the Iraqi government, Lockheed had lost a considerable quantity of money but had learned some very valuable business lessons. The aircraft, regardless of its financial status, proved to be a successful corporate transport. Several versions eventually were built by Lockheed, including the C-140A, the C-140B, and the VC-140B for the military, and the *JetStar 6*, the *JetStar 8*, and the *JetStar II* for the corporate market. The type gave birth to a sizable after-market industry as well, with AiResearch Aviation Company, American Aviation Industries, and K. C. Aviation, among others, offering engine, interior, and systems upgrades to meet ongoing customer needs. Approximately 150 of the 204 aircraft manufactured remain in operational service as of this writing.

*The first JetStar served as the Lockheed corporate jet for a considerable period of time following its use as a prototype. It eventually was donated to a trade school in Canada for use as a maintenance trainer.*

**CL-400-10**

*Representing one of the few major programs undertaken by the Skunk Works that did not reach the full-scale hardware stage, the CL-400, or Project Suntan, was nevertheless a successful exercise in engineering and a precedent setting accomplishment in the field of propulsion.*

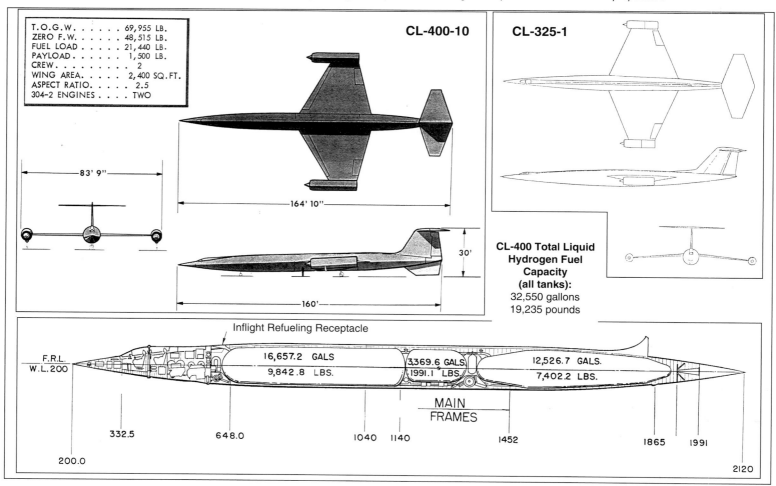

**CL-400-10**

| T.O.G.W. | 69,955 LB. |
|---|---|
| ZERO F.W. | 48,515 LB. |
| FUEL LOAD | 21,440 LB. |
| PAYLOAD | 1,500 LB. |
| CREW | 2 |
| WING AREA | 2,400 SQ. FT. |
| ASPECT RATIO | 2.5 |
| 304-2 ENGINES | TWO |

83' 9"
164' 10"
30'
160'

**CL-325-1**

**CL-400 Total Liquid Hydrogen Fuel Capacity**
**(all tanks):**
32,550 gallons
19,235 pounds

Inflight Refueling Receptacle

F.R.L.
W.L. 200

16,657.2 GALS
9,842.8 LBS.

3,369.6 GALS.
1991.1 LBS.

12,526.7 GALS.
7,402.2 LBS.

MAIN
FRAMES

200.0    332.5    648.0    1040  1140    1452    1865   1991    2120

106

# Chapter 8:
# HYDROGEN FUEL AND *SUNTAN*

*"CL-400 I can talk about, in view of the fact that I think things are declassified after 12 years, it says on the cover a liquid hydrogen airplane. We were well into that model. Fifteen miles of extrusion in the plant, ready to nail 'em together. The cost performance was good. It was a total failure because of poor concept due to logistics. How did you ever haul enough liquid hydrogen anyplace in the world to exploit the short range of the airplane? It had a ceiling of well over 100,000 feet on paper. And it failed because we would not promise the government that it had any performance stretch in it. Neither could we nor Pratt & Whitney, who made the first true hydrogen cycle engine. As far as I know, this was the first time in which Skunk Works procedures were used to build a complete new engine of a modern type."*

**Clarence L. "Kelly" Johnson**

The use of hydrogen as a propellant for aircraft powerplants first surfaced in the US as a viable fuel option near the end of World War 2. A most noteworthy study, conducted by Alexis Lemmon, Jr. of the Office of Scientific Research and Development (OSRD) initiated during 1944 and released during May of 1945, concluded the combination of liquid hydrogen and liquid oxygen offered the highest specific impulse (thrust divided by total propellant flow rate; i.e., the amount of energy generated per quantity of propellant consumed) of any of the many propellants examined.

Lemmon's book became the primary postwar propellant reference and proved particularly timely in light of the many different propulsion options being explored during the immediate post-World War 2 period. German experiments with liquid oxygen and the subsequent evolutionary development of liquid hydrogen, led to the exploration of these fluids as a rocket oxidizer and propellant, respectively. The successes realized were significant, but were achieved with considerable difficulty due to the severe logistical problems surrounding their production, containment, handling, and transport.

A variety of research programs, mostly under the auspices of Ohio State University operating with an Air Force contract, generated a considerable quantity of data related to the use of hydrogen fuel. Though the study concluded hydrogen was a viable option, nothing in the way of full-scale, flightworthy hardware initially was tested.

Concurrent with the Air Force effort, the Navy also pursued the use of hydrogen as a propellant, though specifically as it might be applied to a rocket for launching satellites into near-earth orbit. Retained to do the Navy's research were the Jet Propulsion Laboratory and Aerojet Engineering Corporation which presciently concluded that satellites were feasible and liquid hydrogen-based propulsion systems were practical powerplants.

Word of this effort eventually surfaced in Air Force circles and it was not long before similar studies, undertaken by the RAND Corporation and funded by the Air Force, reached similar conclusions. Aerojet Engineering, the Glenn L. Martin Company, and North American Aviation now contracted both with the Air Force and the Navy to build prototype liquid-hydrogen powerplants and study how they might be used in future satellite launch vehicles. By 1949, both Aerojet Engineering and the Jet Propulsion Laboratory had successfully tested rudimentary liquid hydrogen rockets.

This initial effort proved fruitless, due in part to national economic difficulties and a short-sighted military bureaucracy, but the data

base generated held the industry in good stead until the political climate was forced to change during 1950 as a result of military pressures in Korea and elsewhere. By now, the National Advisory Committee for Aeronautics (NACA) had initiated research into the use of hydrogen as a propulsion system fuel, and several national advisory groups, including the Scientific Advisory Board, had either directly or indirectly expressed interest in further exploring its unique properties.

On March 24, 1954, Randolph Rae, a British engineer, hand carried to the Air Force's new developments offices at Wright Field a proposal he had drafted calling for the development of an aircraft powered by a unique liquid-hydrogen fueled engine he had patented called the *Rex I*. Basically a rocket-type gas generator driving a turbine...which in turn, through a geared transmission, drove a propeller, it required liquid hydrogen and liquid oxygen for fuel and oxidizer. The aircraft for which this engine was designed, described by Rae as "a lightly loaded low-speed plane having an exceptional L/D (lift over drag) characteristic," was optimized to cruise at an altitude in excess of 75,000 feet at a speed of about 500 mph.

Though the combined performance figures were stunning, to say the least, the item of greatest interest to the Wright Field personnel reviewing the proposal was the *Rex I* engine. Over a period of time encompassing reviews by the Air Research and Development Command (ARDC) and many individuals at the Wright Air Development Center, the Rae proposal, and in particular, the *Rex I* engine, became items of considerable controversy.

*Though of extremely poor quality, this is one of the few extant images of the CL-400 mock-up.*

Rae's proposal could not have arrived at Wright Field at a more awkward time. Its broad impact was due in part to the fact it addressed timely issues in many Wright Field offices, not the least of which were those investigating the development of new powerplants, high-altitude airframes, the use of hydrogen fuel, and various subsystems that required high-altitude capability.

During the review of Rae's documents, Wright Field personnel voiced concerns over Rae's ability to bring the hardware to fruition, even in light of his formal association with the Summers Gyroscope Company. In the interim, a subdued but intense battle between the government, Rae, and the Garrett Corporation...which had quietly acquired Summers Gyroscope's interest in the Rae engine in order to obtain access to the *Rex I* patent, surfaced. This tug-o'-war would continue throughout the rest of the *Rex* engine's life.

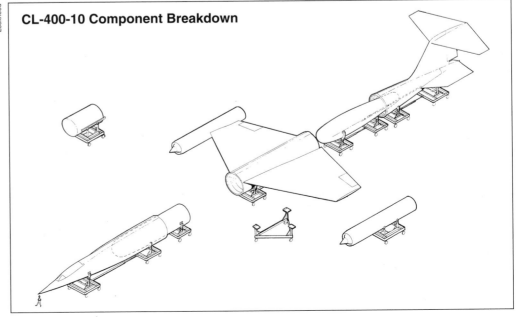

**CL-400-10 Component Breakdown**

Lockheed and the *Skunk Works* first entered this picture during mid-1954, when it was noted in the original Rae proposal that Lockheed would be provided $50-thousand for airframe analysis. Concurrently, work was getting underway in the *Skunk Works* on the Model CL-282...which as noted in Chapter 7 would lead to development of the definitive U-2 reconnaissance aircraft. As this latter program progressed under the direction of the Central Intelligence Agency, Air Force analysts at Wright Field already had deduced its ability to safely execute a mission over unfriendly territory would be time limited as a result of expected advances in anti-aircraft technology and the unknown dependability of the airframe, the powerplant, and experimental electronic countermeasures systems. Even before the U-2's first flight, the Air Force already was assessing replacement options.

During 1954, as work on the first U-2 progressed, of particular concern to Johnson was the problem of fuel loss from evaporation at high altitudes...and the adverse affect this would have on the aircraft's range. Consultations with the Air Force and Pratt & Whitney (builders of the U-2's J57-PW-37 turbojet engine) confirmed that conventional JP4 fuel would slowly evaporate as a result of "boiling" at the altitudes the U-2 was expected to achieve in cruising flight. A low-volatility fuel developed by Shell Oil Company solved the problem, but perhaps more importantly, the meetings leading up to its development also served to expose Johnson to the attributes of hydrogen.

By mid-1955, Rae and Garrett's problems with the Air Force had led to a stalemate resulting from the former's wish to execute both the airframe and powerplant development and the latter's desire to split the program into separate airframe and powerplant components (which was, in reality, the standard approach). Personal issues of patent infringement and division of work responsibility only added to the confusion, and it was not until October of 1955 that contracts finally were let.

Though Rae and the Garrett Corporation assumed their initial problems now were resolved, the actual work statement from Wright Field, when it arrived several weeks later, only served to reopen old wounds. Their belief the proposed aircraft would be a high-altitude, long-range subsonic design had been

mistaken; the Air Force contract called for a supersonic aircraft...with range of secondary importance. Lurking in the background, as it turned out, was the Air Force's desire to create a replacement for the Central Intelligence Agency's still-untried Lockheed U-2.

Garrett, not wanting to forego the funding that had been allocated by the Air Force for the *Rex* engine (by now there were three jet versions being offered, including one for a supersonic cruise aircraft) elected to pursue an airframe study that had been given Rae during the negotiation process. A "Problem Statement for Aircraft Studies" dated November 7, 1955 resulted, and Lockheed's Johnson, because of the initial airframe negotiations conducted during mid-1954, was invited to provide airframe input under a *Skunk Works* contract. Garret would provide size, weight, thrust, and specific fuel consumption figures to Lockheed, as well as engine pod dimension and technical data.

The *Skunk Works* engineering team, upon reviewing the Garrett data, concluded the proposed engines were not capable of providing the thrust levels required to meet the Air Force's performance specification. Agreements were reached with Garrett on extrapolation of the data for engines of larger thrust, and specific fuel consumption as a function of Mach number. A cruise speed of Mach 2.25 was determined obtainable with engines providing 50% more thrust than those originally specified.

The resulting powerplant size increase now forced the Air Force to reevaluate Garrett's ability to build such an engine. The company had long been noted for small, auxiliary power unit-type turbine engines but had never built anything of the size now specified for the proposed hydrogen fueled airplane.

Lockheed's *Skunk Works* study, released during January of 1956, contained two configurations for consideration. Both were powered by *Rex III* engines...which were optimized for supersonic flight. The first, referred to as the CL-325-1, had a straight, thin wing and a long, slender fuselage containing a single liquid hydrogen tank. The second, the CL-325-2, was smaller as a result of the use of jettisonable wing tanks to accommodate part of the liquid hydrogen load. Both were of conventional aluminum construction.

Information describing the two CL-325 configurations and the proposed *Rex III* engine

was presented to the Air Force at Wright Field on February 15, 1956. The Air Force's reaction was unfavorable, not because of the quality of the presentation, but rather because the *Rex III's* complexity was great and the ready availability of liquid hydrogen was decidedly questionable. Because of what now was perceived as an urgent need, Garrett's ability to design and produce an engine as complex as the *Rex III* in a "crash" program was considered highly unlikely. Though the company strongly contested these conclusions, on October 18, 1956, the Air Force issued a directive demanding that all *Rex* engine and all CL-325 work be stopped except for completion of a final summary report.

Interest in hydrogen as an aircraft fuel did not die with the demise of the *Rex* engine program. Behind the scenes, other related programs had begun to gather momentum. A year before the *Rex's* demise, following the completion of the various airframe design studies for Rae and the Garrett Corporation, "Kelly" Johnson and his *Skunk Works* team had begun hydrogen fueled aircraft studies of their own in response to a continuing Air Force interest in developing a U-2 follow-on. During a Pentagon meeting with Lt. Gen. Donald Putt in early January of 1956—as the *Rex* program difficulties mounted—Johnson offered to build two prototype hydrogen-fueled aircraft powered by more conventional propulsion units. He guaranteed a first flight date within 18 months of contract signing. The proposed aircraft—based on the CL-325—would be capable of cruising at an altitude of 99,384 feet and a speed of Mach 2.5 while having a range of 2,529 miles.

The Air Force—already somewhat frustrated at having to play a supporting role in the Central Intelligence Agency's U-2 operation—did not hesitate to confirm their strong interest in this latest *Skunk Works* offering...which potentially could serve as an Air Force-managed U-2 replacement. On January 18, 1956, Lt. Gen. Putt called a meeting to discuss the proposal with Lockheed representatives. In attendance were Lt. Gen. Clarence Irvine, then deputy chief of staff for materiel; Lt. Gen. Thomas Power, then head of the ARDC; and Col. Norman Appold, then head of the Wright Air Development Center's powerplant laboratory.

During the meeting it was decided to fund Air Force studies to verify the feasibility of

*Heavily insulated liquid hydrogen tank test specimen being installed in a simulated CL-400 center fuselage section.*

*One-third scale CL-400 wing and associated control surfaces was heavily instrumented for vibration and structural tests.*

Johnson's proposal and to select a qualified manufacturer to design and develop a hydrogen-fueled engine. Appold, who was assigned the task of determining the latter, quickly narrowed the field to General Electric and Pratt & Whitney. Each company then was given two weeks to put together a proposal. By February 20, the proposals had been received and reviewed; the Pratt & Whitney design was chosen for further study. A six month contract was signed on May 1, and on the same date, Lockheed was similarly given a study contract to pursue airframe configuration and materials options. As both companies already had initiated design work on their own, when the contracts were negotiated they were made retroactive to cover already incurred costs.

Lt. Col. John Seaberg, who by this time already had made his mark as a key figure in the U-2 program, now became involved in the new hydrogen fueled aircraft project, directly under Appold. Seaberg would be responsible for airframe development and total program coordination. He would be assisted by Maj. Alfred Gardner, who would manage engine development, and Capt. Jay Brill, who would manage logistics. The team worked initially at Wright Field before moving to ARDC headquarters in Baltimore, Maryland during mid-1956.

Only twenty-five people were given access to the new program. Specially classified higher than "Top Secret" and codenamed *Suntan*, it was considered militarily and politically sensitive primarily because its mission objectives required overflights of "unfriendly" territory. Additionally, in order for Lockheed's *Skunk Works* to design and build the proposed prototypes in the shortest possible time, it was considered necessary for a "no-constraints" environment to be created and maintained. Access to the program implied scrutiny, and scrutiny implied committee reviews, changes, and increased cost. In essence, and per previous *Skunk Works* practice, it was determined that "too many cooks would spoil the broth". Authorities allowing the *Suntan* team to waive normal procurement procedures and to award contracts directly with minimal review became part of this process. It later was estimated months were cut from the procurement process as a result.

Extraordinary measures were taken to conceal *Suntan* from unauthorized personnel. The ARDC's *Suntan* team periodically changed project numbers, contracts were written through other Air Force offices, and in Burbank, *Suntan* workers in the *Skunk Works* were isolated and guarded from other units and

A Pratt & Whitney Model 304 hydrogen expander engine. Several versions of this engine, each improved over the preceeding model, were built and statically tested by Pratt and Whitney at their Florida facility.

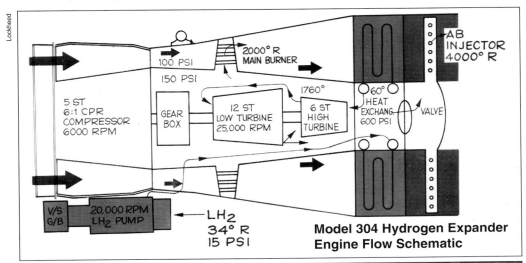

Model 304 Hydrogen Expander Engine Flow Schematic

Lockheed built this dedicated hydrogen fuel test facility at the Burbank plant. Research using liquid hydrogen in real-world environments was conducted here with considerable intensity.

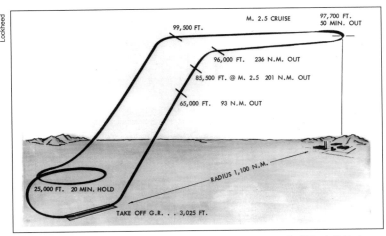

Typical CL-400 mission included a cruise to target speed of Mach 2.5 at an altituded of 90,000 feet. These were impressive figures for the late-1950s.

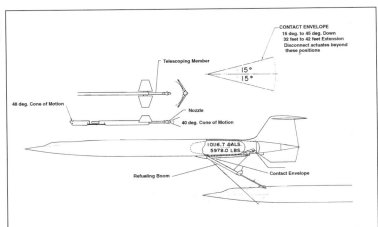

Among the numerous studies conducted during the course of CL-400 development was inflight refueling...perhaps a first for a hydrogen fueled aircraft.

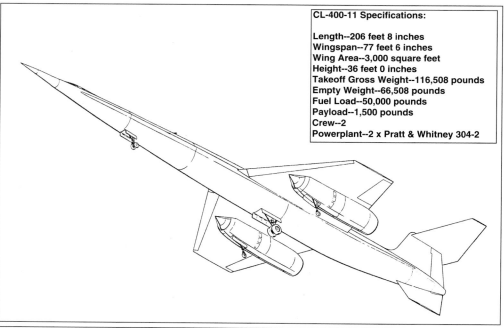

Lockheed

CL-400-11 Specifications:

Length--206 feet 8 inches
Wingspan--77 feet 6 inches
Wing Area--3,000 square feet
Height--36 feet 0 inches
Takeoff Gross Weight--116,508 pounds
Empty Weight--66,508 pounds
Fuel Load--50,000 pounds
Payload--1,500 pounds
Crew--2
Powerplant--2 x Pratt & Whitney 304-2

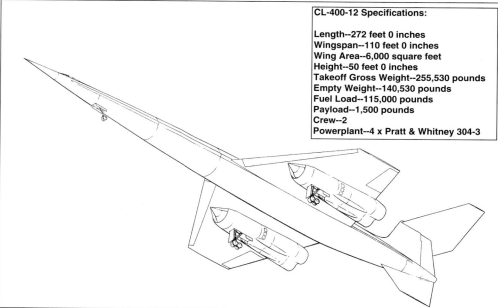

Lockheed

CL-400-12 Specifications:

Length--272 feet 0 inches
Wingspan--110 feet 0 inches
Wing Area--6,000 square feet
Height--50 feet 0 inches
Takeoff Gross Weight--255,530 pounds
Empty Weight--140,530 pounds
Fuel Load--115,000 pounds
Payload--1,500 pounds
Crew--2
Powerplant--4 x Pratt & Whitney 304-3

utilized conventional intake air for the combustion process and liquid hydrogen for fuel. Relatively inefficient, it gave the CL-400 a range of only 2,500 miles...an *Achilles* heel from which the program would never recover.

Pratt & Whitney's design and development work on the Model 304 engine was accommodated at the company's facility in East Hartford, Connecticut. The first engine was completed on August 18, 1957 and shortly was shipped to the company's newly completed factory in West Palm Beach, Florida. Model 304 static tests were initiated there on September 11, 1957 using nitrogen to check the fuel system and rotating machinery such as bearings and seals. Gaseous hydrogen and liquid hydrogen shortly afterwards were used as fuels. The first run series lasted through October and resulted in 4-1/2 hours of running time including 38 minutes on liquid hydrogen. A second run series was started on December 20 following inspection .

Additional runs were continued into July at which time a major bearing, turbine, and heat exchanger failure effectively destroyed the engine. A second Model 304-1 had been placed on the static test stand several months after the first, with a first run being undertaken on January 16, 1958. Work with this engine continued into April, at which time it was disassembled for inspection. An improved engine, the Model 304-2 was run for the first time on June 24, 1958, followed by another Model 304-1 test series and the delivery of several additional test engines in various configurations. In all cases, the tests went exceptionally well and the Air Force and Pratt & Whitney began to have considerable confidence in hydrogen fueled powerplants.

While airframe and powerplant work continued at Lockheed and Pratt & Whitney, the logistical problems associated with the production and transport of liquid hydrogen were confronted by the Air Force's *Suntan* team and Lockheed's *Skunk Works* operation. Special trailers, designated U-1 and U-2 were designed and built by the Cambridge Corporation and a special hydrogen liquefaction plant was placed in operation near Pratt & Whitney's Florida plant during the fall of 1957, and operated under contract by the Air Products Corporation. Two years later, a larger liquefaction plant was built next to this one and placed in operation during January of 1959...though by that date *Suntan* already had come to an untimely end.

Following the initial phase of study and experimentation, *Suntan* proceeded on schedule. About $95 million had been allocated by the Air Force, and construction of miscellaneous components had been initiated by the *Skunk Works*. Lockheed in fact had ordered no less than 2-1/2 miles of aluminum extrusion; Pratt & Whitney was moving ahead with construction and static testing of various Model 304 engines; the Massachusetts Institute of Technology was working on an inertial guidance system; and Air Products Corporation was moving ahead with construction of the large hydrogen liquefaction plant in Florida.

By early-1957, the technological problems lurking in *Suntan's* background had begun to haunt it. Within six months of its formal approval by the Air Force, a difference of technical opinion over achievable range had surfaced as an item of considerable contention between the Air Force and Johnson. Surprisingly, Johnson—the man who had sold the aircraft to the Air Force in the first place—after careful analysis of the airframe, the pow-

operated independently. Special measures were taken to prevent identification of *Suntan* visitors by those not connected to the project. All documentation and related paperwork were kept to a minimum.

During 1956, Air Force enthusiasm for what Lockheed now was calling the CL-400

resulted in a contract for four production aircraft in addition to the original two prototypes and single static test article. Paralleling this, Pratt & Whitney pursued development of their 304-2 engine. Weighing 6,270 pounds and providing 9,450 pounds thrust at sea level (5,940 pounds thrust at Mach 2.5 and 100,000 feet altitude) it

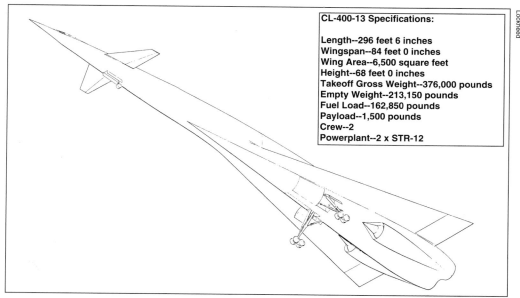

Lockheed

CL-400-13 Specifications:

Length--296 feet 6 inches
Wingspan--84 feet 0 inches
Wing Area--6,500 square feet
Height--68 feet 0 inches
Takeoff Gross Weight--376,000 pounds
Empty Weight--213,150 pounds
Fuel Load--162,850 pounds
Payload--1,500 pounds
Crew--2
Powerplant--2 x STR-12

erplant, the fuel, and the proposed mission requirements had concluded that severe range limitations could not be overcome with extant technology...and that the program should be terminated in favor of a more conventional hydrocarbon-fueled aircraft. During a March 1957 meeting with James Douglas, Jr., then Secretary of the Air Force, and Lt. Gen. Irvine, Johnson had told them bluntly, "we have crammed the maximum amount of hydrogen in the fuselage that it can hold. You do not carry hydrogen in the flat surfaces of the wing..." and he noted that the range growth potential by adding more fuel was only 3%.

Air Force reaction to the meeting was mixed. *Suntan* proponents, particularly Appold and Seaberg, continued to support *Suntan* even in light of Johnson's negative assessment. By late 1958, however, it was apparent the program was in deep trouble.

Johnson apparently had held strong reservations concerning liquid hydrogen almost from the beginning. During *Suntan's* first six months of development, he had concluded a range of 2,500 miles was the maximum that could be expected of a hydrogen-fueled aircraft of this type. Air Force engineers at Wright Field had generated considerably more optimistic figures and had concluded 3,500 miles, if not greater, to be a more realistic range limit. Because of his intimacy with the actual aircraft, however, Johnson became increasingly convinced the CL-400 would not be able to achieve the Air Force's optimistic projections. By mid-1958, others involved in the aircraft's development had reached similar conclusions. During February of 1959, upon Johnson's insistence, the program was terminated...even though national security issues, such as a U-2 successor, remained unresolved.

Approximately a year prior to the actual demise of the CL-400, the Air Force approved a series of follow-on studies to explore potential performance improvements. Boeing, Convair, and North American were invited to participate and the resulting design exercises provided some credibility to Air Force claims. Fourteen configurations were generated by the *Skunk Works* team in response to the study initiative, but they generated little in the way of strong support, other than to verify Johnson's contention that hydro-carbon fuels were considerably more practical.

In the end, *Suntan* and the CL-400 died because of a combination of several factors, not the least of which was Johnson's concerns about range; the logistics of processing, transporting and handling liquid hydrogen; excessive program costs (estimated by some to have required expenditures in excess of $250 million); and other, more practical intelligence gathering options.

Although *Suntan* technology and equipment found no immediate use in the aircraft industry, in 1959, according to retired *Skunk Works* President Ben Rich—who worked on the CL-400 liquid-hydrogen systems and powerplant requirements—"the development data on handling, tank construction, and materials was turned over to Convair who had just won the *Centaur* rocket program. This was the first US liquid hydrogen fueled space vehicle using a Pratt & Whitney rocket engine, developed on the technology acquired developing the Model 304 engine."

Rich, in ending, also noted the program "showed that a large supersonic airplane and engine could be developed on a *Skunk Works* program basis. In addition, concurrent studies

showed that the same mission range could be almost doubled with some altitude loss using a hydrocarbon fuel which does not have the logistics and handling problems of liquid hydrogen. This subsequently led to the *Skunk Works Blackbird* development program."

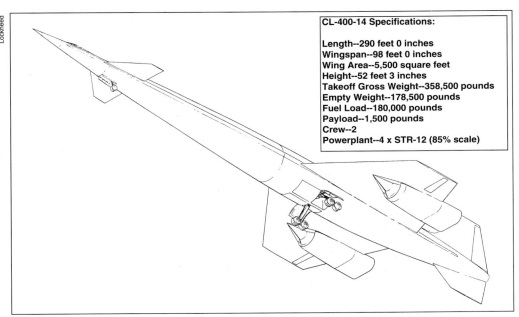

CL-400-14 Specifications:

Length--290 feet 0 inches
Wingspan--98 feet 0 inches
Wing Area--5,500 square feet
Height--52 feet 3 inches
Takeoff Gross Weight--358,500 pounds
Empty Weight--178,500 pounds
Fuel Load--180,000 pounds
Payload--1,500 pounds
Crew--2
Powerplant--4 x STR-12 (85% scale)

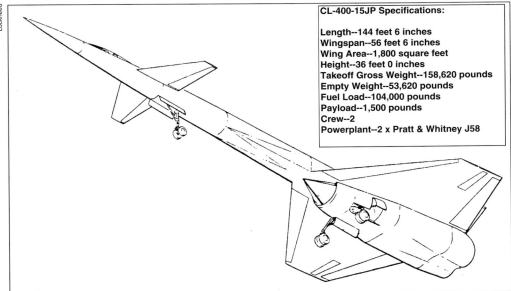

CL-400-15JP Specifications:

Length--144 feet 6 inches
Wingspan--56 feet 6 inches
Wing Area--1,800 square feet
Height--36 feet 0 inches
Takeoff Gross Weight--158,620 pounds
Empty Weight--53,620 pounds
Fuel Load--104,000 pounds
Payload--1,500 pounds
Crew--2
Powerplant--2 x Pratt & Whitney J58

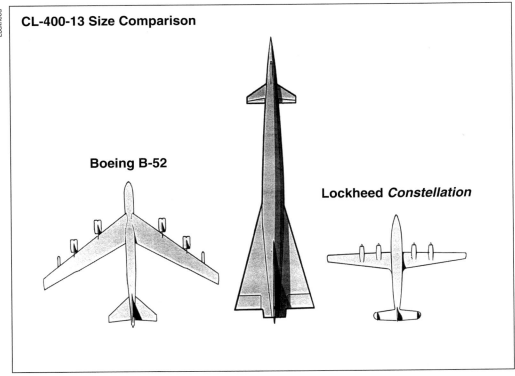

**CL-400-13 Size Comparison**

**Boeing B-52**

**Lockheed *Constellation***

*Missing its nose, the first A-12, No. 121, nears the end of its final assembly process inside the Skunk Works' Burbank facility on January 2, 1962. At the time, it was unquestionably the most advanced jet-propelled aircraft in the world.*

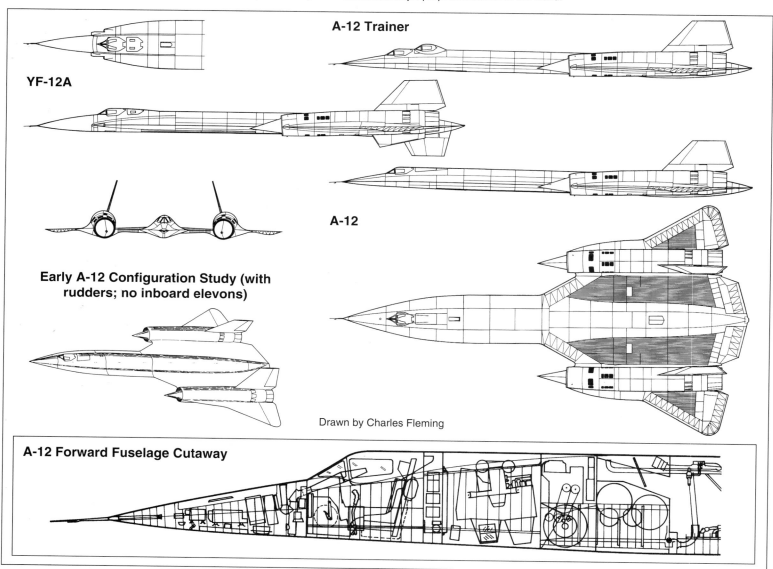

**A-12 Trainer**

**YF-12A**

**Early A-12 Configuration Study (with rudders; no inboard elevons)**

**A-12**

Drawn by Charles Fleming

**A-12 Forward Fuselage Cutaway**

*Then came a number of Mach 3.0 types, the first one of which you'd be familiar would be the YF-12A. Its gross weight is still secret. But the cost performance was excellent. It was a success. Didn't produce any because there wasn't any threat—not until the Backfire bomber showed up..."*

**Clarence L. "Kelly" Johnson**

*Archangel I on October 9, 1957. This was the first of many high-speed reconnaissance aircraft studies leading up to the definitive A-12 configuration.*

Of the many aircraft whose origins can be traced back to Lockheed's renowned *Skunk Works*, none is more significant than the A-12. More than any other aircraft, this titanium masterpiece represented the apex of aeronautical engineering in its day...not only at Lockheed, but at every significant aerospace engineering bureau around the world. Today, over three decades after its first flight, it remains the aircraft by which all others are judged.

As noted in the preceding chapter, *Project Suntan* had given "Kelly" Johnson and the Lockheed advanced development team engineers a significant opportunity to explore the attributes of hydrogen propulsion systems. Equally as important, however, *Suntan* also permitted the exploration of advanced airframes optimized for the first time to cruise at speeds well in excess of Mach 3. Though only paper exercises, the data base represented by these studies would hold the company in good stead until an opportunity to move ahead with a more detailed work, permitted by the demise of *Suntan*, presented itself.

Soon after the U-2's first flight during 1955, Richard Bissell (Dulles' Special Assistant

for Planning and Coordination—so named during 1954) moved quickly to organize the research and development of follow-on systems, including what was to become the A-12. Bissell, as well as various members of the Killian Committee and Johnson had concluded the U-2 would have a period of invulnerability lasting no more than two years from the beginning of *Operation Overflight*.

As noted in the U-2 chapter, one of the first surprises of the overflight program was the ease with which Soviet radar systems found and tracked the aircraft before and after it penetrated Soviet airspace. As a result, considerable effort was put into reducing the U-2's radar cross section (RCS), but with only limited results. In the end, it was concluded the effort and cost far outweighed the advantages and the aircraft's high operating altitude was still its best defense.

Consequent to this conclusion, new studies, conducted under the codename *Gusto*, were initiated exploring the design and possible development of a totally new subsonic reconnaissance platform that would be designed

from the start to incorporate the lowest RCS obtainable. During the fall of 1957, Bissell, still convinced the U-2 would have a short service life, contacted Johnson and asked if the *Skunk Works* team would conduct an operations analysis to determine how far the probability of shooting down an aircraft varied respectively with its speed, altitude, and RCS. Johnson, already immersed in related studies, agreed to accept the project.

The resulting analysis concluded that supersonic speed coupled with the use of radar attenuating materials and radar attenuating design considerations greatly reduced the chances of radar detection...though it did not reduce it to zero. Bissel and Johnson both were impressed with the study's findings and agreed that further exploratory work should be done.

Attention in the CIA now focused on the possibility of building a vehicle which could fly at extremely high speeds and extremely high altitudes, and which also would incorporate the best available radar-attenuating capabilities. Lockheed Aircraft Corporation and the Convair

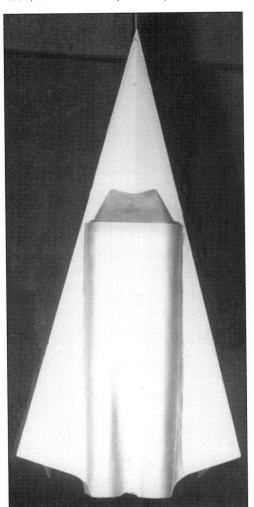

*Arrow I was another of the many initial studies conducted to develop a U-2 replacement.*

*Archangel II was second in the design study series that eventually evolved into the A-12. This configuration was powered by two turbojets (inboard) and two ramjets (outboard).*

Arrow I *model (front) followed by models of* Gusto 2 *and a standard U-2A.*

*Wind tunnel model of the original A-11 configuration illustrates its relatively conventional planform.*

*Final A-12 configuration (left) alongside the ninth version of the A-6 configuration design study.*

Division of General Dynamics during the fall of 1957 were to respond to a general operational requirement calling for a high-speed, high-altitude reconnaissance aircraft...but to do so without a formal contract or government funding. Both companies accepted with the assurance funding would be forthcoming at the appropriate time. For the following year, configurations were developed and refined...all at no expense to the CIA.

Bissell had realized that the development and production of the proposed advanced aircraft would be exceedingly expensive. He also realized there was considerable risk involved, because the performance parameters selected had never previously been attainable with extant technology. The two companies work-

ing on the project, General Dynamics and Lockheed, were not in a position to guarantee success, and it would therefore be necessary for the government to assume most, if not all the liability.

Bissell assumed that to secure the necessary program funding, various high-ranking government officials would have to be cleared for access and consequently be given the best and most authoritative presentations on advances as they occurred. In order to accommodate this, he moved to assemble a panel consisting of people he had identified as some of the most talented and brilliant in their respective fields. Among these was Edwin Land, who was asked to serve as panel chairman.

Between 1957 and 1959, this panel met approximately six times, usually in Land's Cambridge, Massachusetts office. Johnson, and General Dynamic's Vincent Dolson and Bob Widmer were sporadically in attendance and served to address the issues that had caused the panel to come into existence in the first place. The Assistant Secretaries of the Air Force and Navy and select technical advisors usually were on hand as well, these later all but eliminating bureaucratic and jurisdictional feuds that often stem from decision-making processes that have excluded their participation. As it turned out, Air Force and Navy participation

also resulted in valuable assistance and cooperation.

Johnson spent virtually every available minute working on the advanced aircraft program—which he sometimes jokingly referred to as the "U-3". As early as April 21, 1958, he noted in the first entry for what was to become the A-12 log, "I drew up the first *Archangel* proposal for a Mach 3 cruise airplane having a 4,000 nautical mile range at 90,000 to 95,000 feet." Three months later, on July 23, he wrote "I presented this airplane, along with the *Gusto* Model G2A, to the Program Office. It was well received. The Navy mentioned a study they had been making on a slower, higher altitude airplane, on which the Program Office wanted my comments."

Another meeting with the Land panel took place on August 14 and Johnson would note, "They gave me a description of an inflatable airplane which they stated to be capable of 150,000 foot cruise altitude. It was ramjet powered and carried to altitude by a balloon. I made some rapid notes and found the balloon would have to be over a mile in diameter."

Work continued at the *Skunk Works* on the new project. On August 25 Johnson would write, "Have contacted Marquardt and Pratt & Whitney and gotten some ramjet data. Have reconfigured the *Archangel* to include wing tip ramjets as per our proposal on the F-104 to the Air Force in 1954. This appears to give us an airplane which would cruise at Mach 3.2 at 95,000 to 110,000 feet for the full distance. As of today, it looks like the rubber blimp would have a radius of operation of 52 miles."

Obviously not impressed with the Navy's proposal, Johnson continued to work feverishly on what he already was viewing as the *Skunk Works* most important aircraft. Summarizing the period from September 17 through 24, he would write, "Spent considerable time in Washington and ended up in Boston on September 22nd and 23rd to review *Archangel* project. I presented a report on evaluation of Navy inflatable airplane design and also a revised version of the *Archangel* design for higher altitude performance. The inflatable airplane concept appears to have been dropped for our particular mission. Convair proposed a *Super Hustler*, which apparently was a Mach 4 ramjet, piloted, turbojet-assisted on landing, to be launched from the B-58 to do the mission. I presented *Gusto 2A*, which was very well received and also *Archangel II*. This airplane was 135,000 pound gross weight, powered by two J58 turbojets and two 75 inch ramjets. It could do 100,000 foot mission and 4,000 mile range. This airplane was not accepted, because of its dependence on penta-borane for the ramjet and the over-all cost of the system. We left Cambridge rather discouraged with everything."

On the way back, Johnson would note, "I thought it would be worth a try to break one existing ground rule...namely, that we should use engines in being. It was this factor which made the *Archangel II* so large, as we started out with some 15,000 to 18,000 pounds of installed powerplant weight on the J58s (JT12) alone. Because the JT12A is a low-pressure ratio engine, it seemed to me to be well-suited to high Mach number operation. I made a few numbers trying to scale down *Archangel II* to the 17,000 to 20,000 pound gross weight, and it appears feasible."

The General Dynamics team had devoted no less time and energy to their proposal. Developed from a proposed B-58 parasite

Gusto 2 *was a tailless, subsonic, very low radar cross-section configuration proposed as a U-2 replacement when the latter was discovered to be visible to Soviet radar systems.*

*Anachoic chamber model of the A-10 study reveals the design trend in the direction of the chined delta that became the A-12's trademark. This particular model has been optimized for radar cross-section work.*

known in its later stages as *Super Hustler*, it continued to evolve during the one year study period. During its later stages, it was given the strange codename of *Fish*, and then still later, *Kingfish*. In the latter configuration, it was an extraordinary vehicle. Carrying a crew of two (seated side-by-side) and a large sensor package, it was optimized to cruise at Mach 6.25 at an altitude of 125,000 feet. Radically, it was to have been built primarily of pyro-ceram and other related heat-resistant, radar attenuating materials. Two Marquardt ramjets were to propel it throughout the cruise portion of its mission, and two retractable General Electric J85 turbojets were to provide propulsion during takeoff, acceleration to ramjet ignition, and landing.

During late November of 1958, a crucial meeting was held. The miscellaneous studies conducted by General Dynamics and Lockheed had led to the conclusion the advanced aircraft was feasible. This information was relayed to President Eisenhower who was then asked to approve funding for further studies and preliminary hardware development.

President Eisenhower and Killian now met with the panel and reviewed the various design options, and the *Gusto* program in general. At the end of the meeting, Eisenhower agreed that funding—once again from the CIA's special Contingency Reserve Fund—be allocated for the development of definitive proposals from General Dynamics and Lockheed.

Johnson and the various other members of the small *Skunk Works* team assembled to develop the new design, from December of 1958 through July of 1959, worked ceaselessly in an attempt to create the perfect aircraft. According to Ben Rich who would eventually play a key role in the A-12's development, "Initially it was a small cadre composed of Dave Campbell, Dick Fuller, Don Nelson, Dick Cantrell, Ray McHenry, Bob Batista, Henry Combs, Merv Heal, Lorne Cass, Ed Baldwin, and Ed Martin...and we all worked for Dick Boehme, the program manager. Dick Bissell and John Parangosky from the CIA worked closely with Johnson, and Brig. Gen. Leo Geary was the Air Force's liaison with the CIA."

Rich also recalled that, "We calculated everything with a slide rule and a Friden calculator." This was a difficult and laborious process, as computer technology was rudimentary, at best, and capabilities were extremely limited.

Complicating things was the extraordinary security blanket that had been thrown over the project. Rich would note, "The A-12 inhabited the black world for many years. The CIA knew about development of the A-12 as did a few people in the Air Force, a few Congressmen, and of course, President Eisenhower. Security rivaled the *Manhattan Project*.. Those of us on the project never used the name Lockheed, no drawings were stamped, and (later) parts were sent to C&J Engineering ("Kelly's" initials) and we had things mailed to post office boxes all over the city. We maintained perimeter security and even swept out our own offices."

"During this period we studied models from A-3 to A-12," Johnson would write. "Gradually it became evident that we could not obtain radar invisibility and all the other conditions desired for the airplane. In April 1959 I proposed the concept of a single base operation with air-to-air refueling, operating out of Muroc. The A-11 resulted, as an airplane which we made no compromises for radar but which had very good performance, and was a

straight forward twin J58 Mach 3.2 airplane.

"I gave the A-11 pitch and reported on about six months of radar studies which we made, in which we proved, at least to ourselves, that improvements available to radars at the present time would enable detection of any conceivable airplane which would fly in the next three to five years. We specifically computed that the probability of detection of the A-11 was practically 100%.

"I think I made some kind of impression with the radar people, because the ground rules changed shortly after this and it was agreed that the A-11 would make such a strong target that it might be taken for a bomber.

"Nevertheless, on July 3, when the Director of the Program Office visited me again, just at about the time when I thought we were ruled out, they extended our program and agreed to take lower cruising altitudes which we could obtain with a version of the A-11 adapted in shape and treatment to reduce the cross-section. I proposed the A-12 with the J58 engines in a mid-wing arrangement, the use of chines on the fuselage and serrations on the leading edge incorporating radar treatment. This airplane weighs about 110,000 to 115,000 pounds and, by being optimistic on fuel consumption and drag, can do a pretty good mission.

"As of July 8, it seems there is a good chance that, if an airplane will be built for the mission, it will be ours."

Official approval to proceed with the program was granted the CIA on July 20. During a meeting with Eisenhower, it was agreed that either the General Dynamics or the Lockheed proposal should be chosen for construction and flight test. It also was agreed that a final proposal review should be undertaken and that the winning design should be cleared for prototyping as quickly as possible.

On August 20, 1959, the final design submissions from General Dynamics and Lockheed were delivered to a joint Department of Defense/Air Force/CIA selection panel. The two aircraft, though strikingly different, compared favorably in terms of performance:

| | Lockheed | General Dynamics |
|---|---|---|
| Length (feet) | 102 | 79.5 |
| Wingspan (feet) | 57 | 56 |
| Gross weight (pounds) | 110,000 | 101,700 |
| Fuel weight(pounds) | 64,600 | 62,000 |
| Speed | Mach 3.2 | Mach 3.2 |
| Range (nautical miles total) | 4,120 | 3,400 |
| Range (nautical miles @ altitude) | 3,800 | 3,400 |
| Cruise altitude (feet @ start) | 84,500 | 85,000 |
| Cruise altitude (feet @ middle) | 91,000 | 88,000 |
| Cruise altitude (feet @ end) | 97,600 | 94,000 |
| Expected First Flight Date | 22 months | 22 months |

On August 28 Johnson noted in the log, "Saw the director of the program office alone. He told me that we had the project and that Convair is out of the picture. They accept our conditions (1) of the basic arrangement of the A-12 and (2) that our method of doing business will be identical to that of the U-2. He agreed very firmly to this latter condition and said that unless it was done this way, he wanted nothing to do with the project either. The conditions that he gave me were these:

*A-12 tunnel model, photographed during 1960, implies the design was nearing final definitiion.*

(1) We must exercise the greatest possible ingenuity and honest effort in the field of radar.

(2) The degree of security on this project is, if possible, tighter than on the U-2.

(3) We should make no large material commitments, large meaning in terms of millions of dollars.

"We talked throughout the day on problems on security, location, manpower, and aircraft factors. At noon I took nine of the project people out for lunch, in celebration of our new project."

On August 29, 1959, Lockheed was given an official go-ahead on the A-12. Initial funding, for $4.5 million was approved to cover the period from September 1 to January 1, 1960. *Project Gusto* now was terminated and a new codename, *Oxcart*, was assigned. On August 31, Johnson wrote in the log, "Started immediate action in Building 82A to build full-scale mock-up and 1/8 scale mock-up, an elevation post, and engineering reorganization and expansion, and plans for a complete rearrangement of offices and shop. I reported results of the trip to Robert Gross, Courtlandt Gross, Cyril Chappellet, Charlie Barker, and Hall Hibbard."

*Canards were tested unsuccessfully on the A-12 model in an attempt to improve pitch stability.*

**115**

*The second A-12, No. 122, was used as a pole model to test the aircraft's radar cross-section.*

On the next day, he noted, "I consider this to be the first day on our new project, with a flight date set 20 months from today. The original 18-month program will be delayed to allow Pratt & Whitney to make a by-pass version of the J58 engine."

Not surprisingly, the design of the A-12 was clearly dominated by the aircraft's propulsion system. Underscoring this were the engine nacelles, which in fact were larger in diameter than the basic fuselage. The propulsion system consisted of three major elements: the inlet and inlet control; the Pratt & Whitney J58 (civil designation was JT11D-20) and its control; and the self-actuating airframe mounted ejector nozzle. In the actual aircraft, engine access was provided by hinging the outer wing about the upper outboard nacelle split line.

On September 3, the CIA authorized Lockheed to proceed with anti-radar studies, aerodynamic, structural tests, and engineering designs. Johnson would write, one week later, "We will go forward with greater confidence, having in 18 months completed the circle and come back to an airplane very similar to the A-1, which was our first proposal but considered to be too large, inadequate in the anti-radar concept, and to have too low performance. It was actually smaller than the A-12 and had better performance. All of this is now behind us and we have nothing to do but work."

The engineering team continued to remain small. By now, under the supervision of Ed Martin, Dan Zuck had been assigned cockpit design, Dave Robertson had been brought aboard to handle the fuel system requirements, and Henry Combs and Dick Boehme had been

assigned to head-up structures development. Dick Fuller, Burt McMaster, and Ben Rich also were intimately involved, though their time was being spent working at night at the NASA Ames high-speed wind tunnel facility south of San Francisco at Moffett Field, California.

By mid-October the radar-cross-section model was nearing completion and low-speed wind tunnel testing was already underway with a small-scale model. "I had Dick Fuller and Bert O'Laughlin go up to Ames to make arrangements for high-speed tunnel tests...(these) indicated the expected problems in regard to longitudinal stability with chines. We are extending the wing after the afterburner and believe we have usable solutions coming up. The over-all problem of weight, balance, and stability is extremely high."

Work on the wind tunnel models, full-scale mock-up, and initial pieces of full-scale hardware progressed rapidly. By December 7, the RCS model—which had been loaded aboard a special trailer and trucked to the test location during November—had permitted refinement of the design to establish the optimum external configuration for radar attenuation, and Johnson appeared to feel confident the aircraft would meet the promised RCS specification, "We are beginning to get the anti-radar return of the model down remarkably. Inlets are the problem in the forward aspect and the exhaust in the rear, as expected."

The powerplant issue had not been treated lightly, either by the *Skunk Works'* A-12 propulsion system manager, Ben Rich, or the CIA. Not only was RCS an issue of considerable contention, but also the basic design of the engine, its advanced supersonic intake, its nacelle, and its ejector nozzle configuration. As Johnson would note concerning the latter, "This thing is fantastically hard to build, but we must take on the job because it involves so much of the airplane structure."

Pratt & Whitney, almost from the very beginning, had been involved in *Gusto* and its successor, *Oxcart*.. Their J58, which was to be used in the new *Skunk Works* aircraft, had been sponsored originally by the Navy as a conventional, but very advanced turbojet engine providing extraordinarily high thrust with the ability to operate routinely at speeds up to Mach 3.

The J58 had become increasingly difficult and expensive to develop by the advent of the

A-12. Additionally, several of the aircraft for which the J58 was intended, including the Vought F8U-3, had ceased to exist. The Navy, as a result had lost interest. In short, at the beginning of 1959 the engine was without a home or sponsorship.

As originally conceived, the J58 was to use conventional ram compression at supersonic speeds to augment the compressor's moderate pressure ratio. With its conventional afterburner and a convergent-divergent exhaust nozzle, the J58 was expected to be capable of producing up to 45,000 pounds static sea level thrust.

The more radical approach to the A-12's required Mach 3 cruise speed led to a major J58 redesign. The resulting configuration bypassed intake air from the fourth-stage of the high-pressure compressor section and dumped it into the afterburner. This created a highly efficient ramjet *effect* and thus augmented the more conventional thrust being generated by the core engine.

Funding allocated for *Oxcart* by the CIA also included developmental funding for the advanced J58. When, on January 30, 1960, Lockheed received official word that funding for twelve A-12s had been approved, Pratt & Whitney also was informed they were cleared to move ahead with the construction of three "advanced, experimental engines for durability and reliability testing." Additionally, three engines were to be made available for initiation of flight testing during early 1961.

Work on the A-12's sensors also had been initiated. The primary camera manufacturer was Perkin-Elmer. Because of the extreme complexity of the design a decision was quickly made to fund Kodak's proposed back-up system in case Perkin-Elmer ran into difficulty. At the same time, Minneapolis-Honeywell Corporation was selected to provide both the inertial navigation and automatic flight control systems. The Firewell Corporation and the David Clark Corporation became the prime sources of pilot equipment and associated life support hardware.

During early February of 1960 the CIA proposed to Lockheed that it serve to screen a minimum of 60 pilots in an attempt to assemble an initial group of 24. These men would be "sheep dipped"—as had those associated with the CIA's U-2 effort—and they also would be put through a physical review comparable to

*Eighth-scale A-12 radar-cross-section model with radar absorbent panels in place on its chines.*

*The third A-12 forward fuselage section under construction inside the* Skunk Works' *Burbank facility. What appears to be second cockpit is actually "Q-bay" to accommodate camera.*

that developed for the *Project Mercury* astronauts. Johnson did not react to this with great favor, as he felt it would be some time yet before pilots, other than those already in the employ of Lockheed, would be needed. The following April, he picked Lou Schalk to be first flight pilot.

The basic pilot candidate requirements were that they be between 25 and 40 years of age, be under six feet tall, and weigh no more than 175 pounds. Air Force files were screened for potential candidates and a list of pilots was assembled. Psychological assessments, physical examinations, and refinement of criteria eliminated many. Pre-evaluation processing resulted in sixteen potential nominees. This group underwent a further intensive security and medical scrutiny by the CIA. Those who remained were then approached to take employment with the CIA on a highly classified project involving a very advanced aircraft. During November of 1961, commitments were obtained from five of the group. The small number recruited required that a second search be undertaken.

When the final screening was completed, the pilots, other than Lou Schalk, included William Skliar, Kenneth Collins, Walter Ray, Lon Walter, Mele Vojvodich, Jr., Jack Weeks, Ronald "Jack" Layton, Dennis Sullivan, David Young, Francis Murray, and Russell Scott. After the selection, arrangements were made with the Air Force to effect appropriate transfers and assignments to cover their training and to lay the basis for their transition from military to civilian status. Compensation and insurance arrangements were similar to those for the CIA's U-2 pilots.

While work on the A-12 progressed at a steady pace, on-going studies of the basic configuration and its long-term potential continued in the *Skunk Works'* engineering department. On March 16, after several weeks of design and engineering effort, Johnson went to Washington in order to present an A-12 configuration study calling for an interceptor version optimized for air defense work. Specifically targeted was North American's ill-fated F-108 *Rapier*...a one-third scale extrapolation of the forthcoming Mach 3-capable North American XB-70 *Valkyrie* intercontinental heavy bomber.

"I was given information on the Hughes AN/ASG-18 radar and the latest information on the Hughes GAR-9 rocket. Before leaving, the Air Force program office clearly explained that they wanted to know whether we could make use of this equipment in the A-12 and that, if we could, they would propose it as a standby air defense fighter. They said there would not be any immediate order, but they were interested in getting development aspects of the fighter system carried along. I told them we could get them an air defense airplane in a couple of years under our present commitments. This would be A-12 number 6 or 7."

As the jigs began to go together inside the Burbank building where the aircraft were to be built, the manifold difficulties entailed in the A-12's construction began to surface in ever-increasing numbers. The early decision to build the aircraft out of titanium in order to cope with the high temperatures at the Mach 3-plus cruise speeds was a first for the industry. Though miscellaneous aircraft parts had been manufactured from this material on select occasions, an entire airframe had never previously been attempted. Ben Rich would note that the A-12 "was composed of 85% titanium and 15% composite materials."

*The A-12s were constructed inside Building 309/310 at Plant B-6. Construction techniques were complicated by the use of titanium alloys and previously untried metallurgical procedures.*

*The first A-12, No. 121, during engine and fuel system tests. These uncovered a serious leak problem, thus necessitating the use of external tanks in order to accommodate engine static ground runs.*

*The A-12 shortly after lifting off on its first official flight on April 30, 1962. Lockheed test pilot Lou Schalk was at the controls. Aircraft was powered by Pratt & Whitney J75 engines at the time.*

Though strong, relatively light, and capable of retaining its exceptional strength characteristics at very high temperatures, it also suffered from scarcity, high cost, and a reputation for being extremely difficult to work. Initially, over 80% of the titanium delivered to Lockheed had to be rejected for contamination. It was not until 1961 that the problem was brought fully under control.

Learning to work with titanium proved to be a major undertaking. The myriad breakthroughs pioneered by the *Skunk Works* manufacturing team in conquering this metal remain one of the great and unheralded successes of this most incredible program.

Other manufacturing challenges, most too numerous to mention here, included development of fuels that could be safely stored at the A-12's ambient fuel cell cruising speed temperature of 350° F; nitrogen inerting of the fuel tanks as fuel was depleted; development of a special lubricating oil that could be used effectively on parts that had cruising speed stabilized temperatures of 600° F or more while remaining fluid at temperatures of less than 40° F; development of a hydraulic seal capable of maintaining its integrity at high temperatures; and a quartz glass window that could retain its optical qualities while being exposed to the extreme temperatures of the A-12's operating environment (the window, in fact, eventually took three years and $2 million to develop and

pioneered a unique process for metal-to-glass fusion using high-frequency sound waves).

Another major problem was radar-cross-section. The areas causing the most RCS difficulty included the vertical stabilizers and the forward section of the engine nacelles. Lockheed conducted considerable research into the use of ferrites, high-temperature radar absorbing materials, and high-temperature plastic structures to find methods for reducing the RCS. Eventually, the vertical tails, originally of titanium, were replaced by units of high-temperature composites. This was almost certainly the first time such materials had been used for a major part of an aircraft's structure.

The old U-2 test location now was prepared to accept the first aircraft, which originally had been promised for delivery during May of 1961. Considerable work was required to bring the facility up to the standard needed for A-12 operations, and this had been initiated during September of 1960. Though a double-shift scheduled was instigated, the actual upgrade was not finally completed until mid-1964. In the interim, the runway was lengthened to 8,500 feet from the original 5,000; the highway leading to the location was resurfaced; three surplus Navy hangars were obtained, dismantled, and erected at the location's north side; and an additional 100 surplus Navy buildings were moved to the base and rebuilt.

While work on the test location moved

ahead at a rapid pace, the prototype aircraft were being assembled with considerable difficulty at Burbank. A review of Johnson's A-12 log underscores some of the problems:

August 30, 1960—"The stress and flutter boys presented a study on aeroelasticity which was woefully in error. If it had been correct, the airplane couldn't fly at all."

September 14, 1960—"Start design of the bomber version of the A-12."

September 30, 1960—"We are in desperate trouble trying to get extrusions for the wing beams. The material is not acceptable."

October 3/24, 1960—"Continuing to have many shop problems. Can't get material, and it appears that the schedule is slipping some more."

December 20, 1960—"Have a very strong suspicion that Pratt & Whitney are not going to meet their schedule. They have run into trouble on the compressor with tip shrouds. Of course they didn't mention this as being a major problem."

March 6, 1961—"Having trouble with wing load distribution and have to put twist in outboard leading edge."

March 15/April 1, 1961—"Just a great deal of work with the many problems we have trying to get this airplane built. Everywhere you turn there are tremendous problems requiring invention, new systems, and money."

Johnson, during March, informed the CIA that, "Schedules are in jeopardy on two fronts. One is the assembly of the wing and the other is in satisfactory development of the engine. Our evaluation shows that each of these programs is from three to four months behind the current schedule."

To this, the CIA's Bissell replied, "I have learned of your expected additional delay in first flight from 30 August to 1 December 1961. This news is extremely shocking on top of our previous slippage from May to August and my understanding as of our meeting 19 December that the titanium extrusion problems were essentially overcome. I trust this is the last of such disappointments short of a severe earthquake in Burbank."

But it wasn't; Johnson's frustrations continued without let-up:

*The A-12 was by far the most exotic aircraft in the sky at the time of its 1962 debut. This view of the third A-12, No.123, was taken on December 22, 1962. The dark V-shaped panels on the leading and trailing edges of the wing were designed to help reduce the aircraft's radar cross section.*

April 12, 1961—"Fighting a whole host of problems on powerplant, ejectors, plumbing, material shortages, lack of space."

July 10, 1961—"Having a horrible time building the first airplane and we are stopped on the second by a change in the design of the radar configuration of the chines. Have shop meetings often—about three times a week—but it's hard to drive a willing horse. Everyone on edge connected with the production of the A-12 airplane, and we still have a long, long way to go. I told Courtlandt Gross and Dan Haughton how tough our problems are, with no under-estimation on my part of the extreme danger we will encounter in flying this revolutionary airplane. And told them some of the steps we are taking to minimize these dangers."

Concurrently, engine development also was proving a difficult task for Pratt & Whitney. Johnson would note in the log, "Pratt & Whitney told us the story on the engine, and said that the best delivery date we could get for two engines was March 1962 (they admitted this meant April...or March 31)." Realizing the engine problems could push the first flight date back even further, Johnson, on September 29, made a decision..."after a sleepless night, I decided that we should have to try to fly with a J75 engine, doing everything possible to raise the takeoff power, such as using water injection, and higher takeoff temperature and rpm's."

With the delays now causing the cost of the program to soar, the CIA decided to place a top level engineer from the Air Force in residence at the *Skunk Works*. Norman Nelson, as Johnson noted, "brought in Lt. Col. Richmond Miller," on October 3, 1961, "...who had been on the program two weeks. Miller said he was supposed to be their man 'in charge of the airframe,' which neither he nor I understood. We know Miller from work on the U-2 at Edwards AFB. He is competent in the flight test area, but he follows the book religiously. He asked me for an A-12 flight manual, which I told him would be ready in about a year..."

The completion date of the first A-12 now had slipped to December 22, 1961, and the expected first flight date to February 27, 1962. Construction pressures were intense at Burbank and work went on around the clock in three shifts. Engine problems continued, as well. Johnson, following a meeting with Pratt & Whitney in Florida, would note in his log, "Their troubles are desperate. It is almost unbelievable that they could have gotten this far with the engine without uncovering basic problems which have been normal in every jet engine I have ever worked with. Prospect of an early flight engine is dismal, and I feel our program is greatly jeopardized. It's a good thing we went to the J75, although these engines, too, have troubles and require new compressor discs."

At the test location, support aircraft began to arrive during the spring of 1962. Included were eight McDonnell F-101s for chase and training, two Lockheed T-33s for proficiency training, a Lockheed C-130 for cargo transport, a Cessna U-3A for administration purposes, a helicopter for search and rescue, and a Cessna 180 for liaison use. In addition, an F-104 was used as a chase plane.

During January of 1962 an agreement was reached with the Federal Aviation Administration permitting expansion of the restricted airspace surrounding the test location. Select FAA air traffic controllers were cleared for *Oxcart* operations. Additionally,

select military radar facilities were briefed and told not to report radar sightings of high-performance aircraft.

The first A-12 was ready for final assembly during mid-February of 1962. Johnson and the CIA had decided that, in light of the secrecy surrounding the project, the aircraft could not be flown from Burbank to the test location. A special trailer, evolved from the unit built to transport the RCS test specimen, was therefore designed and built to haul the aircraft to the test location by road. A thorough survey of the route during June of 1961 ascertained the hazards and problems of moving the actual aircraft and showed that a package measuring 35 feet wide and 103 feet long could be moved along the road without major difficulty...though some obstructing road signs would have to be removed and select trees would have to be trimmed.

The entire fuselage, minus wings, was crated, covered with canvas, and loaded on the special $100,000 trailer. On February 26, Johnson noted, "The convoy left at 2:30 a.m. to go to the test location. Everything went smoothly and it arrived at 1:00 p.m. on February 28. Dorsey Kammerer did his usual splendid job of organizing the move."

Shortly after its arrival at the test location, reassembly of the first aircraft and installation of the J75 engines was initiated. It was soon discovered, however, that fuel tank sealing compounds had failed to adhere to the titanium fuel tank walls. When the tanks were filled for the first time, the aircraft leaked like a sieve. Johnson counted a total of 68 leaks. The tanks were laboriously stripped and resealed. Johnson would note, "This is a cruel blow, as it will delay us a month or more."

Finally, on April 25, 1962, the aircraft appeared ready for its initial tests. The *Skunk Works'* Lou Schalk, who had joined the program two years earlier, had spent many hours in the cockpit and a rudimentary simulator. By the advent of the first taxi and flight tests, he was as prepared as it was possible to be using available technology.

Johnson had flown to the location to witness the event and noted in his log, "Went to the test location and stayed over night. Made our first flight under very difficult conditions. Flew about 1-1/2 miles at an altitude of about 20 feet. Aircraft got off the ground with lots of right rudder on, and then required change of rudder angle to 24° immediately. This set up lateral oscillations which were horrible to see.

*Main instrument panel of the first A-12, No. 121, photographed on January 2, 1962...several months prior to the aircraft's first fight. Large periscopic viewsight is missing from center top.*

*Though often published, this is one of the few extant photos depicting the standard A-12 in filght. Interestingly, unpainted metal vertical tail surfaces are installed rather than the low-RCS composite fins.*

*Early operational configuration of the A-12 utilized black paint only on the chine areas and around the nose and cockpit (for anti-glare). Radar absorbent properties of specialized paints often attributed to Skunk Works aircraft were in fact not known ever to have been applied.*

Abrams collection

*Inflight refueling capability proved critical to the successful execution of virtually all A-12 operational missions. Here, an early KC-135A, modified to pump JP-7, refuels an A-12 during tests.*

We were all concerned about the ability of Lou Schalk to stop, but he did this very nicely, without severe braking. The lake is soft enough so that we can roll onto it at fantastic speeds and stop readily. Actual trouble was later shown to be due to nose wheel steering problems."

Schalk, in recounting the first flight during a 1993 interview, had a different perspective on what actually happened: "It had a very light load of fuel so it sort of accelerated really fast. Not many people really knew that we were going to lift the airplane off...some of the people in flight test engineering didn't know this. I was probably three to four percent behind the aft limit center of gravity when I lifted off the airplane...so it was unstable...and we fought it longitudinally which translated into lateral and directional problems, too.

"The airplane wallowed through the sky until I finally felt I had it under control enough to put it back down on the ground...which I did. By that time I was over the lakebed. This developed a big cloud of dust and the tower wanted to know if everything was ok. I said 'yes...but I'm going to have to roll out here on the lakebed and I'll turn around and come back'. But they couldn't hear me because the UHF transmitting antenna was on the bottom of the fuselage and that blanked out my transmission...so no one heard what I was saying. So they asked me again and I said there was no problem. I wasn't trying to stomp on the brakes

or anything. Everyone was having a heart attack...I finally made the turn and came out of the cloud of dust and they saw I hadn't run into the mountains on the other side of the lake and blown up the airplane, so there was a big sigh of relief.

"I still didn't know what the devil was wrong with the airplane...why it handled so poorly--it didn't do that way on the simulator and 'Kelly' and I and Fuller--we were talking about what we should do if we fly the airplane the next day. I said I think we should turn on the dampers and fly with the dampers on...they were off when I was taxiing; they said fine. On the second first flight we were going to fly the airplane around with the gear down. The third official flight was the one we pulled up the gear.

"On the second flight with the gear down the airplane took off fairly smoothly...I couldn't wait to get up to about 10,000 feet. I'm flying along below gear speed and I turned one damper off, and then another damper off, and then another damper off--no problem. Then I got the clue as to what had gone wrong on the first flight. There were a sequence of fuel tanks in the fuselage of the airplane...one through six or one through seven--they had all the fuel in the back end...there was nothing up front for the taxi tests. When we actually flew the airplane it was loaded properly and I was in a c.g. that was ahead of the aft limit and the airplane flew fine...I lifted the airplane off the runway for

ten seconds...I never thought to check where all the fuel was. Probably had 12,000 pounds of fuel (all aft) during the taxi tests."

The day following the first flights, Johnson would write, "We decided to fly with the stability augmentor engaged on April 26, which is obviously a day for the A-12, in that 2 x 6 = 12. Everyone was awake just about through the night. We rolled out early and at 07:05 a.m. took off, making a beautiful takeoff. However, due to failure of a forward fillet bracket, we shed almost all the left hand fillets and one on the right side, starting before we left the runway. Fortunately, I had spent the previous day with Lou Schalk, explaining that the fillets were non-structural and that we might have troubles. A beautiful landing was made and in flight we investigated the effect of the stability augmentors. We showed that the first flight troubles were not caused by basic aircraft stability."

An "official" first flight, with appropriate government representatives on hand now was made on April 30. Nearly a year behind schedule, the aircraft became airborne for the first time. With Lou Schalk at the controls, the aircraft lifted off at 170 knots. The landing gear was retracted and a climb was made to 30,000 feet. A top speed of 340 knots was reached during the flight which lasted for 59 minutes. Following an uneventful landing, Schalk expressed satisfaction with the aircraft's stability and the way it handled."

On the second flight, on May 4, the A-12 went supersonic for the first time, reaching Mach 1.1. Problems were minimal and Johnson began to feel confident that the flight test program would progress rapidly...possibly recovering some of the time that had been lost in the drawn-out manufacturing process. Another test pilot, Bill Park, also joined the *Skunk Works* team now to share flight testing with Schalk.

Static testing, by mid-June, had cleared the airframe for initial flight testing, but problems remained with the integrity of the vertical fins. Failures had occurred on numerous occasions and the metal fins, in particular, had

Tony Landis

*Late in their operational careers, the A-12s were painted dull black. This particular A-12 is seen following restoration for display at Blackbird Airpark in Palmdale, California, where it now resides alongside an SR-71, a twin-Buick engine-equipped starter, and a Pratt & Whitney J58 engine.*

proven very susceptible to fatigue-related anomalies. Even more frustrating was the low-RCS composite Narmco fin—which also had failed with surprising regularity.

On June 26, the second A-12 arrived at the test location and was immediately assigned to a three-month-long RCS static test program, even before it was completed and its engines were installed. The third aircraft arrived during August and flew for the first time during October, and the fourth aircraft, a two-seat A-12 trainer, arrived by trailer during November. The fifth aircraft, minus engines, arrived on December 19.

The trainer, with an elevated second seat in the position behind the cockpit normally occupied by sensor gear, was immediately equipped with J75 engines so that flight testing could get underway and flight training could be accommodated as expeditiously as possible. This aircraft flew for the first time during January of 1963.

During mid-August, Johnson brought another test pilot, Jim Eastham, on board. Eastham eventually would become the first pilot to fly the YF-12A.

On October 5, 1962, the first A-12, reengined with the first flightworthy J58 mounted in its left engine nacelle (a J75 was retained in the right), took to the air for the first time. It wasn't until January 15, 1963, that the first flight with two J58s installed took place.

On October 11, Johnson met with Pratt & Whitney representatives to go over the ongoing difficulties with the J58. "We are having a terrible time trying to fly the prototype J58. It is down in thrust; fuel control is inconsistent; there are thrust jumps at different throttle positions; and we have continual trouble with the afterburner lighting system and plugged spray bars."

The Cuban missile crises now reinvigorated the program. The loss of Maj. Rudolph Anderson's U-2 over Cuba on October 27 underscored the increasing vulnerability of this subsonic platform when operating in denied airspace, and this was not lost on intelligence community offices involved with the overflight program. Successful execution of *Oxcart* now became a matter of highest national priority.

On November 14, Johnson met with Pratt & Whitney representatives in Washington, D.C. It appeared the ongoing engine problems were not going to be solved without considerable effort. "The thrust of the engines was down, specific fuel consumption was up. The initial engines would not run well above 75,000 feet. Pratt & Whitney showed their program for getting performance back, but this could not be accomplished until engine #19...due for delivery in April 1963."

On January 5, Johnson noted that Bob Gilliland had been hired as the program's fourth pilot. He was scheduled to arrive at the test location on January 15.

At the end of 1962 two A-12s were in flight test (one powered by J75s and the other powered by one J75 and one J58). A speed of Mach 2.16 and an altitude of 60,000 feet had been achieved. Flight test progress was still slow and the engine delays and thrust deficiencies remained a major concern.

The engine problem had, in fact, led to CIA director John McCone writing Pratt & Whitney, "I have been advised that J58 engine deliveries have been delayed again due to engine control production problems...By the end of the year it appears we will have barely enough J58 engines to support the flight test

*A single two-seat A-12 was built to serve as a dedicated trainer. This aircraft spent its entire life powered by Pratt & Whitney J75s; it was never converted to the considerably more powerful J58s.*

program adequately...furthermore, due to various engine difficulties we have not yet reached design speed and altitude. Engine thrust and fuel consumption deficiencies at present prevent sustained flight at design conditions which is so necessary to complete developments."

By the end of January 1963, ten J58s had been delivered to the test location. The first A-12 flight with two J58s was finally undertaken on January 13. The other aircraft now were retrofitted with J58s and all forthcoming aircraft were flown with J58 propulsion. The only exception became the A-12 trainer, which though intended for conversion to J58s, was left equipped with J75s throughout its life.

On March 20, Johnson wrote in the log, "We have been to Mach 2.5 and as high as 70,000 feet, but we are in trouble from Mach 2.0 up." Problems with the propulsion system continued. On May 2, Johnson "went to the test location to find out why we have not been able to get beyond Mach 2.0 during recent flights. It develops that Hamilton Standard had changed the gain of the spike control, and the main control contributed to the instability. Greatly displeased that the responsible engineers could not find this out on their own, and no one seemed to know which controls gave which performance, until I made a review of the ships' records, and then it became perfectly clear."

On May 24, the third A-12, involved in a subsonic engine test flight and piloted by Ken Collins, crashed 14 miles south of Wendover, Utah. Collins had ejected successfully and was unhurt. The aircraft wreckage was recovered in two days and all persons at the scene were identified and requested to sign a secrecy agreement. A press cover story referred to the crashed aircraft as being a Republic F-105.

The A-12 fleet was temporarily grounded following the accident while an investigation was conducted. A pitot-static system failure due to icing was determined to be the culprit.

By mid-1963 five A-12s were flying. This,

coupled with the loss of a third aircraft, renewed CIA and Air Force concerns over how long the project could be kept secret. The program had gone through development, construction, and a year of flight testing without attracting public attention. But the Department of Defense was having difficulty in concealing its participation because of the increasing expenditure rate which had, till now, gone unexplained. There also was a realization that the technological data would be extremely valuable in connection with feasibility studies for the supersonic transport program...which was rapidly accelerating throughout the US aerospace industry. Finally, there was a growing awareness in the higher reaches of the aircraft industry that something new and remarkable was going on. Rumors were spreading.

The four week period from September 12 to October 10, was summarized by Johnson with, "We have been to Mach 3.0 twice, now, the first time being on July 20. On the second flight, we blew an engine at design speed. It was very difficult to slow down and it rattled Lou Schalk around for three minutes. The aircraft stability augmentation system did precisely as I asked it to do three years ago and no high structural loads were obtained."

By November, the afore-mentioned intake problems were finally being brought under control. "Today we flew the mice installation, to change the subsonic diffusion angles in the duct. This change corrected the roughness encountered at Mach 2.4 and up, and it is the first major improvement in the duct. Collected 25¢ from Rich, Fuller, and Boehme."

Jim Eastham now took the first A-12 out to Mach 3.3 and then cruised at Mach 3.2 for fifteen minutes. "At about this same time, we flew the second aircraft for 53 minutes at Mach 2.65 or above."

President Johnson was briefed on the program a week after taking office during November of 1963. He reacted by directing that a formal announcement be prepared for release shortly after the first of the year. "Kelly" Johnson had been asked to participate in the unveiling process and on February 25 noted, "Plans going forward for surfacing of the AF-12 program. I worked on the draft to be used by President Johnson and proposed the terminology 'A-11' as it was the non-anti-radar version."

In fact, a decision had been made to unveil the YF-12A long-range interceptor version rather than the actual A-12. The YF-12A, referred to initially by Johnson as the AF-12, had come into being during the fall of 1960 as the end product of a proposal to the Air Force for a long range, high-speed interceptor to counter newly perceived Soviet threats. During late October, a letter of intent for $1 million was delivered to Lockheed to "go forward with Plan 3A". The seventh A-12 was marked to become the AF-12 prototype and late in the year, Rus

Daniell became project engineer.

The AF-12, as originally conceived by the *Skunk Works* engineering team, was a modified A-12 incorporating a fire control system integrated with a Hughes radar. A second seat in the original sensor system bay was added to accommodate a fire control system operator. During December of 1960, a separate project group was organized in the *Skunk Works*, working independently of the A-12 team. On January 23 and 24, the first meeting with the Air Force's weapon system project office took place at Burbank and everyone was briefed on the *Skunk Works* aircraft design and development philosophy.

On May 31, the AF-12 mock-up review took place. Johnson noted, "I was very concerned when I learned that some 31 people were coming, but the mock-up group from the

Air Force consisted of about 15 people. The different participants told me any number of times how pleased they were with the status of the mock-up, in general, and the ready answers they were getting from our engineering group."

By June, AF-12 wind tunnel tests had revealed directional stability problems that resulted from the revised nose and cockpit configuration mandated by the massive Hughes AN/ASG-18 radar. For the first time, ventral fins were introduced into the design, two being in the form of fixed surfaces attached to the underside of each engine nacelle, and a third being a large folding fin mounted on the fuselage centerline.

The AN/ASG-18 was the first US coherent pulse Doppler radar design for long-range, look-down, or look-up detection and single target attack. It was intended for use as an air defense interceptor system and was scheduled initially for the North American F-108 *Rapier*. Following termination of the F-108 program, Hughes continued research, development, and flight testing of the system—including the Hughes GAR-9/AIM-47 air-to-air missile—on a specially modified Convair B-58A *Hustler*.

The AN/ASG-18 employed a high average-power, liquid-cooled, traveling wave tube transmitter chain (consisting of two traveling wave tube amplifiers in tandem to provide the desired gain and analog circuitry for generation and processing of the coherent high pulse repetition frequency wave form. This system provided Hughes with much of the basic coherent high pulse repetition wave form experience that later enabled both the AN/AWG-9 and the AN/APG-63 program to be accomplished successfully. The AN/ASG-18 radar consisted of 41 units and weighed 1,380 pounds. The entire package included a solid-state digital computer for navigation, attack, and BIT; integrated controls and displays; missile auxiliaries; an analog attack steering computer; and an infrared search and track set capable of cooperative usage with the radar.

Concurrent to the activity on the AF-12, a bomber version of the A-12, referred to as the RB-12, also was being studied. A forward fuselage full-scale mock-up had been completed and on July 5, along with the AF-12 mock-up, was reviewed by Generals Curtis LeMay and Thomas Power. The two found the mock-ups of considerable interest and asked if either configuration could be modified to carry a terminal radar or an air-to-ground missile. Johnson responded favorably, by stating, "we could do this within the aerodynamic configuration of the A-12 and, for the job that they outlined to do, which was to place a missile within 200 feet of a target, one could not argue about the use of a guided missile rather than our simpler approach in the RB-12 report." The latter referred to the use of conventional free-falling bombs.

The RB-12 study had in fact resulted from the recent development of small, high-yield nuclear warheads. Johnson, in an RB-12 proposal, had noted that the aircraft could result in a "very powerful striking force...with little or no weight or space penalty..." to the aircraft. Four hypothetical 400 pound bombs based on the new warheads, or a single *Polaris*-sized warhead could be accommodated in a fuselage bomb bay while retaining the same fuel load as the reconnaissance A-12. No aerodynamic changes were required and the radar attenuating features of the aircraft could be retained. The latter, coupled with the aircraft's extraordi-

Jim Goodall

*All extant A-12s are now in museums. This beautifully restored example, due in part to the efforts of enthusiast Jim Goodall, is displayed in Minneapolis, Minnesota under the aegis of the Minnesota ANG.*

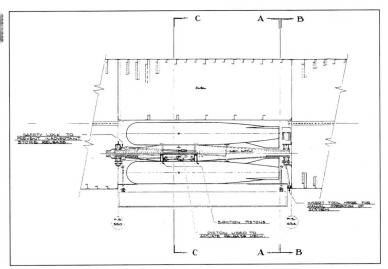
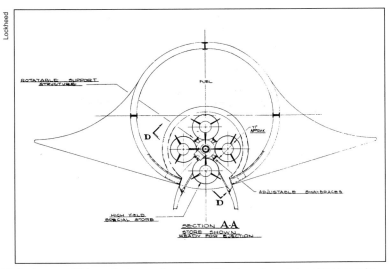

Many bomber A-12s were proposed to the Air Force, most under the RB-, or B-12 designator. This particular configuration utilized a rotary-style release mechanism. Other proposals ejected the bombs from vertical tubes. The Air Force, for various political reasons, never expressed strong interest in these proposals.

nary performance, almost certainly would make chances of detection close to non-existent.

In addition to these queries, it was noted by Johnson that, "While Hughes was giving a presentation on a simplified air-to-ground weapon system, LeMay took me by the arm and we went to another office. He told me that he wasn't very sure that the RB-12 would become a model, but he felt sure 'we would get some fighters'. I asked him, 'what about reconnaissance airplanes like the A-12?' and he seemed surprised that the Air Force were not getting any. He made a note on a yellow paper and asked me how soon we would have to know about A-12s to continue our production. I told him within two to three months."

In fact, the RB-12 program would not reach the hardware stage. This was not as a result of lack of capability, but rather because it was a threat to the on-going North American XB-70A *Valkyrie*...a program with considerable political clout and one on which the Air Force had hung its hat for a Boeing B-52 replacement. Surprisingly, as noted on October 26, 1961, Johnson discovered the Department of Defense found the RB-12 more interesting than the AF-12. He noted, however, "The Air Force, from LeMay down, do want the AF-12."

Through mid-1962, Johnson continued to work on both the A-12 and AF-12 programs simultaneously. This was an intensive and difficult undertaking, primarily because the two programs were mutually exclusive and the security surrounding each required they be handled with great delicacy and little overlap.

The AF-12's fire control system and missile complement were major concerns for Johnson. No one had ever fired an air-to-air missile while flying at Mach 3 speeds, and there seemed to be little agreement as to how to eject the missile from the AF-12's weapon bay. Even the design of the missile pylon and trapeze assembly was ill-defined, and the company overseeing the fire control system, Hughes Aircraft, was as much in the dark as Lockheed. Paper studies verified it could be done, and wind tunnel tests confirmed these, but it would only be through testing of actual hardware that a realistic insight could be gained.

Air Force funding allocations for construction of three AF-12s by now had cleared the way for modification of three of the CIA's original order for ten A-12s, and by August 3, 1962, the major elements of the first AF-12 were in the jig at Burbank. During September,

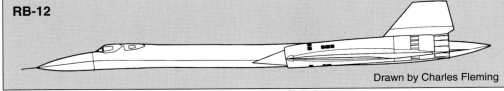

**RB-12**

Drawn by Charles Fleming

Johnson, with Rus Daniell on engineering, began exploring what he called a "common market" A-12, "which would use one airframe to make either a reconnaissance and RS or an AF airplane. This would require folding the fins on the GAR-9 missile and use of a new radar antenna. It turned out very well. This version would simplify our production problems greatly and make a better fighter with more range and a better over-all arrangement. It eliminates the necessity of the Air Force deciding which version they want to buy!"

From December of 1962 through the early spring, construction of the three AF-12s, taking place in a segregated corner of the Burbank manufacturing facility, moved ahead with little difficulty. Discussions concerning the location of the flight test program surfaced as a result of the security surrounding the on-going A-12 program, and it appeared that Edwards AFB would be the best option. Regardless, at the last moment, initial flight test activity was moved to the A-12 test location and the final decision on moving flight testing to Edwards was delayed.

On August 7, 1963 several weeks after being moved by truck to the test location, the first AF-12 (aka YF-12A), with Lockheed's Jim Eastham at the controls, made its first flight. Johnson would note in the AF-12 log, "It is the first airplane I've ever worked on where the fire control system was checked out prior to the

first flight."

Flight testing proceeded without significant difficulty and during January, the aircraft was temporarily grounded while intake system upgrades and newer engines with increased thrust were installed.

Meanwhile, by the end of 1963, the CIA's A-12 flight test program had resulted in 573 flights totaling 765 hours. Nine aircraft were on hand at the test location. As noted earlier, during July Mach 3 had been reached for the first time and during November, design speed—Mach 3.2—had been reached at an altitude of 78,000 feet. The following February 3, an A-12 had cruised at Mach 3.2 at an altitude of 83,000 feet for ten minutes. By the end of 1964 the A-12 fleet—now consisting of eleven aircraft—had logged over 1,214 flights and 1,669 hours of flying time...but only 6 hours and 23 minutes at Mach 3. Only 33 minutes had been logged at Mach 3.2.

These numbers changed drastically within the following year. By late 1965, some 33 hours had been logged at Mach 2.6 or above, and total Mach 3 time was now 9 hours. All Mach 3 time had been logged by test aircraft. The CIA's "operational" aircraft, because of extent propulsion system difficulties, were limited to maximum speeds of Mach 2.9.

On February 29, 1964 the wraps were pulled off the A-12 program, but only partially.

The AF-12 was an interim proposal between the A-12 and the YF-12A. Still retaining the chined nose of the A-12, it integrated a long-range tracking radar with infrared tracking (sensors in chine indention).

*YF-12A wind tunnel model undergoing testing by NASA. Two of the three YF-12As eventually would be placed on loan to the NASA for use as high-speed research testbeds and platforms.*

President Johnson announced, "The United States has successfully developed an advanced experimental jet aircraft, the A-11, which has been tested in sustained flight at more than 2,000 miles per hour and at altitudes in excess of 70,000 feet.

"The performance of the A-11 far exceeds that of any other aircraft in the world today. The development of this aircraft has been made possible by major advances in aircraft technology of great significance to both military and commercial application.

"Several A-11 aircraft are now being flight tested at Edwards AFB in California.

"The existence of this program is being disclosed today to permit the orderly exploitation of this advanced technology in our military and commercial planes. This advanced experimental aircraft, capable of high speed and high altitude, and long-range performance at thousands of miles, constitutes the technological accomplishment that will facilitate the achievement of a number of important military and commercial requirements. The A-11 aircraft now at Edwards AFB are undergoing extensive tests to determine their capabilities as long-range interceptors. The development of supersonic commercial transport aircraft will also be greatly assisted by the lessons learned from this A-11 program, for example, one of the

*The first YF-12A, 60-6934, under construction during early 1963. There were many differences between the F-12s and the A-12s...all as a result of the fire control system and weapon accommodations.*

*The YF-12As were built in a cordoned-off section of Building 309/310. Mock-up is visible upper left.*

*Photograph purportedly taken at the end of the first YF-12A's (60-6934) first flight on August 8, 1963. Lockheed test pilot Jim Eastham was at the controls and no one occupied the aft cockpit. Size of deployed drag chute is noteworthy.*

*The YF-12A was the first of the A-12/F-12/SR-71 family to set official world absolute speed and absolute altitude records for class. These records, including those set by the SR-71A, now have stood essentially unchallenged for over a quarter century.*

most important technological achievements in this project has been the mastery of the metallurgy and fabrication of titanium metal which is required for the high temperatures experienced by aircraft traveling at more than three times the speed of sound.

"Arrangements are being made to make this and other important technical developments available under appropriate safeguards to those directly engaged in the supersonic transport program.

"This project was first started in 1959. Appropriate members of the Senate and House have been kept fully informed on the program since the day of its inception.

"The Lockheed Aircraft Corp. at Burbank, California, is the manufacturer of the aircraft. The aircraft engine, the J58, was designed and built by the Pratt & Whitney Aircraft Division, United Aircraft Corp. The experimental fire control and air-to-air missile system for the A-11 was developed by the Hughes Aircraft Co.

"In view of the continuing importance of these developments to our national security, the detailed performance of the A-11 will remain strictly classified and all individuals associated with the program have been directed to refrain from making any further disclosure concerning this program.

"I do not expect to discuss this important matter further with you today but certain additional information will be made available to all of you after this meeting. If you care, Mr. Salinger will make the appropriate arrangements."

His reference to the A-11 was of course, the result of "Kelly" Johnson's input. There was no A-11, at least in hardware form, and the photographs released in conjunction with the President's announcement actually depicted the first AF-12. Compounding the confusion was the fact the AF-12 now was assigned an official Air Force designation...YF-12A. Regardless, the first and second aircraft, several hours before the actual announcement, were flown from the test location to Edwards AFB in order to give credence to the President's claim they were operating from Edwards AFB. According to Johnson, when the first aircraft arrived and were hurriedly moved into a hangar, they were "so hot that the fire extinguishing nozzles came on and gave us a free wash job."

Now referred to as the YF-12A, test flights continued with increased frequency as confidence in the aircraft grew. On April 16, 1964, the first AIM-47 air-to-air missile was ejected in flight. According to Johnson, "The launching was safe but the angle developed was poor. If

it had been a powered missile, it would have come out through the cockpit. In spite of all our missile ejection tests without airflow, we muffed this one by a factor of three in nose-down pitching moment."

Also during mid-1964, difficulties with the A-12, also reflected in the YF-12, had yet to be fully overcome. Transonic acceleration

remained troublesome and miscellaneous subsystems still required major improvements in dependability. On July 9, Bill Park was forced to eject from an A-12 during final approach to landing at the test location. Bill was uninjured and the cause of the accident was quickly determined to be "a stuck outboard elevon servo valve."

*The Hughes AN/ASG-18 radar and associated fire control system (and infrared tracking system) for the AIM-47 first was flight tested aboard highly modified Convair B-58A, 55-665.*

*Special cartridge starting units for the J58 were developed for the YF-12A to accommodate the Air Force requirement the aircraft be capable of being quickly started while standing on alert.*

125

The YF-12A was the only member of the A-12/F-12/SR-71 to be equipped with a folding centerline ventral fin.

YF-12A flight testing provided convincing arguments the aircraft was a viable long-range, high-speed interceptor. AIM-47 tests also were encouraging.

It should be noted at this point that on July 24, 1964, President Johnson made the first official announcement concerning the forthcoming Lockheed SR-71. As part of the A-12 history, it is necessary to understand that from this point forward, there was a plan to replace the A-12 with Air Force's follow-on aircraft.

Attempts to make the A-12 operational had been short-circuited by the various technological difficulties that continued to surface. During August of 1964, it was determined that the CIA required four operational aircraft to overfly Cuba by November 5. "We have been told by the Soviets that immediately after the election they intend to shoot down every U-2, which we are operating at a rate of 18 sorties per month. Should this be done, we would be unable to find out whether they put missiles back in; the A-12 is vital for this purpose."

Though transition training was taking place at the test location, by November of 1964 there still was no CIA pilot qualified to fly the extremely temperamental A-12—which the CIA now was sometimes referring to under the codename *Cygnus*—on a reconnaissance mission. Johnson volunteered to use Lockheed test pilots to fly over Cuba.

According to Johnson's log, under the then-classified project codename of *Skylark*, the CIA accepted this offer, and on November 10 the first A-12 operational mission and first penetration of denied airspace was successfully accomplished. The CIA record, however, seems to dispute this. Their account is as follows:

"By early 1964 Project Headquarters began planning for the contingency of flights over that island under a program designated *Skylark*. Bill Park's accident in early July held this program up for a time, but on 5 August, acting DCI Marshall S. Carter directed that *Skylark* achieve emergency operational readiness by November 5. This involved preparing a small detachment which should be able to do the job over Cuba though at something less than the full design capability of the *Oxcart*.. The goal was to operate at Mach 2.8 and 80,000 feet altitude.

"In order to meet the deadline set by Gen. Carter, camera performance would have to be validated, pilots qualified for Mach 2.8 flight, and coordination with supporting elements arranged. Only one of several equipments for electronic countermeasures (ECM) would be ready by November and a senior intra-governmental group, including representation from the President's Scientific Advisory Committee, examined the problem of operating over Cuba without the full complement of defensive systems. This panel decided that the first few overflights could safely be conducted without them, but the ECM would be necessary thereafter. The delivery schedule of ECM equipment was compatible with this course of action.

"After considerable modifications to aircraft, the detachment simulated Cuban missions on training flights, and a limited emergency *Skylark* capability was announced on the date Gen. Carter had set. With two weeks notice the *Oxcart* detachment could accomplish a Cuban overflight, though with fewer ready aircraft and pilots than planned.

"During the following weeks the detachment concentrated on developing *Skylark* into a sustained capability, with five ready pilots and five operational aircraft. The main tasks were to determine aircraft range and fuel consumption, attain repeatable reliable operation, finish pilot training, prepare a family of *Skylark* missions, and coordinate routes with North American Air Defense, Continental Air Defense, and the Federal Aviation Administration. All this was accomplished without substantially hindering the main task of working up *Oxcart* to full design capability."

In spite of all this, according to the CIA document quoted, "*Oxcart* was never used over Cuba. U-2s proved adequate and the A-12 was reserved for more critical situations."

While the A-12 situation vacillated back and forth between an operational commitment and continued wait-and-see, flight testing of the YF-12A had continued. On January 9, 1965, *Skunk Works* pilot Jim Eastham had taken the first aircraft out to Mach 3.23, sustaining Mach 3.2 for some five minutes. On the same day, Johnson would note in the log, "The airplane flies well and we actually set several speed records in the process of making a swing over Phoenix. I think we'll shortly get the go-ahead to go for the speed record, using Air Force pilots, of course."

The YF-12A's Hughes AN/ASG-18 pulse-Doppler radar was the most powerful unit of its kind in the world at the time of its debut. Surprisingly, it was completely functional at the time of the YF-12A's first flight.

Work with the YF-12A as an interceptor had remained a program priority. Difficulties with the Hughes fire control system had delayed actual missile firing tests, but finally, on March 18, Johnson wrote, "We finally fired a GAR-9 at a target. We hit it 36 miles away with a closing rate of well over 2,000 mph. We are scheduled to fire against many drones, including those at low altitude, this summer".

The various A-12s and the three YF-12As had routinely broken the world's absolute speed and altitude records during the nearly three years they had been flying. The Department of Defense, aware the extant records were held by Soviet aircraft, on August 12, 1964 informed Johnson of their desire to use the YF-12A to bring the records back to the US. The YF-12A was chosen primarily because it was the model with the greatest public exposure and the one with the least design and technology sensitivity. This proposal languished as a result of on-going technical difficulties, but the following April, the Air Force approved an official assault.

Finally, on May 1, 1965, the first and third YF-12As were used to set the following Class C Group III absolute records: sustained altitude (absolute)—80,258 feet (crew, Col. Robert Stephens/Lt. Col. Daniel Andre); 15/25 kilometer closed circuit (absolute)—2,070.102 mph (crew, Col. Robert Stephens/Lt. Col. Daniel Andre); 500 kilometer closed-circuit (Class C)—1,643.042 mph (crew, Maj. Walter Daniel/Maj. Noel Warner); and 1,000 kilometer closed-circuit without payload and with 1,000 kilogram payload (absolute) and with 2,000 kilogram payload (Class C)—1,688.891 mph (crew, Maj. Walter Daniel/Capt. James Cooney).

Work on the YF-12A now took a slightly encouraging turn when, on May 14, 1965, the *Skunk Works* received a $500 thousand contract for F-12B engineering. This aircraft, the proposed production version of the YF-12A, was configured for operational deployment and had improvements in aerodynamics and select systems. No production go-ahead was received with the engineering contract, but the expression of interest was sufficient to merit some optimism.

On September 28, a GAR-9 was fired from a YF-12A at Mach 3.2 at 75,000 feet, thus causing Johnson to note the program finally was "hitting the high speed corner of the design diagram". The missile missed its target at 40,000 feet and at a range of 36 miles by "6 feet 6 inches...which is a very good shot".

On November 10, another half-million dollar contract for basic F-12B design work kept the program alive. Hughes Aircraft received a $4.5 million contract to continue development of the AN/ASG-18 radar and fire control system.

During 1965, the "critical situation" the CIA's A-12 Detachment had been waiting for finally emerged in Asia. On March 18, 1965,

*The ventral fin folded left for takeoff and landing in concert with landing gear extension and retraction. It compensated for the loss of directional stability resulting from the interceptor's abbreviated chine design.*

the CIA's McCone discussed with Secretary of Defense Robert McNamara and Secretary Cyrus Vance the increasing hazards to U-2 and unmanned drone reconnaissance of Communist China. "It was further agreed that we should proceed immediately with all preparatory steps necessary to operate the *Oxcart* over Communist China, flying out of Okinawa. It was agreed that we should proceed with all construction and related arrangements. However, this decision did not authorize all preparatory steps and the expenditure of such funds as might be involved. No decision has been taken to fly the *Oxcart* operationally over Communist China. This decision can only be made by the President."

Four days later, Brigadier Gen. Jack Ledford, Director of the Office of Special Activities, briefed Mr. Vance on the scheme which had been drawn up for operations in the Far East. The project was called *Black Shield*, and it required the A-12 to operate out of Kadena Air Force Base in Okinawa. In the first phase, three aircraft would stage to Okinawa for sixty day periods twice a year, with about 225 personnel involved. Following this, *Black Shield* would advance to a point of maintaining a permanent detachment at Kadena. Secretary Vance made $3.7 million available to provide support facilities on the island, which were to be available by early fall of 1965.

The deployment of surface-to-air missiles around Hanoi also had caught US forces in the rapidly escalating Vietnam war off guard, as well. Secretary McNamara, after being briefed, called this to the attention of the Under Secretary of the Air Force on June 3, 1965, and inquired about the practicability of substituting A-12s for U-2s. He was told that *Black Shield* could operate over Vietnam as soon as adequate aircraft performance was achieved.

Thus with deployment impending in the fall, the detachment went into the final stages of its program for validating the reliability of aircraft and aircraft systems. It set out to demonstrate complete systems reliability at Mach 3.05 and at 2,300 nautical miles range, with a penetration altitude of 76,000 feet. A demonstrated capability of three aerial refuelings also was part of the validation requirement.

Back at the *Skunk Works*, work continued

on the A-12's propulsion system throughout much of 1965. On January 4, Johnson noted, "It appears that our duct problems at high speed are stemming from excess leakage at the engine face and various bypass doors. Have concluded 10,764 wind tunnel tests on the inlet alone, and every one of them confirms our present design. The addition of mice not only solved the roughness problem but gained us 2% in ram. We will gradually work up to our basic performance, as close as we can expect to get it, considering the engine's overweight and added equipment in the airplane."

On January 27, 1965, an A-12 embarked on the type's first long-range, high-speed flight. Airborne for an hour and forty minutes, it spent an hour and fifteen minutes at Mach 3.1 or above. The mission covered 2,580 nautical miles while cruising at an altitude of between 75,600 and 80,000 feet. Just over two weeks earlier, Jim Eastham had flown the first YF-12A at Mach 3.23, staying there for five minutes.

On March 18, Johnson sent Hamilton Standard a letter saying Lockheed no longer could use the AIC-10 inlet control. "We have spent $17 million on the thing to this point, but it just will not do the job and is totally unpredictable."

Difficulties with the A-12's performance as a result of intake problems had become the aircraft's *Achilles' heel*, particularly in the flight regime between Mach 2.4 and 2.8. On-going studies of the intake and its spike had failed to uncover a solution to airflow anomalies until a review of the Hamilton Standard actuator had determined it was not working. At that point, Ben Rich, who was responsible for the *Skunk Works'* side of the propulsion system package and, in particular, the intake design, concluded the Hamilton Standard hydro-mechanical spike control unit could not be made to work. Garrett Corporation then provided an electrically-powered actuator that, following installation, solved almost all the spike control problems virtually overnight.

YF-12A work had moved ahead with some difficulty during this period as well, though its problems were compounded not only by the propulsion system anomalies, but also by the complexities of the AN/ASG-18 fire control system and the Hughes GAR-9 (AIM-47)

*The Hughes AIM-47 radar-guided air-to-air missile tests were successful. Full-scale targets utilized during the tests included two Boeing B-47 Stratojets. Special camera pods, suspended from the YF-12A's engine nacelles, photographed the launches at Mach 3.*

*YF-12A, 60-6935, seen landing at Edwards AFB, would become the only one of the three YF-12As built to survive the flight test program. It is presently on display at the US Air Force Museum, Wright-Patterson AFB, Ohio.*

air-to-air missile.

The A-12 flight test program had not gone without losses. At the test location, the number six aircraft, piloted by Mele Vojvodich, Jr., crashed on December 28, 1965. It had yawed violently shortly after taking off on a test flight. When additional corrective actions had not stabilized the aircraft, Vojvodich ejected. He landed with only minor injuries, but the A-12 was a total loss. Johnson would note, "Coming down in the airplane with Bill Park and Burt McMaster, we analyzed the situation within a half hour. The SAS gyros were hooked up backwards. This is the first thing I told the accident board to look at. Prior to leaving the test location, Ed Martin cut the gyros out, keeping the wires connected to them. Low and behold—the pitch and yaw gyro connections were interchanged in the rigging, which explained the accident completely."

Continuing concerns about various A-12 systems and their impact on the aircraft's performance were addressed during the fall of 1965 when four A-12s were selected for assignment to *Black Shield*. Johnson took personal responsibility for seeing to the solution of the various problems and assuring the CIA the aircraft would be ready for operational service on schedule. During the tests that ensued, the A-12 achieved a maximum speed of Mach 3.29, an altitude of 90,000 feet, and a sustained flight time above Mach 3.2 of one hour and fourteen minutes. The longest flight lasted six hours and twenty minutes.

On November 20, 1965, Johnson wrote Gen. Ledford, "...over-all, my considered opinion is that the aircraft can be successfully deployed for the *Black Shield* mission with what I would consider to be at least as low a degree of risk as in the early U-2 deployment days. Actually, considering our performance level of more than four times the U-2 speed and three miles more operating altitude, it is probably much less risky than our first U-2 deployment. I think the time has come when the bird should leave its nest."

Ten days later, the 303 Committee received a formal proposal that the A-12 be deployed to the Far East. The proposal was rejected. The Committee did agree, however, that short of actually moving aircraft to Kadena, all steps should be taken to develop and maintain a quick reaction capability, ready to deploy within a 21-day period at any time after January 1, 1966.

In between the various A-12 tests and political maneuverings, work on the YF-12A had continued in spurts. On March 29, 1966, Johnson noted in the log, "Had a long meeting with Col. Benjamin Bellis, Hughes Aircraft Company, test force members, etc., to talk about optimum use of the YF-12A for deriving information for the F-12B. The production airplane possibilities now look very good. At this meeting, Col. Bellis asked if we would take on the job of weapon systems integration going far beyond our normal responsibilities in that we would do major planning and programming not only of the aircraft but also of the missiles, radar, engines, and similar gear."

Johnson thought it over and replied that the *Skunk Works* would, indeed be willing to handle the program from top to bottom. It was, in fact, quite reminiscent of what the *Skunk Works* already had done with the U-2...and what was, in most respects, being done with the A-12. It was to be a precedent the company would emulate for the following quarter century...and which continues to this very day.

YF-12A flight testing had now continued to the point where actual fire control system tests against real targets could be undetaken. On April 25, two aircraft were flown to Eglin AFB, Florida and there used to conduct live target test intercepts. On one mission over the Gulf of Mexico, the attacking YF-12A—piloted by Jim Eastham—while flying at 75,000 feet and Mach 3.2, fired a single AIM-47A at a Boeing B-47 target aircraft flying at 1,500 feet on an opposite heading. The unarmed missile hit and destroyed some four feet of the B-47's horizontal stabilizer. The mission was considered a complete success. Eventually, seven launches were accomplished. All but one was deemed successful (the failure was attributed to a missile gyro system failure)...see table below.

During July of 1966, Johnson wrote in the log, "We were directed to give up further flying of the YF-12As, although we had proposed shooting down a drone at Holloman to get the effect of ground clutter for low altitude targets." The following August 5, he wrote, "We have laid off half of our test crew on the YF-12A and are maintaining only enough people to store the airplane or send it to Burbank. We are very near the end of this program."

Surprisingly, even in light of the declaration concerning continued flight testing of the YF-12As, Johnson remained somewhat hopeful the F-12B would be funded. During November of 1966, he wrote, "The F-12B is being opened up again as a result of a study made by the Air Force to get a modern air defense system." As late as January 27, 1967, he still was awaiting a decision. "In spite of favorable press releases, the President did not specifically spell out F-12B in his budget message, but did say that a start would be made on a new air defense system."

Things continued to heat up. On March 21, a call from Col. Bellis led Johnson to believe that the F-12B proposal had been accepted by the Air Force. And on March 4, Col. Dan Andre visited Johnson in Burbank and began discussing the security that would be required to cover the F-12B program. "I had a basic agreement with Gen. Bellis that externally, for drawings and manuals going to the Air Force, we would comply with DoD security requirements, but internally, we would not. Later on, we were given a thick document which would apply complete DoD security, internally and externally, to the *Skunk Works*. We couldn't begin to function; so I refused to sign our contract."

On November 13, Johnson noted, "We were asked to study the conversion of ten *Oxcart* airplanes to fighters and also ten SR-71s to fighters. We proposed the installation of Westinghouse radars and *Sparrow* missiles. Nothing came of this."

The writing now appeared to be on the wall. There would be no production A-12 interceptor. On December 29, Johnson wrote in the log, "I had a call from the SPO canceling all ADP air defense programs except a portion of the vulnerability study which was transferred to the SR-71. We were instructed to shut down immediately, but I told them it would require at least a month. A termination notice, therefore, was not issued. We were asked to come in with a plan for an orderly shutdown." On January 5, 1968, an official wire "closing down the F-12B" was received from the Air Force. The YF-12A program would be formally ended on February 1. As a parting gesture, Johnson left Air Force representatives with a proposal to convert two of the YF-12As to trainers for SAC use.

In a final disheartening move, the Air Force, on February 5, sent Johnson a letter instructing Lockheed to destroy the A-12/F-12

### YF-12A/AIM-47 Tests @ Eglin AFB, Florida

| Date | YF-12 # | Mach # | Altitude (feet) | Target | Target Alt. (feet) |
|---|---|---|---|---|---|
| 3/18/65 | '935 | 2.20 | 65,000 | Ryan Q-2C | 40,000 |
| 5/19/65 | '935 | 2.30 | 65,000 | Ryan Q-2C | 20,000 |
| 9/28/65 | '934 | 3.20 | 75,000 | Ryan Q-2C | 20,000 |
| 3/22/66 | '936 | 3.15 | 74,500 | Ryan Q-2C | 1,500 |
| 4/25/66 | '934 | 3.20 | 75,000 | Boeing QB-47 | 1,500 |
| 5/13/66 | '936 | 3.17 | 74,000 | Ryan Q-2C | 20,000 |
| 9/21/66 | '936 | 3.20 | 74,000 | Boeing QB-47 | sea level |

*The YF-12A's missile bays, though large, were nevertheless a snug fit for the Hughes AIM-47A. The missile bay doors were hydraulically actuated.*

*The missile bay doors were, like most of the rest of the YF-12A, manufactured of titanium alloys. The aircraft was equipped with three missile bays.*

tooling (by the date of the letter, this also included the SR-71 tooling...the aircraft addressed in Chapter 12). "We have proceeded to store such items as are required for producing spare parts at Norton. The large jigs have now been cut up for scrap and we are finishing the clean-up of the complete area. Ten years from now the country will be very sorry for taking this decision of stopping production on the whole Mach 3 series of aircraft in the USA."

Throughout 1966, the A-12 program had continued to flounder, as well. In effect, it had nothing to do. During the year, repeated requests to authorize the flights over China and North Vietnam were refused. The CIA, the Joint Chiefs of Staff, and the President's Foreign Intelligence Advisory Board favored the overflights, while Alexis Johnson of the State Department, McNamara, and Vance of the Defense Department opposed them. Perhaps most importantly, the President sided with the opposition...agreeing that the political and technological risks were too great.

On May 12, 1966, Johnson wrote in the log, "As of this date, there is still no go-ahead for the deployment, although it seems fairly optimistic. The airplanes are ready to go. We do not yet have the range up to the design value, but two-thirds of the loss has been due to weight changes due to added equipment. One-third of it is due to loss in range cruising. We can do about 3,000 nautical miles, but they, of course, do not get the range that we can."

On October 10, he noted, "Still no deployment. We are making 40 flights a month. The airplane is working quite well. It has not yet obtained its range. We are down to working on duct leakage and basic engine performance."

An impressive demonstration of the A-12's capability occurred on December 21, 1966 when the *Skunk Works'* Bill Park flew the aircraft 10,198 statute miles in six hours. The A-12 had departed the test location and had flown northward over Yellowstone National Park, then east to Bismark, North Dakota, and on to Duluth, Minnesota. It had then turned south and passed Atlanta, Georgia enroute to Tampa, Florida, then northwest to Portland, Oregon, and then back for a pass over the test location. From there, it had headed eastward, passing over Denver, Colorado and St. Louis, Missouri. Turning around at Knoxville, Tennessee, it had passed Memphis, Tennessee for its return to the test location. It was a record unapproachable by any other aircraft in the world.

On January 5, 1967, Walter Ray and the fourth A-12 were lost during the course of a routine training flight from the test location. A fuel gauge apparently failed and the fuel supply had depleted without the pilot knowing it. The engines flamed out shortly before the aircraft reached the runway. Ray ejected but was killed when he failed to separate from the ejection seat before impact.

The CIA's inability to justify using the A-12 operationally, by the end of 1966 had led to concerns the aircraft would soon be placed in storage. As late as January 26, 1967, Johnson made the following comments in the A-12 log, "We are still not clear on going about storing the airplanes. I spent some time yesterday with Larry Bohanan going over the personnel problems in our flight test crew. It is inevitable that we lose half of our good people this year. And there is no flight test activity in CALAC to use them. In spite of the plans to store the airplanes, Headquarters are going ahead with putting changes on the airplanes, because the word hasn't gotten around. I'm trying to get some direction to this program, to prevent further waste of money. I think back to 1959, before we started this airplane, to discussions with the Program Office where we seriously considered the problem of whether there would be one more round of aircraft before the satellites took over. We jointly agreed there would be just one round, and not two. That seems to have been a very accurate evaluation, as it seems that 30 SR-71s give us enough overflight reconnaissance capability and we don't need the additional ten A-12 aircraft."

The plan to place the A-12s in storage continued to accelerate during the first few months of 1967. On March 21, Johnson wrote, "The Air Force and the Program Office are having quite a time about storing the A-12s. It appears that half of them will be stored by the middle of this year and all of them by February of 1968. In the meantime, five airplanes will be kept on alert status for deployment."

With this bleak prognosis, it came as somewhat of a surprise during early May when prospects for operational deployment suddenly took a new turn. Concerns that surface-to-air missiles would be deployed in North Vietnam suddenly provided the small A-12 community with a *raison d'être* during early 1967. The President now asked for a review of the surface-to-air missile activity and what might be done to monitor it.

The CIA, in response, briefed the 303 Committee and once again suggested the A-12 be used. It was noted that its Hycon camera was far superior to those then being used on the various Teledyne Ryan drones and the operational SAC U-2s...and its vulnerability was considerably less.

As a result of this, the State and Defense Department members of the Committee elected to reexamine the requirements and political risks. While this was taking place, the CIA's director, Richard Helms, submitted to the 303 Committee another formal proposal to deploy the A-12. President Johnson, concurrently, granted permission for use of the unique aircraft and on May 16, his assistant, Walt Rostow, formally conveyed the President's decision. *Black Shield* was put into effect immediately.

On May 17, the first support components of *Black Shield* were airlifted to Kadena AB in Okinawa. They were followed on May 22 by the first A-12 which arrived six hours and six minutes after departing the location. A second A-12 followed on May 24, and a third on May 26. The latter, as a result of inertial navigation system and communications system problems, landed at Wake Island enroute before proceeding on to Kadena the next day.

On May 29, 1967, the unit was declared ready to fly its first operational mission. Under the command of Col. Hugh Slater, 260 personnel had been transferred to Kadena as part of the *Black Shield* team. Except for hangars, which were a month short of completion, everything was in shape for sustained operations. Next day, the detachment was alerted for a mission scheduled for May 31.

The A-12 departed on schedule...though in the middle of a heavy rain (a first for the A-12). The flight followed a predetermined route over North Vietnam and the Demilitarized Zone. It lasted three hours and 39 minutes. Cruise legs

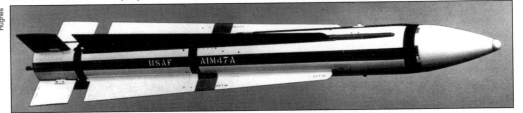

*The 818 pound Hughes AIM-47A, initially referred to as the GAR-9, was a Mach 4 radar-guided air-to-air missile with a range in excess of 125 miles. Its technology later was applied to the successful AIM-54.*

*The* Coldwall *experiments exploring heat transfer phenomenon at high Mach numbers were conducted while the YF-12As were on loan to NASA. The* Coldwall *hardware, in the form of a steel tube and associated thermocouples, was mounted ventrally on the aircraft centerline.*

were flown at Mach 3.1 and 80,000 feet. Results were satisfactory and seventy of the 190 surface-to-air missile sites in North Vietnam were photographed...along with nine other priority targets. There were no radar signals detected—implying the Chinese and North Vietnamese had not known about the aircraft's flyover.

Fifteen *Black Shield* missions were alerted during the period from May 31 to August 15, 1967 and seven were actually flown. Four of these resulted in detectable radar activity, but no hostile action was taken. By mid-July, the A-12 overflights had determined with a high degree of confidence that there were no surface-to-surface missiles in North Vietnam.

All operational missions were planned, directed, and controlled by Project Headquarters in Washington, D.C. A constant watch was maintained on the weather in the various target areas. Each day, at a specified hour (1600 hours local), a mission alert briefing was given to appropriate *Black Shield* personnel. If the forecast weather appeared favorable, the Kadena base was alerted and provided a route to be flown. The alert preceded actual takeoff by 28 to 30 hours. Twelve hours prior to takeoff (H minus 12) a second review of the target area's weather was made. If it continued favorable, the mission generation sequence continued. At H minus 2 hours, a "go-no-go" decision was made and communicated to the field. The final decision depended not solely on weather in the target area but also on conditions in the refueling, launch, and recovery areas.

Operations and maintenance at Kadena began with the receipt of alert notification. Both a primary aircraft and pilot and a back-up aircraft and pilot were selected. The aircraft were given a thorough inspection and servicing, all systems were checked, and the cameras were loaded. Pilots received a detailed route briefing in the early evening prior the day of flight. On the morning of the flight a final briefing occurred, at which time the condition of the aircraft and its systems was reported, last minute weather forecasts reviewed, and other relevant intelligence communicated together with any amendments or changes in the flight plan. Two hours prior to takeoff the primary pilot had a medical examination, got into his suit, and was taken to the aircraft. If any malfunctions developed on the primary aircraft, the back-up could execute the mission one hour later.

A typical *Black Shield* mission route profile over North Vietnam included a refueling south of Okinawa shortly after takeoff, the planned photographic pass or passes, withdrawal to a second aerial refueling in the Thailand area, and return to Kadena. So great was the A-12's speed that it spent only twelve and one-half minutes over North Vietnam in a typical "single pass" mission, or a total of twenty-one and one-half minutes on two passes. Its turning radius of 86 miles was such, however, that on some mission profiles it might be forced during its turn to intrude into Chinese airspace.

Once landed at Kadena, the camera film was removed, boxed, and sent by special aircraft to a processing facility. Film from earlier missions was developed at the Eastman Kodak plant in Rochester, New York. By late summer of 1967, an Air Force Center in Japan began processing it in order to place the photo intelligence in the hands of American commanders in Vietnam within twenty-four hours of a *Black Shield* mission's completion.

Johnson had been kept apprised of A-12 activity and successes. On July 18, 1967, he noted in the A-12's log, "The results of the deployment appear to have been very successful. In six flights, more data was obtained than had been gathered the prior year by all other reconnaissance methods. In spite of this favorable performance, I am shocked and amazed to find that the airplane will be returned in December and be stored at Palmdale. At that time, SAC will be deployed with the SR-71."

Between August 16, and December 31, 1967, twenty-six missions were alerted. Fifteen were flown. On September 17, one surface-to-air missile site tracked the vehicle with its acquisition radar but was unsuccessful with its *Fan Song* guidance radar. On October 23, a North Vietnam surface-to-air missile site for the first time launched a single, albeit unsuccessful missile at an A-12. Photography from this mission documented the event with photographs of missile smoke above the missile firing site, and with pictures of the missile and its contrails. The A-12's electronic countermeasures system appeared to perform well against the missile's systems.

During a flight on October 30, 1967, pilot Dennis Sullivan detected radar tracking on his first pass over North Vietnam. Two sites prepared to launch missiles but neither did. During the second pass, at least six missiles were fired, each confirmed by vapor trails documented on mission photography. Sullivan saw these vapor trails and witnessed three missile detonations. Post-flight inspection of the aircraft revealed that a small piece of threaded metal had penetrated the lower right wing fillet area. The fragment was not a warhead pellet but was probably part of the debris from one of the missile detonations.

Between January 1 and March 31, 1968, six missions were flown out of fifteen alerted. Four of these were over North Vietnam and two were over North Korea. The first mission (flown by CIA pilot Frank Murray) over North Korea on January 26 occurred during a very tense period following seizure of the USS *Pueblo* on January 23. The aim was to discov-

er whether the North Koreans were preparing any large scale hostile moves on the heels of this incident. Chinese tracking of the flight was detected, but no missiles were fired.

The Department of State was reluctant to endorse a second mission over North Korea for fear of the diplomatic repercussions which could be expected if the aircraft came down in hostile territory. Brigadier General Paul Bacalis then briefed Secretary Rusk on the details and objectives of the mission and assured him the aircraft would transit North Korean in no more than seven minutes. He explained that even if some failure occurred during flight the aircraft would be highly unlikely to land either in North Korea or China. Secretary Rusk made suggestions to alter the flight plan, thus becoming the project's highest ranking flight planner.

Between April 1, and June 9, 1968 two missions were alerted for North Korea. Only the mission which flew on May 8 was granted approval. Flown by Jack Layton, it would be the last operational A-12 mission...ever.

During November of 1965, the very month when the A-12 finally was declared operational, the moves toward its retirement had commenced. Within the Bureau of the Budget a memorandum was circulated expressing concern at the costs of the A-12 and SR-71 programs, both past and projected. It questioned the requirement for the total number of aircraft represented in the combined fleets and expressed doubt about the necessity of a separate CIA A-12 fleet. Several alternatives were proposed to achieve a substantial reduction in the forecasted spending, but the recommended course was to phase out the A-12 by September 1966 and stop any further SR-71 procurement. Copies of this memorandum were sent to the Department of Defense and the CIA with the suggestion that those agencies explore the alternatives set out in the paper. The Secretary of Defense declined to consider the proposal, presumably because the SR-71 would not be operational by September of 1966.

Things remained in this state until July of 1966 when the Bureau of the Budget proposed that a study group be established to look into the possibility of reducing expenses on the A-12 and SR-71 programs. The group was requested to consider the following alternatives:

(1) Retention of separate A-12 and SR-71 fleets, i.e., *status quo.*

(2) Co-location of the two fleets.

(3) Transfer of the A-12 mission and aircraft to SAC.

(4) Transfer of the A-12 mission to SAC and storage of the A-12s.

(5) Transfer of the A-12 mission to SAC and disposal of the A-12s.

The study group included C. W. Fisher,

Bureau of the Budget; Herbert Bennington, Department of Defense; and John Parangosky, CIA. It conducted its review through the fall of 1966 and identified three principal alternatives of its own. They were:

(1) To maintain the *status quo* and continue both fleets at current approval levels.

(2) To mothball all A-12 aircraft, but maintain the capability by sharing SR-71 aircraft between SAC and the CIA.

(3) To terminate the A-12 fleet during January of 1968 (assuming an operational readiness date of September 1967 for the SR-71) and assign all missions to the SR-71 fleet.

On December 12, 1966 there was a meeting at the Bureau of the Budget attended by Richard Helms, George Schultze, Cyrus Vance, and Richard Hornig (scientific advisor to the President). Those present voted on the alternatives proposed in the Fischer/Bennington/Parangosky report. Vance, Schultze, and Hornig chose to terminate the A-12 fleet and Helms was in favor of eventually sharing the SR-71 fleet between the CIA and SAC. The Bureau of the Budget immediately prepared a letter to President Johnson setting forth the course of action recommended by the majority. Helms, having dissented from the majority, requested his Deputy Director for Science and Technology to prepare a letter to the President stating the CIA's reasons for remaining in the reconnaissance business.

On December 16, Schultze handed Helms a draft memorandum to the President which requested a decision either to share the SR-71 fleet between the CIA and SAC or terminate the CIA's reconnaissance capability entirely. This time, Helms replied that new information of considerable significance had been brought to his attention concerning SR-71 performance. He requested another meeting after January 1, to review pertinent facts and also asked that the memorandum to the President be withheld pending the meeting's outcome. Specifically he cited indications the SR-71 program was having serious technical problems and that there was real doubt that it would achieve an operational capability by the time suggested for termination of the A-12 program. Helms therefore changed his position from sharing the SR-71 aircraft with SAC to a firm recommendation to retain the A-12 fleet under civilian sponsorship. The Budget Bureau's memorandum was nevertheless transmitted to the President who, on December 23, 1966 accepted the Vance, Hornig, and Schultze recommendation and directed the A-12 program be terminated by January 1, 1968.

This decision meant that a schedule had to be developed for orderly phase-out. After consultation with Project Headquarters, the Deputy Secretary of Defense was advised on January 10, 1967 that four A-12s would be

NASA discovered the heavy folding ventral fin of the YF-12As could be removed without seriously impacting the aircraft's directional stability at high Mach numbers.

placed in storage during July of 1967, two more by December, and the last four by the end of January 1968. During May, Vance directed that the SR-71 assume contingency responsibility to conduct Cuban overflights as of July 1, 1967 and take over the dual capability over Southeast Asia and Cuba by December 1. This provided for some overlap between A-12 withdrawal and SR-71 assumption of responsibility.

Meanwhile, until July 1, 1967, the A-12 Detachment was to maintain its capability to conduct operational missions both from a prepared location overseas and from the US. This included a 15-day quick reaction capability for deployment to the Far East and a seven-day quick reaction for deployment over Cuba. Between July 1 and December 31, 1967, the fleet would remain able to conduct operational missions either from a prepared overseas base or from home base, but not from both simultaneously. A quick reaction capability for either Cuban overflights or deployment to the Far East would also be maintained.

All of these arrangements were made before the A-12 had conducted a single operational mission or even deployed to Kadena. As noted earlier, the first A-12 mission over North Vietnam took place on the last day of May 1967. In succeeding months it demonstrated both its exceptional technical capabilities and the competence with which its operations were managed. As word began to get around the A-12 was to be phased out, high officials began to feel some disquiet. Concern was shown by Walt Rostow, the President's Special Assistant; by key Congressional figures; members of the President's Foreign Intelligence Advisory Board; and the President's Scientific Advisory Committee. The phase-out lagged, and the decision was reexamined.

0these alternatives in a memorandum to Paul Nitze, Richard Hornig, and Al Flax, dated April 18, 1966. In it he questioned why, if eight SR-71s could be stored in one option, they could not be stored in all options, with the resulting savings applied in each case. He questioned the lower cost figures of combining the A-12s with the SR-71s and disagreed, for security reasons, with co-locating the two fleets. Above all, however, he felt that the key point was the desirability of retaining a covert reconnaissance capability under civilian management. It was his judgment that such a requirement existed and he recommended that A-12s continue at their own base under CIA management.

In spite of all these belated efforts, the Secretary of Defense on May 16, 1968 reaffirmed the original decision to terminate the A-12 program and store the aircraft. At his weekly luncheon with his principal advisors on May 21, 1968, the President confirmed Secretary Clifford's decision.

During early March of 1968, SR-71s began arriving at Kadena to take over the *Black Shield* commitment, and by gradual stages the A-12 was placed on standby to back up the SR-71. During April of 1968, Johnson would note in the A-12 log, "The A-12 aircraft are operating with a 30-day overlap with three SR-71s deployed from Beale. The photographic take of the A-12 is considerably better than that of the SR-71s because the Hycon camera in the latter airplane isn't doing its job."

As noted earlier, the last operational mission flown by the A-12 took place on May 8, 1968 over North Korea, following which the Kadena Detachment was advised to prepare to go home. On May 24, 1968, Johnson would write, "The decision was taken to phase out the A-12 by about mid-June." On May 29, 1968 he

All of NASA's YF-12A operations were conducted from NASA's Dryden facility at Edwards AFB. Both NASA and Air Force pilots participated in the various research projects. NASA markings were applied to the aircraft during their NASA tenure.

*The YF-12A's extended centerline ventral fin has not often been seen. Visible under the right engine nacelle is one of the special pylon-mounted camera pods which originally were intended for use while photographing Hughes AIM-47 air-to-air missile launches.*

would note, "Plans were put into effect for storing the A-12 aircraft at Palmdale."

In fact, Project Headquarters had selected June 8, 1968 as the earliest possible date to begin redeployment, and in the meantime, A-12 flights were limited to those essential for maintaining pilot proficiency. After *Black Shield* aircraft returned to the US they were placed in storage at Palmdale. Those already at the location were placed in storage beginning June 4...with the last going into storage three days later.

During its final days overseas the A-12 program suffered a final blow that was as inexplicable as it was tragic. On June 4, an aircraft piloted by Jack Weeks set out from Kadena on a check flight necessitated by an engine change. Weeks last was heard from when 520 miles east of Manila. Then he disappeared. Search and rescue operations found nothing. No cause for the accident was ever ascertained and the Weeks disappearance remains a mystery to this day.

The final A-12 flight took place on June 21, 1968, when the last remaining aircraft, number "131", was ferried from the test location to Palmdale by CIA pilot Frank Murray and placed in storage. It would remain there for the following two decades.

On June 24, Johnson wrote, "While the intelligence community in Washington wanted very much to keep the A-12 program going, the present financial situation cannot stand the strain. It's a bleak end for a program that has been over-all as successful as this."

In summary, the A-12 program lasted just over ten years from its inception during 1957 through its termination during 1968. The *Skunk Works* produced fifteen A-12s and three YF-12As. Five A-12s and two YF-12As were lost in accidents; two pilots were killed, and at least six had narrow escapes. In addition, two F-101 chase aircraft were lost with their Air Force pilots during the A-12 test program.

The main objective of the program—to create a reconnaissance aircraft of unprecedented speed, range, and altitude—was triumphantly achieved. It may well be, however, that the most important aspects of the effort lay in its by-products—the notable advances in aerodynamics, engine performance, cameras, electronic countermeasures, pilot life support systems, and the arcane art of milling, machining, and shaping titanium. Altogether, it was a pioneering accomplishment almost certainly never to be repeated in the history of aviation.

In a ceremony at the test location on June 26, 1968, Vice Admiral Rufus Taylor, Deputy Director of Central Intelligence, presented the CIA Intelligence Star for valor to pilots Kenneth Collins, Ronald Layton, Francis Murray, Dennis Sullivan, and Mele Vojvodich for participation in the *Black Shield* operation. The posthumous award to pilot Jack Weeks was accepted by his widow. The Air Force Legion of Merit was presented to Colonel Slater and his Deputy, Colonel Maynard Amundson. The Air Force Outstanding Unit Citation was presented to the members of the 1129th Special Activities Squadron, Detachment 1 (the A-12 Detachment) and the USAF supporting units. "Kelly" Johnson was a guest speaker at the ceremony and in moving words lamented the end of an enterprise which had marked his most outstanding achievement in aircraft design.

### NASA:

Though NASA facilities and select personnel had been used during the course of early A-12 and F-12 wind tunnel tests, the agency's access to information relating to the highly classified Lockheed program remained decidedly limited until 1967. That year, personnel at NASA Ames initiated dialog with Air Force representatives concerning the possibility of giving the agency access to YF-12A wind tunnel data. In return, NASA would cooperate with and participate in the YF-12A flight test program then underway at Edwards AFB. Coincident to this it was noted also that the proposed activity would complement plans of the Office of Advanced Research and Technology which was tasked with high speed research and its applicability to the proposed US supersonic transport.

Gene Matranga of the NASA now was assigned to the Edwards AFB YF-12A test pro-

*The YF-12A was inflight refuelable. Select NASA missions required lengthy endurance times and the YF-12As were inflight refueled accordingly. KC-135Qs-- modified to carry the JP-7 required for the SR-71's mission--were provided by the Air Force when such capability was required.*

gram. NASA personnel, believing this to be an indicaton of reduced propriety, requested the Air Force provide an instrumented SR-71A for its own purposes. This was declined, along with a NASA request that, instead, a NASA research package be carried by the Air Force's Category II stability and control SR-71A test aircraft. However, the Air Force countered by offering NASA use of the two remaining YF-12As then stored at Edwards AFB.

Using funding that had been coincidentally released following termination of the North American XB-70A and North American X-15 flight test programs, NASA agreed to undertake support of the two YF-12As (with the help of an Air Defense Command maintenance and logistical support team) and physically transferred them to the NASA Dryden Flight Research Center facility.

A memorandum of understanding between the Air Force and NASA was signed on June 5, 1969, and a public announcement followed on July 18. Matranga and his team, several months later, undertook the first of what would be an extensive list of YF-12A modifications that included the installation of strain gauges and thermocouples in the wing and fuselage to permit the measurement of dynamic loads, and the installation of thermocouples along the left side of the aircraft for temperature assessment and analysis.

Acquisition of the two YF-12As proved a windfall not only for the NASA research centers at Edwards AFB and Ames (Moffett Field, California), but also those at NASA Langley (Langley AFB, Virginia...for high-speed aerodynamics and associated structures) and NASA Lewis (Cleveland, Ohio...for propulsion). NASA had developed two computer programs to predict loads and structural responses using finite element analysis. Known as FLEXSTAB and NASTRAN, they were utilized at the very beginning of the NASA YF-12A test program in order to determine the flight dynamics of the aircraft and set up a baseline for future reference.

NASA and Air Force personnel completed three months of modification and test instrumentation installation the second YF-12A during early December of 1969. On December 11, this aircraft, under the auspices of NASA (though manned by an Air Force crew) successfully completed its first post-modification flight. The first flight with a NASA flight test engineer, Victor Horton, occupying the back seat took place the following March 26. The first flight with a NASA pilot, Donald Mallick, flying the aircraft took place on April 1.

Johnson, in contemplating the NASA's YF-12A operation wrote on July 21, 1971, "Had a visit from the NASA test organizations who discussed their research to date. They haven't come up with anything that was new to us, but it seems to be a good program for them to keep up their technical organizations. I am attaching a letter from Gene Matranga indicating our current relationship, which is excellent. I have two objections to the NASA program, the main one is that they will probably publish important data, which the Russians will be happy to receive as they always are with NASA reports. Secondly, they are repeating so many things we pioneered in and I gravely doubt our people will be given any, or sufficient, credit for solving the problems first. We have continued to cooperate to the hilt with NASA in spite of the above."

NASA YF-12A research in fact had been modestly productive during this period, with the aircraft serving to permit exploration of a speed regime that had long been out of NASA's reach with its extant aircraft stable. The YF-12A's ability to cruise at speeds in excess of 2,000 mph made it an ideal platform for studying the unique aerodynamic and heating phenomenon which occurred. A large number of test specimens, systems, and equipment complements were heat-soaked and dynamically loaded at Mach 3 for sustained periods...a capability that had remained elusive until the arrival of Lockheed's retired fighter.

In the interim, flight test work utilizing the second YF-12A had been on-going primarily with Air Force crews. It was being flown in a series of tests where it was being used to simulate the Russian MiG-25 (a Mach 3-capable interceptor) at various speeds and altitudes. On its sixty-third flight, taking place on June 24, 1971, however, an inflight fire in the right engine nacelle (caused by a fatigue failure of a fuel line) led to its crew (Lt. Col. Ronald Layton and Maj. Billy Curtis) ejecting and the aircraft being written-off. Propulsion system studies scheduled for this aircraft now had to be rescheduled for the surviving YF-12A, thus causing schedule delays. A month after this loss, however, a redundant SR-71A was placed on loan to the NASA from the Air Force inventory. This aircraft, at the Air Force's request, was redesignated YF-12C (see Chapter 12). Among the many studies conducted using the surviving YF-12A during its NASA tenure were the *Coldwall* experiments using a ventrally suspended stainless steel tube equipped with thermocouples and a series of pressure sensors. Supported by NASA Langley, *Coldwall* was essentially a heat transfer experiment to acquire data applicable to future high-speed aircraft and transports.

A special insulation coated the covered tube which, prior to flight, was chilled to extremely cold temperatures using liquid nitrogen. During an actual test flight, the insulation was expected to suddenly blow away at Mach 3, thus exposing the tube to the ambient high-temperature environment. The resulting data then was compared with similar data obtained from a similar *Coldwall* tube that had been tested in a wind tunnel. The final flight in this series took place on October 13.

At the beginning of 1977 the two YF-12s (including the afore-mentioned YF-12C) had completed over 175 flights. A sizable percentage had included time at speeds of Mach 3 or greater. Unfortunately, operating expenses for the two high-performance aircraft was becoming ever more difficult to justify as funding became tighter and research missions become more esoteric. Accordingly, during the spring of 1977, a decision was made by NASA directors to retire the YF-12A...though in fact, it would continue to fly sporadically until being turned over to the Air Force Museum at Wright-Patterson AFB, Ohio on November 7, 1979. It flew its last official NASA flight, number 145, on October 31, 1979.

Earlier, residual funding had permitted additional test work with the YF-12C to be conducted through the fall of 1978. On October 27, 1978, however, it also was retired and returned to the Air Force inventory. The last official NASA YF-12C flight, the 88th, had taken place on September 28, 1978.

*Many studies, including this wind tunnel model with a hypersonic ramjet mounted dorsally, were conducted calling for the YF-12A to serve as a testbed carrying operational or test payloads externally.*

*D-21 full-scale mock-up. Black areas were fabricated from composite materials and used to lower the drone's radar cross-section. The actual D-21 differed only in detail from the mock-up. Intake spike and vertical tail differences, however, are noteworthy.*

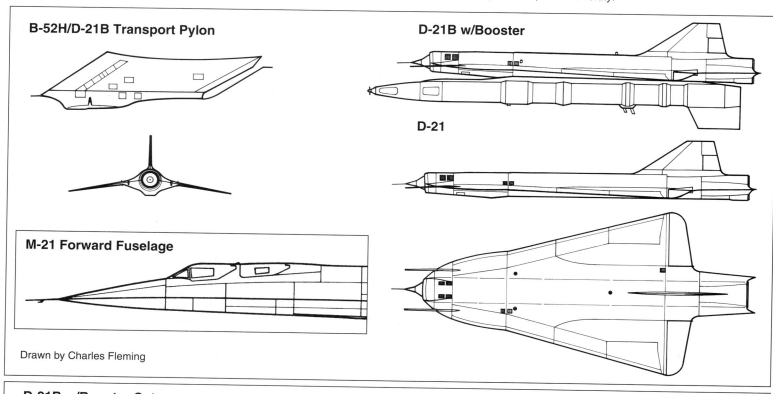

## B-52H/D-21B Transport Pylon

## D-21B w/Booster

### D-21

## M-21 Forward Fuselage

Drawn by Charles Fleming

## D-21B w/Booster Cutaway

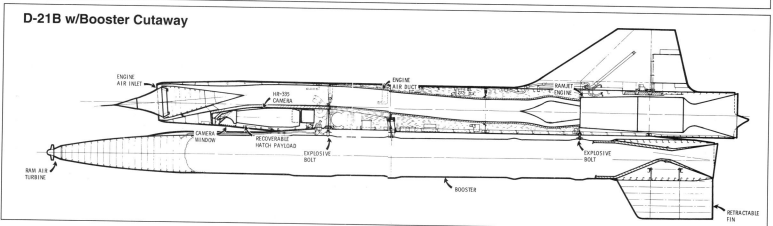

ENGINE AIR INLET

ENGINE AIR DUCT

RAMJET ENGINE

HR-335 CAMERA

CAMERA WINDOW

RECOVERABLE HATCH PAYLOAD

EXPLOSIVE BOLT

EXPLOSIVE BOLT

RAM AIR TURBINE

BOOSTER

RETRACTABLE FIN

# Chapter 10:
# *Senior Bowl* and *Tagboard*

*"The airplane met its performance and its radar cross-section goals but we had difficulty with some of the detailed equipment. It was still an outstanding feat to make a ramjet operate for two hours."*

**Ben Rich**

Of the various *Skunk Works* Mach 3 aircraft programs, the least known to reach the operational hardware stage was undoubtedly the D-21 unmanned strategic reconnaissance drone. Developed and operated by the Central Intelligence Agency and Air Force under a veil of extreme secrecy not penetrated until long after the program had ceased to exist as a viable national reconnaissance asset, it was unveiled only by accident...when seventeen D-21s were discovered in storage at Davis-Monthan AFB's Military Aircraft Storage and Disposition Center by aviation enthusiasts during early 1977. This chance unveiling resulted in the first public disclosure concerning the D-21 and the beginning of a long curiosity about its history and operational service life.

The D-21 was, in fact, an extension of the A-12 program brought to life in response to the US Government's decision to discontinue overflights following the loss of Gary Powers and his U-2 during May of 1960. During October of 1962, "Kelly" Johnson made the first log entry in what was to become this enigmatic aircraft's long-hidden history, "Over the past several years, we have had a number of discussions on the feasibility of making a drone with the A-12 aircraft. I have steadily maintained that we should not do this, as it is a much too large and complicated machine. On several different occasions, we studied the use of a QF-104 air-launched from the A-12. It became obvious at an early date that the CIA were totally uninterested in this project, (but) others wanted to do it very much."

Regardless, on October 10, 1962, authorization for a drone study was received by the *Skunk Works* from the CIA. Johnson would note the event as follows, "We have now configured it to allow the use of plastic blankets over-all for the basic structure. In order to avoid the F-104 problem of a high central vertical tail, I put two on the tips and one in the middle. Besides the aerodynamic benefits of this configuration, they will provide the basis for a landing gear during the flight test operation."

Lockheed's experience with high-speed ramjets was well founded as a result of its previous experience with the X-7 program. Coupled with the propulsion technology developed by Marquardt, it was not difficult for the team to execute a functional reconnaissance platform in a relatively short period of time. Importantly, the experience base being generated by initial flight tests of the A-12 had given the engineering team—under Johnson—considerable confidence in the aerodynamic precedent set by the chined delta. This configuration was applied to the D-21 as its design solidified.

On October 24, Johnson, Ben Rich, and Rus Daniell met with representatives from Marquardt to discuss ramjet propulsion system options. Johnson would write, "It is obvious that we cannot use the *Bomarc* engine without change. We will just do the best we can to use its major parts."

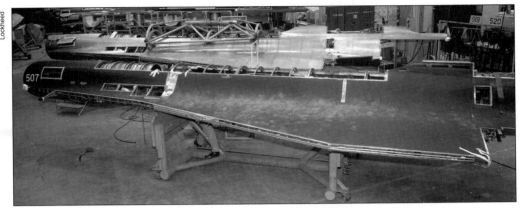

*D-21 in foreground does not yet have composite leading edge surfaces attached. Inner wing surface was manufactured of conventional metal alloys.*

The new project now was assigned to Art Bradley under the supervision of Dick Boehme. A small team was assembled to handle engineering and a piece of the *Skunk Works* shop at Burbank was walled off specifically to accommodate the new drone activity.

During early November of 1962, while preliminary design work (on what now was being referred to in the *Skunk Works* as the Q-12) progressed with considerable rapidity, miscellaneous subsystem problems, including those of the proposed optical sensor system, surfaced to cause concerns about program progress. Johnson had favored the Hycon company to win the contract to build the compact camera, "I am very impressed by their recent design with a fast moving slit shutter arrangement I saw at their factory recently."

On November 5, Johnson would write, "The drone is developing without much discussion between Headquarters and ourselves. I think I know what they want, but no one has spelled it out. We will try to get 6-inch ground resolution photographically, a range of 3,000 nautical miles, and a payload of 425 pounds for the camera. We will attempt to save the expensive elements of the aircraft by parachute recovery of the nose."

The full-scale mock-up was completed on December 7. As it included the "anti-radar" characteristics of the actual drone, on December 10 it was sent to a test facility and for eleven days used for pole model tests to measure radar cross section. When it was returned to Burbank, it was modified to improve its RCS and concurrently used by Hycon to fit check a mock-up of their new camera.

Propulsion system work began to accelerate at this time, also. A Marquardt RJ43-MA-3 *Bomarc* engine was wind tunnel tested at simulated Q-12 operating conditions. "We were all amazed, including Marquardt, that the engine could be shut off as long as 45 seconds and still restart, due to hot engine parts."

CIA and Air Force support, though modest, continued to give Johnson and the rest of the Q-12 team encouragement. On January 3, Johnson wrote in the log, "We are running wind tunnel tests and have revised the model to look exactly like the original proposal with the single tail, except that we have blended the leading edge of the chine into the basic wing. We also

*Radar cross-section and radar reflectivity were major D-21 design concerns. Virtually all of the aerodynamic surfaces missing from this drone under construction were of composite materials.*

*Part of the combustion chamber and all of the exhaust nozzle of an installed Marquardt ramjet engine. This powerplant was the first of its kind in the world capable of sustained Mach 3 operations.*

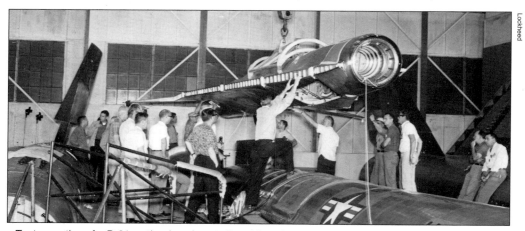

*Test mounting of a D-21 on the dorsal centerline pylon of an M-21. The drone weighed just over 11,000 pounds fully loaded and the engineering concerns of safely transporting it at Mach 3 were significant.*

reduced the size of the vertical tail. We are going to plastics to reduce the anti-radar cross section."

On March 20, a letter contract from the CIA arrived. "It makes us responsible for the navigation system and the ramjet engines, as well as the airframe," Johnson wrote.

All was not copacetic with the new drone, however. On May 9, Johnson noted that engineering was having trouble with aerodynamic loads. "After investigating tunnel data, we find we have a jury-rigged model that does not represent the configuration of either the A-12 or the R-12. Presence of the sting in the tail of the fuselage and a break in the fuselage to move the nose up 1-1/4 inch have resulted in the Q being placed in the wrong flow field and highly confusing loads."

Other difficulties included the size of the Hycon camera. The minor dimensional changes in the drone had led to dimensional changes in the ventral sensor system bay. As a result, Johnson noted that Hycon was going to be forced to change the design of their camera if it were to fit. On August 6, 1963, it was noted that Hycon was successful. The redesign effort had not impacted the quality of the imagery and the camera was dimensionally compatible with the Q-12's sensor bay.

By October, the Q-12's overall configuration had been finalized and the equally difficult tasks of defining the A-12 launch system and its configuration were nearing an end. By now, the somewhat unusual M-21 designation had been assigned the carrier A-12. "M" stood simply for "Mother". Concurrent with this, it was decided to rename the Q-12, D-21—thus making it the "Daughter" aircraft. The numerals "1" and "2" of A-12, Q-12, etc., were simply reversed so as not to confuse the "mother/daughter" combination with other "-12" variants.

Johnson, on October 1, wrote, "I proposed to Boehme that we simplify some of the load problems by letting the D-21 float at a zero moment incidence when attached to the M-21. While this concentrated the loads at one point, it reduces most of them and particularly the effect on the M-21. I also made sure that we can jettison the aircraft without power."

On December 31, 1963, Johnson noted that wind tunnel and paper studies were leading him to believe there would be launching difficulties with the M-21 "mother ship". "Going through the fuselage shock wave is very hard. I am insisting on launching at full power, but there are problems regarding fuel-air ratio to the engine and engine blow-out in this condition."

A month later he would write, "Reviewed launch conditions again, and was very upset by recent tunnel tests which show we must make a pushover to launch. This is due to making the pylon too short. This was done for structural reasons, but it got us into aerodynamic troubles, which weren't recognized at once, although I suspected that we might encounter such troubles when it was done."

By late May of 1964, Johnson's image of the D-21 had improved. "We have launch problems, transonic drag deficiencies in the basic airplane, and equipment problems, as usual. But we can now haul the thing through Mach 1.0, I believe, if we can get performance like A-12 #129. Launching must be done as an automatic pushover maneuver."

Concurrent with the D-21 work, the purpose-building of two M-21s to serve as launch platforms also was underway. A single, dorsally mounted pylon had been developed that was low drag...yet sufficiently strong to support the 11,000 pound D-21 at Mach 3. The pylon contained a series of latches that secured the D-21 to the M-21, provisions for emergency pneumatic jettison of the D-21, and a refuel line that was used to top-off the D-21's tanks prior to launch. D-21 separation was to be accomplished by flying the D-21 off the M-21 during a slight (approximately 0.9 g) pushover maneuver (the D-21 was not *forcibly* ejected from the M-21).

A fit check—using M-21 "134" and D-21 "501"—was completed successfully in the *Skunk Works'* Building 309/310 on June 19, 1964. Few problems surfaced and over the next several weeks, final manufacturing of the first carrier was completed. On August 12, it was sent to the test location to undergo initial post-modification flight testing. Concurrently, the initial D-21 static tests were successfully concluded. Johnson wrote in the log, "Engine

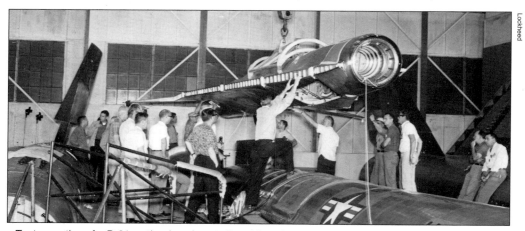

*The D-21 was mounted on the aircraft centerline between the M-21's vertical fins. Noteworthy are the upward folding outer wing panels of the M-21...which permitted engine access for maintenance.*

deliveries are in good shape but equipment, particularly cameras, is not so good. Trying to get out seven drones this year."

On December 22, the first flight of the D-21/M-21 combination was successfully completed from the test location. "Bill Park flew at the end of the day. It flew well and, in spite of having low-powered engines, went supersonic on the first flight." Interestingly, on this same day, the first SR-71A successfully completed its first flight from Lockheed's Palmdale, California facility.

Interest in the project, though supported by the CIA and the Air Force, remained difficult to ascertain. Johnson, however, doggedly pursued successful execution. "We are aiming to launch one by my birthday—February 27, 1965."

Johnson's wish was not to be. His birthday came and went with little fanfare...and no D-21 launch. "We have all kinds of troubles," he wrote, "Minneapolis-Honeywell came in with a terrible story on the Kollsman star tracker which they had purchased for the M-21 guidance system. It was a complete shambles from beginning to end."

Further flight testing of the mated M-21/D-21, in the meantime, continued...though without a launch. During April of 1965, Johnson noted that one flight resulted in the loss of "both elevons on the D-21 due to flutter. We are going to put on balance weights, and add control surface locks, etc."

By May, the two-aircraft combination had been flown out to Mach 2.6. The flutter anomaly had been overcome but problems continued with the M-21's two J58s. "We are ready to light the engine of the drone, but we must get a new course to run as we can not accelerate sufficiently in a turn. We are being restricted by lack of suitable test areas."

On October 21, 1965, Johnson noted, "We have had great difficulties in getting *Tagboard* to speed and range. We tried to run to Point Mugu for launch practice, but couldn't make the range. Transonic acceleration is very poor, particularly with high air temperatures. As of this day, we are putting in 34,000 pound thrust engines. Have had to convert from the Hamilton Standard inlet control to our own, and are having trouble blowing the nose cone and keeping parts out of the inlet. I believe I found a solution yesterday, involving the use of an aluminum ring. We are driving for a launch date of November 15. We seem to have the recovery system in hand, and have taken good pictures from the 'hot pod' (an externally mounted pod with special high-temperature glass ports for photography) on #134. All D-21s have been built, but I cannot recommend construction of more until we prove the bird in flight.".

*Initial flights with the D-21 in position were conducted with the frangible nose and tail cones in place. The unsuccessful attempt to pyrotechnically remove the cones in flight curtailed their further use.*

*Part of the M-21 mission profile included inflight refueling to extend range. The D-21 was a heavy, high-drag payload and it adversely affected the M-21's normally exceptional performance.*

*Once it was determined the frangible nose and tail cones were not practical, the D-21 was flown without them and in fact was used as a third engine to help accelerate the mated aircraft to launch speed.*

*The D-21 was conceived as an extension of the original A-12 reconnaissance capability at a time when the Nixon Accords dictated the elimination of further manned overflights of countries such as China. The unmanned drone was viewed as a legitimate, albeit controversial means of circumventing the Accords.*

Lockheed

*The leading edge of the D-21's ogival delta wing was severely damaged during the first, and as it turned out, last attempt to pyrotechnically remove the aerodynamic cone fairing from the D-21's intake.*

Jim Goodall collection

*The seventh D-21 is utilized to test compatibility with the special pylon designed and built by the* Skunk Works *to permit transport and launch of the drone from two specially modified Boeing B-52Hs.*

By November, the transonic acceleration problems had yet to be overcome. Further complicating the situation was the inability of the instrumentation system strain gauges to measure separation forces accurately at the high temperatures associated with the Mach 3-plus launch conditions. Johnson noted that "we will not go until we know for certain what the separation maneuver will consist of."

The solution to the frangible inlet cone problem was to eliminate it altogether. In addition to pieces of the cone entering the D-21's inlet, they also caused unacceptable damage to the drone's wing leading edges, as well as the fuselage of the M-21. By discarding the nose cone (and the aluminum exhaust nozzle fairing), the D-21's Marquardt ramjet engine now could be used to supplement the propulsive effort of the M-21's J58 engines during the acceleration to launch conditions. The ramjet was started at Mach 1.24, and immediately prior to launch, fuel was transferred from the M-21 to the D-21 to replenish that used during the acceleration.

By late January, most of the difficulties had finally been overcome. "We have now established that the separation forces, engine operation, and parachute recovery system work properly, and we have practiced the launch maneuver." With the exception of the Minneapolis-Honeywell inertial navigation system (critical to any operational D-21 mission, but not critical for the envisioned test launch),

the time finally appeared ripe for an attempted D-21 launch. February 7 was declared the target date.

Delays inevitably set in and the February date came and went. Finally, on March 5, 1966, the first D-21 launch was successfully accomplished. "It was a great success," according to Johnson, "in terms of the launch. The airplane was lost 120 miles from the launch point. Mainly, we demonstrated the launch technique, which is the most dangerous maneuver we have ever been involved in any airplane I have worked on. Bill Park and Keith Beswick flew it. Everyone was greatly encouraged by the launch."

CIA and Air Force interest, even in light of the modestly successful first flight, remained luke warm. Johnson had continued to emphasize the D-21 concept to the Air Force, and SAC officials had been kept apprised of progress. On April 22, 1966, Johnson wrote in the log, "Had a meeting with two SAC officers. We talked of using the D-21 and how to get it into service. If necessary, Lockheed will launch the early operational birds. We have been very strapped for money in the whole program, and training is difficult and time consuming."

The second flight now was successfully undertaken on April 27. "Boehme and I went to Pt. Mugu for the second launching...this was a dandy flight, going over 1,200 nautical miles and holding course within a half mile for the whole flight. It reached 90,000 feet, Mach 3.3, and finally fell out of the sky when a hydraulic pump burned out. It turned out that the pump had been run unpressurized several times during checkout. At this time I have proposed the use of the D-21 with a rocket launch from the B-52. Our problem now will be to get wide usage of this new bird at low cost."

A second batch of fifteen D-21s was ordered on April 29, 1966 and the following month, Johnson made a formal proposal to SAC to launch the new drone from Boeing B-52Hs. "This was based on greater safety, lower cost, and greater deployment range."

On June 16, the third D-21 was successfully launched. "It flew about 1,600 nautical miles, making 8 programmed turns, to stay within sight of the picket ship. It did everything but eject the package, due to some electronic failure."

The fourth launch, attempted on July 30, 1966, was a disaster. The second M-21, piloted by Bill Park and with Ray Torick in the launch system operator's position, was lost over the Pacific Ocean off Point Mugu, California when D-21 #504 collided with the carrier moments after release. Observed by the first M-21—which was flying chase—the D-21 and the M-21 were seen to make contact at the moment of drone release. At Mach 3.25, as the M-21 pitched up, its nose broke off. Park and Torick ejected, but by the time a rescue helicopter arrived on the scene, Torick had drowned because his suit had filled with water. Park was recovered 150 miles at sea after floating for an hour.

Though additional studies of the M-21/D-21 combination were conducted, after the accident it was concluded that Mach 3 launches of a large vehicle like the D-21 were difficult to justify from a safety standpoint. The Interim studies calling for the use of boosters to accelerate the D-21 to ramjet ignition speed (ala' the X-7) now were given renewed emphasis. On August 15, after returning from a trip to Washington wherein the accident was discussed primarily with the Air Force, Johnson

**B-52H Flight Deck Modifications for D-21B**

| | |
|---|---|
| 1 STELLAR INS RACK | 6 DUAL TM RECEIVERS, L/R |
| 2 STAR TRACKER PLATFORM | 7 LCO'S SEAT, LEFT HAND |
| 3 LCO'S SEAT, RIGHT HAND | 8 4-TRACK TAPE RECORDER |
| 4 PERISCOPE, D-21B OBSERVATION, L/R | 9 FLEXWRITER UNIT |
| 5 LCO CONTROL PANELS, L/R | 10 FLEXWRITER DRIVER UNIT |

noted, "I proposed going to the B-52 and I believe we will get a go-ahead on this program." The D-21 now was grounded for a year while the new launch system was developed.

As modified for B-52H carriage, the new D-21 configuration (now with dorsal mounting hooks rather than ventral) was referred to as the D-21B. The 4200th Test Wing at Beale Air Force Base assumed responsibility for the two B-52Hs modified for the D-21B program. These aircraft—the first of which arrived at Palmdale on December 12, 1966, for modification—were operated initially from the test location and then moved to Beale AFB for operational missions. The latter were usually flown under cover of darkness and rarely observed by unauthorized personnel.

In its proposed operational configuration, the D-21B was to be launched from its carrier aircraft after arriving at any launch destination. The capabilities of the system were made possible by the 3,000 nautical mile range of the D-21B and the B-52H's innate ability to fly to virtually any spot on the globe.

Following air-launch, the D-21B was accelerated to Mach 3.3-plus and an altitude of 80,000 feet by a solid propellant booster rocket developed by Lockheed Propulsion Company of Redlands, California. The booster then was jettisoned and the D-21B commenced a 3,000 nautical mile cruise over a course which was pre-programmed in the inertial guidance system. At the end of the flight, a controlled descent was made to a lower altitude where the hatch containing the special Hycon camera and the inertial navigation unit was ejected. The hatch payload then was decelerated and lowered by parachute to an altitude where an air retrieval was executed by a Lockheed JC-130B *Hercules*.

The operational D-21B consisted of three major elements: (1) the airframe and engine; (2) the recoverable hatch containing the camera and the high value electronic equipment; and (3) the booster including associated antenna, electrical and hydraulic power systems, and a folding ventral fin.

The recoverable hatch contained the reconnaissance camera, the inertial navigation system, the automatic flight control system, the command and telemetry electronics, the recov-

*The first D-21, No. 501, undergoes systems checks during conversion to D-21B status. The D-21Bs required dorsal, rather than ventral suspension gear in order to be accommodated by the B-52H.*

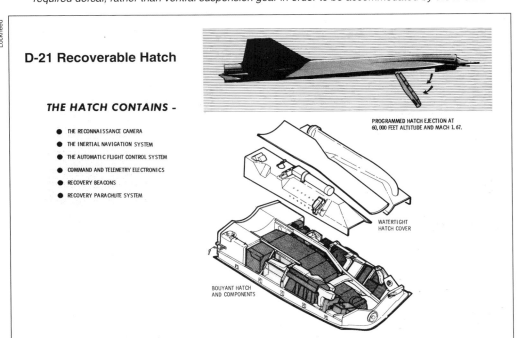

**D-21 Recoverable Hatch**

**THE HATCH CONTAINS -**

- THE RECONNAISSANCE CAMERA
- THE INERTIAL NAVIGATION SYSTEM
- THE AUTOMATIC FLIGHT CONTROL SYSTEM
- COMMAND AND TELEMETRY ELECTRONICS
- RECOVERY BEACONS
- RECOVERY PARACHUTE SYSTEM

PROGRAMMED HATCH EJECTION AT 60,000 FEET ALTITUDE AND MACH 1.67.

WATERTIGHT HATCH COVER

BOUYANT HATCH AND COMPONENTS

ery beacons, and the recovery parachute system. Hatch ejection took place automatically at 60,000 feet and Mach 1.67.

The booster had a length of 531 inches, a case diameter of 30.16 inches, a weight of 13,286 pounds, an average thrust of 27,300 pounds, a burn time of 87 seconds, and an impulse of 2,371,600 pound seconds. The booster was ignited shortly after release at an altitude of about 38,000 feet. It would accelerate the D-21 out to Mach 3.2-plus at which time the functioning ramjet would assume the propulsion requirement.

Boost phase trajectory was pre-pro-

*The B-52H was carrying a payload with a total weight of 48,572 pounds (exclusive of miscellaneous support and communications equipment) when it tookoff with two D-21Bs and their solid fuel boosters suspended from its underwing pylons. D-21 ventral fin folded to right side of aircraft.*

*View from a KC-135A "boomer's" position of the left D-21B. B-52H pylon suspension unit was reminiscent of that utilized for carrying and launching the North American X-15 research aircraft.*

grammed in the inertial navigation system. Boost phase time was approximately 90 seconds. Maximum forward acceleration during boost was 1.5 g.

Modifications to the B-52Hs consisted principally of the following:

(1) Addition of a D-21B attach pylon to each wing. Each pylon bolted to the underside of the wing at existing attachment points and no structural modifications to the B-52H were required.

(2) Alteration of the flight deck area to accommodate two launch control officer (LCO) stations. The two stations were completely independent of each other and were located in the area normally occupied by the electronic warfare officer and the gunner.

(3) Addition of a stellar inertial navigation system and of telemetry and command systems. Telemetry receiving and recording systems, including antennas, were duplicated for reliability.

(4) Addition of an air conditioning system to supply air at the proper temperature and pressure to the D-21B for cooling and heating and for driving the auxiliary power unit.

The inertial navigation system was accurate to 4.7 nautical miles over the course of an 18 hour 35 minute flight. During the course of its flight, the D-21B INS position error accumulation was periodically updated to the B-52H's stellar INS.

The D-21B telemetry system provided space-positioning and speed data to the LCO aboard the B-52H launch vehicle during the boost phase for the first ten minutes of cruise. At this time, the telemetry system was turned off by an INS discrete and the mission was flown in radio silence. During the final phase of the mission, the telemetry system was turned on again by an INS discrete and the transmitted data was received by the recovery aircraft.

In addition to providing immediate data to the launch and recovery aircraft, the telemetry system transmitted other data, forty-one items in all, which were recorded for post mission analysis. These items consisted of the following: automatic flight control measurements; propulsion system, fuel system, booster and hydraulic pressures; engine and equipment temperatures; electrical system voltages and frequencies; D-21B Mach number, direction, and location; and various systems event mark signals

The command system consisted of two command transmitters plus two antennas in the B-52H, and one command receiver plus two antennas in the D-21B. This system provided the launch and recovery aircraft with the means to command eight post launch functions which were normally automatic (programmed in the INS) plus a destruct capability. The system provided a backup in the event of failure of any of the preprogrammed signals and it afforded the means to change the sequence or timing of the events should this become desirable. The functions provided included: fuel shutoff; engine ignition; destruct arm; beacons and TM on; booster jettison; hatch ejected; TM off; destruct disable; and destruct fire.

On January 18, 1967, Johnson met with Deputy Secretary of Defense Cyrus Vance for one-and-a-half hours in Washington, D.C. "He was very much for *Tagboard* and asked that we press forward vigorously on it. He also said we would never again fly a manned aircraft in peacetime over enemy territory, confirming the *Oxcart* decision."

During February, problems with longitudinal stability and control at Mach 1.4 surfaced. These were all booster related and not easily rectified. On September 28, a D-21 was accidentally dropped from a B-52H as a result of what Johnson referred to as "poor workmanship...a stripped nut in the forward right attachment to the pylon." Johnson noted that it was "very embarrassing". The booster in fact fired after the inadvertent launch, and was "quite a sight from the ground".

The first actual launch attempt from a B-52H took place on November 6. Johnson noted that it was not successful. "The rocket took it to altitude but it nosed over and dived in within 150 miles." On November 28, a B-52H was flown for the first time with two D-21s (#'s 508 and 509) suspended from its wing pylons. This equated to a total payload weight of 24 tons...which was within the limits of the B-52H's capabilities, but an extremely heavy load nevertheless.

Launches and launch attempts now followed with some regularity. Failures occurred on December 2 and January 19, and in-between there were several aborts. On February 5, Johnson wrote, "I feel we must make this thing work on the next flight or the project will be canceled." In frustration, he convened a *Skunk Works* review of the failures that lasted from January 22 through February 14, 1968. "We made a careful study of all available data which ended up showing two things. The launches, whether from the *Oxcart* airplane or the B-52, got to identical altitudes but higher speeds with the rocket. The B-52 launch aircraft, however, flew 6,000 to 10,000 feet lower than they should have, compared to the *Oxcart* launches."

Another failure occurred on April 30, but on June 16, 1968, a successful flight was finally accomplished with D-21 #512. "It flew its design range, 3,000 nautical miles," Johnson wrote, and it reached an altitude of "over 90,000 feet and the package was recovered satisfactorily. The engine blew out in turns, but reignited in climb back."

*D-21B shortly after release from the B-52H. Solid fuel rocket booster had not yet ignited. Telemetry data was transmitted to the launch and recovery aircraft periodically during the course of the D-21's mission.*

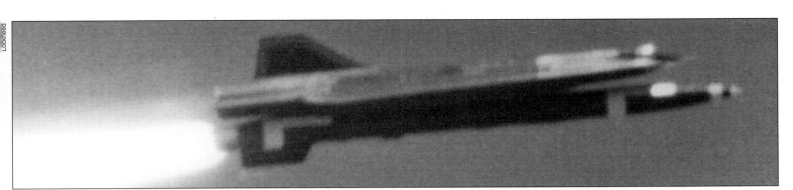

The D-21B solid fuel booster generated 27,300 pounds of thrust for 87 seconds following ignition. It was not recoverable. At the point of booster fuel exhaustion, both the drone and the booster were traveling at approximately Mach 3.2...a speed sufficient to sustain the Marquardt ramjet combustion processes.

More attemped flights followed, including several that Johnson flew to Hawaii to witness in person, and this continued to frustrate him. "We are overrunning costs obviously, working not only for zero budgets, but putting Lockheed money into the program. The *Tagboard* shows a great deal of promise, but it is a very tough technical job."

Still another failed flight took place on February 11...this being the first to attempt a "Capt. Hook" mission wherein the inertial navigation system was programmed per an operational sortie. "Our best analysis for the reason was water in the autopilot, but we cannot definitely prove this."

A successful launch and flight took place on May 10 with modestly good photography resulting. Another good launch and flight took place on July 10. Johnson noted, "We have now met our design objectives to the point where the Air Force can consider the program successful and completed up to the operational phase. The remaining job will be to put the other birds in the same configuration as the last successful launch."

These successes now gave the *Skunk Works*, the CIA, and the Air Force renewed confidence in the program. On September 25, Johnson noted that the "decision to use *Tagboard* on a hot mission has now gone to President Nixon. I think there is a good probability that it will be used within the next six months. If we successfully do this, *Tagboard* should have a good future. We are studying how to recover the complete vehicle and it appears feasible." As an afterthought he would note, "I am very pleased with the technical success we have had with the bird since putting it on the B-52 for launching and I am very glad that we took our medicine at the time."

On November 9, 1969, the first operational mission was launched but did not succeed. The D-21 simply disappeared. Johnson wrote, "It was lost. Subsequent to this failure, we went into the navigation system again and changed the programming to something I have wanted since the beginning of the program. This enables the airplane to miss a destination check point, but to continue to the following ones."

A non-operational mission was flown on February 20, 1970, this time with considerably more success, "We ran another "Captain Hook" mission with the new navigation programming flying over 3,000 nautical miles. The aircraft performed superbly reaching altitudes over 95,000 feet, hitting all its check points within two to three miles. We were told to standby for another hot mission in March."

Political and other considerations now stepped in to curtail further D-21 activity. Between February 20 and mid-December, no further launches were attempted and the air-

craft sat idle. Finally, after nearly a year of relative inactivity, a second "hot" mission was attempted on December 16. The D-21 apparently flew successfully, but the hatch was not recovered and no imagery resulted. Nearly three months later, on March 4, 1971, a third operational mission was flown resulting in a successful flight but a poorly managed hatch recovery effort. "The parachute was damaged during descent with the hatch, it fell slowly into the water. The hatch floated—the Navy got there with a ship. During the recovery operation the hatch was damaged to the point where it sank. Another Navy ship found the *Tagboard* vehicle floating, but was unable to get cables around it before it sank."

Sixteen days later, the fourth operational mission was flown. The mission was a failure. The D-21 was lost "three-quarters of the way through...over a very heavily defended area". This was to be the last D-21 mission ever...though Johnson and the *Skunk Works* team did not know it at the time.

The D-21's problems had been many, and not easily resolved. Progress had been made throughout the course of the program, but four modestly successful missions out of a total of twenty-one flown did not a good track record make. This, when coupled with the ambivalence that had been shown by the CIA from the very beginning, spelled doom for the D-21 by mid-1971. On July 15, Johnson received word of the program's cancellation, "Received wire canceling Tagboard. The birds will be placed in dead storage. We will work out the details of storing the aircraft later. We were already returning the birds and equipment from Beale AFB to ADP by means of a C-5A. We were

ordered to destroy tooling, not only here, but at our vendors."

The real end came on July 23 when a very low key, but official termination get-together took place at Beale AFB near Sacramento, California. Johnson summarized the event with, "I flew up to Beale to make a speech to the 4200th Air Support Squadron who are being disbanded in SAC. It was a sad occasion for all. I have four major feelings regarding the *Tagboard* program: (1) We will probably see the day when we will greatly rue the decision taken to scrap the program; (2) we did an excellent job on a program of the most difficult nature and at very low cost; (3) We had excellent cooperation from the Air Force, including SAC and our friends in the Pentagon; and (4) I am sad to see such a program, which actually had its inception back on the X-7 ramjet test vehicle, which developed the *Bomarc* engine and was based on some 20 odd years of technical development be canceled. The remarkable part of the program was not that we lost a few birds due to insufficient launches to develop reliability, but rather that we were able to obtain such a high degree of performance with such low cost compared to any other system."

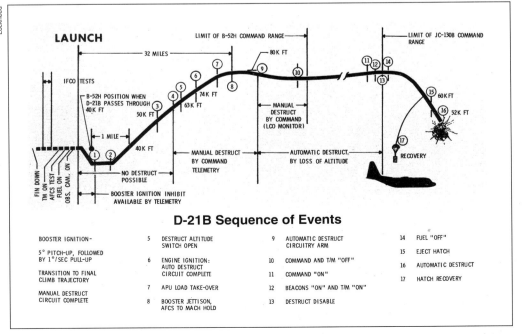

## D-21B Sequence of Events

| | | | | |
|---|---|---|---|---|
| | BOOSTER IGNITION- | 5 DESTRUCT ALTITUDE SWITCH OPEN | 9 AUTOMATIC DESTRUCT CIRCUITRY ARM | 14 FUEL "OFF" |
| | 5° PITCH-UP, FOLLOWED BY 1°/SEC PULL-UP | 6 ENGINE IGNITION: AUTO DESTRUCT CIRCUIT COMPLETE | 10 COMMAND AND T/M "OFF" | 15 EJECT HATCH |
| | TRANSITION TO FINAL CLIMB TRAJECTORY | 7 APU LOAD TAKE-OVER | 11 COMMAND "ON" | 16 AUTOMATIC DESTRUCT |
| | MANUAL DESTRUCT CIRCUIT COMPLETE | 8 BOOSTER JETTISON, AFCS TO MACH HOLD | 12 BEACONS "ON" AND T/M "ON" | 17 HATCH RECOVERY |
| | | | 13 DESTRUCT DISABLE | |

*Stunningly attractive from almost any angle, the SR-71 was particularly striking when viewed head-on. This profile was not illusory...as the low frontal area it represented was an important ingredient among the many that gave the world's most famous reconnaissance aircraft its extraordinary performance.*

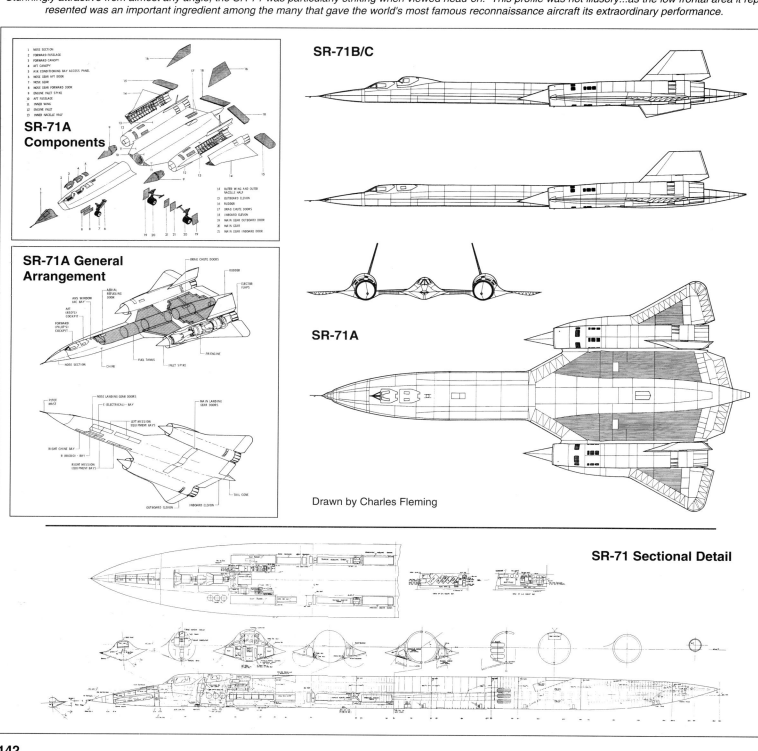

### SR-71A Components

1 NOSE SECTION
2 FORWARD FUSELAGE
3 FORWARD CANOPY
4 AFT CANOPY
5 AIR CONDITIONING BAY ACCESS PANEL
6 NOSE GEAR AFT DOOR
7 NOSE GEAR
8 NOSE GEAR FORWARD DOOR
9 ENGINE INLET SPIKE
10 AFT FUSELAGE
11 INNER WING
12 ENGINE INLET
13 INNER NACELLE HALF

14 OUTER WING AND OUTER NACELLE HALF
15 OUTBOARD ELEVON
16 RUDDER
17 DRAG CHUTE DOORS
18 INBOARD ELEVON
19 MAIN GEAR OUTBOARD DOOR
20 MAIN GEAR
21 MAIN GEAR INBOARD DOOR

### SR-71A General Arrangement

### SR-71B/C

### SR-71A

Drawn by Charles Fleming

### SR-71 Sectional Detail

# Chapter 11:
# SR-71...THE *SENIOR CROWN*

*"The YF-12A developed into the SR-71. And in that case, again, the cost performance was excellent as we gave back to the government well over 19 million dollars on the contract. And we consider it to be a success."*

**Clarence L. "Kelly" Johnson**

During the course of the A-12 program the Air Force had been exceedingly helpful to the CIA. It provided financial support, conducted the refueling program, provided operational facilities at Kadena, and air-lifted A-12 personnel and supplies to Okinawa for the operations over Vietnam and North Korea. Through it all, however, the Air Force remained frustrated that a strategic reconnaissance mission—historically its provenance—had been given to another government agency. This umbrage had in fact been ongoing for nearly a decade by the advent of the R-12—later formally designated SR-71—and could be traced back directly to the Lockheed U-2 program and President Eisenhower's decision to turn control over to the CIA.

"Kelly" Johnson had first mentioned working on a "reconnaissance/strike" variant of the A-12 for the Air Force during April of 1962...though preliminary discussions relating to a configuration of this type had been ongoing almost from the beginning of the program during 1958 and 1959. During March of 1962, the Air Force had been cleared to give Lockheed a study contract wherein the various Air Force mission options—including the ability to destroy ground targets—could be more precisely identified. The basis for the proposed aircraft was to be the CIA's A-12.

By April, two different mock-ups, an R-12 and an RS-12 (as Johnson referred to them), were under construction and mission definition work was well underway in the *Skunk Works*. On May 14, Johnson noted in the log, "Had mock-up review of RS-12 mock-up. Flew a simulated mission using 'quick check' radar photographs. The fifteen people we have had on this 90-day study under Daniell have done a most excellent job."

On June 4, the ninety day study that had been granted the *Skunk Works* was reviewed by "Rus Daniell, Templeton, and a large number of aerial reconnaissance people." This was concluded satisfactorily, but no firm commitment to move ahead with hardware was immediately forthcoming...which frustrated the sometimes impatient Johnson.

On December 6, Johnson would note, "Working on R-12 *Universal* airplane, using company work order. Can get no decision on any military version of the aircraft, but there does seem to be considerable interest in it. "

The idea of the *Universal* A-12—which fundamentally could be field optimized to accommodate either reconnaissance or strike missions, had continued to appeal to Johnson. This utilitarian A-12 did, in fact, make sense, though political ramifications (i.e., one aircraft and one aircraft company doing all things for all requirements) eventually would prove too much for such pragmatism to prevail.

Seven days later, the *Skunk Works* was visited by SAC personnel. "They wanted to see what kind of a reconnaissance version would meet SAC's needs. There is a group of Air Force people who seem to be anxious that we

do not exploit the A-12 to its maximum capability as a reconnaissance airplane. However, after they were here for a day or so, I believe we convinced them that we could carry all the reconnaissance gear that SAC felt was required. There is still a feeling that a reconnaissance/strike airplane larger than the R-12 is required, but I am going to be sure that our *Universal* airplane can do that job. We prepared our proposal for a 140,000 pound reconnaissance airplane capable of carrying 4,300 pounds of reconnaissance gear and gave it to Col. Templeton with a forwarding letter."

One week after SAC's visit, Johnson and several other *Skunk Works* engineers were off to Washington to continue their contract pursuit. "Presented our R-12 version, which Templeton and group presented to the Air Force in a closed session the next day. The outcome was that we were proposing too heavy an aircraft, with too much equipment, so we were requested to scale it down to 1,500 pounds of payload."

During this period, the *Skunk Works*, primarily under Rus Daniell, went through many exercises in order to perfect the "R" model's design. Finally, on February 18, 1963 they were given precontractual authority to build six aircraft, with the understanding that an additional 25 aircraft would be ordered by July 1.

Interestingly, the first six aircraft were part of the A-12 order for the CIA and the contract was through that agency and not the Air Force. Not coincidentally, the R-12 order eased the path of A-12 development by allowing the Air Force to share the program financial burden. Thus the cost per aircraft was somewhat reduced by the larger production quantity. In the long run, however, the funding of the R-12 spelled doom for the A-12. As noted in the A-12 chapter, government budgetary agencies determined two independent reconnaissance systems with basically similar capabilities could not be justified.

Col. Leo Geary was assigned as Weapon System Program Officer for the RS-12 in the

*The first SR-71A forward fuselage under construction. Chine structure is noteworthy.*

Pentagon, and—after prolonged debate—Col. Templeton and the AF-12 project group became the project group on the R-12.

By the advent of the R-12 the CIA had begun to diverge into other sensor platforms of a considerably more clandestine nature, including the first of the super-high-resolution optical systems then being merged for the first time with satellite technology. As the A-12s had been supported via Air Force (and Lockheed) expertise it was not surprising when the CIA capitulated to Air Force demands that the airborne strategic reconnaissance mission be returned to its jurisdiction.

*The first SR-71 forward fuselage during weight and center of gravity measurements inside Building 309/310 of Plant B-6. Each fuselage component was measured in this fashion before final assembly.*

*The first SR-71 in final assembly at the* Skunk Works' *Palmdale Site 2 facility. All members of the A-12/F-12/SR-71 family had the unique hinged outer wing panels permitting engine access.*

*Though superficially resembling its A-12 predecessor, the SR-71 differed in many important ways including the chine, the fuselage, and miscellaneous subsystems.*

In light of the Air Force's strong support for their mission-optimized R-12, it is surprising to note the CIA's A-12 remained the more capable aircraft in many respects. Its single-man crew left room for a much larger and higher resolution camera as well as other collection devices which at the time could not be carried by the proposed R-12. At the time, the A-12 was certainly the most effective reconnaissance aircraft in existence. Also, perhaps most importantly, it was operated by civilians and thus could be employed covertly, or at least without the number of personnel and amount of fanfare normally attending an Air Force operation.

Once the Air Force had been approved to take over the A-12 mission, Johnson and his *Skunk Works* team moved ahead with the slightly stretched and reconfigured A-12—which still was being referred to as he R-12. The new aircraft would differ from its predecessor in one major respect...and several minor; it would be given a pressurized aft cockpit for a second crew member in the "Q-bay" position normally occupied by sensor equipment. A slight fuselage stretch would result from adding another fuselage fuel tank—along with other changes in the way sensors were carried.

On March 19, 1963, after receiving the Air Force go-ahead, Johnson would write in the log, "Having considerable problem with choosing the guidance system vendors. I have cautioned both Geary and Templeton not to proceed too fast in making hasty judgments. They are under pressure to use the Nortronics system from the GAM-87, which has been canceled. This leaves us with a problem on Motorola, Hughes, and Litton, who have pro-

posed a system."

As the construction process gathered momentum and the first aircraft began to go together at Burbank, Bob Murphy had been sent to Site 2 at Palmdale in order to make arrangements with the Air Force and occupant Rockwell International to take over the facility. The *Skunk Works* needed the site for its own production program and it became Murphy's job to wrest it away.

A shortage of thin titanium sheet brought to light the sensitivity of this aspect of the program. Titanium had, in fact, been a source of major concern for the *Skunk Works* from the very beginning. As it was far and away the single most important material utilized in the A-12 family, extraordinary means were used to control every facet of its manufacture and implementation. Johnson would summarize this in a paper written for *Lockheed Life* during December of 1981, "The *Skunk Works* traditionally avoids the snarls of excess report writing. However, with titanium, for an outfit that hated paperwork, we really deluged ourselves with it. Having made 13 million titanium parts to date, we can trace the history of all but the first few back to the mill pour and, for about the last 10 million of them, even the direction of the grain in the sheet from which the part was cut has been recorded."

During the initial phases of the A-12 program, the *Skunk Works* engineering team discovered that titanium wing panels spot welded during the summer failed early in life, but those made in the winter lasted indefinitely. "We finally traced this problem to the Burbank water system, which heavily chlorinated water in the summer to prevent algae growth, but not in the winter. Changing to distilled water to wash the parts solved this problem."

Johnson also remained concerned about the crucial navigation system, noting, "I am not at all sold on the Nortronics guidance system. This device is not nearly as far along as Templeton and his people think. I look for nothing but trouble with this unit." And as a side note he added, "The mock-up is progressing well."

The first mock-up review took place on June 13 and 14, 1963. "Over-all, it was a very successful meeting in all regards, including the flight test phase with Col. "Fox" Stephens," Johnson recalled. "I think the Air Force are well impressed with our operation to this point and I am very pleased at the high caliber of people Leo and Templeton are getting on the program."

Air Force interest in the strike capability of the new aircraft continued, even at this late date. On June 29, Johnson traveled to SAC Headquarters at Offutt AFB, Nebraska and met with Gen. Thomas Powers, then Commander of SAC. "We went over the problems of converting the R-12 aircraft to the RS version. I described the structural changes required and presented some Hughes Aircraft Company data on the new missile and side-looking radar. We also talked of several other items, such as the U-2 for satellite search, and the current status of the A-12 program."

Another mock-up conference took place on December 11, 1963 and was deemed a success by Johnson. By March 18, 1964, R-12 construction was moving along with considerable rapidity, but contract negotiations had yet to be concluded with the Air Force. Johnson noted in the log, "Spent several days...on...the first six R-12s. It is extremely difficult to get a

*To maintain program security, the SR-71 prototype, like its A-12 and YF-12 predecessors, was transported from Burbank to Palmdale inside large trailers designed specifically for the task.*

reasonable profit for what we do and no credit is given for the fact we operate more cheaply than others."

All activity relating to the R-12 and RS-12 configurations had, of course, been kept completely under wraps in the *Skunk Works* and within the confines of the involved Air Force and CIA offices. On July 24, 1964, however, President Johnson made his memorable announcement revealing to the world the existence of Lockheed's Mach 3-capable reconnaissance aircraft. The full context of Johnson's speech was:

"I would like to announce the successful development of a major new strategic manned aircraft system, which will be employed by the Strategic Air Command. This system employs the new SR-71 aircraft, and provides a long range advanced strategic reconnaissance plane for military use, capable of worldwide reconnaissance for military operations. The Joint Chiefs of Staff, when reviewing the RS-70, emphasized the importance the strategic reconnaissance mission. The SR-71 aircraft reconnaissance system is the most advanced in the world. The aircraft will fly at more than three times the speed of sound. It will operate at altitudes in excess of 80,000 feet. It will use the most advanced observation equipment of all kinds in the world. The aircraft will provide the strategic forces of the United States with an outstanding long-range reconnaissance capability.

"The system will be used during periods of military hostilities and in other situations in which the United States military forces may be confronting foreign military forces.

"The SR-71 uses the same J58 engine as the experimental interceptor previously announced, but it is substantially heavier and it has a longer range. The considerably heavier gross weight permits it to accommodate a multiple reconnaissance sensors needed by the Strategic Air Command to accomplish their strategic reconnaissance mission in a military environment. This billion dollar program was initiated in February of 1963. The first operational aircraft will begin flight testing in early 1965. Deployment of production units to the Strategic Air Command will begin shortly thereafter.

"Appropriate members of Congress have been kept fully informed on the nature of and the progress in this aircraft program. Further information on this major advanced aircraft system will be released from time to time at the appropriate military secret classification levels."

Though President Johnson's announcement had no impact on the status of the program, Air Force pressure was great to get the first aircraft completed and shipped to Lockheed's Palmdale facility by October 21. Difficulties with vendors continued to plague the program, however, and as predicted by Johnson, the Nortronics guidance system was becoming a "big mess".

Finally, on October 29, 1964, the first R-12 was surreptitiously delivered by truck from Burbank to Palmdale for final assembly and pre-flight preparations. Much to everyone's surprise—in particular, Johnson's—the first aircraft, by now being referred to by its official Air Force SR-71 designation, initiated engine runs on December 18, 1964. Three days later, the first taxi tests were undertaken. Johnson would write in the log, "A large number of SAC people were here to see taxi tests of airplane #2001. They were very much impressed with the smooth operation. I delayed the flight on

*The first SR-71A undergoing static propulsion system testing at Palmdale prior to its first flight. By late 1964, most of the Pratt & Whitney J58's difficulties had been overcome.*

*With an F-104C flying chase, the first SR-71A, 17950, on December 22, 1964, departs Palmdale on its first flight. Lockheed test pilot Bob Gilliland was at the controls.*

*The SR-71A's chine profile changed following flight testing of the first aircraft. The nose was tilted up 2 degrees to reduce drag at cruise flight conditions.*

*Like its A-12 predecessor, the SR-71A was highly dependent on the dedicated KC-135Q tanker fleet assigned specifically to accommodate its mission requirements.*

*At least four nose options permitted carriage of an opitcal bar camera, either of two side-looking airborne radar systems, or an essentially empty nose that served only to accommodate aerodynamic requirements. Eleven bays, including the nose, were available for electromagnetic and optical sensors.*

*SR-71A (17961, shown) nose chine is particularly pronounced from this angle. At least four different nose options were available for the SR-71, with all but one containing different sensor types or configurations*

the aircraft one day, due to unfavorable weather and to get it in better shape to fly."

The next day, December 22, the first SR-71, with *Skunk Works* test pilot Bob Gilliland at the controls, took to the air for the first time. Departing from Lockheed's Air Force Plant 42 Site 2 facility at Palmdale, it remained airborne for just over an hour and reached a speed in excess of 1,000 mph..."which", Johnson noted,

"is some kind of record for a first flight."

As a perturbation of the now seemingly defunct RS-12, Johnson and the rest of the *Skunk Works* engineering team had continued to pursue an armed version of the A-12 configuration...in the form of a bomber SR-71. Referred to in-house at Lockheed as the B-71, on April 21, 1965, it was presented by Johnson to a small contingent of Air Force generals.

Johnson had seen an opportunity in the form of the demise of the North American XB-70 and its proposed replacement with a bomber version of the still-experimental and highly controversial F-111. As Johnson so modestly described it, "I wanted them to know about our studies so they would not go too fast on the FB-111".

Though the SR-71 first flight had been completed with few difficulties, ongoing flight testing of the aircraft had not been comparably problem free. During April of 1965, fuel and hydraulic plumbing difficulties lead to numerous test flight cancellations. "We are using a new fitting for better field installation", Johnson would note, "but poor workmanship due to our high labor turnover has rocked us back hard. We have made several landings with no hydraulic fluid in the left or right hydraulic system. Thank gosh we have an A and a B system to fly the airplane, or we would have been in real trouble. I put all the airplanes except one on the ground and we are doing a complete replumbing job. On one airplane we found 100 cases where tubes didn't fit, no seals were placed in the fittings, or two seals were in a fitting, bad scratches on the mating surfaces and every conceivable type of poor practice. This is a hard blow to take at this stage of the game, because we are delivering airplanes at almost one per month and we have really barely begun Category I testing. In April and again on May 11 I called numerous meetings with our shop and inspection personnel to set up ways and means for correcting and curing both the plumbing and the wiring problems due to workmanship."

Problems continued into October. "...We have gone through very expensive reworks of the electrical system and tank sealing on the SR-71s. Category I tests are way behind schedule, but so are Category II tests. The Air Force are very understanding. Our major problem now has to do with range, where we are about 25% short. We have made our speed, altitude, and are getting good results with the sensor packages."

On January 7, 1966, the first trainer SR-71—with its elevated aft cockpit and associated flight controls and instrumentation changes—referred to as the SR-71B, was delivered to Beale AFB from Palmdale. Daniell and Johnson flew to Beale to attend the acceptance ceremony.

This aircraft was the first to enter the operational Air Force inventory. It was the seventh aircraft completed and the first to go to the 4200th SRW at Beale AFB, California. Following service introduction this unit was reorganized six months later as the 9th SRW at the same base. This occurred officially on

*Though a highly complex and sophisticated aircraft, the SR-71A could be operated from a variety of Operating Locations around the world with little difficulty.*

*Special starting equipment was required for the SR-71A because its J58s were not starter equipped. Triethyl borane, used because of its spontaneous combustion characteristics, served as the fuel igniter.*

June 22, 1966, and two squadrons, the 1st and the 99th SRS reformed to operate the SR-71A and SR-71B. Boeing KC-135Q tankers continued to be operated by the 456th Bomb Wing's 907th Air Refueling Squadron.

The SR-71 flight test program, conducted at Palmdale, like that of its A-12 predecessor, was not without its accidents. The first, involving the third SR-71A, occurred on January 25, 1966 when *Skunk Works* pilot Bill Weaver miraculous escaped without using his ejection seat. His back seater, Jim Zwayer, was not so lucky and was killed.

At the time of the accident, the aircraft was in a right turn and the right inlet forward bypass doors were being controlled manually by Weaver. Approximately 15° into this turn, at between 77,000 and 78,000 feet and Mach 3.17, he experienced a right inlet unstart and bank angle immediately increased from 35° to 60°, and the aircraft started to pitch up. Weaver attempted to regain control, but to no avail. The aircraft continued to pitch up until "the horizon disappeared and there was nothing left but blue sky to look at..." and then the nose broke off.

The first operational SR-71A, the ninth aircraft completed, was delivered to Beale AFB on April 4, 1966. Problems, however, continued to plague the program, and thus delayed actual operational integration of the aircraft into the activities of the military intelligence community. Johnson, in recounting this period, would write in the log, "We have a backlog of airplanes at Palmdale for many reasons, particularly fuel leaks, plumbing problems, etc. The Air Force is very understanding and sympathetic to our problems."

The following month, the program took a turn for the better. "We have broken the log

*SR-71A, 17955, was operated exclusively by the Skunk Works as a flight test aircraft. It was flown first on January 6, 1971 and flown last on January 24, 1985. It was one of two primary dedicated test SR-71As.*

*Following the removal of the SR-71A from the operational Air Force inventory, this aircraft, 17968, was one of three aircraft placed in inviolate storage at Lockheed's Site 2 facility in Palmdale.*

*Distinctive chined delta of the SR-71 and its predecessors was a shape unlike any other aircraft of its day. The SR-71 was a successful engineering exercise both aerodynamically and volumetrically...and even more extraordinary when viewed in light of the fact titanium alloy was the basic working material.*

*"Big Tail" aircraft, 17959, was conceived to generate stereoscopic imagery by carryng an optical bar camera in its nose and a similar camera in its extended tail. The tail, which could be raised and lowered for takeoffs and landings, was never outfitted with its camera or a proposed electronic countermeasures system.*

Tony Landis collection

jam and are getting airplanes to Beale, with tank leaks being our biggest problem. They are released to go to Mach 3.0. This includes the second trainer, aircraft number 8. We have not completed our Category I or II tests, but have made good progress." On June 15, a small but notable change also was made to the aircraft's aerodynamics, "Laid out a program for changing the nose tilt on the SR-71 2° up to improve the trim characteristics."

Though SR-71s finally were beginning to enter the operational Air Force inventory, the miscellaneous subsystem problems remained difficult to overcome. Tank sealing and range deficiencies continued to plague the aircraft, including those considered operational at Beale AFB, and corrective action was painfully slow in overcoming them.

On January 10, 1967, the first SR-71 was accidentally written-off during a brake testing exercise. The drag chute failed on an artificially wetted surface. According to Johnson, "The airplane ground off the right-hand wheels until they had a one-foot-long flat spot. Going out on the overrun at 100 knots, the right gear broke off, then all the others. The airplane burned completely. Art Peterson escaped with a cracked disc in his back." Braking on wet surfaces would continue to be a problem with the initial production aircraft.

On April 13, another SR-71, aircraft number 17, crashed in New Mexico. Johnson noted it in the log with, "After a night refueling, the pilot had some engine stalls and let the airspeed drift down to about 170 knots at 37,000 feet. Both crew members escaped. It was a bad time to have another accident."

Another aircraft, SR-71 number 16, crashed in Nevada on October 25. "The pilot became completely disoriented. The crew bailed out safely, but a large part of the problem came about due to confusion between the

crew members and their inability to read the standard Air Force standby attitude indicator, which is really not suited for night flying."

The Air Force had maintained a position of patience with Lockheed from the SR-71's inception. There was no question it was a major rework of the original A-12 and in many respects, because of the operational criteria around which it had been conceived, it was a significantly different aircraft. These factors had adversely impacted the flight test program and problems had resulted.

Though select aircraft were operational at Beale AFB, the Air Force had long envisioned deploying the SR-71 to detachment facilities near critical hot spots around the world. First among these was Kadena Air Force Base, Okinawa, which would permit quick response overflights of sensitive areas. Flights into denied airspace required not only the SR-71's superior performance, but also a host of advanced electronic countermeasures systems. Installation of the latter proved a difficult, if not demanding task and it was not until late 1967 that the first effective systems were tentatively installed.

On December 4, 1967, Rus Daniell, Dan Haughton, and Johnson went to SAC Headquarters in Omaha, Nebraska and made a presentation on yet another A-12 model, the FB-12. A common airframe for an air defense fighter *or* bomber, it was noted by Johnson as being, "...a strong case for high altitude bombing." Though the trio were well received, the FB-12, like its other *Universal* predecessors, proved short-lived. There were simply too many other bomber projects with stronger lobbying teams in Congress.

By late 1967, all thirty-one SR-71s on order from Lockheed had been completed and delivered. On February 14, 1968, Johnson wrote in the log that Col. Benjamin Bellis was

"trying to have us store SR-71 tools". *Skunk Works* activity related to the SR-71 was then limited to getting the aircraft ready for their initial deployment to Kadena AFB and keeping them serviced in the field. On March 4 and 5, the final SR-71 construction contract termination negotiations were concluded and the company concomitantly was given an on-going service contract.

On July 31, the number eleven SR-71 was severely damaged after flying 300 miles with an engine fire. It was repairable, but not without great expense. On April 11, 1969, the number five SR-71 also was severely damaged. Like number eleven, it was repairable, but the cost was estimated to be $5 million. In both cases, the crews escaped without injury.

By late September of 1969, the SR-71 was well on its way to a long a illustrious operational career. SAC already had flown well over one-hundred "hot missions" out of Kadena.

NASA, for the first time, formally inquired into having an SR-71 for test purposes on December 29, 1970, when a query was received by the *Skunk Works* concerning possible use of the aircraft to launch test scale models of the forthcoming *Space Shuttle*. This query was the result of general acknowledgment that SR-71 assets were greater than the intelligence community's needs...or the Air Force's operating budget, and that redundant aircraft might be made available to the NASA if funding could be found.

Funding was indeed found and during July of 1971 a single SR-71A was transferred from the Air Force inventory to the NASA...where it was promptly and ironically redesignated YF-12C. Underscoring the airframe redundancy problem, however, was a decision to store six select aircraft at Palmdale. Johnson attributed the decision to a "lack of missions and money".

On July 28, 1971, Johnson noted in the

Lockheed

*A family portrait documenting eleven of the remaining SR-71s at Beale AFB several months after the Air Force's November 22, 1989 decision to remove the type from the active inventory. Most of these aircraft now have been shipped to museums and placed on static display.*

log, "Nothing new on the SR-71 operation. SAC made a ten hour flight a short time ago on which about half the time was over Mach 3 and 80,000 feet. They flew 10,000 miles."

The Vietnam war had successfully justified the SR-71's existence from the time of its operational debut during 1968 through 1973. But as the war wound down, additional aircraft were placed in storage, even after their return to Beale AFB. Some 600 missions had been logged during the course of Vietnam operations, and the aircraft had logged an enviable record of dependability and mission successes.

SR-71 deployments to Kadena and to RAF Mildenhall in the United Kingdom were made at regular intervals during the 1970s, and 1980s and a permanent facility maintaining at least two SR-71As on a round-the-clock availability level eventually was activated at the latter. Temporary deployment to Forward Operating Locations (FOLs) worldwide were undertaken with considerable alacrity and during the course of its service career, the aircraft overflew almost every major political and militarily significant hot spot in the world...gathering intelligence data of inestimable political and military value. At least one mission in excess of 14,000 miles was flown, and though unrefueled range continued to be a limiting tactical factor, the availability of the large KC-135Q fleet allowed the aircraft to overfly targets anywhere on the globe.

Johnson and the *Skunk Works* team, in the meantime, had continued to pursue alternative missions for the SR-71 in an attempt to keep the program alive and justifiable. One study, dated November 9, 1970, called for "experimental development of an airborne system to destroy heavily defended point targets". This called for a modification of the SR-71 which had "proven to be invulnerable to the types of surface-to-air missiles and interceptors used by Soviet satellite countries and Communist China." The *Skunk Works* engineering team estimated that with laser guided bombs, the circular error probable (CEP) was about fifteen feet against fixed targets and mobile radiating targets such as surface-to-air missile radars.

On October 23, 1973 Johnson spoke with representatives from the Defense Advanced Research Projects Agency (DARPA) about the possibility of using the SR-71 as a Mach 3 bomber "for dropping a streamlined iron bomb with a guidance system on hard targets." As Johnson envisioned it, the aircraft would have become a "national crises control force". A

*Striking portrait of the NASA's first SR-71A (aka YF-12C), 17951, which was acquired for use on July 16, 1971, following the loss of YF-12A, 60-6936, on June 24, 1971.*

small study contract was issued, but no hardware resulted.

The last log entry was dated June 26, 1974. Johnson wrote, "Generally in 1974 the SR-71s played a vital role in the *Yom Kippur War* flying missions out of the east coast in the US over the eastern Mediterranean battle lines.

In fact, based on SR-71 photographic and other takes, the Israelis were advised where to strike. Made many missions using several refuelings. Aircraft and crews operated very well."

The previously mentioned YF-12A speed and altitude records were eclipsed by the SR-71A during a series of Federation Aeronautique

*Flown for some six years by the NASA, 17951, the second production SR-71A, eventually was placed in storage at Palmdale until the demise of the Air Force's operational SR-71 program. Following that, it was released to the Pima County Aviation Museum near Tucson, Arizona and there placed on static display.*

*SR-71A, NASA 844, during formation photo flight with General Dynamics (now Lockheed Martin) F-16XL, NASA 849. F-16XL has ogival delta wing and is being used for a variety of NASA test programs.*

*Of the two SR-71Bs, one, 64-17957, was written-off on January 11, 1968. The single SR-71C proved a hangar queen and was used infreqently. The surviving SR-71B, 64-17956, remains in use with NASA.*

International (FAI) monitored flights during 1976. As of this writing, all of these records still stand, including the world's absolute speed and sustained altitude records. The attempt had been approved by the Air Force during early 1976 and on July 27, the following records were set: height in sustained horizontal flight— 85,069 feet (crew, Capt. Robert Helt/Maj. Larry Elliot); speed in a straight line—2,193.17 mph (crew, Capt. Eldon Joersz/Maj. George Morgan, Jr.); and speed over a 1,000 kilometer closed circuit—2,092.294 mph (crew, Maj. Adolphus Bledsoe, Jr./Maj. John Fuller). Other records set by the SR-71A include, on April 26, 1971, a non-stop 15,000 mile mission flown in 10.5 hours (crew, Maj. Thomas Estes/Maj. Dewain Vick—awarded the 1971 Harmon and McKay Trophies); on September 1, 1976, a non-stop flight from Beale AFB to RAE Farnborough in which the New York to London (3,490 miles) segment was flown in 1 hour 55 minutes 42 seconds (crew, Maj. James Sullivan/Maj. Noel Widdifield); and a non-stop flight on September 13, 1976, from London to Los Angeles (5,645 miles) in 3 hours 45 minutes 39 seconds at an average speed of 1,487 mph including inflight refuelings (crew, Capt. Harold Adams/Maj. William Machorek).

During the late 1980s, as major international political and economic changes began to manifest themselves throughout the world, the US intelligence community began to reassess priorities and in particular, the way it was going to spend its limited financial resources. Virtually every program, including the SR-71, was reviewed with the intent of determining its long-term viability and in particular, its simple cost effectiveness.

As a result of this review, and in light of advances in other sensor system programs, on October 1, 1989, all SR-71 activities, with the exception of crew proficiency training and associated training flights, were suspended while the Air Force awaited release of the 1990 Fiscal Year budget. When revealed several weeks later, funding for the SR 71 program had been eliminated. Accordingly, all Air Force SR-71 operations were terminated officially on November 22. The SR-71 was officially retired during an emotional ceremony at Beale AFB the following January 26. Many of the Lockheed, Air Force, and CIA personnel who had been involved in the program during the preceding twenty-four years were on hand to say farewell to what many viewed as the single most significant military aircraft of the post World

War Two period.

Lockheed, Pratt & Whitney, and in particular, the Skunk Works could take great pride in their many accomplishments relative to the SR-71. Besides the more noteworthy aerodynamic, subsystems, materials, and airframe advances, the Skunk Works demonstrated highly successful systems engineering/integration on the SR-71. Included were optical film cameras (both visual and infrared); imaging radar systems; electronic intelligence equipment; air-to-ground data linking; analog and digital recording devices; design of a real-time satellite data link; design of a global positioning system (GPS); captive test of radar for reentry vehicles; and laser communications systems. Other successful tests and demonstrations included: overland sonic boom characterization; Space Shuttle reentry flight path emulation; extended high-heat profile development; digital automatic flight/inlet control development; advanced sensor/electronic warfare interoperability; high-altitude turbulence characterization; and high-temperature structure and thermal-protection materials.

The SR-71's record in service had been inspiring, to say the least. SAC operations had resulted in 53,490 flight hours, 17,300 missions, 3,551 operational missions, 11,008 operational hours, 25,862 inflight refuelings, and a staggering 11,675 hours of operation at Mach 3 or greater. No other conventional fixed-wing aircraft in the world had ever sustained speeds of Mach 3-plus and 80,000 feet—much less operated routinely for long periods at such velocities and altitudes.

High-time crew member of the program was Lt. Col. Joseph Vida, a reconnaissance systems operator who had first flown in the SR-71 on June 18, 1975. At the end of the program, he had logged no less than 1,392.7 flight hours in the aircraft. High time pilot was Col. Robert Powell, who had first flown the aircraft on July 5, 1967. He had logged no less than 1,020.3 flight hours and received two Distinguished Flying Crosses by the time the program ended.

Of the thirty-one original aircraft, twenty had survived to the program's finish. With the formal termination during January of 1990, fourteen of those remaining were released to the jurisdiction of the US Air Force Museum at Wright-Patterson AFB, Ohio where plans were placed in motion to allocate them to various aviation museums around the US.

On March 6,1990, the 1974 record-setting SR-71A, 64-17972, was given to the Smithsonian Institution's National Air & Space Museum in Washington, D.C. During its delivery flight from Beale AFB, to Dulles International Airport, Maryland, this aircraft set four world class records, including: US coast-to-coast in 67 minutes 54 seconds with an average speed of 2,124.5 mph; Los Angeles, California to Washington, D.C. in 64 minutes 2 seconds with an average speed of 2,144.8 mph; Kansas City, Kansas to Washington, D.C. in 25 minutes 59 seconds with an average speed of 2,176.1 mph; and St. Louis, Missouri to Cincinnati, Ohio in 8 minutes 32 seconds with an average speed of 2,189.9 mph. All four records were set on the same flight. The Air Force crew consisted of Lt. Col. Edward Yielding and Lt. Col. Joseph Vida.

Of the six aircraft not assigned to various museums (see Appendix A), three were placed in storage at Lockheed's Site 2 facility at Palmdale and three were assigned to the NASA at their Dryden Flight Research Center at Edwards AFB, California. The former, as of this writing, are being retained by the Air Force for contingency situations and almost certainly eventually will find their way into museums (it is highly unlikely they ever will fly again); and the latter (which consists of two SR-71As and the SR-71B trainer) are being groomed (with Lockheed's cooperation) for a variety of research programs including National Aerospace Plane propulsion system studies (specifically, the external burning attendant to the design of supersonic combustion ramjets), and future supersonic transport technology issues.

*NASA's SR-71A, "844", is being modified to accommodate the Linear Aerospike SR-71 Experiment (LASRE). A 1/10th Lockheed Martin X-33 Reusable Launch Vehicle will be attached to a dorsal pylon.*

Proponents of the SR-71's use by NASA argue that the aircraft could become a cost-effective high-altitude platform for scientific experiments and engineering development of space instruments. They feel it's much cheaper to conduct operational tests at 85,000 feet than to launch them aboard the Space Shuttle and have them fail in space.

The first official NASA project utilizing the SR-71's unique capabilities was undertaken on March 9, 1993 when the aircraft flew the first of a series of high-altitude ultraviolet spectrometry missions from Edwards AFB. At this writing, flights planned or being planned include: evaluations of two ultraviolet spectrometers; a University of California physics department study of Aurora Borealis; the testing of sensors specifically optimized for volcano plume and lava-flow studies; chasing a planned 1994 launch of the Strategic Defense Initiative Organization's Clementine lunar fly-by module while carrying special ultraviolet spectrometers; studies of atmospheric pollutants; and combining the most recent advances in laser resonant fluorescence techniques with ultraviolet spectrometry to sense substances such as chlorine monoxide.

As noted previously, a single SR-71A (aka YF-12C during its NASA tenure) was operated by the NASA following the loss of one of two YF-12As on loan from the Air Force. This aircraft had been turned over to NASA during July of 1971 and NASA pilots Fitz Fulton and Don Mallick, along with flight test engineers Victor Horton and Ray Young had been assigned as crew members. Both underwent flight instruction at Beale AFB using the Air Force's SR-71 simulator there. On May 24, 1971, Fulton and Horton successfully completed the first official NASA YF-12C flight. Consequently, this was the first SR-71A flight under the auspices of NASA.

At this writing, one of NASA's SR-71As and the SR-71 B are flyable. It is almost certain the second SR-71A will be reserved as a spare parts source. Besides the three aircraft, the NASA also received the Air Force's cockpit simulator. This unit initially has facilitated crew transitions but long term plans include utilizing it to explore specific mission objectives without exposing crews to hazardous flight conditions. At present, NASA's SR-71 program manager is David Lux. Project pilots are Stephen Ishmael and Rogers Smith. Flight test engineer include NASA's first husband and wife flight test engineering team, Robert Meyer and Mart Bohn-Meyer.

### Update:

During 1994, the U.S. Congress, noting a shortfall in intelligence gathering capability, elected to return the SR-71 to operational status. Accordingly, three SR-71As were picked for refurbishment and upgrading, with two coming from Lockheed long-term storage at Palmdale, and a single aircraft being recalled from the NASA.

Congress has tentatively approved a total budget of $100-million for the refurbishment project. Successful reconditioning of the first aircraft

*During 1996 NASA will test Rocketdyne's linear aerospike engine aboard NASA SR-71A, "844".*

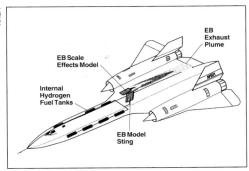

*Proposed NASA SR-71A modification as External Burning (EB) Scramjet testbed.*

*The first SR-71A to be returned to operational Air Force service since the type was removed from the inventory during 1990 is 64-17971, seen during a post-refurbishment test flight from Palmdale.*

(64-17971) was completed during mid-1995, and it was handed over to the Air Force at Palmdale on June 28. The second aircraft (64-17967) is due for delivery during August of 1995. Funds for the third aircraft (64-17968) are tentatively committed for inclusion in the fiscal year 1996 budget with the aircraft being delivered during that year.

The first and second SR-71As planned for reintegration into the Air Force under the auspices of the 9th Reconnaissance Wing will remain at Palmdale until September 1. At that time, they will be delivered to Edwards AFB. It is from there that they will fly their operational missions, rather than the 9th's home base at Beale AFB.

The second SR-71A will be the first of the three to be equipped with a Unisys air-to-ground data link which will allow its intelligence gathering systems to work in concert with those found in *Senior Span*-configured U-2Ss. At a later date, the first SR-71A also will be upgraded to the Unisys system.

The Unisys unit accepts digital input from a Loral advanced synthetic aperture radar system (ASARS) and associated digital and analog electronic intelligence system inputs from the other parts of the reconnaissance system. This permits the near-real-time down-linking of collected data to appropriate analysis entities.

The first refurbished SR-71A reached a speed of Mach .94 on its initial flight following modification on April 26. On May 23, it reached a speed of Mach 3.3 at 81,000 feet...just 13.5 knots short of its world speed record set during July of 1976.

*Another view of SR-71A, 64-17971, following refurbishment at the Skunk Works' Palmdale facility. Aircraft is on final approach and is in conventional landing configuration. Serial number and 9th Reconnaissance Wing code are barely visible in red on vertical tail.*

*The X-27, referred to for promotional purposes as the Lancer, was a thinly-guised attempt to acquire prototype funding from the Air Force for what Lockheed hoped would be the service's choice to fill a lightweight fighter requirement. In the end, General Dynamics F-16...now a Lockheed product...proved the winner.*

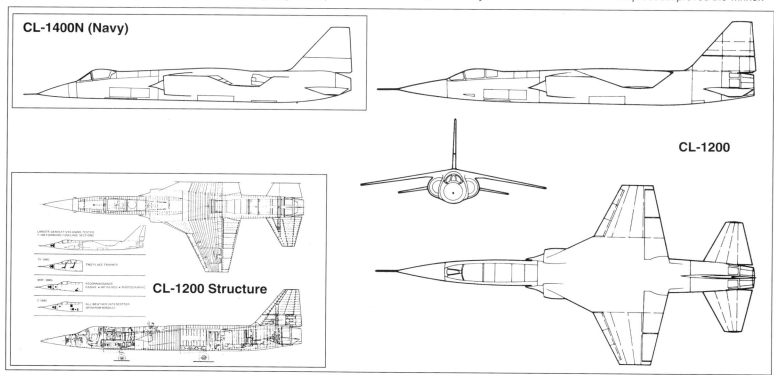

**CL-1400N (Navy)**

**CL-1200**

**CL-1200 Structure**

# Chapter 12:
# THE LIGHTWEIGHT FIGHTERS

*"The F-104 was never accepted by the Air Force as a concept because its relatively light weight automatically excluded many pet programs in armament and missions. In today's environment of multi-service missions, no risk development, and fiscal rather than performance goals, the lightweight fighter may have become an elusive dream."*

**Willis Hawkins**

*The X-27 was designed to accommodate several different engine options...and thus was offered with several different intake design choices. Ramp-style intake shown was for the Pratt & Whiteny F100.*

As the initial successes of the F-104 production program continued to lead to ever increasing orders, Lockheed, and in particular, "Kelly" Johnson and his *Skunk Works* team, began to think in terms of developing an F-104 follow-on. Believing the basic premise on which the original aircraft had been designed to be good, the new fighter was to be more of an evolutionary development of the basic *Starfighter* rather than a totally new aircraft.

During mid-1961, Johnson initiated an in-house study calling for the development of a vastly improved, yet remarkably unchanged F-104. He approached the new aircraft with caution, as preservation of the original F-104 airframe, wherever possible, was considered mandatory in order to underscore salability. Major fuselage changes were religiously avoided and relocation of the F-104's distinctive, trapezoidally-configured wing became the primary objective of the redesign effort.

Powerplant options, by the advent of the new initiative, proved a key factor in assessing the performance improvements that were expected. The high thrust-to-weight ratios being obtained using static test engines, coupled with improved specific fuel consumption figures, now became suitable justification to merit a fuselage redesign from behind the cockpit area, aft.

Over a period spanning some twenty-four months, numerous design studies, assigned Lockheed Temporary Design Designations CL-900 to CL-1200, were generated by the *Skunk Works* engineering team at Burbank. Numerous single- and twin-engine configurations were analyzed for their F-104 commonality and relative performance merits.

Concurrent to this, the lucrative European and other miscellaneous world fighter markets had not gone unnoticed by Lockheed and other western aircraft manufacturers. Coupled with the 1966 Air Force announcement a new fighter competition, acronymed F-X (Fighter Experimental), was underway, almost all initiated intense in-house design development efforts to meet forthcoming US Department of Defense and expected foreign sales needs.

"Kelly" Johnson's log on this project would note the *Skunk Works*, "...worked on small...study contracts for the Air Force, and eventually on Lockheed research money; studied variable sweep wings, fixed wings, and other types of fighters to requirements sent out by Wright Field. Maj. John Boyd and Col. Robert Titus were in charge of the early editions of the competition."

Initial configurations were designed to meet a very broad performance envelope, including low-altitude and low-speed operations and Mach 3 at over 90,000 feet . Involved in the basic concept was the use of a straight, thin wing of light wing loading, a turbofan engine to get good subsonic performance, nacelle installation of engines to provide good inlet and exhaust conditions, and the use of simplified, high-temperature titanium construction.

These studies continued into 1968, but during October, Johnson made a decision to withdraw from the competition based on concerns over the future of the program, performance and weight requirements, political issues, and the need to concentrate on the Air Force's Advanced Technology Fighter (ATF) requirement for which Lockheed was a sole source supplier. A contract for this latter aircraft came within hours of being consummated. Questions from Air Force personnel in the Pentagon killed it, however, and by late September of 1969, it was a non-issue.

Developing new fighters during the mid-1960s was not an easy task. Several new philosophical schools of thought already had begun to influence the aircraft design process, and the differences in the various approaches were significant. The "Fighter Mafia"—essentially representing perhaps the most important of these salients—was the product of a team consisting of Maj. John Boyd, analyst Pierre Sprey, Col. Everest Riccioni, and analyst Charles Myers. This team had argued convincingly that the next generation fighter following the F-X (which led to the McDonnell Douglas F-15), and the Navy's VF-X (which led to the Grumman F-14) should be austere and lightweight. This belief would eventually result in the General Dynamics F-16...considered by many to be the finest operational air combat fighter in the world at the time of its 1974 debut, but not before Lockheed and several other major players had fought vigorously with the Air Force to bring the program to life.

During early 1971, Lockheed, at "Kelly" Johnson's recommendation, headed a procession of contractors with proposals to prototype an advanced fighter design. Lockheed submitted theirs on January 14, Northrop followed on January 31, Boeing submitted one during February, and LTV (Vought) delivered theirs during June.

There was considerable doubt in the DoD that the prime motivation for this flood of unsolicited proposals was a desire for the Air Force to evaluate potential new weapon systems. DoD felt the interest was being generated by the "Fighter Mafia's" fear the forthcoming F-X and A-X (F-15 and A-10, respectively) would monopolize, and in fact consume, the Air Force's tactical aircraft budget for the next ten years. Additionally, concern was expressed that the short supply of funds would kill any chance a US fighter might have to compete in the European market when a decision was made to find a replacement for the F-104.

By the spring of 1971, *Skunk Works* design efforts had focused on the company's CL-1200 *Lancer*. In order to obtain prototype funding , the company, with Johnson spearheading the effort, resorted to some unusual tactics. Johnson secured letters of intent from two European air forces as well as several US

*Earlier* Lancer *studies included advanced J79 propulsion and utilization of the original F-104-style half-cone intakes. A major selling point of the* Lancer *and CL-1200 project was its F-104 origins.*

*One of the earliest CL-1200 studies coupled an F-104C forward fuselage and intakes with a virtually new aft fuselage, wing, empennage, and tail surfaces. There were several powerplant options.*

## CL-1200-1

equipment vendors to provide, at little or no cost, major aircraft components, subsystems, and miscellaneous support for the proposed prototypes. The Luftwaffe, for instance, had agreed to contribute a two-seat TF-104G and the Dutch had tentatively agreed to complement this with a single-seat F-104G. Significant cost savings were expected to be realized with the CL-1200 because the nose, cockpit area, and many miscellaneous sub-systems were virtually identical to those of the F-104G (or Italian F-104S).

Besides the proposed European contributions, in the US Pratt & Whitney agreed to convert three Air Force TF30-PW-100 turbofan engines (from General Dynamics F-111Fs) for CL-1200 use while also providing parts and maintenance support for any hardware testing. Similarly, Hughes agreed to supply a radar and

gunsight; Minneapolis-Honeywell agreed to donate a flight control system and autopilot; and Garrett agreed to contribute an environmental control system.

With these substantial commitments in hand, and assuming the Air Force would provide the engines promised via Pratt & Whitney, Lockheed proposed to fabricate and test two "research" *Lancer* prototypes for $30 million. The proposed eighteen month project would be undertaken by the *Skunk Works*.

Johnson cited many possible benefits to the Air Force if they were to approve a *Lancer* go-ahead: test data on a fighter configuration capable of countering the projected threat; information on automatic leading and trailing edge maneuvering flaps; and a performance evaluation of an aircraft which could be produced at roughly half the cost of an F-X and

which could out-perform the latest French Dassault *Mirage* variants.

The latter statement was of particular importance to NATO as Johnson also had set his sights once again on cornering the European fighter market. Johnson considered NATO a *de facto* Lockheed territory and refused to turn it over to any competitor (not the least of which was Northrop with their various advanced F-5 proposals and their forthcoming P-530 *Cobra*..which later would come to fruition as the YF-17). The feeling was underscored by Johnson's desire to acquire political and financial support for the CL-1200 while forcing the development of interest in countries that initially did not support the prototype venture.

Once word of Johnson's tactics reached the Air Force, proponents of the F-X and VF-X programs became concerned the CL-1200 could lead to incursions into their funding allocations. Teams were assembled to evaluate the Lockheed offer...and if possible, sidetrack Johnson's claims. Some advantages were too strong to deny however, as the design represented, (1) another contemporary fighter for the 1970s at very reduced development cost; (2) a second production source in the event of a crises; (3) a potential Dassault *Mirage* competitor; and (4) yet another step forward in the concept of prototyping.

Johnson's innovation was not long in being adopted by other companies. Northrop followed with a similar effort based on its P-530, and Vought, with several advanced A-7 and V-1000 designs on the drawing board, was not far behind. Concurrent to this, the Air Force continued to study the Lockheed fighter and by 1971, had trumped up a number of acquisition problems. For one, the US had no F-104Gs on inventory to use as spare parts bins; for another, the Air Force was reluctant to accept two aircraft, at no cost, from its allies since "strings" no doubt were attached; and for another, the proposed eighteen month development program provided for only a six month flight evaluation with three months set aside for Lockheed and three months set aside for the Air Force. Coupled with the fact Lockheed wanted the two prototypes returned so they could be used as demonstrators—presumably to the Dutch and Germans—it appeared obvious that the desire to sell the aircraft to the Air Force was not as strong as to sell it to NATO.

Growing pressure now dictated that Johnson revise some of his requirements if he had any hope of generating even moderate Air Force backing. Among the complaints emanating from the DoD were fears the flight testing period was too short; that after spending at least $30 million the Air Force would have no hardware in hand; and that to return the aircraft to Lockheed would open the door to a charge from competitors the Air Force had assisted the company in developing a prototype aircraft for foreign sales.

These concerns, coupled with a number of related questions from high level Air Force officials, prompted Johnson, during early March of 1971, to significantly modify his proposal. The Air Force, he decided, would be allowed to keep the two prototypes after flight evaluation; the program would be more research oriented; and the aircraft would not be equipped with a fire control system or other weapons-related avionics and subsystems.

As a result of this CL-1200 program reorientation, the Air Force and Lockheed agreed to assign the aircraft the official model designator X-27. This implied the experimental or

## Lightweight Fighter #2

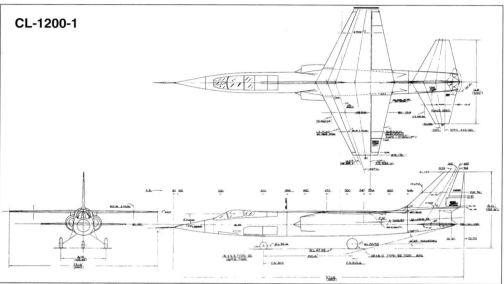

research nature of the project and artificially assured the Air Force the aircraft would not compete directly with the forthcoming F-X (F-15). On March 12, 1971, Johnson wrote Brig. Gen. John Burns a letter in which he stated, "As per our discussions last week, I am submitting a specification on the X-27 aircraft. I believe it can be used for contractual purposes. This specification clearly defines the single-place airplane, but has an addendum which makes the fundamental characteristics of the single-place airplane the basis for the specification on the two-place aircraft." He continued, "I believe it is necessary for us to describe it (the two-place aircraft) as we can not obtain the objectives of the research program unless we keep constantly in mind the fact that evaluation of the maneuvering flaps, for instance, will require the presence of a gunsight, etc."

Though the Air Force now had conceded Johnson the "right" to build the CL-1200/X-27, funding was not forthcoming from Congress and there was no guarantee it ever would. Somewhat surprisingly, Lockheed corporate picked this very moment to inform Johnson his *Skunk Works* design team, perhaps the most innovative and prestigious in the world, soon was to be disbanded unless it could be restructured to carry its own financial weight.

Johnson took this revelation to the Air Force and—in a masterstroke—effectively threatened the service with the possibility of a world without its most innovative advanced design team. The ploy had an immediate effect; during April of 1971, the Air Force prepared to request official approval to proceed with the X-27. A contract was drafted and signing was declared imminent.

The Lightweight Fighter Request for Proposals was released to nine aerospace companies on January 6, 1972. It was requested that responses to the RFP be returned no later than February 18. The RFP was short, being only 21 pages long, and rather unique in that it asked for the contractors to design to goals rather than specifications.

According to Johnson's log on Lockheed's response, the following chain of events now took place, beginning on the day the RFP was released:

"I talked with Ray Crandall prior to the RFP being released and he suggested I talk to Col. Larry Welch, now going to War College, but who was one of Gen. Kent's most excellent officers. Larry said that it was his advice that we go all out for performance. There will be no credit for producibility or use of the aircraft for NATO or other export purposes. It would certainly be necessary to win the basic competition before there would be any talk of producing the aircraft in quantity. The number one requirement was to have extremely good maneuverability, acceleration, and climb. I asked him about the creditability of various co-contractors entered in the competition and he said all were creditable. I questioned whether Boeing, who has never built a modern fighter, lit an afterburner, or had a supersonic airplane could be considered creditable, and he said that would be based on their transport reputation ( I did not make any snide remarks about the supersonic transport fiasco). Larry said the Air Force is split up the middle on the desirability of the lightweight fighter because it definitely was a threat to the F-15. The research, development, test and engineering (RDT&E) cost of the F-15 will exceed $1.7 billion and the obvious implication is that if a smaller, cheaper airplane would do the air superiority mission, the

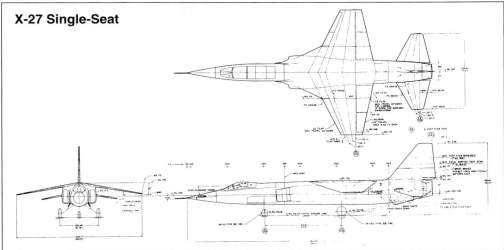

**X-27 Single-Seat**

Air Force would be in a very untenable position.

"I have the feeling that a group of young officers like Larry Welch, John Boyd, and Mike Loh are struggling to get an aircraft that we definitely need, but they are being kept under wraps because of the F-15 political problems."

On January 7, Johnson wrote, "We received the RFP for the Lightweight Fighter Proposal and went to work on it immediately." Four days later he noted, "Met with Dan Haughton, Carl Kotchian, John Cavanaugh (corporate lawyer), Willis Hawkins, and Giff Myers to discuss the program. I pointed out the pitfalls in the Data Requirements clause, particularly in that the Air Force required signing over all design rights including all the work we had done on our own money over the past two years up to this date. I pointed out specifically how the program was dragged out, with great emphasis on low speed performance and the lack of credit for anything above Mach 1.6. I noted the engine cost as being at least $500-thousand more than for the Pratt & Whitney TF30-P-100, which is rated at 4,000 pounds thrust more, but weighs 1,200 pounds more installed. I commented on our competition, which consists of Northrop, Boeing, LTV, General Dynamics, and possibly North American. We are informed that the Boeing proposal weighs at least 2,000 pounds less than our comparable design, and noted also that probably Boeing and Northrop will submit both one and two engine designs. I commented on the situation of the development of the General Electric YJ101 engine rated at 14,500 pounds thrust and which they quote will be available in approximately a year at a cost of $40-million. They do not state, as they previ-

ously told me, that an additional $252-million will be required in three more years to qualify the engine in the normal way.

"Haughton was so mad about the obvious stupidity of the Air Force and DoD in not pushing for the best they can get immediately that he seemed to be for not going into the competition.

"I told them also that all the work we had done with the NATO nations and others, for a follow-on to the F-104 was essentially 'down the drain' because of the characteristics of the lightweight fighter, particularly in its ability to carry external stores, range, and use of a proven engine certified for export now made our discussions invalid. I had previously called Walt Smith, Al White, Bob Tillman, Lynn Pitchford, and Lou Caton over to inform them of the change of status of our NATO sales plan. We are currently working on a response to the Australian RFP for a new fighter for them. This has been based entirely on the CL-1200.

"As of January 12, 1972, we have received an RFP from the Air Force calling for the design and development of two prototype Lightweight Fighter aircraft. Fundamentally this aircraft is developed from the CL-1200, on which we have worked about a year and a half. It is almost an even year since I submitted a letter proposal to Air Force Secretary Robert Seamans and Deputy Secretary of Defense David Packard, proposing a lightweight fighter which would be complementary to the F-15.

"The CL-1200 plowed the ground for both the prototype system and development espoused by Packard, and obviously by many for a long period of time. There has been a desperate struggle in the Air Force, which con-

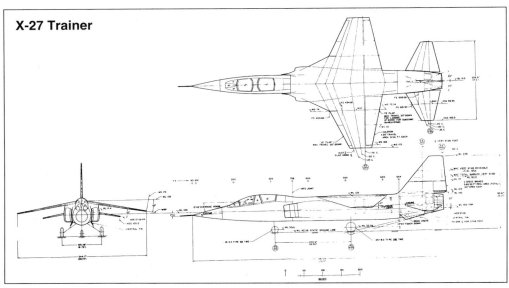

**X-27 Trainer**

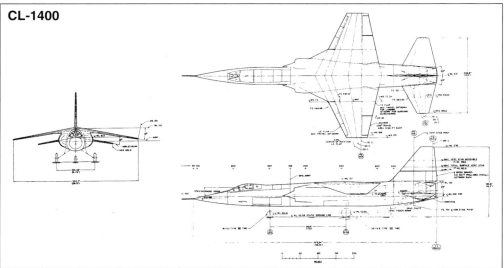

CL-1400

tinues, in an effort to prevent a lightweight fighter from competing with the F-15. The CL-1200 was a first line fighting aircraft with a developed engine and equipment, weighing essentially half of the F-15, but having higher performance in practically all categories. The Air Force successfully stopped development of this aircraft because of its threat to the F-15, but there were enough Air Force people, particularly at the Colonel level, who fought the battle to get a simple, cheaper, high-performance fighter which the country desperately needs and which has led to the RFP.

"It is clear that Sec. Seamans, Gen. John Ryan, Gen. John Meyer and, of course, the whole F-15 crowd, including Gen. Chapman and possibly Gen. Brown, Commanding Officer of the Air Force Systems Command, are quite worried about the competition presented by the lightweight fighter approach.

"At the current time, the F-15 is slated to cost between 9 and 11 million dollars a piece, in production for 700 aircraft. The CL-1200, in quantities of 300, could be built for under $4-million a piece. With a requirement now to use the F-15 engine we can probably still hit the number because of simplicity of equipment, and about a 14,000 pound empty weight.

"The Air Force funding is so projected that we can fly as soon as we would desire, mainly within a year. This is again due to the desire to not have another fighter flying when the F-15 is in the service stages. I called Bill Brown at Pratt & Whitney regarding the status of the F-15 engine. Bill always gives me an honest answer to our questions, and has done so for many years in our prior projects. He said the F-15 will be a good one, even though it is extremely complex and expensive. The production run engine is currently 110 pounds overweight. The F-15 project has ordered 21 engines for the first buy with a potential second buy of 59. The engine performance is optimized for 0.90 Mach at 30,000 feet. He said it was 'not too good at Mach 2.2 through 2.4'. McDonnell have base drag problems, but he did not know any details on this situation. They have agreed on a specification for inlet distortion, but when I told him the definition of this factor leaves a great deal to be desired, he agreed. He said, however, the F100 engine is less sensitive to circumferential distortion, but is sensitive to radial distortion. He said, 'Kelly, you must win the lightweight fighter'. I assured him of our best efforts and that we desired an engine price. He could not give me any information on this subject as this will be set by the

project officer, Gen. Ben Bellis, who does not want to reveal the true cost of the F-15 at this time. Our old friend, Ed Rifenbark, is following the engine problems. I expect to call Ed and try to get an honest cost. If I had to guess, I would expect it to be $1-1/2 million each in production compared to the TF30 at $1 million. We will have our problems in getting an export license for the F100 engine when the proper time arrives to consider that factor."

In still another January 12 entry, Johnson recounted, "Reviewed our design efforts to date to obtain optimum performance of the lightweight fighter. I disagreed with Ben and others on shortening the airplane by 6 feet, which would lead to a questionable weight saving, in my view, and very poor flight and buffet characteristics. After going over all design elements, I set a design empty weight of 13,900 pounds for the long fighter, which does have good flying characteristics and much greater ground attack potential than the one 6 feet shorter.

"We will submit the single-engine airplane with the aerodynamic configuration of the CL-1200 as our basic bid. We set a new design number for the lightweight fighter, which will be the CL-1600, to divorce it from our prior studies. I called Rus Daniell, Larry Billups, Dick Adair, Ben Rich, Jack Prosser, and Bob Murphy and told them the schedule and approach I want to take on the CL-1600. Essentially with the Feb. 18, 1972 date for turning in our proposal and following the Air Force statement that they would decide the program in about 45 days. I proposed that if we are one of the two winners, that in June we start tooling the aircraft with part of the $3 million available, and we aim for a flight date of June 1973."

Johnson, in releasing the new design number, had written several of his *Skunk Works* team members with the following notation:

"It is advisable to change the design number of our Lightweight Fighter from the CL-1200 to another serial. The reason for this is to impress the Air force with the fact this is truly a new aircraft and responsive reaction to their request for bid on the subject aircraft. We have been advised to play down the fact that our Lightweight Fighter is derived from the CL-1200, the X-27, or the F-104. In response to this suggestion, I have obtained the design number CL-1600 for our proposed aircraft. Rationale for this number has to do with our desire to avoid the 1300 and 1500 series for obvious reasons, the latter of course being conflict with the F-15."

"I want to propose one of the two aircraft

as a two-place trainer and essentially want to speed up the program by at least a year, compared to the Air Force desire. I will have to sell this program after February 18, 1972. I want to study how much, or how close we can come to flying under the funding restrictions outlined in the RFP. I must get our partners in the CL-1200 proposal together and release them from their commitments on sharing development costs on the CL-1200 and reorganize the program to get their help on the CL-1600.

"I talked to Erik Nelson, Dallas Cederberg, and Lou Caton. Cederberg is our Australian Sales Rep and Nelson our Canadian one. I told them that any sales effort starting today must be held in limbo awaiting the outcome of the lightweight fighter. I showed them the mock-up and said we would probably not respond to the Australian RFP except with an overall letter. Regarding any visit on my part, to either Australia or Canada, this is quite indeterminate. In the case of Australia, it might be tried to sell them U-2s for ocean surveillance."

On January 20, Johnson continued his log, "Had a bidder's conference at Wright-Patterson AFB to define requirements and application of prototype systems. Gen. James Stewart gave the introduction stating that there should be no 'buy-ins' and outlined clearly the financial funding available. It was perfectly evident that the whole pitch was aimed at making an airplane that would not be competitive to the F-15. Everything was aimed toward maneuverability and rate of turn, encouraging consideration of the smallest and lightest possible aircraft. We were definitely told not to consider production factors in the aircraft, to which I objected. We were allowed to use the F-15 engine, but later General Electric came up with a 15,000 pound thrust new type which Northrop used.

"I liked the way the presentation was limited to 10 pages on management procedures, 50 pages on the technical aspects, but limitation on cost data. I was very well impressed with Col. Lyle Cameron, who was to be the SPO, and the contracts officers, a civilian named Fred Wood.

Somewhat less than four weeks later, on February 16, 1972, Johnson flew to Dayton and delivered the *Skunk Works* lightweight fighter proposal by hand. The prototype *JetStar* was used for the flight, it made possible the delivery to Ohio and return to California all in one day.

Some four weeks after that, on March 13, Johnson made the following log entry, "We were visited by Lt. Gen. James Stewart, Col. Cameron, Col. John Boyd, Col. Robert Parsons, Mr. Fred Wood, Maj. Loh, and Maj. Gordon England. We discussed our lightweight fighter and the ability of the *Skunk Works* to produce the prototypes. They were on a tour to visit all bidders who were, besides ourselves, General Dynamics, Northrop, Boeing, and LTV. I am sure we answered all their questions well, but I am greatly concerned about the horrible situation facing Lockheed with regard to the C-5A, AH-56, SRAM, and our L-1011 situation. It seems almost impossible for them to give us a contract in view of Sen. Proxmire's almost daily attacks on Lockheed, compounded by the fact that our design out-performs the F-15 at approximately 40% of its cost. "

On April 13, 1972 Johnson got the final word on the lightweight fighter program, "We were not a winner. The winners were: General Dynamics and Northrop. This was a very bad shock to take in view of the fact that in all honesty I believe I started both the lightweight fighter and the prototyping program with my letter to Seamans back in January of 1971." Later, he would offer the following observations, "In the debriefing it was perfectly clear that we never had a chance to win the lightweight fighter. The Air Force maintained a very rigid position of not having anything interfere with the F-15. They liked no part of the rapid schedule I proposed, nor the fact that our aircraft was large enough to take sophisticated equipment, which the others could not."

Finally, on June 14, Johnson summarized the program and its demise:

"Between the period of the debriefing and the present time it has been confirmed to me from many sources that out CL-1600 was too good, too honest, too soon, and too cheap. When you combine these factors with the overall Lockheed image today, it is easily understood why we were not a winner. Some interesting factors developed worthy of note in the time period stated. Boeing were very mad at their not placing. Ray Utterstrom from Boeing came down to see whether or not we could join together in a joint program to build a fighter incorporating some of their ideas and some of ours. When he saw what we had in the CL-1600 and we compared wind tunnel data, wherein our wing beat theirs by 20% in lift and buffet boundary. He went away completely shaken, saying that we should have won.

"It is interesting that he admitted to legislating 1,000 pounds of weight out of the airplane, which put their airplane at 16,600 pounds. Our CL-1600 was originally 2,000 pounds heavier than our proposal.

"Utterstrom stated that of course to build a realistic airplane with the pilot sitting up instead of reclining, and with proper equipment in it, their airplane would grow to our size. He made an interesting statement about the activities of General Electric who came to Boeing and offered to pay them up to one-quarter of a million dollars if they would submit a two-engine version around their projected new YJ101 turbojet. Northrop was the second winner using the twin engine version based the General Electric engine. It is greatly evident that G.E. went all out to buy into the engine business in the lightweight fighter competition.

"It is interesting that immediately upon conclusion of the lightweight fighter evaluation, Col. John Boyd, who pushed hard to get some competition for the F-15, was sent on a combat tour to Southeast Asia, and Maj. Mike Loh was taken out of the Pentagon and assigned other duties.

"I was told that in the final meeting between Sec. Seamans, Gen. Ryan, Gen. Stewart, and others in the Pentagon, that when the choice was finally made and Lockheed's name came up, Seamans said he didn't want to hear anything about it. So it wasn't even discussed in that particular meeting. I had tried to get with Mr. Packard prior to the final notice of award and get his advice on anything we might do to carry forward our program.

"It is very interesting that I was told by Col. Cameron that we were given no credit for our ground attack capability and ferrying range, and the fact that we required only 125 pounds of added equipment to make a production aircraft.

"Starting early in June of 1972 I was forced to practically disband our fighter project group. Prior to doing this, we revised the aircraft to meet Navy requirements. I presented this to Adm. Hank Suerstedt on May 11, but the Navy had no interest whatsoever in anything

competitive to the F-14.

"It was Adm. Suerstedt, incidentally, who went to see Gen. Chapman of Air Force Systems Command (AFSC) after I first presented the aircraft to the Air Force a number of months ago, and was told by Chapman that the CL-1200 was a 'hell of an airplane', but that the Air Force would only give it 'lip service' in the prototyping program, because of its competitive effect on the F-15. And furthermore stated that the Admiral had better watch it as a competitor for the F-14, which he did."

As of June 15, 1972, the CL-1600 lightweight fighter was dead. What little additional work remained was done so under the auspices of the CL-1200 for potential foreign sales. The General Dynamics YF-16 and the Northrop YF-17 prototypes, during mid-1974, began their respective flight test programs and associated fly-off at Edwards AFB, California. Johnson would observe both with considerable interest, noting in his log, "The G.D. aircraft appears to be quite good, but the Northrop aircraft is in considerable trouble. In any case, both of these aircraft are being peddled in competition to the Lancer in Europe as heavy lightweight fighters, as they must be modified to do the NATO mission. After they add a proper radar and more internal fuel and meet NATO load factors, the heavy lightweight fighters will be in the same category as the CL-1600...there is no reward for righteousness."

His last gasp comments on this program were, "There will be no further entries on the CL-1600 beyond this date (June 15) and in all likelihood the Lancer program is completed also."

On August 1, 1973, Johnson made the following log entry:

"After the cancellation of the CL-1600 for the Air Force our efforts shifted to the CL-1200, a Lancer for export, and a study of an adaptation of the Lancer for the Navy, known as the CL-1400N. We spent a considerable amount of time to interest Aeritalia in paying for the development of a version of the aircraft known as the F-204 (which would have been powered by a single TF30-P-100). We proposed that two or three prototypes be built at ADP (the Skunk Works) and that production be undertaken by Aeritalia. During the last month after lengthy negotiations this situation does not look promising for the F-204. Both their Government and Company management continually change. We worked with the California Division under Bob Tillman, to try to arrive at a contract for approximately $50 million to build the prototypes. In mid-July 1973 there was a major management change in Aeritalia and the

whole situation is in limbo as of today. "

Work continued on the Lancer throughout the rest of the year, but support continued to be difficult to come by. Lockheed's corporate interest, though flagging, continued, but only with superficial funding. What kept it alive was the potential for sales in Europe. A heated competition for the International Fighter to replace NATO's extensive fleet of F-104s continued to entice companies like Lockheed with sales that could potentially amount to several thousand aircraft. During March of 1974 Johnson and several assistants briefed several representatives in Holland, Norway, and Belgium on the Lancer program. Upon returning to Burbank, Johnson, noted, "Our plans for complete production of an aircraft and engine in Europe were extremely well received at the highest level, but the big question remains...when are we going to have a prototype?"

By June, Johnson felt it was a foregone conclusion Lockheed's Lancer would not be a contender in the European fighter market. "In all likelihood, we are now out of the fighter business for lack of $35 million to develop a demonstrator. This, in spite of our fine efforts in Europe and Turkey to cash in on our fine F-104 program. It is very probably that there is no way for us to get back in the business in the foreseeable future."

Unsupported and floundering, the Lancer now was pulled form the limelight by Lockheed and declared a dead project. Not surprisingly, predictions of the Skunk Works demise proved somewhat premature. The operation not only survived the Lockheed corporate crises that ensued, but managed to move on to bigger and substantially more lucrative projects.

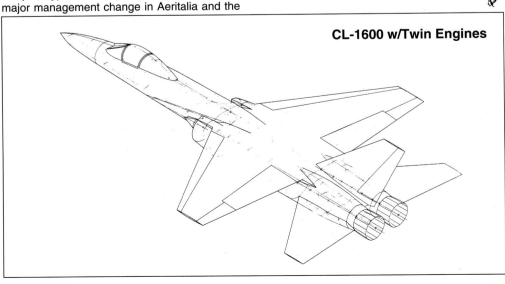

**CL-1600 w/Twin Engines**

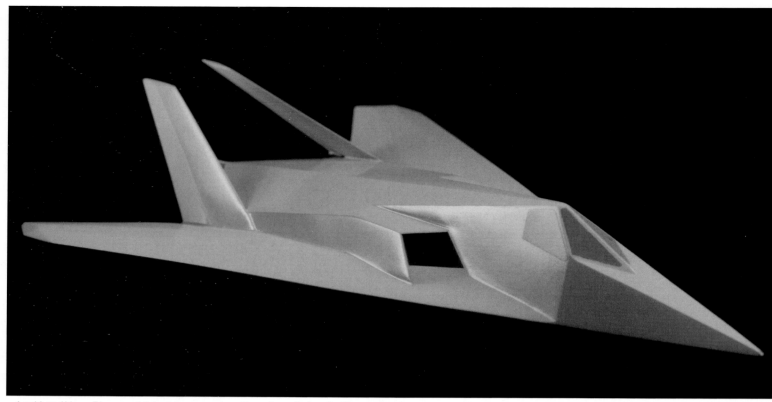

*Lockheed* Have Blue *model depicts general configuration of aircraft. Faceted surfaces are readily apparent, as are inward-canted vertical tail surfaces and extreme wing sweep angle. Noteworthy in this early study is use of conventional rudders rather than all-moving vertical tails as in actual aircraft.*

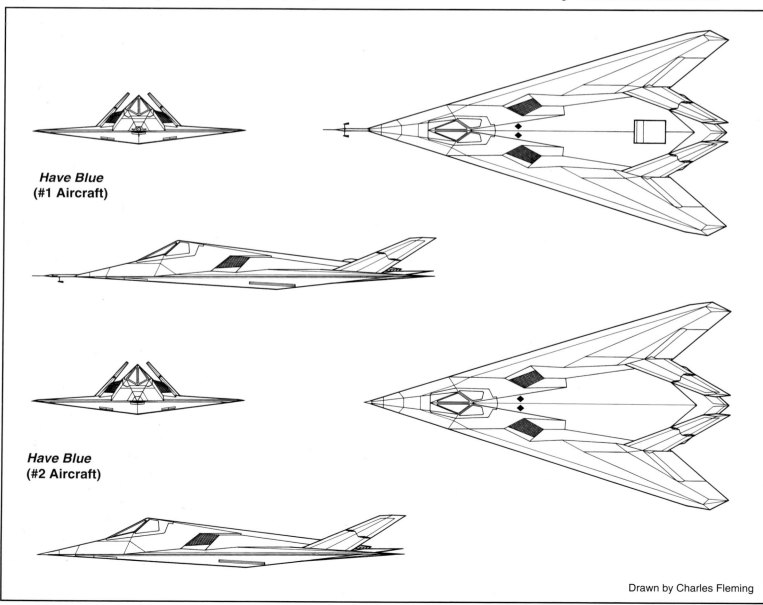

**Have Blue
(#1 Aircraft)**

**Have Blue
(#2 Aircraft)**

Drawn by Charles Fleming

# Chapter 13:
# *Have Blue*

*"To build* Have Blue *we needed $10 million. One can't imagine what goes through your mind when you have to ask the Board of Directors to invest $10 million at a time when the Corporation was considering declaring bankruptcy. That $10 million investment brought the Company several billion dollars of sales and a reputation of technical superiority in stealth technology."*

**Ben R. Rich**

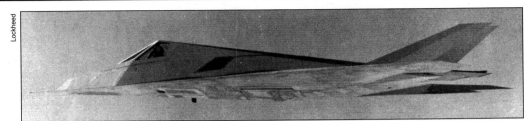

*The second* Have Blue *was flown a total of 52 times. It joined the flight test program during July of 1978 and differed from the prototype in being dedicated to airborne radar cross-section testing.*

The advantages of *low observables* or *stealth technology* have been a military matter of considerable interest for decades. Applicable not only to aircraft, but to all other forms of military equipment as well, attempts to camouflage, or reduce the visibility of hardware and personnel have been on-going since the beginning of recorded military history.

Due primarily to the three-dimensional environment in which they operate and the degree of exposure to which they are subjected, aircraft in particular have been appropriate candidates for the application of low observables technology. As early as World War One, attempts to visually camouflage aircraft with paint met with a modicum of success. There were even examples of aircraft being provided transparent wing and fuselage coverings to reduce their detectability.

During World War Two, the application of camouflage paint patterns was studied with considerable intensity. Scientifically conducted research helped generate patterns that genuinely reduced an aircraft's visibility both in the air and on the ground. Polished aluminum, for instance, was criticized for its notable ability to reflect sunlight and increase the detection distance of a target aircraft. Dull, non-glare, matte-type paints eliminated this problem, but not without increased expense and some cost in performance.

World War Two also provided the first opportunity to utilize the new technology of radar to locate and target moving objects.

Particularly vulnerable were aircraft, because of the lack of background clutter and their tendency to be built of highly reflective materials. Paint had no discernible effect on radar's ability to track an aircraft in flight.

Radar proved a menace of vast importance to all combatants during the war. For the first time, a means to accurately bomb surface targets in all weather conditions and at any time of the day or night was provided. It also permitted the tracking of a target aircraft under similar conditions, and it basically removed the security that had long been represented by an aircraft's speed and altitude.

The first attempts to counter the effect of radar were crude, at best. Metallic foil strips known as chaff, cut to specific lengths (determined by the frequency of the radar being countered), were found to temporarily blind radar when dispensed from aircraft in large quantities in the form of a cloud.

Though effective...and used with considerable regularity as a radar countermeasure to

this very day...the foil strips had their failings. Limited suspension times, dispersion difficulties, and enemy radar frequency considerations were all shortcomings that led to exploration of more effective alternatives.

The exigencies of war curtailed extensive research into the development of airworthy, non-radar-reflective structural materials, but some attempts were nevertheless made. The Germans, in particular, placed emphasis on lowering the radar return of select aircraft...including the notable Horton Ho 229. This extremely advanced all-wing jet fighter, built primarily of wood over a steel-tube load-bearing structure, in some production models was to have utilized a wood-sandwich ply with a core material of granulated charcoal. Presumed to have absorbed radar energy, the charcoal was calculated to reduce the aircraft's radar return by a not-insignificant margin. The war ended before the technology could be fully exploited.

Advances in radar not only continued after

*The second* Have Blue *prior to its first flight on July 20, 1978. Unlike the first aircraft, it incorporated all the various coatings and other radar absorbent materials required to permit its use as a full-scale RCS test specimen. It also had nose wheel steering (unlike the first aircraft) to improve ground handling characteristics.*

*An inverted pole model illustrates one of the earliest* Have Blue *configurations. Vertical tails were smaller and less swept than those ultimately found on the actual aircraft.*

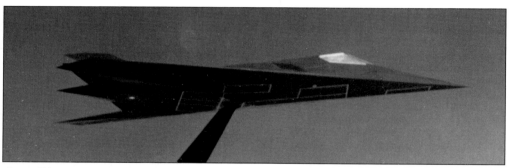

*Several* Have Blue *pole models were built. Construction materials were similar to those used on the actual aircraft...aluminum covered with radar absorbent materials.*

the war, but accelerated at a break-neck pace. Countermeasures, on the other hand, were considerably slower to evolve. In fact, during the 1950s and 1960s, little if any emphasis was placed on reducing an aircraft's radar return or on electronically countering radar energy. Electronic countermeasures (ECM) systems—what there were of them—were few in number and limited in capability.

It was not until the advent of the Vietnam war that a conscientious effort to develop truly effective ECM was undertaken. The availability of radar-guided surface-to-air and air-to-air missiles could not be discounted as in previous conflicts, and their very real threat to the viability of the US offensive effort required a most serious reassessment of the technology. Funding for the development of add-on systems such as ECM pods and chaff dispensers expedited the availability of these interim systems to accommodate near-term needs. More advanced integral systems and design-from-start-low-observables aircraft were considerably longer in coming to fruition.

Commencing with the U-2 program in the mid-to-late 1950s and continuing on with the A-12 and SR-71 aircraft series during the 1960s, Lockheed gained considerable experience in the development and application of anti-radar and other low observable features for high-performance aircraft.

These were pioneering efforts in the use of special materials and coatings, electronic devices and shaping of the aircraft to reduce radar signature along with special paint schemes and other techniques to reduce the visual signature.

During 1974, the Defense Advanced Research Projects Agency (DARPA) requested five major US military aircraft manufacturers to generate preliminary studies calling for a fighter optimized to have significantly reduced radar delectability. As Lockheed had not produced a fighter for nearly ten years, it was not invited to participate.

Consequent to this, the *Skunk Works'* Ben Rich, then deputy to "Kelly" Johnson, asked Johnson to obtain a letter from the CIA granting the *Skunk Works* permission to discuss the SR-71's (and A-12's) low observable charac-

teristics in order to petition for Lockheed to be included in the DARPA project. As a result, the *Skunk Works* was cleared to release information and participate in classified symposia to share the knowledge gained from the A-12 and SR-71 programs. This led to an invitation by DARPA to participate in conceptual studies of low observable techniques, known at the time as *Harvey*.

While Rich, along with the *Skunk Works'* Ed Martin was maneuvering to get Lockheed approved to participate in *Harvey*, during 1974 and 1975 Lockheed, using internal research and development funds, refined a technique of flight vehicle external shaping that reduced its RCS by several orders of magnitude. This accomplishment was made possible by the development of *Echo I*, the first practical computer program to very accurately predict the RCS of an air vehicle Developed by software engineer Denys Overholser and retired Lockheed mathematician Bill Schroeder, it was a major breakthrough...and it gave Lockheed a distinct advantage over any of its competition.

Schroeder had created *Echo I* by intellectually revisiting a century-old set of mathematical formulas originally derived by Scottish physicist James Clerk Maxwell and refined by turn-of-the-century German electromagnetics expert Arnold Johannes Sommerfeld. These calculations predicted the manner in which a given geometric configuration would scatter (or reflect) electromagnetic radiation.

Russian physicist Pyotr Ufimtsev had taken this early work a step further, developing a more simplified approach that concentrated on electromagnetic currents at the edges of geometric shapes. The Maxwell, Sommerfeld, and Ufimtsev equations were available to anyone but had been considered too cumbersome to be applied to anything but simple geometric forms.

Lockheed's breakthrough was Schroeder's concept of reducing the complex shape of a traditional aircraft to a finite set of two-dimensional surfaces that could be reasonably analyzed using these calculations. The result was "faceting"—creating a three-dimensional aircraft, not out of smooth, gracefully curved surfaces, but out of a collection of flat panels.

Schroeder realized that by using groups of triangular panels to form a vehicle surface, the number of individual radar reflection calculations could be limited to a manageable number. If each flat surface could then be angled in a way that would reflect any incoming radar beam away from its source, and if the combined shape could still create lift, a "stealth" aircraft might be achieved.

In the rush of competition, Overholser's team was asked to quickly create a revolutionary computer code to solve for the radar cross-section (RCS) of the shape Schroeder envisioned. They arrived at a clever system able to accurately predict the way a faceted aircraft shape would appear on radar. In just five weeks, *Echo I* had been born.

To validate the approach a simple, idealized aircraft model, nicknamed the *Hopeless Diamond* by its creators, was built and tested at *Skunk Works* electromagnetics facility in Burbank. Its RCS proved far lower than any shape Lockheed had previously tested. Since range testing of signatures being obtained was beyond the capability of then existing facilities, Lockheed concurrently developed special mounting devices and testing methods to evaluate its new design.

*Small-scale* Have Blue *radar cross-section model in Lockheed's Rye Canyon anachoic chamber. Some empennage detail is discernible, though platypus exhaust nozzle details are not readily visible.*

In August of 1975, Lockheed, along with two other contractors (Boeing and Northrop), was invited by DARPA to participate in a competitive effort to develop and test an aircraft known as the Experimental Stealth Testbed (XST) (some sources indicate the acronym stood for Experimental Survivable Testbed). In April of 1976 Lockheed was chosen to proceed with detail design, development, and test of this new aircraft. The program was given the name *Have Blue*.

Preliminary design responsibility for the new aircraft at Lockheed was given to Dick Scherer, Warren Gilmour, and Leo Celniker. Program Manager was Norm Nelson and the principle engineers assigned were Ed Baldwin, Alan Brown, Dick Cantrell, Henry Combs, Bob Loschke, the afore-mentioned Denys Overholser, and Bill Taylor. Manufacturing was placed under the direction of Bob Murphy.

*Have Blue* was a subsonic, single-place aircraft powered by two General Electric J85-GE-4A engines. The aircraft was 47 feet 3 inches in length, 7 feet 6-1/4 inches high, and had a wingspan of 22 feet 6 inches with a resultant wing area of 386 sq. feet. The wing planform was a modified delta with a sweep of 72.5°. There were no flaps, speed brakes, or high lift devices incorporated in the design. The structure was aluminum alloy with steel and titanium utilized in the hot areas. The surface controls were elevons, located inboard on the wings, and two all moveable fins at the wing root that were swept back some 35° (leading edge) and canted inboard some 30°. A side stick controller and conventional rudder pedals operated the control surfaces through a fly-by-wire command and stability augmentation system without mechanical back-up. Elevon nose-down pitch control was augmented by a large, two-position flap called the *platypus*, which was deflected downward automatically whenever 12° angle-of-attack was exceeded.

The aircraft had a tricycle landing gear with main gear antiskid braking. Nose wheel steering was installed on the second aircraft. While the forward retraction insured reliable emergency gear extension, it also meant that takeoff and landing would always occur at the most aft center-of-gravity location.

The test gross weight of the aircraft ranged from approximately 9,200 to 12,500 pounds. Zero fuel weight was 8,950 pounds. Fuel weight was 3,500 pounds and all fuel was carried in fuselage and wing tanks.

The unorthodox Have Blue configuration was designed to provide a highly maneuverable fighter aircraft with Verly Low Observable (VLO) characteristics. As a result, the external shape evolved from VLO and controllability characteristics. This resulted in a relaxed static stability (RSS) aircraft which required a quad-redundant, fly-by-wire flight control system (FCS) to provide handling qualities throughout the flight envelope.

The restrictions imposed by VLO requirements were unprecedented and demanded new approaches to preserve efficient propulsion system performance. Each inlet duct was equipped with a flat, RCS treated grid who porosity was sized for the cruise condition. The airflow was augmented at takeoff with blow-in doors mounted on the upper fuselage surface. There was concern that the inlet grids would create problems with engine performance, but these worries proved unfounded. The grids actually had a beneficial side effect in that they helped straighten the vortex disturbed inlet airflow from the highly swept wing leading edges, especially at high angles of attack.

The General Electric J85-GE-4A non-afterburning engines were obtained as Government Furnished Equipment (GFE) from the United States Navy North American T-2B trainer stores. No engine modifications except coating of the spinners was made.

The exhaust system design was likewise driven by VLO requirements. To prevent radar energy from penetrating to the turbine face, the tailpipe was transitioned from a round duct to a 17 to 1 flattened slot convergent nozzle. The trailing edge of each nozzle was terminated on a 54° scarf angle to correspond to the airframe aft closure. Vanes which were interposed and angled in the slot exit helped straighten the exhaust flow back to the longitudinal axis, although some thrust vector "toe-in" remained. Sufficient bypass air was passed over the tailpipe to cool the aft fuselage structure.

The *Have Blue* test program was clearly outlined in the original Development and Demonstration test plan to include: radar cross section and wind tunnel model tests of the prototype design; qualification and proof tests for various systems and subsystems; preflight testing of the assembled aircraft and systems; and finally, flight tests of the aircraft.

As previously stated, the basic configuration was developed utilizing the *Echo* program. A one-third scale RCS model of the *Have Blue* configuration was tested during December 1975 at the Grey Butte Microwave Measurement facility and a small model in the Lockheed Anechoic Chamber. A second series of one-third scale model tests were conducted at Grey Butte in January of 1976. These tests confirmed significant RCS improvements made with a few minor configuration changes.

On the basis of these tests, low and high speed wind tunnel models were fabricated. Only 1920 hours were used to tailor and define aerodynamic and propulsion characteristics.

A full-scale RCS model was constructed and used at the Air Force Ratscat Backscatter Measurement Range at White Sands, New Mexico to further develop and validate the VLO design. Many detail problems were resolved during this stage, allowing manufacture of the two test aircraft to proceed rapidly.

The initial engine runs were accomplished on the first *Have Blue* aircraft on November 4, 1977 at Lockheed's Burbank facility. In order to maintain security, the aircraft was parked between two semi tractor-trailers over which a camouflage net had been installed. The runs were performed at night after the airport was closed. The biggest problem experienced was a phone call for a local resident who wanted to know what was making all the noise. Following the engine runs, the aircraft was partially disassembled (the wings were removed) and readied for shipment. It was delivered to the test location, via C-5A, on November 16, 1977. Since this was the first time a C-5A had operated from the Burbank airport, the morning traffic became substantially more congested as people strained to see this "aluminum overcast" that appeared to hover over the city during its departure.

The aircraft was off-loaded at the test location and reassembled. Since most of the systems had been checked out in Burbank, only a few System Check Outs (SCOs) needed to be accomplished prior to first flight...which would be conducted under the direction of *Have Blue* Flight Test Manager Dick Miller. Engine thrust runs were performed and a series of four low and high speed taxi tests were conducted. During the third taxi test a problem developed that would become a nuisance throughout the program. In particular, overheated brakes which caused the wheel fuse plugs to melt. Flight control system performance was carefully monitored during the taxi tests and some minor changes were made to the yaw gains. Successful drag chute operation was verified and, following the fourth taxi test, the aircraft was deemed ready to fly.

*Initial ground tests of* Have Blue *took place at Lockheed's Burbank, California facility. Engine runs were accomplished outdoors at night after the Burbank airport was closed. Following the runs, the aircraft was partially disassembled and delivered to the test location via Lockheed C-5A on November 16, 1977.*

Lockheed

*Built from aluminum,* Have Blue's *construction was relatively simple. The low observables capability came from the prismatic surface arrangement and the use of radar absorbent materials.*

On December 1, 1977, with Lockheed test pilot Bill Park at the controls, *Have Blue* lifted into the air. A new era in military aviation had just begun. Only twenty months had passed since contract award,

As previously noted, the primary objective of the test program was to demonstrate VLO technology. Towards this end, *Have Blue* 1001 would demonstrated loads/flutter, performance handling qualities, and stability and control. *Have Blue* 1002 was designated as the RCS test vehicle.

*Have Blue* 1001 accomplished 36 flights over the next 5 months and successfully expanded the flight envelope sufficiently to allow the RCS testing to be performed. Unfortunately, on May 4, 1978, the aircraft sustained major damage during an attempted landing at less than design landing speed and had to be abandoned in flight by Park.

*Have Blue* 1002 joined the program during July 1978 and flew for the first time on July 20 with Air Force pilot Norman "Ken" Dyson at the controls. This aircraft differed from *Have Blue* 1001 in that it possessed a "real" airspeed system (no nose boom) and did not have a drag chute installed. It also incorporated nose wheel steering, to improve ground handling, and was adorned with all the coatings and materials required to perform its intended task. Following some airspeed calibration flights, the aircraft accomplished 52 flights during the following 12 months and completed the low observable testing.

*Have Blue's* pitot static system consisted of three separate static sources on the upper and lower forebody surfaces and three total pressure probes; one at the nose tip and two on the windshield center post. *Have Blue* 1001 also had a flight test nose boom which included pitot-static pressure sources and angle-of-attack and sideslip vanes. A flight path accelerometer (FPA) also was included as part of the basic airspeed probe and was located inside the probe at the angle-of-attack vane position. The forebody static pressure position error, determined from flight tests, agreed very well with wind tunnel data. The gear down position error, however, was less than the wind tunnel results. It should be noted that the design concepts of this airplane severely limited the choices of static and total pressure locations and, as a result, the static pressure position errors were quite large but were consistent.

The flight test measured pitch stability coefficient confirmed the prediction that the aircraft was marginally stable to unstable at and below 0.3 Mach number in 1 g flight. Pitch stability was not affected by landing gear extension at normal landing gear angles of attack, again as predicted. The change in lift with angle-of-attack was also as predicted.

The aircraft's static directional stability was significantly less than predicted at middle to high Mach numbers with the aircraft being directionally unstable above 0.65 Mach number. As a result, the FCS directional axis gain was increased to improve the augmented directional stability.

Sideforce with sideslip coefficient values, extracted from yaw doublets and steady sideslips indicated that this derivative was one-half the predicted level, possibly as a result of thrust effects. The increase as a result of landing gear extension was as predicted.

Dihedral effect, roll damping, and yaw damping were all substantially as predicted. The only exception was roll damping which was weaker than predicted around 0.3 Mach number.

Engine out characteristics were unusual in that rolling and yawing moments were in the direction of the operative engine, and more control effort was required in the roll axis than the yaw axis.

Baseline inflight RCS testing was completed during September of 1978. After several modifications required by the results of the baseline testing were completed, penetration testing against ground based radars and IR systems was begun. IR detections matched predictions well. When a T-38 participated in or duplicated the test profiles, it was tracked to the maximum range of the terminal system.

The final phase of testing in a simulated integrated air defense environment was completed during July of 1979. The aircraft demonstrated its VLO capabilities against ground and airborne systems during these tests. Its low acoustic signature was also verified. Measured RCS data correlated well with those measured at Ratscat.

The project management of the *Have Blue* program for both the government and Lockheed can be characterized as small, close knit, streamlined, and tailored to the specific needs of the program objectives.

The project was accomplished with daily verbal and secure electronic communications between Lockheed and government program managers supplemented by frequent visits and more formal program reviews. Technical, schedule and cost performance tracking and reporting, although in simplified form, was accurate, timely, and responsive to customer needs.

Evidence of good contingency planning activity on *Have Blue* included actions taken to recover from: the non-availability of significant GFAE items, workarounds and rapid recovery from a three month IAM strike, and reactivation of flight test operations at the test location.

Contractor interfaces were limited, but very important and well managed on the *Have Blue* program. General Electric was a subcon-

tractor for J85 engine installation and performance interface. Lear Siegler was the principle subcontractor responsible for manufacture and field support of the flight control system.

Lockheed's security program was also quite successful during the *Have Blue* program. The program initially started as a "white world" program with minimum security classification requirements. This security posture remained until early 1977 when the government realized that a major breakthrough had been achieved in VLO technology, with great potential to national defense. Subsequently, the program was placed under the "special access required" (SAR) security umbrella. From that point forward Lockheed maintained total secrecy of the program.

The *Have Blue* program was made possible by a great deal of contractor/customer cooperation in successfully achieving technical breakthroughs. The ability to reduce high risk technical areas on an accelerated basis and in a cost effective manner was demonstrated by the fact that design, manufacture, and test of this innovative aircraft was accomplished in three years. The VLO aircraft, including engine inlets and exhausts, featured faceted surfaces covered with RAM. Adequate stability and control of the basically unstable aircraft was provided by a quad-redundant fly-by-wire flight control system, with unique *Have Blue* features and some basic components adapted from the F-16 system. The radical design involved breakthroughs in virtually all disciplines of aircraft design.

Areas of improvement for follow-on programs were defined by the flight test results. In particular: door closure designs were modified during the flight test program to provide more positive closing forces; fin and rudder installations were improved by relocating at the centerline instead of outboard (heat input was then reduced and potential gaps were eliminated); air data probes were placed further forward to reduce air data correction factors; the handling quality requirements in Mil-F-8785B were inadequate for the design of the FCS required for the *Have Blue* aircraft (*Have Blue's* fixed side stick control was not totally satisfactory for many piloting tasks; lack of stick motion, stick orientation relative to seat location, and the need for lateral constraints for the pilots were all identified as areas requiring improvement); the large flat plate upper surface of the *platypus* was unevenly heated when engine power settings were changed and the resulting differential expansion caused distortions which warped the surface (this distortion combined with manufacturing tolerances associated with the nozzles to make the thrust vector toe-in angles asymmetric; the side forces generated by the asymmetry were picked up by the lateral accelerometer used in the FCS for directional stability augmentation; the resulting commands to the fins caused the aircraft to fly "crabbed", thus requiring the pilot to retrim the aircraft directionally each time that the flight condition changed; the automatic yaw trim feature in the FCS was a partial solution, but the final solution involved elimination of the lateral accelerometer and substitution of a direct measurement of the side slip angle for directional stability augmentation; and the aerodynamic stability and control parameters derived from flight test results with the modified maximum likelihood estimator (MMLE) technique were in good agreement with wind tunnel predictions except for directional stability which was lower than predicted (aircraft with unortho-

*The second* Have Blue *prototype undergoing flight test. This aircraft differed from the first in several significant ways, not the least of which was the elimination of the flight test nose boom and the deletion of the drag chute housing between the vertical tails.*

dox nozzle configurations and low inherent directional stability require special wind tunnel testing techniques, including flowing nozzles and inlets).

The *Have Blue* program was a low cost demonstration of a radically new concept in VLO aircraft design. This program represents the ultimate example of Lockheed/customer cooperation to perform fast track risk reduction, concept definition, and demonstration of a fighter capable, VLO aircraft.

*Have Blue* program accomplishments included from a technical standpoint: lowest RCS aircraft in the world by several orders of magnitude; VLO Infrared signature; VLO visual signatures; VLO acoustic signature; and confirmation of complex aerodynamics. From a schedule standpoint: 20 months from prototype contract award to first flight; and 88 test sorties. From a cost standpoint: $43.0 million total; $32.6 million US Air Force/DARPA funding;

and $10.4 million from Lockheed. In conclusion, it was determined VLO tactical and strategic aircraft could be designed, produced,

and operated.

Have Blue *differed in many significant areas from its F-117A successor. Most noticeable from the aft perspective was the inward cant to the vertical tail surfaces...which was exactly opposite the F-117A.*

*The first* Have Blue *was equipped with a conventional nose boom for airspeed, altitude, angle-of-attack, and sideslip sensing. Primarily an aerodynamic prototype, it served to prove the viability of the configuration's flightworthiness. It was the only one of the two prototypes to wear camouflage paint.*

*The full-scale F-117 wood mock-up under construction during late 1979 inside Building 309/310 at Plant B-6. Faceted surface detail echoing the technolgy gener-*
*ated from the* Have Blue *program already was apparent. F-117 program at this time was referred to by its codename of* Senior Trend.

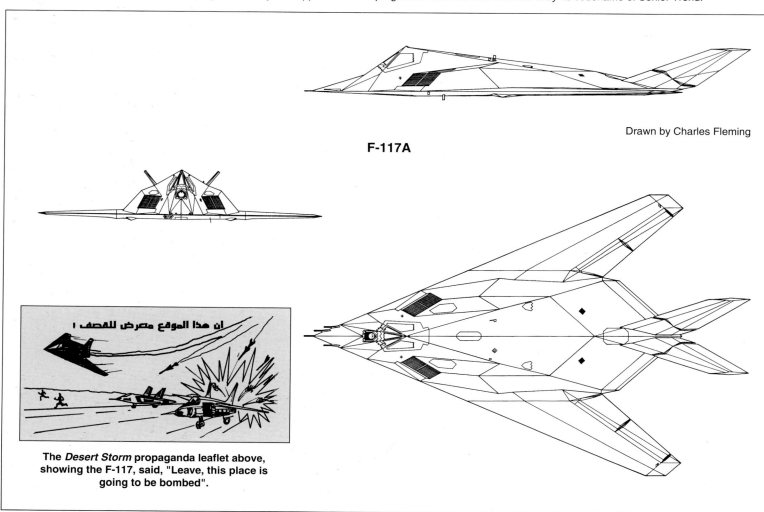

Drawn by Charles Fleming

**F-117A**

The *Desert Storm* propaganda leaflet above,
showing the F-117, said, "Leave, this place is
going to be bombed".

# Chapter 14:
# F-117A...the *Nighthawk*

*"I always felt it would perform very well...but I never expected it to perform as well as it did. We had not involved the airplane operationally, and therefore the operators didn't know how to use the airplane. It's like having a new tool...I was worried we hadn't operated it enough"*

**Ben Rich**

The advantages of very low observables or stealth technology, once successfully demonstrated by Lockheed's *Have Blue* prototypes, quickly led to a full-scale engineering development contract award from the Air Force on November 16, 1978. The fixed price production contract was signed thirteen months later. It called for five full-scale development (FSD) and fifteen production models of a single-seat, subsonic attack aircraft to be officially designated F-117A. Under Program Manager Norm Nelson (working under the direction of the *Skunk Works'* Vice President and General Manager, Ben Rich), engineering on the new aircraft proceeded at a rapid pace, utilizing the data base that had been developed under *Have Blue*. Principle engineers assigned to the new aircraft were Ed Baldwin, Alan Brown, Dick Cantrell, Bob Loschke, and Bill Taylor...all veterans of the earlier *low-observables program*. Bob Murphy again was tapped to direct manufacturing.

The resulting unusual shape of the F-117A is the end product of the low-observables goals set for the aircraft at the program's beginning. Not surprisingly, it provided the aerodynamic and stability and control engineers with a significant challenge. A major effort was instituted to minimize performance penalties and provide satisfactory flight characteristics. In the end, these efforts were quite successful.

The F-117A incorporates a variety of design features to significantly reduce aircraft signature. There are seven different types of observable signatures of concern: radar, infrared, visual, contrails, engine smoke, acoustics, and electromagnetic emissions. The three signature characteristics providing the greatest potential for exploitation by threat systems are radar, infrared and electromagnetic emissions. The F-117A was designed to minimize these signatures. Techniques utilized include highly swept surfaces, radar absorbing structure and materials, gridded inlets, high-aspect-ratio two-dimensional exhaust nozzles, internal weapons carriage, special antennas, and radio frequency transmission techniques.

Since the F-117A was a departure from normal aerodynamic design, a significant effort was made to reduce development risk by using several proven systems from existing aircraft. Examples of this are: the General Electric F404 turbofan engine used in the McDonnell Douglas F/A-18 fighter; cockpit components from the General Dynamics (now Lockheed) F-16 and the McDonnell Douglas F/A-18; navigation and attack systems; computer and electronics; off-the-shelf weapons; and a modified fly-by-wire F-16 flight control system.

All aircraft designs are a compromise in one form or another, with the primary mission objective dominating these characteristics. The primary mission of the F-117A is to penetrate enemy airspace, destroy high value targets and survive. As a result, low observability became the dominant design factor. Instead of an aerodynamic shape optimized for high speed or

*A full-scale F-117A pole model for radar cross-section studies was built to emulate the return signature of the actual aircraft. This gave credence to what had previously been only computer generated numbers.*

*The full-scale F-117A pole model under test. Most pole model work of this kind was conducted at night to prevent the aircraft being observed by anyone lacking proper clearance.*

The first F-117A, No. 780, nears final assembly at the test location. This aircraft would fly for the first time on June 18, 1981, with Locheed test pilot Hal Farley at the controls. Some difficulties were experienced during the initial flight including a noticeable insufficiency in vertical tail surface area.

F-117A, No. 780, being prepared for its first flight. Static engine runs like this were conducted under cover of a hangar in order to prevent reconnaissance satellites from acquiring usable imagery.

long range, the shape was faceted for purposes of lowering the radar cross section.

Once Dick Cantrell, the *Skunk Works'* chief aerodynamicist, recovered from the initial shock that Alan Brown, the *Skunk Works* 'low observables expert, had given him, he set out to achieve the desired compromises and still have a flyable aircraft. This proved a sizable challenge.

Since low observability—or stealth—was the primary goal, it established the external configuration and in particular the sweep angles of the wings and tail. One of the larger challenges was to provide as much sweep as possible and still have sufficient aspect ratio for the needed lift-over-drag (L/D) to achieve the required range. This was accomplished by carrying the wing as far aft as possible in order to increase the span. The trailing edge of the delta was notched-out both for low observables considerations as well as to reduce wetted area.

Another major challenge was to provide adequate control to achieve the desired maneuverability within a reasonable angle-of-attack range for an unstable aircraft in both pitch and yaw. Since horizontal tails were not to be used, large full-span elevons were provided for both pitch and roll control. These were sized to handle the pitch instability which resulted in more roll control power than was needed.

The highly-swept V-tail surfaces were another concession to low observability. The objective was to reduce the height and size yet still provide adequate control for the unstable yaw axis. This required all-movable surfaces.

Alternate means of directional control were investigated, such as split elevon tips, but the V-tail was preferred to provide adequate control power and reduce drag.

The resulting control configuration was not conducive to low takeoff and landing speeds. The full-span elevons could not be drooped for landing without leading edge devices or another means of pitch control. The solution was to use a drag chute for landing and accept a longer takeoff roll. The brake system capacity was subsequently improved reducing reliance on the drag chute.

Another low observability design consideration was to provide very sharp leading edges. This is good for a supersonic airfoil, but not optimum for a subsonic aircraft.

Since this was the first aircraft designed by electrical engineers, it was not surprising that a number of aerodynamic "sins" were committed. In fact, when unaugmented, the F-117A exhibits just about every mode of unstable behavior possible—longitudinal and directional instability, pitch-up, pitch-down, dihedral reversal, and various other cross-axis couplings. Because of these characteristics, there was no question about what kind of flight control system was required. Piloted simulation showed it had to be a full-time, fly-by-wire command augmentation system. Any mechanical back-up flight control system would just add weight since pilot control was impossible without stability augmentation.

When the F-117A program started, the F-16 was just being introduced into squadron service and the F/A-18 was just beginning flight test. Since there was already enough risk in the new *Skunk Works* program, it proved prudent to use developed, off-the-shelf components to the maximum extent possible not only to reduce risk but also to reduce costs even if it meant some weight penalty. It was decided that the technology developed for the F-16 fly-by-wire flight control system was the only one mature enough to be low risk and also relatively low cost due to the volume of production. The F-16 actuators, the flight control computer chassis, and power supplies were modified slightly to adapt them to the F-117A. New control laws had to be developed for implementation in the flight control computer, new interfaces for the new air data sensors defined, and a different actuator failure detection and redundancy management scheme developed. The

F-117A, No. 780, differed in many ways from follow-on aircraft. The most distinctive item was the flight test nose boom which was fitted with sensors to calibrate the production flight control system sensors.

air data probes and pilot's control stick were developed especially for the F-117A.

The pitch axis was implemented as a g-command system optimized for flight path control to support the ground attack mission. An angle-of-attack (AoA) limiter was incorporated to prevent departures and the elevons were sized to provide the necessary pitch control power. Because the pitch axis control required large elevons, the available roll control power was much more than needed and the flight control computer incorporated authority limiters to keep the roll rate down to minimize structural loads. The four elevons are used for roll control, and roll rate feedback is used to improve the roll damping.

The directional axis control is of particular interest since the F-117A is directionally unstable over large parts of its operational envelope. Operating the weapon bay doors makes it more unstable so that two large all-moveable fins were required to provide the necessary control power. Because of its shape, the aircraft has very low side force...which means that use of a conventional lateral accelerometer feedback for directional stability augmentation was not practical. The air data probes measure differential pressure and the flight control computer acting through the fins literally keeps the nose aligned with the relative wind. Yaw rate and roll rate are fed back to give the desired levels of dutch roll damping and the product of pitch rate and roll rate is fed back to cancel inertia coupling. The directional axis also incorporates an automatic yaw trim when the gear is up and the pilot is not using the rudder pedals. This feature greatly simplified emergency procedures following an engine failure at lift-off since the pilot only has to retract the gear and concentrate on maintaining AoA and bank angle at the desired values.

Series trim is implemented in all three axes; that is, the stick and pedals are at neutral when the aircraft is in trim. Also, the stick does not move when the autopilot is operating. The autopilot incorporates pitch and roll attitude hold and heading hold with control stick steering (CSS). The CSS disables the autopilot while the pilot maneuvers to a new attitude or heading with the stick and then holds the new attitude when the stick is released. The autopilot also incorporates altitude hold, Mach hold, and automatic navigation.

The net result of the F-117A's flight control system development is an aircraft with comparable pitch and roll response to that of conventionally shaped contemporary fighter and attack aircraft within certain boundaries. It is very maneuverable and fully aerobatic.

The F-117A flight test program began with a series of flights in the Calspan NT-33A where the suitability of the flight control laws was checked and where the effects of some aerodynamic variations were investigated. One of the variations assumed that the directional stability was even worse than predicted so that the pilot could see the effects and get some experience.

The actual first flight of the F-117A, under the direction of program Flight Test Manager Dick Abrams, took place on June 18, 1981 with *Skunk Works* test pilot Harold "Hal" Farley, Jr. at the controls. Since the air data probes were of a new design and had exhibited some pitch yaw coupling during vibration testing, it was decided to ballast the aircraft to a forward center of gravity location and turn off the AoA and beta measurements to the FLCC to prevent any possible coupling. Switches were incorporated in the cockpit for the pilot to activate the

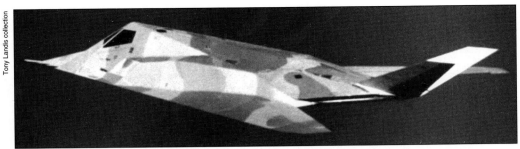

*A three-tone camouflage paint scheme was applied to F-117 No. 780 shortly after its first flight in an attempt to disguise its facets. It quickly proved ineffective and the aircraft was repainted light grey.*

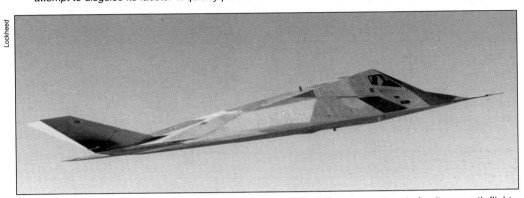

*The small vertical tail surfaces initially installed on F-117A No. 780 were replaced after its seventh flight when it was determined the aircraft's directional stability and control power were less than predicted.*

AoA and beta feedbacks after attaining a stabilized flight condition at 15,000 feet. Extenders were installed on those switches so they could quickly be turned on if needed.

Immediately after lift-off, it became apparent that the directional stability was significantly worse than predicted and the beta feedback to the flight control computer was immediately switched on. Fortunately, the probes worked exactly as predicted, the aircraft stiffened up directionally, and the rest of the flight was more or less routine. This experience once again showed the value of using in-flight simulation to investigate possible aerodynamic variations prior to first flights. As it turned out, both the directional stability and directional control power were less than predicted and the fins were increased in size by 50% to get back up to the original predicted levels of stability and control power.

Stealthy air data sensors were a unique design challenge. Ideally, flush-mounted "invisible" sensors such as pressure ports on the forebody could be used. Unfortunately, *Skunk Works* engineers could not find four independent locations for AoA and beta (actually sixteen places on the aircraft) without all variables being functions of all others (AoA, beta, Mach, and q) which would require too many correction coefficients in the flight control system. As a result, four probes (for quadruple redundancy) are utilized.

These probes were made of special materials in an unconventional shape which required a lot of test flying to get good position error calibrations on AoA, beta, airspeed, and altitude. Initial designs cracked when the heat was turned on, calibrations shifted, and quality control problems in probe manufacture required testing and retesting until deficiencies were identified and eliminated.

High angle-of-attack flight test to verify the

*F-117A No. 780's centerline-mounted flight test nose boom and light gray paint scheme were easily discerned when the aircraft was viewed from overhead. Slotted exhaust arrangement is noteworthy.*

Four of the F-117A's Combined Test Force fleet of five--Nos. 781, 782, 783, and 831--are seen in formation during March of 1991. By the date of this photograph, No. 780, the first Full-Scale Development (FSD) F-117A, had been retired from active flight testing.

Leading edge extensions were evaluated on F-117A No. 780 late in its career in an attempt to reduce the F-117A's takeoff and landing speeds. The speed reduction proved too small to warrant fleet retrofit.

ery chute. The high AoA test plan that was implemented was as follows:

The testing began 10° below the predicted pitch-up AoA. The AoA limiter was set slightly higher than this value, the aircraft was trimmed at the test AoA, and small inputs were made to obtain data for analysis. If the results agreed with the wind tunnel predictions, the AoA limiter would be set down to the test AoA and on the next flight, the pilot would do slow pulls to full aft stick in wind-up turns If the results did not agree with the wind tunnel prediction (and they sometimes did not) the flight simulator was programmed with the new data and extensive piloted simulation with many aerodynamic variations were made before accomplishing the next flight test point. Every high AoA test flight was rehearsed in the flight simulator and various failures simulated at the most critical points so that the pilots would not be surprised. This test procedure was repeated increasing the AoA limiter a degree at a time until the AoA envelope was opened up as far as required to give mission capability. Literally hundreds of full aft stick yanks, full stick rolls, etc., were performed to verify the adequacy of the AoA limiter design. The AoA limiter was modified as the testing was accomplished to improve performance and safety margins.

There was one free, unscheduled high AoA test that exercised the AoA limiter before the formal high AoA tests were completed. On May 23, 1983, when returning from a mission avionics test flight, an F-117A encountered a very large clear air gust at low altitude. The aircraft was left wing down turning final in light to moderate turbulence when the gust hit. Later simulation matches showed the gust was mostly horizontal but it was large enough to instantaneously increase AoA and beta to levels higher than had been tested to date. The AoA limiter responded with full down elevon in less than 0.4 seconds and the fins deflected to 90% of full travel to control sideslip. *Skunk Works* engineers were very pleased with these results...which showed that the new probes worked properly and that the flight controls were able to maintain control in a severe gust.

Flutter testing became a bigger effort than originally planned as a result of a chain of events that started with the aircraft's original design. The big surprise came when an Air Force test pilot was flying a stores compatibility test mission. While performing a sideslip

adequacy of the AoA limiter was approached with extreme caution and took a lot of test time to complete. There were two reasons for this. The first was that all the wind tunnel tests showed that pitch-up would occur at high AoA. Free flight testing of unpowered models verified that pitch-up and deep stall were possible, but that there were no identifiable spin modes. The second reason was that the high AoA tests

were done without a recovery chute. There was never any intention to deliberately depart the aircraft because the small model free flight tests showed that all departures eventually wound up in a deep stall. Since there was a possibility that the normal drag chute would effect a recovery from that condition, it was decided that the high AoA testing could go forward without the installation of a special recov-

maneuver, explosive flutter of the left fin occurred. The fin was almost completely lost and the pilot brought the F-117A home with difficulty...and with considerably less directional stability than before. As noted earlier, the original fin was 50% smaller than the final version due to directional stability considerations. The corrective action was to increase the fin area by extending the fin edges, but without changing the size of the fin box structure. The net result was a reduction of fin stiffness.

Prior to this incident, an extensive flight flutter clearance program had been conducted, the results of which indicated there were no aeroelastic problems of any significance. Analysis performed subsequent to the incident revealed the problem to be a flutter mode, known as the "hump" mode, that was considered at first to have a flat damping trend that was actually found to be potentially flutter critical. In fact, the aircraft had been cleared to and flown many times at the incident flight conditions before the fin flutter problem was encountered.

The subsequent investigation also revealed that this critical mode, along with others, was highly affected by rudder post bearing friction, which had masked the criticality of the mode in earlier flutter testing. In order to test the absolute worst case (no friction) low friction roller bearings were installed in the test aircraft replacing (for test purposes only) the standard journal bearings on the rudder posts. The testing continued and verified satisfactory stability levels of the fin modes out to the desired speeds.

However, the flutter test results did show a significant loss of damping in sideslips. This loss, when coupled with the masking effect of the bearing friction, led to the fin flutter incident. Since then, the fins have been replaced with new fins made of graphite-thermoplastics. These new fins are much stiffer and have demonstrated a very large flutter margin.

The requirements for structural flight tests were fairly typical of a normal aircraft. All of the standard maneuvers had to be performed out to the structural limits of the aircraft. Two problems arose. The first was due to a change in fuel transfer sequencing which reduced the inertia relief provided by wing fuel. This stopped flight testing until a strengthening of the aft wing attach points was accomplished. The second problem occurred when the aft fuselage loads measured in flight test turned out to be significantly higher than predicted by analysis. After much speculation without a reasonable explanation, it was decided to install pressure taps on the rear of the aircraft and compare the pressure distribution results from flight test with those from the wind tunnel. The tunnel data matched the flight test results. This led the *Skunk Works* engineers to look for other sources of loading...which turned out to be the effect of the unusual exhaust system. Trying to take the thrust and squeeze it out of a high-aspect-ratio two-dimensional nozzle resulted in some unusual down bending moments which had not been accounted for in the analysis.

Engine tests also were conducted due to the unorthodox design of the exhaust nozzles. Problems were known to occur when a circular thrust pattern is expelled from a round engine then turned and flattened to exhaust out of a long, flat, two-dimensional nozzle. Hot spots, loads, tailpipe distortion, etc. had to be overcome requiring many tests and engineering exercises before a suitable exhaust configura-

*Several different weapons, including this GBU-10 laser guided bomb with refined targeting capability, have been developed specifically for the F-117A.*

*F-117A, No. 780, in final assembly at Burbank. It was one of five pre-production series full-scale development F-117As that served to explore the performance, stability and control, and mission envelopes.*

*F-117A production inside Plant B-6 at Burbank. These aircraft would become the last Skunk Works aircraft manufactured at the old Burbank site as all new production would afterwards take place at Palmdale.*

*The F-117A's faceted surfaces result in an extraordinarily unorthodox aerodynamic configuration. Without a fly-by-wire flight control system, the aircraft would be virtually impossible to fly.*

*Extreme sweep angle of wing is strikingly apparent when the F-117A is viewed from underneath or above. Asymetric placement of air data probes on nose is easily discerned from either vantage point, as well.*

were tunnel tested before an acceptable one was found.

Airborne results proved the systems worked well. The only real modification required was the repositioning of the icing detector within the engine inlet.

The development of the F-117A avionics systems continues to be an ever-evolving program of changes, upgrades, and improvements. Early FSD testing brought the initial avionics architecture to an initial operational capability during October of 1983. Full capability development after initial operational capability brought most avionics systems to maturity. The Weapon System Computer Subsystem (WSCS) upgrade brought needed computational capability improvements to the F-117A while the Offensive Combat Improvement Program (OCIP) brought additional pilot situational awareness and reduced workload to the night single-seat attack mission. Ongoing programs and planned future capabilities will continue the evolutionary process.

The F-117A avionics systems development followed the same principles as the main airframe program: minimize development risks by using off-the-shelf hardware where possible, modify existing equipment where feasible, and invent new systems only when absolutely required. In this regard, the program was highly successful; however, some of the off-the-shelf and modified systems provided inadequate performance until additional improvements were made.

The stealth requirement for avionics design was just as stringent as the basic airframe and required substantial integration of airframe/avionics design. Stealth requires that the signature of the aircraft be reduced in the areas of radar, infrared, acoustic, and visual observables. Avionics system designs must also be aware that electromagnetic emissions from the aircraft, such as radar, are just as vulnerable to detectability as any of the other observables.

Considerable effort went into the incorporation of features to preclude any emission from the F-117A. In the aircraft's stealthy mode, the F-117A is incapable of any emission which may cause detection; i.e., UHF, IFF, radar altimeter, TACAN, etc. The laser target designator is the only exception and considerable forethought went into the amount of time and conditions under which it may fire. As a result, the avionics design of the F-117A operates independently of any active emission and relies completely on passive systems for navigation, target acquisition, and weapon delivery.

tion was developed.

One other area of concern also was the distortion produced by the inlet grids and the engines' ability to tolerate this. Analysis indicated the grids should be no problem, but a little skepticism remained. The distortion levels in fact proved to be less than expected and the grids actually acted as flow straighteners giving a consistent source of air to the engine throughout the entire AoA and beta range of the aircraft.

A great deal of icing tunnel work was conducted as a result of inlet icing concerns. This indicated that the inlet grids not only looked like a giant ice cube tray, but acted like one, as well. Later, inflight icing tests using the normal buildup approach were undertaken. It was concluded that a special de-icing system would have to be devised. As a result, the aircraft was equipped with a special wiper system complete with alcohol dispensing capability.

With the F-117A's handling qualities so dependent on good air data, the criticality of pitot-static probe deicing was obvious. Requirements forced upon the aircraft by the low-observables engineering group made the design of the probes and their deicing system a serious challenge. Many different designs

*Configuration of F-117A as it enters final approach into Tonapah. Extended communications antenna are noteworthy. The aircraft's extremely low reflectivity dictates the need to attach special temporary radar reflectors to the fuselage sides when operating in a controlled airspace environment.*

As a result of the need to minimize development risks and maximize the use of off-the-shelf equipment, the cockpit became a mix of then state-of-the-art glass cockpit technology and Century series aircraft type switches, lights, and dials. Much of the equipment came from front line aircraft, such as the F/A-18, but the aircraft includes components from practically every aircraft built since the T-33. Examples include parts taken from the SR-71, the P-3, the C-130, the L-1011, the S-3, the F-104, the P-2, and many others.

The main cockpit layout is the now familiar arrangement of Multifunction Displays with a HUD and center sensor display. During F-117A conceptual design, the F/A-18 was the only US fighter using a similar arrangement. Due to limitations within the computer system and for risk reduction, most of the warning lights, indicators, and aircraft systems switches are external to the avionics architecture and have no provisions for control from the displays.

Most of the cockpit systems are derived from the F/A-18. These include the early multifunction display indicators, the HUD, fuel gauge, engine instruments, stick grip, and throttles. The sensor display is provided by Texas Instruments and is derived from the Vietnam-era OV-10D and P-3C programs.

The original avionics architecture was a distributed real-time processing system which used three Delco M362F computers from the F-16 interconnected with a dual redundant MIL-STD-1553 data bus. The computers interface with the displays, controls, INS, autopilot, stores management system (SMS), and the sensor systems. The weapon delivery computer (WDC) was the system executive. Beside providing over-all control, the WDC serviced and updated the cockpit displays, performed the weapon delivery ballistics calculations, interfaced to the various sensor systems, and controlled the data distribution. The navigation control computer performed all navigation and control functions including the inertial measurement unit, the control display unit, navigation steering, flight director steering, position update, attitude heading reference system integration, and the TACAN and ILS interface. The third computer provided control and data processing for an additional sensor system and was used as a back-up computer if one of the other two should fail. A data transfer module interface unit was provided to load preflight mission data via a data transfer module from the mission data planning system.

The underlying operating principle of the avionics system is the cueing of the sensor to the target via a precision navigation system thus providing updated target information for accurate weapons release.

Given suitably accurate information about the location of a target and given the excellent accuracy of the onboard inertial system, the computer system cues the infrared (IR) system to the target. The field of view of the IR system being small, requires not only that the position accuracy of the INS be very good but also that the target location data be very accurate so that the IR system can be pointed very accurately. This was the critical program issue for the avionics system. Would sufficiently good target information be available and would system performance be good enough to be able to find a target at night looking only through a small IR window? And, of course, could weapons be delivered accurately enough to destroy the target? Given that the desired tar-

*The F-117A was publicly unveiled for the first time on April 21, 1990, at Nellis AFB, Nevada. Two aircraft were made available following a media brief and fly-by.*

*The F-117A's participation in* Desert Storm *was considered critical to the successes enjoyed by the Allied combatants. Saudi Arabian air force facilities provided ideal accommodations for aircraft and crew.*

get is within the field of view of the IR system, i.e., the pilot can see it on the sensor display, the pilot refines the aiming, designates the target, and consents for weapon release, which occurs via the SMS at the appropriate time.

The infrared acquisition and detection system (IRADS) was built by Texas Instruments. This was an off-the-shelf single turret system that was adapted to a twin turret design due to the unique "in contour" mounting requirements of the F-117A. Stealth characteristics of the F-117A required that the unique exterior shape be maintained. Since there was a need to be able to see from just above the horizon to well behind the aircraft, a forward-looking IR (FLIR) turret and a downward-looking IR (DLIR) were required. This need doubled the size of the servo controller unit and the video tracker unit. Due to the mounting arrangement in the aircraft, the DLIR is inverted relative to the FLIR and thus required the video to be inverted electronically when displayed to the pilot. This led to some interesting calibration and alignment problems. But, any turret may still be mounted in either position.

The F-117A employs screens over the FLIR and DLIR cavities to maintain its low observable signature. The original screens were to be etched metal units from a process not unlike printed circuit boards. These

screens proved unable to take the acoustic environment of the cavities, in particular the DLIR cavity where the screen broke on its first flight. This breakage led to a vibration and acoustics investigation of the cavities and a redesign of the screens. Both FLIR and DLIR cavities now feature acoustic shrouds to limit acoustic affects. The screens are redesigned woven wire units capable of handling the acoustic loads.

The weapon bays are each equipped with a trapeze for loading and raising the weapons. Early concerns for possible damage to the aircraft and bay doors from fin scheduled weapons, like the GBU-10, required that these weapons be dropped trapeze down. This was a major detectability problem for the aircraft. Early weapon certification was performed in this configuration. Later efforts by the aerodynamics department indicated that adequate clearance could be maintained with the trapeze up. This reduced the exposure times by more than a factor of 5. However, some weapons did end up with small speed restrictions due to weapon bay dynamics or airflow disturbances in the near flow field.

The Delco M362F computers were long known to be just adequate for the computational tasks of the F-117A. At the time of their selection, the MIL-STD-1750A instruction set

*F-117As operated from King Khalid Air Base in Saudi Arabia during* Desert Storm. *The base's hangars...designed to take the brunt of a nuclear attack...could accommodate two F-117As each.*

*A Desert Storm F-117A is uploaded with one of two GBU-27 laser guided bombs it is capable of carrying internally. The GBU-27 is a 2,000 pound bomb coupled to a* Paveway 3 *seeker.*

computers that were on the horizon were still too big a risk. The first several years of software development prior to first flight were just as involved with getting the OFP to fit and run in the computer as much as with implementing capabilities.

During 1984, the weapon system computational subsystem (WSCS) upgrade program was started to replace the Delco M362F computers. The IBM Federal Systems AP-102 MIL-STD-1750A computer was selected. This was a repackaged version of the same computer used in the Rockwell International *Space Shuttle*.

The architecture for the WSCS computer upgrade was similar to the WDC version with some improvements. Three AP-102 computers were used with each computer controlling a dual redundant MIL-STD-1553 bus for a total of three in the system. The onboard systems were divided between buses 1 and 2 with the third computer and bus held as spares for growth. A unique high speed bus was incorporated for direct communications between the three AP-102s and the expanded data transfer module interface unit.

The aircraft was also enhanced by the decision to expand the weapon release capability from the use of a single weapon bay per pass to the ability to use both weapon bays. This was a significant change as the weapon bay doors, actuators, hydraulics, SMP, and cockpit controls all required redesign and modification.

With the growth potential of the WSCS

computers, the program was positioned to embark upon introducing a number of new capabilities. Among the first of these was the incorporation of a significant new weapon capability. The GBU-27 laser guided bomb (LGB) brought new levels of accuracy and target penetration to the guided weapon inventory.

The GBU-27 was the marriage of a modified GBU-24 low level laser guided bomb seeker, sometimes known as *Paveway 3*, and the BLU-109 improved 2,000 pound warhead. Changes to the GBU-24 seeker included modified canards to fit inside the F-117A weapon bays and a firmware change for trajectory shaping.

The GBU-27 features two guidance modes, each optimized to achieve the best penetration angle for horizontally or vertically oriented targets. The trajectory for vertically developed targets is essentially the ballistic path. For bunkers, rooftops, or any other target of horizontal orientation, the GBU-27 flies a commanded pitch down after release to strike the target in as near a vertical attitude as possible. These modes, coupled with the penetrating warhead and excellent accuracy of the weapon, caused the GBU-27 to become the primary F-117A weapon in *Desert Storm*. While the exact circular error probable (CEP) of the GBU-27 is not presently releasable, the video tape aired during *Desert Storm* depicts weapons consistently striking the center of the crosshairs.

The most recent major avionics develop-

ment is the offensive combat improvement program (OCIP). Based on the WSCS computer system, a number of new systems and capabilities were added. These were color cockpit displays, a digital tactical situation display or moving map, a 4D flight management system (FMS), a new data entry panel, a display processor, autopilot improvements for vertical flight path control, an autothrottle system, and a pilot activated automatic recovery system.

The OCIP program provides no new capabilities for target acquisition and attack. What it does do, is provide the pilot greater situational awareness, reduces pilot workload by allowing the FMS system to fly complex profiles automatically, provides automatic speed and time over target control, and provides unusual attitude recovery upon pilot command.

For the future, a number of major new systems are planned for the aircraft. A new IRADS system is now in production retrofit. Goals for this program are to double the acquisition range of the IRADS system and to increase the range and life of the laser. To replace the aging, out of production SPN-GEANS inertial navigation system, a ring laser gyro (RLG) system will be installed. This system will be supplemented by the addition of a global positioning system (GPS) unit.

Although it incorporated many new technologies, the F-117A, typical of a *Skunk Works* product, was developed in significantly less time and for less cost than a comparable conventional fighter. This was achieved within the tight security of a special access program using streamlined management methods. The Air Force's Aeronautical Systems Division and *Skunk Works* personnel worked in a non-adversarial, problem solving atmosphere with a minimum number of people. In addition, the use of proven components from other aircraft reduced risk and gave the confidence to proceed concurrently with development and low rate production.

Original F-117A program costs can be broken down as follows: Total development to date—$2 billion; Procurement—$4.265 billion (Total flyaway—$2.515 billion; Unit flyaway—$42.6 million); Military construction—$295 million; Total program cost—$6.560 billion. These costs include all government furnished equipment, including engines.

During March of 1984, Ben Rich left the *Skunk Works* for a two year assignment as president of the Lockheed Advanced Aeronautics Company. During his absence, Dick Heppe took over the *Skunk Works'* reigns. Heppe retained this position until June 1, 1984, when Lockheed California Company president C. Graham Whipple retired and Heppe was named to replace him. Norm Nelson, the *Skunk Works'* vice president for engineering and program manager then took over the *Skunk Works* until Rich returned during August of 1986.

With production concurrence at an average rate of eight aircraft per year, initial operational capability was achieved during October of 1983, only twenty-eight months after the F-117A's first flight. The last of fifty-nine aircraft was completed and delivered to the Air Force's Tactical Air Command during June of 1990.

On October 5, 1989, the 37th Tactical Fighter Wing (TFW) was formed at Tonopah Test Range, Nevada, to take up the role as the Air Force's only stealth fighter unit. Since assuming the stealth mission, the unit has twice taken part in combat operations. The wing's F-117As led the attack against Panama

*Virtually all F-117A combat missions are flown at night...increasing the "stealthiness" of the aircraft. When operational, no continuous emissions of any kind eminates from onboard systems.*

on December 21, 1989 during Operation *Just Cause*. Pinpoint bombing stunned and disrupted the Panamanian infantry at Rio Hato and paved the way for US paratroopers to land and eventually overcome the Panamanian opposition. This operation, though successful, did not test the aircraft from a low-observables standpoint as Panama had no radar defense network.

The F-117's second combat tour began on August 17, 1990 when the 37th TFW received its deployment order to Saudi Arabia for Operation *Desert Shield*. On August 21, eighteen F-117As from the 37th's 415th Tactical Fighter Squadron (TFS) arrived at King Khalid Air Base. These aircraft had departed from Tonapah on August 19 and after a brief stop enroute at Langley AFB, Virginia, had continued on to Saudi Arabia.

On August 23, the 415th TFS launched eight orientation sorties with the Saudis. Three days later, the F-117A assumed alert duty for the first time in its history.

On December 3, eighteen F-117As from the second 37th TFW squadron, the 416th TFS, deployed to King Khalid Air Base from Langley AFB. They arrived at their destination the following day.

The following several weeks were spent involved in various training exercises and bringing the unit up to full operational readiness. In the meantime, the international political situation involving the confrontation between Iraq and the US continued to deteriorate. On January 16, the 37th TFWP (now Tactical Fighter Wing *Provisional* for purposes of alignment with other coalition forces) received orders to execute its D-day tasking against targets in Iraq; however, the first wave of F-117As did not depart on their first combat mission until after midnight.

Twenty-two minutes after midnight, on January 17, ten F-117As from the 415th TFS launched against a combined integrated operations center/ground control intercept site at Nukhayb, two air defense control sector headquarters facilities, and the Iraqi Air Force Headquarters building in Baghdad, a joint integrated operations center/radar facility at Al Taqaddum, a telephone center at Ar Ramadi and two in Baghdad, an integrated operations center at Al Taji, a North Taji military related facility, and the Presidential grounds at Abu Ghurayb.

A second wave of twelve F-117As (three from the 415th and nine from the 416th) left shortly afterwards to repeat strikes against the Iraqi Air Force Headquarters, air defense sector headquarters, and telephone exchanges in Baghdad; the Alo Taqaddum integrated operations center/ground control intercept facility; military related facilities at North Taji, and the Presidential grounds at Abu Ghurayb. New targets included the Salmon Pak troposcatter station; a television transmitter station, international radio transmitter, and the Presidential bunker in Baghdad; Rasheed Airfield; a joint integrated operations center/ground control intercept site at Ar Rutbah; a troposcatter station at Habbaniyah; and the communications satellite terminal at Ad Dujayl.

On January 25, 1991, six more F-117As flew from Langley AFB to King Khalid Air Base, where they were assigned to the 416th TFS. Their arrival resulted in a total contingent of 42 combat ready F-117As.

Operation *Desert Storm* thus became the first combat environment wherein the F-117A was utilized in a real-world test against a mod-

*The F-117A is reasonably agile in spite of its exotic appearance and unorthodox aerodynamics. Elevons provide pitch and roll control and the all-moving vertical tail surfaces provide directional control.*

ern, integrated air defense. The *Nighthawks* of the 37th TFW repeatedly flew into and through intense anti-aircraft artillery and surface-to-air missile fire, accurately delivering 2,000 tons of precision-guided munitions during 1,300 combat sorties. Wing pilots scored 1,600 direct hits against enemy targets in nearly 400 locations. Without suffering a single loss, or experiencing any damage, they destroyed hardened command and control bunkers, aircraft shelters, production and storage facilities for nuclear, biological, and chemical weapons, and other heavily defended targets of the highest military and political significance.

Employing just 2.5% of the Air Force assets in theater, the 37th TFW not only led the UN coalition force against Iraq, but also hit nearly 40% of the Iraqi targets that came under fire in the first three days. Twenty-nine F-117As hit twenty-six high value targets on the first night alone. The F-117As were so effective that the Iraqi air defense system virtually collapsed. Iraq's command, control, and communications network never recovered.

Thereafter, the 37th TFW constantly hit key political and military targets to further weaken Iraqi resistance and to prepare for the ground campaign. Early on, and employing only four F-117As, Baghdad's nuclear research facility was attacked, completely destroying its three reactor cores. Noteworthy is the fact the F-117s were the only coalition aircraft tasked to fly over Baghdad during the entire *Desert Storm* operation.

During another strike, the 37th TFW destroyed a whole network of surface-to-air missile sites in central Iraq in the space of one hour, thus enabling B-52s to carpet-bomb Republican Guard positions without fear of

interception. Immediately prior to the start of the coalition's ground campaign, the F-117As destroyed a complex of pumping stations and a distribution network that fed oil into anti-personnel fire trenches in southern Kuwait. The attack earned strong praise and the gratitude of the multinational ground forces.

At 0015 hours on February 28, 1991, the 37th TFWP received good news: all operations relating to Desert Storm combat were suspended in order to give the Iraqis an opportunity to sign a cease fire agreement. Combat for the 37th TFWP had come to an end.

Statistically, during the course of *Desert Storm*, the 37th TFW compiled a record that is unparalleled in the chronicles of air warfare. The *Nighthawks* achieved a 80% hit rate on pinpoint targets (1,669 direct hits and 418 misses) while destroying nearly 40% of all strategic targets attacked by the coalition forces.

The 37th TFW's performance also drew high praise from military and political leaders. In particular, Senator Sam Nunn, Senate Armed Services Committee Chairman, stated, the F-117A to be "the heart of our offensive power and targeting capability." Brigadier General "Buster" Glossen, Fourteenth Air Division Commander, called the 37th TFW "the backbone of the strategic air campaign." General Colin Powell, Chairman of the Joint Chiefs of Staff, commented, "You are showing the nation what it's all about—the combination of the very highest technology with the very best kind of people we can put together in the field as a team." Secretary of Defense Richard Cheney stated, "You have gone far beyond anything anybody envisioned...it has been phenomenal."

*The first F-117A, No.780, today can be seen as a gate guardian near the entrance to Nellis AFB, Nevada. The second full-scale development aircraft , No. 781, is displayed at the US Air Force Museum.*

*Perhaps representing the most advanced fighter technology in the world today, the two YF-22A technology demonstrators brought a broad spectrum of air combat and technology disciplines together in one airframe for the first time ever.*

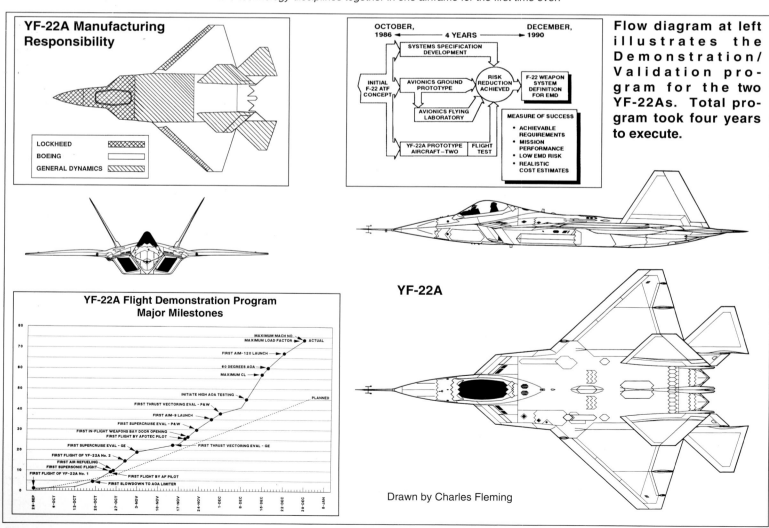

## YF-22A Manufacturing Responsibility

LOCKHEED

BOEING

GENERAL DYNAMICS

OCTOBER, 1986 ◄— 4 YEARS —► DECEMBER, 1990

SYSTEMS SPECIFICATION DEVELOPMENT

INITIAL F-22 ATF CONCEPT

AVIONICS GROUND PROTOTYPE

AVIONICS FLYING LABORATORY

RISK REDUCTION ACHIEVED

F-22 WEAPON SYSTEM DEFINITION FOR EMD

YF-22A PROTOTYPE AIRCRAFT—TWO

FLIGHT TEST

MEASURE OF SUCCESS
- ACHIEVABLE REQUIREMENTS
- MISSION PERFORMANCE
- LOW EMD RISK
- REALISTIC COST ESTIMATES

**Flow diagram at left illustrates the Demonstration/ Validation program for the two YF-22As. Total program took four years to execute.**

### YF-22A Flight Demonstration Program Major Milestones

MAXIMUM MACH NO.
MAXIMUM LOAD FACTOR ► ACTUAL

FIRST AIM-120 LAUNCH

60 DEGREES AOA

MAXIMUM CL

INITIATE HIGH AOA TESTING

FIRST THRUST VECTORING EVAL - P&W

PLANNED

FIRST AIM-9 LAUNCH

FIRST SUPERCRUISE EVAL - P&W

FIRST IN-FLIGHT WEAPONS BAY DOOR OPENING

FIRST FLIGHT BY AFOTEC PILOT

FIRST SUPERCRUISE EVAL - GE

FIRST THRUST VECTORING EVAL - GE

FIRST FLIGHT OF YF-22A No. 2

FIRST AIR REFUELING

FIRST SUPERSONIC FLIGHT

FIRST FLIGHT OF YF-22A No. 1

FIRST FLIGHT BY AF PILOT

FIRST SLOWDOWN TO AOA LIMITER

29-SEP 6-OCT 13-OCT 20-OCT 27-OCT 3-NOV 10-NOV 17-NOV 24-NOV 1-DEC 8-DEC 15-DEC 22-DEC 29-DEC 6-JAN

## YF-22A

Drawn by Charles Fleming

# Chapter 15:
# THE F-22

*"In many ways the F-22 advanced tactical fighter is the true daughter of the F-117. Stealth will be a major factor in the USA remaining a superpower in the 21st Century. We worked very hard with the F-22 to integrate stealth into a supersonic supermaneuverable fighter, and we succeeded. After our last day of YF-22A flight demonstrations from Edwards late on December 28, 1990, I said to my wife Judia, "we won"...and we did. Our team delivered results. It was a privilege to lead this team."*

**Sherm Mullin**

The requirement for a new air superiority fighter, given the acronym ATF (Advanced Tactical Fighter) and codenamed *Senior Sky* by the Air Force, formally was identified during November of 1981. A detailed requirements definition and operational concept was developed and the resulting document focused on a clear need for an air superiority fighter designed specifically to replace the McDonnell Douglas F-15...and consequently capable of countering the sophisticated threats projected to exist during the early years of the next century.

ATF engineering studies had been started in the *Skunk Works* during the early 1980s. The first configurations were considered to be fairly unconventional, because they were based on the successes of the F-117A, which had not yet been publicly disclosed. Senior Air Force personnel were adamant that an outstanding fighter was mandatory, in addition to low observability. By mid-1985 a respectable design had evolved which was definitely low observable, but also highly maneuverable across the speed range, and with the supersonic drag levels required for supercruise.

During October of 1985, the Air Force issued the ATF Demonstration/Validation (Dem/Val) phase Requests for Proposal (RFP) to Boeing, General Dynamics, Grumman, Lockheed, McDonnell Douglas, Northrop, and Rockwell International (Grumman and Rockwell eventually dropped out of the competition). One month later, more stringent low observable requirements were issued by the Air Force.

The Dem/Val proposals were submitted to the Air Force during February of 1986. During May, however, the total program was restructured to meet the Packard Commission recommendations, and prototype aircraft and avionics systems were added.

With the advent of the decision to prototype the two contending aircraft, the purpose of

YF-22A, N22YF, during fly-off against Northrop YF-23A. The aircraft's configuration was optimized to not only give it exceptional stealth characteristics, but also superior performance and maneuverability.

the revised Dem/Val phase now was focused on risk reduction and demonstrating that the advanced technologies required for successful accomplishment of the ATF's mission were feasible and practical and could be moved successfully into Engineering and Manufacturing Development (EMD). Dem/Val was composed of three major elements:

(1) System specification development, which would utilize effectiveness analysis, design trade studies, tests, simulation, technology evaluations, and other efforts to refine the

weapon system characteristics and operational requirements.

(2) Avionics prototypes, which would be used to demonstrate the achieveability of the fully integrated avionics suites, first in a series of ground based demonstrations, and then in avionics flying laboratories.

(3) ATF prototypes, which would be used to demonstrate the capabilities on which the ATF EMD proposals would be based.

At Lockheed the decision to team was made during early 1985. At that time it was felt

*YF-22A, N22YF, was the first of the two prototypes completed. Powered by two General Electric YF-120 turbofan engines, it later would become the first of the two YF-22As to fly. Small Skunk Works logo is visible at base of vertical fin ahead of the rudder.*

*The Pratt & Whitney F119-powered second prototype, N22YX, during engine runs at Palmdale, California prior to its first flight. Articulated exhaust nozzles are noteworthy.*

**1/12 SCALE SPIN MODEL**

*A 1/12th-scale spin test model was one of many produced to accommodate analysis of the aircraft's stability and control characteristics throughout its flight envelope.*

*A composite wing section for the YF-22A during assembly at Boeing Military Airplanes' facility in Seattle, Washington. Jig rotates about its axis to provide accessability to all surfaces and edges.*

that one of the initial Dem/Val contracts could be won alone, but in order to win the final competition, teaming would be required. During June of 1986, after a year of analysis and discussions with potential teaming partners, Lockheed, Boeing, and General Dynamics signed a teaming Memorandum of Agreement, but also continued to compete. Northrop and McDonnell Douglas followed suit a few weeks later.

The modified Dem/Val proposals were submitted to the Air Force during July of 1986. Lockheed and Northrop were selected on October 31, 1986 to build two prototypes each to compete in the revised Dem/Val phase. Lockheed, under a $691 million contract, would build two of what later would become its Model 1132 aircraft under the official Air Force designation YF-22A and Northrop, under a similar $691 million contract, would build two of its design under the official Air Force designation YF-23A.

Prior to this, a similar propulsion system competition had been initiated, pitting Pratt & Whitney against General Electric. The engine RFP, then referred to simply as the Advanced Fighter Engine (AFE) and later as the Joint Advanced Fighter Engine (JAFE) was released to the manufacturers during May of 1983. The following September, both were awarded $550 million contracts to build and test static prototypes. General Electric's engine was known in-house as the GE37 and Pratt & Whitney's as the PW5000. Later they would be designated F120 and F119, respectively, by the Air Force.

As stipulated in the Lockheed, Boeing, and General Dynamics teaming agreement, lead would go to the company whose proposal was selected. Lockheed, therefore, took the lead with Sherman Mullin as General Manager of the ATF Team Program office. Under Mullin, Lockheed assigned Jack Gordon as company program manager. Micky Blackwell would later become program manager during December of 1987 when Gordon returned to the *Skunk Works* as the assistant general manager. At General Dynamics in Ft. Worth, Randy Kent was given program manager responsibilities, and at Boeing Military Airplanes in Seattle, Dick Hardy became program manager there. Under them came Lockheed's YF-22A Program Manager Joe Donaldson who headed up a group of principle engineers that included Dick Cantrell, Bud Ohrenstein, and Bart Osborne. Manufacturing and final assembly became the responsibility of the *Skunk Work's* Paul Schumacher.

As part of Lockheed Aeronautical Systems Company, *Skunk Works* involvement in the YF-22A would be as follows:

(1) The original Lockheed design team would be drawn from *Skunk Works* design engineering organizations; (2) the YF-22A's forebody would be *Skunk Works* manufactured; (3) YF-22A final assembly operations would be accommodated at the *Skunk Works* facility in Palmdale; (4) all Lockheed flight test mechanics, technicians, quality assurance, and logistical support personnel (who made up the bulk of the YF-22A flight test team maintenance organization) would be *Skunk Works* personnel; (5) *Skunk Works* pilots would represent Lockheed on the test team; and (6) all Lockheed flight test engineering personnel (including the flight test program manager) would be recent transfers from the *Skunk Works* to Lockheed Aeronautical Systems Company for the express purpose of working on the YF-22A flight test program.

During early November of 1986, Lockheed, Boeing, and General Dynamics finally were able to exchange their preliminary design data. The job at hand now was to develop a winning team configuration. This proved to be no simple task. By the middle of July 1987, the existing aircraft configuration was determined by the team to be technically and competitively unacceptable, and new configuration design and development work was initiated on July 13. It was not until January of 1988 that this task was completed.

With the Lockheed/Boeing/General Dynamics consortia, each company brought substantial, applicable experience to the partnership: Lockheed's experience in the F-117A program design and production; Boeing's strength in military avionics development/integration and advanced materials development; and General dynamics expertise as a designer and builder of the F-16 and its advanced fly-by-wire flight control system.

The over-all distribution of work between the team partners was based on the dollar value of work performed, rather than on a man-hours to weight equation, etc. In simple terms, the program was divided into thirds. This proved difficult as interfaces required by these arrangements were extremely complex.

Lockheed's responsibilities included weapon system, air vehicle, and avionics system design integration, the forward fuselage (including the cockpit and air intakes, the wing leading edge flaps and tips, the vertical stabilizer leading edges and tips, the horizontal stabilator edges, and final assembly of the complete aircraft. Boeing's responsibilities included the wing, the aft fuselage, and propulsion system integration. General Dynamics' responsibilities included the mid-fuselage, the empennage, most subsystems, the armament system, the landing gear, and the vehicle management system integration (including flight controls).

Four years after contract signing, the prototype ATFs were ready for flight. The first of these, Northrop's YF-23A, N231YF, was rolled out on June 22, 1990. It was followed on August 29, by the roll-out of the first YF-22A, N22YF. The first of the new ATF prototypes to take to the air was again the Northrop aircraft, this occurring with the first hop of N231YF from Edwards AFB on August 27, 1990.

The primary focus of the Lockheed half of the Dem/Val flight test program, under the direction of Lockheed's Flight Test Manager Dick Abrams, was on those objectives the contractor team felt would provide the Air Force with quantitative data that clearly demonstrated YF-22A performance capabilities directly relatable to the F-22A EMD design. A flight test strategy then was developed to use the prototypes to satisfy this objective by demonstrating the following capabilities: super maneuverability/controllability (sometimes referred to as agility); supercruise (i.e., supersonic cruise without the use of afterburner) with both engine options (i.e., Pratt & Whitney and General Electric); high AoA flight characteristics; live missile firing of both the AIM-9M *Sidewinder* and the AIM-120 Advanced Medium Range Air-to-Air Missile (AMRAAM).

In order to accomplish these specific objectives in the limited time available, it was mandatory that an efficient and aggressive test approach be utilized. This included: ensuring the required resources were available to support a high sortie rate; utilize inflight refueling to the maximum extant possible; only conducting those envelope expansion tests that were absolutely required to demonstrate the specified performance capabilities; planning for, and utilizing multi-discipline test techniques; and early check-out of both the Air Force Flight Test Center (AFFTC) and Air Force Operational Test and Evaluation Center (AFOTEC) pilots and their participation in the Dem/Val program.

Flight testing of the YF-22A prototypes was conducted at Edwards AFB by a combined test team made up of personnel from each of the three contractors along with representatives from the two engine companies, avionics suppliers, vendors, and the Air Force.

The Lockheed consortium had the over-all responsibility for the planning and execution of the YF-22A flight test demonstration program. In a departure from the standard AFFTC practice, the Flight Test Center's dual role during the ATF Dem/Val program was that of facilitator and to provide safety oversight, rather than performing in its traditional test manager role.

The overall flight test plan was developed by the contractor team. The engine manufacturers provided inputs to this plan for their

*The General Electric-powered YF-22A prototype following successful completion of high speed taxi tests at Lockheed's Palmdale facility. Lockheed test pilot Dave Ferguson was at the controls.*

*The prototype Boeing 757 commercial transport, N757A, was utilized by the Lockheed ATF team as an airborne YF-22A avionics, radar systems, electronic warfare systems, and related technologies testbed.*

*Though relatively evenly matched in performance, the YF-22A and YF-23A were decidedly different approaches to the Air Force's new Advanced Tactical Fighter requirement. Northrop's aircraft was somewhat more radical in planform with its unconventional tail surfaces and diamond-shaped wing.*

*Landing following successful first flight. Aerodynamic braking is a common, but important part of the landing routine for most high performance combat aircraft, including the YF-22A. The YF-22A was equipped with conventional leading and trailing edge flaps but no drag chute.*

*Though giving the impression of being relatively small, the YF-22As were, in fact, approximately the same size as the largest current Air Force fighter, the McDonnell Douglas F-15.*

propulsion system related test requirements. The only guidelines set forth by the Air Force were that the prototype aircraft should be flown for the purpose of EMD risk reduction. The capabilities to be demonstrated during flight test were left to the discretion of the contractor team.

The test plan review and approval cycle differed significantly from the norm for the Dem/Val program in that the AFFTC did not have approval authority. Therefore, there was no AFFTC test plan Technical Review Board (TRB) coordination, only that of the Safety Review Board (SRB). However, the ATF SPO did have review and approval authority for all of the flight test plans and they frequently looked to the AFFTC for their opinions regarding the plans.

In some respects, the program had to be structured somewhat differently than a "normal" development flight test program. Both YF-22A prototypes were treated as the first of the type, not only because of the immaturity of the airframe, but because each was powered by different prototype engines (since the first Northrop YF-23A had flown with the Pratt & Whitney F119 engines, it was assumed that by the first flight date of the No. 2 YF-22A, the engine type had effectively already been flown).

Much of the testing intended to be accomplished on the first prototype was planned to be repeated on the second in order to obtain as much comparative data as possible with both engines. The first prototype was tasked with accomplishing the high AoA tests. The second YF-22A prototype was equipped with a stores management system (SMS) and missile launchers and it would be used for weapons bay environment and armament tests. From the beginning it was intended the AFOTEC would conduct their Early Operational Assessment (EOA) utilizing both aircraft.

Low and medium speed taxi tests were performed on both prototypes prior to their first flights. The primary objectives of these tests were to evaluate ground handling characteristics, braking dynamics, longitudinal control capacity, FLCC air data accuracy, nose wheel steering characteristics and to ensure there was no landing gear shimmy or adverse interaction between the aircraft structural bending modes and the flight control system.

The first flight of the number one YF-22A, N22YF, powered by the General Electric YF120-GE-100 engines was made by Lockheed test pilot Dave Ferguson from Lockheed's Palmdale facility to Edwards AFB on Saturday, September 29, 1990. Flight duration was shorter than originally planned

because the takeoff had been delayed while a ground station problem was rectified. The long static time on the ground consumed considerable fuel, and thus flight duration was affected.

The landing gear were not retracted during the first flight. It probably would not have retracted anyway, as difficulties with what the F-22 Program Manager termed "Fascist Software" prevented retraction until the fifth flight. As it turned out, the landing ear extension command was hardwired, but the retraction cycle was controlled by the integrated vehicle subsystem control (IVSC). Bypassing the IVSC landing gear retraction control with independent hardwiring solved the problem.

Once the landing gear retraction anomaly was corrected, the pace of the flight test program increased rapidly. Initial tasks for N22YF were to complete its initial airworthiness tests in order to establish a reasonable level of confidence with the aircraft's flying qualities, performance, and engine and systems operation. Concurrently with the accomplishment of those objectives, the plan was to expand the flutter envelope clearance up to Mach 1.6 at 40,000 feet (450 KEAS). This goal was achieved approximately one month into the program on the fourteenth flight of the aircraft. By this time, the KC-135 tanker qualification tests also had been completed. These all were flown by the AFFTC YF-22A project pilot, Maj. Mark Shackelford.

A short down time now followed permitting incorporation and checkout of a new FLCC operational flight program (OFP) that would enable the use of thrust vectoring. Shortly thereafter, high AoA testing was initiated. The objective in this phase was to reach 60° AoA and be able to perform pitch and rolling maneuvers at this flight condition. This was accomplished in one week. The majority of test effort for the remainder of the Dem/Val program was devoted to supersonic envelope expansion

*The Pratt & Whitney powered YF-22A, N22YX, averaged nearly three-and-one-half flights per week during the DemVal flight test program at Edwards AFB. This aircraft continued to be flown after DemVal, unlike N22YF which was ferried to Lockheed's Marietta, Georgia facility and used for EMD development.*

along with performance, flying qualities, propulsion system and loads testing out to maximum speed.

The first flight of the second YF-22A, N22YX, was made by Lockheed test pilot Tom Morgenfeld on October 30, 1990. Once initial airworthiness testing was completed, the thrust of its program was directed toward the completion of all the prerequisite testing that was required prior to conducting a live AIM-9M *Sidewinder* missile launch. This task was completed approximately one month after first flight and the AIM-9M live launch was accomplished successfully on November 28, 1990. The AIM-120 AMRAAM live launch was accomplished just before Christmas, on December 20, 1990. The remainder of the second prototype's flight test program was devoted to supersonic envelope expansion along with performance, flying qualities, and propulsion system testing. The YF-22A flight test program was completed on December 28, 1990.

The integration of thrust vectoring into the flight control system went very smoothly, beginning with the first thrust vectoring flight on November 15, 1990. This was in spite of the fact two separate sets of control laws were required because of the two different airframe/engine combinations. Thrust vectoring was reported as being transparent to the pilot as far as handling qualities were concerned.

The increased performance gained through thrust vectoring was very evident both at high AoAs and in increased maneuverability at supersonic speeds. In fact, supersonic agility was widely praised by the pilots who likened the YF-22A when supersonic to other fighters when subsonic. In all, the YF-22A was judged by all the pilots who flew it to be a very pleasant aircraft to fly.

Supercruise performance was evaluated with both the General Electric (achieved for the first time on November 3, 1990) and Pratt & Whitney engines (achieved for the first time on December 27, 1990).

*Deep-V of YF-22A fuselage cross-section is just one of several physical concessions to the low radar cross-section requirement. Intake ducts shielding the engine faces also reflect this objective.*

The specific supercruise test results are classified, but in general terms, the YF-22A proved quite capable of maintaining level flight in supersonic cruise conditions using intermediate thrust for as long as desired. This capability was demonstrated on several occasions during the Dem/Val program at altitudes between 37,000 feet and 40,000 feet.

Outstanding low speed agility was considered a hallmark of the YF-22A design. Therefore, early in the development of the Dem/Val flight test plan it was deemed appropriate to devote a relatively significant amount of the flight test effort to demonstrating the aircraft flight characteristics at low-speed, high AoA flight conditions. Historically, however, high AoA flight testing has been full of surprises due to the complexities of predicting the results. For this reason, and the inherent hazardous nature of these tests, the test methods to accomplish this testing were thoroughly scrutinized before testing began on December 10, 1990.

All planned Dem/Val high AoA tests were completed in nine flights (14.9 hours) over a period of one week with the end of testing on December 17, 1990. These were the critical tests used to demonstrate basic aircraft aerodynamics, thrust vectoring, flight control system design, aircraft handling qualities, and to verify correct operation of the air data and inertial navigation systems.

The pilots were very pleased with the aircraft's handling qualities at high AoA. Light airframe buffet was noted at 22° and increased slightly at 24°. The buffet intensity or frequency did not change after this point up to 60° and may actually have started to decrease. Of particular note was the precise pitch control at all AoA. Both pitch attitude and AoA could be held to within 1/2° with thrust vectoring on. With thrust vectoring off, control was less precise due to control law changes and the obvious loss of control power, and AoA could be maintained only to within 1° to 2°.

The high AoA program was very aggressive. Wind tunnel and simulator predictions were confirmed in a very complex portion of the envelope, while demonstrating the aircraft's outstanding high AoA capabilities. The YF-22A's high AoA handling qualities were best summarized by General Dynamics' test pilot Jon Beesley when he said, "It always did what I wanted it to do and never did anything that I didn't want it to do."

*After being declared the victor in the brief but intense DemVal competition, Lockheed elected to continue flight testing of the aircraft with the objective of exploring parts of the flight envelope that had not been explored earlier. The Pratt & Whitney powered aircraft was retained at Edwards AFB for this purpose.*

*YF-22A, N22YF, was used for spin tests. Accordingly, it was equipped with an anti-spin chute, canister, and associated mounting assembly. Spin chute height was dictated by the exhaust plume size.*

*Inflight refueling, once the envelope was cleared, was used routinely by the YF-22As during the course of the Dem/Val fly-off. Pilots had few problems with the center-aft-positioned receptacle.*

Internal weapons carriage was fundamental to the YF-22A's stealth characteristics and design and the team felt it was important to demonstrate live firings of both the AIM-9 and AIM-120 air-to-air missiles.

The second YF-22A, N22YX, was utilized for the armament test program. Two of the three bays (left hand and main) were fitted with launchers. A stores management system also was incorporated. Contrary to what one might expect to find in a prototype aircraft missile launch system (i.e. pilot activated toggle switch

that is hardwired to the launch mechanism), the YF-22A incorporated an essentially production type software-controlled stores management system (minus sensors).

Both missile firings were accomplished at .70 Mach and 20,000 feet The AIM-9M test was conducted on November 28, 1990 at the China Lake Naval Weapon Test Center and was successful in all respects. The missile separated as predicted. There was no evidence of rocket exhaust impingement on the aircraft structure, nor engine exhaust plume

ingestion.

The AIM-120 firing, which took place on December 20, 1990, also was an unqualified success. This test was accomplished utilizing the Navy's Pacific Missile Test Center range at Pt. Mugu. Missile separation and ignition was as predicted and it flew its intended trajectory.

The AFOTEC participated in the YF-22A Dem/Val flight test program and conducted an early operational assessment (EOA) of the YF-22's capabilities with regard to its ultimate operational role.

At the conclusion of the Dem/Val program an independent assessment was prepared by the AFOTEC team and briefed by them up through the Tactical Air Command (TAC) chain of command. The YF-22A team's AFOTEC pilot, Lt. Col. Willie Naigle, stated the YF-22A was a "mighty fine machine at this phase of development".

In the course of a three-month flight test program, the YF-22As were able to clear a demonstration flight envelope of over 7 gs, 82 KCAS to over Mach 2, and 50,000 feet. An aggressive flight test plan included the demonstration of supercruise capability with both the Pratt & Whitney and General Electric engines, flight control development (specifically thrust vectoring), demonstration of unequaled maneuverability across the airspeed spectrum from extremely low speed to high supersonic Mach numbers, and weapon separation from internal weapons bays. Despite the limited time available, all of these primary test objectives were accomplished without encountering any major snags.

From first flight of a new aircraft design to a cleared demonstration envelope in 91 days is an unequaled achievement in the modern history of aviation. Additionally, this was accomplished with two new engine designs and with the most advanced cockpit/avionics architecture ever flown in any fighter. Throughout this high intensity testing there was no foreign object damage (FOD) or safety incidents. Upon conclusion of the flight test program, 43 flights and 52.8 hours had been logged on N22YF and 31 flights and 38.8 hours had been logged on N22YX.

Lockheed's EMD proposal was flown to Wright-Patterson AFB, Ohio aboard a specially chartered Convair transport on December 31, 1990. The following day, on January 1, 1991, Sherm Mullin left the YF-22A program and rejoined the *Skunk Works* as its president. On that same day, Ben Rich formally retired from the *Skunk Works*. Ten days earlier, the entire aviation community had been saddened to learn that the *Skunk Works'* founder, the great "Kelly" Johnson, had died on December 21 at the age of 80 following a lengthy illness. "Kelly" later was interred at Forest Lawn Memorial Park in Hollywood Hills, California.

After a three-month-long review of the Dem/Val results and the associated EMD proposals from Northrop and Lockheed, then-Secretary of the Air Force Donald Rice announced on April 23, 1991 that the Lockheed, Boeing, and General Dynamics consortium had been selected to proceed with the EMD F-22A. At the same time, the Pratt & Whitney YF119-PW-100 engine was selected as the preferred powerplant. Rice noted the Lockheed and Pratt & Whitney designs "clearly offered better capability at lower cost, thereby providing the Air Force with a true *best value*".

The second YF-22A, N22YX (the Pratt & Whitney-powered prototype) resumed flight testing at Edwards AFB, California on October

*With nearly 70,000 pounds of thrust and a normal takeoff weight of approximately 60,000 pounds, the YF-22As were capable of exceptional performance...particularly in terms of acceleration and climb.*

30, 1991. Lockheed and the Air Force had elected to continue exploration of the YF-22A's performance and flight envelopes beyond what had been accomplished during the fly-off. This follow-on work was planned to include 100 hours of flying time (approximately 25 flights) to expand the flight envelope and selected envelope segments in greater detail. Unfortunately, follow-on flight testing was abruptly terminated on April 25, 1992, when N22YX was severely damaged during a landing accident at Edwards AFB.

Prior to the accident, the first YF-22A, N22YF (the General Electric-powered prototype) had been flown to Lockheed's Marietta, Georgia facility where it is being used as a full-scale mock-up for EMD systems and hardware integration.

One month later than originally planned, on August 3, 1991, the Air Force signed contracts totaling $9.55 billion with the Lockheed consortia and $1.375 billion with Pratt & Whitney consummating initial agreements leading to the manufacture and flight test of nine single-seat, two two-seat, and two fatigue and static test EMD aircraft. Pratt & Whitney will furnish 33 F119-PW-100 engines for the flight-worthy aircraft. Lockheed's Marietta, Georgia plant, as these words are written, remains the facility of choice for F-22A final assembly.

*Cockpit of YF-22A, N22YF. At the time of the YF-22A's first flight, this was probably the most technologically advanced cockpit in the world. Finger-on-glass (FOG) system eliminated conventional push buttons.*

*On December 20, 1990, a single AIM-120 was launched from N22YX, utilizing the ventral centerline weapons bay. Tom Morgenfeld was the pilot.*

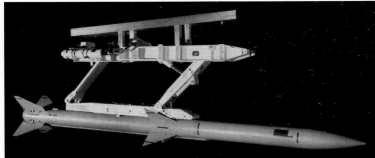

*EDO's dedicated AIM-120 launcher is accommodated in the YF-22A's ventral bay only. Up to four AIM-120s will be carried by production F-22As.*

*The EMD F-22A, expected to represent in most significant respects the production F-22A configuration, is compared in this image of two models to the Dem/Val YF-22A (left). There are surprisingly few differences between the prototypes and the proposed production aircraft.*

*Latest navalized F-117 configuration study is the A/F-117X. It utilizes many F-117A fuselage components, but virtually everything else, including the canopy, is new. The aircraft is equipped with slab-type horizontal tail surfaces, a new wing, and a revised exhaust nozzle configuration, among other changes.*

*Among other changes currently planned for the proposed A/F-117X is an extended ventral weapons bay which will permit internal carriage of weapons and a doubling of weapons payload capacity. Among the weapons slated for the A/F-117X's repertoire are the AIM-120 and AIM-9...for self-defense.*

Lockheed Martin

*One of the earliest views of the A/F-117X was released under the original F-117N designator. All navalized F-117 studies include folding wings.*

*Artist's rendering of A/F-117X flaring for a carrier landing. Noteworthy are extended flaps and tailhook.*

# Chapter 16:
# TODAY AND TOMORROW

*"We have the heritage, the tools, and the talent to compete with anyone. Reduced business opportunities have forced our competitors to improve, and modern computer technology has allowed them to make great strides. We have to continue to improve our performance to keep our competitive edge. "*

**Jack Gordon**

As the *Skunk Works* heads into the 21st Century, it does so with considerable confidence and cautious optimism. The company remains profitable, intensely competitive, and technologically innovative, and contracts—both confirmed and pending (many of a classified nature)—indicate substantial financial viability for years to come.

Perhaps most importantly, the merger of two of the world's largest and most dynamic aerospace companies, Lockheed and Martin Marietta, has opened an entirely new era for the world's foremost high-technology aerospace production facility. The merger, officially consummated during mid-March of 1995, only serves to enhance the stature of what will henceforth be known as the "Lockheed Martin Skunk Woirks".

Lockheed Martin Corporation (the LMADC's parent company) President, Norm Augustine, has long been an admirer of the *Skunk Works*. During his long association with Martin Marietta, he brought a similar operation to life there under the auspices of the company's Advanced Development Organization at Rancho Bernardo, near San Diego.

On the occasion of the Lockheed/Martin merger, Jack Gordon, who took over as President of the *Skunk Works* during Sherm Mullin during February of 1994, in part had the following comments to make:

"By now you have all heard or read a great deal about the merger that has resulted in forming the Lockheed Martin Corporation. At the risk of providing an overdose, I would like to share my views.

"It comes as no surprise that the defense industry is shrinking. Department of Defense (DoD) budgets have declined from $350 billion to $250 billion over the last several years—not counting the impact of inflation. The sales and income we are earning today reprsent a budget authorized several years ago. So as an industry, we have not yet seen the end of the needed reductions. Fortunately, we at the *Skunk Works* have enjoyed sales for the past several years that have not declined as rapidly as the rest of the industry. We have also benefited from our consolidation in Palmdale that has enhanced our competitive posture.

"The merger has created an opportunity for us to be one of the surviving aerospace corporations. Senior DoD leadership has stated that future budgets will only support two manufacturers of tactical aircraft and two producers of satellites and launch vehicles. In strategic missiles, only one will survive. We intend to be one of the survivors!"

Major international fiscal and political changes continue to positively affect the company's ability to compete in an environment adversely impacted by an ever-tightening federal budget and a world that, at least for the short term, is not threatened by Armageddon. In part because of the *Skunk Works'* track record of producing highly functional products on time and at—or under—cost, it is in an enviable position among peers in being at the right place at the right time with the right capability and philosophy.

The ability to produce extraordinary aircraft in relatively small production quantities for a reasonable price has been the *Skunk Works'* strong point for fifty years. In today's economic climate, that ability is a legacy that cannot be matched by any other aerospace company in the world. The days

*Model depicting one of the earliest navalized F-117 configurations under the original F-117N designator. Noteworthy is hinge-line for wing fold and decreased wing leading edge sweep angle.*

of massive production runs calling for thousands of aircraft are long gone...and along with them, simplistic approaches to highly complex tactical, military, and commercial problems.

By intent, the *Skunk Works* today is in a unique position to respond rapidly to contemporary military and commercial requirements. As a result of its 1990 decision to move all *Skunk Works* engineering and manufacturing facilities to Palmdale it now can lay claim to world-class facilities that include Plant 10 where its headquarters and engineering offices are located; Site 2 where U-2 modification and flight test take place; Site 7 where F-117 modification and flight test take place; the Helendale facility which is a state-of-the-art radar cross-section range; and the Rye Canyon (now named after "Kelly" Johnson) research facility with its state of-the-art anachoic chamber. With the present focus on prototyping and limited production, no aerospace company in the world is better suited than the *Skunk Works* to provide such "full service" capability. This includes research and development, advanced design,

prototyping and development, low-rate manufacturing, modification, and logistical support.

As with any company heavily involved in highly classified military and government programs, a overview describing its present and future activities must, of necessity, remain both abbreviated and exclusive. Accordingly, only the following programs have been deemed releasable at this time:

**A/F-117X Attack Aircraft**—Initially referred to by the *Skunk Works* as the F-117N, the A/F-117X is an upgraded and improved Navy derivative of the original F-117A. Inherent structural features of the F-117 fuselage enable it to be effectively modified specifically for Navy use. It possesses three primary Navy characteristics not normally found in Air Force aircraft. These are: a full-depth center line keel from nose gear to tail hook; three full-depth fuselage frames for wing carry through; and the main landing gear being attached directly to a major bulkhead. These features allow maximum utilization of existing F-

*Twin V-type vertical tail surfaces and horizontal tail surfaces are two of the most noticeable external configuration changes on the A/F-117X. Single-piece low-RCS canopy is also distinctive.*

**183**

*The 86%-scale model of the JAST demonstrator aircraft under construction at Lockheed Martin's* Skunk Works *facility at Palmdale. The model is built of glass-reinforced plastics and steel.*

117A tooling. Existing F-117 structure is beefed up for carrier landing and catapult launches. This results in lower program cost and lower associated risk.

Carrier suitable aerodynamic qualities are achieved through the integration of a larger, reduced-sweep wing and the addition of horizontal tail surfaces. The fuselage is unchanged with the exception of the canopy configuration, ventral weapons bay fairing, and new aft fuselage design to accommodate afterburning engines. All aerodynamic modifications are achievable with no degradation to existing signature levels. Survivability will actually improve in many areas. F-117A landing gear are replaced with modified F-14 landing gear reducing development costs and increasing commonalty with rolling stock already in inventory aboard carriers.

As stated previously, the A/F-117X leverages significantly off of the investment already made in the F-117A. Beyond the new electro-optical /infrared, and radar sensors, avionics are relatively unchanged, requiring only the addition of an off-the-shelf automatic carrier landing system (ACLS). Propulsion system integration, all major subsystems, application of low observable technology, the air data system, the precision weapon delivery system, and all primary aircraft software are all drawn from the F-117A...resulting in a quick, efficient and affordable development program.

With the retirement of the Grumman A-6 fleet during 1997, the Navy will lose the capability to place regional trouble spots at risk from the sea. Modification to existing conventional aircraft or increased use of the *Tomahawk* cruise missile will not guarantee target destruction with minimum collateral damage. Stealth and precision, will. The A/F-117X can provide these requisite capabilities long before the Navy variant of JAST—the replacement for the A-6—becomes operational some fifteen years from now.

The A/F-117X has gone through a number of design studies alongside the Air Force's F-117A+ and F-117B. Each of these has been configured to accommodate a specific tactical need. The F-117A+ was a proposed modification of existing Air Force aircraft that would have led to the incorporation of 18 advanced low-observables technologies and other improvements. The current A/F-117X for the Navy, for which the Senate Armed Services Committee has earmarked $175 million to initiate a program definition phase and flying demonstrator, would involve new production aircraft. It would feature a beefed-up fuselage to accommodate carrier landings, a folding wing, a carrier-qualified tailhook, and access to equipment weapons bays with "tail over water" and/or one engine running. Flyaway cost was estimated to be $70 million per aircraft in 1994, based on a 250 aircraft production run.

The F-117B, which like the A/F-117X would involve new production aircraft, would capitalize on commonalty with the A/F-117X while leveraging the investment made in the F-117A. The result would be a superior attack aircraft with a higher maximum gross takeoff weight than the F-117A (73,200 pounds v/s 52,500 pounds), an increased combat radius (1,000 n. miles v/s 570 n. miles), and double the internal payload (10,000 pounds v/s 5,000 pounds). The Navy's A/F-117X would have a wing with a reduced sweep angle of 42°, a span increased by 21.45 ft., and a new tail (conventional horizontal tail surfaces would be added).

A new wing also would give the F-117B a distinct shape and all-weather sensors, advanced signature characteristics, improved aerodynamics, and twin General Electric F414 afterburning turbofan engines would press the state-of-the-art for low-observable aircraft.

In a push for modular production and further cost savings, the *Skunk Works* is proposing the Navy and Air Force execute a joint program to build both the A/F-117X and the F-117B together. Common hardware would include fuselage, engines, inlet, nozzle, and horizontal and vertical tails. The aircraft would differ in some individual components such as landing gear and select avionics.

A five-year Offensive Combat Improvement Program (OCIP) to improve the standard F-117A was completed during mid-1995. This program, under a $250 million Air Force contract, began in 1990 when aircraft "805" arrived at Palmdale. The retrofit involved integration of an expanded computer memory and throughput with state-of-the-art avionics to significantly improve pilot situational awareness and reduce pilot workload. The upgrade enhances mission effectiveness by allowing the pilot to focus on target acquisition and weapons delivery while the F-117A flies its complex profiles automatically. Automatic time control throughout the flight ensures time-over-target and bomb impact within one second of what is planned. Another feature gives pilots the ability to command automatic recovery from unsafe attitudes. It is the first use of four-dimensional flight management and automatic recovery in any Air Force tactical fighter.

Lockheed Martin has briefed the British Ministry of Defense on a proposed derivative of the Air Force's F-117B. It is being suggested to meet the Staff Target (Air) 425 deep-strike requirement that will otherwise remain unfulfilled when the RAF's Panavia *Tornado* GR4s are retired by the end of this century. The proposed RAF variant could potentially have GEC-Marconi-supplied avionics, Eurojet EJ200 engines, and some structural content indigenous to Great Britain in the form of structure produced by British Aerospace.

Interestingly, discussions with Britain also have included the possibility of selling the Royal Air Force U-2Ss. As many as a dozen aircraft could be needed for British intelligence and proposed military tactical missions.

On a final note, the name *Nighthawk* was officially adopted for the F-117A during 1994.

**Joint Advanced Strike Technology (JAST)/Advanced Short Takeoff and Vertical Landing (ASTOVL)**—The Advanced Research Projects Agency (ARPA...it was Defense Advanced Research Projects Agency or DARPA) selected the *Skunk Works* and McDonnell Douglas Aerospace as Contractors for the critical technology validation phase of the ASTOVL technology demonstration program during March of 1993.

Under this three year project, ARPA intended to incrementally demonstrate the feasibility of developing a modular, affordable, lightweight fighter that could be used by the Air Force, Navy, and Marine Corps of the future.

The *Skunk Works* received a $40-million contract (including $8-million of UK Mod funding) for its shaft-driven lift fan concept. In this, the aircraft engine is mechanically connected to a vertically mounted lift fan during takeoff and landing. The lift fan is used to augment the main engine thrust, thus enabling the aircraft to takeoff in very short distances and land vertically, not unlike the McDonnell Douglas AV-8B *Harrier*. The *Skunk Works* was teamed with Pratt & Whitney, Allison, and Rolls Royce.

McDonnell Douglas received a $28-million

*The JAST test stand vehicle is primarily a wind tunnel model designed to explore aerodynamics and the viability of the mixed-capability horizontal and vertical flight propulsion system.*

**184**

contract (including $4-million of UK Mod funding) contract for their gas-coupled lift fan concept. With a gas coupled lift-fan, a portion of the exhaust gas from the main aircraft engine is ducted forward to drive a lift fan. Like the shaft-driven concept, the lift fan is used to augment main engine thrust to enable very short takeoffs and vertical landings. McDonnell Douglas is teamed on ASTOVL with General Electric Aircraft Engines and British Aerospace.

Both contractors will refine the design of an operational aircraft concept using their lift technology, and analyze and demonstrate affordability-enhancing technologies and processes. They are also to conduct large-scale wind tunnel model testing and develop a project plan for a full-scale technology demonstration aircraft.

As envisioned, an Air Force version of the advanced aircraft could be a single-engine, single-seat, conventional strike fighter powered by a derivative of the Advanced Tactical Fighter engine. The Marine Corps version of the advanced aircraft would share a common airframe, engine, and avionics with the Air Force aircraft. The Marine Corps version would also include propulsive lift hardware and software to enable it to takeoff and land from ships and expeditionary airfields without the use of catapults or arresting gear. With the above capabilities, this common aircraft could be considered by the services as a replacement for the Lockheed Martin F-16, the McDonnell Douglas F/A-18, and the McDonnell Douglas AV-8B (as well as *Harriers* serving with foreign air forces). Future aircraft decisions would be made by the services based on budget and force structure considerations at the time. A decision whether to build a demonstrator aircraft will be made based on the results of this phase.

During 1994, Lockheed, McDonnell Douglas, Boeing, and Northrop/Grumman during 1994, began independent work on a common tactical aircraft familiy under the JAST program. The JAST and ASTOVL program since have been merged and the ASTOVL concept has been adopted for the Marine Corps JAST variant. It is planned that technology demonstrators will be built under the X-32 designator. Two variants are planned. The X-32A will employ conventional takeoff and landing (CTOL) capability and the X-32B will employ short takeoff and vertical landing (STOVL) capability.

An 86% scale X-32B model, built by the *Skunk Works*, was completed during September of 1994 and was shipped to Pratt & Whitney in West Palm Beach, Florida for F100-PW-220+ engine installation and integration. The engine provides jet thrust for conventional flight and can be converted to provide shaft horsepower to drive an Allison lift fan installed behind the cockpit. Total thrust is about 17,000 pounds. For vertical landings, the thrust of the lift fan is balanced by deflecting the engine thrust at the rear of the aircraft with a Rolls Royce thrust vectoring nozzle (the *Skunk Works* receiveda patent for this innovative, convertible propulsion concept). During February through April of 1995, Pratt & Whitney conducted engine ground runs and then returned the aircraft to Lockheed for wing, canard, and tail surface installation. A month later, it was shipped to NASA Ames in Mountain View, California.

Lockheed Martin began outdoor hover and ground effects testing of the near-full-scale demonstrator at NASA Ames during July of 1995. The fiberglass and steel model is 45 feet long and has a wingspan of 30 feet. Testing will include measurements of jet thrust, airframe suckdown, hot gas ingestion, and ground pressures and temperatures. The hover tests will be followed during November by wind-tunnel tests of transition from hover to conventional wing-borne flight in NASA's 80 foot by 120 foot wind tunnel.

Lockheed Martin Tactical Aircraft Systems Ft. Worth is leading Lockheed's combined JAST efforts, which involve the *Skunk Works*, Lockheed Martin Aeronautical Systems Co., and Lockheed Sanders. A request for proposal to design and

*As built, the JAST testbed is unmanned and equipped only with dedicated propulsion system and aerodynamic research equipment. Aircraft is seen during tests at NASA Ames, California.*

build two full-scale, manned technology demonstrator aircraft is expected during December of 1995.

The JAST aircraft is being designed as a lightweight, multirole aircraft for use by the Air Force, Navy, Marine Corps, and key allies. Lockheed Martin is competing with Boeing and McDonnell Douglas/Northrop Grumman/British Aerospace for the flight demonstrator phase, which will begin during 1996. Actual flight testing is to take place before 2000.

**Single Stage To Orbit (SSTO)/Reusable Launch Vehicle (RLV)**—The *Skunk Works* is leading a Lockheed Martin team into the 21st Century space launcher arena with an AeroBallistic Rocket (ABR) concept. Designed to provide affordable access to space, the ABR is a single-stage-to-orbit (SSTO), vertical launch vehicle optimized to deliver payloads to low earth and other orbits, utilize lifting reentry, and land horizontally. It was conceived by the *Skunk Works* during the summer of 1992 to combat losing the space launch industry to subsidized foreign and non-free-market launchers. Developed in the rapid *Skunk Works'* process, the AeroBallistic Rocket is expected to revolutionize transportation before the turn of the century.

The ABR combines a Lockheed Missiles & Space Company lifting body design concept developed for the Assured Crew Return Vehicle with a linear aerospike rocket engine developed over twenty years ago by the Rocketdyne Division of Rockwell Corporation.

The seven liquid hydrogen/liquid oxygen rocket engine modules are expected each to develop about 250,000 pounds thrust to lift the million pound-plus vehicle directly to orbit. Once in

orbit, huge 15 foot by 56 foot payload bay doors will open and payload items weighing up to twenty tons would be launched.

The ABR's unique lifting body shape was designed to permit a relatively cool lifting reentry and horizontal landing without the weight penalty of wings. Once landed, the vehicle will be towed conventionally (in a horizontal attitude) into a hangar and processed just like a normal aircraft.

The payload bay, based on the payload requirements of the *Titan IV* launchers, was designed to permit delivery of 40,000 pounds to low earth orbit or, with the addition of an upper stage, transfer smaller payloads to other orbits.

The vehicle's design concept would permit ground handling with common aircraft support equipment and horizontal processing using standard palletized payloads. This, combined with a design emphasis on reliability, maintainability,

*There have been hundreds of JAST studies conducted by Lockheed Martin's Ft. Worth division.*

*As with most aircraft that include low-observables technology in their design, the production JAST aircraft will be configured for internal weapons carriage. This is one of several early JAST studies.*

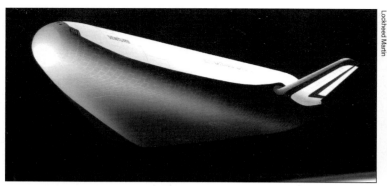

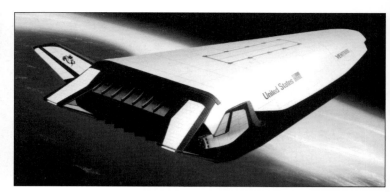

Lockheed has actively studied Reuseable Launch Vehicles for a number of years and this configuration represents one of the most recent.

The merging of Lockheed and Martin has brought together two major engineering talents in the quest for a viable single-stage-to-orbit vehicle.

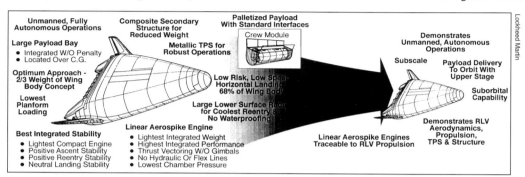

The Lockheed Martin Reuseable Launch Vehicle combines several different propulsion, aerodynamic, and materials disciplines to create a practical single-stage-to-orbit vehicle.

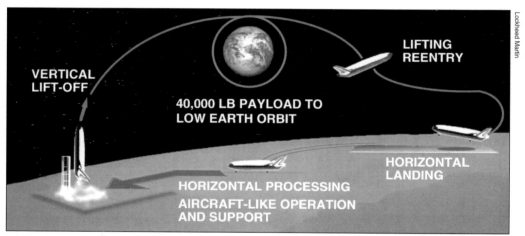

Simple in concept and in execution, the Reuseable Launch Vehicle as Lockheed Martin envisions it will allow a twenty-ton payload to be placed in low earth orbit at minimal cost.

and supportability, is to provide a standard turn-around time of less than seven days...a key component in affordable access to space.

With this concept, the *Skunk Works* hopes to foster the creation of a new and less expensive space transportation capability which, if it was successful, could finally open space to profitable commercial use for the benefit of mankind.

The emphasis of the *Skunk Works'* ABR design is affordability. Nothing is thrown away or

The linear aerospike engine has been tested and proven viable for the proposed RLV.

expended to achieve orbit except the fuel itself. Single-stage operation combined with aircraft like reliability, and maintainability resulted in truly low cost space access. The ABR could be launched at one-one-hundredth the cost of existing launchers.

During March of 1995, the *Skunk Works* was informed by NASA that it was one of three contractor teams that had been selected to enter into negotiations for reusable launch vehicle (RLV) studies. The *Skunk Works*-led team, McDonnell Douglas, and Rockwell were selected for Phase I studies involving concept definition and design. The new space launch and recovery system will be initially referred to as the X-33 and will be tested in the form of a scale vehicle that will be significantly smaller than the full-scale transport. Government funding has been set at $24 million ($8 million for each team plus additional technology development funds). Phase I is expected to last fifteen months.

Lockheed's vehicle will be powered by the linear aerospike engine with liquid hydrogen and liquid oxygen as propellants. The vehicle has high volumetric efficiency, a moderate lift-over-drag body shape, a low drag aft body, combined aft body and thrust structure (one of the attributes of the linear aerospike engine), and upper and lower

body flaps with canted vertical tail surfaces. Length of the current configuration is 126 feet, span (body width) is 85 feet, height is 31 feet, and the payload bay is 45 feet by 15 feet.

One aspect of the technical demonstration part of the contract involves full-scale development of a linear aerospike propulsion system with plug-type nozzles that adjust aerodynamically with changes in altitude. The Rocketdyne J2-S unit will be tested while attached to a dorsal pylon on NASA SR-71A "844". This aircraft, during mid-1995, was undergoing modification at Palmdale to accommodate the Rocketdyne unit.

Based on a 1996 go-ahead from NASA, first flight of an X-33 technology demonstrator could occur as early as March of 1999.

***Tier III Minus***—During June of 1994, the *Skunk Works*, in a partnership with Boeing's Military Airplanes Company received a contract for $106 million from the Department of Defense's Advanced Research Projects Agency (ARPA) that called for the development of a low-observable, high-altitude Unmanned Aerial Vehicle (UAV). Codenamed *Tier III Minus*, the system would be optimized to be an affordable, continuous, all-weather, wide-area surveillance vehicle to support military operations. It would be complementary to the U-2S and planned *Tier II Plus* conventional UAV.

The *Tier III Minus* program is the first project to be executed under the "Section 845 Authority" granted to ARPA for prototype weapons development projects. This authority has paved the way for unprecedented government-industry collaboration by removing the burden of specialized Defense procurement regulations and statutes. The program represents a new way of doing business--one that is based on teamwork and mutual trust.

The agreement stipulates completion of the two proof-of-concept vehicles and one launch control and recovery ground station within 21 months (ten months after go-ahead). However, the *Skunk Works* is on a fast track and roll-out of the first aircraft took place on June 1, 1995...only eleven months after go-ahead. This aircraft--and the second--represent proof-of-concept prototypes under Phase II of the program. Phase III—operational evaluation—will include the manufacture of two to four additional air vehicles and one additional launch control and recovery ground station. Phase IV includes the acquistion of an unspecified number of operational systems.

Other tactical and endurance UAV systems, including a high-altitude endurance UAV without low observable features (designated *Tier II Plus*) are being contracted for by the Advanced Research Projects Agency (ARPA) and the Defense Airborne Reconnaissance Office (DARO).

Work on the two *Tier III Minus* prototypes is split fifty/fifty between Boeing and Lockheed with Lockheed having overall system responsibility. The *Skunk Works* designed and built the composite body along with the subsystems that fit inside. Boeing built the bonded wing and is responsible for the fuel system and avionics integration. Final

As a result of the low-observables requirement in the Tier III Minus *design specification,* DarkStar *is one of the more unorthodox aerodynamic configurations ever to be designed for flight. Heavy reliance has been placed on high-strength composite structures and materials.*

DarkStar *is basically a flying wing design. The wing has a slight forward sweep . Some lift and considerale stability is imparted by the abbreviated fuselage. All sensors are located in the fuselage, as is the Williams turbofan engine. Emphasis has been placed on exhaust design to lower the aircraft's infrared signature.*

assembly is at Palmdale. Lockheed's Missiles & Space Company Space Systems Division in Sunnyvale procured and integrated the data management and storage system, the electro-optical camera, and both data link systems.

The UAV is now officially named *DarkStar.* It is powered by a single Williams International (Wall Lake, Michigan) FJ44 turbofan engine rated at 1,900 pounds thrust. Basically a flying wing, it has a length of 15 feet, a wingspan of 69 feet, and a height of 5 feet. Maximum gross weight is 8,600 pounds. Construction is primarily composites with emphasis placed on efficiency and low radar cross section. The aircraft's design and systems approaches were dictated by a unit cost limit of $10 million based on production units 11 through 20.

Miscellaneous performance characteristics exceed design goals. Endurance is well over eight hours; cruising speed at altitude is 250 knots; loiter altitude is over 45,000 feet; and operating radius is greater than 500 n. miles. Miscellaneous features include a UHF Milsat (Fleetsatcom) compatible communication and and control system and a sensor package that includes a synthetic aperture radar, an electro-optical camera system with night infrared capability, and a 20 meter CEP geo-location accuracy. Coverage per mission is

14,000 sq. n. miles in the form of 600 spot image frames each covering 2 km by 2 km. Sensor data transmission rates are narrow band comsat: 1.5 megabytes per second line-of-sight; wide band 137 Mbps.

*DarkStar's* first flight is tentatively planned before year-end, 1995.

**The *Skunk Works* Today**—The decision to establish the Skunk Works as an independent company (the Lockheed Advanced Development Company) was announced by Lockheed Chairman and CEO Dan Tellep during May of 1990. Accordingly, from a financial and accounting viewpoint LADC became a true separate company on January 1, 1991. As *Skunk Works* President at that time, Sherman Mullin noted during late 1992, "We are no longer a company within a company...which we had been from 1943 to 1990."

Tellep, offered the following comments on the *Skunk Works'* future following the 1990 decision: "I feel very positive about the decision we made to set up the *Skunk Works* as its own company...the *Skunk Works* exists and it is going to stay as it is."

Recalling recent international events that saw the demise of the Soviet Union and the threat it posed, Tellep noted that "Lockheed, more than

any other company, contributed to the end of the Cold War. The Cold War's end has triggered radical changes in aerospace's business environment." He then went on to predict another three to four years of declines in US Government defense budgets, with annual spendinq stabilizing at about $220 billion per year.

Among the opportunities Tellep envisioned for the *Skunk Works* was the proposed ASTOVL (now combined with JAST) advanced short takeoff and vertical landing aircraft. He cited the F-117A as "a reminder of the singularly unique skills the *Skunk Works* possesses....there is an aura about the *Skunk Works*—it really adds luster to the corporation."

"The latest five-year forecast of Lockheed projects growth in *Skunk Works* sales of 16 to 17 percent over the half-decade period." Tellep continued, "My commitment is that the corporation will support the *Skunk Works* with all of the resources it will need for future success."

The extraordinary vehicles described thus far were conceived during the *Skunk Works'* first fifty years—from its inception during 1943 to the present. We'll have to wait, now, for the next *Skunk Works* revolutionary breakthrough...

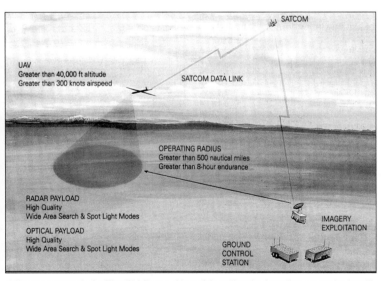

*Mission scenario for* Tier III Minus. *Aircraft is utilized primarily to acquire intelligence data and relay it to ground commanders in real time.*

DarkStar *is a very unorthodox design. Slight forward sweep angle of both leading and trailing edges is readily discernible in this image.*

## Glossary:

ABR—*AeroBallistic Rocket*
ACLS—automatic carrier landing system
AEW—anti-electronic warfare
AFE—advanced fighter engine
AFFTC—Air Force Flight Test Center
AFOTEC—Air Force Operational Test and Evaluation Center
AIM—air intercept missile
AMRAAM—advanced medium range air-to-air missile
AoA—angle-of-attack
ARPA—Advanced Research Projects Agency
ASARS—advanced synthetic aperture radar system
ASTOVL—advanced short takeoff and vertical Landing
ATF—advanced technology fighter
ATSC—Air Technical Service Center
A-X—attack experimental
B—Bomber
BLC—boundary layer control
C—Cargo
C&J—Clarence and Johnson
CAA—Civil Aeronautics Authority
CAT—clear air turbulence
CEP—circular error probable
CIA—Central Intelligence Agency
CPC—current program calculator
CSS—control stick steering
DARPA—Defense Advanced Research Projects Agency
Dem/Val—demonstration/validation
DLIR—downward looking infrared
DoD—Department of Defense
ECM—electornic countermeasures
ELINT—electronic intelligence
EMD—engineering manufacturing development
EOA—early operational assessment
EP-X—electronic patrol experimental
F—Fahrenheit
F—Fighter
FAA—Federal Aviation Administration
F.A.I.—*Federation Aeronautique International*
FCLP—field carrier landing practice
FCS—flight control system
FLCC—flight control computer
FLIR—forward looking infrared
FMS—flight management system
FOD—foreign object damage
FOL—forward operating location
FPA—flight path accelerometer
F.S.—Federal Standard
FSD—full-scale development
F-X—Fighter Experimental
GAR—guided aerial rocket
GBU—guided bomb unit
GE—General Electric
GFE—government furnished equipment
GOR—general operational requirement
GPS—global positioning system
HALO—high-altitude launch option
HAMB—high-altitude missions branch
HASP—High-Altitude Sampling Program
HICAT—high-altitude clear air turbulence
HUD—head up display
HVAR—high-velocity aerial rocket
IAM—International Association of Machinists
ICBM—intercontinental ballistic missile

IFF—identification friend or foe
ILS—instrument landing system
INS—inertial navigation system
IR—infrared
IRADS—infrared acquisition and detection system
IRAN—inspect and repair as necessary
IRBM—intermediate range ballistic missile
IVSC—integrated vehicle subsystem control
JAFE—joint advanced fighter engine
LADC—Lockheed Advanced Development Company
LCO—launch control officer
L/D—lift over drag
LGB—laser guided bomb
LSO—landing systems officer
MIDAS—missile defense alarm system
MMLE—modified maximum liklihood estimator
MRBM—medium range ballistic missile
NACA—National Advisory Committee for Aeronautics
NASA—National Aeronautics and Space Administration
NASM—National Air & Space Museum
NATO—North Atlantic Treaty Organization
OCIP—offensive combat improvement program
OFP—operational flight program
OL—operating location
OSRD—Office of Scientific Research and Development
P&W—Pratt & Whitney
PLSS—precision location strike system
RAAF—Royal Australian Air Force
RAE—Royal Aeronautical Establishment
RAF—Royal Air Force
RAM—radar absorbent material
RB—reconnaissance bomber
RCS—radar cross-section
RDT&E—research, development, test and engineering
RFP—request for proposals
RLG—ring laser gyro
RSS—relaxed static stability
SAMOS—satellite and missile observation system
SAR—special access required
SCO—system check-out
SMS—stores management system
SPO—system program office
SR—strategic reconnaissance
SRB—Safety Review Board
SSF—short takeoff, vertical landing strike fighter
T—Trainer
TACAN—tactical area navigation
TEB—tetra-ethyl-borane
TFS—Tactical Fighter Squadron
TFW—Tactical Fighter Wing
TFWP—Tactical Fighter Wing *Provisional*
TM—telemetry
TRB—Technical Review Board
U—Utility category
UCX—utility cargo experimental
UHF—ultra-high frequency
UN—United Nations
UTX—utility trainer experimental
VF-X—navy fighter experimental
VHF—very-high frequency
VLO—very low observable
WDC—weapon delivery computer
WSCS—weapon system computer subsystem
XST—experimental stealth testbed

# *SKUNK WORKS* COLOR PORTFOLIO

*XP-80 following restoration at the Smithsonian Institution's National Air & Space Museum's Paul Garber facility at Silver Hill, Maryland.*

*An original P-80A has been refurbished by volunteers to externally resemble the long-deceased first XP-80A, the Gray Ghost..*

*Lockheed's enormous* Constitution *was one of the world's largest aircraft at the time of its late-1940's debut.*

*The prototype YF-94, 50-955, over the Mojave Desert. This aircraft originally was flown under the YF-97A designator.*

*The second YC-130, 53-3397, was the first of the* Hercules *family to fly.*

*The X-7A was transported by and launched from a modified Boeing B-29A.*

*The JetStar, though a well-known corporate jet and military transport, is not well known as a Skunk Works project.*

*The number and variety of U-2 modifications was--and is--astounding. This aircraft, U-2A 56-6692, is configured to accommodate* Project TRIM.

*Two U-2As were modified to incorporate instructor's cockpits in the Q-bay, thus becoming U-2CT trainers.*

*NASA's two U-2Cs were removed from the Administration's inventory during 1987 and 1989.*

*The prototype U-2R during the course of its first flight on August 28, 1967. The flight began and ended at Edwards AFB.*

*A U-2R banks over Beale AFB, California. Visible on the ground below is a statically displayed SR-71A*

*Several U-2Rs have been modified to the Senior Span configuration. Aircraft of this type were critical to combat during the Gulf War.*

*The A-12 was the least-known of the acclaimed* Blackbird *family and was operated only by the Central Intelligence Agency.*

*A single two-seat A-12 was built to accommodate training requirements. It was powered by Pratt & Whitney J75s throughout its service career.*

*The three YF-12As were the only armed members of the* Blackbird *family to reach the full-scale hardware stage.*

Lockheed

*During initial flights attached via dorsal pylon to the M-21, the D-21 was equipped with a frangible nose cone.*

Lockheed

*When launched from Boeing B-52Hs, D-21s required Lockheed-developed boosters with folding ventral fins.*

Lockheed

*YF-12A pilot's panel had both vertical and round dial instrumentation.*

Lockheed

*YF-12A back cockpit panel was dedicated to Hughes AN/ASG-18.*

*SR-71s were highly dependent upon tankers.*

*Distinctively marked first SR-71A, 617950.   This aircraft was used extensively by Lockheed.*

*Distinctive chined delta configuration of SR-71A was typical of Skunk Works engineering innovation and genius.*

*The CL-1200 (aka X-27) was to have utilized many F-104 parts...thus making it more appealing to the many foreign F-104 customers.*

*Second* Have Blue *prototype differed from the first in being optimized for radar cross-section tests and having radar absorbent materials applied..*

*The F-117A was the production end-product of the technology verified by* Have Blue.

*Both YF-22As were assembled at the Skunk Works'* Palmdale facility.

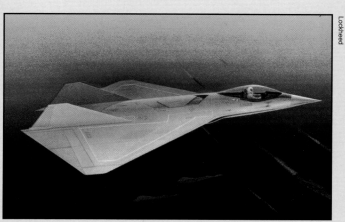

*Skunk Works ASTOVL concept study with lift fan aft of cockpit.*

**Appendix A: PRODUCTION, SPECIFICATION, AND PERFORMANCE TABLES**

**XP-80 Specifications/Performance:**
**Construction:** conventional aluminum monocoque
**Length:** 32 feet 10 inches
**Wingspan:** 39 feet 0 inches
**Wing Area:** 240 square feet
**Height:** 11 feet 3 inches
**Empty Weight:** 6,287 pounds
**Max. Gross Takeoff Weight:** 8,600 pounds
**Maximum Speed:** 506 mph @ 20,000 feet
**Operational Ceiling:** unknown
**Maximum Unrefueled Range:** 915 miles @ 35,000 feet/430 mph
**Fixed Armament:** 6 x .50 cal. machine guns w/200 rpg
**Powerplant Data:** 1 x de Havilland *Halford* H-1B centrifugal flow turbojet rated at 3,000 pounds thrust

**XP-80 Production/Disposition**

| Model/Designation: | Ser. # | Manu. # | Comment: |
|---|---|---|---|
| **140/XP-80** | 44-83020 | none | Restored for static display at the Smithsonian Institution's National Air & Space Museum Paul Garber Storage and Restoration Facility @ Silver Hill, Maryland |

**XP-80A Specifications/Performance:**
**Construction:** conventional aluminum monocoque
**Length:** 34 feet 6 inches
**Wingspan:** 38 feet 10-1/2 inches
**Wing Area:** 237.6 square feet
**Height:** 11 feet 4 inches
**Empty Weight:** 7,225 pounds
**Max. Gross Takeoff Weight:** 13,780 pounds
**Maximum Speed:** 500 mph @ 5,700 feet
**Operational Ceiling:** 48,500 feet
**Maximum Unrefueled Range:** 1,200 miles
**Fixed Armament:** 6 x .50 cal. machine guns w/300 rpg
**Powerplant Data:** General Electric I-40 centrifugal flow turbojet rated at 4,000 pounds thrust

**XP-80A Production/Disposition**

| Model/Designation: | Ser. # | Manu. # | Comment: |
|---|---|---|---|
| **141/XP-80A** | 44-83021 | none | Written-off on March 20, 1945 |
| **141/XP-80A** | 44-83022 | none | unknown |

**Model 75 *Saturn* Specifications/Performance:**
**Construction:** conventional aluminum monocoque
**Length:** 51 feet 7 inches
**Wingspan:** 74 feet 0 inches
**Wing Area:** 502 square feet
**Height:** 19 feet 10 inches
**Empty Weight:** 11,782 pounds
**Max. Gross Takeoff Weight:** 16,000 pounds
**Maximum Speed:** 252 mph @ 10,600 feet
**Operational Ceiling:** 27,700 feet
**Maximum Unrefueled Range:** 1,940 miles w/45 min. reserves
**Fixed Armament:** none
**Powerplant Data:** initially powered by 2 x 600 hp Continental GR9-A nine-cylinder radials; later powered by 2 x 700 hp Wright Cyclone 744C-7BA-1 seven-cylinder radials

**Model 75 *Saturn* Production/Disposition**

| Model/Designation: | Civil Reg. # | Manu. # | Comment: |
|---|---|---|---|
| **75/*Saturn*** | NX90801 | none | Scrapped upon program termination |
| **75/*Saturn*** | NX90802 | none | Scrapped upon program termination |

**Model 89/XR6O-1/XR6V-1 *Constitution* Specifications/Performance:**
**Construction:** conventional aluminum monocoque
**Length:** 156 feet 1 inch
**Wingspan:** 189 feet 1-1/4 inches
**Wing Area:** 3,610 square feet
**Height:** 50 feet 4-1/2 inches
**Empty Weight:** 114,575 pounds
**Max. Gross Takeoff Weight:** 184,000 pounds
**Maximum Speed:** 303 mph @ 20,000 feet
**Operational Ceiling:** 27,600 feet
**Maximum Unrefueled Range:** 6,300 miles (w/o payload)
**Fixed Armament:** none
**Powerplant Data:** initially powered by 4 x 3,000 hp Pratt & Whitney R4360-18 28-cylinder radials; later powered by 4 x 3,500 hp Pratt & Whitney R4360-22W radials

**XR6O-1/XR6Y Production/Disposition**

| Model/Designation: | BuNo. | Manu. # | Comment: |
|---|---|---|---|
| **89/XR6O-1/XR6Y** | 85163 | none | Scrapped at Las Vegas, Nevada; civil registered N7672C |
| **89/XR6O-1/XR6Y** | 85164 | none | Scrapped at Opa Locka, Florida |

**TP-80C/T-33 Specifications/Performance:**
**Construction:** conventional aluminum monocoque
**Length:** 37 feet 9 inches
**Wingspan:** 38 feet 10-1/2 inches
**Wing Area:** 234.8 square feet
**Height:** 11 feet 8 inches
**Empty Weight:** 8,365 pounds
**Max. Gross Takeoff Weight:** 15,061 pounds
**Maximum Speed:** 600 mph @ sea level
**Operational Ceiling:** 48,000 feet
**Maximum Unrefueled Range:** 1,275 miles
**Fixed Armament:** 2 x .50 cal. machine guns w/300 rpg
**Powerplant Data:** 1 x 4,600 pound thrust Allison J33-A-23 centrifugal flow turbojet

**TP-80C/T-33 Production/Disposition**

| Model/Designation: | Ser. # | Manu. # | Comment: |
|---|---|---|---|
| **580/TP-80C** | 48-356 | 5001 | Built from P-80C airframe. Later modified to become unofficial YF-94 prototype. Presently on loan to LADC from the Air Force Flight Test Center Museum at Edwards AFB, California. |

**YF-94 Specifications/Performance:**
**Construction:** conventional aluminum monocoque
**Length:** 40 feet 1 inch
**Wingspan:** 37 feet 6-1/2 inches w/o tip tanks
**Wing Area:** 234.8 square feet
**Height:** 12 feet 7 inches
**Empty Weight:** 10,064 pounds
**Max. Gross Takeoff Weight:** 16,844 pounds
**Maximum Speed:** 606 mph at sea level
**Operational Ceiling:** 48,000 feet
**Maximum Unrefueled Range:** 905 miles
**Fixed Armament:** 4 x .50 cal. machine guns
**Powerplant Data:** 1 x 4,400 pound thrust (dry)/6,000 pound thrust (afterburner) Allison J33-A-33 centrifugal flow turbojet

**YF-94 Production/Disposition**

| Model/Designation: | Ser. # | Manu. # | Comment: |
|---|---|---|---|
| **780/YF-94** | 48-356 | 5001 | Built from P-80C airframe. Served as TP-80C/T-33A prototype. YF-94 designation never officially assigned. Presently on loan to LADC from the Air Force Flight Test Center Museum at Edwards AFB, California. |
| **780/YF-94** | 48-373 | 5018 | Second prototype. |

**YF-94B Specifications/Performance:**
**Construction:** conventional aluminum monocoque
**Length:** 40 feet 1 inch
**Wingspan:** 37 feet 6-1/2 inches w/o tip tanks
**Wing Area:** 234.8 square feet
**Height:** 12 feet 8 inches
**Empty Weight: 10,064 pounds**
**Max. Gross Takeoff Weight:** 16,844 pounds
**Maximum Speed:** 606 mph at sea level
**Operational Ceiling:** 48,000 feet
**Maximum Unrefueled Range:** 905 miles
**Fixed Armament:** 4 x .50 cal. machine guns
**Powerplant Data:** 1 x 4,400 pound thrust (dry)/6,000 pound thrust (afterburner) Allison J33-A-33 centrifugal flow turbojet

**YF-94B Production/Disposition**

| Model/Designation | Ser. # | Manu. # | Comment: |
|---|---|---|---|
| **780YF-94B** | 49-2497 | 7019 | Modified 19th F-94A. |

**L-188/YF-97A/YF-94C Specifications/Performance:**
**Construction:** conventional aluminum monocoque
**Length:** 41 feet 5 inches
**Wingspan:** 37 feet 3 inches
**Wing Area:** 232.8 square feet
**Height:** 14 feet 11 inches
**Empty Weight:** unknown
**Max. Gross Takeoff Weight:** unknown
**Maximum Speed:** est. 640 mph @ sea level w/J48
**Operational Ceiling:** est. 52,000 feet w/J48
**Maximum Unrefueled Range:** unknown
**Fixed Armament:** 24 x 2.75 FFARs
**Powerplant Data:** initially equipped w/1 x 6,250 pound thrust (afterburner) Rolls Royce *Tay* centrifugal flow turbojet; later refitted w/6,000 pound thrust (dry)/8,000 pound thrust (afterburner) Pratt & Whitney J48/P-3 centrifugal flow turbojet

**YF-97A/YF-94C Production/Disposition**

| Model/Designation: | Ser. # | Manu. # | Comment: |
|---|---|---|---|
| **188/YF-94C** | 50-877 | 7183 | Second prototype but first built to F-94C standard. Officially redesignated YF-94C on September 12, 1950. |
| **188/YF-94C** | 50-955 | 8000 | Privately funded L-188 prototype for YF-94C; civil registered N94C; initial military designation was YF-97A. Officially redesignated YF-94C on September 12, 1950. |

**XF-90 Specifications/Performance**
**Construction:** conventional aluminum
**Length:** 55 feet 11-1/2 inches
**Wingspan:** 39 feet 11-1/2 inches
**Wing Area:** 350 square feet
**Height:** 15 feet 9 inches
**Empty Weight:** 18,050 pounds
**Max. Gross Takeoff Weight:** 31,060 pounds
**Maximum Speed:** 668 mph @ 1,000 feet w/XJ34-WE-15 engines
**Operational Ceiling:** 39,000 feet
**Maximum Unrefueled Range:** 2,300 miles
**Fixed Armament:** 6 x .50 cal. machine guns
**Powerplant Data:** 2 x 3,000 pound thrust Westinghouse XJ34-WE-11 axial flow turbojets initially; later equipped w/2 x 3,600 pound thrust (dry)/4,200 pound thrust (afterburner) Westinghouse XJ34-WE-15s

**XF-90 Production/Disposition**

| Model/Designation: | Ser. # | Manu. # | Comment: |
|---|---|---|---|
| **90/XF-90** | 46-687 | none | Used by NACA Langley for structural test work; eventually scrapped |
| **90/XF-90** | 46-688 | none | Test specimen during 1952 nuclear tests at Frenchman's Flat, Nevada; still exists, but too radioactive to retrieve |

**RB-69A Specifications/Performance**
**Construction:** conventional aluminum
**Length:** 91 feet 8 inches
**Wingspan:** 103 feet 10 inches
**Wing Area:** 1,000 square feet
**Height:** 29 feet 4 inches
**Empty Weight:** est. 50,000 pounds
**Max. Gross Takeoff Weight:** est. 80,000 pounds
**Maximum Speed:** 403 mph @ 14,000 feet
**Operational Ceiling:** 22,000 feet
**Maximum Unrefueled Range:** est. 3,750 miles
**Fixed Armament:** unknown
**Powerplant Data:** 2 x 3,500 hp Wright R3350-32W 18-cylinder turbo-compound radials and 2 x 3,400 pound thrust Westinghouse J34-WE-36 turbojets

**RB-69A Production/Disposition**

| Model/Designation: | Ser. # | Manu. # | Comment: |
|---|---|---|---|
| **726/P2V-7U/RB-69A** | 54-4037 | 7047 | No information |
| **726/P2V-7U/RB-69A** | 54-4038 | 7097 | No information |
| **726/P2V-7U/RB-69A** | 54-4039 | 7099 | No information |
| **726/P2V-7U/RB-69A** | 54-4040 | 7101 | No information |
| **726/P2V-7U/RB-69A** | 54-4041 | 7105 | No information |
| **726/P2V-7U/RB-69A** | 54-4042 | 7185 | No information |
| **726/P2V-7U/RB-69A** | 54-4043 | 7186 | No information |

There appears to be some indication that three additional aircraft, 54-4044 through 54-4046 were canceled.

**X-7A/X-7B/XQ-5 Specifications/Performance**
**Construction:** steel and aluminum
**Length:** X-7A = 32 feet 10 inches (booster 19 feet 10 inches) w/nose spike; X-7A-3/X-7B = 35 feet 0 inches w/nose spike; XQ-5 = 37 feet 1 inch w/nose spike
**Wingspan:** X-7A = 12 feet 0 inches (booster = 21 feet 6 inches); X-7A-3/X-7B = 10 feet 0 inches; XQ-5 = 10 feet 0 inches
**Wing Area: X-7A =** 52.3 square feet; X-7A-3/X-7B = 60 square feet; XQ-5 = 60 square feet
**Height: X-7A =** 7 feet 0 inches (booster = 10 feet 5 inches); X-7A-3/X-7B = 7 feet 5 inches
**Empty Weight:** X-7A = 2,636 pounds; X-7A-3/X-7B = 3,345 pounds
**Max. Launch Weight:** X-7A = 8,108 pounds (including booster which weighed 5,010 pounds); X-7A-3/X-7B w/28 inch engine approx. 8,350 pounds (with boosters)/w/36 inch engine approx. 8,900 pounds (with boosters)
**Maximum Speed:** X-7A-3 = Mach 4.3
**Operational Ceiling:** X-7A-3 = 106,000 feet
**Maximum Unrefueled Range:** X-7A-3 = 134 miles
**Fixed Armament:** none
**Powerplant Data:** The following includes all known ramjets tested during the course of the X-7 program:

| Manufac. | Size | Designation | Flts. | Comments |
|---|---|---|---|---|
| Wright | 20 inch | XRJ47-W-1 | 2 | 1 partial success |
| Wright | 20 inch | XRJ47-W-3 | 5 | 1 successful; 2 partially successful; 3 failures |
| Marquardt | 20 inch | XRJ43-MH-1 | 2 | 2 failures (not engine related) |
| Marquardt | 28 inch | XRJ43-MA-3 | ? | |
| Marquardt | 28 inch | XRJ43-MA-20B | 5 | |
| Marquardt | 28 inch | XRJ43-MA-20C | 13 | |
| Marquardt | 28 inch | XRJ43-MA-20-XF-1 | 23 | |
| Marquardt | 28 inch | XRJ43-MA-20-XF-4 | 6 | |
| Marquardt | 28 inch | XRJ43-MA-20-XF-6 | 11 | |
| Marquardt | 28 inch | XRJ43-MA-20-XF-8 | 3 | |
| Marquardt | 28 inch | XRJ43-MA-20-XP-1 | 9 | |
| Marquardt | 28 inch | XRJ43-MA-20-XP-3 | 9 | |
| Marquardt | 28 inch | XRJ43-MA-3 | ? | |
| Marquardt | 28 inch | XRJ43-MA-20ZF-5 | 1 | |
| Marquardt | 28 inch | XRJ43-MA-5 | ? | |
| Marquardt | 28 inch | XRJ43-MA-20-XF-7 | 8 | |
| Marquardt | 28 inch | XRJ43-MA-20-XF-9 | 3 | |
| Marquardt | 28 inch | XRJ43-MA-7 | ? | |
| Marquardt | 28 inch | XRJ43-MA-20-XS-1 | 11 | |
| Marquardt | 28 inch | XRJ43-MOD 11 | 3 | |
| Marquardt | 28 inch | XRJ43-M-9 | ? | |
| Marquardt | 28 inch | XRJ43-MA-20-XS-2 | ? | |
| Marquardt | 28 inch | XRJ43-MA-11 | ? | |
| Marquardt | 28 inch | XRJ43-MA -20-XS-3 | ? | |
| Marquardt | 36 inch | XRS-59-MA-1 | ? | |
| Marquardt | 36 inch | XRS-59-MA-24-C | 6 | |
| Marquardt | 36 inch | XRS-59-MA-24-D | 2 | |

There were 12 additional flights with unknown engine configurations
Booster units used include
For the X-7A: 1 x 105,000 pound thrust Allegheny Ballistics Lab X202-C3
For the X-7A-3/X-7B: 2 x 50,000 pound thrust Thiokol 5-KS-50,000 (XM-45)s
For the X-7A-3/X-7B: 2 x 50,000 pound thrust Aerojet 5-KS-50,000 (XM-62)s
For the X-7A-3/X-7B: 2 x 50,000 pound thrust Grand Central Rocket 5KS-50,000s

**X-7A/X-7B/XQ-5 Production/Disposition**
Air Force serial numbers assigned the X-7 program include the following: X-7A: 55-3167/3173; 56-4045/4052; 57-6295/6307, XQ-5: 56-4054; 58-1025. All Manufacturing Numbers for all X-7 versions and serial numbers assigned to the X-7A-3, X-7B, and XQ-5 missiles remain unverifiable.

**R7V-2/YC-121F *Constellation* Specifications/Performance**

**Construction:** conventional aluminum monocoque
**Length:** 116 feet 2 inches
**Wingspan:** 119 feet 1 inch
**Wing Area:** 1,615 square feet
**Height:** 24 feet 9 inches
**Empty Weight:** 76,162 pounds
**Max. Gross Takeoff Weight:** 150,000 pounds
**Maximum Speed:** 506 mph
**Operational Ceiling:** 28,700 feet
**Maximum Unrefueled Range:** 3,140 miles
**Fixed Armament:** none
**Powerplant Data:** delivered w/4 x 5,550 shaft horsepower Pratt & Whitney YT34-P-12A turboprops; YC-121Fs converted to 4 x 6,000 shaft horsepower Pratt & Whitney T34-P-6 turboprops

**R7V-2/YC-121F *Constellation* Production/Disposition**

| Model/Designation: | BuNo. | Manu. # | Comment: |
|---|---|---|---|
| **1249A/R7V-2** | 131630 | 4131 | Ordered as R7V-1 |
| **1249A/R7V-2** | 131631 | 4132 | Ordered as R7V-1 |
| **1249A/R7V-2/YC-121F** | 131660 | 4161 | Ordered as R7V-1; delivered to the Air Force as YC-121F, 53-8157 |
| **1249A/R7V-2/YC-121F** | 131661 | 4162 | Ordered as R7V-1; delivered to the Air Force as YC-121F, 53-8158; later modified as testbed for Allison 501 turboprop |

**L-245Specifications/Performance:**
**Construction:** conventional aluminum
**Length:** 37 feet 9 inches
**Wingspan:** 38 feet 10-1/2 inches
**Wing Area:** 234.8 square feet
**Height:** 11 feet 8 inches
**Empty Weight:** 8,500 pounds
**Max. Gross Takeoff Weight:** 12,250 pounds
**Maximum Speed:** 600 mph at sea level
**Operational Ceiling:** 47,500 feet
**Maximum Unrefueled Range:** 1,250 miles
**Fixed Armament:** none
**Powerplant Data:** 1 x 5,400 pound thrust Allison J33-A-16 centrifugal flow turbojet

**L-245 Production/Disposition**

| Model/Designation: | Civil Reg. | Manu. # | Comment: |
|---|---|---|---|
| **1080/L-245** | N125D | none | Ex-Air Force T-33A, 52-9255 (Manu. # 7321); referred to in-house at Lockheed as the L-245; it was informally referred to as the T-33B. |

**T2V-1/T-1A Specifications/Performance**
**Construction:** conventional aluminum
**Length:** 38 feet 6-1/2 inches
**Wingspan:** 42 feet 10 inches
**Wing Area:** 240 square feet
**Height:** 13 feet 4 inches
**Empty Weight:** 11,965 pounds
**Max. Gross Takeoff Weight:** 16,800 pounds
**Maximum Speed:** 580 mph at sea level
**Operational Ceiling:** 40,000 feet
**Maximum Unrefueled Range:** 970 miles
**Fixed Armament:** none
**Powerplant Data:** 1 x 5,400 pound thrust Allison J33-A-16 centrifugal flow turbojet

**T2V-1/T-1A Production/Disposition**

| Model/Desig | Civil Reg. | Manu. # | Comment |
|---|---|---|---|
| **1080/T2V-1** | N125D | 7321 | Ex-Air Force T-33A, 52-9255; following test work as the L-245, this aircraft was aerodynamically modified to later production T2V-1/T-1A standards. |

**YC-130 Specifications/Performance**
**Construction:** conventional aluminum monocoque
**Length:** 95 feet 2-1/2 inches
**Wingspan:** 132 feet 6 inches
**Wing Area:** 1,745 square feet
**Height:** 38 feet 0 inches
**Empty Weight:** 57,500 pounds
**Max. Gross Takeoff Weight:** 124,200 pounds
**Maximum Speed:** 383 mph @ 20,400 feet
**Operational Ceiling:** 41,300 feet
**Maximum Unrefueled Range:** 3,215 miles
**Fixed Armament:** none
**Powerplant Data:** 4 x 3,750 shaft horsepower Allison T56-A-1 turboprops

**YC-130 Production/Disposition**

| Model/Designation: | Ser. # | Manu. # | Comment: |
|---|---|---|---|
| **82/YC-130** | 53-3396 | none | Second aircraft to fly |
| **82/YC-130** | 53-3397 | none | |

**XF-104 *Starfighter* Specifications/Performance**
**Construction:** conventional aluminum monocoque
**Length:** 49 feet 2 inches (w/o nose boom)
**Wingspan:** 21 feet 10 inches (w/o tip tanks)
**Wing Area:** unknown
**Height:** 12 feet 8 inches
**Empty Weight:** 11,500 pounds
**Max. Gross Takeoff Weight:** 15,700 pounds
**Maximum Speed:** Mach 1.79
**Operational Ceiling:** 50,500 feet
**Maximum Unrefueled Range:** 900 miles
**Fixed Armament:** 1 x 20 mm General Electric M61A-1 (second aircraft only)
**Powerplant Data:** first aircraft equipped with 1 x Buick-manufactured 7,200 pound thrust Wright J65-B-3 axial flow turbojet without afterburner; first aircraft refitted and second aircraft delivered with 7,800 pound thrust (dry)/10,200 pound thrust (afterburner) Wright XJ65-W-6 axial flow turbojet

**XF-104 *Starfighter* Production/Disposition**

| Model/Designation: | Ser. # | Manu. # | Comment: |
|---|---|---|---|
| **83/XF-104** | 53-7786 | none | During 1955, the first aircraft logged 334 flights; during 1956, it logged a total of 167 flights; and during 1957, it logged a total of 20 flights |
| **83/XF-104** | 53-7787 | none | Written-off on April 18, 1955; it had logged a total of 31 flights |

**XFV-1 Specifications/Performance**
**Construction:** conventional aluminum
**Length:** 36 feet 10-1/4 inches
**Wingspan:** 30 feet 10-7/64 inches (w/tip tanks)
**Wing Area:** 246 square feet
**Height:** unknown
**Empty Weight:** 11,599 pounds
**Max. Gross Takeoff Weight:** 16,221 pounds
**Maximum Speed:** 580 mph (w/YT40-A-14)
**Operational Ceiling:** 43,300 feet
**Maximum Unrefueled Endurance:** 1 hour 10 minutes
**Armament:** 4 x 20 mm cannon or 48 x 2.75 inch FFARs (proposed, none ever actually installed)
**Powerplant Data:** 1 x 5,850 shaft horsepower Allison XT40-A-6 turboprop; the intended engine, though never installed, was the 7,100 shaft horsepower Allison XT40-A-14 turboprop

**XFV-1 Production/Disposition**

| Model/Designation: | BuNo. | Manu. # | Comment: |
|---|---|---|---|
| **81/XFV-1** | 138657 | none | Displayed at Naval Aviation Museum, Pensacola, Florida |
| **81/XFV-1** | 138658 | none | Never completed; served as gate guardian at NAS Los Alamitos, California |

**U-2A/U-2C/U-2D Specifications/Performance**
**Construction:** conventional aluminum monocoque
**Length:** 49 feet 8 inches
**Wingspan:** 80 feet 2 inches
**Wing Area:** 600 square feet
**Height:** 15 feet 2 inches
**Empty Weight:** 14,250 pounds
**Max. Gross Takeoff Weight:** 24,150 pounds
**Maximum Speed:** over 430 mph
**Operational Ceiling:** over 70,000 feet
**Maximum Unrefueled Range:** over 3,000 miles
**Armament:** none
**Powerplant Data:** 1 x 10,500 pound thrust Pratt & Whitney J57-P-37/J57-P-37A or 1 x 11,200 pound thrust J57-P-31/J57-P-31A or 1 x 15,800 pound thrust J75-P-13/J75-P-13A or 1 x 17,000 pound thrust J75-P-13B axial flow turbojet
**U-2A Production/Disposition:** The first aircraft were delivered in two batches; the first was under contract SP-1913 and the second was under contract SP-1914. **It should be noted that, for reasons of national security, the following serial number list and associated information has been gathered from non-Lockheed sources.**

| Model/Designation: | AF Ser. # | Manu. # | Comment: |
|---|---|---|---|
| **none/U-2A** | none | none | Static test article; delivered May 21, 1955 |
| **none/U-2A** | none | 341 | Delivered July 24, 1955; written-off during April of 1957 |
| **none/U-2A** | 56-6675 | 342 | Delivered September 11, 1955; first aircraft to be converted to U-2C configuration; first flight as U-2C on May 13, 1959; during test program, flew 54 flights and 140 hours 36 minutes as fully instrumented test aircraft; remained at Edwards AFB as U-2 test aircraft |
| **none/U-2A** | 56-6676 | 343 | Delivered October 16, 1955 |
| **none/U-2A** | 56-6677 | 344 | Delivered November 20, 1955; written-off @ Edwards AFB |
| **none/U-2A** | 56-6678 | 345 | Delivered December 16, 1955 |
| **none/U-2A** | 56-6679 | 346 | Delivered January 13, 1956 |
| **none/U-2A** | 56-6680 | 347 | Delivered February 8, 1956; first aircraft to make overflight of the Soviet Union; converted to U-2F configuration; flown in Vietnam with "rams horn" antennas; first all-black Air Force U-2; as U-2C displayed in the Smithsonian Institution's National Air & Space Museum, Washington, D.C. |
| **none/U-2A** | 56-6681 | 348 | Delivered March 5, 1956; civil registered N801X; converted to U-2G for carrier operations; as U-2C flown by the 4080th SRW; transferred to the NASA as N708NA during June of 1971; as U-2C displayed at NASA Ames Research Center, NAS Moffett Field, California |
| **none/U-2A** | 56-6682 | 349 | Delivered March 29, 1956; civil registered N802X; converted to U-2G for carrier operations; transferred to the NASA as N709NA during June of 1971; as U-2C displayed @ Robins AFB, Georgia |
| **none/U-2A** | 56-6683 | 350 | Delivered April 24, 1956; civil registered N803X; written-off following Cuban overflight |
| **none/U-2A** | 56-6684 | 351 | Delivered May 18, 1956; civil registered N804X; U-2C development test aircraft; flew 15 flights during test program and 93 hours 18 minutes; deployed operationally on August 12, 1959 |
| **none/U-2A** | 56-6685 | 352 | Delivered June 13, 1956; civil registered N805X |
| **none/U-2A** | 56-6686 | 353 | Delivered July 6, 1956; civil registered N806X |
| **none/U-2A** | 56-6687 | 354 | Delivered July 27, 1956; civil registered N807X; converted to U-2F configuration |
| **none/U-2A** | 56-6688 | 355 | Delivered August 16, 1956; civil registered N808X; converted to U-2F configuration |
| **none/U-2A** | 56-6689 | 356 | Delivered September 5, 1956; civil registered N809X |
| **none/U-2A** | 56-6690 | 357 | Delivered September 21, 1956; written off on October 8, 1966 near Ben Hoa Air Base, South Vietnam |
| **none/U-2A** | 56-6691 | 358 | Delivered October 8, 1956; U-2C development test aircraft; flew 37 flights during test program and 147 + 13 hours; deployed operationally on August 12, 1959; as U-2C in Taiwanese AF markings, wreckage displayed at PRC Military Museum, Beijing, China |
| **none/U-2A/U-2CT** | 56-6692 | 359 | Delivered October 22, 1956; as U-2C displayed at RAF Alconbury, England |
| **none/U-2A** | 56-6693 | 360 | Delivered on November 5, 1956; as U-2C damaged at Fugisawa Airfield near Atsugi Airport, Tokyo, Japan on September 24, 1959; aircraft flown by Francis Gary Powers on May 1, 1960 |
| **none/U-2A** | 56-6694 | 361 | Delivered during September of 1956; written-off near Del Rio, Texas |
| **none/U-2A** | 56-6695 | 362 | Delivered during November of 1956; participated in Cuban Missile Crises overflight program |
| **none/U-2A** | 56-6696 | 363 | Delivered during December of 1956; as U-2A used for HASP missions; converted to U-2C; participated in Cuban Missile Crises overflight program; written-off near Del Rio, Texas |
| **none/U-2A** | 56-6697 | 364 | Delivered during January of 1957; written-off near Del Rio, Texas |
| **none/U-2A** | 56-6698 | 365 | Delivered during January of 1957; written-off near Del Rio, Texas |
| **none/U-2A** | 56-6699 | 366 | Delivered during February of 1957; written-off during 1957 in New Mexico |
| **none/U-2A** | 56-6700 | 367 | Delivered during February of 1957; as U-2A used for HASP missions; written-off near Winterberg, West Germany on May 29, 1975 |
| **none/U-2A** | 56-6701 | 368 | Delivered during March of 1957; as U-2C displayed at SAC Museum, Offutt AFB, Nebraska |
| **none/U-2A** | 56-6702 | 369 | Delivered during March of 1957; written-off near Del Rio, Texas |
| **none/U-2A** | 56-6703 | 370 | Delivered during April of 1957; converted to U-2F; written-off near Davis-Monthan AFB, Arizona |
| **none/U-2A** | 56-6704 | 371 | Delivered during April of 1957; written-off near Del Rio, Texas |
| **none/U-2A** | 56-6705 | 372 | Delivered during April of 1957; as U-2A used for HASP missions |
| **none/U-2A** | 56-6706 | 373 | Delivered during May of 1957; participated in Cuban Missile Crises overflight program |
| **none/U-2A** | 56-6707 | 374 | Delivered during May of 1957; converted to U-2F; as U-2C displayed at Laughlin AFB, Texas |
| **none/U-2A** | 56-6708 | 375 | Delivered during June of 1957 |
| **none/U-2A** | 56-6709 | 376 | Delivered during June of 1957 |
| **none/U-2A** | 56-6710 | 377 | Delivered during June of 1957; written-off |
| **none/U-2A** | 56-6711 | 378 | Delivered during July of 1957; written-off as a result of surface-to-air missile contact over Cuba during October of 1962 |
| **none/U-2A** | 56-6712 | 379 | Delivered during July of 1957; participated in Cuban Missile Crises overflight program; written-off in Idaho |
| **none/U-2A** | 56-6713 | 380 | Delivered during July of 1957; written-off in New Mexico |
| **none/U-2A** | 56-6714 | 381 | Delivered during August of 1957; as U-2A used for HASP missions; as U-2C displayed at Beale AFB, California |
| **none/U-2A** | 56-6715 | 382 | Delivered during August of 1957 |
| **none/U-2A** | 56-6716 | 383 | Delivered during September of 1957; as U-2A used for HASP missions; as U-2C displayed at Davis-Monthan AFB, Arizona |
| **none/U-2A** | 56-6717 | 384 | Delivered during September of 1957; as U-2A used for HASP missions |
| **none/U-2A** | 56-6718 | 385 | Delivered during September of 1957; as U-2A used for HASP missions |
| **none/U-2A** | 56-6719 | 386 | Delivered during October of 1957; written off in Latin America |
| **none/U-2A** | 56-6720 | 387 | Delivered during October of 1957; written-off near Del Rio, Texas |
| **none/U-2D** | 56-6721 | 388 | Delivered during October of 1957; assigned to Edwards AFB as Air Force Flight Test Center aircraft; as U-2D displayed at March AFB, California |
| **none/U-2A** | 56-6722 | 389 | Delivered during November of 1957; assigned to Edwards AFB as Air Force Flight Test Center aircraft; became HICAT aircraft; as U-2A displayed at the US Air Force Museum, Wright-Patterson AFB, Ohio |
| **none/U-2A** | 56-6950 | 390 | No information |
| **none/U-2A** | 56-6951 | 391 | Written-off near Davis-Monthan AFB, Arizona |
| **none/U-2A** | 56-6952 | 392 | Written-off near Davis-Monthan AFB, Arizona |
| **none/U-2A/U-2CT** | 56-6953 | 393 | As U-2CT displayed at Edwards AFB, California |
| **none/U-2D** | 56-6954 | 394 | Assigned to Edwards AFB as Air Force Flight Test Center aircraft; written-off near Davis-Monthan AFB, Arizona |
| **none/U-2A** | 56-6955 | 395 | Written-off near Boise, Idaho on August 14, 1964 while piloted by a Nationalist Chinese |

**Note:** U-2A was the basic "A" configuration; U-2A-2LO was the basic "A" configuration equipped with a nose sampler (Manufacturer's Nos. 381 to 385); U-2B was a proposed U-2 bomber equipped with tricycle landing gear, two hardpoints under each wing for external weapons carriage, and a single M60 machine gun mounted in the "Q-bay" for self-defense (it was mounted on a trapeze-type mechanism so that it could be lowered out of the "Q-bay" for firing); U-2C-1-LO were "A" models w/J75 engines and bigger intakes (U-2C flight testing using Nos. 342, 351, and 358 required a total of 106 flights and 381 hours 7 minutes flying time); U-2D-1LO was purpose-built two-place aircraft (manufacturer's model nos. 388 and 394); U-2E-1LO was the U-2A converted to inflight refueling system (3 aircraft); U-2F-1LO was the U-2C converted to inflight refueling system (5 aircraft); U-2G-1LO was the U-2C converted for carrier compatibility with an arresting hook and other modifications (3 aircraft); U-2H-1LO was the U-2C converted for carrier compatibility with an arresting hook and other modifications including inflight refueling system; U-2CT was U-2C converted to trainer; miscellaneous registrations and serial numbers assigned to U-2s but not attributable to select aircraft include: NASA 55741; NACA 320; NACA 331; NACA 357; NASA 405; NASA 432; NASA 449; NASA 464; 55891; N800X; N802X; N803X; N804X; N806X; N807X; N808X; N809X; 320; 3512; 3514; etc.

3512; 3514; etc.

**U-2R/U-2RT/TR-1A/TR-1B Specifications/Performance**
**Construction:** conventional aluminum monocoque w/some composites
**Length:** 62 feet 10-1/2 inches
**Wingspan:** 103 feet 0 inches
**Wing Area (gross):** 1,000 square feet
**Height:** 16 feet 0 inches
**Empty Weight:** classified
**Max. Gross Takeoff Weight:** classified
**Maximum Speed:** over 430 mph
**Operational Ceiling:** over 70,000 feet
**Maximum Unrefueled Range:** over 3,000 miles
**Armament:** none
**Powerplant Data:** 1 x 17,000 pound thrust Pratt & Whitney J75-P-13B or 1 x 18,000 pound thrust class General Electric F118-GE-101
**U-2R/TR-1A Production/Disposition: It should be noted that, for reasons of national security, the following serial number list and associated information has been gathered from non-Lockheed sources.**

| Model/Designation: | Ser. # | Manu. # | Comment: |
|---|---|---|---|
| **none/U-2R** | 68-10329 | 051 | Registered N803X during flight test; assigned to 9th SRW @ Beale AFB, California |
| **none/U-2R** | 68-10330 | 052 | Registered N810X during flight test; written-off at Akrotiri, Cyprus on December 7, 1977 |
| **none/U-2R** | 68-10331 | 053 | Assigned to 9th SRW @ Beale AFB, California |
| **none/U-2R** | 68-10332 | 054 | Assigned to 9th SRW @ Beale AFB, California |
| **none/U-2R** | 68-10333 | 055 | Assigned to 9th SRW @ Beale AFB, California |
| **none/U-2R** | 68-10334 | 056 | No information |
| **none/U-2R** | 68-10335 | 057 | No information |
| **none/U-2R** | 68-10336 | 058 | Flight test at Palmdale |
| **none/U-2R** | 68-10337 | 059 | Assigned to 9th SRW @ Beale AFB, California |
| **none/U-2R** | 68-10338 | 060 | Assigned to 9th SRW @ Beale AFB, California; one of two EP-X testbed aircraft |
| **none/U-2R** | 68-10339 | 061 | Assigned to 9th SRW@ Beale AFB, California; one of two EP-X testbed aircraft |
| **none/U-2R** | 68-10340 | 062 | Assigned to 9th SRW @ Beale AFB, California |
| **none/U-2ER/ER-2** | 80-1063 | 063 | Assigned to NASA Ames Research Center, NAS Moffett Field, California as N706NA, arriving on June 10, 1981; first flight took place on May 11, 1981 w/Art Peterson @ the controls |
| **none/U-2RT** | 80-1064 | 064 | Assigned to 9th SRW @ Beale AFB, California; delivered as TR-1B; first flight took place on February 23, 1983 w/Art Peterson @ the controls; delivered to Beale AFB on March 25, 1983 |
| **none/U-2RT** | 80-1065 | 065 | Assigned to 9th SRW @ Beale AFB, California; delivered as TR-1B; first flght took place on May 5, 1983 w/Ken Weir @ the controls; delivered to Beale AFB on May 23, 1983 |
| **none/U-2R** | 80-1066 | 066 | Assigned to 9th SRW @ Beale AFB, California; delivered as TR-1A; first flight took place on August 1, 1981 w/Ken Weir @ the controls; delivered to Beale AFB on September 15, 1981 on 15th flight |
| **none/U-2R** | 80-1067 | 067 | Delivered as TR-1A and retained by Lockheed at Palmdale; first flight took place on December 1, 1981 w/Art Peterson @ the controls |
| **none/U-2R** | 80-1068 | 068 | Assigned to 9th SRW @ Beale AFB, California; delivered as TR-1A; first flight took place on April 14, 1982 w/Ken Weir @ the controls |
| **none/U-2R** | 80-1069 | 069 | Temporarily assigned to NASA Ames Research Center, NAS Moffett Field, California as N708NA; on loan from Air Force; delivered as TR-1A; first flight took place on July 13, 1982 w/Art Peterson @ the controls |
| **none/U-2R** | 80-1070 | 070 | Assigned to 9th SRW @ Beale AFB, California; delivered as TR-1A; first flight took place on October 18, 1982 w/Ken Weir @ the controls |
| **none/U-2R** | 80-1071 | 071 | Assigned to 9th SRW @ Beale AFB, California; first flight took place on July 25, 1983 w/Ken Weir @ the controls; first U-2R of new production run; delivered to Beale AFB on August 17, 1983 |
| **none/U-2R** | 80-1072 | 072 | No information |
| **none/U-2R** | 80-1073 | 073 | assigned to 9th SRW @ Beale AFB, California; delivered as TR-1A |
| **none/U-2R** | 80-1074 | 074 | Assigned to 9th SRW @ Beale AFB, California; delivered as TR-1A |
| **none/U-2R** | 80-1075 | 075 | No information |
| **none/U-2R** | 80-1076 | 076 | Assigned to 9th SRW @ Beale AFB, California |
| **none/U-2R** | 80-1077 | 077 | Assigned to 9th SRW @ Beale AFB, California; operated by 17th RW RAF Alconbury; delivered as TR-1A |
| **none/U-2R** | 80-1078 | 078 | Assigned to 9th SRW @ Beale AFB, California; operated by 17th RW RAF Alconbury; delivered as TR-1A |
| **none/U-2R** | 80-1079 | 079 | Assigned to 9th SRW @ Beale AFB, California; operated by 17th RW RAF Alconbury; delivered as TR-1A |
| **none/U-2R** | 80-1080 | 080 | Assigned to 9th SRW @ Beale AFB, California; delivered as TR-1A |
| **none/U-2R** | 80-1081 | 081 | Assigned to 9th SRW @ Beale AFB, California; operated by 17th RW RAF Alconbury; delivered as TR-1A |
| **none/U-2R** | 80-1082 | 082 | Assigned to 9th SRW @ Beale AFB, California; delivered as TR-1A |
| **none/U-2R** | 80-1083 | 083 | Assigned to 9th SRW @ Beale AFB, California; by 17th RW RAF Alconbury; delivered as TR-1A |
| **none/U-2R** | 80-1084 | 084 | Assigned to 9th SRW @ Beale AFB, California; delivered as TR-1A |
| **none/U-2R** | 80-1085 | 085 | Assigned to 9th SRW @ Beale AFB, California; operated by 17th RW RAF Alconbury; delivered as TR-1A |
| **none/U-2R** | 80-1086 | 086 | Assigned to 9th SRW @ Beale AFB, California; operated by 17th RW RAF Alconbury; delivered as TR-1A |
| **none/U-2R** | 80-1087 | 087 | Assigned to 9th SRW @ Beale AFB, California; delivered as TR-1A |
| **none/U-2R** | 80-1088 | 088 | Assigned to 9th SRW @ Beale AFB, California; operated by 17th RW RAF Alconbury; delivered as TR-1A |
| **none/U-2R** | 80-1089 | 089 | Assigned to 9th SRW @ Beale AFB, California; delivered as TR-1A |
| **none/U-2R/U-2ER** | 80-1090 | 090 | Delivered as TR-1A and retained by Lockheed at Palmdale; now NASA N708NA |
| **none/U-2RT** | 80-1091 | 091 | Assigned to 9th SRW @ Beale AFB, California |
| **none/U-2R** | 80-1092 | 092 | Assigned to 9th SRW @ Beale AFB, California; operated by 7th RW RAF Alconbury; delivered as TR-1A |
| **none/U-2R** | 80-1093 | 093 | Assigned to 9th SRW @ Beale AFB, California; operated by 7th RW RAF Alconbury; delivered as TR-1A |
| **none/U-2R** | 80-1094 | 094 | Assigned to 9th SRW @ Beale AFB, California; operated by 7th RW RAF Alconbury; delivered as TR-1A |
| **none/U-2R** | 80-1095 | 095 | Assigned to 9th SRW @ Beale AFB, California |
| **none/U-2R** | 80-1096 | 096 | Assigned to 9th SRW @ Beale AFB, California |
| **none/ER-2** | 80-1097 | 097 | Assigned to NASA Ames Research Center, NAS Moffett Field, Californai as N709NA |
| **none/U-2R** | 80-1098 | 098 | Assigned to 9th SRW @ Beale AFB, California |
| **none/U-2R** | 80-1099 | 099 | Assigned to 9th SRW @ Beale AFB, California; operated by 17th RW RAF Alconbury; delivered as TR-1A |

**Note:** serial numbers assigned to U-2R program but not used include 68-10346 through 68-10353; miscellaneous registrations and serial numbers assigned to U-2Rs but not attributable to select aircraft include: N809X; 3925, etc.

**Model CL329 *JetStar* Specifications/Performance**
**Construction:** conventional aluminum
**Length:** 58 feet 10 inches
**Wingspan:** 53 feet 8 inches
**Wing Area:** 523 square feet
**Height:** 20 feet 6 inches
**Empty Weight:** 15,139 pounds
**Max. Gross Takeoff Weight:** 38,841 pounds
**Maximum Speed:** 613 mph @ 36,000 feet
**Operational Ceiling:** unknown
**Maximum Unrefueled Range:** 1,725 miles w/max. payload
**Fixed Armament:** none
**Powerplant Data:** 2 x 4,850 pound thrust Bristol *Orpheus* 1/5 axial flow turbojets or (second prototype only) 4 x 3,000 pound thrust Pratt & Whitney JT12A-6 axial flow turbojets
**Model CL329 *JetStar* Production/Disposition**

| Model/Designation: | Civil Reg. | Manu. # | Comment: |
|---|---|---|---|
| **CL329/*JetStar*** | N329J | 1001 | Flown only w/*Orpheus* engine; now serving as a maintenance trainer in Canada |
| **CL329/*JetStar*** | N329K | 1002 | Second prototype; only one of two prototypes to be equipped w/JT12A-6 engines, though first flown with *Orpheus* |

**A-12 Specifications/Performance**
**Construction:** titanium (Beta-120/Ti-13V-11Cr-3A1) monocoque w/some super-high-temperature plastics
**Length:** 102 feet 3 inches
**Wingspan:** 55 feet 7 inches
**Wing Area:** 1,795 square feet
**Height:** 18 feet 6 inches
**Landing Weight:** 52,000 pounds
**Max. Gross Takeoff Weight:** 117,000 pounds
**Maximum Speed:** Mach 3.2 above 75,000 feet
**Operational Ceiling:** unknown
**Maximum Unrefueled Range:** unknown
**Fixed Armament:** none
**Powerplant Data:** 2 x 17,000 pound thrust Pratt & Whitney J75 (approx. first five aircraft only during flight test) or—in production configuration—2 x 20,500 pound thrust (dry)/31,500 pound thrust (afterburner) Pratt & Whitney JT11D-20A (J58) high-bypass ratio turbojets (some later engines generated 34,000 pounds thrust)
**A-12 Production/Disposition**

| Mode/Designation: | Ser. # | Manu. # | Comment: |
|---|---|---|---|
| **none/A-12** | 60-6924 | 121 | Completed 322 flights/418:12 hours of flying time; displayed @ Palmdale in Blackbird Airpark |
| **none/A-12** | 60-6925 | 122 | Completed 122 flights/177:52 hours of flying time; delivered to test location on June 26, 1962; displayed aboard USS *Intrepid* museum, New York City |
| **none/A-12** | 60-6926 | 123 | Completed 79 flights/135:20 hours of flying time; delivered to test location during August 1962; written-off on May 24, 1963 near test location |
| **none/A-12** | 60-6927 | 124 | Completed 614 flights/1,076:25 hours of flying time; only trainer A-12; sometimes referred to as the *Titanium Goose*; stored at Lockheed's Palmdale Plant 10 but eventually to be displayed @ California Museum of Science, Los Angeles, California |
| **none/A-12** | 60-6928 | 125 | Completed 202 flights/334:55 hours of flying time; delivered to test location on December 17, 1962; written-off on January 5, 1967 near test location |
| **none/A-12** | 60-6929 | 126 | Completed 105 flights/169:15 hours of flying time; written-off on December 28, 1965 near test location |
| **none/A-12** | 60-2930 | 127 | Completed 258 flights/499:10 hours of flying time; displayed @ Space and Rocket Center Museum, Huntsville, Alabama |
| **none/A-12** | 60-2931 | 128 | Completed 232 flights/453 hours of flying time; displayed by Minnesota Air National Guard following delivery on October 27, 1991 |
| **none/A-12** | 60-6932 | 129 | Completed 268 flights/409:55 hours of flying time; written-off on June 5, 1968 near Philippine Islands |
| **none/A-12** | 60-6933 | 130 | Completed 217 flights/406:20 hours of flying time; displayed @ San Diego Aerospace Museum, San Diego, California |
| **none/A-12** | 60-6937 | 131 | Completed 177 flights/345:45 hours of flying time; first aircraft to Kadena; stored @ Lockheed's Palmdale Plant 42 |
| **none/A-12** | 60-6938 | 132 | Completed 197 flights/369:55 hours of flying time; displayed @ USS Alabama memorial, Mobile, Alabama |
| **none/A-12** | 60-6939 | 133 | Completed 10 flights/8:19 hours of flying time; written-off on July 9, 1964 near test location |
| **none/M-21** | 60-6940 | 134 | Completed 80 flights/123:55 hours of flying time; purpose built to M-21 configuration for D-21 carriage; displayed @ Museum of Flight, Seattle, Washington (D-21 recently made available for companion display) |
| **none/M-21** | 60-6941 | 135 | Completed 95 flights/152:46 hours of flying time; purpose built to M-21 configuration for D-21 carriage; written-off on July 30, 1966 over the Pacific Ocean |

**Note:** A batch of serial numbers spanning from 60-6924 to 60-6948 was assigned the A-12 program; 60-6942 through 60-6948 were not used.

**D-21/D-21B Specifications/Performance**
**Construction:** titanium (Beta-120/Ti-13V-11Cr-3A1) monocoque w/some super-high-temperature plastics
**General:** Titanium and composite construction
**Length:** 42 feet 10 inches
**Wingspan:** 19 feet 1/4 inch
**Wing Area:**
**Height:** 7 feet 1/4 inch
**Empty Weight:** ?
**Max. Gross Takeoff Weight:**11,000 pounds
**Maximum Speed:** Mach 3.35/ Mach 3.25 cruise at 80,000 to 95,000 feet
**Operational Ceiling:** 95,000 feet
**Maximum Unrefueled Range:** 3,000 n. miles
**Fixed Armament:** none
**Powerplant Data:** Marquardt RJ43-MA-11 ramjet rated @ 1,500 pounds thrust
**D-21/D-21B Production/Disposition**

| Model/Designation: | Manu. # | Comment: |
|---|---|---|
| **none/D-21** | 501 | After manufacture, modified to D-21B standard; accidentally dropped on September 28, 1967 from B-52H; no mission flown |
| **none/D-21** | 502 | After manufacture, modified to D-21B standard; stored at Davis-Monthan AFB, Arizona following D-21 program termination |
| **none/D-21** | 503 | Launched on March 5, 1966 from M-21 and flew a total distance of 150 nautical miles; Lockheed crew was Bill Park and Keith Beswick |
| **none/D-21** | 504 | Launched on July 30, 1966 from M-21; immediately collided with carrier aircraft ending M-21 program; Lockheed crew was Bill Park and Ray Torick |
| **none/D-21** | 505 | Launched on June 16, 1966 from M-21 and flew a distance of 1,550 nautical miles; Lockheed crew was Bill Park and Keith Beswick |
| **none/D-21** | 506 | Launched on April 27, 1966 from M-21 and flew a total distance of 1,120 nautical miles; Lockheed crew was Bill Park and Ray Torick |
| **none/D-21B** | 507 | Launched on November 6, 1967 from B-52H and flew a total distance of 134 nautical miles |
| **none/D-21B** | 508 | Launched on January 19, 1968 from B-52H and flew a total distance of 280 nautical miles |
| **none/D-21B** | 509 | Launched on December 2, 1967 from B-52H and flew a total distance of 1,430 nautical miles |
| **none/D-21B** | 510 | Stored at Davis-Monthan AFB, Arizona following D-21 program termination |
| **none/D-21B** | 511 | Launched on April 30, 1968 from B-52H and flew a total distance of 150 nautical miles |
| **none/D-21B** | 512 | Launched on June 16, 1968 from B-52H and flew a total distance of 2,850 nautical miles; hatch was recovered but no camera was carried |
| **none/D-21B** | 513 | Stored at Davis-Monthan AFB, Arizona following D-21 program termination |
| **none/D-21B** | 514 | Launched on July 1, 1968 from B-52H and flew a total distance of 80 nautical miles |
| **none/D-21B** | 515 | Launched on December 15, 1968 from B-52H and flew a total distance of 2,953 nautical miles; hatch recovered; fair photos |
| **none/D-21B** | 516 | Launched on August 28, 1968 from B-52H and flew a total distance of 78 nautical miles |
| **none/D-21B** | 517 | Launched on November 9, 1969 from B-52H and flew a total distance of ? nautical miles; this was the first operational mission; the hatch with camera was not recovered |
| **none/D-21B** | 518 | Launched on February 11, 1969 from B-52H and flew a total distance of 161 nautical miles |
| **none/D-21B** | 519 | Launched on May 10, 1969 from B-52H and flew a total distance of 2,972 nautical miles; hatch recovered; fair photos |
| **none/D-21B** | 520 | Launched on July 10, 1969 from B-52H and flew a total distance of 2937 nautical miles; hatch recovered; good photos |
| **none/D-21B** | 521 | Launched on February 20, 1970 from B-52H and flew a total distance of 2,969 nautical miles; hatch recovered; good photos |
| **none/D-21B** | 522 | Stored at Davis-Monthan AFB, Arizona following D-21 program termination |
| **none/D-21B** | 523 | Launched on December 16, 1970 from B-52H and flew a total distance of 2,448 nautical miles; second operational mission; hatch not recovered |
| **none/D-21B** | 524 | Stored at Davis-Monthan AFB, Arizona following D-21 program termination |
| **none/D-21B** | 525 | Stored at Davis-Monthan AFB, Arizona following D-21 program termination |
| **none/D-21B** | 526 | Launched on March 4, 1971 from B-52H and flew a total distance of 2,935 nautical miles; third operational mission; hatch not recovered |
| **none/D-21B** | 527 | Launched on March 20, 1971 from B-52H and flew a total distance of 2,935 nautical miles; fourth operational mission; hatch not recovered; last mission of D-21 program |
| **none/D-21B** | 528 | Stored at Davis-Monthan AFB, Arizona following D-21 program termination |
| **none/D-21B** | 529 | Stored at Davis-Monthan AFB, Arizona following D-21 program termination |
| **none/D-21B** | 530 | Stored at Davis-Monthan AFB, Arizona following D-21 program termination |

**none/D-21B** 531 Stored at Davis-Monthan AFB, Arizona following D-21 program termination

**none/D-21B** 532 Stored at Davis-Monthan AFB, Arizona following D-21 program termination

**none/D-21B** 533 Stored at Davis-Monthan AFB, Arizona following D-21 program termination

**none/D-21B** 534 Stored at Davis-Monthan AFB, Arizona following D-21 program termination

**none/D-21B** 535 Stored at Davis-Monthan AFB, Arizona following D-21 program termination

**none/D-21B** 536 Stored at Davis-Monthan AFB, Arizona following D-21 program termination

**none/D-21B** 537 Stored at Davis-Monthan AFB, Arizona following D-21 program termination

**none/D-21B** 538 Stored at Davis-Monthan AFB, Arizona following D-21 program termination

**YF-12A Specifications/Performance**
**Construction:** titanium (Beta-120/Ti-13V-11Cr-3A1) monocoque w/some super-high-temperature plastics
**Length:** 101 feet 8 inches
**Wingspan:** 55 feet 7 inches
**Wing Area:** 1,795 square feet
**Height:** 18 feet 6 inches
**Landing Weight:** 68,000 pounds
**Max. Gross Takeoff Weight:** 124,000 pounds
**Maximum Speed:** Mach 3.2 above 75,000 feet
**Operational Ceiling:** unknown
**Maximum Unrefueled Range:** unknown
**Fixed Armament:** 3 x Hughes GAR-9/AIM-47A air-to-air radar-guided missile (max. speed, Mach 4)
**Powerplant Data:** 2 x 20,500 pound thrust (dry)/31,500 pound thrust (afterburner) Pratt & Whitney JT11D-20A (J58) high-bypass-ratio turbojets

**YF-12 Production/Disposition**

| Model/Designation: | Ser. # | Manu. # | Comment: |
|---|---|---|---|
| **YF-12A** | 60-6934 | 1001 | 80.9 total hours logged; written-off on August 14, 1966; parts utilized to build SR-71C, 64-17981 |
| **YF-12A** | 60-6935 | 1002 | 534.7 total hours logged; displayed @ US Air Force Museum, Wright-Patterson AFB, Ohio |
| **YF-12A** | 60-6936 | 1003 | 439.8 total hours logged; written-off on June 24, 1971 |

**SR-71A/SR-71B/SR-71C Specifications/Performance**
**Construction:** titanium (Beta-120/Ti-13V-11Cr-3A1) monocoque
w/some super-high-temperature plastics
**Length:** 107 feet 5 inches
**Wingspan:** 55 feet 7 inches
**Wing Area:** 1,795 square feet
**Height:** 18 feet 6 inches
**Landing Weight:** 68,000 pounds
**Max. Gross Takeoff Weight:** 140,000 pounds
**Maximum Speed:** Mach 3.2 above 75,000 feet
**Operational Ceiling:** 85,000 feet
**Maximum Unrefueled Range:** 3,200 miles
**Fixed Armament:** none
**Powerplant Data:** 2 x 34,000 pound thrust Pratt & Whitney JT11D-20A (J58) high-bypass-ratio turbojets

**SR-71 Production/Disposition**

| Model/Designation: | AF Ser. # | Manu. # | Comment: |
|---|---|---|---|
| **none/SR-71A** | 64-17950 | 2001 | Primary Lockheed test aircraft; manufacture date was September of 1963; assembly was started on October 10, 1963; roll-out took place on August 25, 1964; first flight took place on December 23, 1964 w/Gilliland as pilot; written-off @ Edwards AFB, California on January 10, 1967 |
| **none/SR-71A** | 64-17951 | 2002 | Systems testbed flown primarily from Palmdale; manufcture date was January of 1965; assembly was started on December 6, 1963; roll-out took place on October 20, 1964; first flight took place on March 5, 1965 w/Gilliland/Zwayer as crew; loaned by Air Force to NASA and redesignated YF-12C; assigned fictitious serial number (60-6937) during NASA tenure; following last flight on December 22, 1978 and after removal from Air Force inventory, placed on permanent loan to the Pima County Air Museum near Tucson, Arizona; total time logged was 796.7 hours |
| **none/SR-71A** | 64-17952 | 2003 | Lockheed test aircraft; manufacture date was January of 1965; assembly was started on January 27, 1964; roll-out took place on December 8, 1964; first flight took place on March 24, 1965; written-off near Tucumcary, New Mexico on January 25, 1966; pilot Bill Weaver survived but the RSO Jim Zwayer did not |
| **none/SR-71A** | 64-17953 | 2004 | Manufacture date was April of 1965; assembly was started on March 4, 1964; roll-out took place on January 19, 1965; first flght took place on June 4, 1965 w/Weaver/Andre as crew; Lockheed and service test aircraft; written-off near Shoshone, California on December 18, 1969 |
| **none/SR-71A** | 64-17954 | 2005 | Manufacture date was May of 1965; assembly was started on April 8, 1964; roll-out took place on February 23, 1965; first flight took place on July 20, 1965 w/Weaver/Andre as crew; Lockheed and service test aircrfaft; written-off @ Edwards AFB, California on April 11, 1969 |
| **none/SR-71A** | 64-17955 | 2006 | Lockheed test aircraft operated from Site 2 @ Palmdale; manufacture date was June of 1965; assembly was started on May 13, 1964; roll-out took place on March 24, 1965; first flight took place on August 17, 1965 w/Weaver/Andre as crew; following last flight on January 24, 1985, placed on display at the Air Force Flight Test Center Museum at Edwards AFB, California; total time logged was 1,993.7 hours |
| **none/SR-71A STATIC TEST** | none | none | Assembly started on June 18, 1964; final assembly was initiated on December 10, 1964 |
| **none/SR-71B** | 64-17956 | 2007 | Manufacture date was September of 1965; assembly was started on June 18, 1964; roll-out took place on May 20, 1965; f irst flight took place on November 18, 1965 w/Gilliland/Belgau as crew; operational aircraft with the 9th SRW; now operational with NASA Dryden Flight Research Center at Edwards AFB, California as NASA 831; upon turn-over to NASA, had logged 3,760 hours flying time |
| **none/SR-71B** | 64-17957 | 2008 | Manufacture date was October of 1965; assembly was started on August 28, 1964; roll-out took place on June 21, 1965; first flight took place on December 18, 1965 w/Gilliland/Eastham as crew; operational aircraft with the 9th SRW; written-off as a result of an approach accident at Beale AFB, California on January 11, 1968 |
| **none/SR-71A** | 64-17958 | 2009 | Manufacture date was October of 1965; assembly was started on October 1, 1964; roll-out took place on July 22, 1965; first flight took place December 15, 1965 w/Weaver/Andre as crew; operational aircraft with the 9th SRW; following last flight on February 23, 1990 and removal from Air Force inventory, placed on permanent display at Robins AFB, Georgia; holder of official world's absolute speed record for class of 2,193.167 mph; total time logged was 2,288.9 hours |
| **none/SR-71A** | 64-17959 | 2010 | Lockheed test aircraft operated from Site 2 @ Palmdale; manufacture date was November of 1965; assembly was started on November 3, 1964; roll-out took place on August 19, 1965; first flight took place on December 20, 1974 w/Weaver/Andre as crew; following last flight on October 29, 1976 and removal from Air Force inventory, placed on permanent display at Air Force Armament Museum, Eglin AFB, Florida; only aircraft modified to "big tail"; made first flight in this configuration on December 3, 1975; total time logged was 866.1 hours |
| **none/SR-71A** | 64-17960 | 2011 | Manufacture date was December of 1965; assembly was started on December 8, 1964; roll-out took place on September 20, 1965; first flight took place on February 9, 1966 w/Weaver/Andre as crew; operational aircraft with the 9th SRW; following last flight on February 27, 1990 and removal from Air Force inventory, placed on permanent display at Castle AFB, California; total time logged was 2,669.6 hours |
| **none/SR-71A** | 64-17961 | 2012 | Manufacture date was February of 1966; assembly was started on January 13, 1965; roll-out took place on October 19, 1965; first flight took place on April 13, 1966 w/Weaver/Andre as crew; operational aircraft with the 9th SRW; following last flight on February 2, 1977 and removal from Air Force inventory, placed in storage for the Chicago Museum of Science and Industry at Beale AFB, California; total time logged was 1,601 hours |
| **none/SR-71A** | 64-17962 | 2013 | Manufacture date was February of 1966; assembly was started on February 15, 1965; roll-out took place on November 17, 1965; first flight took place on April 29, 1966 w/Weaver/Belgau as crew; operational aircraft with the 9th SRW; following last flight on February 14, 1990 placed in flyable storage at Lockheed's Air Force Plant 42, Site 2; total time logged was 2,835.9 hours |
| **none/SR-71A** | 64-17963 | 2014 | Manufcture date was April of 1966; assembly was started on March 16, 1965; roll-out took place on December 16, 1965; first flight took place on June 9, 1966 w/Weaver/Belgau as crew; operational aircraft with the 9th SRW; following last flight on October 28, 1976 and removal from Air Force inventory, placed on permanent display at Beale AFB, California; total time logged was 1,604.4 hours |
| **none/SR-71A** | 64-17964 | 2015 | Manufacture date was March of 1966; assembly was started on April 14, 1965; roll-out took place on January 19, 1966; first flight took place on May 11, 1966 w/Weaver/Belgau as crew; operational aircraft with the 9th SRW; following last flight on March 20, 1990 and removal from the Air Force inventory, placed on permanent display at Strategic Air Command Museum, Offutt AFB, Nebraska; total time logged was 3,373.1 hours |
| **none/SR-71A** | 64-17965 | 2016 | Manufacture date was April of 1966; assembly was started on Mary 13, 1965; roll-out took place on February 17, 1966; first flight took place on June 10, 1966 w/Weaver/Moeller as crew; operational aircraft with the 9th SRW; written-off over Lovelock, Nevada on October 25, 1967 |
| **none/SR-71A** | 64-17966 | 2017 | Manufacture date was April of 1966; assembly was started on June 14, 1965; roll-out took place on March 21, 1966; first flight took place on July 1, 1966 w/Gilliland/Belgau as crew; operational aircraft with the 9th SRW; written-off over Las Vegas, New Mexico on April 13, 1967 |
| **none/SR-71A** | 64-17967 | 2018 | Manufacture date was June of 1966; assembly was started on July 14, 1965; roll-out took place on April 18, 1966; first flight took place on Augst 3, 1966 w/Weaver/Andre as crew; operational aircraft with the 9th SRW; following last flight on February 14, 1990, placed in flyable storage at Lockheed's Air Force Plant 42, Site 2; total time logged was 2,636.8 hours |
| **none/SR-71A** | 64-17968 | 2019 | Manufacture date was August of 1966; assembly was started on August 12, 1965; roll-out took place on May 17, 1966; first flight took place on October 10, 1966 w/Weaver/Andre as crew; operational aircraft with the 9th SRW; following last flight on February 12, 1990, placed in flyable storage at Lockheed's Air Force Plant 42, Site 2; total time logged was 2,279 hours |
| **none/SR-71A** | 64-17969 | 2020 | Manufacture date was August of 1966; assembly was started on September 13, 1965; roll-out took place on June 16, 1966; first flight took place on October 18, 1966 w/Weaver/Belgau as crew; operational aircraft with the 9th SRW; written-off near Korat Royal Thai Air Force Base on May 10, 1970 |
| **none/SR-71A** | 64-17970 | 2021 | Manufacture date was September of 1966; assembly was started on October 12, 1965; roll-out took place on July 18, 1966; first flight took place on October 21, 1966 w/Weaver/Belgau as crew; operational aircraft with the 9th SRW; written-off near El Paso, Texas on June 17, 1970 |
| **none/SR-71A** | 64-17971 | 2022 | Manufacture date was September of 1966; assembly was started on November 10, 1965; roll-out took place on August 16, 1966; first flight took place on November 17, 1966 w/Weaver/Moeller as crew; operational aircraft with the 9th SRW; now operational with NASA Dryden Flight Research Center at Edwards AFB, California as NASA 832; upon turn-over to NASA, had logged 3,512.5 hours flying time |
| **none/SR-71A** | 64-17972 | 2023 | Lockheed test aircraft operated from Site 2 @ Palmdale; manufacture date was October of 1966; assembly was started on December 13, 1965; roll-out took place on September 15, 1966; first flight took place on December 12, 1966 w/Weaver/Belgau as crew; this aircraft was used to set various world speed and altitude records for class including New York to London; following last flight on March 6, 1990 and after removal from the Air Force inventory, placed In storage at Dulles International Airport for the Smithsonian Institution's National Air & Space Museum; total time logged was 2,801.1 hours |
| **none/SR-71A** | 64-17973 | 2024 | Manufacture date was December of 1966; assembly was started on January 14, 1966; roll-out took place on October 17, 1966; first flight took place on February 8, 1967 w/Weaver/Greenamyer as crew; operational aircraft with the 9th SRW; following last flight on July 21, 1987 and after removal from the Air Force inventory, placed on display at the *Blackbird* Airpark at Palmdale, California; total time logged was 1,729.9 hours |
| **none/SR-71A** | 64-17974 | 2025 | Lockheed test aircraft operated from Site 2 @ Palmdale; manufacture date was December of 1966; assembly was started on February 14, 1966; roll-out took place on November 14, 1966; first flight took place on February 16, 1967 w/Weaver/Belgau as crew; written-off on April 21, 1989 |
| **none/SR-71A** | 64-17975 | 2026 | Lockheed test aircraft operated from Site 2 @ Palmdale; manufacture date was February of 1967; assembly was started on March 15, 1966; roll-out took place on December 15, 1966; first flight took place on April 13, 1967 w/Greenamyer/Belgau as crew; following last flight on February 28, 1990 and after removal from the Air Force inventory, placed on display at March AFB, California; total time logged was 2,854 hours |
| **none/SR-71A** | 64-17976 | 2027 | Manufacture date was March of 1967; assembly was started on April 13, 1966; roll-out took place on January 18, 1967; first flight took place during May of 1967 w/Gillaland/Belgau as crew; operational aircraft with the 9th SRW; following last flight on March 27, 1990 and after removal from the Air Force inventory, placed on display at the US Air Force Museum, Wright-Patterson AFB, Ohio; flew first operational SR-71 mission; total time logged was 2,985.7 hours |
| **none/SR-71A** | 64-17977 | 2028 | Manufacture date was April of 1967; assembly was started on May 12, 1966; roll-out took place on February 16, 1967; first flight took place on June 6, 1967 w/Gilliland/Greenamyer as crew; operational aircraft with the 9th SRW; written-off at Beale AFB, California on October 10, 1968 |
| **none/SR-71A** | 64-17978 | 2029 | Manufacture date was May of 1967; assembly was started on June 13, 1966; roll-out took place on March 20, 1967; first flight took place on July 5, 1967 w/Weaver/Belgau as crew; operational aircraft with the 9th SRW; written-off at Kadena AB on July 20, 1972 |
| **none/SR-71A** | 64-17979 | 2030 | Manufacture date was June of 1967; assembly was started on July 13, 1966; roll-out took place on April 17, 1967; first flight took place on August 10, 1967 w/Greenamyer/Belgau as crew; operational aircraft with the 9th SRW; following last flight on March 6, 1990 and after removal from Air Force inventory, placed on display at Lackland AFB, Texas; total time logged was 3,321.7 hours |
| **none/SR-71A** | 64-17980 | 2031 | Manufacture date was July of 1967; assembly was started on August 11, 1966; roll-out took place on May 16, 1967; first flight took place on September 25, 1967 w/Gilliland/Belgau as crew; operational aircraft with the 9th SRW; now operational with NASA Dryden Flight Research Center at Edwards AFB, California as NASA 844; upon turn-over to NASA, had logged 2,255.6 hours flying time |
| **none/SR-71A/SR-71C** | 64-17981 | 2000 | Manufacture date was January of 1969; first flight took place on March 14, 1969 w/Gilliland/Belgau as crew; hybrid aircraft from salvaged parts of YF-12A, 60-6934 (rear half), and an SR-71A forward fuselage static test article; stored at Beale AFB for use as a spare parts aircraft during operational SR-71 program, but after removal from Air Force inventory, placed on display at Hill AFB, Utah; had logged 556.4 hours of flying time |

**Note:** Serial numbers for four additional SR-71As, 64-17982 through 64-17985 were canceled when no further orders for the aircraft were forthcoming.

***Have Blue* Specifications/Performance**
**Construction:** conventional aluminum w/some composites
**Length:** 47 feet 3 inches
**Wingspan:** 22 feet 6 inches
**Wing Area:** 386 square feet
**Height:** 7 feet 6-1/2 inches
**Empty Weight:** 8,950 pounds
**Max. Gross Takeoff Weight:** 12,500 pounds
**Maximum Speed:** Mach .8
**Operational Ceiling:** unknown
**Maximum Unrefueled Endurance:** 1.0 hour
**Fixed Armament:** none
**Powerplant Data:** 2 x 2.950 pound thrust General Electric J85-GE-4A axial-flow turbojets

***Have Blue* Production/Disposition**

| Model/Designation: | Manu. # | Comment: |
|---|---|---|
| **none/*Have Blue*** | 1001 | Written-off on May 4, 1978 @ test location; 36 flights completed |
| **none/*Have Blue*** | 1002 | Written-off on July 11, 1979 @ test location; 52 flights completed |

**F-117A Specifications/Performance**
**Construction:** conventional aluminum and titanium w/some composites
**Length:** 65 feet 11 inches
**Wingspan:** 43 feet 4 inches
**Wing Area:** 913 square feet
**Height:** 12 feet 5 inches
**Empty Weight:** 29,500 pounds
**Max. Gross Takeoff Weight:** 52,500 pounds
**Maximum Speed:** high subsonic
**Operational Ceiling:** classified
**Maximum Unrefueled Range:** classified
**Fixed Armament:** various free-falling and laser guided weapons
**Powerplant Data:** 2 x 10,800 pound thrust General Electric F404-GE-F1D2 low-bypass-ratio turbofans

**F-117A Production/Disposition**

| Model/Designation: | AF Ser. # | Manu. # | Comment: |
|---|---|---|---|
| **none/F-117A** | 780 | 780 | Full-scale development aircraft; displayed @ Nellis AFB, Nevada |
| **none/F-117A** | 781 | 781 | Full-scale development aircraft; displayed @ US Air Force Museum, Wright-Patterson AFB, Ohio following arrival on July 17, 1991 |
| **none/F-117A** | 782 | 782 | Full-scale development aircraft |
| **none/F-117A** | 783 | 783 | Full-scale development aircraft |
| **none/F-117A** | 784 | 784 | Full-scale development aircraft |
| **none/F-117A** | 785 | 785 | Written-off on April 20, 1982 prior to Air Force acceptance; first production aircraft |
| **none/F-117A** | 786 | 786 | |
| **none/F-117A** | 787 | 787 | |
| **none/F-117A** | 788 | 788 | |
| **none/F-117A** | 789 | 789 | |
| **none/F-117A** | 790 | 790 | |
| **none/F-117A** | 791 | 791 | |
| **none/F-117A** | 792 | 792 | Written-off on July 11, 1986 |
| **none/F-117A** | 793 | 793 | |

| | | | |
|---|---|---|---|
| none/F-117A | 794 | 794 | |
| none/F-117A | 795 | 795 | |
| none/F-117A | 796 | 796 | |
| none/F-117A | 797 | 797 | |
| none/F-117A | 798 | 798 | |
| none/F-117A | 799 | 799 | |
| none/F-117A | 800 | 800 | |
| none/F-117A | 801 | 801 | Written-off on August 4, 1992 |
| none/F-117A | 802 | 802 | |
| none/F-117A | 803 | 803 | |
| none/F-117A | 804 | 804 | |
| none/F-117A | 805 | 805 | |
| none/F-117A | 806 | 806 | |
| none/F-117A | 807 | 807 | |
| none/F-117A | 808 | 808 | |
| none/F-117A | 809 | 809 | |
| none/F-117A | 810 | 810 | |
| none/F-117A | 811 | 811 | |
| none/F-117A | 812 | 812 | |
| none/F-117A | 813 | 813 | |
| none/F-117A | 814 | 814 | |
| none/F-117A | 815 | 815 | Written-off on October 14, 1987 |
| none/F-117A | 816 | 816 | |
| none/F-117A | 817 | 817 | |
| none/F-117A | 818 | 818 | |
| none/F-117A | 819 | 819 | |
| none/F-117A | 820 | 820 | |
| none/F-117A | 821 | 821 | |
| none/F-117A | 822 | 822 | |
| none/F-117A | 823 | 823 | |
| none/F-117A | 824 | 824 | |
| none/F-117A | 825 | 825 | |
| none/F-117A | 826 | 826 | |
| none/F-117A | 827 | 827 | |
| none/F-117A | 828 | 828 | |
| none/F-117A | 829 | 829 | |
| none/F-117A | 830 | 830 | |
| none/F-117A | 831 | 831 | Flight test aircraft |
| none/F-117A | 832 | 832 | |
| none/F-117A | 833 | 833 | |
| none/F-117A | 834 | 834 | |
| none/F-117A | 835 | 835 | |
| none/F-117A | 836 | 836 | |
| none/F-117A | 837 | 837 | |
| none/F-117A | 838 | 838 | |
| none/F-117A | 839 | 839 | |
| none/F-117A | 840 | 840 | |
| none/F-117A | 841 | 841 | |
| none/F-117A | 842 | 842 | |
| noneF-117A | 843 | 843 | Last production aircraft; delivered July 12, 1990 |

**YF-22A Specifications/Performance**
**Construction:** conventional aluminum w/some composites
**Length:** 64 feet 2 inches
**Wingspan:** 43 feet 0 inches
**Wing Area:** est. 830 square feet
**Height:** 17 feet 8-3/4 inches
**Empty Weight:** est. 34,000 pounds
**Max. Gross Takeoff Weight:** est. 60,000 pounds
**Maximum Speed:** Mach 2.0+
**Operational Ceiling:** unknown
**Maximum Unrefueled Range:** unknown
**Fixed Armament:** 1 x short-range air-to-air missile (AIM-9); 1 x long-range air-to-air missile (AIM-120); etc.
**Powerplant Data:** #1 aircraft flown w/2 x 35,000 pound thrust class General Electric YF120-GE-100 afterburning turbofans; #2 aircraft flown w/2 x 35,000 pound thrust class Pratt & Whitney YF119-PW-100 afterburning turbofans

**YF-22A Production/Disposition**

| Model/Designation: | AF Ser. # | Manu. # | Comment: |
|---|---|---|---|
| Model 1132/YF-22A | none | 1001 | Civil registered N22YF; presently used as a static mock-up at Air Force Plant 6, Marietta, Georgia |
| Model 1132/YF-22A | 87-700 | 1002 | Civil registered N22YX; written-off @ Edwards AFB, California on April 25, 1992 |

**Appendix B: MISCELLANEOUS LOCKHEED AND *SKUNK WORKS* DESIGN STUDIES AND PROJECTS**

**P-80A with Ramjet Engines**—At the request of the Army Air Force during 1947, an investigation into the use of a P-80A as a testbed for the Marquardt Aircraft Company's subsonic ramjets was undertaken. As a result, an initial decision to modify a single P-80A, 44-85214, Manufacturer's No. 1237, to accommodate a single Marquardt ramjet of either 20 inch (XJ30-MA-1), 30 inch (XRJ31-MA-1), or possibly 48 inch diameter on each wing tip. As noted in Lockheed Report No. 6221 of September 5, 1947, this particular aircraft had been "previously outfitted for speed runs". Particular care had been given to surface smoothness and to the choice of a high-thrust Allison J33 turbojet engine. The aircraft was modified to incorporate a higher strength horizontal stabilizer, and higher strength vertical stabilizer, and a stronger aft fuselage in anticipation of higher dynamic loads. The design loads were 15,400 pounds for the horizontal stabilizer and 10,000 pounds for the vertical fin...which was in contrast to the standard P-80A's 7,750 pounds and 3,300 pounds, respectively. Externally, the modified aircraft differed from a stock P-80 only in having modified wing tips to accommodate the ramjet engines. Fuel for the 20 inch and 30 inch ramjet engines was contained in the two 44-gallon outboard leading edge tanks. The 48 inch ramjets were expected to require more fuel and thus had a self-contained 100-gallon tank in the intake spike. Fuel was non-leaded gasoline (Type AN-F-24 or AN-F-23A). Fuel was supplied by pumps to the 20 inch and 30 inch engines and by pressure bottle in the 48 inch engine. During the Lockheed tests, the average weight of the modified P-80A was 12,600 pounds with the 20 inch engines and 13,200 pounds with the 30 inch.

Modifications to the wing tips in order to accommodate the ramjet engines included replacing the standard tip tank support castings with welded steel fittings which were made to accommodate both the 20 inch engine which weighed 130 pounds and the 30 inch engine which weighed 335 pounds. Provision also was made for installation of a special fitting used to measure thrust and drag. The engines were not jettisonable. Two sets of fairings were manufactured, one for the 20 inch engines and one for the 30 inch.

In order to provide room for an observer in the space behind the pilot, a small rear sit installation was undertaken. Space was provided by installing a smaller fuselage fuel tank and partially eliminating the bulkhead directly behind the pilot. A safety belt, oxygen system, intercom unit, and other necessary items were provided. A fuel tank in the nose peculiar to this aircraft also was removed and replaced by ramjet engine fuel pumps and test equipment. The radio also was repositioned.

Other features of note included warnings the engine would not ignite above 20,000 feet...but if they were ignited below that altitude, they would continue to function to much higher altitudes; that the ramjets would blow out at approximately 12° of yaw or pitch; and that the fuel/air ratio was adjustable on the ground with automatic compensation for altitude and speed.

The following projections for each engine type also were made:

48 inch ramjet—A level flight Mach number of .865 can be attained at 20,000 feet. However, to stay within the P-80A's performance limits, the dive flaps must be lowered and the engine must be throttle back. Rates of climb as high as 28,400 feet per minute can be attained at sea level with a flight Mach number of .75 (570 mph at sea level). This represents a climb angle of 34.5°. Depending on the altitude and the type of flight, sufficient fuel is available to "fire" these ramjets from 1 to 3 minutes. The time to accelerate from a "cold" to a "hot" ramjet high speed is approximately 45 seconds. This consumes from 120 gallons of fuel at sea level to 67 gallons of fuel at 20,000 feet. The distance to takeoff and climb to 50 feet with these ramjets will be as high as 5,800 feet with the normal loading of 13,800 pounds. Extreme difficulty will be experienced in controlling the aircraft in both the initial firing and in a flame-out. Since the thrust coefficient is relatively independent of altitude and Mach number, the equilibrium angle of sideslip for an asymmetric thrust condition is also independent of altitude and Mach number. This angle corresponds to approximately 15.5°. However, the overswing angle is sufficiently great to stall and fail the vertical tail. To provide protection against the dynamic overswing angle, a design proposal has already been made to have automatic shut-off of the live ramjet for the flameout condition. For the firing condition, separate firing switches are proposed with *initial* rudder being held to reduce the angle of sideslip. Further, a reduction of rudder angle to improve the pilot's mechanical advantage in making this maneuver is proposed.

30 inch ramjet—A level flight Mach number of .83 is attainable. By using zero thrust on the J33 turbojet or by using dive flaps the speed can be kept under Mach .8. The maximum rate of climb is only 12,400 feet per minute in contrast to 28,400 feet per minute of the 48 inch ramjets. Fuel also is available for 1 to 3 minutes of flight with about 45 seconds required to accelerate from the "cold" to "hot" level flight speed. Control on flameout or on firing should be obtained without the use of rudder as time sequence may increase the total tail load. After equilibrium sideslip angle of approximately 8° has been reached, the airplane is brought to zero sideslip by a slow application of the rudder. Flight with the 30 inch ramjets will be satisfactory providing flutter considerations are satisfactory.

20 inch ramjet—Level flight speed will not exceed Mach 0.8 with the J33 turbojet at rated rpm (11,000). Flight endurance is expected to be from 2 to 4 minutes with 60 seconds required to accelerate from "cold" to "hot" ramjet speed. Control and aircraft strength should be highly satisfactory for both firing and flameout.

Concerns over high speed flutter, particularly as might be confronted with the use of the more powerful 48 inch ramjets eventually led to studies calling for attaching the large engines to clipped wings (thus increasing wing torsional stiffness)) or mounting a single engine dorsally, behind the cockpit on the aircraft centerline. Clipping the wings also called for elimination of the ailerons. This could be offset by using differential flap actuation, but tunnel testing would have been required. Additionally, clipping the wings would have led to a 40% increase in takeoff distance.

Carrying the engine dorsally would have required a stainless steel vertical fin. Major difficulties were expected with longitudinal trim, directional stability, and pilot emergency egress. In any event, flight testing of the 48 inch engines was never undertaken.

As of April 16, 1948, some 14 hours of flying time during 28 flights had been accomplished testing the 20 inch engines and 4.6 hours during 10 flights had been accomplished testing the 30 inch engines. During these tests, airflow, fuel flow, and thrust versus Mach number relationships were determined. At 0.68 Mach number and 10,000 feet altitude the 20 inch engines produced 480 pounds thrust each and the 30 inch engines produced 1,160 pounds thrust each. During the tests, the 20 inch units were flown up to 0.78 Mach and as high as 31,000 feet.

Operation was smooth except at lean mixtures and intermediate speeds. Starting was a problem throughout the test program, though spark plug ignition (versus ignition via flares) proved the most dependable. The 30 inch engines proved more difficult to start than the 20 inch. Starting speeds were limited to 150 to 160 knots...or below 0.3 Mach. Richer mixtures were required for the 30 inch engines than for the 20 inch. The 30 inch engines, by April 16, 1948, had been to 20,000 feet and 0.75 Mach. To that date, all flying had been accomplished by Lockheed test pilots.

The first flight of the program, without ramjet engines installed, took place on November 21, 1947 with Tony LeVier as pilot. On the second flight, taking place three days later, LeVier was joined by Ernie Joiner in the observer's seat. The first flight with the 20 inch engines installed, the third of the program, took place on November 25. No attempt was made to ignite the engines. On December 3, 1947, LeVier, with Joiner in the back seat, flew the aircraft for the first time with both 20 inch engines operating. Ignition took place at 10,000 feet. The final 20 inch engine flight took place on March 22, 1948 with Roy Wimmer as pilot and Glen Fulkerson as observer. On April 1, 1948, the first 30 inch engine flight was conducted with Herman Salmon as pilot (there was no observer). There was no attempt to ignite the engines. On the second flight with the 30 inch engines, they were ignited for the first time at 10,000 feet. Speed achieved with the engines running was 0.45 Mach.

On the 49th flight of the ramjet engine program, the P-80A was reengined. The original J33-A-9 was replaced by a J33-A-21 which offered more thrust for takeoff and acceleration. A water-alcohol injection system also was installed.

A second aircraft was converted for additional Marquardt flight test work. The program continued into late 1948 at which time sufficient data had been gathered on the 20 inch and 30 inch ramjet engines to merit an accurate assessment of their applicability to forthcoming propulsion requirements.

Miller collection

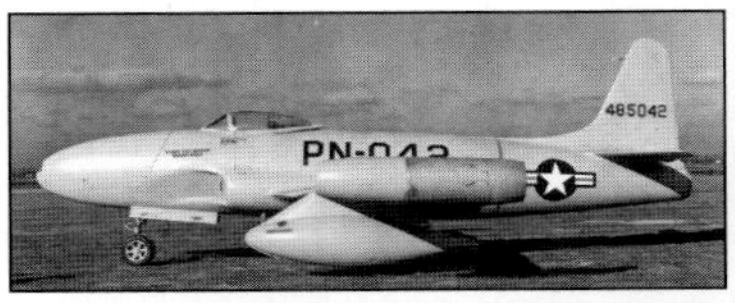


Miller collection

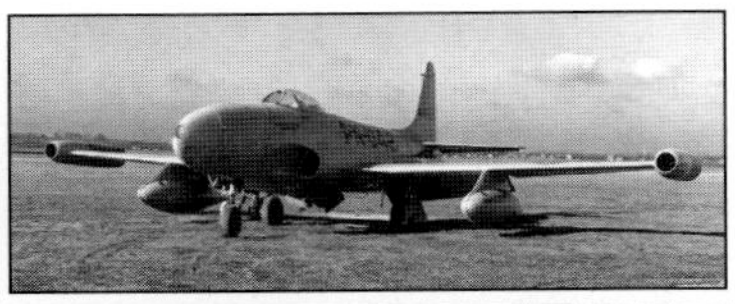

Miller collection

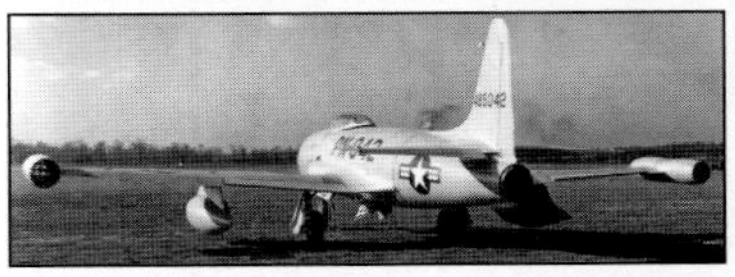

Lockheed

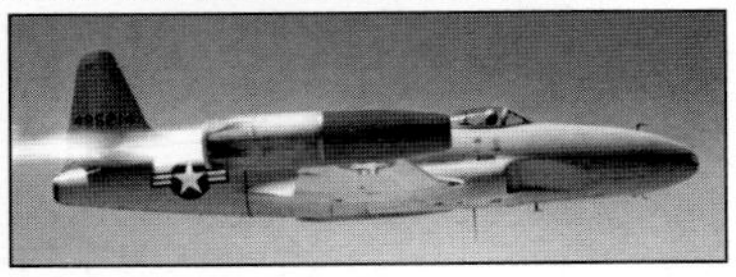

Lockheed

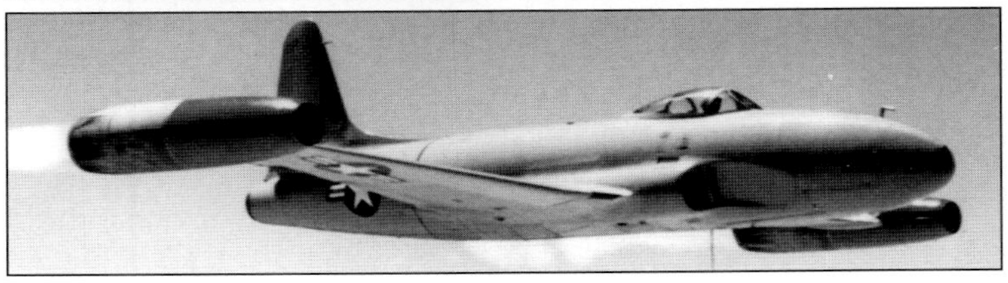

*Two P-80As were modified to serve as Marquardt ramjet engine testbeds. The first three photos depict 44-85042; the last two depict 44-85214.*

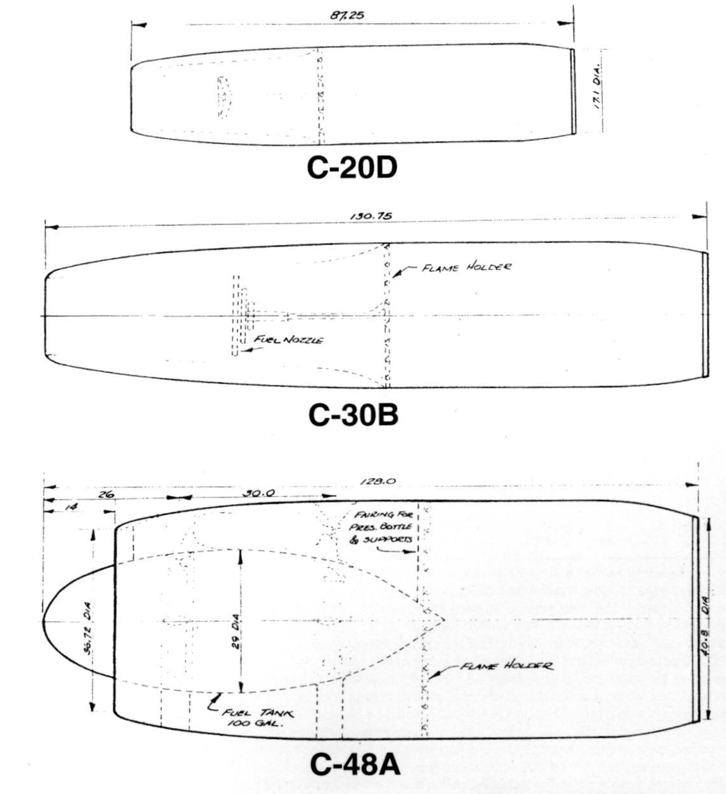


**Marquardt Ramjet Engines For P-80A**

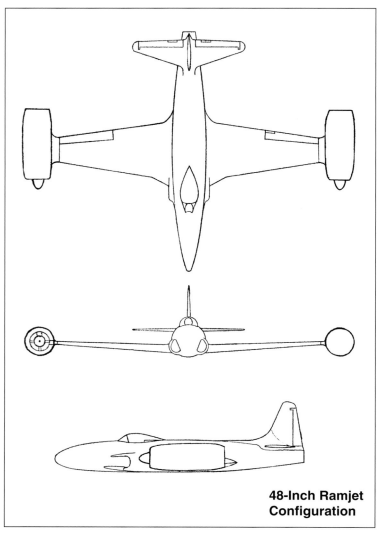

**48-Inch Ramjet Configuration**

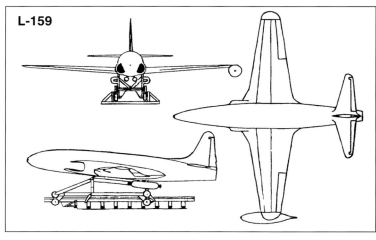

L-159

**L-168**---Perturbations of the basic *Constitution* airframe were studied with considerable intensity by Lockheed during the immediate post-World War Two period. Among these was the L-168-5 which was optimized to carry a large cargo pod under its immense fuselage. The versatility of the pod provided many mission options, but interest proved non-existent during a time when surplus military transports were available at minimal cost. The L-168 utilized many *Constitution* components, including its outer wing panels, its upper fuselage, and its horizontal and vertical tail surfaces. Powerplant options also were similar to those offered on the *Constitution*.

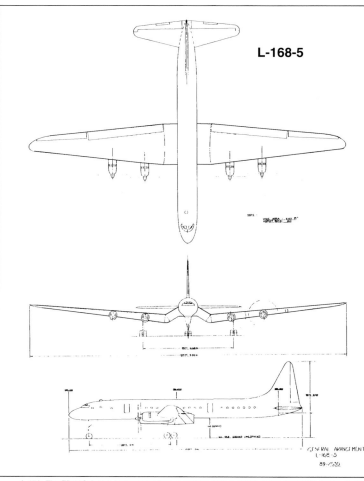

L-168-5

**L-153**—Numerous paper studies preceded the actual design, development, and construction of the XF-90—or L-153. Among the earliest were the L-153-1, the L-153-2, and the L-153-3. These P-80 perturbations differed as follows: -1—flush intakes and a thinner wing section; -2—same as the -1 but with a swept wing; and -3—a major revision of the basic design including a new engine and modest wing sweep. Some aspects of these designs eventually reached the hardware stage, including the flush intake—which was tested on the original XP-80R. Though found somewhat wanting, it remained an item of contention on many forthcoming L-153 configuration studies. Another L-153 technological concern became the design of the engine tail pipe...or "augmentor tailpipe". This was to provide a suction source for boundary layer control near the intakes and at the same time provide cooling air for the engine compartment; to provide a tailpipe that had no engine mechanical connection...thus eliminating heat-created expansion problems and an associated requirement for expandable, sealed interfaces; to form a plenum around the engine which would serve to control fires by diverting them down the exhaust tunnel and out the exhaust pipe nozzle area; and to provide cooling air for the exhaust pipe in order to keep pipe temperatures within safe limits. An augmentor of this type later was successfully demonstrated on the second XP-80A. The -2 and -3 L-153 studies proved short-lived primarily because of the lack of confidence in swept wings to bring about a significant performance improvement. Accordingly, all three of these early L-153 studies were set aside for the many to follow.

L-153-1, -2, -3 comparison:

|  | L-153-1 | L-153-2 | L-153-3 |
|---|---|---|---|
| Length | 35 feet 0 inches | 35 feet 0 inches | 39 feet 0 inches |
| Wingspan | 40 feet 0 inches | 40 feet 0 inches | 40 feet 0 inches |
| Height | 11 feet 11 inches | 11 feet 11 inches | 12 feet 0 inches |
| Wing area | 280 square feet | 280 square feet | 280 square feet |

L-153-1

L-153-2

L-153-3

**L-170**--The TP-80C (which became the T-33A) evolved from a series of two-seat P-80 design studies under the company designator of L-170. Several different versions were proposed, these differing primarily in type and number of powerplants. The L-170-3, for instance, had two Westinghouse X-19XB-3 engines and the L-170-2 and heavier L-170-4 were powered by a single Allison J33C-5 engine. Performance using the Allison engine eventually convinced Lockheed engineers it was the better choice.

**L-159**—Initiated during 1946 as an attempt to explore the P-80's potential as a long-range, high-speed, guided missile carrying a powerful high-explosive warhead. It was to have been used against both strategic and tactical targets. The performance of the missile was expected to make it extremely difficult to intercept. Major changes from the standard P-80 included removal of the cockpit and all associated accouterments, removal of the landing gear, an increase in internal fuel capacity to 830 gallons (1,160 gallons with tip tanks), and the addition of a 2,000 pound warhead in the nose bay area just above the original gun bay. The gun bay, in turn, would be converted to the radio control equipment bay. Aft of the radio control equipment bay was to be the hydraulic control actuator bay which was interfaced with the original control stick and rudder pedal assemblies. Single instead of dual controls would be utilized and all trim tabs would be deleted. For short range missions, the fuselage fuel tank could be reduced in size to accommodate a larger warhead. Range with the 2,000 pound warhead was projected to be approximately 3,000 miles at a cruising speed of 520 mph. With water injection, cruising speeds over short ranges were expected to be 600 mph at sea level. Launching was to be via a statically positioned surface-based 300-foot-long launch rail and associated carriage unit or from a modified transport aircraft (among the latter, it was projected to use the Lockheed R6O-1 *Constitution* with a single L-159 suspended from wing pylons attached to each outer wing panel). Remote control would be from a ground station, a ship, or the carrier aircraft. The advent of more advanced systems and an historical dislike of remotely piloted aircraft eventually killed any further development of the L-159.

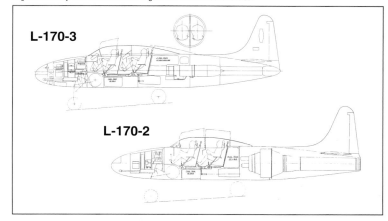

L-170-3

L-170-2

**L-171**--The predecessor design study leading up to the X-7. Information pertaining to this program is outlined in Chapter 4 under the X-7 section. The following drawings and photo illustrate just a few of the L-171 configurations explored by Lockheed:

L-171B Wind Tunnel Model

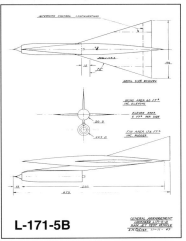

**L-171-5B**

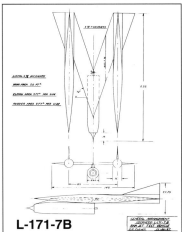

**L-171-7B**

**L-181**—Proposed low-cost (minimal change) follow-ons to the P-80C included the L-181-1...which was allocated the formal Air Force P-80E designation and the L-181-2...which was allocated the formal Air Force P-80D designation. Both were expected to benefit from the improvement in performance noted in the TF-80C (T-33) as a result of its better fineness ratio (fuselage cross sectional area to fuselage length). Studies were initiated during 1948. The P-80D utilized the TF-80C fuselage redesigned to accommodate an afterburner-equipped engine and a single-seat cockpit. The P-80E utilized the fuselage and related cockpit and propulsion changes and coupled them to a new, swept wing and a swept horizontal stabilizer. Both aircraft, though viable, were not pursued as there were many more advanced configurations already under development.

Specification and Performance comparisons were as follows:

| | P-80C | P-80D | P-80E |
|---|---|---|---|
| Length | 34 feet 6 inches | 38 feet 10.3 inches | 38 feet 10.3 inches |
| Wingspan | 39 feet 0 inches | 38 feet 10.5 inches | 37 feet 0 inches |
| Wing area | 237.6 square feet | 237.6 square feet | 248.0 square feet |
| Max. speed at sea level (knots) | 508 | 537 | 575 |
| Max. speed at 35,000 feet (knots) | 456 | 484 | 519 |
| Speed at maximum continuous power at sea level (knots) | 425 | 481 | 487 |
| Rate of climb at sea level with afterburner (feet/minute) | 6,650 | 15,400 | 15,200 |
| Rate of climb at sea level with maximum continuos power (feet/minute) | 3,150 | 3,820 | 3,720 |
| Service ceiling with maximum continuous power (feet) | 40,200 | 41,200 | 37,800 |
| Combat ceiling with maximum continuous power (feet) | 44,500 | 50,400 | 51,800 |
| Time-to-climb from sea level to 35,000 feet (minutes) | 12.1 | 3.6 | 3.5 |
| Clean performance takeoff weight (pounds) | 12,400 | 13,122 | 13,500 |
| Tip tank performance takeoff weight (pounds) | 15,336 | 16,722 | 17,100 |

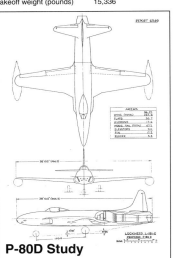

**P-80D Study**

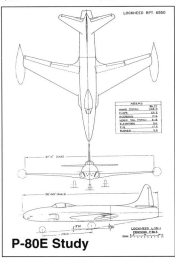

**P-80E Study**

| | | | |
|---|---|---|---|
| Stalling speed in "dirty" configuration, no power (knots) | 106 | 111 | 113 |
| Powerplant "dash" number (J33-) | -A-23 | -A-27 | -A-27 |
| Combat radius (nautical miles) | 543 | 710 | 590 |
| Combat range (nautical miles) | 1,260 | 1,744 | 1,530 |

**L-204**—By the time F-94C contractor trials had been completed and the flight test program was assimilated by the Air Force, the *Skunk Works*, as it existed at that time, had become involved in a totally different aircraft program. Concurrently, Hall Hibbard and "Kelly" Johnson had elected to carry the basic F-94—and by default, the original P-80 configuration—to its ultimate level of development. The resulting L-204 variants, though stillborn, are worthy of mention. These studies, initiated during July of 1950, and assigned temporary design designations from L-204-1 to L-204-3, were conducted by Willis Hawkins with the intent of improving the aircraft's performance (specifically top speed and range). The resulting designs were all single-seat configurations with the normal back seat position replaced with a 143.5 gallon saddle tank. All three configurations were equipped only with air-to-air rocket armament, an E-5 fire control system, and Pratt & Whitney's 8,750 lb. thrust J48-P-5 engine.

The L-204-2 was to be equipped with a new 6% thickness/chord ratio wing similar in planform to its predecessors, while the L-204-3 was to have a 6% thickness/chord ratio wing with a low-aspect ratio and high taper ratio. Even more interesting was the L-204-1 which was to be equipped with a variable-geometry wing having a 0°- to 55° sweep capability. At each pivot point the sweep angle was to be controlled by a hydraulically-operated screw drive. Two horizontal tail configurations were proposed. In one, the single-piece horizontal tail was to be mounted at the extreme end of the empennage above the exhaust; in the other, the horizontal tail was to be rigidly attached to the vertical tail, which in turn was hinged and hydraulically moved around a hinge point—thus changing the horizontal tail incidence.

Principle characteristics and calculated performance are as follows:

| | L-204-1 | L-204-1 | L-204-1 | L-204-2 | L-204-3 |
|---|---|---|---|---|---|
| Wing Sweep | 0° | 35° | 55° | n.a. | n.a. |
| Length (feet/inches) | n.a. | n.a. | n.a. | 42.7 | 42.5 |
| Span (feet/inches) | 37.6 | 30.9 | 25.3 | 37.3 | 31.0 |
| Wing area (square feet) | 233 | 254 | 271 | 392 | 275 |
| Zero fuel weight (pounds) | 14,573 | n.a. | n.a. | 13,316 | 12,305 |
| Combat weight (pounds) | 18,330 | 18,380 | 18,750 | 18,390 | 16,190 |
| Max. Takeoff weight (pounds) | 22,186 | n.a. | n.a. | 24,098 | 20,345 |
| Internal fuel (gallons) | 665 | 665 | 665 | 812 | 730 |
| External fuel (gallons) | 460 | n.a. | n.a. | 750 | 460 |
| Vmax at sea level (mph) | 654 | 739 | 765 | 704 | 706 |
| Combat climb rate (feet/minute) | 3,500 | 3,800 | 6,200 | 4,100 | 4,150 |
| Combat ceiling (feet) | 50,000 | 48,800 | 44,500 | 49,500 | 49,000 |
| Combat radius (miles) | 575 | 560 | 455 | 760 | 540 |

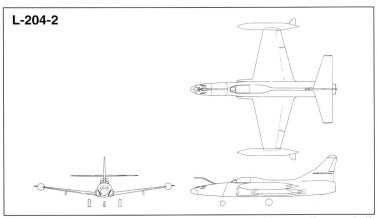

**L-204-2**

**L-206**--In effect an evolutionary development of the L-168, the L-206--with its removable cargo pod-- differed in being somewhat smaller and powered by turboprop rather than reciprocating engines. Perhaps most interesting is the fact the L-206 and the several perturbations of its basic design eventually gave birth to the most successful Lockheed transport of all...the C-130 *Hercules*. This lineage is most noticeable in the wing design and the use of Allison turboprop engines. Eventually, design complexity and compromised performance and payload cooled Air Force interest in the L-206.

The following table provides a performance comparison of alternate L-206 medium cargo transport designs:

| | L-206-1 | L-206-2 | L-206-3 | Air Force Requirement |
|---|---|---|---|---|
| Wing area (square feet) | 1,744.6 | 1,206 | 1,744.6 | |
| Takeoff weight (pounds) | 109,500 | 99,500 | 120,000 | |
| Equipment included (pounds) | 6,218 | 1,516 | 1,518 | 6,216 |
| Max. fuel required (pounds) | 28,000 | 27,500 | 29,660 | |
| Takeoff distance over over 50 foot obstacle (feet) | 2,435 | 2,910 | 3,060 | 3,000 |
| Landing distance over 50 foot obstacle (feet) | 2,425 | 3,120 | 2,660 | |
| Average cruise speed; typical mission (knots) | | 313 | 323 | 305 |
| Max. cruise speed (knots/altitude) | 319/29,000 | 330/26,000 | 307/22,500 | |
| Rate of climb--sea level takeoff weight (feet/minute) 4 engines | 2,175 | 2,400 | 1,890 | 1,500 |
| 3 engines | 1,400 | 1,500 | 1,175 | 500 |
| Service ceiling (feet) 3 engines | 28,400 | 26,800 | 24,500 | 16,000 |
| Range w/20,000 pound payload (nautical miles) | 2,270 | 2,200 | 2,050 | 2,200 |
| Load at above range w/full equipment (pounds) | 20,000 | 15,300 | 15,300 | 20,000 |

**Airfoil section data:**
Wing--NACA 64A318 root/incidence of 3 degrees
    NACA 64A412 tip/incidence of 0 degrees
    M.A.C. = 164.5 leading edge at F.S. 487.39
    Horizontal stabilizer: NACA 64A015
    Vertical stabilizer: NACA 64A015
**Total surface areas and control surface angular movements:**
Wing area--1,744.6 sq. feet (aspect ratio 10.09)
Aileron area (2)--110 sq. feet (plus 15 degrees/minus 25 degrees)
Aileron tab area (2)--8 sq. feet (plus 20 degrees/minus 20 degrees)
Flap area (4)--345 sq. feet (plus 35 degrees)
Horizontal tail--415 sq. feet (plus 3 degrees/minus 12 degrees incidence)
Elevator (2)--97.0 sq. feet (plus 15 degrees/minus 30 degrees)
Elevator tab (2)--4.4 sq. feet (1 per degree of stab. incidence change)
Vertical tail--300 sq. feet
Rudder--75 sq. feet (30 degrees left/30 degrees right)
Rudder tab--50 sq. feet (25 degrees left/25 degrees right)
**Weight data:**
Equipped weight empty (minus pod)--58,620 pounds
Weight of pod--11,720 pounds
Design useful load--49,660 pounds
Design gross weight--120,000 pounds
Engines: 4 x Allison T38 turboprops; single unit of XT40-A-8/Allison Model 501-02; propeller--Hamilton Standard 3-blade (16 foot diameter), blade no. 2H17Q3-14/hub 23260

# L-206

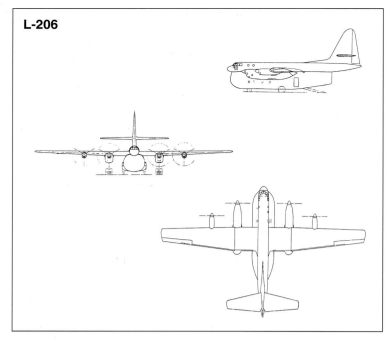

**F-90 Delta:** There were a large number of studies conducted prior to a definitive decision concerning the final configuration of the XF-90. Perhaps the design given most serious consideration was that of the tailed delta...which "Kelly " Johnson, Willia Hawkins, and Hall Hibbard all found very appealing. Johnson, however, in the end opted for a more conventional design and the delta configuration was removed from contention.

# F-90 Delta

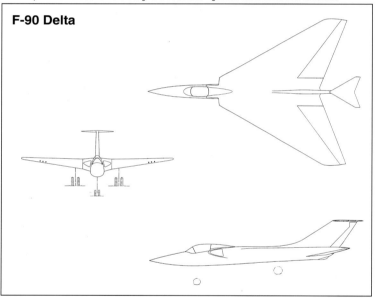

**F-90A:** One of the many production F-90 configurations studied by Lockheed. Most noticeably, this aircraft would have featured a pronounced--and somewhat unorthodox for its day--ventral intake. Noteworthy is the pinwheel pattern to the missile ports in the nose.

# F-90A Study

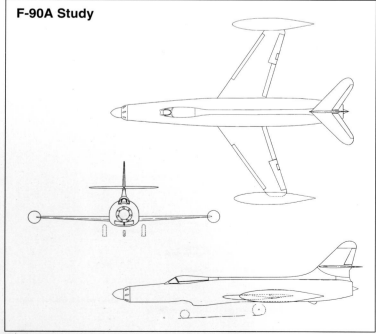

**CL-288 and CL-320**--The CL-288 and CL-320 represent just two examples of a large family of late 1960s studies conducted by Lockheed's *Skunk Work's* calling for intermediate and long-range, high-speed interception capability. Transitional design characteristics between the F-104 and the A-12 are readily discernible.

## CL-288-1

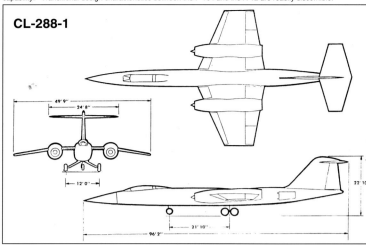

## CL-320

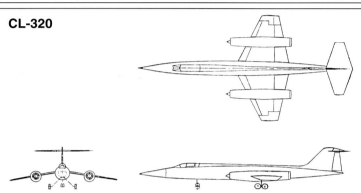

**Airborne Astronomical Laboratory**--One of a family of studies for the NASA calling for an aircraft capable of long range, high-altitude cruising. These designs varied in having different numbers and types of engine. The version illustrated was equipped with no less than ten turbofan engines. Mission was to serve as a reserch vehicle carrying optical and electromagentic spectrum sensors for astronomical research.

## Airborne Astronomical Laboratory

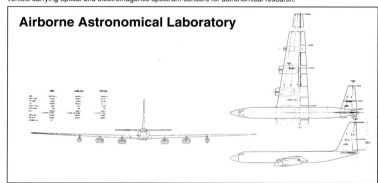

**AMSA Studies**--The Advanced Manned Strategic Aircraft (AMSA) studies beginning during 1965 eventually led to the Rockwell International B-1. Two of Lockheed's losing studies, developed by the *Skunk Works*, are illustrated.

## AMSA-1968

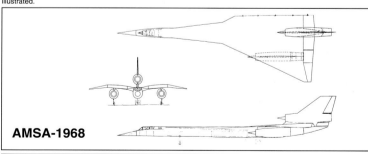

## AMSA-1969

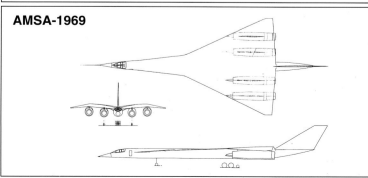

**L-1400**--The Air Force issued requests for proposals to fill a need for a new attack aircraft during 1967. Lockheed responded with the L-1400 series. Republic's A-10 and Norfthrop's A-9 were picked for prototyping during 1970. Republic's A-10 eventually was picked the winner.

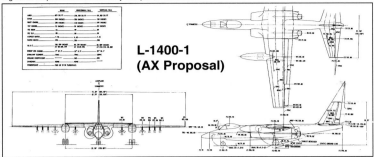

### L-1400-1 (AX Proposal)

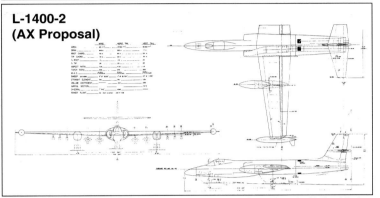

### L-1400-2 (AX Proposal)

**CL-1980**--After losing the Air Force Lightweight Fighter Program to General Dynamics (F-16) and Northrop (F-17), Lockheed undertook to design a lightweight fighter for the Navy. The first attempt, illustrated in Chapter 12, was the CL-1400N powered by a single Pratt & Whitney 401. Through an evolutionary design process, the CL-1980 followed during 1973, this being an effort coupling the talents of Ben Rich, Henry Combs, and "Kelly" Johnson. The aircraft had many novel features, not the least of which were flyable chines, gun installation in the left chine to provide more armament capability, minimal parts usage, and the same planform and basic aerodynamics embodied in the successful A-12/SR-71 family. Both single-seat and two-seat versions were proposed. Maximum speed was estimated to be Mach 2 at 58,000 feet. Armament consisted of 2 x AIM-9s and a gun. Navy interest in the program, though initially strong, eventually proved insufficient to merit a prototype or production contract.. Ongoing development and production of the Grumman F-14 also proved difficult to overcome.

CL-1980 (Air Force)

### CL-1980 (Navy)

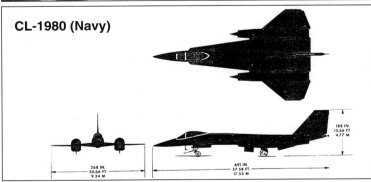

**915-Series**--Preceding the CL-1980 and setting precedent for its design was a lengthy series of design studies under the "915" designator. The configurations, as depicted in the various three-view drawings that follow, covered a wide range of design options from the convention to the unorthodox. Virtually all of these were configured to meet the somewhat ill-defined parameters that had been established for the forthcoming lightweight fighter. Accordingly, they were all small, highly maneuverable aircraft optimized for maneuverability, ease of maintenance, and a top speed of from Mach 1.4 to Mach 2.0. Maximum gross takeoff weights were limited to approximately fifteen tons...though some of these designs were obviously considerably lighter. In the end, "Kelly" Johnson and his design team settled on the CL-1200 series and pursued that to no avail.

### CL-915

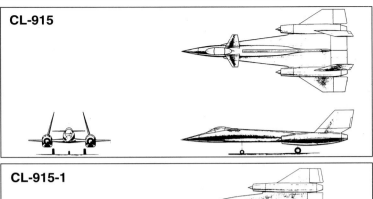

### CL-915-1

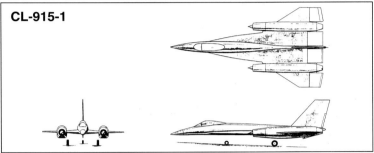

### CL-915-2

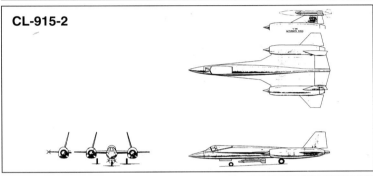

### CL-915-3

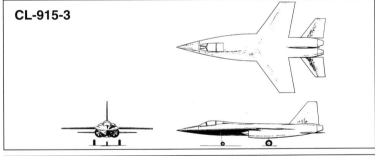

### CL-915-4

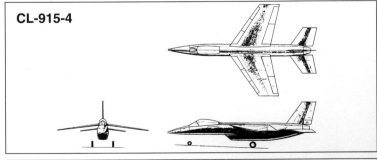

### CL-915-5

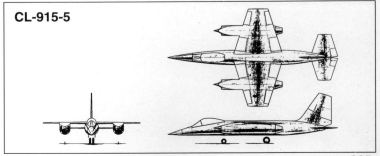

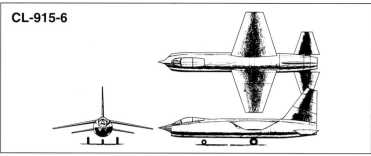

**CL-915-6**

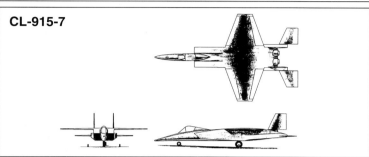

**CL-915-7**

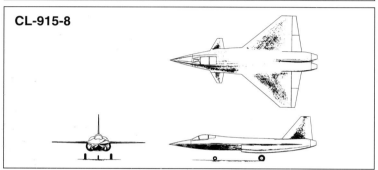

**CL-915-8**

**AEW P-3--**The *Skunk Works* has completed work on a P-3 *Orion* airborne early warning aircraft to be used by the US Customs Service for air operations against drug smugglers along the southern borders on the US. The fourth of its kind produced by Lockheed, the aircraft was delivered to the USCS on May 12 at Lockheed's Palmdale Plant 10 following its first flight on May 11 bound for the USCS Southern Surveillance Center at NAS Corpus Christi, Texas.

With the addition of this P-3 AEW, the USCS now will operate a fleet of eight *Orions*—four in early warning configuration with the rotating dome antenna, and four others outfitted with special surveillance equipment but without the dome.

All four of the P-3 AEW aircraft were created from P-3B *Orions* through modifications performed by Lockheed in California . The initial two modifications were accomplished by LASC in Burbank before corporate restructuring consolidated that Lockheed division in Marietta, Georgia. Rather than relocate work on this program out of state, the *Skunk Works* completed the current commitment under contract to LASC, delivering the third P-3 AEW from Burbank during July of 1992 and finishing with the May 1993 delivery of the fourth aircraft, which was modified wholly in Palmdale.

Along with the addition of a 24 -foot dome antenna mounted atop the *Orion's* fuselage, the aircraft interior was essentially remanufactured for its unique Customs Service mission. Naval acoustical systems were removed, flight controls refurbished, and new avionics, sensors, and communications equipment installed.

Lockheed P-3 AEW aircraft give the Customs Service an unprecedented capability to monitor illegal airborne smuggling activities over the Caribbean Sea, Gulf of Mexico, and other air routes into the country.

With each sweep of its antenna, the P-3 AEW's APS-138 surveillance radar can survey 196,000 square miles of airspace from sea level to 100,000 feet. An operator can monitor up to 2,000 potential targets at once with the help of an enhanced AN/AYK-14 central computer and Lockheed Sanders displays.

LADC Star May 20, 1993.

Over the course of the half-century the *Skunk Works* has built and modified aircraft, an immense assortment of types have been run through the company's various facilities for miscellaneous systems and airframe upgrades. Among these have been Martin RB-57Ds, P2Vs (P-2s), aircraft for foreign customers, and ships.

**ES-3A:** LADC conducted a flight test program on the prototype fully-mission-capable ES-3A aircraft between January and August of 1991. The aircraft design and manufacturing were accomplished by the Lockheed Aeronautical Systems Company under contract to the United States Navy. All tests were conducted at Lockheed Plant 10 in Palmdale, California.

The S-3 originally was configured for the mission of antisubmarine warfare. As an ES-3A, the aircraft took on an entirely new mission, that of electronic surveillance. To accomplishing this transformation, all of the ASW avionics and wiring were removed and replaced by a sophisticated suite of electronic surveillance avionics. The aircraft essentially was stripped bare and completely rebuilt within the pressure vessel.

The test program actually consisted of several phases involving contractor and Customer tests. Following delivery of the aircraft to the Navy during August of 1991, the navy continued to test many aspects of the ES-3A and its mission at the Naval Air Test Center, Patuxent River, Maryland, such as carrier suitability and mission avionics integration.

### Appendix C: *SKUNK WORKS* NAME ORIGINS

Lockheed's Advanced Development Company, long known by its unofficial, but considerably more famous *Skunk Works* moniker, is unquestionably the best known advanced aircraft development operation of its kind in the world. The origin of its nickname, accordingly, often is the subject of considerable discussion.

There is little doubt the *Skunk Works* name can be traced back to noted cartoonist Al Capp's extraordinarily popular "Li'l Abner" newspaper comic strip and its infamous brewery, the "Skonk Works". Already well known during the early 1940s, the Capp strip was read with considerable regularity by many Lockheed employees, including more than a few who were involved in the highly-classified XP-80 project. Among these was Irving Culver, then chief engineer in charge of the aircraft's fuselage design.

Culver, over the past fifty years, has been the person most often credited with giving birth to the popular, now trademarked pseudonym.

Culver, when interviewed during 1993 by Richard Abrams, recalled that World War Two secrecy required anyone associated with the XP-80 project not to identify their location when answering the phone. The resulting isolation reminded Culver of the "Skonk Works" in Capp's comic strip.

One day, during mid-1943, Navy officials in Washington, D.C. were trying to establish a conference call connection with Lockheed's W. A. "Dick" Pulver, probably in connection with the *Constitution* program. The Lockheed operator mistakenly though they wanted to speak to Irv Culver, and when his phone rang, Culver answered by stating, "Skonk Works, inside man Culver". After an awkward pause, one of the officers asked, "What?", and Culver repeated, "Skonk Works". The name proved perfectly appropriate, and it stuck...but "Kelly" Johnson was not happy about it. According to Culver, "Kelly eventually got to like the name, but when he first heard about the incident he told me I was fired. Of course he fired me about twice a day anyway..."

Later, in the 1960s, Al Capp objected, so 'Skonk' was changed to 'Skunk', eliminating the cartoonist's unique spelling. By that time, the term *Skunk Works* was identified with success that many companies and people, including Pres. Lyndon Johnson, used it generically to connote well-managed programs accomplished in short spans of time and at low cost, following "Kelly" Johnson's *Skunk Works* motto: 'Be quick, be quiet, be on time'.'

The words *Skunk Works* over time became so identified with Lockheed that during 1973, the company applied for and received from the US Patent and Copyright Offices a copyright on the name and a trademark on the cartoon skunk logo. The latter was developed in-house by a Lockheed art department employee and has become the official symbol of the *Skunk Works*. Few variations have evolved from this cartoon...which can be utilized facing either left or right. Lockheed's legal department requires use of the copyright symbol with the skunk wherever it appears. Permission to use the skunk must be obtained from Lockheed.

One of the few skunk variations, developed for Navy program promotional purposes, follows:

### Appendix D: *SKUNK WORKS* FACILITIES AT BURBANK AND PALMDALE LOCATIONS:

Shortly after the start of the P-80 flight operations at Lockheed's Van Nuys, California facility it was recognized that although the Van Nuys area was less populated than Burbank, problems would surface and ultimately their solutions would be necessary. The difficulties basically evolved around the noise and vibration that were anticipated to result from run-up operations on the flight line and from takeoff and landing of aircraft over the residential areas. As production rates increased and advanced engine designs were incorporated in the various aircraft rolling from the production and experimental aircraft operations, the noise levels and vibrations problems increased almost exponentially. An attempt to attenuate the sound and associated vibrations through the use of blast chutes and silencers met with limited success and it was soon realized that with the increasing population around the airport and the high cost of such measures, the problem had to be solved in some other manner.

As early as 1945, Lockheed initiated contact with the Palmdale Irrigation District regarding possible use of the Palmdale airport. Negotiations continued with Los Angeles County through 1946 and 1947, and on December 19, 1950, a five-year lease of 237-plus acres was made for area on the Palmdale facility. Construction of one hangar for flight functions was begun and Building 401 was occupied during December of 1951. This formed the nucleus of flight operations at Palmdale. With this facility established, the F-94C program was set up so that work pre-flight work was performed at Van Nuys. After first flights, all aircraft landed at Palmdale for the balance of flight operations and delivery. This program aided the Van Nuys problem by reducing the quantity of run up operations and flights.

On the basis of this program, further planning for complete final assembly and flight facilities was undertaken with Los Angeles County and the Air Force. During October of 1952, a site plan for the F-94C at Palmdale was approved by the Air Force and during April of 1953 construction was begun. During the period from April of 1953 to October of 1953, the F-94C contract picture changed. Due to no follow-on for the F-94C, a proposed plan was submitted to the Air Force during October for modification of the site for a T-33 program. Upon approval of this request a T-33 program was authorized. As of March 25, 1954, some three T-33s per day were being delivered and plans were being finalized for relocation of final assembly from Burbank. It was expected that by the first week of May, final assembly of the T-33 would be undertaken at Palmdale. Final relocation of all flight operations was expected to be completed by May 24, 1954.

Dirromg a ceremony at the Palmdale facility on December 22, 1992, Lockheed Advanced Development Company celebrated the official relocation of the *Skunk Works'* headquarters to the Antelope Valley after 50 years

Lockheed

in Burbank. California Lt. Gov. Leo McCarthy joined Lockheed Corporation Chairman Dan Tellep and LADC President Sherm Mullin in dedicating the newly reconstructed Bldg. 608, which new houses *Skunk Works* headquarters operations. Also on hand at the ceremony were Howard "Buck" McKeon, the newly elected congressman for the Antelope Valley; the mayors and other city officials from Palmdale and Lancaster, and US Air Force representatives.

"This is a major milestone in the transition of the *Skunk Works* from Burbank to Palmdale," Mullin said. "The *Skunk Works* is a world aerospace leader partly due to our cost effectiveness. This consideration will make us even more competitive in capturing future contracts."

With the headquarters staff in place, LADC began the new year with approximately 2,100 employees in Palmdale. More than 200 occupy Bldg. 608, a two-story, 61,000 square foot edifice that was formerly an administrative and training facility. At the time of the official opening ceremony, about 2,200 other Lockheed workers were expected to transfer to the Antelope Valley as other facilities became available.

General contractor and designer for the headquarters building reconstruction project was the Austin Company (Western District,) of Santa Ana, California.

Additional construction projects in progress at the 677 acre LADC Plant 10 were expected to add another 260,000 square feet of floor space by the spring of 1994. Plant 10 already included 41 buildings comprising more than 2 million square feet.

*USAF Plant 42 as it appeared during the early 1950s. T-33 and F-94 final assembly and production flight test operations were conducted at Site 7.*

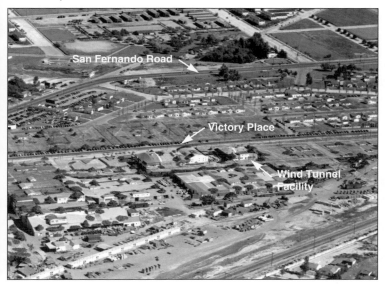

*The* Skunk Works *was located in Plant B-1 from June of 1943 through January of 1944 in a facility that was attached to the rear of the wind tunnel.*

*During January of 1944 the* Skunk Works *was relocated to Plant B-5 where it remained through April of 1945. It then was moved to Plant B-6.*

*The move to Plant 10 was initiated during mid-1992 and is expected to be completed by mid-1994. U-2 depot and flight test facilities are at Site 2; the F-117 depot and flight test facilities are at Site 7. Human resources and other unclassified organizations occupy Unit 10.*

*The* Skunk Works' *world-class full-scale aircraft radar cross-section test facility at Helendale, California. Stations with retractable pylons are at 1,400, 5,000, and 7,500 feet from the radar emitters.*

*Oildale facility was used for U-2A production during the U-2 production program. Aircraft were trucked to Burbank for delivery to the test location.*

### Appendix E: *SKUNK WORKS* PERSONALITIES

No history of the *Skunk Works* could be written without interfacing at least a brief biography of its founder, the late **Clarence L. "Kelly" Johnson**. Standing 5 feet 11 inches tall and with blue eyes, he was undeniably the driving force behind what became the most heralded advanced design bureau in the world under his guidance and control.

Johnson was born on February 27, 1910 in Ishpeming, Michigan, the seventh of nine children. His father, a bricklayer and carpenter who died about 1943, was Peter Johnson born in Sweden in 1862 and arrived in the US about 1890. His mother, who died in 1940, was Christine Johnson who also was born in Sweden in 1868 and who also arrived in the US about 1890. Johnson had one brother, Arthur Johnson of Flint, Michigan.

Johnson attended grammar school in Ishpeming and went to Flint Central High School in Flint, Michigan where he graduated in 1928. He then attended Flint Junior College before entering the University of Michigan at Ann Arbor. He graduated from the latter in 1932 with a bachelor of science degree in aeronautical engineering. In 1933 he received his master of science degree in aeronautical engineering, also from the University of Michigan. During 1948 he completed the requirements for and received a private pilot's license.

Johnson joined Lockheed as a tool designer earning $83 a month on August 21, 1933. During 1953, he became Lockheed's chief engineer and was appointed corporate vice presidnet-research and development during

1956. During 1964 he became a member of Lockheed's board of directors and on December 1, 1969, he became a senior vice president. He retired from Lockheed during 1975 but was retained by the company as a senior advisor. He died fifteen years later on December 21, 1990.

Both during his working years and afterwards Johnson was showered with awards and accolades. Among the more significant were two Collier Trophies. two Theodore on Karman Awards, the Wright Brothers Memorial Trophy, two Sylvanus Albert Reed Awards, and the Daniel Guggenheim Medal. During 1964 President Lyndon Johnson presented him the nation's highest civilian honor... the Medal of Freedom. President Ronald Reagan also honored Johnson with the National Security Medal during 1983 and the National Medal of Technology during 1988. Johnson also was enshrined in the National Aviation Hall of Fame during 1983. That same year, Lockheed renamed its Rye Canyon California facility the "Kelly" Johnson Research and Development Center.

**Other *Skunk Works* directors/presidents past and present include:**

**Richard Heppe** was born in 1923 and received his bachelors degree in mechanical engineering from Stanford University during 1944. He received a masters degree in aeronautics at Stanford in 1945. This was followed by a professional engineer's degree from the California Institute of Technology during 1947. Heppe joined Lockheed in 1947 as an aerodynamicist. He held a series of engineering positions for the following 25 years, becoming a member of general management during 1972. He became a company vice president in 1974. In 1984 he became president of Lockheed California Company which then employed 18,000. Heppe was intimately involved in the conception and development of every new aircraft Lockheed produced during the 41 years he was with Lockheed.

Heppe is a Fellow of the American Institute of Aeronautics and Astronautics and the recipient of their 1987 Reed Award as Aeronautics Man of the Year He was elected to the National Academy of Engineering during 1982 after having won the Admiral Charles Weakley Award for National Defense Contributions during 1979. He has served on the American Defense Preparedness Association, the National Security Industry Association, the Naval Aviation Museum, numerous NACA and the NASA committees, the Aeronautics and Space Engineering Board, and was chosen by the American Management Association as a Silver Knight of Management during 1986. During his Lockheed tenure Heppe served as vice president and general manager of the *Skunk Works* prior to becoming company president. He formally retired during 1988, but worked essentially full time until the F- 22 contract was won. He is actively assisting the *Skunk Works* on several new programs.

**Norman Nelson** was born In Chicago Illinois during 1918. During 1941 he earned a bachelors degree in aeronautical engineering and an advanced degree in the same discipline from the University of Cincinnati. Both as an officer and as a civilian Nelson served in the Air Force's research and development efforts. He was separated from the service as a captain during 1953. He subsequently held a position as vice president of engineering at Doak Aircraft Company; engineering consultant to Lockheed Advanced Development Products company; chief of advanced design at Lockheed's rotary wing branch; vice president engineering and operations at McCulloch Corporation; and engineering consultant to the Hughes Tool Company on the Hughes *Glomar Explorer* program. He left Hughes to rejoin ADP during January of 1976 and later that year became program manager and chief engineer of the Lockheed stealth fighter programs (i.e. the *Have Blue* concept demonstrator during 1976 and the F-117 during 1977). During 1984 he became vice president and general manager of ADP, a position he held until 1988, when Ben Rich returned. Nelson retired from Lockheed during 1987.

**Ben Rich** was born in Manila, Philippine Islands on June 18, 1925. He received his bachelor of science degree in mechanical engineering from the University of California at Berkeley and his masters degree in the same discipline from the University of California at Los Angeles. He was graduated from Harvard University's advanced management program during 1966. Rich joined Lockheed during 1950 as an engineer participating in the aerodynamic, thermodynamic, propulsion, and preliminary design aspects of the F-104, the U-2, the YF-12, the SR-71, and numerous other technologically sophisticated programs. He was named senior engineer for advanced programs during 1963 and served as Advanced Development Projects program manager and assistant chief engineer. He became vice president for fighter programs and preliminary design during 1972. He became president of the Lockheed Advanced Development Company upon its creation during May of 1990. Prior to that he was ADP's vice president and general manager beginning during January of 1975 (except for a two year interim assignment as president of the Advanced Aeronautics Company from March of 1984 to August of 1986). He was elected a vice president of Lockheed Corporation during May of 1977.

Rich was a Fellow of the American Institute of Aeronautics and Astronautics and the winner of that organization's national aircraft design award during 1972. He is also a Fellow of the Institute for the Advancement of Engineering and a member of the Tau Beta Pi honorary professional engineering society.

Rich received many awards during his years as an aeronautical engineer. Among these was the 1969 Collier Trophy shared with other members of the F-117 team; the Peter Recchia Omni Memorial Award; the 1962 UCLA Alumnus Engineer of the Year; the AIAA/Royal Aeronautical Society Wright Brothers Lecturer; Gold Knight of Management; and the 1988 *Aviation Week & Space Technology* Aero Propulsion Laurel Award.

Rich officially retired from Lockheed on January 1,1991. He died on January 5, 1995. His anecdotal book, *Skunk Works*, was published during 1994.

**Sherm Mullin** was born In Somers, Connecticut on October 12, 1935. He attended Princeton and several other universities and later completed the Stanford Executive Program during 1984. He served in the US Army from 1954 to 1957 and was on the faculty of the US Army's Guided Missile School from 1955 to 1957. During 1959, Mullin joined the Lockheed Electronics Company as an electronics engineer specializing in the design of military electronics systems including pioneering work on real time digital systems and antisubmarine warfare system engineering. Transferring to Lockheed-California Company during 1968, Mullin played a major role in the development of the P-3 and S-3 antisubmarine warfare aircraft. He became chief engineer on the P-3 program during 1974. From 1976 to 1980 he was P-3 program manager directing all domestic and international program activities. He was director of planning and advanced programs from 1981 to 1982.

During March of 1982, Mullin was appointed a vice president for Advanced Development Projects and program manager for the F-117A. Mullin was a member of the F-117A team awarded the 1989 Collier Trophy. During October of 1985 Mullin became vice president and general manager of Advanced Tactical Fighter Programs leading the Lockheed team that was awarded the YF-22 DemVal prototype contract by the Air Force during October of 1986.

Mullin is a Fellow of the Institute for the Advancement of Engineering; an associate fellow of the American Institute of Aeronautics and Astronautics; a senior member of the Institute of Electrical and Electronics Engineers; a member of the American Association for the Advancement of Science; a member of the Association of Computing Machinery; a member of the Air Force Association; a member of the US Naval Institute; and a member of the Tailhook Association. He was also the AIAA 1992 Wright Brothers Lecturer in Aeronautics. Mullin has served as the chairman of the Flight Test Museum Foundation and a trustee of the Naval Aviation Museum Foundation.

**Jack Gordon** was born in Whittier, California on October 19, 1940. He holds bachelor's and master's degrees in mechanical engineering from Stanford University awarded during 1962 and 1963, respectively. During 1976 he received a second master's degree after completing the executive engineering program at UCLA.

Gordon joined Lockheed during August of 1963 as a propulsion engineer and worked on Lockheed's initial supersonlc transport proposal. He transferred to the *Skunk Works* during March of 1964 where he participated in the design and development of the SR-71, the U-2 and later the F-117. He has held a number of executive positions In ADP including deputy program manager and chief engineer on the F-117 from 1981 to 1986 and program director for the Lockheed portion of the advanced tactical fighter from 1986 through 1987.

Between 1979 and 1981 Gordon was assistant to the Lockheed Corporation s vice president for engineering during an executive training assignment. He was responsible for coordination of Lockheed' s corporate independent research and development effort. He was named executive vice president of the Lockheed Advanced Development Company on May 8, 1990, when the company was created out of the Advanced Development Projects (*Skunk Works*) division of the Lockheed Aeronautical Systems Company. Gordon had been ADP s assistant general manager since December of 1987 and was named an LASC vice president during March of 1989.

Gordon is an Associate Fellow of the American Institute for Aeronautics and Astronautics, a Fellow of the Institute for Advancement of Engineering, a member of the Society of Automotive Engineers (SAE), and a member of the Security Affairs Support Association.

During January of 1994, Lockheed announced that Gordon would be replacing Sherm Mullin as President of the *Skunk Works.* He was offically named president on March 1, 1994. Gordon had been the *Skunk Works* assistant general manager since December 1987 and was appointed a vice president in March of 1989. He was named executive vice president of LADC in May of 1990.

Gordon is active with youth sports and is an elected school board member. He also serves on the board of directors of the Henry Mayo Newhall Memorial Hospital.

**Other Skunk Works Personalities:**

**Willis Hawkins**, Senior Advisor, Lockheed Corporation, was born in Kansas City, Missouri on December 1, 1913. He was graduated from the University of Michigan during 1937 with a bachelor of science degree in aeronautical engineering. He received an honorary doctor of engineering degree from the University of Michigan during 1965, and an honorary doctor of science degree from Illinois College during 1966. He was awarded the National Medal of Science by President Reagan during 1966.

Hawklns was hired by Lockheed during 1937 as a senior detail engineering draftsman in the company's engineering department. He advanced through a number of key positions becoming engineering department manager during 1944 and chief preliminary design engineer during 1949. From 1953 to 1957, Hawkins was director of engineering at Lockheed Missiles ~ Space Company and during 1959 was appointed assistant general manager of that division. He was elected a vice president of Lockheed Corporation during 1960.

Before assembling duties as the corporation s vice president-science and engineering during 1962, Hawkins served 'or more than a year as vice president and general manager of the Lockheed Missiles ~ Space Company s Space Systems Division. He served as Assistant Secretary of the Army for Research and Development for nearly three years beginning during 1963. He returned to Lockheed during July of 1966, to resume his duties as vice president of science and engineering and remained In that position until December of 1969.

During December of 1969, Hawkins was advanced to senior vice president-science and engineering of Lockheed Corporation and was a member of the company's board of directors from 1972 through May of 1980. In fact, Hawkins had taken early retirement from the company during May of 1974, but had stayed on as senior vice president of the corporation and as president of the Lockheed-California Company...a position he retained until April of 1979. During 1979 and early 1980, Hawkins served the corporation as senior vice president-aircraft from which position he retired a second, and final, time.

*Willis Hawkins*

***Skunk Works* Test Pilots 1943 Through 1993:**

Stan Beltz; Milo Burcham; John Christensen; Ernie Claypool, Ray Crandal, Jim Eastham; Harold Farley, Jr.; Dave Ferguson; Bob Gilliland; Ray Goudey; Darryl Greenameyer; Skip Holm; Harold Johnson; Dave Kerzie; Tony LeVier; Ted Limmer; Bud Martin; Sammy Mason; Bob Massey; Bob Matye; George McEntire; "Slim" Menefee; Tom Morgenfeld; "Red" Mulvahil; Joe Ozier; Bill Park; Art Peterson; Frank Powers; Bob Riedenauer; Herman "Fish" Salmon; Lou Schalk; Bob Schumacher; Bob Sieker; Bill Thomas; Jim Thomas; Joe Towle; Bill Weaver; Ken Weir; Jim White; and Roy Wimmer.

*Stan Beltz*

*Milo Burcham*

*Bob Christensen*

*Ray Crandall*

*Jim Eastham*

*Hal Farley, Jr.*

*Dave Ferguson*

*Bob Gilliland*

*Ray Goudey*

*"Kelly" Johnson*

*Dick Heppe*

*Norm Nelson*

*Ben Rich*

*Sherm Mullin*

*Jack Gordon*

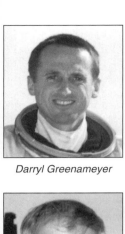
Darryl Greenameyer

Skip Holm

Harold Johnson

Lou Schalk

Bob Schumacher

Bob Sieker

Dave Kerzie

Tony LeVier

Ted Limmer

Jim Thomas

Joe Towle

Bill Weaver

Bud Martin

Sammy Mason

Bob Massey

Ken Weir

Jim White

Roy Wimmer

Bob Matye

Tom Morgenfeld

"Red" Mulvahill

*YC-130 first flight crew included (from l. to r.) Dick Stanton, Jack Real, Stan Beltz, "Kelly" Johnson (flew chase), and Roy Wimmer.*

Joe Ozier

Bill Park

Art Peterson

*Lou Schalk is greeted by government and company representatives following successful completion of the A-12's first official flight on April 30, 1962.*

Frank Powers

Bob Riedenauer

Fish Salmon

**Skunk Works Directors of Flight Test 1943 Through 1993**
Dick Abrams; Keith Beswick; Larry Bohanan; Ernie Joiner; Dick Miller

Dick Abrams          Keith Beswick

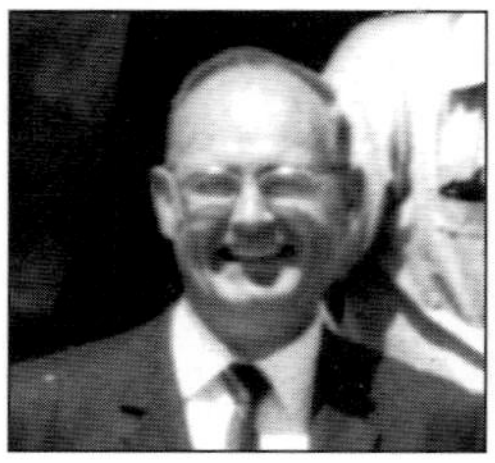

Larry Bohanan

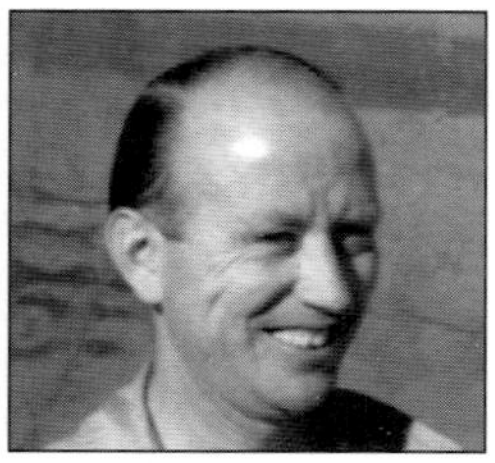

Ernie Joiner

**Appendix F:**
**PRINCIPLES OF THE *SKUNK WORKS***

During August of 1992, the Lockheed Advanced Development Company released a summary document entitled, ***The Skunk Works Approach to Aircraft Development, Production and Support.*** Its contents follow:

**Introduction:**

Over the past few years, we have witnessed sweeping geopolitical changes and revolutionary events that are triggering major changes in our nation's defense requirements. Clearly, in future years, the Defense Department and services will be operating with much smaller force structures and budgets. The resulting challenge will be to maintain a viable, responsive defense infrastructure in the face of budget reductions. To meet this challenge, both the Defense Secretary and Congress are proposing new approaches to DoD acquisition that emphasize research and advanced technologies; technology demonstrators and prototypes; selective upgrading of existing systems; and selective/low rate procurement of new systems.

But not only will we have to develop new technology and systems, we must implement acquisition strategies and management approaches that will enable development and fielding of new systems in a more timely and less costly manner. For the past half century, the Lockheed *Skunk Works* and its government customers have employed specialized management methods that have done just that. The purpose of this paper is to describe what this *Skunk Works* approach is...and why it should be used more broadly today.

**The *Skunk Works* Approach:**

The Lockheed *Skunk Works* has demonstrated a unique ability to rapidly prototype, develop and produce a wide range of highly advanced aircraft for the US armed forces and intelligence agencies. The P-80, U-2, F-104, SR-71 and, more recently, the F-117 are widely recognized as among the most significant achievements of the aerospace industry. These and other *Skunk Works* aircraft have incorporated breakthrough technology to achieve new thresholds in aircraft and systems performance. The common thread among these aircraft is that they were created by men and women working together employing a unique approach to aircraft development—the *Skunk Works* approach. This management approach, developed by the founder of the *Skunk Works*—C. L. "Kelly" Johnson, fosters creativity and innovation, and has enabled prototyping and development of highly complex aircraft in relatively short time spans and at relatively low cost. It has also demonstrated efficient, economical production of complex systems in small quantities and at low production rates.

**The *Skunk Works* Operating Rules:**

Based on lessons learned from early *Skunk Works* programs, Kelly Johnson developed and wrote the Basic Operating Rules of the *Skunk Works.* These fourteen "rules" address program management, organization, contractor/customer relationships, documentation, customer reporting, specifications, engineering drawings, funding, cost control, subcontractor inspection, testing, security, and management compensation. Although the language does not sound as if it would be applicable in today's environment, the basic principles are relevant and are applied in present *Skunk Works*' operations on a regular basis (Parenthetical comments expand the reasons behind the rules):

(1) The *Skunk Works'* manager must be delegated practically complete control of his program in all aspects. He should report to a division president or higher (*It is essential that the program manager have authority to make decisions quickly regarding technical, finance, schedule, or operations matters.*)

(2) Strong *but small* project offices must be provided both by the customer and contractor (*The customer program manager must have similar authority to that of the contractor.*)

(3) The number of people having any connection with the project must be restricted in an almost vicious manner. Use of a small number of good people (10 to 25 percent compared to the so-called normal systems). (*Bureaucracy makes unnecessary work and must be controlled brutally.*)

(4) A very simple drawing and drawing release system with great flexibility for making changes must be provided. (*This permits early work by manufacturing organizations, and schedule recovery if technical risks involve failures.*)

(5) There must be a minimum of reports required, but important work must be recorded thoroughly. (*Responsible management does not require massive technical and information systems.*)

(6) There must be a monthly cost review covering not only what has been spent and committed, but also projected costs to the conclusion of the program. Don't have the books ninety days late and don't surprise the customer with sudden overruns. (*Responsible management does require operation within the resources available.*)

(7) The contractor must be delegated and must assume more than normal responsibility to get good vendor bids for the subcontract on the project. Commercial bid procedures are very often better than military ones. (*Essential freedom to use the best talent available and operate within the resources available.*)

(8) The inspection system as currently used by the *Skunk Works,* which has been approved by both the Air Force and Navy, meets the intent of existing military requirements and should be used on new projects. Push more basic inspection responsibility back to subcontractors and vendors. Don't duplicate so much inspection. (*Even the commercial world recognizes that quality is in design and responsible operations—not inspection.*)

(9) The contractor *must* be delegated the authority to test his final product in flight. He can and must test it in the initial stages. If he doesn't, he rapidly loses his competency to design other vehicles. (*Critical, if new technology and the attendant risks are to be rationally accommodated.*)

(10) The specification applying to the hardware must be agreed to in *advance* of contracting. The *Skunk Works* practice of having a specification section stating clearly which important military specification items will not knowingly be complied with and reasons therefore is highly recommended. (*Standard specifications inhibit new technology and innovation, and are frequently obsolete.*)

(11) Funding a program must be *timely* so that the contractor doesn't have to keep running to the bank to support government projects. (*Rational management requires knowledge of, and freedom to use, the resources originally committed.*)

(12) There must be mutual trust between the customer project organization and the contractor with very close cooperation and liaison on a day-to-day basis. This cuts down misunderstanding and correspondence to an absolute minimum. (*The goals of the customer and producer should be the same—get the job done well.*)

(13) Access by outsiders to the project and its personnel must be strictly controlled by appropriate security measures. (*This is a program manager's responsibility even if no program security demands are made—a cost avoidance measure.*)

(14) Because only a few people will be used in engineering and most other areas, ways must be provided to reward good performance by pay *not based on the number of personnel supervised.* (*Responsible management must be rewarded, and responsible management does not permit the growth of bureaucracies.*)

Since it inception in 1943, the *Skunk Works* has completed a significant number of projects that have resulted in development and/or production hardware. These programs vary significantly in terms of type of product, technologies, customer, contracts, specifications, support requirements, and other parameters. However, there are some general characteristics that emerge:

- Need to rapidly field a new capability
- Requirement for new technology breakthroughs
- Willingness to accept risk—contractor and customer
- Use of prototyping to reduce development risk
- Low rate and low quantity production
- Specialized management methods required and accepted
- Need and/or desire to maintain tight security

The *Have Blue* stealth technology demonstrator and F-117 stealth fighter are two recent highly successful *Skunk Works* programs that have these general characteristics.

More than ever, the current environment demands that each acquisition dollar be spent wisely and efficiently. The *Skunk Works* management approach offers a proven, quick, efficient way to: develop new technology through prototyping; execute engineering and manufacturing development (EMD) programs; procure limited production systems at low rates; and upgrade current systems with new technology.

**Program Management:**

A *Skunk Works* program is organized around a program manager who is given total control of all program aspects including engineering, test, manufacturing, quality assurance, security, plans and schedules, budget control, etc. Thus, the program manager has the ability to control his costs and meet rational program milestones and objectives.

The organization structure is simple and has its own built-in checks and balances. For example, engineering and flight test report separately to the program office, as do manufacturing and quality assurance.

Other functional organizations within the *Skunk Works* (Lockheed Advanced Development Company) such as human resources, information service, facilities, environmental health and safety, and legal provide "on demand" support to the program managers. Furthermore, staff support in any specialty area of the corporation is available to the program manager if needed. As a program grows and transitions into development and production, additional functions are added such as product support, training, and assistant program managers for specific program end items as needed.

*Skunk Works* program offices are small. For example, at the height of F-117 development and production, the *Skunk Works* management team was 20 to 30 people total, and the Air Force's System Program Office (SPO) was similar in size. The objective is to establish a "one-on-one" relationship between the *Skunk Works* and customer procurement teams, with clear lines of responsibility and full authority for all managers, both contractor and customer.

The *Skunk Works* approach also demands the use of a small number of high quality individuals staffing each function. Individuals are given broad responsibility and have a substantial workload. Our experience has shown that under these circumstances individual achievement is most often much higher than management's expectations. The F-117 is a program that achieved excellent results while using a relatively small number of people. The maximum number of direct *Skunk Works* employees during each phase follows:

*Have Blue* Demonstrator...340
Full-Scale Development....2,500
Production.........................4,000
Sustaining Support............1,200

The benefits of keeping both management and total personnel at a minimum are: greater individual responsibility and satisfaction; better communications; high productivity; and reduced costs.

The key to success is a cohesive team working closely together to achieve well-defined objectives. Tasks, responsibilities and progress are measured and tracked in a series of integrated plans and schedules developed by the contractor and customer to meet the program/system requirements.

Individual managers have access to all plans and schedules and understand how their part contributes to the total program. Progress is measured in formal weekly program reviews with the total program directorate. Other smaller or individual meetings are used to iron out differences of opinion or improve operating procedures.

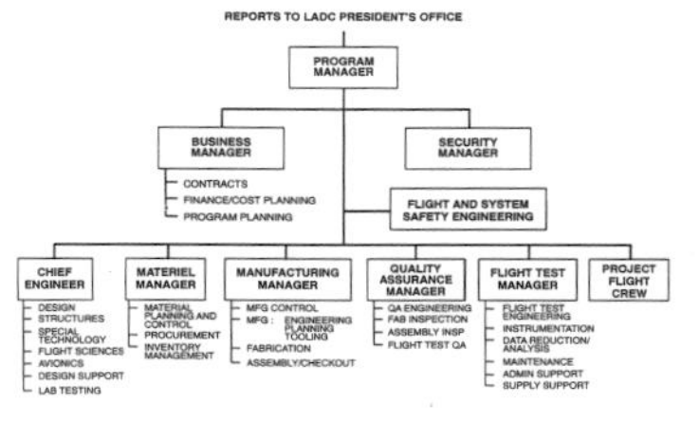
REPORTS TO LADC PRESIDENT'S OFFICE
PROGRAM MANAGER
BUSINESS MANAGER
CONTRACTS
FINANCE/COST PLANNING
PROGRAM PLANNING
SECURITY MANAGER
FLIGHT AND SYSTEM SAFETY ENGINEERING
CHIEF ENGINEER
DESIGN
STRUCTURES
SPECIAL TECHNOLOGY
FLIGHT SCIENCES
AVIONICS
DESIGN SUPPORT
LAB TESTING
MATERIEL MANAGER
MATERIAL PLANNING AND CONTROL
PROCUREMENT
INVENTORY MANAGEMENT
MANUFACTURING MANAGER
MFG CONTROL
MFG: ENGINEERING PLANNING TOOLING
FABRICATION
ASSEMBLY/CHECKOUT
QUALITY ASSURANCE MANAGER
QA ENGINEERING
FAB INSPECTION
ASSEMBLY INSP
FLIGHT TEST QA
FLIGHT TEST MANAGER
FLIGHT TEST ENGINEERING
INSTRUMENTATION
DATA REDUCTION/ ANALYSIS
MAINTENANCE
ADMIN SUPPORT
SUPPLY SUPPORT
PROJECT FLIGHT CREW

When expanding technical capability, failures are inevitable and changes must be incorporated. In specific situations, special task teams are formed to develop solutions to critical problems. Progress is reviewed frequently by management, and decisions are made on a weekly or even daily basis for critical problem areas. In summary, individual commitment and performance is at its peak when the team believes in the objectives, recognizes his or her individual responsibility, and shares in the progress towards meeting those objectives.

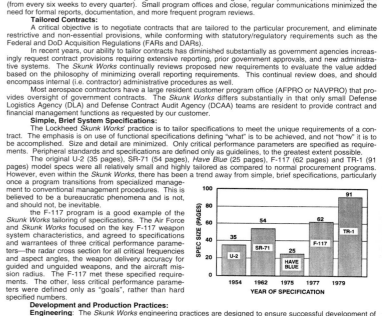

**Contractor-Customer Relationship:**

Successful implementation of a *Skunk Works* management approach requires that the program customer be strongly committed to operating in a similar manner. This should not be a unique management approach; it is a rational way to develop new products containing advanced technology components. The starting point is a small, high quality, highly responsive customer program office, and a small supporting organization only as needed. The customer program manager must be given singular authority and broad responsibilities. The program manager should report directly to a senior decision-capable management level free of external "staff" direction.

During the F-117 development, a small SPO at Wright-Patterson AFB was augmented by small supporting organizations at Headquarters USAF, Headquarters TAC, Air Force Flight Test Center - Edwards AFB, Sacramento ALC, and Nellis AFB. This SPO director reported directly to the Commander, Aeronautical Systems Division, who was a Lieutenant General.

Successful development, production and fleet operations were achieved by building mutual trust over time among the contractor, Air Force, and supporting subcontractors. The Air Force and Lockheed program team maintained daily, open communications on program issues which resulted in teamwork, rapid joint problem solving, and mutual trust, rather than adversarial relationships.

Frequent technical and program reviews were conducted, but only important work and decisions were documented. Formal contractor-customer program reviews were held regularly and keyed to the pace of the program (from every six weeks to every quarter). Small program offices and close, regular communications minimized the need for formal reports, documentation, and more frequent program reviews.

**Tailored Contracts:**

A critical objective is to negotiate contracts that are tailored to the particular procurement, and eliminate restrictive and non-essential provisions, while conforming with statutory/regulatory requirements such as the Federal and DoD Acquisition Regulations (FARs and DARs).

In recent years, our ability to tailor contracts has diminished substantially as government agencies increasingly request contract provisions requiring extensive reporting, prior government approvals, and new administrative systems. The *Skunk Works* continually reviews proposed new requirements to evaluate the value added based on the philosophy of minimizing overall reporting requirements. This continual review does, and should encompass internal (i.e. contractor) administrative procedures as well.

Most aerospace contractors have a large resident customer program office (AFPRO or NAVPRO) that provides oversight of government contracts. The *Skunk Works* differs substantially in that only small Defense Logistics Agency (DLA) and Defense Contract Audit Agency (DCAA) teams are resident to provide contract and financial management functions as requested by our customer.

**Simple, Brief System Specifications:**

The Lockheed *Skunk Works*' practice is to tailor specifications to meet the unique requirements of a contract. The emphasis is on use of functional specifications defining "what" is to be achieved, and not "how" it is to be accomplished. Size and detail are minimized. Only critical performance parameters are specified as requirements. Peripheral standards and specifications are defined only as guidelines, to the greatest extent possible.

The original U-2 (35 pages), SR-71 (54 pages), *Have Blue* (25 pages), F-117 (62 pages) and TR-1 (91 pages) model specs were all relatively small and highly tailored as compared to normal procurement programs. However, even within the *Skunk Works*, there has been a trend away from simple, brief specifications, particularly once a program transitions from specialized management to conventional management procedures. This is believed to be a bureaucratic phenomena and is not, and should not, be inevitable.

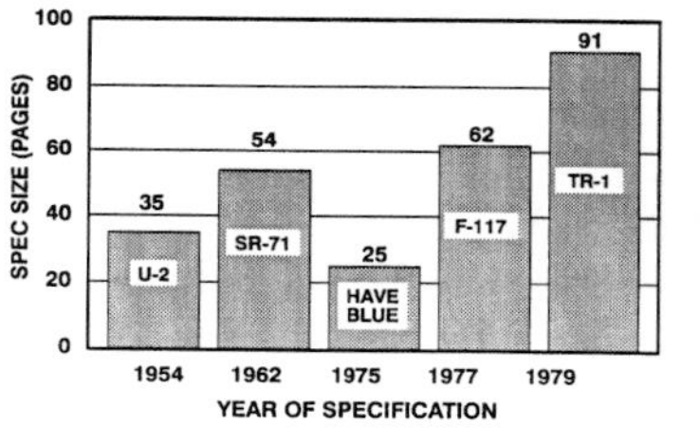
SPEC SIZE (PAGES)
100
80
60
40
20
0
35
U-2
54
SR-71
25
HAVE BLUE
62
F-117
91
TR-1
1954
1962
1975
1977
1979
YEAR OF SPECIFICATION

the F-117 program is a good example of the *Skunk Works* tailoring of specifications. The Air Force and *Skunk Works* focused on the key F-117 weapon system characteristics, and agreed to specifications and warrantees of three critical performance parameters—the radar cross section for all critical frequencies and aspect angles, the weapon delivery accuracy for guided and unguided weapons, and the aircraft mission radius. The F-117 met these specified requirements. The other, less critical performance parameters were defined only as "goals", rather than hard specified numbers.

**Development and Production Practices:**

**Engineering**: The *Skunk Works* engineering practices are designed to ensure successful development of advanced technology prototypes and limited production aircraft at low cost and in minimum time. Projects are staffed with a minimum number of multi-disciplined designers and engineering specialists.

The focus is on engineering design, yet the other engineering disciplines have key development roles in support of the design process. Manufacturing and quality assurance are involved early, working with the design, structures and materials engineers to ensure highly producible products.

It is the intent that the designer be responsible for his or her portion of the vehicle through manufacturing, test, and into service operation. Completing this cycle ensures that lessons-learned are applied to future projects. Materiel and subcontractors also are involved early in the program to ensure that all procured items meet technical, schedule and cost requirements. In today's acquisition terminology, the *Skunk Works* utilized a concurrent engineering or Integrated Product Development (IPD) process to assure that performance, quality, producibility and affordability requirements are met.

A simple engineering drawing system that readily accommodates change is utilized. Each drawing provides all necessary information for procurement, manufacture, test, inspection, acceptance and maintenance of a particular item. Drawing release approval is accomplished quickly, usually within one day. Primarily, design, weights and the program office approval are required to release a drawing. As necessary, approval may also include the stress and materiel organizations.

In addition, the number of controlled drawing copies is kept to a minimum to speed release and simplify the change cycle. Designers have a direct interface with manufacturing and materiel, and if changes are required, drawings can be "red marked" to eliminate delays. Re-release of a revised drawing occurs when five "red markings" have been made or four weeks have passed.

**Manufacturing:** The *Skunk Works* is organized and facilitized to be an efficient, high quality, quick-response prototype and low-rate manufacturer. As part of the *Skunk Works* process, manufacturing is directly involved in aircraft development—from concept through delivery. Working with engineering, the assembly sequence and tooling concepts are defined early to ensure the most cost-effective approach for prototyping or limited production. The *Skunk Works* seldom makes use of elaborate mock-ups, but does construct simple mock-ups for space allocation or fit and function requirements. Today's use of modern computer aided design and manufacturing systems (CADAM and CATIA) has contributed to a reduced need for mock-ups.

A minimum tooling concept is employed on all prototype programs. Shop aid fabrication tools are utilized whenever possible, and hard tools are only used where critical dimensions must be maintained. For production programs, tooling requirements are carefully defined to meet the desired production rates and quantities while minimizing cost.

Working closely together, engineering, manufacturing and materiel establish the engineering release, material order, subcontractor delivery, fabrication and assembly schedules that result in minimum time from go-ahead to delivery for flight. Problems in fabrication and assembly are quickly analyzed and resolved by manufacturing, quality assurance, and engineering teams. "Red marked" drawings minimize manufacturing delays.

The *Skunk Works* also employs a variety of automated manufacturing systems that provide bill-of-materiel, inventory, order location, tool control, order writing, and scheduling functions.

**Quality Assurance:** Maintaining quality is a continuous, active process throughout all phases of development and production. Early in the design, the *Skunk Works*' quality assurance organization (QA) works with engineering and manufacturing to design inspectability and testability into the aircraft and its subsystems.

The effort includes ensuring that all subcontractor furnished items meet the engineering requirements.

The *Skunk Works* avoids duplicate inspections and tests of incoming materials by pushing that responsibility back to qualified and approved suppliers.

During fabrication, assembly and flight test, QA establishes methods by which critical inspections are performed and compliance of processes to engineering requirements are verified. Accurate configuration status records are verified and maintained from released drawings and "red marked" documents. When necessary, simplified material review procedures are utilized to document and process nonconforming materials. Again, the approach is to have a minimum amount of paperwork, but highly relevant and focused.

**Laboratory and Ground Test:** Extensive testing of all subsystems and the completed aircraft is conducted to validate performance and safety. The *Skunk Works* philosophy is to get to first flight quickly through an aggressive design, development and ground test program with subcontract support. In all cases, system and flight safety are independently reviewed and uncompromised.

Extensive testing is planned and conducted to validate aerodynamics, propulsion/integration, low observables, materials/structures, aircraft subsystems and avionics subsystems. The flight control system performance is thoroughly proven through extensive pilot-in-the-loop flight simulation and "iron bird" testing of flight control hydraulic system components under simulated flight loads.

The *Skunk Works* focuses on early integrated laboratory testing of system avionics, including sensors, core avionics, cockpit controls/displays, and software to validate performance and reliability. The objective is to test end-to-end performance as early as possible to uncover problems early so that changes can be implemented with minimum impact to the program.

Structural testing during prototype development is generally limited to selected critical load carrying components. In full-scale development, complete static load and fatigue testing is conducted to ensure structural integrity and service life requirements are met.

Functional tests and system checkout procedures are performed on completion of functional systems, subassemblies, or major assemblies. The tests and procedures are developed by the design organization, conducted by manufacturing, and monitored by QA to assure conformance with engineering criteria. Upon completion of these tests, the prototype or development aircraft is transferred to flight test.

**Flight Test:** Prototype and full-scale development aircraft testing is conducted under the direction of a flight test manager reporting directly to a program manager. Functions include test planning, ground test, flight test, data acquisition, data reduction/analysis, flight vehicle maintenance/supply support, and test data documentation.

The primary objective is to minimize the time required to obtain flight test results. This is accomplished by procuring reliable instrumentation, using proven data processing methods, and minimizing the total number of data parameters. In addition, written reports and documentation are kept to a minimum. Formal test reports are written after the conclusion of the test program, using the contractor preferred format, but closely following accepted customer reporting guidelines.

The customer flight test organization and involvement varies depending on the program phase, but like the *Skunk Works*, must be a relatively small organization. During prototype development, the *Skunk Works* has full responsibility and authority for testing. However during full-scale development, flight testing is accomplished by a team that includes both *Skunk Works* and customer personnel.

**Cost and Schedule Control**

The *Skunk Works* closely monitors and controls cost and schedule performance on all programs. The extent of cost and schedule tracking and reporting is determined by customer-contractor negotiation of requirements specific to each program.

An automated cost reporting system that meets the customer's requirements for cost/schedule status reporting (CSSR) has been in place for ten years, and is used on all major programs. This system also provides cost reporting on a weekly basis to *Skunk Works* managers. Budgets, actual expenditures and variances are provided by Work Breakdown Structure (WBS) element thereby allowing manager at all levels to track and evaluate cost and schedule performance.

It is the *Skunk Works*' practice to conduct detailed monthly program reviews of cost and schedule status that address expended, committed, and projected costs, including those of subcontractors. Critical cost and schedule issues are highlighted for more frequent, close scrutiny by program management.

**Logistics Support Approach**

The *Skunk Works* approach to logistics support has broadened in scope in recent years in response to changing customer needs, and varies depending on program requirements. A systems engineering approach is used for requirements definition, allocation, design-to criteria, and "designing-in" reliability, maintainability, and supportability (RM&S) early in the development process. Logistic support analyses are performed which identify and quantify the required resources (support equipment, personnel, spares, technical publications, training, skill levels, etc.).

The *Skunk Works* produces and delivers small numbers of aircraft that perform specialized missions and operate from relatively few base locations. As a result, customers have found it cost effective to contract for proportionately greater levels of field service support than that found with many weapons systems.

The level of support and organizational structure varies. For example, like other tactical aircraft, the F-117 is a complete Air Force "blue suit" maintenance and support operation, with the *Skunk Works* providing only a few contractor field service representatives at the F-117 operating base. Working with the Air Force the *Skunk Works* provided all initial maintenance training and materials, support equipment, maintenance publications, and extensive field service representative support to facilitate this start-up.

In contrast, the U-2 program employs a mix of Air Force and contractor maintenance organizations. Some operating locations are largely "blue suit" with a few contractor personnel in key skill areas while other locations employ complete hands-on contractor maintenance support with Air Force personnel occupying required supervisory and military essential positions.

**Maintaining Security**

*Skunk Works* programs have met very stringent security requirements. Many of these programs, such as the U-2, A-12, *Have Blue*, and F-117, have been Special Access Programs or covert "black" programs. The *Skunk Works*, together with its subcontractors and customers, have been able to work within these security constraints and meet challenging technical, cost and schedule requirements.

A key to maintaining security is the practice of granting program access only on a strict "need to know" basis. When implemented by the *Skunk Works*, subcontractors and the customer, this access policy reduced interference from "outsiders" and greatly improves productivity. This restrictive access policy can be employed effectively on all programs, including unclassified, to improve efficiency and reduce costs.

The *Skunk Works* is presently working on a broad range of programs from unclassified to covert, and maintains competent, experienced staff that meets the physical, technical, personnel, communications, information systems, and documentation security requirements.

**Facility Considerations**

Co-location of all program functions in a minimum number of dedicated facilities is the *Skunk Works* approach on all programs. However when programs increase in size and scope, a variety of facilities are utilized for engineering, development test, fabrication, assembly, flight test and other functions.

Early in prototype and full-scale development, the *Skunk Works* co-locates program management, engineering, business management, materiel, security, and flight test functions. The production sub-assembly and final assembly are located close to the above functions to insure tight coordination. Flight test is accomplished at a separate location with appropriate runway and aircraft maintenance and support facilities. These types of facility arrangements were used on both the *Have Blue* and F-117 programs.

Extensive teaming among contractors on recent procurements is revolutionizing the way aircraft are being developed and produced. For example, detail design of the YF-22 Advanced Tactical Fighter prototype was accomplished in three geographic locations—Lockheed in Burbank, Boeing in Seattle, and General Dynamics in Fort Worth. Issues of communications were addressed early, and systems were implemented to enable secure electronic transmission of CADAM and CATIA drawings among the three locations to facilitate communications among team members.

The *Skunk Works* was responsible for fabrication and assembly of the YF-22 forward fuselages and perimeter edges, and final assembly of the forward fuselages with segments received from Boeing and General Dynamics. The end result was that the segments came together almost perfectly, just as if they had been built in the same facility.

**The *Skunk Works* Payoff**

The success of a *Skunk Works* approach is that it provides an environment that fosters individual creativity and innovation within both the contractor and customer organizations. The payoff is the ability to develop and deliver high technology aircraft in relatively short time spans and at relatively low costs. The Lockheed *Skunk Works* ability to create leading technology aircraft developments attests to the success of this approach over the past half century.

Furthermore, a *Skunk Works* management approach enables prototyping, development and production of high technology products in significantly less time than normal DoD management methods. It is also apparent that as aircraft complexity has increased, aircraft development spans have correspondingly increased. The significance of the technology advancements incorporated in the A-12 and SR-71 Mach 3+ strategic reconnaissance aircraft of the 1960s is also evidenced by the greater time to first flight, 32 and 24 months respectively.

| AIRCRAFT | FIRST FLIGHT | DOMINANT TECHNOLOGY |
|---|---|---|
| XP-80 | 1944 | JET PROPULSION |
| XF-104 | 1954 | SUPERSONIC AERODYNAMICS AND PROPULSION |
| U-2 | 1955 | HIGH ALTITUDE AERO/PROPULSION, LIGHTWEIGHT STRUCTURE |
| A-12 | 1962 | MACH 3 AERO PROPULSION, TITANIUM STRUCTURE |
| HAVE BLUE | 1977 | STEALTH |
| F-117 | 1981 | OPERATIONAL STEALTH - PASSIVE FIRE CONTROL PRECISION WEAPONS |
| YF-22 | 1990 | STEALTH, SUPERCRUISE, AGILITY |

The *Have Blue* stealth technology demonstrator and F-117 stealth fighter are recent examples of the *Skunk Works* ability to get new technology into flight test quickly. Under DARPA and USAF sponsorship, the *Skunk Works* was competitively selected in April 1976 to design, build and flight test two *Have Blue* demonstrator aircraft, following initial studies and RCS testing. The *Have Blue* first flight was in December 1977—only 18 months after go-ahead. The success of this technology demonstrator program led to development of the F-117—the first operational stealth aircraft.

The *Skunk Works* was awarded the F-117 FSD contract on 16 November 1978 and, through an intensive cooperative team effort with the USAF and subcontractors, achieved first flight on 18 June 1981—less than 31 months after go-ahead. Furthermore, with concurrency between development and production, the *Skunk Works* and USAF were able to achieve an initial operational capability (IOC) for the first operating squadron in only 59 months from go-ahead.

The *Skunk Works* has also consistently developed and produced high technology aircraft at comparatively low costs. A good example is the F-117 stealth fighter—the program costs being:

| | |
|---|---|
| Development | $2,000 M |
| Procurement (59 aircraft) | $4,265 M |
| *Total Flyaway | $2,515 M |
| *Unit Flyaway $ 42.6 M | |
| Military Construction $ 295 M | |
| Total Program Cost | $6.560 M |

* Then Year Dollars in Millions

* Includes Government Furnished Equipment

The total development costs were only $2 billion including the initial full-scale development effort, follow-on development of weapon system upgrades, and some Air Force related costs. Total procurement costs for the 59 F-117 production aircraft were also relatively low—$4.3 billion. The flyaway portion totals $2.5 billion, and the remaining portion ($1.8 billion) was for training devices, ground support equipment, tech orders, initial spares, and some government costs. The average unit flyaway cost for the 59 production aircraft was only $42.6 million in then-year dollars including GFE. This flyaway cost compares favorably with other twin engine fighter produced at significantly higher rates during the same period. Additional allocated costs are the $295 million in construction costs for a dedicated base—the Tonopah Test Range Airfield. Thus, total program costs including all non-recurring development, procurement and military construction were only $6.5 billion.

Focusing on F-117 procurement, this program demonstrates how the *Skunk Works* approach facilitates highly efficient, low-rate production. The 59 production aircraft were produced over an eight year span. Peak production rate was just eight aircraft per year, and decreased to just "one per season" near the end. Conventional wisdom suggest that these low rates would yield inefficient production and high flyaway costs, but that was not the case. Manufacturing initially proceeded on an 82% learning curve through the initial 29 aircraft, and then further improved over the remaining production run, in part due to implementation of a highly effective USAF-sponsored producibility program. In the end, the 59 production aircraft were delivered on an average 78% learning curve.

To illustrate that our F-117 performance is not an anomaly, the airframe unit flyaway cost and manufacturing hour history for the TR-1 included 37 aircraft produced at a rate of 4 to 6 per year, and an average 82% learning curve was achieved. Spikes in the learning curve reflected the three two-seat trainer aircraft that were produced.

The conclusion is that efficient production can be achieved at low rates using *Skunk Works* management methods, and careful up-front planning, facilitizing, and tooling, together with customer willingness to organize and delegate authority to match the *Skunk Works* process.

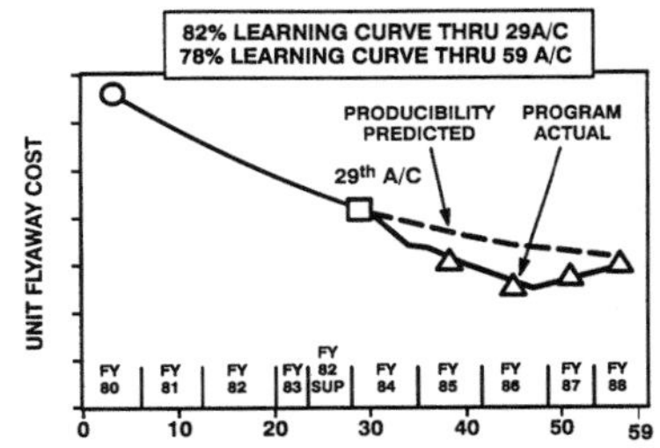


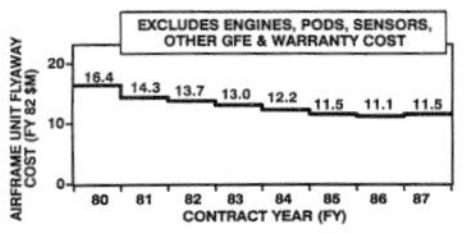


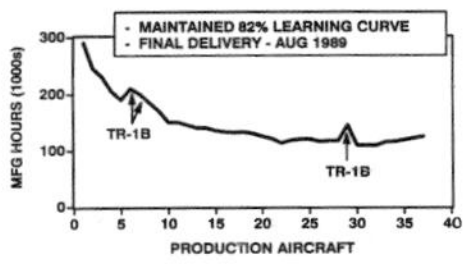


**A *Skunk Works* Approach Has Broad Application**

The *Skunk Works* management methods can be applied to a wide variety of programs—not just aircraft programs. A good example is the Lockheed *Skunk Works* program known as RAMS, or the RATSCAT Advanced Measurement System.

The *Skunk Works* was selected to design and construct this new radar backscatter test range at the White Sands Missile Test Range, as quickly as possible and at a reasonable cost. Although it was not a special access program, the *Skunk Works* and its customer organized and operated RAMS as if it were so, to eliminate unwanted, unproductive oversight.

A key to the program's success was the team spirit that developed between the small *Skunk Works* and customer program offices (5 people each), and the extensive subcontractor team. They were confronted with and overcame a number of major challenges. For example, differing site conditions (rock vs. the expected gravel); disruptions created by the need to evacuate the site due to test missile firing (more than projected); and state authorities claiming the right to impose state taxes (a mutually agreed set aside as a cost reimbursable item).

The program was a total success in terms of system performance, schedule, and cost. The range was built, equipment was installed, and the system was fully operational in 24 months as scheduled. The completed system met or exceeded all performance requirements. At the outset, Air Force civil engineers believed construction would take considerably longer, and the cost would be considerably greater than in our proposed CPFF contract price. Consequently, the customer and the *Skunk Works* negotiated a fixed price contract with an $80.1 million ceiling, and a target of $64.6 million. In the end, the *Skunk Works* underran the target price by $2.1 million. The RAMS program has been subsequently represented as the only construction contract in the history of the Air Force Development Test Center to underrun target or ceiling price.

**Conclusions**

For the past half century, the Lockheed *Skunk Works* has employed a unique management approach that fosters creativity and initiative, and has prove to be a highly effective means for:

- Creating new technology and concepts
- Rapid prototyping of advanced vehicles
- Engineering and manufacturing development (EMD) of new systems
- Low rate and small quantity production
- System upgrades with new technology

The *Skunk Works* and its customers have consistently met program objectives. Success has been achieved by:

- Establishing small, but strong, program office teams.
- Giving a program manager total control of all program functions and thereby the ability to meet technical, cost and schedule objectives.
- Minimizing the size of program staffs, and maximizing individual responsibility.
- Maintaining daily, open communications focused on joint problem-solving.
- Restricting program access to "outsiders" while ensuring appropriate, but minimum, oversight.
- Establish challenging, but achievable requirements, and minimizing changes.
- Setting tight schedules while recognizing that delays/setbacks will occur.
- Keeping tight control over all expenditures, and reviewing costs regularly and thoroughly.
- Tailoring contracts to eliminate restrictive/non-essential provisions.
- Minimizing the size and detail of specifications.
- Minimizing paperwork—formal reports/documentation and formal contractor-customer program reviews.
- Focusing on the engineering design and utilizing manufacturing, QA, test, materiel, and logistics support early in the process.
- Using a simple engineering drawing system with "red marking" to eliminate delays in fabrication and assembly.
- Allowing the contractor to conduct the flight testing of his products.
- Maintaining security consistent with the program requirements.
- Co-locating personnel to the maximum extent possible.

By following these practices, the *Skunk Works* has demonstrated a consistent ability to prototype, develop and produce highly advanced aircraft in minimum time and at low cost.

The current environment demands that the DoD and industry adopt practices that shorten the acquisition cycle and increase efficiency. And with the future emphasis on technology development, prototyping/advanced technology demonstrators, selective/low rate procurements and system upgrades, consideration should be given to broader application of a *Skunk Works* approach.

**Appendix G: SOME DEVELOPMENT ASPECTS OF THE YF-12A INTERCEPTOR AIRCRAFT** by Clarence L. "Kelly" Johnson, Vice President, Lockheed Aircraft Corporation, Burbank, California, July 1969

**Abstract:**

In this paper, problems encountered in the development and testing of the Lockheed-USAF Mach3+ interceptor aircraft are discussed. The application of high strength titanium alloys, some system development aspects and a number of aerodynamic and thermodynamic problems are briefly reviewed. Flight tests at very high speeds and altitudes involved development of new escape systems, cooling and navigation equipment, among many others.

**Introduction:**

In the early 1960s, the Advanced Development Projects Group, (the *Skunk Works*), of Lockheed, was given the task of development of an advanced interceptor.

The aircraft was to have a continuous cruising speed above Mach 3.0, at altitudes over 80,000 feet. It was to incorporate a Pratt & Whitney turbo-ramjet powerplant and the Hughes ASG-18/GAR-9 fire control and missile system. The engine had never been flown previously and was, and is, a very advanced concept in all respects.

The Hughes system, involving advanced Doppler radar and many other features, was undergoing tests, along with the GAR-9 missile, on a B-58 testbed. It is interesting to survey the status of design and equipment availability for the continuous cruising speed at the conditions noted at the time of conception of the YF-12A.

While there was a considerable amount of experience with the aluminum fighter aircraft at Mach numbers of approximately 2, these aircraft had very short durations of only a few minutes at such speeds, and neither the temperature nor the altitude factors gave much help or experience required for the design of Mach 3 aircraft.

The North American B-70 was in its design stages. It was expected that a large amount of fall-out would result from this program and the NASA tests on the X-15. Both of these conditions did not apply however; the YF-12A rapidly passed the development status and took different paths than followed for the B-70. The X-15 with its very short duration of flight, even though at higher Mach numbers and altitudes, did not encounter problems of air breathing powerplant inlet design, ejectors or steady state temperature conditions.

In fact, in terms of cooling of the cockpit, the problem turned out to be at least seven times as hard on the YF-12A due to the steady state heat flux, than it was for the X-15. It is also true that, in the whole series of research aircraft from the X-1 though the latest types beyond the X-015, there are no powerplant problems even remotely resembling those we encountered on the YF-12A. Most of the high speed X-series aircraft were either rocket powered, or followed conventional design, current at the same time on military fighter aircraft.

We considered various advanced materials, particularly steels and new titanium alloys for a considerable period before deciding on the most modern of the titanium alloys.

In studying the B-70 honeycomb approach, it was evident very shortly that the *Skunk Works* was not smart enough to make use of steel honeycomb with its very involved and precise tooling and difficulties in quality control. We decided to use the unconventional alloys of titanium in a construction which was open for inspection and construction. When one speaks of titanium, it should be realized that approximately 93% of the structural weight of the YF-12A is built of advanced alloys of this material. Certainly, our whole industry had used titanium in it lower strength and, particularly, in its annealed conditions for certain applications on many aircraft, including our jet transports (where it is used for rip stoppers as well as certain hot areas in the engine installations). There is, however, a vast difference in using material with ultimate strengths of 120,000 pounds per square inch and those of up to 200,000 pounds per square inch, which we finally used on the YF-12A and its follow-on aircraft.

Lockheed had worked with titanium on a research basis since 1949. We attempted to attain high strength-weight ratios, good ductility, and relatively cheap structures, which did not develop very rapidly, however.

In the field of equipment there was an amazing lack of high temperature electronic gear, particularly in the areas of wires, plugs, transducers, etc. Many vendors told us they had transducers good for 1,000° F. operating temperatures, but when we tested the gear we found it had mainly been designed for rocket testing and its life span was very short. Due essentially to temperature lag, the inside of the unit seldom got hot.

There were no hydraulic fluids or pumps that could take operating temperatures continuously of approximately 600° F. There were no hydraulic seals, suitable for such an environment.

The navigation problem was particularly important in that at such high speeds, which we were designing for, it was absolutely mandatory to depend on automatic navigation, which we chose to be of the inertial type.

The cooling for the electrical black boxes, armament and cockpit led us into a new area of design.

Starting with bleed air from the engine at a temperature between 1,300° F. and 1,400° F., it was necessary to develop equipment such as the turbine units, as well as heat exchangers for both air-to-air and air-to-fuel types, which would provide cooling air to the cockpit at -30° F. to maintain the temperature between 30° F. to 100° F. maximum.

There were no escape parachutes, drag chutes, rocket-eject propellants and similar equipment available that could take the range of temperatures, altitudes, and speeds which would develop after continuous thermal soaking at high speeds and altitudes.

There were no control cables which would take the required number of cycles safely. So we had to have special ones made of Elgiloy, the material used for watch springs.

There was no fuel available which could take the continuous high temperatures, particularly having the characteristics of low vapor pressures at high temperatures and low coking characteristics to prevent clogging of the engine fuel system.

The use of plastic for radomes at these temperatures required the development of new materials and new processes for their construction.

A whole host of antennas had to be developed for high temperatures and high altitude operations in air density only slightly greater than one per cent of the sea level values.

I believe I can truly say that everything on the aircraft from rivets and fluids, up through materials and powerplants had to be invented from scratch.

**The Design Effort:**

It is rather amazing that with all these problems to be solved, that using the so-called *Skunk Works* approach, the number of engineers in the design effort at ADP was considerably less than 200 at its peak. These were very experienced personnel who performed well in producing the advances weapon system.

A similar system was followed by Pratt & Whitney in the design of the J58 engine and their performance, as well as that of Hughes, was remarkably good. We could only do such a job by having the closest possible liaison among our associates and vendors. They responded uniformly with the greatest dedication in taking on the problems outlined above.

In fact, the J58 was perhaps the single most important aspect driving the design of the aircraft. Consisting of three major elements (inlet and inlet control; engine and its control; and self-actuating airframe mounted ejector nozzle) it was a complex and highly integrated system without peer at the time of its debut.

The inlet was an axisymmetric design with a translating spike. When the spike was retracted to its high Mach number position, the inlet contained an internal throat typical of a mixed compression design. Boundary-layer control on the spike was provided by a porous centerbody bleed with the bleed air passing overboard through louvers located at the ends of the centerbody support struts. Cowl boundary layer bleed was taken off through a "shock-trap" bleed, oversized to provide sufficient pressure to feed the air through the engine secondary compartment and into the ejector. This cowl bleed air served the dual purpose of stabilizing the terminal shock and cooling the engine and nozzle. The inlet was fitted with a forward bypass door, controlled by an inlet control to pass excess airflow overboard, matching the inlet to the engine. Aft bypass airflow joined the cowl bleed air passing through the ejector. This flow had to be limited in order to avoid backing up the bleed and unstarting the inlet (when supersonic flow entering an inlet breaks down due to the expulsion of a normal shock, the inlet is said to have unstarted). It was manually scheduled. The aft bypass was added after initial flight tests indicated forward bypass airflow was insufficient to allow idle operation. Also, judicious use of the aft bypass during acceleration reduced the drag of the forward bypass flow.

The Pratt & Whitney JT11D-20, referred to in the military by its original J58 Navy designator, was a single-spool afterburning turbojet with a fourth-stage bleed bypass which ducted air into the afterburner. This bleed system was operated at high Mach numbers to provide increased compressor stall margin. The bleed air reentered the engine ahead of the afterburner where the air was used for cooling and increased thrust augmentation. The engine fuel control maintained a ratio of primary fuel flow to burner pressure as scheduled by compressor inlet temperature, rotor speed, and power lever. Fuel flow ratio was trimmed by exhaust gas temperature to maintain high cycle efficiency. Engine airflow was controlled by scheduling engine rpm as a function of inlet total temperature. Engine rpm was maintained by modulating the exhaust nozzle. This arrangement provided nearly constant airflow at a given Mach number from below military power to maximum afterburner, which was very desirable when operating behind a supersonic mixed compression inlet. The J58 was unique in being designed to operate continuously in afterburner.

Interestingly, there were no igniters of any kind in the J58. Instead, tetra-ethyl-borane (TEB) was used. This chemical, which self-ignited upon contact with the atmosphere, served not only to ignite the standard JP-7 kerosene-based low-volatility fuel in the burner section of the engine, but also to ignite the afterburners. Enough TEB was provided to allow ten ignitions.

The ejector nozzle was a blow-in-door ejector design with free floating trailing edge flaps developed by Pratt & Whitney and modified as required to install it on the airframe. Airframe mounting of the ejector facilitated the passage of large secondary airflows and allowed aircraft structural provisions to pass through the ejector. Airframe mounting allowed a smooth transition from the aircraft contours into the ejector contours and facilitates engine removal. The blow-in-doors provided tertiary air to fill the ejector nozzle at airspeeds below Mach 1.1. The trailing edge flaps opened up between Mach 0.9 and Mach 2.4, in order to provide a divergent shroud around the primary nozzle and the secondary stream at high Mach numbers.

The propulsion system was optimized to provide maximum thrust at relatively high angles of attack for maximum altitude capability while operating at high Mach number cruise. The inlet was sized to provide good transonic performance and excellent high speed cruise performance, With increasing flight Mach number, the engine air inlet became a potentially more significant part of the propulsion system and could affect the aircraft flying qualities.

Each inlet centerbody had a spike which moved forward at low speeds to provide a large throat area required to match engine airflow and spill excess airflow ahead of the inlet. As the Mach number increased above Mach 1.6, the spike was retracted to capture more airflow and restrict the throat as required to slow the flow for efficient compression. The inlet control sensed flight mach number at the nose boom of the aircraft. Angle-of-attack and angle-of-sideslip were sensed by an attitude probe on the left side of the pitot static boom. Spike position was scheduled by Mach number and biased by angle-of-attack, angle-of-sideslip, and normal acceleration. Normal acceleration was selected in order to compensate for the effects of structural bending. The nose of the aircraft containing the angle-of-attack sensor deflected up or down during elevated g conditions depending upon fuel loading in the aircraft.

When an inlet unstarted, a sensor was provided to note the rapid drop in duct pressure. This unstart signal overrode both inlet spikes and drove them forward in order to remove the internal contraction sufficiently to allow the inlet to restart. The spike then returned to its normal position. Both inlets were restarted in order to balance the forces produced upon the airframe by the unstarted inlet.

In the event of a control system malfunction, the spike could be set manually in accordance with a Mach schedule on the cockpit control provided hydraulic pressure was available and the spike linear voltage differential transducer (LVDT) was functional. If the spike LVDT failed, the spike could be moved forward with a solenoid.

With the spike properly positioned, the inlet was capable of producing a pressure ratio of 40:1 at Mach 3.0-plus, provided the terminal shock was properly positioned within the inlet. The terminal shock moved in response to changes in airflow. The forward bypass door in each inlet consisted of a series of openings in a rotating band located a short distance aft of the inlet throat. Rotation of the band uncovered matching openings in the inlet duct and allowed airflow to pass overboard through louvers.

Operating automatically , the bypass doors were open on the ground to allow additional air to enter the inlet at static conditions. The doors were closed upon retraction of the landing gear. At Mach 1.4, the bypass sometimes moducated as required to produce a scheduled pressure ratio between a duct wall static pressure slightly aft of the inlet throat and a cowl pitot pressure. The single pressure ratio, like the spike position, was scheduled as a function of Mach number, biased by angle-of-attack, angle-of-sideslip, normal acceleration, and in addition, spike position error. If the signal pressure was below the pressure ratio set by the control cam, the bypass door would close, reducing the airflow from the duct.

During rapid transients, if the spike was out of position as indicated by a large voltage to the spike electro-hydraulic valve, an open bias was applied to the forward bypass door. This added tolerance during dynamic situations and made provision for the fact the spike was out of its scheduled position.

When the bypass door was commanded closed beyond its stop, the hydraulic valve and electronics would tend to integrate to a condition which would not allow rapid response to a door open transient. This tendency was overcome by providing a capacitor circuit which changed in response to a large door closed signal and opposed the door closed signal.

Large unsatisfied forward bypass door open commands were sensed and used to double the door open signal gain and provide added response to the bypass doors in a direction to avoid unstarts.

In the event of a malfunction of the bypass control, manual control of the door was possible by cockpit control knob or an open override solenoid switch.

The *Skunk Works'* system provides for minimum paperwork, but does require good documentation on all important developments. I can assure you that one does not develop an aircraft like the YF-12A on the "back of an envelope", a term sometimes used in a derogatory sense regarding our operation. The fact is, that in such a large program, our operating techniques were investigated many times by various groups of Government-technical, contractual and audit types, and we were given excellent marks for performance and in the discipline we were able to maintain in our various systems and controls.

I will touch briefly on a few interesting items in the design effort. We made ample use of full scale mock-ups and test rigs. The whole fuel system from the refueling pump into the engine fuel control and afterburner booster pump was represented and run for hundreds of hours simulating fuels at various temperatures and altitudes up to 100,000 feet. The fuselage angle could be simulated up to 35° inclination as well as for the dive conditions, and the complete fuel gauging system, refueling and dump systems were represented accurately.

When it was understood that the fuel temperature and pressure of final injection to the engines takes place at a temperature of 600° F. and a pressure of 130 psia, the fuel characteristics as well as the purging system and pumping system required a very considerable amount of development.

Obtaining satisfactory grease for high temperature bearings turned out to be extremely difficult. We evaluated dozens of different types. Two of the best for high temperature use froze up the grease guns at normal temperatures!

A full scale hydraulic system was also mocked up and operated many hundreds of hours.

When I first wrote to various vendors to get hydraulic oils, as well as other gear, one enterprising firm sent me a free sample of a fluid good for operation at 600° F. When I opened up the package, I noticed it was enclosed in a canvas bag. It was a white powder at normal room temperatures and up to 200° F.! Not being desirous of thawing out the system with a blow torch every time we had a flight, we did not use this material, The petroleum based fluid which we did use was an initial development at Penn State College, in which we placed a considerable number of additives to get proper lubricity. We finally arrived at a suitable specification and were able to get a supply of material which has given us excellent results to date.

I must say that the original cost of something like $130 per gallon led us to spend another fifty cents to ship the material in one gallon cans, to avoid the risk of destroying larger containers in service.

We had need for a complete cockpit installation which could be tested at high temperatures, so we built a forward fuselage which was of interest to us also from a structural point of view. This section of the aircraft, which makes use of the minimum gauge materials, includes, of course, the windshield glass, and has many pieces of double curved structure. This gave us an opportunity to check our production methods, which was indeed fortunate. We found of the first 6,000 pieces we fabricated of the Beta B-120 titanium, we lost 95%. With the help of Titanium Metals Corporation, we attacked the problem vigorously, investigating such factors as hydrogen embrittlement, heat treatment procedures, forming methods, and design for production. We solved these problems, but at considerable cost.

We were very concerned about the method of building the wing box, with particular reference to the difference of heating rate between the thin outer skin and the heavy spars. We built a section approximately 4 feet wide by 6 feet long and subjected it to the temperature flux which would be encountered during typical climb and acceleration maneuvers. We had taken the usual steps to provide the smoothest possible external surface. On the first test using heat lamps to develop the proper heat flux rate—as well as we were able to—the skin curled up like a dish rag. It was therefore necessary to provide a means for allowing the skin temperatures to climb exactly with the Mach number, and yet not to wrinkle in a manner that would provide low strength and high drag. This was done by using chord-wise corrugations and a few tricks with how we attach the wing surface to the spars. We have had no difficulties due to the time difference in heating up of various aircraft components which vary from a few seconds for the thin skins to an hour for the landing gear.

We were very concerned about temperatures for the tires during long missions. Here, Air Force programs sponsored by Wright Field, gave us a good lead in tire design. When we retracted the wheels into the fuselage fuel tank area, we were able to provide enough insulation and radiant cooling so that tire temperatures in-flight have not been a problem.

We set ourselves a very high goal in providing crew escape systems. We were determined to develop a system good for escape at zero velocity on the ground and through the complete flight spectrum, having speeds above Mach 3 at 100,000 feet. The unit was towed by an automobile on the lakebed. We did achieve our design goals, but it took several years of constant improvement of parachute design, the seat itself, the rocket ejectors, and every element of the escape system, including substantial work on all aspect of personal equipment.

I have never been convinced that a capsule ejection is required for anything other than high velocity reentry from outer space. Our escape system in a very important sense really provides a capsule, which is the pressure suit, which is surely capable of meeting the speeds and temperatures likely to be encountered in the near future of manned aircraft.

The area of such escape systems which needs more work at the present time has to do with water recovery, particularly in high waves, but in this regard excellent progress is being made to date.

**Aerodynamic Testing:**

Obviously, very sophisticated wind tunnel testing was required in the design of the YF-12A. Besides the usual lift, drag, and stability testing, very careful measurements transonically had to be made. The testing of the inlet and the ejector, took by far, the most effort. Million s of test points were taken to develop the internal compression inlets. Basic to the concept of the YF-12A was to get the inlet away from the wing and fuselage effects within the limits of the shock patterns developed by the fuselage nose, and to get the ejector to work in a field where we had a chance of minimizing base drag.

Early designs involving engines buried in the fuselage were discarded for these reasons. We faced the problem of high, offset thrust and drag during engine failure or blowout. It was decided to account for this by using a stability augmentation system that in a few milliseconds would provide the proper rudder angle to compensate for any duct or engine blow out. This device has been so successful that it was several years after the initial flights before the pilot knew which engine would blow during an inlet unstart. It is absolutely impossible to depend on manual reaction to account for such disturbances, but the stability augmentation system designed to our requirements by Minneapolis-Honeywell has been extremely good.

Test of the ejector, which is of the blow-in door type, were run in several facilities, including the Pratt & Whitney wind tunnel. We made a fundamental error in not providing for the presence of the wing, fuselage, and vertical tail, which affected the ejector performance. This was particularly true in the transonic speed range.

As soon as aerodynamic data were available, NASA modified the X-15 flight simulator which was used to very good effect to study the flight characteristics of the aircraft in advance of its first flight.

The simulator, in fact, gave conservative results in terms of emergency conditions, as the pilot was not subjected to the various accelerations and vibrations, which developed and which assist him in taking proper corrective action. The device was very useful in development of the stability augmentation and control system.

**Construction Phase:**

Tooling for the type of construction used in the YF-12A was quite straightforward, except that, fabrication tools were a much higher percentage of the overall cost of tooling than they normally would be for aluminum structures.

In an effort to save weight, the basic structure contained many small pieces, which in aluminum could have been combined readily to reduce the parts count. Hot forming of the B-120 alloy was very expensive and slow, but an excellent product was obtained in the end.

We found that the machinability of titanium was of great importance to our overall cost, as the rate of metal removal from the high strength titanium alloys was initially 5% of what could be done on aluminum parts. Likewise, it was necessary to invent new drills, cutting machinery, powerheads for profilers, and cutting lubricants to increase the rate of metal removal.

We were not able to obtain die forgings to final dimensions, or extrusions in the finished form. On certain large rings, which were cut on tape controlled profilers, approximately 90% of the forging weight had to be removed by machining.

When you consider the miles of extrusions required for an aircraft the size of the YF-12A, it is obvious that every effort had to be made to improve titanium machining, not only at Lockheed, but with all our vendors who did approximately 60% of the work.

We set up training classes for machinists, a complete research facility for developing tools and procedures, and issued research contracts to competent outside vendors to develop improved equipment. This was very successful in all its phases. We were able to improve the rate of metal removal from three to ten times the industry average rate at the conclusion of the program, and we increased drill life from ten holes per grind to an average of over 119.

There is still a great deal to do, as titanium construction is still very expensive compared to dural in aircraft.

Very careful records were kept of all processes of making titanium parts. In fact, it is possible to track back the construction of all parts to the output at the rolling mills. These data include strength information on the parts, the direction of grain in the sheet metal used, and such factors as the critical bend radius, at which the coupon sample would break. We found it more important to make what is described as, a notch bend test on the material sample, than it was to try to correlate ductility with elongation factors.

One of the hardest items we had t construct was titanium rivets. This was basically because of inability in the early days to obtain pure enough samples of materials in wire form. Initially, the cost of titanium fasteners, such as bolts of different types, were extremely high, but today with their greater use in other aircraft, the price has been reduced considerably.

**Flight Test Phase:**

After completion of very thorough structural tests, the flight test phase was undertaken.

Great difficulty existed in obtaining instrumentation satisfactory for measuring pressures and air velocity over the speed altitude spectrum. This is particularly true of conditions in the engine air inlet and ejector. This necessitated the development of water cooled instrumentation packages, which were quite clumsy, but did provide a means for making the millions of pressure measurements required through the development tests.

I would say the greatest problem encountered in-flight, had to do with the transonic speed region, where it was extremely difficult to correlate the results from wind tunnel tests and flight tests.

The next greatest problem had to do with the development of the air inlet control system, which involved scheduling the air inlet spike position, and various bypass door arrangements, to maintain the optimum shock position on the cowl, and minimum drag. Operating forces as high as fourteen tons can develop on the spike. This requires massive hydraulic power and extremely fast sensing of the various design parameters to restart the inlet.

Effective bleeding of the boundary layer, both on the outside of the inlet and the spike itself, must be done with minimum drag and carefully balanced to obtain optimum stability of the air flow pattern.

It is most interesting to note that at high speed the thrust developed by the engine, which shows up on the engine mounts, is only 17% of the propelling force of the aircraft. The remainder of the thrust is provided by the pressure distribution integrated around the inlet and the ejector for the complete nacelle. Note that the inlet alone provides 70% of the thrust, the spike is 14%, and the ejector pushes with 27% to make up the total thrust for the aircraft.

My good friends at Pratt & Whitney do no like me to say, that at high speeds, their engine is only a flow inducer, and that after all, it is the nacelle pushing the airplane!

The aircraft showed itself to have excellent flight characteristics throughout its speed range, particularly on takeoff and landing. Visibility was good, but the pilots initially complained of a very high glare flying at high altitudes. The use of non-reflective coatings on instruments, and other areas, definitely helped this condition.

We looked with great interest on the test program to see whether we would ever reach an altitude where there was no clear air turbulence at all. Unfortunately, this situation does not exist, although the frequency of encountering turbulence, and the load factors therefrom, are substantially less at high altitudes than at low altitudes under 50,000 feet.

The sonic boom experience encountered provided a shotgun pattern of ground pressures, which showed the computed values to be good, but variations therefore, particularly in the transonic region, to be about plus or minus 200% from the theoretical value.

During the initial test stages, an unforeseen problem cropped up, and this was, —how to get the airplane down! If power was retarded too quickly, and a high rate of descent established, it was possible for the engine case to cool much faster than the compressor disk, which resulted in rubbing the compressor blades in the case.

The testing of the Military equipment is classified and can not be discussed in this paper.

**Conclusions:**

As a result of our experience on the YF-12A, the following conclusions are noted:

(1) It was proven again, that it is absolutely impossible to foresee all problems in advance, when making large steps forward in the speed altitude regime. We need prototype programs now, more than ever, since the beginning of manned flights, in my view.

(2) There was, and still is, a lack of an industrial base to produce Mach 3+ aircraft. In fact, the nineteen requirements, which I outlined in my Panel Discussion on Advanced Precepts of Aircraft Technology at the AIAA aircraft and Technology Meeting in 1965, still apply, almost unchanged.

(3) Good agreement exists between properly run wind tunnel tests, engine stand tests, and flight tests, after the problems of instrumentation were solved.

(4) There is a completely new breakdown in the cost of manufacturing a Mach 3+ aircraft considering material, parts fabrication, tooling assembly and testing, from what we encounter in low speed aircraft (under Mach 2.2).

(5) There are great opportunities for cost reduction in building titanium aircraft from the procedure used to build the YF-12A, but inflation is rapidly eroding these potential savings in terms of actual dollar costs per aircraft.

(6) Improved machining methods, forging and extrusion presses are vitally needed for high production of either steel or titanium aircraft.

(7) The sonic boom is quite unpredictable with ground pressures varying greatly from flight to flight and from day to day, particularly in the transonic region.

### Appendix H: THE LOCKHEED DESIGNATION SYSTEM

The L-series designators (today they usually are identified as CL for Lockheed-California), which came into being during 1938, are temporary designations assigned when a project (usually an aircraft, but not always) has entered the preliminary design stage. They are used until a project reaches a point wherein detail drawings are authorized and prototype or production funding has been allocated. A model number then is assigned. Because they are mostly design studies and because they can be voluminous in quantity, most CL-series studies do not progress to the Model number assignment stage.

During the forties, fifties, and sixties, the system used by Lockheed for its manufacturer's designations consisted of (1) a Basic Model Number or Modified Basic Model Number, (2) a Powerplant Identification Number, and (3) an Interior Arrangement Identification Number. With the F-94, for instance, the Modified Basic Model Number 780 indicated it to be the seventh proposed version of the Basic Model 80 which eventually included the single-seat P-80/F-80 fighters (Models 80, 180, 280, 380, and 480), the two-seat TP-80/TF-80/T-33 trainers (Model 580), the single-seat F-80D ground attack fighter (Model 680), the two-seat F-94 fighters (Models 780 and 880), the single-seat F-94D ground attack fighter (Model 980), and the two-seat T2V-1/T-1A/T-33B trainers (Model 1080). The fact that the same number, 80, was used by Lockheed for its first jet fighter and by the Air Force for the F-80 series is believed to be coincidental.

### Appendix I: CL-282 HIGH ALTITUDE AIRCRAFT; LOCKHEED REPORT LR 9732

**Summary:** This report presents information on the design of an aircraft capable of flight at an average altitude of 73,000 feet with a combat radius of 1,400 nautical miles. The objective of the design is to accomplish this performance with a relatively small airplane and with a non-jettisonable military payload of 600 pounds. The airplane has a normal takeoff gross weight of 13,768 pounds including 4,966 pounds of fuel which is sufficient for the basic mission. With an overload gross weight of 14,815 pounds, the radius is increased to 1,720 nautical miles.

It is a conventional turbojet design except for the relatively high aspect ratio of 10.0 and wing area of 500 square feet. The airplane has no landing gear; takeoff being accomplished by use of a ground cart. Due to the design shape of the bottom of the fuselage a belly landing can be accomplished without damage to the airplane. The wing design is entirely new. Otherwise the airplane configuration is identical to the Lockheed XF-104 Day Fighter except for the removal of a straight 62 inch section of forward fuselage. This makes very minor local changes in the loft lines. The detail parts are lighter and somewhat different than in the XF-104 in order to incorporate the maximum possible structural simplification and efficiency. This simplification is made possible by the elimination of all requirements pertinent to the XF-104 not necessary for this design, such as fighter load factor, armament, landing gear, etc. However, the nature of the detail design is such as to utilize the maximum of XF-104 design and manufacturing experience. All basic tooling jigs and most detail jigs for the XF-104 are used for the CL-282.

The basic mission diagram includes takeoff from a ground cart in 1,062 feet, climb to initial cruising altitude of 65,000 feet, the 1,400 nautical mile flight to the radius point at which the altitude is 73,000 feet, and return. The overload mission results in a higher combat weight at the radius point due to the additional fuel required for the cruise home. This higher combat weight reduces the altitude at the radius point to 71,500 feet.

The basic performance objective is to obtain a capability for very high altitude flight, and therefore the high speed of this airplane is limited. With the General Electric J73-X52 engine the airplane has a maximum speed of 495 knots at 73,000 feet, and 518 knots at 35,000 feet at combat gross weight. The limiting speed below 35,000 feet is determined as a function of the relative gust velocity which may be experienced. The ability of the airplane to withstand gusts is increased by the incorporation of upward deflecting ailerons used at altitudes up to 35,000 feet. Thus the limit speed is 150 knots at sea level for a 30 foot per second gust and 300 knots for a 15 foot per second gust at both normal and overload gross weights with ailerons deflected up. With ailerons in the normal position these speeds are 115 knots and 230 knots, respectively. The airplane is designed for a maneuver load factor of 2.5.

**INTRODUCTION:** There is a need for an airplane capable of flight at extreme altitudes, higher than any tactical airplane is capable of flying today. It is possible to design such an airplane by the utilization of present day powerplants plus the aerodynamic features required for minimum wing induced drag. This report shows such an airplane. The utilization of the turbojet engine has been found to result in an over-all airplane size and weight superior to that obtainable with any other currently available powerplant. Furthermore, the turbojet engine greatly simplifies the design and allows the elimination of such items as the landing gear, while maintaining a possibility of takeoff and landing without damage.

It has always been known that an airplane can be designed for the highest speed or the highest altitude, but to obtain the maximum of both these factors in one airplane is difficult. With the advent of supersonic flight capablities it has now become impossible to obtain one airplane with both the maximum speed and the maximum altitude capabilities. The Lockheed Corporation has constructed the XF-104 airplane to have high speed capabilities equal or superior to any aircraft in the world. This was possible through the use of an advanced turbojet engine with afterburner in a fuselage of high fineness ratio, and with a low aspect ratio, extremely thin straight wing. The result is that the XF-104 has a flight ceiling similar to that of other current airplanes but still considerably lower than could be obtained if extreme ceiling was the design objective.

The XF-104 design is such that the wing panels are attached to the sides of the fuselage. The mid-wing configuration which resulted in the minimum drag supersonic airplane also makes possible the minimum drag high altitude airplane. The substitution of high aspect ratio wings of greater thickness and area, on the same attachments of the XF-104 present wing, can change this airplane to one which has high altitude characteristics with reduced speed.

This report presents the results of an investigation in which this airplane is changed in such a way that the basic airframe configuraiton is maintained in terms of fuselage structural arrangement, empennage characteristics and powerplant installation. The design is capable of accomplishing a mission which no other aircraft can perform today.

**OBJECTIVE:** The basic performance objective is to accomplish a 1,400 nautical mile radius mission, the entire distance being flown at altitudes above 65,000 feet with a minimum altitude at the radius point of 72,000 feet. It is desired to achieve this performance with a relatively small airplane of minimum practical strength which carries a non-jettisonable military load of 600 pounds.

This performance is to be attained with a conventional airframe of refined design using present engineering and manufacturing experience. The engine to be used must be a current development which can be obtained in the near future. Design and construction of such an airplane must be of such a nature that it could be started today.

**ENGINE SELECTION:** The three engines which have been considered for this high-altitude aircraft are as follows:

G.E. J73-X52: it weighs 3,150 pounds; it produces 8,920 pounds thrust; specific fuel consumption (#/hr./# th.) is .917; its thrust at 75,000 feet and Mach 0.75 is 398 pounds; its specific fuel consumption (#/hr./th.) at 75,000 feet is 1.377.

Rolls Royce *Avon* RA.14: it weighs 2,897 pounds; it produces 9,500 pounds thrust; specific fuel consumption (#/hr./# th.) is .840; its thrust at 75,000 feet and Mach 0.75 is 385 pounds; its specific fuel consumption (#/hr./# th.) at 75,000 feet is 1.372.

Wright TJ31B1: it weighs 2,720 pounds; it produces 7,800 pounds thrust; specific fuel consumption (#/hr./# th.) is .880; its thrust at 75,000 feet and Mach .075 is 339 pounds; its specific fuel consumption (#/hr./# th.) at 75,000 feet is 1.340.

Thrusts available for the General Electric J73-X52 engine were obtained from the G.E. Specification No. E-615a revised March 16, 1953. For the Rolls Royce *Avon* 14 engine, the data were obtained from T.S.D. Publication 394 (issue 2) dated November, 1952. Performance of the Wright TJ31B1 engine was obtained from the Wright dimensionless performance curves SP1268-1 through SP 1268-9.

The extreme importance of careful thrust determination in the range of altitudes at which the design airplane cruises is exemplified by the fact that five pounds of thrust at 75,000 feet is worth nearly 100 pounds of airplane weight. Consequently, Reynolds number effects were applied to the chart thrusts and specific fuel consumptions of all engines. These are included above.

Although the *Avon* engine shows superior performance on the basis of sea level static ratings, the General Electric J73-X52 engine was chosen for the CL-282 airplane on the basis of its superior performance at altitude and the ease of adaptation to the existing XF-104 fuselage.

**FUSELAGE CONFIGURATION:** In order to accomplish the design mission it is essential that the airplane be at the absolute minimum practical weight over the target. With the relatively large wing area the physical size of the wing is such that basically all fuel may be carried in the wing resulting in airplane weight advantage.

No armament is required and the payload is a 600 pound non-jettisonable item.

In the interest of economy in both engineering and manufacturing a consideration of the adaptability of existing Lockheed fighter models was made. This led to an evaluation of the fuselage and tail sections of the F-80 and XF-104 and the eventual selection of the XF-104 fuselage and tail section as a basis for the CL-282 design. In either fuselage appreciable detail changes of material gages, etc. would be required in the interest of minimum weight. The advantages of the XF-104 type fuselage include the following:

1. The engine may be more readily moved forward in the XF-104 to compensate balance-wise for fuselage fuel and armament removal. The wing-to-fuselage intersection arrangement makes this possible.

2. The resilient wing construction of the XF-104, with no solid bulkhead in the aft and center sections of the fuselage, lends itself more readily to landing directly on the fuselage bottom.

3. The mid-wing arrangement of the XF-104 is much less subject to wing damage, during landing on the belly, than a low wing type.

The fuselage for the CL-282 is basically similar to the XF-104 fuselage in that it utilizes a considerable amount of XF-104 design and actual components.

The strength requirements for flight on the CL-282 fuselage are greatly reduced from those on the XF-104 for reasons including the following:

1. The CL-282 is designed for a maneuvering load factor of 2.5 g as compared to 7.33 g on the XF-104.

2. The elimination of 3,990 pounds of fuel weight from the forward fuselage made it possible to shorten the fuselage forebody approximately 62 inches. In order to reestablish balance the engine is moved forward 562 inches to a position essentially riding directly on the wing. Thus the 1g bending moments on the fuselage are well below those for the XF-104. With the fuel in the wing the center of gravity travel is much less than on the XF-104, so that the tail loads are beneficially affected.

The external shape of the fuselage is identifical to the XF-104 except for the removal of a 62 inch length of fuselage taken from the straight faired area forward of the wing. The shape and position of the engine air inlet ducts is modified to acommodate the more forward engine location and to provide more efficiency at lower speeds as well as to take advantage of weight reduction and simplification associated with much lower design pressures than on the XF-104.

The shift of the engine forward is readily acommplished by eliminating the landing gear cavity and making all the main frames resemble the present two aft main frames.

A 75 gallon fuel sump tank is incorporated in the crotch between the engine air intake ducts. The forward bulkhead for this tank serves also as did the station 378.5 bulkhead, on the XF-104, to transfer fuselage shear loadings to the outside contour of the ducts.

The basic fuselage joints, both service and production, including the wing mating joints and tail mating joints are held the same as on the XF-104.

The fuselage aft of the service joint (Station 508) is the same as on the XF-104 with the exception of gage reductions and the elimination of the drag chute provisions. The dive brakes are retained as on the XF-104 except for some gage reductions.

In the forward end of the fuselage the XF-104 escape hatch, nose landing gear, wheel well, armament and emergency hydraulic pump are eliminated. Therefore the XF-104 split lower longeron is replaced by a simpler single longeron along the bottom centerline.

An abrasion resistant scuff strip approximately 15 inches wide extends the full length of the fuselage beginning at the front pressure bulkheads and is given back-up support by the lower longeron and fuselage rings.

The crew accomodation are revised somewhat from the present XF-104 as a result of the change in mission. Seat ejection, and consequently the escape hatch, are not required because of the low bail-out velocities and therefore are replaced with a simple bucket seat. The aft hinging canopy as used on the XF-104 ship No. 2 is used. The cockpit is pressurized to the present design pressure differential (5 psi limit) and thereby results in a 25,000 foot cockpit altitude at 75,000 feet. The pressurization air is supplied by direct engine bleed. The J73-X52 engine is capable of suppying 4 pounds of air per minute at 5.22 pounds per square inch differential at 75,000 feet and Mach 0.70. A cockpit altitude of 25,000 feet required the use of a pressure-demand oxygen system for the complete flight duration. Therefore, a supply of oxygen is included for seven hours of flight. For emergency use, the pilot is equipped with a paressure suit which is inflated automatically in the event of an emergency by an integral supply of air and oxygen.

The cockpit pressure carrying structure is considerably simplified with the elimination of the escape hatch and gun blast tube provisions. The sides and bottom are changed to a simple carry-through of rings and skin.

**WING SELECTION:** A limited wing configuration study was made to determine the minimum wing area and aspect ratio required to obtain an altitude of 75,000 feet over the target amenable to the weight requirements of the balanced aircraft. A further refinement of this study to determine the optimium wing planform (i.e., the advantages of increase aspect ratio in permitting additional allowable airplane weight) will be included in an appendix to this report at a later date.

The results indicate a wing aspect ratio of 10 with 500 square feet of area would attain the desired altitude over the target with the smallest and lightest airplane. However, it should be noted that in the determination of the feasibility of an extremely high altitude aircraft such as the Lockheed CL-282, one thousand feet of altitude is equivalent to the order of 550 pounds of allowable aircraft weight. Therefore, the altitude requirement becomes of utmost importance in a design selection of this type.

**STABILITY AND CONTROL:** A preliminary examination of the stability and control problems inherent in a design such as the Lockheed CL-282 airplane has been made. These considerations indicate that a tail retaining the present geometric characteristics and size of that of the XF-104 airplane will provide satisfactory longitudinal, directional, and lateral characteristics. Because of the considerably different appearance of the airplane, particularly with respect to the wing size, many of the coefficients do not appear to have their characteristic magnitude, but they nevertheless indicate satisfactory stability qualities.

The wing of the CL-282 airplane has been located with respect to the center of gravity such that the relatively small tail volume supplies a minimum longitudinal static stability margin of 5% mean aerodynamic chord. The most aft center of gravity position is 18.4% chord, and the 5% margin is satisfactory inasmuch as it has been possible to so locate the fuel in the wing that very small travel results as the fuel is burned out in the basic mission. These pitch characteristics were estimated using the Lockheed low speed wind tunnel tests of the XF-104 airplane. Corrections were applied to reflect the shortened fuselage, wing camber and incidence, and reduction in tail volume. In the overload mission configuration, fuel has been placed in tanks located in the aft section of the wing panels. This location of the fuel reduces the minimum static margin to zero longitudinally and will require further study before it can be deemed entirely satisfactory.

The vertical tail contribution to directional stability was determined using the effective lift-curve slope for the XF-104 vertical tail as obtained from Lockheed wind tunnel data. The fuselage directional stability contribution has been calculated based on a Lockheed empirical formula and a series of parametric curves which have given reasonable estimates for the directional stability of wing-body configurations comparable to the present design. The wing-body stability is assumed constant over the Mach number range, while the tail contribution varies with Mach number as the vertical tail lift-curve slope. Thus, a positive static directional stability is inidcated throughout the design speed range.

For the unswept mid-wing configuration, the wing-body contribution is assumed to be very small for zero degrees wing dihedral. The vertical tail contribution was determined using the wind tunnel XF-104 data for vertical tail effective lift-curve slope and the new tail volume. The vertical tail center of pressure position also was determined from wind tunnel data. The resulting dihedral effect is positive for all flight conditions.

The dihedral angle of the wing to provide the lateral stability was selected to obtain a ratio of directional stability to lateral stability of unity. Such a ratio has usually been found to be satisfactory for conventional aircraft in the past in that the lateral dynamic stability and handling qualities are approximately as desired in Air Force Specification 1815-B. Further study of the CL-282 aircraft should be made including extensive dynamic analysis in order to establish the most suitable dihedral angle.

**DESIGN CRITERIA:** The airplane is designed to land on its belly in glider fashion and therefore has no landing gear except for the fuselage structure itself. In order to most efficiently withstand this landing shock the fuselage structure is basically the XF-104 and consists of simple barrel-like construction with flexible rings and no solid bulkheads aft of Station 354.75. A single lower longeron along the full length of the bottom centerline acts as a back-up member for the scuff-strip. The wing is center-mounted to the fuselage main rings so as to divide wing bending moment over the top and under the bottom of the fuselage without destroying fuselage shell resilience for landing. The fuselage is of the three longeron type with two top longerons and one bottom longeron.

The cockpit is pressurized for a 25,000 foot cabin altitude at 75,000 feet (5.0 pounds per square inch differential).

The wing is of conventional two-cell construction with the beam at approximately 48% of chord. The wing bending moment is resisted in each surface by spanwise stringers which originate at the fuselage main frame joints. A root rib in the wing distributes wing torsion to the fuselage frames. The fuel tanks in the wing are of nylon bladder construction and are subjected to vapor pressure. In order to keep these vapor pressures from excessively distorting the airfoil contour, the upper and lower surfaces of the fuel cell are internally tied together by means of molded-in ties. Small replaceable wing tip skids protect the end of the wing and the aileron against abrasion damage.

The empennage is of the same general description as for the XF-104 except that the airfoil thicknesses are increased for structural efficiency. The basic structural support points are identical to those in the XF-104.

The airplane is designed to standard CAR 04 transport structural stength requirements. Accordingly, the basic maneuvering load factor is 2.5 g limit for normal design gross weight:

Normal takeoff gross weight = 13,768 pounds
Normal design gross weight = 13,190 pounds
Overload design gross weight = 14,815 pounds

The overlaod fuel is located in the wing near the spanwise center of pressure location so as to minimize the increase in wing bending moments. On the basis of the strength set up for the normal design gross weight the overload maneuvering load factor is 2.25 g limit.

The speed restrictions for encountering gusts are based on not allowing the gust conditions to exceed strength requirements as set by the 2.5 g maneuvering load factor. The gust velocities are taken as the CAA standard 20 foot per second gust at Vc and 15 feet per second at Vd. In order to minimize these speed restrictions the ailerons are both deflected upward approximately 20 degrees so that in effect the span wise location of the center of pressure is moved inboard. Ample differential deflection is still available for lateral control. This angle is held throughout any period in flight under 35,000 feet and can be used at any other altitude should air turbulence indicate it to be necessary. On this basis the speed restriction, up to 35,000 feet altitude, is 150 knots indicated for a 30 foot per second gust and 300 knots indicated for a 15 foot per second gust.

The design landing strength for the airplane landing in glider fashion is sufficient for up to a 5 foot per second sinking speed with the airplane at a minimum landing speed of 1.2 Vs and being landed on reasonable terrain other than a hard surfaced runway.

**WEIGHT DATA:** The weight estimate for the CL-282 for the most part, is based on comparative data from Lockheed fighters and from estimates of differences with respect to the present XF-104. The resulting group weight and balance summary for the CL-282 is as follows:

Wing: Inasmuch as the wing configuration and loadings are completely different than the XF-104, a complete Rand analysis was made to determine the weight. The critical loading is the design gross weight at 2.5 limit load factor. The wing also accounts for the complete lack of high lift devices.

Fuselage: The fuselage weight is determined by modifying the existing fuselage weight compatible with the fuselage changes dictated by the CL-282 design requirements. All provisions for landing gear, armament, and drag chute are removed. Because the principal fuel tanks are moved from the fuselage into the wings, a 62 inch long barrel section is removed. Weight allowance is made for reduction in intake duct length. In addition to the above changes, a 316 pound weight allowance is made for a general weight reduction of the fuselage structure made possible by the revised design criteria.

Tail: The estimated weight for the tail group is consistent with those for airplanes of equivalent speed and size. The empennage planform configuration for the XF-104 is retained, but the thickness ratio has been increased to 8 percent.

Powerplant: the powerplant group weight was revised to incorporate the J73-X52 engine and to incorporate the principal fuel tanks in the wing instead of the fuselage.

Group Weight and Balance:

| | % MAC | Weight | Horiz. Arm |
|---|---|---|---|
| Wing | | 1,297 | 441.9 |
| Tail | | 200 | 622.3 |
| Fuselage | | 1,600 | 423.0 |
| Surface controls | | 180 | 430.0 |
| Powerplant | | 3,719 | 451.0 |
| Instruments | | 75 | 275.0 |
| Hydraulics | | 50 | 429.0 |
| Electrical | | 300 | 350.0 |
| Electronics | | 150 | 300.0 |
| Furnishings | | 91 | 304.3 |
| Air conditioning | | 125 | 345.0 |
| Weight empty | 30.0 | 7,787 | 435.6 |
| Pilot (incl. pres. suit) | | 300 | 290.0 |
| Military load | | 600 | 325.0 |
| Residual fuel | | 60 | 436.6 |
| Oil | | 23 | 453.0 |
| Oxygen (7 x D-2 bottles) | | 32 | 220.0 |
| Zero fuel weight | 16.2 | 8,802 | 422.4 |
| Fuel/fuselage (75 gallons) | | 488 | 366.0 |
| | 13.0 | 9,290 | 419.4 |
| Fuel/wing (600 gallons) | | 3.900 | 436.6 |
| Design gross weight | 18.4 | 13,190 | 424.5 |
| Fuel/aft wing (89 gallons) | | 578 | 467.0 |
| Takeoff gross weight | 21.0 | 13,768 | 427.0 |
| Fuel/aft wing (161 gallons) | | 1,047 | 467.0 |
| Overload gross wt. | 23.2 | 14,815 | 429.1 |

Fixed equipment: In general, the fixed equipment group weights were estimated from comparison of weight data for the XP-80, F-80C, T-33A, F-94C, and XF-104 airplanes.

The CL-282 has only one hydraulic function, namely the dive brake. From the weight data comparison of Lockheed fighter airplanes it is determined the weight of a hydraulic system per function is 34 pounds. Therefore, a hydraulic weight of 50 pounds is allocated for the CL-282.

Because the power requirements for the military load are unknown a good estimate of the electrical system cannot be made. A 300 pound allotment is provided. This is representative of the F-80C electrical system.

The electronics group is assumed to consist of on ARN-6 and one ARC-34.

The furnishing groups weight is representative of a typical non-jettisonable installation, and includes fire detector system and oxygen provisions.

The air conditioning and pressurization system weight is based on the present system exclusive of the refrigerator. It is assumed that under the design operating conditions only the heat exchanger will be required for cooling cockpit air.

The surface controls estimate accounts for the lack of hydraulic boost and for the absence of high lift devices. Reducing the surface controls weights of five Lockheed fighters to the similar condition, the average resultant group weight is 155 pounds. An allotment of 180 pounds is made for the CL-282.

Useful load: The useful load items include a 300 pound allotment for a pilot with pressure suit, a 600 pound military load, and an allotment for seven D-2 oxygen bottles. This oxygen supply is sufficient for a seven hour flight duration using a pressure demand system with the maximum cabin altitude of 25,000 feet.

**FLIGHT PERFORMANCE:** Following is a brief summary of the methods and sources used to estimate the pertinent performance characteristics of the airplane. While a complete performance analysis has not been made, the maximum speeds, rates of climb, and fuel requirements for the design mission are demonstrated.

Drag Estimation: The drag estimation procedures are adequately described in the Lockheed XF-104 performance report LR 8973. These procedures have been substantiated at low speeds by tests in the Lockheed wind tunnel and at high speeds by tests in the NACA wind tunnels.

Since the fuselage is externally identical to that of the XF-104 but with a 62 inch straight section removed just aft of the canopy, the XF-104 fuselage drag coefficients were used, subtracting the friction drag accountable to the removed section and referenced to the new wing area. In the case of the fuselage a skin friction coefficient of .0030 is used for transitional conditions while at higher Reynolds numbers, the turbulent reduction of skin friction is applied. The effect of Mach number in reducing skin friction has also been incorporated. This is the only airplane component on which this reduction is included.

Inasmuch as the XF-104 tail geometry was maintained except for thickness ratio and all speeds considered are sub-critical, the empennage drags are identical to those of the XF-104.

Based on Lockheed wind tunnel tests of wings of comparable thickness and aspect ratio, a skin friction coefficient of .00325 is indicated which, when applied to the wing wetted area, gives a wing Cdp-min of .0058. It is believed that the variation shown is conservative and that such a highly cambered round-nose section as has been selected will result in smaller Cdp increments than used herein. From these data a maximum low speed lift-drag ratio of 26.8 is indicated, while at cruise Mach numbers and altitudes, maximum lift-drag ratios of 24 to 25 are attained.

Thrust and Drag: The thrust required curves were calculated for a range of weights using appropriate drag coefficients.

Thrust available curves were determined, using the chart thrust of General Electric Specification No. E-615a for the G.E. J73-X52 engine, assuming 98% pressure recovery, and correcting for Reynolds number effects as per the methods used in G. E. Specification R53AGT78.

Speed and Climb: The severe limitations on maximum speed imposed by gusts (due to the low design load factor) are reflected in these curves below 35,000 feet. The speeds depicted are for military power only.

For the climb performance calculations, weight of the airplane has been reduced with altitude according to the amount of fuel burned. Climb speeds up to 35,000 feet conform to the gust limitations indicated. These rates of climb include the kinetic energy correction where applicable. This information is the basis for the radius calculations for the missions discussed herein.

**MISSION ANALYSIS:** Basic Mission: In the basic mission, the combat radius is 1,400 nautical miles. The fuel allowance for warm-up and takeoff is computed as one minute at normal rated power.

A climb to 65,000 feet is made at military power at the speeds indicated.

A climbing cruise out is performed from 65,000 feet to 73,000 feet over the target at a constant cruise Mach number of .75, while cruise-back is maintained at constant altitude for 1,250 nautical miles. The remaining distance is covered by throttling back to idle thrust and descending with dive brakes extended in the remaining 150 nautical miles.

Twenty-five gallons of fuel are maintained for reserve.

Overload Mission: For the overload mission, 250 gallons of additional fuel are carried in the aft wing tanks. For this mission, an altitude of 71,500 feet is attained over the target with a combat radius of 1,720 nautical miles.

**TAKEOFF AND LANDING:** The aircraft is designed to accomplish its mission without a landing gear and to land on its belly in glider fashion after completion of the mission.

Takeoff for Design Mission: Takeoff is accomplished by means of a three-wheeled "takeoff cart". This cart is designed for ease of ground handling of the airplane and is not a flying cart. After a belly landing the aircraft may be drawn onto the cart, directly from the ground, by means of a winch built into the cart. No other special equipment is required. The cart has its own shock absorbing system and supports the airplane by three points, one under each wing and one under the nose just aft of the cockpit. The airplane is mounted on the cart at takeoff angle and lifts off when takeoff speed is attained. A lanyard type attachment to the cart applies brakes on the cart when the aircraft is clear. For convenience during ground handling, the airplane attitude on the cart may be adjusted to any desired angle between level and the takeoff angle.

The airplane takes off in 1,062 feet at 100 knots at sea level.

Takeoff for Practice and Flight Test Missions: Even though the airplane is designed for belly landings it is desirable to minimize unnecessary wear on the airplane by using a detachable landing cart. This detachable landing cart could be designed to fly with the airplane and accordingly be streamlined. The three mounting points for the landing cart are the same points used for the takeoff cart. The landing cart would not have the self-loading feature as does the takeoff cart and the airplane would be hoisted into postion.

The landing strength characteristics of the airplane with the landing cart would be as per conventional landing gear designs for 10 feet per second sinking speeds.

Landing Method: For the basic mission the airplane lands directly on its belly in conventional glider fashion. The barrel structure of the fuselage is designed for maximum possible distributed resilience along the bottom to take the landing shock. A replaceable scuffing strip along almost the full length of the fuselage bottom provides maximum protection against abrasion. Replaceable tip skids on the wing protect the wing and aileron against abrasion damage.

The minimum landing speed, at basic mssion landing weight is 84 knots (1.2 Vs) at sea level.

**CONCLUSIONS:** 1. The Lockheed CL-282 design can accomplish the desired mission of a 1,400 nautical mile radiius at cruising altitudes above 65,000 feet with a final altitude of 73,000 feet at the radius point.

2. By the addition of overload fuel the radius is extended to 1,720 nautical miles with a final altitude of 71,500 feet at the radius point.

3. The desired performance is attained with a relatively small airplane whose takeoff gross weight is 13,768 pounds including a 600 pound non-jettisonable military load.

4. The airframe design and construction is so similar to the Lockheed XF-104 that many of the actual parts, most of the basic tooling jigs, and many of the detail part jigs can be used.

5. Of the engines investigated, the General Electric J73-X52 turbojet is the most suitable to achieve the desired performance.

6. The design of the CL-282 is of such nature that with the present engineering and manufacturing experience this airplane could be started today.

**SPECIFICATIONS:**

Horizontal tail area = 47.5 square feet; vertical tail area = 34.7 square feet ; wing aspect ratio = 10; horizontal tail aspect ratio = 2.98; vertical tail aspect ratio = 1.10; wing taper ratio = .25; horizontal tail taper ratio = .31; vertical tail taper ratio = .50; wing root chord = 136 inches; horizontal tail root chord = 73 inches; vertical tail root chord = 112.5 inches; wing tip chord = 34 inches; horizontal tail tip chord = 22.7 inches; and vertical tail tip chord = 43 inches The wing root section = NACA 64A409 with an incidence of plus 3°; the wing tip section = NACA 64A406 with an incidence of plus 1°; and the tail surfaces = a NACA 64A008 section.

**Appendix J: LOG OF XFV-1 BUNO. 138657 FLIGHTS (COMPLETE)**

**All flights flown by Herman Salmon**

| FLIGHT | TEST NO. | DATE | DURATION | PURPOSE |
|---|---|---|---|---|
| 1 | 54 | 6/16/64 | 0.5 | Initial flight |
| 2 | 55 | 6/23/54 | 0.5 | Rudder spring and stall evaluation |
| 3 | 56 | 7/1/54 | 0.7 | Low-speed handlng;zone 2 cooling |
| 4 | 57 | 7/7/54 | 0.8 | Slow-speed and cooling tests |
| 5 | 58 | 7/13/54 | 0.5 | Low-speed and longitudinal stability |
| 6 | 59 | 7/15/54 | 0.3 | Low-speed and longitudinal stability |
| 7 | 60 | 7/20/54 | 0.8 | Airspeed comparison and long. stab. |
| 8 | 61 | 7/21/54 | 0.8 | Propeller vibration |
| 9 | 63 | 10/26/54 | 0.6 | Shakedown; propeller vibration |
| 10 | 64 | 10/27/54 | 0.7 | Low-speed maneuvers; control |
| 11 | 65 | 10/28/54 | 0.8 | Low-speed maneuvers |
| 12 | 66 | 10/28/54 | 0.2 | Low-speed maneuvers |
| 13 | 68 | 11/15/54 | 0.5 | Propeller vibration; practice transitions |
| 14 | 69 | 11/17/54 | 0.6 | Propeller vibration; practice transitions |
| 15 | 70 | 11/17/54 | 0.7 | Propeller vibration; practice transitions |
| 16 | 71 | 12/13/54 | 0.6 | Practice transitions |
| 17 | 72 | 12/15/54 | 0.5 | Practice transitions; descent rate eval. |
| 18 | 74 | 1/11/55 | 0.1 | Descent rate eval. |
| 19 | 75 | 1/25/55 | 0.4 | Surge investigation; descent rate eval. |
| 20 | 76 | 1/26/55 | 0.2 | Surge investigation |
| 21 | 78 | 2/22/55 | 0.1 | Surge investigation |
| 22 | 80 | 3/15/55 | 0.6 | Surge investigation |

Total flight time logged: 11.5 hours

**Appendix K: XP-80 FIRST FLIGHT (JANUARY 8, 1944) LOG**

"I made a normal takeoff using 9,500 engine rpm, and breaking ground at approximately 100 I.A.S. Immediately after takeoff, I noticed that it was difficult to keep the ship level, laterally, due to the extreme sensitivity of the aileron booster. Otherwise all controls seemed very good. I tried to raise the landing gear but the handle wouldn't come up, so I decided to proceed back to the landing area and terminate the flight. I turned the aileron boost off and noted that the aileron forces were extremely heavy but manageable. Turned the boost back on for landing and again experienced difficulty to keep from rocking the ship. I then made the landing approach and put the flap switch in the down position. The ship seemed to come in fairly fast as if the flaps were not fully down. The elevator forces felt good in landing. On the landing roll, I raised the nose wheel to clear a small depression and the bottom of the aft fuselage scraped the ground. I noticed in taxiing that at low speeds it is difficult to maneuver the airplane. Turning can only be accomplished with the brakes and a little braking will almost stop the airplane. The application of considerable power is necessary to get the ship moving again. Note: It was found after landing that the flaps had partly retracted. The reason that the landing gear handle wouldn't come up was because of malfunctioning of the landing gear scissors switch."

A second flight took place shortly after the first. It is recorded by Burcham as follows:

"I took off at 9,500 engine rpm, running on the fuselage fuel tank. Engine speed was reduced to 9,000 rpm and the climb continued to approximately 11,000 feet at 260 I.A.S. Climbing at such high speeds was quite impressive and the ship seemed to get up very fast. In the climb I felt out the ailerons. The forces are very good and the effectiveness is excellent. In fact, it was so satisfactory that I made several rolls on the way up. Readings were taken at termination of the climb. R. Bearing temp. = 60 degrees C. Jet temp. = 600 degrees C. The longitudinal stability in climb seemed to be satisfactory, but I want to verify this later after feeling it out more. I stalled the airplane, gear up, flaps up, and power off at 95 I.A.S. The ship stalled with no warning. It was sharp, but inoffensive, with no tendency to roll. I repeated this about two or three times with the same results. I put gear down and 50% flaps and stalled at approximately 93 to 95 I.A.S., about the same as before. Then with full flaps, gear down, made a stall at 87 I.A.S. On this one I got a bad right wing stall and the airplane fell off to the right. However, recovery was fairly easy. During the descent, I worked the speeds up slowly. The airplane felt good. I reached a maximum of 490 I.A.S. and everything felt solid. The cockpit was quiet and there were no shrieks from the canopy. Visibility is good. Maneuverability seemed normal as far as I investigated. I noticed some effect on rudder forces, as I had to hold light left or right rudder, depending on speed. I made a low pass across the field with full power, 9,500 rpm, and reached 475 I.A.S. After pulling up I made a series of rolls, in both directions. The airplane rolls extremely well, and has a very fast rate of roll. Longitudinal stability builds up considerably with speed and quite a bit of nose-down tab is needed to maintain trim. In general, engine operation was normal, except that the rear bearing temperature was near the maximum limit of 100 degrees C. most of the time. I made a normal approach for landing with flap switch in down position. Again the airplane seemed to land too fast. Note: After landing it was found that the flaps had partly retracted." Milo Burcham, January 8, 1944.

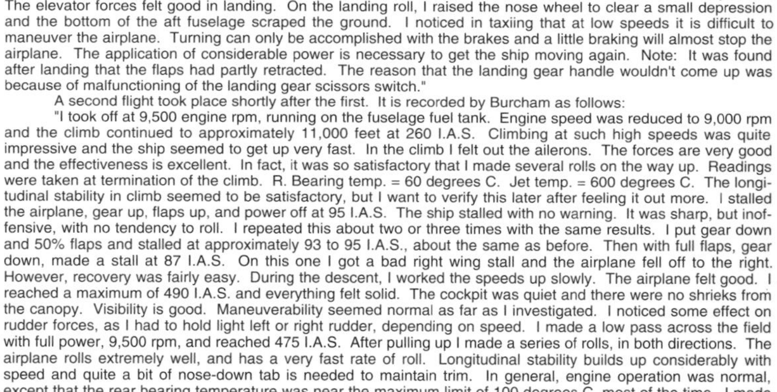

Lockheed

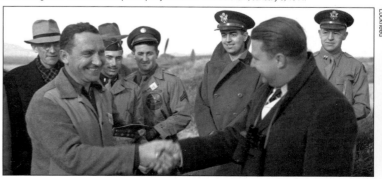

*Milo Burcham and "Kelly" Johnson exchange congratulations following successful completion of the XP-80's first flight at Muroc on January 8, 1944.*

**Appendix L: BIBLIOGRAPHY**


**Books:**

***Aircraft, Engines, and Airmen, A Selective Review of the Periodical Literature, 1930-1969***, August Hanniball, The Scarecrow Press, Inc., Metuchen, New Jersey, 1972

***Aircraft Engines of the World, 1957***, Paul Wilkinson, 1957, Paul Wilkinson, Washington, D.C.

***Central Intelligence Agency, History and Documents, The***, William Leary, 1984, The University of Alabam

***Development of the Lockheed P-80A Jet Fighter Airplane***, Clarence Johnson, 1946,, Lockheed Aircraft Corporation, Burbank, California

***Dragon Lady, The History of the U-2 Spyplane***, Chris Pocock, 1989, Airlife Publishing Ltd., Shrewsbury, England

***Flame Powered, The Bell XP-59A Airacomet and the General Electric I-A Engine***, David Carpenter, 1992, Jet Pioneers of America, Edwards AFB, California

***German Jets in Combat, The***, Jeff Ethell and Alfred Price, 1979, Jane's Publishing Company, London, England

***Encyclopedia of U. S. Air Force Aircraft and Missile Systems, Vol. 1***, Marcelle Knaack, 1978, Office of Air Force History, Washington, D.C.

***Flying the Frontiers, NACA and NASA Experimental Aircraft***, Arthur Pearcy, 1993, Naval Institute Press, Annapolis, MD

***General Dynamics Aircraft and Their Predecessors***, John Wegg, 1990, Putnam Aeronautical Books, London, England

***General Dynamics F-16 Fighting Falcon, Aerofax Aerograph I***, Jay Miller, 1982, Aerofax, Inc., Arlington, Texas

***Gloster Aircraft Since 1917***, Derek James, 1971, Putnam, London, England

***Jet Aircraft of the World, The***, William Green and Roy Cross, 1957, Hanover House, Garden City, New York

***Kelly, More Than My Share of It All***, Clarence L. Johnson and Maggie Smith, 1985, Smithsonian Institution Press, Washington, D.C.

***Liquid Hydrogen as a Propulsion Fuel 1945-1959***, John L. Sloope, 1978, National Aeronautics and Space Administration, Washington, D.C.

***Lockheed Aircraft Since 1913***, Rene' Francillon, 1982, Putnam, London, England

***Lockheed Aircraft Since 1913***, Rene' Francillon, 1987, Putnam, London, England

***Lockheed Constellation***, M. J. Hardy, 1973, Arco Publishing Inc., New York, NY

***Lockheed F-94 Starfire***, Rene' Francillon and Kevin Keaveney, 1986, Aerofax, Inc., Arlington, Texas

***Lockheed F-117 Stealth Fighter***, Jay Miller, 1991, Aerofax, Inc., Arlington, Texas

***Lockheed (General Dynamics/Boeing) F-22***, Richard Abrams and Jay Miller, 1992, Aerofax, Inc., Arlington, Texas

***Lockheed SR-71 (A-12/YF-12/D-21)***, Jay Miller, 1985, Aerofax, Inc., Arlington, Texas

***Lockheed U-2***, Jay Miller, 1983, Aerofax, Inc., Arlington, Texas

***Lockheed U-2R/TR-1***, Jay Miller and Chris Pocock, 1988, Aerofax, Inc., Arlington, Texas

***Messerschmitt Me 262, Arrow to the Future***, Walter Boyne, 1980, Smithsonian Institution Press, Washington, D.C.

***Northrop F-89 Scorpion, Aerofax Datagraph 8***, Gerald Balzer and Mike Dario, 1993, Aerofax, Inc., Arlington, Texas

***Pilot***, Tony LeVier, 1954, Harper & Brothers, Publishers, New York, NY

***P-80 Shooting Star, Evolution of a Jet Fighter, The***, E. T. Wooldridge, Jr., 1979, Smithsonian Institution Press, Washington, D.C.

***Rockwell International B-1A/B***, Don Logan and Jay Miller, Aerofax, Inc., Arlington, Texas

***U-2 Affair, The***, Thomas Ross and David Wise, 1962, Random House, New York, New York

***United States Military Aircraft Since 1908***, Peter Bowers and Gordon Swanborough, 1971, Putnam, London, England

***United States Navy Aircraft Since 1911***, Peter Bowers and Gordon Swanborough, 1990, Putnam, London, England

***U. S. Intelligence Community***, Jeffrey Richelson, 1985, Ballinger Publishing Co., Cambridge, Massachussetts

***Vehicles of the Air***, Victor Loughead, 1909, The Reilly and Britton Company, Chicago, Illinois

***World Encyclopedia of Aero Engines***, Bill Gunston, 1986, Patrick Stephens, Wellingborough, England

***X-Planes, The***, Jay Miller, 1988, Aerofax, Inc., Arlington, Texas

**Magazines**:

**Lockheed Miscellaneous:**

Flying, March 1960, p. 24-27
Flying, April 1960, p. 44-48
Flying, May 1960, p.42-46
Interavia, June 1957, 582-583
Naval Aviation News, July 1957, p. 12-15
Popular Aviation, October 1937, p.16-18
Western Flying, February 1934, p. 18-20

**P-80 *Shooting Star*:**

Aero Digest, September 1, 1945, p.60-61
Aeroplane, May 7, 1948, p.526-527
Aeroplane, October 21, 1949, p.557
Aircraft Engineering, March 1948, p.75-86
Air News, October 1945, p.30
Airpower Historian, July 1962, p.180-183
Air Progress, April/May 1963, p.75
Aviation, July 1945, p.149-151
Aviation Age, December 1950, p.17-18
Aviation Week, July 19, 1948, p.22-26
Aviation Week, August 2, 1948, p.13
Canadian Aviation, September 1945, p.58-59
Commercial Aviation, August 1945, p.78-80
Flight, April 12, 1945, p.392-394
Flight, August 9, 1945, p.152
Flight, June 26, 1947, p.596-597
Flight, May 6, 1948, p.495
Flight, August 17, 1950, p.197
Flying, October 1945, p.31
Flying, April 1946, p.44-45
Flying, March 1956, p.28-29
Flying, December 1948, p.33-35
Interavia, July 1947, p.15-17
Interavia, May 1948, p.276-277
Interavia, November 1948, p.610-613
Skyways, July 1945, p.20-21
Skyways, August 1946, p.20-21
Skyways, July 1948, p.30-31
Skyways, January 1949, p.30-32
U.S. Air Services, September 1945, p.22
U.S. Air Services, February 1946, p.26-28
U.S. Air Services, July 1947, p.21-22
U.S. Air Services, May 1948, p.25
U.S. Air Services, July 1948, p.21
U.S. Air Services, July 1953, p.18
U.S. Air Services, December 1954, p.22
Western Flying, March 1945, p.68
Western Flying, September 1945, p.48-49
Western Flying, March 1946, p.34
Western Flying, May 1946, p.25
Western Flying, May 1948, p.8
Western Flying, October 1948, p.13
Western Flying, October 1949, p.22

**Model 75 *Saturn*:**

Air Force, September 1946, p.28-29
Aviation, January 1945, p.169
Aviation, August 1946, p.93
Canadian Aviation, September 1946, p.85
Commercial Aviation, January 1945, p.45-46
Interavia, June 1946, p.41-47
Skyways, February 1945, p.92
Western Flying, December 1944, p.76
Western Flying, August 1946, p.56

**XR6O-1/XR6V-1 *Constitution*:**

Aeroplane, June 20, 1947, p.652-653
Air Progress, February 1967 p.31-33
Aviation, October 1946, p.86
Aviation Age, February 1952, p. 36-37
Aviation Week, March 1, 1948, p.20-21
Aviation Week, March 8, 1948, p. 29
Aviation Week, August 30, 1948 p.20-27
Canadian Aviation, October 1946, p.100
Flight, September 5, 1956, p. 248
Flying, December 1946, p.51-53
Interavia, June 1946, p.20-27; April 1949, p. 191-193
Naval Aviation News, October 1946, p.11
Naval Aviation News, January 1947, p.9
Naval Aviation News, September 1947, p.16
Naval Aviation News, May 1948, p.23
Naval Aviation News, April 1949, p.20-21
U.S. Air Services, December 1946, p.25
U.S. Air Services, June 1948, p.15
U.S. Air Services, November 1948, p.15
Western Flying, October 1946, p.70
Western Flying, June 1951, p.16

**T-33:**

Aeroplane, August 21, 1953, p.225-228
Flying Review International, January 1968, p.50

**F-94 *Starfire*:**

Aero Digest, August 1951, p.20-23
Aero Digest, November 1954, p.32-33
Air Pictorial, April 1956, p.126-127
Aviation Week, June 26, 1950, p.13
Aviation Week, June 25, 1951, p.20-23
Aviation Week, July 7, 1952, p.16-17, 61-64
Aviation Week, November 23, 1953, p.19
Aviation Week, August 16 1954, p.380-381
Bee-Hive, Summer 1952, p.31-32
Flight, July 11, 1952, p.46
Flying, August 1951, p.22-23
flying, October 1952, p.29
Flying, February 1954, p.37
RAF Flying Review, October 1962, p.57
Skyways, October 1949, p.19
Skyways, April 1953, p.10-11
Western Aviation, November 1951, p.12
Western Aviation, July 1952, p.11
Western Aviation, December 1953, p.26
Western Flying, October 1950, p.18

**F-90:**

Aeroplane, July 1, 1949, p.18-21
Aviation Week, May 23, 1949, p.12-13
Aviation Week, December 25, 1950, p.27-29
Flying, June 1950, p.14-15
Naval Aviation News, September 1949, p.1
Naval Aviation News, February 1950, p.12
RAF Flying Review, January 1957, p.13
RAF Flying Review, September 1960, p.21
Skyways, August 1949, p.30-31
Skyways, May 1950, p.14-15
Western Flying, June 1949, p.9
Western flying, August 1950, p.22

**R7V *Constellation*:**

Aviation Week, September 13, 1954, p.18
Western Aviation, January 1953, p.19
Western Aviation, October 1954, p.4

**T2V-1 *SeaStar*:**

Aviation Age, May 1956, p.20-25
Aviation Week, April 11, 1955, p.15
Aviation Week, April 23, 1956, p.62-66
Flying Review International, January 1968, p.50
RAF Flying Review, February 1958, p.26-29
U.S. Air Services, January 1956, p.18
Western Aviation, March 1956, p.32

**F-104 *Starfighter*:**

Aeroplane, April 20, 1956, p.284-285
Aeroplane, June 20, 1958, p.841
Air Force, August 1960, p.60-64
Air Pictorial, July 1956, p.232-233
Air Pictorial, August 1958, p.277-279
Air Progress, February/March 1965, p.17-23
Aviation Age, July 1956, p.26-31
Aviation Age, May 1958, p.60-67
Aviation Week, July 12, 1954, p.15
Aviation Week, August 9, 1954, p.21-24
Aviation Week, December 3, 1956, p.32-33
Aviation Week, February 18, 1957, p.81
Aviation Week, February 10, 1958, p.66-84
Aviation Week, October 27, 1958, p.73-85
Canadian Aviation, July 1956, p.45-46
Canadian Aviation, August 1959, p.20-23
Flight, April 20, 1956, p.440-443
Flight, November 23, 1956, p.824
Flight, May 30, 1958, p.739-743
Flying, January 1956, p.34-35
Flying Review International, June 1964, p.21-25
Flying Review Internationa, October 1965, p.120-122
Interavia, May 1956, p.360-361
Interavia, June 1956, p.439
Interavia, April 1958, p.326-327
Lockheed Horizons, Summer 1965, p.20
RAF Flying Review, April 1956, p.17-18
RAF Flying Review, February 1957, p.31-32
Space & Aeronautics, November 1958, p.132-133
Western Aviation, May 1956, p.18
Western Aviation, September 1959, p.18-19

**XFV-1:**

Air Power, Autumn 1954, p.6-10
Aviation Week, March 22, 1954, p.14-18
Aviation Week, March 29, 1954, p.16-17
Interavia, May 1954, p.295-297
Naval Aviation News, May 1954, p.20-21
RAF Flying Review, June 1962, p.43
U.S. Air Services, April 1954, p.8-9

**YC-130 *Hercules*:**

Aeroplane, August 20, 1954, p.253-254
Aeroplane, May 20, 1956, p.16-22
Aviation Age, November 1955, p.30-31
Aviation Week, September 6, 1954, p.26-28
Aviation Week, July 30, 1956, p.72
Aviation Week, December 3, 1956, p.50-67
Aviation Week, August 12, 1957, p.37
Aviation Week, May 19, 1958, p.60-77
Flight, August 13, 1954, p.205
Flight, December 10, 1954, p.842-844
Flight, September 14, 1956, p.491-494
Flying, January 1958, p.28-30
Interavia, February 1957, p.125-127
RAF Flying Review, May 1957, p.34-37
U.S. Air Services, August 1955, p.21
U.S. Air Services, July 63, p.42-43
Western Aviation, September 1954, p.13

**U-2:**

Aeroplane, May 27, 1960, p.639
Air Progress, Fall 1960, p.58-59
Aviation Week, February 11, 1957, p.30
Aviation Week, May 2, 1960, p.158
Aviation Week, May 16, 1960, p.28-29
Aviation Week, May 23, 1960, p.32-37
Aviation Week, August 12, 1963, p.72-77
Aviation Week, November 18, 1963, p.53-57
Canadian Aviation, June 1960, p.55
Flight, November 23, 1956, p.809
Flying, July 1960, p.49
Flying Review International, February 1966, p.331-332
Lockheed Horizons, Summer 1965, p.21
RAF Flying Review, July 1957, p.32
RAF Flying Review, July 1960, p.18-19
Smithsonian Air & Space, August/September 1993, p.22-31
Western Aviation, June 1960, p.37
Western Aviation, February 1961, p.6-8

***JetStar*:**

Aeroplane, November 29, 1957, p. 815-817
Aeroplane, January 16, 1959, p.72-74
Aviation Week, September 30, 1957, p.108-113
Aviation Week, May 5, 1958, p.78-99
Aviation Week, January 8, 1962, p.67-74
Aviation Week, January 15, 1962, p.70-75
Aviation Week, December 16, 1968, p.31-33
Bee-Hive, Fall 1960, p.1
Flight, September 20, 1957, p.490
Flight, March 29, 1962, p.484-485
Flight, August 20, 1964, p.297-299
Flying, October 1957, p.38-39
Flying, October 1958, p.32-34
Flying, March 1961, p.24-27
Flying, March 1965, p.94-95
Flying, April 1968, p.60-64
Flying Review International, July 1969, p.50-51
Interavia, July 1958, p.711-715
RAF Flying Review, January 1963, p.30-33

**"A-11":**

Air Force, April 1964, p.33-37
Aviation Week, March 9, 1964, p.16-19
Flight, March 12, 1964, p.377-379
Flying Review International, May 1964, p.6-7
Interavia, April 1964, p.421-422

**YF-12A:**

Air Force, November 1964, p.46-47
Air Force, June 1965, p.50-51
Air Force, September 1969, p.34
Air Force, July 1965, p.36-37
Air Progress, January 1965, p.50-51
Air Progress, October 1965, p.60-62
Aviation Week, October 5, 1964, p.16-17
Aviation Week, October 12, 1964, p.30-33
Aviation Week, October 19, 1964, p.54-63
Aviation Week, March 15, 1965, p.181
Aviation Week, August 11, 1969, p.65-68
Aviation Week, December 22, 1969, p.22
Bee-Hive, Fall 1964, p.10-12
Flight, October 15, 1964, p.667-669
Flying Review International, January 1965, p.16-21
Interavia, December 1964, p.1806-1807

**SR-71:**

Aviation Week, December 14, 1964, p.20-21
Aviation Week, January 17, 1966, p.33-34

**F-117:**

Lockheed Horizons, May 1992, p.1-60

**Papers/Miscellaneous Documents**:

***A-12 Log***, Lockheed Advanced Development Company

***AF-12 Log***, Lockheed Advanced Development Company

***CL-282 High Altitude Aircraft, Report No. 9732***, P. E. LeVeille, Lockheed Aircraft Corporation, Burbank, California, March 5, 1954

***Design Features of the Lockheed L-133***, Willis Hawkins, Jr., Lockheed Aircraft Corporation, Burbank, California, February 24, 1942

***Design History of the XP-90 Airplane***, Willis Hawkins, Jr., Lockheed Aircraft Corporation, Burbank, California, February 27, 1947

***Development of the Lockheed F-104 Supersonic Fighter***, Clarence L. Johnson, Lockheed Aircraft Corporation, Summer Meeting of the Institute of the Aeronautical Sciences at Los Angeles, California, June 18, 1957

***Development of the Lockheed* JetStar *Transport Airplane***, Clarence L. Johnson, Lockheed Aircraft Corporation, National Summer Meeting of the Institute of the Aeronautical Sciences at Los Angeles, California, July 10, 1958

***F-117A Flight Test Program***, Richard Abrams and Harold Farley, Jr., Lockheed Advanced Development Company, Palmdale, California, 1991

***Final Report of Development, Procurement, Performance, and Acceptance XP-80 Airplane***, Army Air Forces Air Technical Service Command, Air Corps Technical Report No. 5235, June 28, 1945, by Bastian Hello, Wright Field, Dayton, Ohio

***Flight Tests of the Lockheed XFV-1 Airplane***, James Billo, Lockheed Aircraft Corporation, Burbank, California, June 15, 1955

***Have Blue Program Overview***, Richard Burton, Lockheed Advanced Development Company, Palmdale, California, 1993

***Index of Serial Numbers Assigned to Aircraft Through Fiscal Year 1958 (with 1978 Update)***, United States Air Force, 1978, Washington, D.C.

***Lockheed's P-80, The Shooting Star Story***, Lockheed, no date

***Lockheed-California Company's Skunk Works Traces Name Back to 1940 Era Comic Strip***, Richard Stadler, Lockheed-California Co., no date

***Nighthawks Over Iraq, A Chronology of the F-117A Stealth Fighter in Operations Desert Shield and Desert Storm***, Harold Myers, Office of History, Headquarters 37th Fighter wing, Twelfth air force, Tactical Air Command, 1992

***Overview of the F-117A Avionics Flight Test Program***, Richard Sitz, Lockheed Advanced Development Company, Palmdale, California 1992

***Oxcart Story, The***, Thomas McInich, Central Intelligence Agency, December 15, 1986

***Preliminary Design Study of Proposed Lockheed P-80D***, Willis Hawkins, Jr., Lockheed Aircraft Corporation, Burbank, California, May 27, 1948

***Prelminary Design Study of Proposed Lockheed P-80E***, Willis Hawkins, Jr., Lockheed Aircraft Corporation, Burbank, California, May 24, 1948

***Prerequisites for a Successful Skunkworks***, "Kelly" Johnson, Lockheed Advanced Development Company, Burbank, California, 1965

***Progress Report, Ramjet Flight Tests***, E. L. Joiner, Lockheed Aircraft Corporation, Burbank, California, April 20, 1948

***Subsonic Ramjets on P-80A Serial 1237***, Hong, Lockheed Aircraft Corporation, Burbank, California, September 6, 1947

# Index: